INTELLIGENT OFFICES

Object-Oriented Multi-Media Information Management in Client/Server Architectures

Setrag Khoshafian
A. Brad Baker
Razmik Abnous
Kevin Shepherd

John Wiley & Sons, Inc.
New York • Chichester • Brisbane • Toronto • Singapore

In recognition of the importance of preserving what has been written, it is a policy of John Wiley & Sons, Inc. to have books of enduring value published in the United States printed on acid-free paper, and we exert our best efforts to that end.

Actor® is a registered trademark of The Whitewater Group, Inc. Screen shot(s) ©1985-1989 The Whitewater Group. Reprinted with permission from The Whitewater Group.

FullWrite™ and FullWrite Professional™ are trademarks and FullPaint® is a registered trademark of Ashton-Tate Corporation. Copyright © Ashton-Tate Corporation 1986, 1987, 1988. All rights reserved. Reprinted by permission.

MacApp™ is a trademark of Apple Computer, Inc. Screen shots and graphic illustrations © Apple Computer, Inc. Used with permission.

Macintosh® is a registered trademark of Apple Computer, Inc. Screen shots and graphic illustrations ©Apple Computer, Inc. Used with permission.

Metaphor® and CAPSULE® are registered trademarks of Metaphor Computer Systems. Screen capture(s) ©1989 by Metaphor Computer Systems. Reprinted with permission from Metaphor Computer Systems. Figures 1.13*a*, 1.13*b*, 8.32*a*, 8.32*b* courtesy of NeXT, Inc.

Microsoft Windows®, MS Paint®, MS Write® are registered trademarks of Microsoft Corporation. Screen shot(s) ©1985-1989 Microsoft Corporation. Reprinted with permission from Microsoft Corporation.

NetWare® and Novell® are registered trademarks of Novell, Inc.

NewWave® is a registered trademark of Hewlett-Packard Company. Screen shot(s) ©1989 Hewlett-Packard. Reprinted with permission from Hewlett-Packard.

NeXT™, NeXTStep™ are trademarks of NeXT, Inc. Screen shot(s) ©1989 NeXT Inc. Reprinted with permission from NeXT, Inc. Figures 1.14*b*, 8.42, 8.43, and 8.44 courtesy of Metaphor Computer Systems.

Designations used by companies to distinguish their products are often claimed as trademarks. In all instances where John Wiley & Sons, Inc. is aware of a claim, the product names appear in initial capital or all capital letters. Readers, however, should contact the appropriate companies for more complete information regarding trademarks and registration.

This publication is designed to provide accurate and authoritative information in regard to the subject matter covered. It is sold with the understanding that the publisher is not engaged in rendering legal, accounting, or other professional service. If legal advice or other expert assistance in required, the services of a competent professional person should be sought. FROM A DECLARATION OF PRINCIPLES JOINTLY ADOPTED BY A COMMITTEE OF THE AMERICAN BAR ASSOCIATION AND A COMMITTEE OF PUBLISHERS.

Copyright © 1992 by John Wiley & Sons, Inc.

All rights reserved. Published simultaneously in Canada.

Reproduction or translation of any part of this work beyond that permitted by Section 107 or 108 of the 1976 United States Copyright Act without the permission of the copyright owner is unlawful. Requests for permission or further information should be addressed to the Permission Department, John Wiley & Sons, Inc.

Library of Congress Cataloging-in-Publication Data

Khoshafian, Setrag
Intelligent offices : object-oriented multi-media information management
  in client/server architectures / Setrag Khoshafian ... [et al.].
      p. cm.
    Includes bibliographical references and index.
    ISBN 0-471-54699-2. – ISBN 0-471-54700-X (pbk.)
    1. Office practice–Automation. 2. Offices–Technological innovations. 3. Management information systems. 4. Optical data processing. 5. Object-oriented programming (Computer science)
  6. Data base management. 7. Information storage and retrieval systems. I. Khoshafian, Setrag.
    HF5547.5.I5455 1992
    651.8'5133–dc20   91-42335
                                                                                                         CIP

Printed in the United States of America
10 9 8 7 6 5 4 3 2 1

To a Free and Independent Armenia

ABOUT THE AUTHORS

Dr. Setrag Khoshafian is the Vice President of Development and Chief Scientist at Portfolio Technologies Inc., where he designs and supervises delivery of imaging and intelligent information management products on client/server architectures. Previously he was the architect and manager of the intelligent database engine project at the Walnut Creek Advanced Development Center of Ashton-Tate. He is the principal designer of Intelligent SQL and has made significant contributions in the areas of object-oriented and intelligent database technologies. Prior to that he was the manager and architect of one of the earliest object-oriented database implementations at MCC. As an internationally recognized expert, Dr. Khoshafian has presented various seminars on client/server and object-oriented technologies. He is a coauthor of *Intelligent Databases* (Wiley) and *A Guide to Developing Client/Server SQL Applications* (published by Morgan Kaufmann) and the lead author of *Object Orientation* (Wiley). He received his M.Sc. and Ph.D. in Computer Science from the University of Wisconsin, Madison. He also holds an M.Sc. in mathematics from the American University of Beirut. His current research interests span imaging systems, intelligent offices, object-oriented systems, and intelligent user interfaces.

A. Brad Baker is currently the Vice President of Engineering with Pegasus Disk Technologies, Inc., in Walnut Creek, California. Prior to this he was a senior software designer at Ashton-Tate, in charge of Optical Storage Development for the intelligent database engine. Mr. Baker is a world expert in optical disk storage and multimedia data type manipulation technologies. From 1988 to 1989, he was a senior consultant to the federal government in Washington, D.C., designing and developing a network optical jukebox file server for document storage and retrieval of presidential papers. Mr. Baker has an A.A. from Diablo Valley College.

Razmik Abnous is a Senior Software Architect at Documentum, Inc. Previously, he was a senior software designer and a project loader at Ashton-Tate. He received his B.S. and M.E. degrees in Applied Mathematics and Computer Science from the University of Louisville. Also, he teaches object orientation at University of California, Berkeley.

Prior to Ashton-Tate, he was a principal software engineer in the Artificial Intelligence Technology Group of Digital Equipment Corporation. In the past several years, he has been a designer of database systems applying object orientation, inferencing, and the client/server model. His current research interests are in object orientation, intelligent databases, client/server databases, and user interfaces. He is also a coauthor of *Object Orientation*.

Kevin Shepherd is currently a Senior Software Engineer at Portfolio Technologies, Inc., where he is responsible for the design and development of the compound document, multimedia data types and multimedia peripheral support portions of the intelligent information management system products. Prior to this, he was a system designer at Hisoft Computer Systems Division in Melbourne, Australia, specializing in Document Management and Imaging. Previously, he was a Scientific Officer at the National Physics Laboratory in London, UK, designing and developing computer-controlled optical metrology equipment. Mr. Shepherd has an M.A. in Physics and Mathematics from Cambridge University, England.

PREFACE

Dr. Smith works in a medium-sized clinic, which she shares with three colleagues. They have two secretaries and two nurses. On an average day Dr. Smith and each of her colleagues treat about 20 patients. Each visit generates (on the average) five pages ($8\frac{1}{2}'' \times 11''$) of information. Recently Dr. Smith has been quite frustrated because some patient information has been missing. And this has not been the first time. In fact, in the past three months Dr. Smith has been spending about 15 percent of her time dealing with "paper" shuffling and communication with her staff just to maintain consistency of patient information. During a recent meeting with her colleagues, Dr. Smith realized that they, too, suffered from the same inefficiencies in organizing, accessing, and correctly retrieving their data files. Something has to be done. The current situation is becoming very expensive and irritating.

This scenario is typical of many offices. Some businesses use computers primarily for word processing. Most of the information exists either in word processor files, in spreadsheets, in databases, or on paper. The management of the paper information is not integrated within the computerized information bases. In fact, there is often little, if any, electronic data sharing among the different word-processing, database, and spreadsheet applications. If there are more than one workstation in the office, these workstations are typically not connected. To share information, employees use sneaker-net: Information (files) is stored on floppies and carried from one system to another.

The diversity and complexity of existing software products and hardware systems are overwhelming. Pick up a recent issue of a computer magazine (e.g., *Byte, PC Magazine, PC World, COMPUTE!*), imagine yourself a novice, and try to make some sense of the maze of similar sounding products and systems. Products compete with each other, each claiming more features and better performance than the others. But sometimes, having more features available confuses the user. In many cases the majority of the features offered will not be understood, much less needed or used. There are too many cases of offices that use obsolete systems. We have encountered many situations where even the software (in most cases word processors) used on these old systems are the initial releases of the products. The reasoning: "Why should we upgrade? The system we have now is doing its job and we do not want to confuse our employees!"

The good news is that the following are enabling technologies that can be integrated to develop powerful intelligent office systems:

1. Information sharing (through local area networks and database servers)
2. Multi-media management systems (graphical user interfaces; text, voice, image data types)
3. Easy-to-use/easy-to-understand object-oriented work-flow models

Companies must realize that affordable imaging solutions can provide convenient and economically viable solutions to their office information overload problems. Briefly, document management (also known as *document imaging, imaging systems,* or simply *imaging*) is the storage, processing, and retrieval of electronic documents. The term *imaging* connotes the use of scanning technologies to digitize (in other words, convert into computer files) paper or microfilm documents. The images are typically stored on optical media and optical jukeboxes. If designed and integrated carefully, document management for small offices can save time and money, reduce office space, and provide a much more reliable mechanism for storing, accessing, and sharing information.

In fact, some large businesses, such as large banks, insurance companies, travel agencies, and law firms, have chosen document-imaging solutions for economic reasons. Until recently, most existing document-imaging systems were stand-alone, proprietary, high-cost turnkey systems. However, recent advances in hardware and software technologies have evolved to the point that the "dream" of affordable intelligent office solutions based on imaging can (and in many situations *has*) finally become a reality. The maturity of the hardware peripherals and software components of office automation systems means that it is possible to construct powerful systems that (1) are built from standard modules, and (2) integrate and work well with existing systems, such as PCs.

The primary goal of this book is to present a powerful intelligent office model that integrates the technologies mentioned in these paragraphs. This will help management information systems (MIS) managers, system integrators, and vertical application developers make wise decisions when purchasing and integrating the necessary hardware/software components of an automated office system.

Simply stated, we attempt to answer the following questions:

- What are the hardware and software enabling technologies for intelligent office solutions?
- What are the hardware and software components that a department needs in order to provide intelligent office solutions?
- What are the various object categories for intelligent offices?
- What are the different communication and group-collaboration alternatives in intelligent offices?
- How will an intelligent office system be integrated with existing word-processing, spreadsheet, and database systems?
- How cost-effective will an intelligent office system be for the business?
- How easy will it be to change over to such a system?

- How will the system help the office worker automate routine office tasks and processes?

Another goal of the book is to demonstrate how mature database management systems, office automation, and graphical user interface software systems can be integrated with imaging/multi-media hardware to construct affordable document-imaging solutions on PCs. More specifically, we illustrate how a client/server model in a local area network (LAN) of PCs can provide the necessary functionality for concurrently storing and accessing office objects.

The underlying conceptual model of intelligent offices is object-oriented. This means that the user interacts with a collection of metaphors that represent office objects and office activities. Visually, these metaphors are presented to the user through familiar icons: forms, folders, cabinets, and even graphically represented work-flow models. The office objects are stored in database servers. This means a user can lock and grab an object, such as a file, perform updates to it, and put it back. This is very similar to the physical acquisition of a folder from a file cabinet and its subsequent replacement.

Another fundamental aspect of the intelligence in intelligent offices is the ability to scan, store, and retrieve image and voice data objects. As the saying goes, "a picture is worth a thousand words" (a favorite of Microsoft Corporation is "seeing is believing"). Compared to text, pictures are much easier to comprehend and interact with. They provide a more natural interface to the user. In the intelligent office environment, images will be used for the different metaphors of the office environment, for the office objects (such as files, folders, and cabinets), for the objects of business (such as buildings, construction sites in an engineering office), scanned images of forms, and so on.

Voice data is also a natural and effective communication medium in an office environment. Voice data can be used to send messages or as annotations to documents. Similar to all other objects, the multi-media objects (voice and image data) are also stored in the database server. A third aspect of the intelligence of intelligent offices is the controlling model of information flow. Intelligent offices provide work-flow modeling tools that allow the user to describe the relationships and filtering of documents. Work-flow models associate actions (operations) that need to be performed on documents by users, in a specific order.

The rest of the book is organized as follows. After the overview in Chapter 1, Chapters 2 through 8 discuss the various hardware and software enabling technologies for intelligent offices. Chapter 9 presents the multi-media objects used in intelligent offices. Chapters 10 and 11 concentrate on the overall organization and flow of information in intelligent offices, respectively. Finally, Chapter 12 presents a summary. Here is a more detailed description of each chapter.

Chapter 1 gives an overview of current office environments. It illustrates the integration of various technologies in intelligent offices and provides a basic introduction to the different hardware and software components of intelligent office systems. This chapter also provides a simple scenario illustrating the application of intelligent office solutions in office environments.

The heterogeneous information accessed and manipulated in intelligent office environments is space-intensive. One enabling technology that provides the ability to store and retrieve vast amounts of information on-line is optical storage, which is discussed in Chapter 2. The storage capacity of optical media is at least an order of magnitude higher than that of more conventional magnetic media. There are many types of optical storage: CD-ROM, CD-I, WORM, and erasable optical disks. Optical jukeboxes allow the organization an on-line access of trillions of bytes (terabytes) of information stored on many optical disks.

Office models are interconnected environments that employ work-group and workflow paradigms to accomplish different projects. To achieve this, the workstations in an office must be networked. Chapter 3 is dedicated to a clear exposition of the different aspects of networking: bus architecture, token-ring networks, network operating systems, networking protocols, file servers, and database servers, to name a few. The chapter also summarizes the various features of client/server architectures over local area networks.

Integration of environments and networking of computers are geared toward the sharing of information or data across multiple products and by multiple users. Database management systems enable the concurrent and consistent sharing of data in an interconnected network of computer systems. Chapter 4 is dedicated to a tutorial on the most important component of an intelligent office: the database management system. Besides the sharing of data, database management systems provide other features such as querying, transactions, recovery, and security. All these concepts are illustrated in Chapter 4.

Database management systems are excellent for searching collections of records with the same number and type of attributes. However, in many situations it is desirable to search the content of textual documents. In Chapter 5 we discuss full-text retrieval software. These systems enable the retrieval of relevant textual documents from large document collections.

Chapter 6 describes the imaging components for document imaging in intelligent offices. An important element in document imaging is a scanner. Scanners, which are attached to the workstation, scan and digitize paper documents. A scanned $8\frac{1}{2}'' \times 11''$ image can consume anywhere from 20 kbytes to 500 kbytes of (hard disk) storage. The images can therefore be compressed. Since compression and decompression can be time-consuming, compression boards are used to perform the processing in hardware. Because the scanned images are often text documents, it is very desirable to recognize characters in an image document. Therefore, the chapter also discusses optical character recognition (OCR) systems. Other hardware components and their software systems discussed in this chapter include voice digitizers and fax boards. Imaging systems initially started as stand-alone turnkey systems. These are proprietary systems comprising a workstation with high-resolution monitor, a scanner, an optical disk system, and a laser printer. This chapter also discusses the characteristics, advantages, and drawbacks of such systems.

Object-oriented technologies are dedicated to the modeling of the office environment as close to a user's perspective as possible. Chapter 7 provides an overview of the fundamental concepts of object orientation, including the object/message paradigm, classification of objects, inheritance, and compound documents.

Database management systems are the repositories of the shared objects in intelligent offices. The front end, or the human-computer interaction, for these automated/computerized offices is effected through graphical user interfaces (GUIs). Chapter 8 is dedicated to a comprehensive description of these emerging graphical environments. It demonstrates how object-oriented models permeate the object-message and "point and click" paradigms. It discusses the graphical interfaces of such popular systems as

Apple's Macintosh, Microsoft Windows 3.0, the OS/2 Presentation Manager, and so on. It also discusses some emerging tools in these environments, including Hewlett-Packard's NewWave and IBM's Office Vision. This chapter also demonstrates how hypermedia links could be used to integrate different application software and navigate from one application to another.

Chapter 9 defines the multi-media object types in intelligent offices. Multi-media objects can be multi-media data types (images, voice, video, and so on) or peripherals and processes (such as FAX, Scanner, or OCR). The chapter discusses the various classes and the class hierarchy of multi-media objects and illustrates how the functionality of multi-media processing is partitioned in a client/server architecture.

Based upon the multi-media data and peripherals discussed in Chapter 9, Chapter 10 discusses the "container" office objects: files, documents, folders, cabinets, communication objects, and so on. For each object we present

- The attributes
- The operations (methods)
- The containment hierarchies

Chapter 10 also illustrates how the objects are stored in database servers and shared by multiple office workers concurrently. This chapter shows the locking and querying capabilities provided by the underlying database management system. Users can define and modify the structure (attributes) and operations of office objects. These correspond to database schema modifications.

Chapter 11 specifies work-flow models for intelligent offices. The work flow operates on the office objects, and different types of manipulations can trigger actions (or send messages) on office objects. It uses the familiar object/message paradigm of object-oriented systems. This chapter also describes how information retrieval (especially full-text retrieval), record/database management, and multi-media environments are integrated in the intelligent office environment. It illustrates how rule-based systems are used to establish hypermedia links between objects dynamically.

Chapter 12 gives an overall summary of the book.

ACKNOWLEDGMENTS

We would like to extend our appreciation to the people who helped us with this book. First and foremost we would like to thank our spouses—Silva Khoshafian, Jill Baker, and Suzanne Abnous—for their patience and support. Also special thanks go to Catherine Shepherd for her love of Science and Engineering and to Richard Shepherd for the literary skill to express it. We would also like to express our special gratitude to Dr. Ted Marr, president and CEO of Portfolio Technologies, for his numerous contributions and support. We would also like to thank our editors, Pam Dillehay and Dianne Cerra, her assistant Terri Hudson; the copy editor Jerome Colburn, Melissa Madsen Blankenship, and others at Publication Services; and many others involved in the editing process.

Finally, we would like to express our deepest gratitude to numerous companies and corporations (cited throughout the book) who gave us support, materials, illustrations, and in some cases systems. These contributions greatly enhanced the scope, the depth, and the overall quality of our book.

CONTENTS

1 INTRODUCTION   1

    1.1   Introduction to Intelligent Offices   /   1
          1.1.1   Chapter Organization   /   3
    1.2   Information Backlog   /   3
    1.3   Integrating Technologies   /   5
          1.3.1   Graphical User Interfaces   /   6
          1.3.2   Object-Oriented Office Model   /   7
          1.3.3   Multi-Media Data Types and Peripherals   /   7
          1.3.4   Communication   /   8
          1.3.5   Local Area Network Client/Server and Peer-To-Peer Architectures   /   9
          1.3.6   Optical Storage Technologies   /   10
          1.3.7   Intelligent Databases and the Intelligent Office   /   10
    1.4   The Analogy of Nonelectronic Offices   /   11
    1.5   The Intelligence in Intelligent Offices   /   13
    1.6   Scenario   /   14
    1.7   Summary   /   16

2 OPTICAL STORAGE TECHNOLOGIES   17

    2.1   Introduction   /   17
          2.1.1   Chapter Organization   /   18
    2.2   CD-ROM   /   18
          2.2.1   CD-ROMs in the Intelligent Office   /   21
    2.3   WORM   /   21
          2.3.1   History   /   21

              2.3.2   The Technology / 22
              2.3.3   Optical Media / 24
                      2.3.3.1   Media Format / 26
                      2.3.3.2   CLV versus CAV / 27
              2.3.4   WORM Technology in the Intelligent Office / 27
       2.4 Erasable Optical Disks / 28
              2.4.1   History / 28
              2.4.2   Magneto-Optics / 29
              2.4.3   Phase Change / 30
              2.4.4   Dye-Polymer / 31
       2.5 Performance / 31
              2.5.1   Error Correction / 32
              2.5.2   DRAW versus DRDW / 34
              2.5.3   Clustering / 34
              2.5.4   Elevator Seeking / 35
              2.5.5   Caching / 36
              2.5.6   High-Performance Directory Structures / 36
              2.5.7   File Striping / 38
              2.5.8   Multi-Volume Sets / 39
              2.5.9   Disk Software Format / 39
              2.5.10 SCSI Performance / 40
       2.6 Optical File System Strategies / 40
              2.6.1   Tape Emulation: The First Wave / 40
              2.6.2   Optical Device Drivers: The Second Wave / 41
                      2.6.2.1   Winchester Emulation / 41
              2.6.3   Nontransportable Optical File System (Dedicated System):
                      The Third Wave / 43
              2.6.4   General-Purpose Transportable Optical File Systems:
                      The Fourth Wave / 44
              2.6.5   Future Optical File Systems: The Fifth Wave / 47
       2.7 Optical Jukeboxes / 47
       2.8 Future Optical Technology / 48
       2.9 Optical Technology in Intelligent Offices / 51
       2.10 Summary / 51

3
NETWORKING   53

       3.1 Introduction / 53
              3.1.1   Chapter Organization / 54
       3.2 Networking Topologies / 54
              3.2.1   Network Cabling / 56
              3.2.2   Ethernet / 57
              3.2.3   Token Ring / 59
              3.2.4   OSI/ISO and SNA Network Standard Models / 60

Contents ■ xv

        3.2.5   Data Transport Protocols / 63
        3.2.6   Client/Server and Peer-to-Peer Network Models in the Intelligent Office / 64
  3.3 Network Operating Systems / 66
        3.3.1   Novell NetWare / 67
        3.3.2   Microsoft LAN Manager / 68
        3.3.3   Banyan Vines / 69
  3.4 Network Administration Issues / 70
        3.4.1   Network Management Software and the Intelligent Office / 70
        3.4.2   Security and Authorization / 72
        3.4.3   Backup / 73
  3.5 Network Servers / 74
        3.5.1   File Servers / 75
        3.5.2   Database Servers / 76
        3.5.3   Communications Servers / 77
        3.5.4   Network File Systems / 78
  3.6 Summary / 79

4

DATABASE MANAGEMENT SYSTEMS   81

  4.1 Introduction / 81
        4.1.1   Chapter Organization / 81
  4.2 Database Capabilities / 82
        4.2.1   Persistent Storage / 82
        4.2.2   Transactions / 82
        4.2.3   Concurrent Access / 83
        4.2.4   Query Languages / 83
        4.2.5   Recovery / 83
        4.2.6   Integrity and Security / 84
        4.2.7   Performance / 84
  4.3 Evolution of Database Management Systems / 84
  4.4 Relational Data Model / 90
        4.4.1   Data Independence / 91
        4.4.2   Entity and Referential Integrity / 91
        4.4.3   Data Manipulation / 92
                4.4.3.1   Selection / 92
                4.4.3.2   Projection / 93
                4.4.3.3   Product / 93
                4.4.3.4   Join / 93
                4.4.3.5   Union / 93
                4.4.3.6   Intersection / 93
                4.4.3.7   Difference / 94
        4.4.4   SQL Language / 95
                4.4.4.1   Data Definition / 96

              4.4.4.1.1   Tables and Data Types   /   96
              4.4.4.1.2   Indexes   /   97
              4.4.4.1.3   View Definition   /   97
              4.4.4.1.4   Security and Privilege   /   98
     4.4.4.2   Data Manipulation   /   99
              4.4.4.2.1   SELECT statement   /   99
                         4.4.4.2.1.1   Support for Relational
                                      Algebra   /   100
                         4.4.4.2.1.2   Retrieval Using
                                      Subqueries   /   101
              4.4.4.2.2   INSERT Statement   /   102
              4.4.4.2.3   UPDATE Statement   /   102
              4.4.4.2.4   DELETE Statement   /   102
              4.4.4.2.5   Cursor-Based Operations   /   103
     4.4.4.3   Embedded SQL   /   104
  4.4.5   Relational Database Design   /   104
     4.4.5.1   Normalization   /   106
     4.4.5.2   Integrity Constraints   /   107
  4.4.6   Client/Server Architecture   /   109
  4.4.7   SQL Server: A Case Study of a Client/Server Relational
          Database System   /   111
     4.4.7.1   Transact-SQL   /   112
     4.4.7.2   dblibrary   /   113
4.5   Intelligent Databases   /   114
  4.5.1   The Deductive Object-Oriented Data Model   /   118
     4.5.1.1   Deductive Rules and SQL   /   118
     4.5.1.2   The Object-Oriented Constructs in Intelligent SQL   /   120
              4.5.1.2.1   Abstract Data Types   /   120
              4.5.1.2.2   Inheritance   /   121
              4.5.1.2.3   Tuple-Valued Attributes   /   123
              4.5.1.2.4   Object Identity   /   124
     4.5.1.3   Multi-Media Data Types   /   125
              4.5.1.3.1   Text Data   /   126
              4.5.1.3.2   Image Data   /   127
4.6   Summary   /   128

5
FULL-CONTENT RETRIEVAL   131

5.1   Introduction   /   131
  5.1.1   Chapter Organization   /   134
5.2   Quality of Information   /   134
  5.2.1   Data Refinement   /   135
     5.2.1.1   Raw Data   /   135
     5.2.1.2   Recognition   /   135

Contents ■ xvii

              5.2.1.3   Understanding / 136
              5.2.1.4   Intelligent Content Retrieval / 137
                      5.2.1.4.1   Knowledge Bases / 137
                      5.2.1.4.2   Rules / 139
      5.2.2   Refinement vs. Compression / 141
  5.3   Document Collections / 141
  5.4   Full-Text Retrieval / 142
      5.4.1   Document Parsing / 142
      5.4.2   Organizing Words / 142
            5.4.2.1   Term Frequencies / 143
            5.4.2.2   Stems / 143
      5.4.3   Indexing Methods / 143
            5.4.3.1   Inversion of Terms / 144
                      5.4.3.1.1   Inverted Indices / 144
                      5.4.3.1.2   Inverted Index Creation / 146
            5.4.3.2   Signature Indexing / 147
                      5.4.3.2.1   Signature Index Creation / 148
            5.4.3.3   Concept Indexing / 150
                      5.4.3.3.1   Concept-Indexing Techniques and Strategies / 150
                      5.4.3.3.2   Indexing Domain / 152
            5.4.3.4   Clustering / 152
      5.4.4   Query Definition / 153
            5.4.4.1   Boolean / 154
            5.4.4.2   Full-Text Query Language / 154
  5.5   DataBase Support / 156
      5.5.1   Dictionary / 156
      5.5.2   Stop (Noise) Word List / 156
      5.5.3   Rare Word List / 157
      5.5.4   Document Object Descriptors / 157
      5.5.5   Document Storage / 157
      5.5.6   Index Storage / 157
      5.5.7   Implementation Techniques Using Frames / 158
            5.5.7.1   Fixed Frame Support / 158
            5.5.7.2   Amorphous Frame Support / 158
            5.5.7.3   Frame Compression Utility / 158
            5.5.7.4   Rules and Goals / 158
  5.6   Full-Content Retrieval in the Intelligent Office / 159
  5.7   Summary / 159

6
IMAGING SYSTEMS   161

  6.1   Introduction / 161
      6.1.1   Chapter Organization / 163

xviii ■ Contents

- 6.2 Scanners / 164
  - 6.2.1 The Four Scanner Designs / 164
  - 6.2.2 Optical Subsystem / 165
- 6.3 Compression Boards / 166
- 6.4 High-Resolution Display Monitors / 167
- 6.5 OCR Systems / 168
  - 6.5.1 Recognizing a Character / 170
  - 6.5.2 Preserving Format / 171
- 6.6 Fax Boards / 172
  - 6.6.1 The Fax Process / 172
  - 6.6.2 Background Operation / 173
- 6.7 Voice Boards / 173
  - 6.7.1 Digitizing Sound / 174
  - 6.7.2 Voice Synthesis / 175
  - 6.7.3 Speech Recognition / 176
- 6.8 Video Boards / 176
  - 6.8.1 Animation / 177
  - 6.8.2 Video Capture and Overlay / 177
  - 6.8.3 Compression / 178
- 6.9 Laser Printers / 178
- 6.10 Turnkey Imaging Systems / 179
  - 6.10.1 Single-Workstation System / 179
  - 6.10.2 Multi-Component System / 179
  - 6.10.3 Image Workstation / 180
  - 6.10.4 Scan Station / 181
  - 6.10.5 Database Server / 182
  - 6.10.6 Storage / 182
  - 6.10.7 Print Service / 183
  - 6.10.8 Other Services / 184
- 6.11 Forms / 184
  - 6.11.1 Database Interface / 185
  - 6.11.2 Searching / 185
  - 6.11.3 Indexing / 186
  - 6.11.4 Input Format / 188
  - 6.11.5 Reporting / 188
- 6.12 Retrieval Software / 189
  - 6.12.1 Image Decompression / 190
  - 6.12.2 Image Manipulation / 190
  - 6.12.3 Markup and Editing / 190
  - 6.12.4 Archiving Images / 191
  - 6.12.5 Imitating Paper Flow / 192
  - 6.12.6 Host Interface / 192
  - 6.12.7 Other Capabilities / 193
- 6.13 Typical Applications / 194
  - 6.13.1 Insurance / 194

          6.13.2   Banking / 194
          6.13.3   Government / 195
          6.13.4   Accounting / 196
          6.13.5   Engineering / 197
   6.14 Imaging Systems and the Intelligent Office / 197
   6.15 Summary / 198

7

OBJECT-ORIENTED CONCEPTS 199

   7.1 Introduction / 199
        7.1.1   What Is Object Orientation? / 199
        7.1.2   The Evolution of Object Orientation In Programming
                Languages / 201
                7.1.2.1   Extensions, Dialects, and Versions of
                          Smalltalk / 204
                7.1.2.2   Object-Oriented Extensions of Conventional
                          Languages / 204
                7.1.2.3   Strongly Typed Object-Oriented Languages / 205
                7.1.2.4   Object-Oriented Extensions of LISP / 205
                7.1.2.5   Object-Oriented Languages in the 1990s / 206
        7.1.3   The Three Fundamental Concepts of Object Orientation / 206
        7.1.4   Chapter Organization / 206
   7.2 Object-Message Paradigm / 206
        7.2.1   Abstract Data Types / 207
        7.2.2   Classes / 208
        7.2.3   Containers and Class Extensions / 210
        7.2.4   Overloading and Dynamic Binding / 211
        7.2.5   Constraints / 213
        7.2.6   Advantages of Abstract Data Typing / 214
   7.3 Inheritance / 214
        7.3.1   Inheriting Instance Variables / 217
        7.3.2   Inheriting Methods / 218
        7.3.3   Method Overriding / 219
        7.3.4   Multiple Inheritance / 220
        7.3.5   Inheriting the Interface / 222
        7.3.6   Advantages of Inheritance / 223
   7.4 Object Identity / 223
        7.4.1   Path Names in Operating Systems / 223
        7.4.2   Identity Through Identifier Keys / 225
        7.4.3   The Type-State-Identity Trichotomy / 227
        7.4.4   Object Spaces With Identity / 230
        7.4.5   Advantages Of Object Identity / 231
   7.5 Summary / 233

8 GRAPHICAL USER INTERFACES — 235

- 8.1 Introduction / 235
    - 8.1.1 Chapter Organization / 235
- 8.2 History / 236
- 8.3 Common User Interface Terms / 241
- 8.4 GUI on PCs / 249
    - 8.4.1 Microsoft Windows / 249
        - 8.4.1.1 Feature Overview / 250
        - 8.4.1.2 Creation and Manipulation of a Window / 250
            - 8.4.1.2.1 Structure of a Window / 250
            - 8.4.1.2.2 Creating Windows / 250
        - 8.4.1.3 Pop-up and Child Windows / 252
        - 8.4.1.4 Resources / 256
        - 8.4.1.5 Graphics Device Interface / 257
    - 8.4.2 Macintosh Toolbox / 258
        - 8.4.2.1 Functional Overview / 258
        - 8.4.2.2 The Window Manager / 258
        - 8.4.2.3 The Resource Manager / 260
        - 8.4.2.4 The Menu Manager / 260
        - 8.4.2.5 The Control Manager / 261
        - 8.4.2.6 The Dialog Manager / 263
        - 8.4.2.7 The Scrap Manager / 263
        - 8.4.2.8 QuickDraw / 263
- 8.5 Object-Oriented User Interfaces / 265
    - 8.5.1 Actor / 265
        - 8.5.1.1 Overview / 265
        - 8.5.1.2 Class Hierarchy / 267
            - 8.5.1.2.1 Window Classes / 269
            - 8.5.1.2.2 Control Classes / 271
            - 8.5.1.2.3 Dialog Classes / 271
            - 8.5.1.2.4 Existing Dialog Class Hierarchy / 272
        - 8.5.1.3 Extending the Class Hierarchy / 276
    - 8.5.2 MacApp / 277
        - 8.5.2.1 Overview of MacApp Capabilities / 277
        - 8.5.2.2 User Interface Class Hierarchy / 278
            - 8.5.2.2.1 TApplication / 278
            - 8.5.2.2.2 TDocument / 278
            - 8.5.2.2.3 TView / 278
            - 8.5.2.2.4 TCommand / 283
            - 8.5.2.2.5 TList / 283
        - 8.5.2.3 Extensibility / 283

Contents ■ xxi

        8.5.3   NeXT / 284
                8.5.3.1   Overview of NeXT Software / 284
                8.5.3.2   NeXT User Interface / 285
                8.5.3.3   Application Kit / 286
                8.5.3.4   Designing User Interfaces with Interface Builder / 287
    8.6   ToolBook: A Hypermedia GUI Application / 290
        8.6.1   Overview / 290
        8.6.2   ToolBook Objects / 291
                8.6.2.1   Books / 292
                8.6.2.2   Pages / 293
                8.6.2.3   Fields / 294
                8.6.2.4   Buttons / 294
                8.6.2.5   Graphics / 294
        8.6.3   OpenScript Language / 294
    8.7   NewWave / 295
        8.7.1   Overview of NewWave Software / 296
        8.7.2   NewWave Architecture / 297
        8.7.3   Object Management Facility / 300
                8.7.3.1   Objects / 300
                8.7.3.2   Links and Views / 301
    8.8   Summary / 304

9
MULTI-MEDIA OBJECTS IN THE OFFICE   305

    9.1   Introduction / 305
        9.1.1   Chapter Organization / 307
    9.2   Multi-Media Objects / 307
        9.2.1   Structure and Interactions of Multi-Media Objects / 309
    9.3   Multi-Media Data Types / 310
    9.4   Text Data / 312
    9.5   Image Data Types: Attributes and Organization / 313
        9.5.1   Image File Formats / 313
        9.5.2   Image Compression / 314
        9.5.3   Dithering / 316
        9.5.4   Images in the Intelligent Office / 316
        9.5.5   Optical Image Recognition and Neural Network Technology / 317
    9.6   Voice in the Intelligent Office / 318
        9.6.1   Speech Recognition / 319
        9.6.2   Potential Uses of Speech / 320
    9.7   Video and Animation / 321
        9.7.1   Digital Video Interactive / 323

9.7.2 Video, Animation, and the Intelligent Office / 323
9.8 Summary / 325

10
OFFICE OBJECTS AND THE OFFICE OBJECT REPOSITORY 327

10.1 Introduction / 327
    10.1.1 Chapter Organization / 328
10.2 The Intelligent Office Environment / 328
    10.2.1 Issues to Resolve / 330
        10.2.1.1 Office Workers and Office Objects / 330
        10.2.1.2 Heterogeneous Information / 330
        10.2.1.3 Concurrent Sharing / 330
        10.2.1.4 Procedures and Policies / 331
        10.2.1.5 Collaborative Work / 331
    10.2.2 The Object Categories / 331
    10.2.3 Organizing the Office Environment / 332
10.3 Buildings and Corporations / 333
    10.3.1 Security and Resilience / 335
    10.3.2 Corporation Policies and Procedures / 335
        10.3.2.1 Procedures and Policies as Objects / 335
        10.3.2.2 Policy and Procedure Hierarchies / 336
10.4 The Floor/Department / 338
10.5 Cabinets, Drawers, Folders, and Documents / 338
    10.5.1 Cabinets / 340
    10.5.2 Drawers / 340
    10.5.3 Folders / 341
    10.5.4 Documents / 342
    10.5.5 Links / 344
    10.5.6 Design for Extensibility / 346
10.6 The Office / 347
10.7 Organizing the Office Workers / 348
10.8 Managing Paper Information / 351
10.9 Object Repository for Office Objects / 352
    10.9.1 Relational Database Design / 354
        10.9.1.1 Maintaining Object Numbers / 356
        10.9.1.2 Populating the Database / 356
    10.9.2 Query Forms / 357
        10.9.2.1 Folder Navigation / 357
        10.9.2.2 Accessing Objects in the Current Folder / 357
        10.9.2.3 Accessing Objects in the Document Database / 358
        10.9.2.4 Updating Objects / 359
    10.9.3 Locking Shared Objects / 360

10.10 Change Management / 361
10.11 Check-Out/Check-In of Office Objects / 363
10.12 Summary / 365

11
COLLABORATIVE WORK AND WORK FLOW IN INTELLIGENT OFFICES   367

11.1 Introduction / 367
    11.1.1 Groupware: An Overview / 369
        11.1.1.1 Groupware Research / 371
    11.1.2 Work Flow: An Overview / 372
    11.1.3 Intelligent Collaboration / 374
11.2 Electronic Messaging and Mail Systems / 374
    11.2.1 Electronic Messaging in Intelligent Offices / 376
    11.2.2 Launchers, Viewers, and Object Linking / 378
    11.2.3 Rules and Messages / 378
        11.2.3.1 Message Filters / 378
        11.2.3.2 Message Forwarding / 379
11.3 Schedulers and Calendars / 380
11.4 Conferences and Meetings / 381
11.5 Work Flow in Document Management Systems / 382
11.6 Work Flow in Intelligent Offices / 383
    11.6.1 Intelligent Work Flow / 386
    11.6.2 Components of Work Flow in Intelligent Offices / 387
11.7 Summary / 388

12
SUMMARY   391

12.1 Optical Storage Technologies / 392
    12.1.1 CD-ROMs / 393
    12.1.2 WORMs / 393
    12.1.3 Erasable / 393
12.2 Networking and Client/Server Architectures / 394
12.3 Database Management Systems / 394
12.4 Full-Content Retrieval / 395
12.5 Imaging Systems / 396
12.6 Object Orientation / 397
    12.6.1 Abstract Data Typing / 398
    12.6.2 Inheritance / 398
    12.6.3 Object Identity / 399

12.7 Graphical User Interfaces / 399
12.8 Multi-Media Data Types and Peripherals / 401
12.9 Intelligent Offices: A Prescription for the Office of the Future / 402

REFERENCES 405

INDEX 415

1

INTRODUCTION

■ 1.1 INTRODUCTION TO INTELLIGENT OFFICES

Rapidly advancing technologies in the computer industry are revolutionizing the way in which information is managed in office environments. Office environments of the 1990s and the early twenty-first century will be very different from those of previous decades. At a minimum, these technological advances will enable office workers to successfully manage the information glut they encounter in the offices of today.

Most of the information flowing through offices today is still stored on paper. Estimates have been made (Wang, 1989) that about 95 percent of all information managed in a corporation is in paper form. Only 1 percent is on-line information managed by a computer system, and about 4 percent is archived information stored in computer tapes or on microfiche. Furthermore, most of the information stored electronically is in alphanumeric form.

The vast amount of information in typical office environments is very difficult to organize and locate. Office workers frequently have to search numerous cabinets (if the information is in paper format) or navigate several directories (if the information is in electronic format) to locate needed information. Although indexing expedites the process of locating information, often the information is not adequately indexed. In fact, estimates have also been made that office workers spend between 15 to 30 percent of their time (depending on their respective tasks) trying to locate information. Of course, the vast majority of the search time is spent trying to locate paper documents.

Another problem with most office environments is the process by which office workers communicate. Again, depending on the individual's rank and responsibility, office workers spend considerable percentages of their time in meetings (usually the higher the rank, the more the time in meetings). Ironically, one of the most powerful tools available in the office for streamlining communications—personal computers—is used least to handle communication-intensive tasks. In recent years a number of powerful products have offered solutions that enhance the communications between workers who use internetworked PCs. Interestingly enough, however, these solutions often face stiff resistance from managers even within the most technologically advanced corporations (Perin, 1991).

2 ■ Introduction

The concept of the intelligent office provides a model showing how information can be easily searched, organized, and moved through the office. Intelligent office solutions enhance the communication between workers, without challenging existing organizational structures. This concept encompasses two fundamental issues of paramount importance in office automation today:

1. How to model and organize information
2. How to communicate and transport information

These are illustrated in Figure 1.1. These two issues apply to all types of information in the office, from the alphanumeric data stored in corporate databases to the multimedia data (including images and voice data) in office information systems. Figure 1.1a illustrates an office that belongs to a worker and contains a desktop. The desktop contains folders and a scanner. The office worker can also access corporate databases through the desktop. Figure 1.1b illustrates a work flow that captures the main elements of an "intelligent" fax server. The fax server sends the arriving fax to a purchasing agent. The agent forwards it to an optical character recognition (OCR) process, which then organizes the scanned document into various folders.

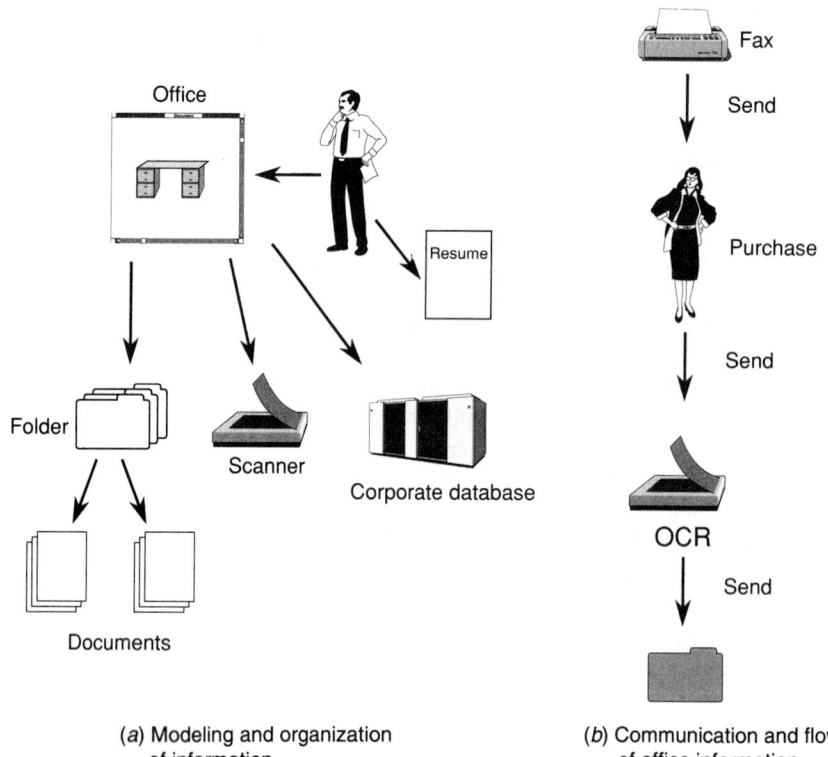

(a) Modeling and organization of information

(b) Communication and flow of office information

Figure 1.1 The two issues in intelligent offices.

In intelligent offices, information about many aspects of the office environment must be stored, transported, accessed, updated, and communicated. This information generally pertains to

1. The domain and information ("knowledge base") of the business: accounts, purchase orders, invoices, and so on
2. Office workers: name, social security number, salary, rank, department, and so on
3. Office tools, resources, devices, and peripherals: scanners, printers, fax machines, OCR processes, and so on
4. Policies and procedures: résumé tracking, raises, relocation packages, and so on

The model of the intelligent office addresses these needs by organizing data within container hierarchies built with such objects as tables, documents, folders, and cabinets. These object types can be private, belonging to one particular office worker or a group, or they can be public, allowing access to many office workers and departments.

In the intelligent office environment, the system stores and coordinates concurrent accesses to all types of information in the office. As we shall see, the intelligent office provides a uniform object-oriented environment to access, update, version, and manipulate these heterogeneous multi-media object types in local area network client/server architectures.

1.1.1 Chapter Organization

Section 1.2 of this chapter discusses the information backlog and the information glut in the typical office. Section 1.3 describes the problems of communication in office environments and also outlines the various technologies that are integrated in intelligent office systems; an analogy is drawn to nonelectronic offices in Section 1.4. Section 1.5 outlines the characteristics of intelligent offices that make them "intelligent." Section 1.6 presents a scenario of a "real-life" application that uses the technologies of the intelligent office.

■ 1.2 INFORMATION BACKLOG

Figure 1.2 depicts the sources of the information that constantly bombard the office worker. These information sources include

> Electronic mail messages
> Electronic documents
> Departmental databases (stored on a LAN server)
> Text files
> Application files: word processor files, spreadsheets, and so on.
> Faxes
> Voice mail
> Scanned images

4 ■ Introduction

Figure 1.2 Information overload.

Corporate databases (stored in a mainframe)
Resource information stored on CD-ROM
Books, articles, and other resources stored on paper

A number of observations can be made about this information backlog:

1. The information comes from many sources.
2. A large quantity of information is involved.
3. The different types of information are heterogeneous: text, graphics, video, image, voice, and so on.
4. Information originates from heterogeneous sources: electronic documents, voice mail, paper, and so on.
5. At a very "global" (that is, officewide) level, information is either in paper, analog audio, analog video, or digital form. Digital information can take the form of database tables, alphanumeric data, word processor data, spreadsheets, images, or digitized voice data.
6. The assumption that all information will be computerized in the future is unrealistic. Paper documents will still play a role in the office environment. The concept of the intelligent office attempts to provide the indexing tools for organizing and locating the paper information.

The way in which information is organized is a fundamental aspect of intelligent offices. Given the vast amounts of different types of information bombarding the office professional, locating the required information often becomes an arduous task. The tools in the intelligent office allow the business professional (office worker) to search and filter through the massive volume of information in the office and obtain the information that he or she needs.

■ 1.3 INTEGRATING TECHNOLOGIES

Although office environments today are faced with an overwhelming information glut and astounding information management–processing needs, the good news is that the following mature technologies can be integrated to develop powerful intelligent office systems. Intelligent office environments allow the sharing of information in local area network client/server architectures. The information shared is both structured alphanumeric (for example, relational database tables) and multi-media (such as images, voice, animation). Object orientation is used to model the information structure and behavior: "everything" in the system is an object. As much as possible, the objects are metaphors of "real-life" entities. Similar to the way interactions happen in the real world, each object has a state and responds to a prescribed set of messages (the "protocol," or interface, of the object). The objects of the intelligent office worker's universe are organized and presented to him or her through easy-to-use object-oriented graphical user interfaces.

The integration of these technologies in the model of the intelligent office is illustrated in Figure 1.3 and introduced briefly in the following sections. In-depth discussions of these technologies are presented later in this book.

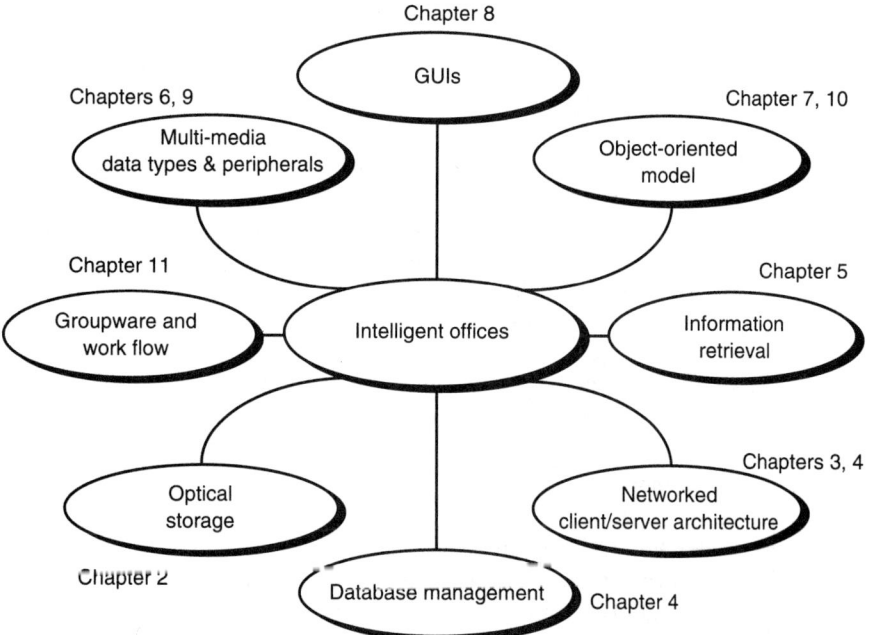

Figure 1.3 The integrated technologies in intelligent offices.

In many aspects the integration of technologies in intelligent offices resembles those of intelligent document management systems (Michalski, 1991). These systems extend imaging systems into more general hypermedia environments, supporting collaborative work (or groupware) over internetworked workstations. Intelligent offices extend the scope and model of intelligent document management systems. They also

- Provide a more uniform model for organizing the various information types: Information exists in many forms and types, not just document images. Some other types of information include structured databases, application files, word processor files, and spreadsheets.
- Provide a model for the corporation and office environment. Thus, intelligent offices support office workers (organizing them in groups, providing access privileges, and so on), office policies, office procedures, as well as various localities of office objects (documents, corporate databases, and so on).
- Supports inferencing rules to filter office objects: message filters, rules for creating folders, rule bases for office policies and procedures, and so on.

Besides intelligent document management systems, there are other systems that are also similar to intelligent offices. One such prototype is Object Lens from MIT (Lai *et al.*, 1989). In Object Lens (and intelligent offices, for that matter) the office worker's environment is organized in objects, which represent familiar entities such as people (office workers), machines, tasks, and containers. The processes and procedures in intelligent offices are like the semi-autonomous "agents" of Object Lens. These agents automate and partition the various tasks (such as tracking a résumé) of the office. When an agent gets "triggered" (for example, due to an external event such as a résumé arriving), it applies a collection of rules to office objects (for example, send the résumé to all relevant departments, where "relevance" is defined through rules).

Intelligent offices also integrate electronic messaging systems. However, the "value added" provided by intelligent office and other similar systems is the ability to dynamically filter and route (or forward) messages using rules. Object Lens and a number of other systems, such as the messaging systems developed at University of Toronto (Mazer and Lochovsky, 1989), have incorporated this useful feature.

Therefore, intelligent offices integrate a number of technologies and provide a model for the next generation of office applications. The next sections explain some of the technologies integrated in intelligent offices. Much more detailed discussions will be devoted to most of these concepts in the following chapters.

1.3.1 Graphical User Interfaces

In the intelligent office environment, employees interact with high-resolution graphical user interface (GUI) environments. These environments present the office worker with icons, which represent physical metaphors for familiar office objects (forms, folders, cabinets, and even graphically represented work-flow models).

In addition, the GUI environment of intelligent offices goes beyond the level of the "personal" workstations used by individuals to streamlining the organization and flow of shared information in the office. In this scenario, the user interacts with metaphors that represent physical office objects (such as printers, conference rooms, and other office workers) and office activities. These office objects are stored in server databases in order to be accessible to the office workers.

Chapter 8 discusses graphical user interfaces in detail and analyzes several present-day GUI systems (such as Windows, Macintosh, and NeXTStep).

1.3.2 Object-Oriented Office Model

The underlying conceptual model of the intelligent office is object-oriented. Each object in the intelligent office (whether a cabinet, fax machine, or person) pertains to a class. The interaction between these objects occurs when they send messages to and request services from one another. The object-oriented concept that makes this possible is abstract data typing.

Classes are organized in inheritance hierarchies, and office workers can specialize or generalize the classes of their office objects. Thus, they can categorize container objects as folders or cabinets, office workers as managers or sales people, and office peripherals as printers or scanners.

Finally, the application of object orientation to the intelligent office allows objects to share other objects referentially. For instance, the intelligent office model can represent the fact that a particular document is contained in many folders by allowing the folders to reference the same object. This referential sharing is supported by the concept of object identity.

These object-oriented concepts are explored in detail in Chapter 7. The categorization of objects in intelligent offices is discussed in Chapters 9 and 10 (Chapter 9 concentrates on multi-media objects and Chapter 10 examines the organization of objects in the intelligent office). Chapter 11 examines the object–message paradigm as it relates to the flow of information in office environments.

1.3.3 Multi-Media Data Types and Peripherals

Another fundamental aspect of the intelligence in intelligent offices is the ability to scan, store, and retrieve image and voice data objects. As the saying goes: "A picture is worth a thousand words."

Compared to text, images are much easier to comprehend and interact with because they provide a more natural interface for the user. In the intelligent office environment, images represent the different physical metaphors of the office environment: the office objects (such as files, folders, and cabinets), the objects of the particular business (such as construction sites in an engineering office), scanned images of forms, and so on.

Voice data is also a natural and effective communication medium in office environments, and it can be used to send messages or to create voice annotations to documents. Other increasingly popular multi-media technologies used in the intelligent office model are animation and videos. Office workers can incorporate video and animation in their documents, so that a multi-media document may have some text-based components, other components that are images, others that are voice annotations, and yet others that are video or animation clips.

8 ■ Introduction

Image, voice, and other multi-media data processing technologies are becoming viable because of several significant technological advances:

- Storage (magnetic, optical, and magneto-optic) has become less expensive. This enables the storage and retrieval of large image/multi-media bases. Optical disk technologies are discussed in more detail in Chapter 2.
- The hardware components for the I/O (input/output) and processing of multi-media data has also become less expensive. Devices such as scanners, high-resolution display monitors, laser printers, and high-resolution printers have become affordable and commonplace. These are discussed in Chapters 6 and 9.
- Software to display, link, store, model, and process multi-media data has also matured and become common. When Microsoft launched Windows 3.0, the company released studies that showed that end users were able to learn, use, and adapt much easier to graphical user interfaces than to character-based interfaces.
- Multi-media development tools for such systems as Microsoft Windows, IBM's OS/2, System 7 from Apple, or NeXTStep from NeXT have enabled third-party developers to build powerful software systems and products that support multi-media data types and peripherals.

In the environment of the intelligent office, multi-media peripherals and data types are defined as persistent and concurrently accessed objects. Some of the attributes and operations of these objects are detailed in Chapters 9 and 10.

1.3.4 Communication

The communication and flow of information through an office can take many forms, such as electronic mail messages, conference calls, meetings for project management, and document routing in the office. It has been observed that an inverse relationship exists between the percentage of work dedicated to communications and computer usage. In other words, the more communication is involved in an office task, the less the likelihood a computer will be used to automate the task. This relationship is illustrated in Figure 1.4.

Of course, one could argue that high-level executives do not like to work with a computer, but a more fundamental and serious problem exists. The networked computer systems in today's offices concentrate on the sharing of information, but no agreed-upon methodologies and products have been developed to assist office workers and executives with communicating that information.

To be sure, electronic office solutions that enhance and automate communication and information flow will not replace human interaction. However, these solutions can assist with the process of communicating information between workers, especially with respect to searching for and navigating through information, performing project management, and handling task (work) assignment. The following scenarios present needs that can be successfully addressed by implementing electronic office solutions:

> Communicating and coordinating the tasks involved in building a complex system

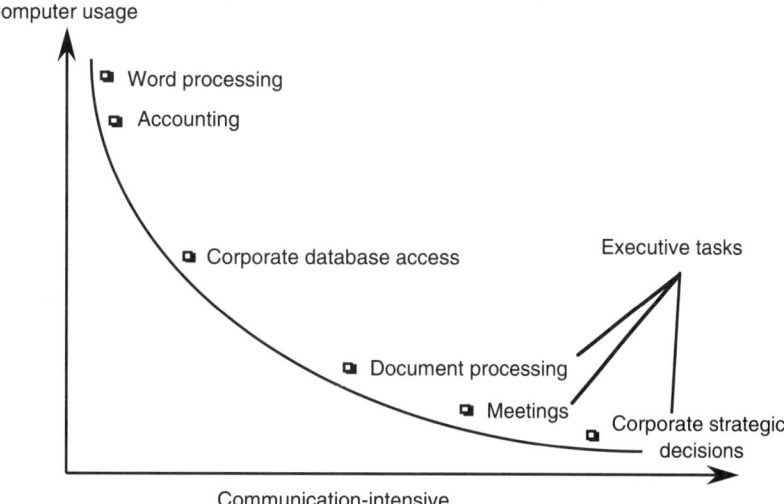

Figure 1.4 Inverse relationship: computer usage versus communication-intensive tasks.

Creating folders and documents from existing individual components or documents, based on certain quantifications (such as creating a folder of all invoices generated by selected office workers)

Enhancing communications in order to maintain consistency between several information sources

In all of these examples, "automation" could successfully meet the needs for enhancing both the communication of information and the flow of information through the system. Throughout this book, other examples will illustrate the power of the intelligent office model.

1.3.5 Local Area Network Client/Server and Peer-to-Peer Architectures

Client/server computing is the latest trend in the development of advanced information systems accessed through local area network (LAN) technology. As LANs have found broader acceptance in business enterprises, users have been busy finding new and different ways to use and concurrently share the data.

Driven by the need for more efficient ways to share and access information, client/server computing seems to be "an idea whose time has come." Client/server computing allows applications to store and access data stored on a LAN-based database server.

With respect to the intelligent office environment, the client/server model provides a number of distinct advantages. Foremost is the fact that client/server technology allows the office applications to optimize the use of hardware and software resources at both the "front end" (the client computer application) and the "back end" (the database server that provides a centralized "repository" of shared database information). Client/server architecture improves the performance of accessing shared office data in a LAN environment and allows more office workers to access the same data, often using their existing personal computer (PC) software.

Local area network technologies are discussed in Chapter 3, and client/server architectures are examined in Chapters 3 and 4. The storage and retrieval of intelligent office objects in concurrently shared client/server environments is explored in Chapter 10.

1.3.6 Optical Storage Technologies

The multi-media information stored and accessed in intelligent office environments is extremely data-intensive. Optical storage provides cost-effective media for the storage of large volumes of data, such as those encountered in multi-media applications. Optical storage is an essential member of the intelligent office storage hierarchy, which is designed to retrieve information for the entire corporation. In the intelligent office, this technology will be used to store and retrieve the data-intensive, multi-media object types.

Mass storage through optical technologies has engendered a whole new way of thinking about text, image, data, and their manipulation. The removal of memory limitations in mass storage allows a great amount of information to be stored for easy access, even if this information requires gigabytes of space on the storage device. Thus, multiple representations of information can exist at different points in information networks or hierarchies. These multiple representations of information can be linked to each other in a variety of ways. In one type of application (hypertext), associative links are constructed that allow the user to browse through information in a highly flexible fashion.

Compared with magnetic media, optical storage provides a number of features that are ideal in intelligent office environments. These include removability, higher storage densities, lower cost, and longer archival life.

1.3.7 Intelligent Databases and the Intelligent Office

The underlying technology of intelligent offices is that of intelligent databases. In a sense, the intelligent office model can be thought of as an application of the concept of intelligent databases. What are intelligent databases?

As described by Parsaye *et al.* (1989), intelligent databases represent a new technology for information management that has evolved from the integration of traditional approaches to databases with more recent fields such as

- Object-oriented concepts
- Expert (or inferencing) systems
- Multi-media information retrieval

The primary emphasis of this book will be on the object-oriented and multi-media functionalities of intelligent databases. Nevertheless, rule-based inferencing does add considerable power to a database engine. It allows the client applications to express complex relationships between database objects through high-level declarative rules. Rules and "predicates" can be attached to various database objects. Upon accessing or updating attributes of the database objects, these rules could "fire" and trigger various actions (including firing other rules). In intelligent offices, rule or predicate attachments could be used to enhance the integrity of various office objects. Rules can also be used to "program" the communication or work flow between various office objects. Although no particular chapter is dedicated to inferencing, we shall illustrate the use of rules and inferencing as applied to various intelligent office features.

As far as the "database" capabilities are concerned, intelligent database servers provide the following:

1. *Persistence*: the ability of objects to persist different program invocations
2. *Transactions*: execution units, which are executed either entirely or not at all
3. *Concurrency control*: the algorithms which control the concurrent execution of transactions to guarantee serializability
4. *Recovery*: the ability of the database management system to recover from transaction, system, or media errors
5. *Querying*: high-level declarative constructs that allow users to qualify what they want to retrieve from the persistent databases
6. *Versioning*: the ability to store and retrieve multiple versions of the same persistent database object
7. *Integrity*: the predicates that specify and define consistent states of the persistent databases
8. *Security*: the mechanisms that control the user access rights of persistent databases
9. *Performance issues*: the constructs and strategies that are used to enhance the response time and the throughput of database management systems

By combining these database capabilities together with object-oriented concepts, expert systems, and multi-media information retrieval, intelligent databases represent the merging of a number of distinct paths of technological development. Until recently, these technologies were treated in isolation, with each technology only weakly linked to others. For instance, expert systems have relied on little more than file transfer protocols to gather data from databases.

Now these mature technologies can be united by the overall unifying structure of intelligent databases. This structure allows a common approach to be used for accessing and using information for the purposes of analysis and decision making. The intelligent office model, constructed on top of the concept of the intelligent database, organizes information itself, and the dynamic communication of that information, in client/server internetworked office environments.

Functionalities and detailed descriptions of object-oriented and intelligent databases are presented in Chapter 7. The application of database functionalities to intelligent office objects is discussed in Chapter 12.

■ 1.4 THE ANALOGY OF NONELECTRONIC OFFICES

One way to understand and capture the office worker's "universe" is by analyzing the characteristics of the "nonelectronic" office. Figure 1.5 illustrates a "nonelectronic" office

12 ■ Introduction

Figure 1.5 A nonelectronic office.

that contains various physical objects: a typewriter, a telephone, documents, a clock, and so on.

Figure 1.6 illustrates another view of an office with a common area where several offices share a space. This office holds a number of "shared objects," such as a fax machine, a library, and shared bookcases.

The physical objects in the office environment area are accessed according to specific privileges and policies, which are assigned to office workers.

The office environment is thus organized by partitioning information and office objects, with specific privileges assigned to office workers to operate on the information (data) or other office objects. These privileges are given to office workers according to their titles (ranks) and/or roles.

The following factors directly affect the workers in an office environment:

- The office workers' organization within the office
- The varied and heterogeneous nature of the information types managed by various departments and the organization of the information
- The need to share information
- The need to handle information according to certain procedures and policies
- The procedures and policies controlling the flow of information within the office

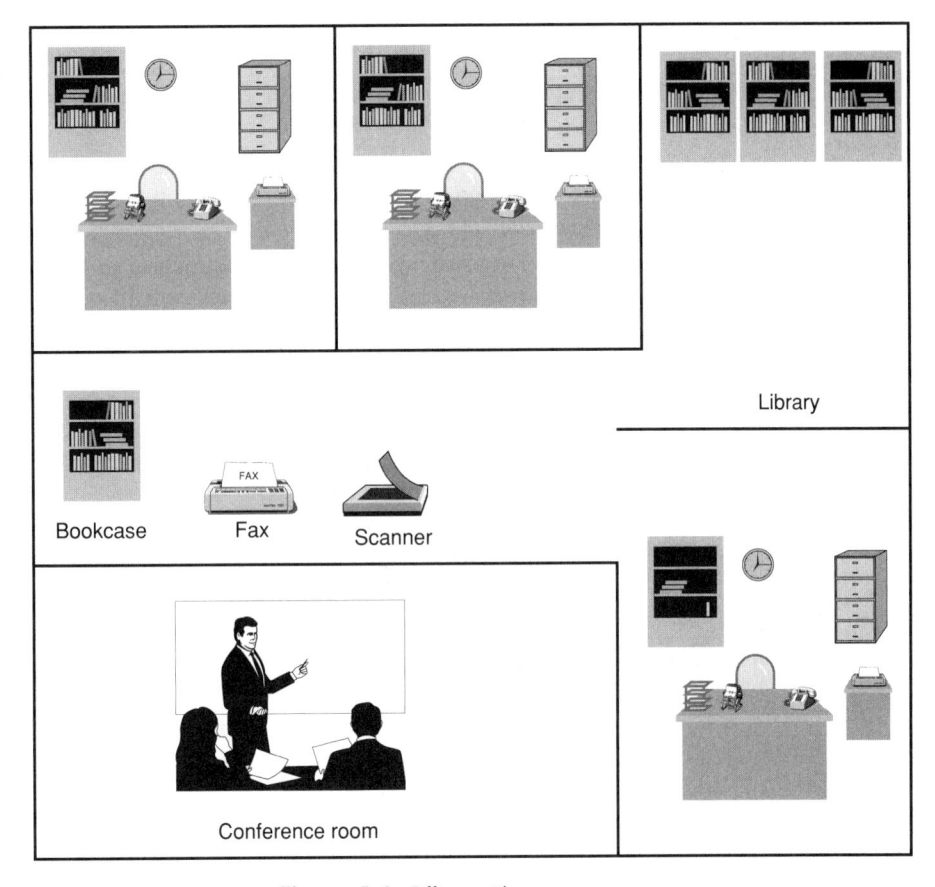

Figure 1.6 Offices with a common area.

The intelligent office environment provides well-understood policies and models for information organization, privileges, and information bases for office workers, groups, and departments. The most natural model is an object-oriented model of office information and objects.

All of the factors just listed hold true in a corporate office environment. The model of the intelligent office provides the tools that make it possible to represent these factors electronically as objects.

In addition, the intelligent office environment surpasses the electronic, computerized modeling and representation of familiar office objects. It provides the added value of supporting and encouraging novel and intelligent ways of organizing and accessing information. The key question is, what makes the intelligent office model intelligent?

■ 1.5 THE INTELLIGENCE IN INTELLIGENT OFFICES

By integrating a number of mature technologies (both software and hardware), intelligent offices provide a natural and easy-to-understand way to capture and automate the office environment. Intelligent offices have the following characteristics:

- *A uniform object-oriented model.* Most objects in the intelligent office environment are represented graphically by icons that reflect the metaphor of the underlying object. The natural structure and behavior of objects is reflected directly in the intelligent office model. The "intelligence" of the intelligent office model originates in its organization, management, and search of objects.
- *Powerful database functionalities for office objects.* Intelligent offices are an application of intelligent databases.
- *Distributed processing.* An important aspect of "intelligence" is the ability to access distributed information bases uniformly, as if the information resided in a single (logical) database. The intelligent office environment provides a distributed database model for office data.
- *Integration of heterogeneous data.* A true intelligent office environment blurs the distinction between record management, document imaging, and database management systems. Through a single integrated intelligent office environment, office workers can manipulate any type of data.
- *Programming the flow of information and office policies.* The intelligent office environment incorporates office policies and procedures as objects that can be instantiated and can respond to their "interface" or protocol. As a result, they can be manipulated by office workers.
- *Support of the intelligent office rather than the intelligent desktop model.* Most existing desktop products do not have icons representing office objects, the interconnection between offices, the organization of information in offices, or the allocation of office workers to offices. By contrast, an intelligent office model must provide a direct representation of the real-world office environment.
- *Expert system rules with office objects.* Rules can be associated with any object within the intelligent office environment and can be used to filter messages, prioritize electronic mail, trigger work flow, and so on. Office workers use high-level declarative rules to "build" expert systems in the intelligent office.

These technologies and their integration in intelligent offices are explored at greater depth in the coming chapters.

■ 1.6 SCENARIO

The following scenario demonstrates the usage and integration of these technologies in the intelligent office model. This office environment is a composite of several real-life corporate information management situations. The central character is Derek, the MIS manager.

The company's board of directors has discovered that an ever-increasing number of their employees are spending much of their time sorting and processing paper documents. The documents arrive by fax, courier, and mail from branch offices and customers.

The company is successful, and the volume of paperwork is growing. To handle the increasing volume, the company can either hire more employees or use current employees more efficiently. Derek has the task of researching this second alternative.

1.6 Scenario ■ 15

He contacts his computer dealers and attends the AIIM (Association of Information and Image Management) show—the retail shelves offer nothing. He is reassured by the confident smile of systems sales reps and by all those amazing things he saw at AIIM. (As yet, he is happily innocent of the subsequent conversation between the rep and the systems engineer (SE), or the months of work that went into the solutions demonstrated at the show.)

His first step with the SE is to interview the managers and employees involved in the current paper-flow system. They map out a detailed flowchart of the current system, including projected volumes and sources. At this point it becomes clear that more than one solution is necessary—in fact, the following independent components are needed, and they all must work together seamlessly:

- *Storage*: Currently, papers that have completed their journey are sorted by date and number in order to be stacked downstairs in the overcrowded file room. Each paper waits for its sister documents, identified by the same ID number, to arrive, be matched up, and then be sorted into an even bigger mountain in the basement. In the company's prime city location, the lease on this storage space does not bear thinking about. When exceptions crop up, unlucky employees must make a pilgrimage to the file room or the basement.
- *Corporate Databases*: Many employees have two machines on their desks: an IBM PC for word processing and spreadsheet and a terminal connected to a host database server used for entering thousands of keystrokes daily from the papers. Many of the terminals are 3270-based systems. If the information in the papers is to be stored on computers, then naturally these computers should talk to those computers (shouldn't they?), eliminating this part of the data entry process entirely.
- *Scanning*: The papers arrive in the mail room. Before they can be used in a computer-based work flow, they must first be converted into electronic form. This need has been met through volume scanning in the mail room, including rescanning of error-filled images and back-file conversion! (This last step frequently is more expensive than the cost of purchasing an entire computer network and software to handle the work flow.)

Fortunately, some branch offices fax their papers, allowing faster response and potentially direct input to the work flow. These branches could send hard copies of the papers via second-class mail for archival.

- *Raw Data to Information to Knowledge*: Having established the benefits of optical storage over mountains of paper for archive, the papers need to be in electronic form. Why not automate the data entry process by using OCR and then use that text data to update the corporate database link?
- *Perusal*. All of the data stored in text form should be stored on optical media to provide access for multiple employees and to allow exception handling (the order was delayed two weeks—now where is the original invoice?). Tools must be provided to access the data from a server and to create reports and summaries. Currently, one

employee's entire job is to read all of the weekly output from the host system, wade through it, and enter certain figures into a spreadsheet.
- *Hard Copy*: Sometimes copies of papers need to accompany correspondence sent back to the source of those papers. Reports also need to be regularly generated for the managers and board.

Finally, if the system is successful, the board of directors intend to plan an entirely new service and want it to be controlled electronically from scratch, with the pilot scheme to start next month.

The needs described in the above "scenario" application could be met by some of the technologies of intelligent offices, including imaging, indexing, OCR, tighter integration with corporate/server data, and integrated environment.

■ 1.7 SUMMARY

The model of the intelligent office provides integrated solutions to solve the information glut of today's offices. These solutions are achieved by incorporating multi-media object spaces and allowing office workers to share information concurrently in client/server architectures. Besides organizing the heterogeneous information in offices, intelligent office solutions also facilitate the communication and flow of information in office environments. The intelligent office uses object-oriented modeling and programming paradigms to represent and model the "universe" of office workers electronically. This modeling and computerized representation of the office worker's environment is as close to the real world as possible.

The model of the intelligent office utilizes a wide range of powerful hardware and software technologies, described in the following chapters.

2

OPTICAL STORAGE TECHNOLOGIES

■ 2.1 INTRODUCTION

The world is currently in the midst of an information explosion the likes of which has never been seen. Entire warehouses are being filled with critical corporate data. This information explosion has driven hardware manufacturers to develop storage devices with ever-increasing capacities.

This chapter describes the state of the art in optical disk mass storage technology. Optical storage is an essential member of the intelligent office storage hierarchy, which is designed to retrieve information for the entire corporation. In the intelligent office, this technology will be used to store and retrieve the data-intensive, multi-media object types.

Mass storage has engendered a whole new way of thinking about text, image, and data and their manipulation. The removal of memory limitations in mass storage allows a great amount of information to be stored for easy access, even if this information requires gigabytes of space on the storage device. Thus, multiple representations of information can exist at different points in information networks or hierarchies. These multiple representations of information can be linked to each other in a variety of ways. In one type of application (hypertext), associative links are constructed that allow the user to browse through information in a highly flexible fashion.

Getting all this information into memory in the first place is made possible on a grand scale because of optical scanning and electronic publishing. Optical scanning and electronic publishing provide data in a machine-readable form. Without these technologies, text and data must be input through the keyboard. This creates a bottleneck where it is almost impossible for new information to be added to a database as fast as it is produced. Optical scanning is discussed at length in Chapter 6.

Optical disks provide cost-effective media for the storage of large volumes of data, such as those encountered in hypermedia applications. Compared with magnetic media, the characteristics of optical disks can be summarized as follows:

    1. *Removability and transportability*: Although some magnetic media, such as floppy disks and magnetic tapes, share these characteristics, optical disks are more rugged and can be transported without fear of data loss.

17

2. *Higher storage densities*: Compared to magnetic technologies, optical disks are much denser. Magnetic bit densities, measured in bits per square inch (bpsi), are about 4×10^7 bpsi. Optical (write-once) bit densities are two orders of magnitude greater at better than 10^9 bpsi.

3. *Lower cost*: One of the results of the higher density of optical disks is their lower storage costs. Optical disks are orders of magnitude cheaper in bit-per-dollar terms than magnetic disks. This ratio will continue to improve in favor of optical disks in the future.

4. *Longer archival life*: Archival life of magnetic media is about 2 to 3 years. In comparison, the archival life of optical media is from 30 to 100 years. Recent improvements in optical media technology have significantly improved the life of the media. Sony now guarantees that its media will last a minimum of 100 years, the current standard for media longevity, and other manufacturers will soon follow suit. As the technology continues to mature, the life expectancy of optical media will continue its upward climb.

Optical disks do have several drawbacks:

1. *Slower access*. Although it depends upon the particular drive and technology, optical disk drive seek times may be significantly longer than those of magnetic disks.

2. *Higher error rates*. The high error rates encountered with optical media necessitate the use of special error detection and correction mechanisms to improve data quality.

2.1.1 Chapter Organization

This chapter describes the characteristics of existing and forthcoming optical media technologies with respect to CD-ROMs (compact disc read-only memory), WORMs (write-once, read-many), and erasable optical media. The discussion will emphasize the technology per se and will not delve into the applications that will use this technology. The use of this technology in the intelligent office is presented. Opportunities for applying the technology to the intelligent office are also described in Chapters 3, 4, 5, and 6.

After the characteristics of the media and hardware itself are described, the algorithms and strategies required to yield high-performance optical storage systems will be discussed. Section 2.5 examines issues of optical disk performance issues, and Section 2.6 describes the optical disk file system solutions. Section 2.7 presents optical jukebox technology, which plays a key role in office storage solutions. Section 2.8 provides a brief overview of the future of optical disk systems. Section 2.9 discusses how optical technologies will be used in the office.

■ 2.2 CD-ROM

CD-ROM (Compact Disc Read-Only Memory) is by far the best-known optical technology, due to the overwhelming acceptance of the compact disc (CD) by the music recording industry.

The CD-ROM media utilizes a 120-mm plastic substrate, which protects the inner, reflective layer. The data, in digital format, is physically stamped into the substrate of the disk. The digital data can be seen under a microscope as a series of flat spots and bumps or indentations. The flat spots generate a binary zero, while the bumps or indentations generate a binary one. This data is permanent and cannot be changed; the user cannot write data to the CD-ROM.

The CD-ROM discs are created through a process known as "mastering." The original data, stored on multiple nine-track tapes, is sent to the premastering facility, where it is downloaded to disk and converted into the proper format for CD-ROM. The premaster is then sent to the mastering facility.

Figure 2.1 illustrates an example of the CD-ROM mastering process. The premaster is used to produce the master, from which the actual production disks are made. The disk substrate (the outside sandwich layers) are injection molded from the master using polymethylmethacrylate, a plastic polymer compound. A reflective metallic alloy, generally based on gold or silver, is coated onto the inner surface of the substrate.

As with all optical technology, the data is read through the use of lasers. The bumps or pits created during the mastering cause a change in the reflectivity of the disk. The

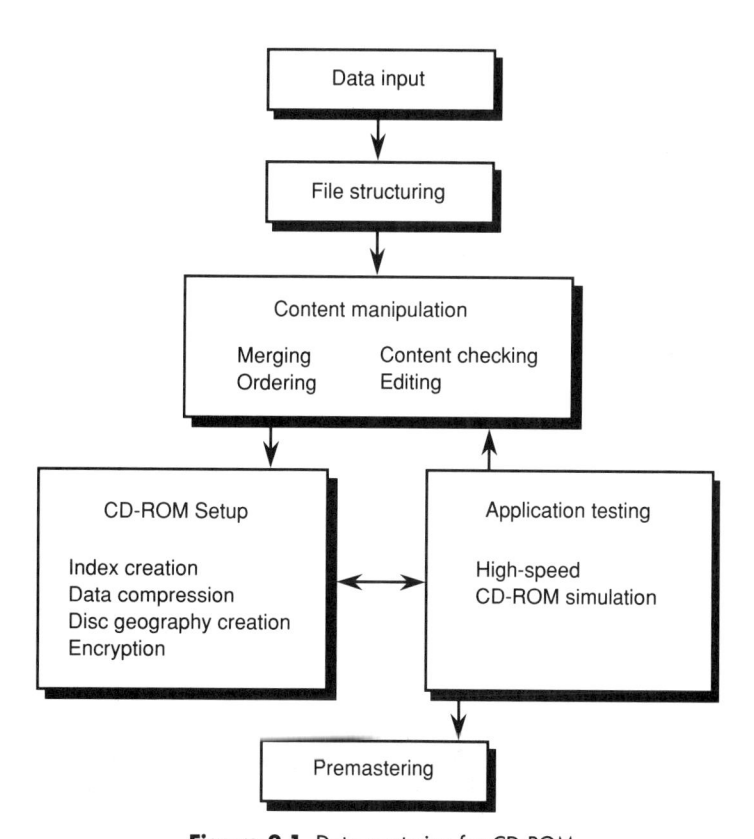

Figure 2.1 Data mastering for CD-ROM.

reflective change is found by precisely focusing the laser in the spiral groove. The change in reflectivity is then perceived as digital data by a photodetector.

CD-ROMs use a laser that produces light in the blue part of the spectrum, far more powerful than the red spectrum lasers used by WORM and erasable drives. The blue-light laser achieves data densities far superior to that of the red, allowing over 800 megabytes of storage on a single side of the CD-ROM disk. Figure 2.2 illustrates how the photodetector reads optical data.

Interfacing the CD-ROM drive to a host computer is accomplished through the use of the SCSI (Small Computer Systems Interface) interface. SCSI was derived from SASI (Shugart Associates Standard Interface) and has become the de facto standard interface for optical technology.

The CD-ROM industry has been very successful in the area of establishing standards. A formal group comprised of industry experts was formed to bring these standards into existence. This committee, known as the High Sierra Group, created strict guidelines for disk, drive, and file formats. These guidelines, known as the High Sierra format, serve as a de facto standard that allows CD-ROM disks and data to be interchanged regardless of the drive or host computer system and is a major factor in the widespread acceptance of CD-ROM by corporate America.

CD-ROMs are currently in widespread use as a distribution medium for infrequently changing reference data (such items as magazines, encyclopedias, and catalogs). CD-ROMs have quite literally become libraries for the computer industry. Many large companies are placing company information (such as employee lists) onto CD-ROM for distribution.

Since the music and computer versions of CD-ROM use the same mastering and production equipment and the sales volume of music CDs has been so great, CD-ROMs have become inexpensive. A CD-ROM drive, complete with software and SCSI interface

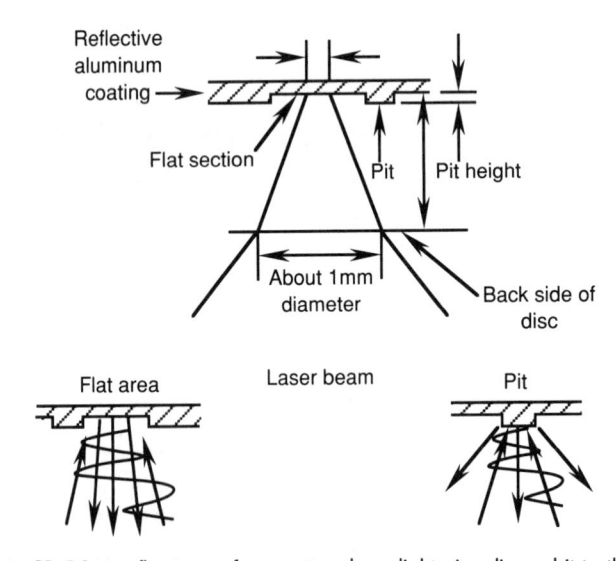

Figure 2.2 Pit in CD-ROM reflective surface scatters laser light, signaling a bit to the photodetector.

equipment, can be purchased for $800 to $1000, giving CD-ROM mass market appeal. Dataquest of San Jose, California, has predicted that more than 1.3 million CD-ROMs will have been delivered for calendar year 1991.

2.2.1 CD-ROMs in the Intelligent Office

CD-ROM will play an important role in the Intelligent Office by meeting the vital need to mass-replicate static information cheaply. CD-ROM allows information to be widely distributed and replicated, thereby improving the accessibility of that information.

Entire libraries of books and information can be placed on-line at each office. These on-line libraries, combined with the ability to perform full-text searches, greatly enhance the office workers' ability to glean useful information.

The distribution of corporate employee phone directories is another area where CD-ROM contributes to the intelligent office. In large corporations it becomes extremely difficult to determine who is in charge of what, where they are located, and how they can be reached. CD-ROM allows a corporate-wide employee "yellow pages" to be installed at each office of the corporation. This phone directory can be connected to the E-mail and fax services, allowing information to be sent to all employees.

■ 2.3 WORM

WORM (write-once, read many) technology differs from CD-ROM in that the data is not prestamped but written during run time. A WORM sector may be written only once; it cannot be overwritten. Capacities range from 115 megabytes per side up to 5 gigabytes per side. WORM drives come in various physical sizes ranging from $5\frac{1}{4}''$ up to 14''.

WORM drives use a single read/write head, unlike Winchester drives. This is due mainly to the high cost of the optical head assembly as well as to media format concerns. Most optical disks in use today are double-sided. To access the data on the other side, the disk must be physically flipped over.

2.3.1 History

Write-once technology, developed from a concept first conceived in the 1930s, has been commercially available for approximately 10 years. The technology was pioneered in the mid-1970s by Acatel Thomsom Gigadisc at Toulouse, France; Philips in the Netherlands; and Xerox at Palo Alto, California. These companies built the foundation on which current optical technology is based.

In 1981, Toshiba Corporation of Tokyo, Japan, contracted SRI International to develop a document-filing system based on optical storage. In 1983, Optimem, then a division of Xerox, announced a 12'' drive. Acatel Thomson Gigadisc (ATG) also announced its 12'' drive the same year. Drives were available in production quantities by 1984. All were in 12'' format. Other companies, such as Laser Magnetic Storage International (LMSI), formerly Optical Storage International, released their own 12'' WORM drives. Olympus Optical Co. Ltd. and Fujitsu Ltd., during this same time frame, began a joint venture that resulted in one of the first commercially available write-once products.

The early drives were all based on a 12'' platform. With the increase in popularity of the personal computer, work began on a smaller, $5\frac{1}{4}''$ form for write-once storage.

January 1985 saw the first $5\frac{1}{4}''$ drive released by Information Storage Inc (ISI) of Colorado Springs, Colorado, with 115 megabytes of storage. Optotech, also of Colorado Springs, announced a 200-megabyte drive, which began shipping in late 1985. Much of the disk manufacturing and format techniques used by WORM technology were first developed by the video disk industry.

The early years of write-once optical storage were plagued with unreliable drives, bad media, poor performance, and limited commercial quantities. End users were not convinced that the technology was real and were unwilling to entrust their data to WORM media.

Today's optical market paints an entirely different picture. There are currently over 17 manufacturers offering $5\frac{1}{4}''$ products and 6 manufacturers offering $12''$ drives. The technology has matured and is now very reliable, while improvements in the optical head design have reduced seek times from 250 milliseconds to under 50 milliseconds.

2.3.2 The Technology

Write-once drives are based on the use of a solid-state diode laser to physically "burn" large quantities of digital data into the active inner layer of the media. Optical drives generally come with the following subassemblies:

- A logic unit, which controls the power output of the diode laser, the drive servos, and disk access mechanisms
- A linear motor, which moves the optical head assembly
- Solid-state diode laser and photodetector
- A single optical head assembly that is actuated for both vertical and radial positioning of the optical head assembly
- High-powered error correction circuitry that enables multiple data errors to be corrected in real time
- Servo units, which control the laser focusing, tracking, seeking, and disk spin functions
- An intelligent drive controller, which implements the interface between the host and the drive

Figure 2.3 illustrates a typical optical laser assembly.

Data can be accessed randomly or sequentially. Reading is accomplished through the principles of light diffraction of the laser beam. The lasers used for WORM drives, such as the 20 mW gallium-aluminum-arsenide (GaAlAs) semiconductor diode laser, produce a coherent beam of red light that focuses on the active layer of the disk. The laser writes data at about 8 to 12 milliwatts, reads data at 1 milliwatt, and idles at around .01 milliwatt.

Writing data is accomplished by thermal alteration of the thin film, generally composed of a rare earth metal, inside the disk. In one method the laser beam creates gases under the surface of the heat-sensitive film, forming bubbles or pits, which alter the disk's reflectivity. Other methods include using the laser to burn a pit or hole into the active

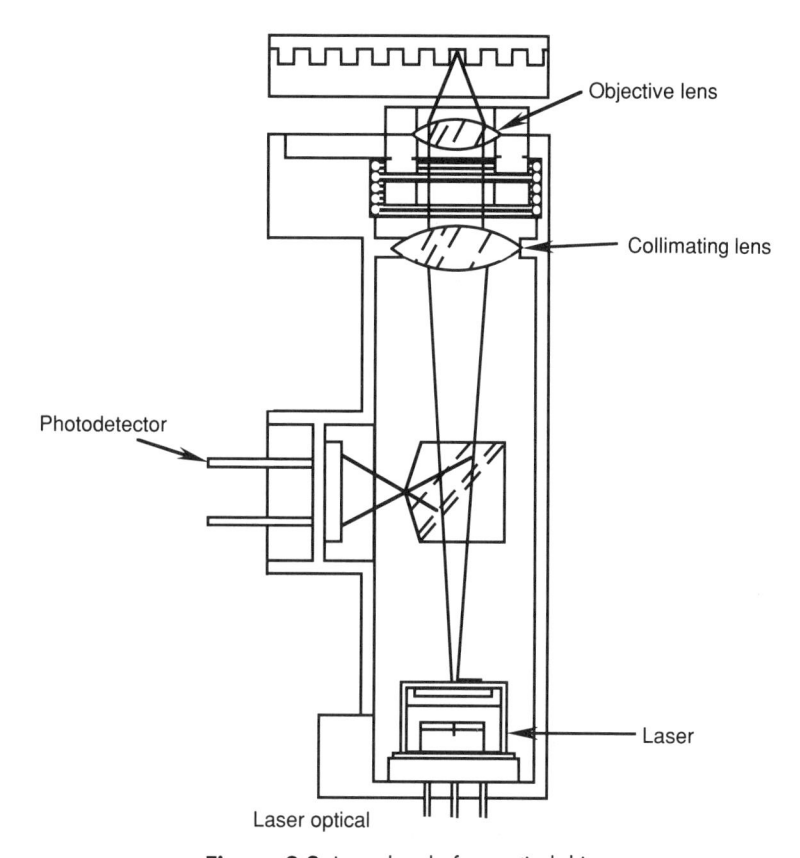

Figure 2.3 Laser head of an optical drive.

layer or to change the molecular structure by fusing two compounds together. Figures 2.4a and b compare the ablative (pit) and thermal (bubble) recording methods.

Reading of data is accomplished when the laser, at low power and combined with a sophisticated decoder, detects changes in the reflectivity of the active layer. Generally, a lowering of the reflectivity indicates a binary one, while the normal disk surface is interpreted as a zero. Some drives, such as the LMSI LD1200, use a proprietary coding scheme where a zero is also encoded with a sequence of pits and not the absence of them.

Perhaps the most notable feature of WORM technology is the incredible data densities that are achievable. The high-intensity laser records one bit of information on the optical medium in a space that is approximately one micron in diameter. Recording densities range from 15,000 bits per inch (bpi) up to 32,200 bpi. Sector sizes range from 256 bytes to 4K bytes.

Disks are formatted with a continuous, logical address scheme, with up to 1.6 million sectors per disk side and 40,000 to 50,000 tracks. The tracks are spaced about 1.6 microns apart, yielding a density range of 15,000 to 16,000 tracks per inch (tpi). Disk capacities range from 230 megabytes per disk to over 10 gigabytes.

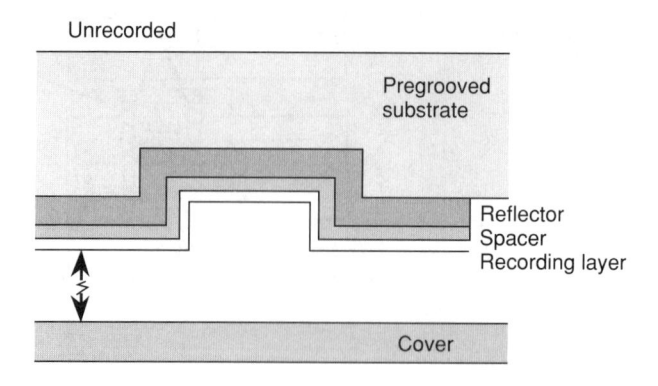

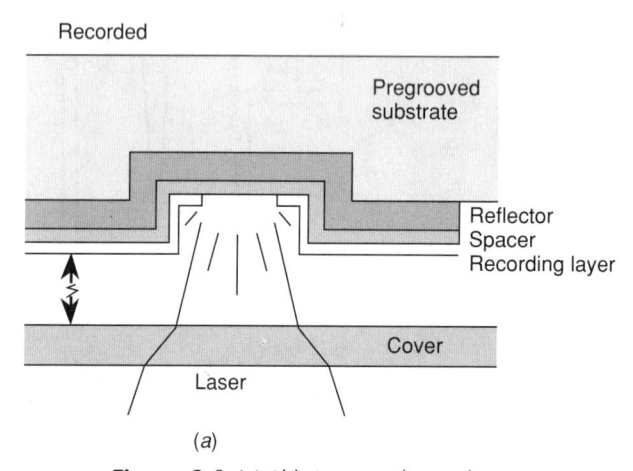

Figure 2.4 (a) Ablative recording technique.

2.3.3 Optical Media

Media technology varies widely in the write-once arena. The write-once media varieties can be broken down into three major categories: pit-forming, bubble-forming, and molecular change. The disks consist of an active inner layer, which is sandwiched between layers of a glass or plastic substrate. The following media types are currently in popular use:

- *Tellurium oxide/tellurium alloy*: This medium was the first write-once recording film developed and is currently the most widely used. A thin film of a tellurium alloy, generally tellurium, chrome, and silver, is coated onto this interior of the substrate in a process called "sputtering".

  Tellurium, a rare earth metal, is used because it heats rapidly, allowing relatively low-power lasers to create pits or bubbles in the recording surface. Tellurium is also very resistant to oxidation even at melting temperatures, thereby greatly extending

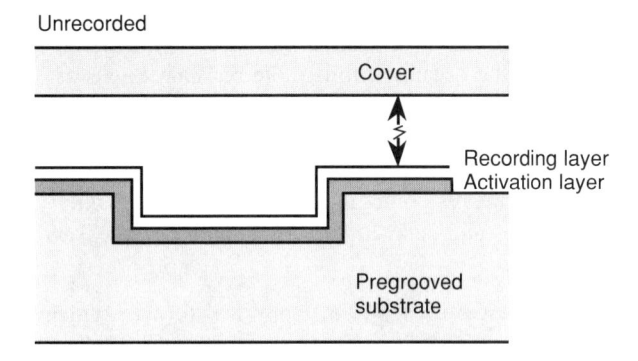

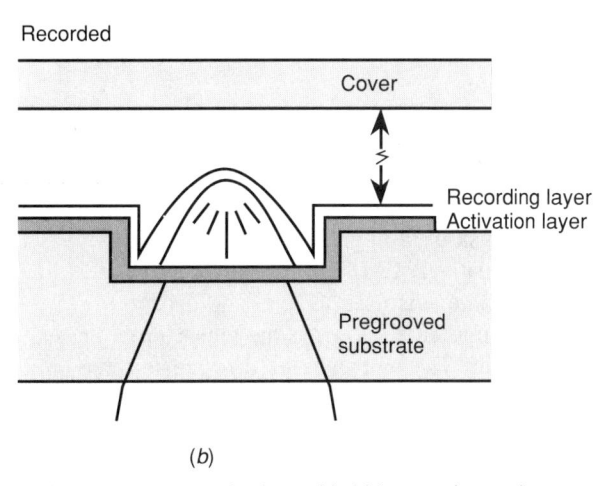

Figure 2.4 (cont) (b) Thermal-bubble recording technique.

the archival life of the media. The drawbacks of this recording film are the toxicity of tellurium and the expense of sputtering to create the disk.

- *Bimetallic alloy*: This recording technique, first developed by Sony, is based on the principles of metal fusion. The medium is created by successively sputtering two different metals, generally bismuth and a sodium-based metal, onto the substrate.

  During the writing process, the laser, in its high-power mode, fuses the two metals together, creating an alloy with a different albedo (reflectivity) factor. The archival life of this medium is claimed to be superior to that of tellurium, but the process of sputtering two different metals onto the substrate make it more costly.

- *Dye-polymer*: Dye-polymer technology is the latest development in optical recording films. The dye-polymer, created from organic-based compounds such as methine, is placed on the substrate using spin-coating equipment. (Spin coating is currently in widespread use for manufacturing magnetic floppy and Winchester media.)

Data marks are created when the laser burns the dye polymer, causing bubbles to form and thereby changing its reflectivity. This medium claims the best archival life, since the organic film is more resistant to corrosion from oxidation.

The reflective layer is sandwiched within the substrate. The seal created is airtight to prevent oxidation of the metals. The laser focuses through the substrate, a distance of about 1.2 millimeters, onto this reflective layer, making the optical disk immune to surface scratches and dust. Figure 2.5 illustrates typical write-once media.

2.3.3.1 Media Format

Optical media come with a "hard" physical format, which is pressed into the substrate during mastering. The format impressed into the substrate is used for such things as addressing, servo synchronization, tracking, and error correction.

Two types of substrates are in use for optical media: plastic and glass. The plastic is composed of an optical-grade polymer known as polymethylmethacrylate (PMMA). The format, known as pregroove, is embossed on the plastic substrate via injection molding with the master.

Glass substrate disks are virtually identical to plastic disks except that the material used is a chemically tempered glass. The pregroove is created by pressing the glass sustrate, coated with a PMMA resin, against a master disk, containing the negative of the pregroove, and polymerizing the resin with ultraviolet light.

The master disk used in creating the glass pregroove is very expensive to make, and they wear out relatively fast. To increase the productive life of the master, a hierarchical parent-child technique is used for pressing disks.

The original master is known as the father. From the father another master is created, called the mother. The mother is used to create three children master disks. The third child is used to create production disks. When the third child wears out, the second child is used to recreate it. This process is repeated on up the hierarchy. Whenever a master disk wears out, the hierarchically superior master is used to recreate that master.

Figure 2.5 Typical write-once disks.

A typical optical pregroove contains information for synchronization, radial tracking, laser focusing, sector addressing, and rotational control. Data is written in the valley of the groove, while the top of the groove is used for tracking. The pregroove information controls the intensity of the laser, produces various signals needed for sampling the tracking and laser focus, and triggers the drive clock for read/write operations. The sector size is fixed and may not be changed.

Two forms of pregroove track are used by the WORM industry: concentric and continuous spiral. Some manufacturers arrange sectors into concentric tracks, in an arrangement similar to that used by magnetic disks. This presents a disadvantage for sustained data transfers, because the data flow must be interrupted to physically move the write head to the next track, reducing the transfer rate. The advantage of this method is that multi-head, multi-platter disk systems are easier to implement.

Since most current WORM drives use a single read/write head (LMS has released a dual-headed optical drive), an innovative scheme was developed to maximize the sustained data transfer rates. This scheme, involving the use of a single pregroove track spiraling from the center of the disk outward, is now used by the majority of WORM drives. This allows long data transfers to occur without interruption, giving WORM drives an advantage over Winchester drives for massive data transfers.

The disadvantage is that the head must constantly be repositioned to remain on the same track. This fact eliminates the use of sector interleave when recording data on WORM drives. It will also make the future development of multi-head systems a bit more tricky (the direction of the spiral would be reversed on one side).

2.3.3.2 *CLV versus CAV*

There are currently two basic methods for spinning the disk to store data with write-once drives. One method is to spin the disk with constant angular velocity (CAV), or the same rotational speed in revolutions per minute (RPM) at all times. The second method is to spin the disk with constant linear velocity (CLV). This method ensures that the speed of the medium spinning directly under the read/write heads is the same at all time. Figures 2.6 and 2.7 illustrate the difference between CLV and CAV media.

The data density varies in CAV, with the number of bpi on the outside edge of the disk being the lowest. This implies that CAV media store less data than CLV. Its main advantage is faster transfer rates. With CLV media, the drive must vary the RPM with head distance from the disk outer edges. Data density is the same throughout the disk, but data transfer becomes slower the further the head gets away from the center. This is a classic tradeoff of transfer rate versus density.

2.3.4 WORM Technology in the Intelligent Office

As mentioned at the beginning of the chapter, optical storage is the vital piece of technology that allows the intelligent office to incorporate the new, data-intensive multi-media objects. Without the storage capacities of optical disks, data types such as images, video, or sound would not be practical. (These data types are discussed in detail in Chapter 9.)

The use of optical media as the primary form of archival storage for all the office objects is perhaps its most important contribution. The storage hierarchy of the intelligent office allows for infrequently used office objects, such as documents and folders, to be archived onto optical storage. At this point the archive may be stored in a jukebox if

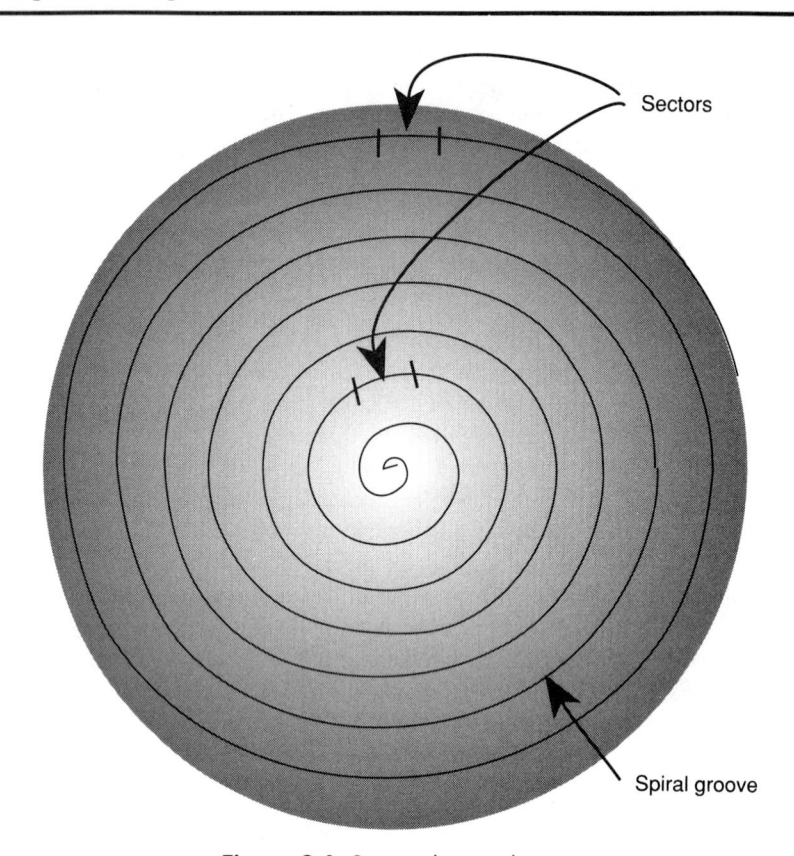

Figure 2.6 Constant linear velocity.

more frequent access is needed, or it may be stored off-line and be brought back on-line if the need ever arises.

■ 2.4 ERASABLE OPTICAL DISKS

The newest arrival on the optical technology scene is the erasable optical drive. Erasable optical drives offer the same rewrite capabilities currently offered by magnetic media. This breakthrough allows optical technology to enter new markets and fill the requirements of new applications.

2.4.1 History

As with WORM technology, the theory behind erasable optical media was discovered back in the 1930s. The hurdle that has prevented erasable technology from being commercially available till now is the recording film. It has taken years of research to develop a medium that can be successively written and erased thousands of times.

Phase-change technology was patented by Energy Conversion Devices (EDC), a media manufacturer based in Troy, Michigan, in the 1960s. Matsushita of Japan (mother company of Panasonic) and IBM both licensed the phase-change technology from EDC

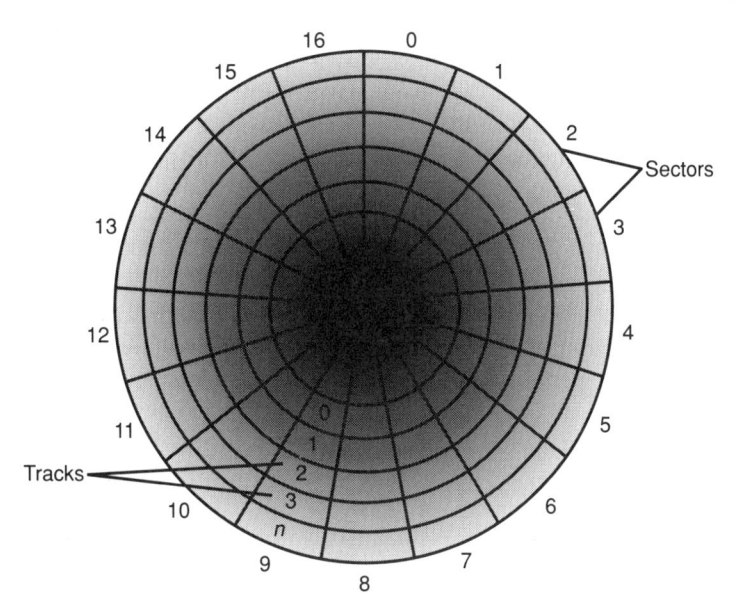

Figure 2.7 Constant angular velocity.

in the early 1980s. Matsushita produced a prototype erasable disk by 1983 and demonstrated an improved version in 1991. No word of IBM's plan has been heard, but analysts believe that the company is also experimenting with magneto-optics.

The erasable drives currently on the market are all based on magneto-optics. Sony appears to be the leader at the moment, but other manufacturers, such as Maxtor and Pioneer, have begun shipping production quantities of erasable drives.

The other two major technology players are Canon and Olympus. Canon is supplying the drives that used to be the primary rotating media for Steve Jobs's NeXT computer (a 660-megabyte Winchester drive has, due to transfer rates, since replaced the erasable optical disk as the primary storage unit). Olympus is supplying its engine to other drive manufacturers such as Ricoh, allowing those companies to bring a product to market without years of R&D. Maxtor has begun shipment of its Tahiti line of magneto-optical drives in quantity.

There are three distinct technologies for erasable optics: magneto-optics, phase change, and dye-polymer.

2.4.2 Magneto-Optics

Magneto-optics, the only commercially available erasable technology, combines the principles of WORM technology with that of magnetics. The recording film is based on a combination of rare earth and transition metals, such as cobalt, gadolinium, terbium, and dysprosium, that possesses a vary stable magnetic field at normal temperatures. It is unaffected by even the strongest external magnetic field.

The data is written by using a solid-state diode laser, similar to those used by WORM technology, to heat a spot on the recording layer to 150° Celsius, energizing the molecular structure of the film to the point that the magnetic field becomes volatile—where the Curie temperature (the temperature above which the net magnetization is zero) is exceeded. At this point a large magnetic coil is passed underneath the medium, creating highly differentiated regions of opposite magnetization.

This magnetization difference creates a laser beam light polarization known as the Kerr effect. The change in polarity effects a change in the reflectivity of the recording film. This change is detected by the optical decoder and interpreted as data.

The major hurdle in creating a commercially viable product was the development of a recording film whose magnetic field became unstable at tolerable temperature. Early films required temperatures of over 300° Celsius to destabilize the field, causing the recording surface to burn up after a minimal number of erasures. Today's films have overcome the problem and have been certified to be erasable over one million times.

A performance bottleneck exists with the current magneto-optic technology. A sector cannot be directly overwritten, requiring data to be written in three passes. The sector must be erased on the first pass, the data written on the second pass, and the sector verified on the third pass. Even though magneto-optic drives boast access times shorter than 30 sub-thirty milliseconds, superior to that of WORM, the effective transfer rate is quite slow and will prevent these drives from competing with Winchester technology for the present.

This problem will eventually be solved in a two-phase process. Phase 1 will see a two-laser optical head developed, so that the first laser will erase the sector while the second laser writes the data in the same pass. Phase 2 will see the development of new recording films that will eliminate the need to erase the sector first.

2.4.3 Phase Change

Phase change technology is based on the crystalline properties of certain chemical polymers. A phase change medium contains a smooth, amorphous recording film, using various combinations of tellurium, gadolinium, selenium, antimony, and germanium, which can be altered by the diode laser.

Data is written to the phase change disk by rapidly modulating the power output of the laser as it records. High-intensity bursts from the laser cause the polymer to form a crystalline structure, around 1 micron in diameter, which is light-absorbent (less reflective), while a low-power shot from the laser will cause a spot on the recording film to relax the crystaline structure and return to the more stable amorphous state, one which reflects light.

Phase change offers an advantage over magneto-optics in that a sector may be directly overwritten, providing for much higher transfer rates. It also uses recording materials that are very similar to write-once media, allowing multifunction drives to be produced.

Pioneer has recently released the first of the true multifunction drives—those that can handle both erasable and write-once disks. Other companies, such as Sony, have claimed to have a multifunction drive, but it is actually an erasable drive that has a switch the user can set to treat the erasable disk as write-once.

The problem that prevented phase change from being commercially available in the past is that of media erasure longevity. Phase change media tended to break down after a few thousand erasures. Pioneer, a leader in optical technology, has completely scrapped its magneto-optics project and has recently released a phase change erasable drive in the belief that magneto-optics is merely an interim technology that will be replaced by phase change.

2.4.4 Dye-Polymer

There is yet a third erasable technology, which employs various dye-polymer recording materials. This technology utilizes the heat generated by a solid-state diode laser to create light-refracting bubbles within a thermoplastic layer, which define individual bits of data. To erase the data, a second laser or a different wavelength is used to relax the bubbles, returning the dye polymer to its original state. This technology is still very much in its infancy and is at least several years away from being commercially available.

2.5 PERFORMANCE

Optical drives have unique performance characteristics that must be taken into account when developing software around this technology. Structures used in managing magnetic media must often be forgotten.

The following are the performance-related characteristics of optical disks:

1. High storage densities
2. Longer archival life
3. Slower access times
4. Higher error rates (discussed in Section 2.1)

CD-ROM is the slowest performer in the optical arena. This is due to the fact that CD-ROMs are treated as byte-addressable devices, a notion that works fine for the music industry but makes for a poor-performing file system. CD-ROM also uses CLV media, giving maximum storage at the cost of performance. The average access times are from 500 to 1000 milliseconds.

Erasable optical drives are next on the performance list. They offer the fastest access times, between 29 to 40 milliseconds, but slow transfer rates. The transfer rates are adversely affected by the need to erase a sector (magneto-optics) before writing it, as discussed in Section 2.4.2.

WORM drives offer the best performance and longest media archival life. WORM drives offer access times of from 65 to 180 milliseconds. Sustained transfer rates range from 100 to 650Kbytes per second, with burst rate capabilities reaching 1 megabyte per second or better.

The terms "seek time" and "access time" are frequently and incorrectly used interchangeably when referring to both Winchester and optical drives. Seek time is the time required for the head to move from one random track to another. Access time is defined as the seek time plus the latency of the drive. Latency time is defined as the time required for the first byte of desired data to pass underneath the read/write head.

Optical drives generally suffer slower seek times than Winchester drives due to the mass of the optical head assembly (between 50 and 200 grams). Long seeks should be minimized with optical drives.

Optical drives use both a coarse seek and a fine seek, which is superior to that of Winchester drives, when accessing a sector. The coarse seek requires the entire head assembly to be moved to a given location, an expensive operation. Fine seeks are accomplished through the use of a radial lens motor to reposition the laser beam, via a tilting mirror, to a certain number of tracks on either side of the current track without moving the optical head assembly.

Fine seeks have an access time of from 1 to 5 milliseconds, much faster than any Winchester drive. This "data window" is a significant advantage that should be incorporated into any optical access software.

The single-spiral format of optical disks gives optical drives a distinct advantage for the transfer of large data files. The reading of large data files, in particular, can be accomplished with better transfer rates than on Winchester drives.

2.5.1 Error Correction

All types of optical media suffer from a very high raw bit error rate. This is due to the laser's sensitivity to any imperfections in the recording film. For the optical medium to be error free, the surface of the film would have to be flawlessly smooth, uniformly thick, and with no impurities in the alloy or polymer. The format embossed in the substrate would have to be flawless as well.

Current manufacturing techniques cannot come close to those specs; therefore, optical media suffer from an unacceptable raw bit error rate, with one byte out of every thousand bits read being in error. This error rate is eight orders of magnitude greater than that experienced by magnetic media.

In order to compensate for this error rate, optical drives employ sophisticated error correction codes (ECCs) using a mathematical technique known as the Reed-Solomon code, reducing the error rate from 1 in 10^{-4} down to 1 in 10^{-12} or 10^{-14}, equaling or bettering the error rates of Winchester drives.

There are various different Reed-Solomon formulas in use today, known by such names as "long-distance codes" or "product codes." The ECC is computed as a function of all the data in the sector. Before the block is written, the ECC (a Reed-Solomon polynomial) is calculated in real time using hardware error detection and correction (EDAC) circuitry. The ECC is stored after the last data byte in the sector. Figure 2.8 shows the structure of an optical sector.

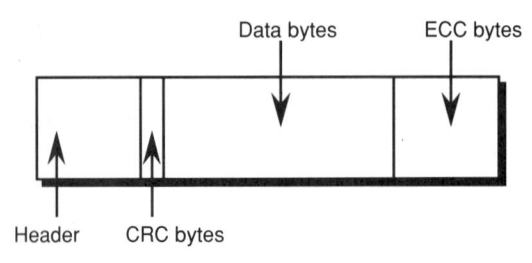

Figure 2.8 Structure of an optical disk sector.

When the sector is read, the ECC is recalculated and compared against the original ECC written in the sector. If differences are found, the original data can be reconstructed even if multiple bits or even bytes are in error.

The exact number of bytes that may be corrected depends both on the Reed-Solomon algorithm used and on the number of ECC bytes employed. The more bytes used for ECC, referred to as "redundancy," the more errors can be corrected. Some manufacturers employ Reed-Solomon algorithms that use 100 percent redundancy, allowing the data to be correctly read even if the entire sector is in error. The ECC bytes themselves are generally protected by multiple Cyclic Redundancy Check (CRC) bytes.

The Reed-Solomon ECC is not capable of correcting every sector written. Some sectors, due to irregularities in the substrate or recording film, cannot be written at all. This fact imposes a requirement that all data written to optical media must be verified. There are two technologies for verification currently in use: direct read after write (DRAW) and direct read during write (DRDW).

Error correction code (ECC) is its own industry within the optical technology field. Companies such as Cyclotomics of Berkeley, California, specialize in developing ECC hardware and software. All optical drives come equipped with advanced ECC firmware, eliminating the need for optical file systems to implement their own ECC.

Other aspects of ECC affect both performance and reliability. All optical media contain bad sectors. Write-once media cannot be mapped, as most bad sectors cannot be found until written to. In light of this, many drives come equipped with a feature known as automatic sector reallocation. In the process of writing data to a sector, if the sector should fail verification, the controller will automatically rewrite or reallocate the data to a new area, called the "spare area." Sectors are reserved on the disk that are only accessible by the controller. This gives the optical medium the appearance of a perfect address space. The manner in which reallocation is implemented greatly affects the performance of disk I/O.

Some manufacturers place the reallocation area on the outermost tracks. Every time a sector is reallocated, the optical head must jump to the outside track, write the data, and then jump back. Subsequent reads of the data cause the same head jumps. In this situation, performance can be significantly improved by implementing bad sector reallocation within the file system (the controller reallocation can be disabled). Sectors should be reallocated within the same data window to prevent the head jumps.

A second aspect of ECC is redundancy. Optical file systems must take steps to ensure the archival safety of data. Sectors on the disk can go "bad" after a period of time due to oxidation; long-term shifting of the substrate, known as "creeping;" and repetitive reads. The heat from the laser during reads can eventually break down the reflective layer.

The file system should not fail just because a single directory link is lost. All critical information, such as directory structures, data pointers, and allocations, must be stored repetitively, in such a manner that if one structure fails, a redundant copy can be used to retrieve the needed information. Redundant data should be stored apart from its twin to reduce the chance that the same disk flaw will destroy both copies. Added safety can also be obtained by placing headers in front of all files so that data may still be retrieved should the entire directory and its redundancy be destroyed.

2.5.2 DRAW versus DRDW

Direct read after write (DRAW) technology performs verification by writing data on the first pass and reading/verifying the data on the second pass of the laser. This method suffers from a serious performance penalty. Each write requires two passes, one for writing and one for verification, cutting the effective transfer rate in half. Drives that use DRAW technology will always have write rates that are half the read rates. Verification is not done automatically. The controller must be commanded to verify the data. DRAW is the only verification method available on Winchester technology.

Direct read during write (DRDW) is a newer technology that allows data to be verified while it is being written. This is accomplished through the use of a two-laser optical head assembly. The first laser is responsible for writing the data. The second laser follows right behind the first laser and verifies each bit immediately after it has been written. This technology eliminates the verification latency, allowing sectors to be verified with no impact on the transfer rates.

Unfortunately, very few optical drives on today's market support DRDW. This is mainly due to the expense of the DRDW optical head. Improvement in laser technology will soon lower the price of the head assembly, and DRDW will become the standard for optical technology.

2.5.3 Clustering

Clustering concerns the optimal method of storing and retrieving data segments from the disk. In the optimal sense, all files should be stored contiguously on the optical disk. Due to the size of the optical head, any fragmentation in a file will cause degradation in transfer rates. Figure 2.9 illustrates the structure of a file when it becomes fragmented.

The algorithm to accomplish this becomes very complex when multiple files or multiple users are allowed to write to the disk at the same time. In fact, the only method to guarantee that all data files will be written contiguously is to allow only one file at a

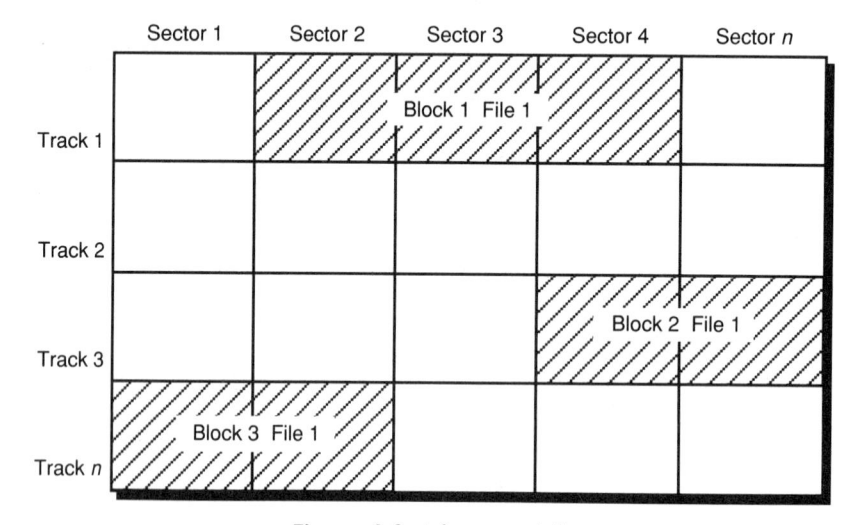

Figure 2.9 A fragmented file.

time to be written to disk. Some systems in fact do this, but it is too large a constraint on the user to be useful.

Two major methods are used to minimize the fragmentation of a file: caching, described later in this chapter, and preallocation.

The preallocation of data blocks allows data to be allocated prior to being written. Data may be dumped directly to disk, since an optimal block size has been allocated. Data may also be appended to a file using this method, keeping new data contiguous with the old. The drawbacks of this method are that data space may be wasted and that allocation tables must be kept and rewritten, adversely affecting performance and disk overhead.

Another important aspect of clustering is that optical data should always be allocated and transferred in large blocks for both reading and writing. Data transfers across the SCSI interface have a set amount of overhead regardless of block size, averaging about 100 milliseconds per transfer. This overhead drastically decreases the effective transfer rate if small block sizes are used. A minimal block size should be 16Kbytes, and block sizes of 64K and above are preferred.

An additional aspect of clustering is that related information, that is, sets of data that will be accessed together, should be stored together on the disk, eliminating long seeks where possible. Figure 2.10 illustrates the concept of storing related information contiguously.

2.5.4 Elevator Seeking

Elevator seeking is an algorithm used to reduce thrashing of the optical head. Multiple requests are placed in a linked list and organized in ascending or descending order from the current head position. This allows all requests to be satisfied with a single unidirectional sweep of the disk head instead of by randomly thrashing back and forth.

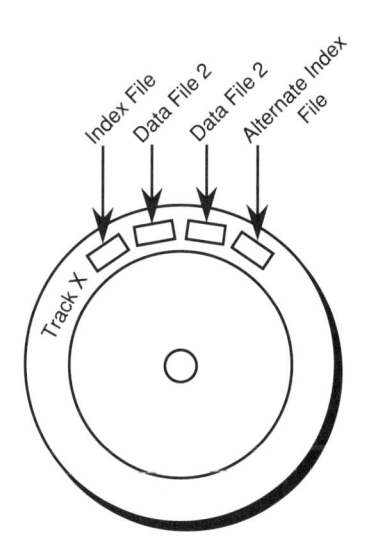

Figure 2.10 Clustering related files.

2.5.5 Caching

Caching is the practice of storing directory information and data blocks in "fast" memory when compared to the original storage. Caching algorithms involve the use of doubly linked lists, which point to, and give information about, directory and data blocks stored in the cache.

Cache memory for optical disks consists of both volatile RAM and high-speed Winchester drive storage. The cache manager routine maintains a list of free cache blocks. When a block is taken off the list to cache data, the block address of the data is put through a hash algorithm to determine which list the block has been assigned to. Figure 2.11 illustrates an example of optical disk caching.

The cache is recycled by using the least-recently-used (LRU) algorithm. When a cache block is accessed, it is placed at the top of the list. Stale data filters its way to the bottom of the list and is either discarded or, if the cached block is "dirty" (has been modified by the application), flushed to the optical disk.

In the case of writing information to the optical disk, caching involves storing data intended for the optical disk on magnetic disk until the file is closed or an optimal block size is filled. At this time the entire data block is dumped to optical in one shot using "lazy allocation" (sectors are allocated when they are written). This method offers minimal file fragmentation and the elimination of all sector allocation tables, but it can be complex to code and will slow performance if improperly designed.

Caching is mandatory for a high-performance optical disk system. New data should be written to cache and flushed asynchronously. Directory information should be obtained from cache whenever possible. Data which is read should also be cached unless the request is for a large block. Large read requests should be dumped directly to user memory.

2.5.6 High-Performance Directory Structures

The capacities of optical media mandate that new approaches be taken in the design of directory structures. Millions of files can be stored in a single optical system. Access to a given file and the data within that file must be within the user's tolerance range. Standard magnetic file system structures (such as found in UNIX, where directories are implemented as files and must be searched sequentially), will deliver very poor performance.

Directories should be implemented as objects, not as files. Each directory is assigned a unique ID, or surrogate, which cannot be reassigned. Files and subdirectories are

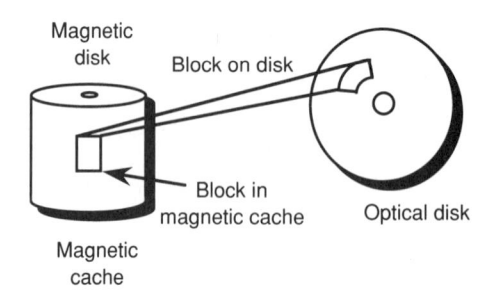

Figure 2.11 Magnetic cache of optical data.

assigned a subordinate membership to the parent directory. This algorithm eliminates sequential searching of directory files and allows for more flexible, high-performance access methods.

The concept of file allocation tables (FATs) must be eliminated from optical structures. FATs are based on the notion that data sectors are erasable and reclaimable. They present a serious overhead on performance. The data pointers for a given file should be stored contiguously with the directory entry for that file so that all information needed to perform file operations may be obtained with a single read. Chaining through a singly linked or indexed FAT table is not acceptable for performance.

Optical structures must support both preallocation and lazy allocation. Allocation operations must be geared in favor of lazy allocation, as this method obtains the high sustained transfer rates, but they must include minimal preallocation structures for improved file update performance. This structure need only define the next available sector on the heap. The directory structure for the file must include information on which data sectors are written and which are preallocated.

Searching techniques for optical technology are numerous. The optical media type lends itself very well to various hashing algorithms. File names and directory names are run through the hash function, based on the binary value of the text strings. A pointer to a directory bucket is placed in the hash table as needed. Files and directories are hashed into the buckets. Figure 2.12 illustrates the concepts of hashed directory access.

Collision overflow can be resolved through the use of linked lists or, alternatively, a binary tree. The hash table must be rewritten and linked together as entries are updated. Old versions of the hash table are used for the history function. The hash table must be stored in memory for acceptable access time.

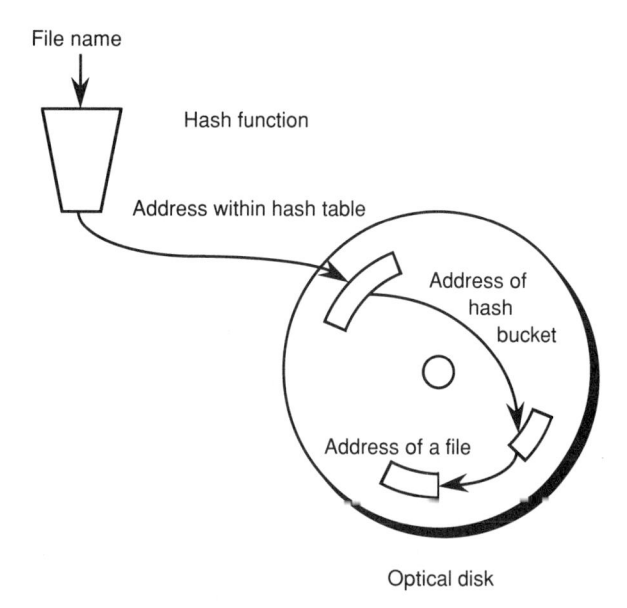

Figure 2.12 Hashed optical directory.

38 ■ Optical Storage Technologies

B-trees can be implemented onto write-once media with good success, given some extra considerations. The node size should be larger than usual, inducing a tree that is bushy while minimizing the number of levels in the tree. The lower the number of levels, the less costly updates are in terms of disk overhead. It also allows more information to be obtained with a single read.

As many index nodes as possible should be stored in cache, minimizing optical accesses. The order in which nodes are written must be adhered to when the B-tree is updated. The leaf node must be written first, followed by each preceding index node from lowest to root. This is necessary because with optical media, successful pointing is only guaranteed when pointing to a sector that has already been written. If the system generates a pointer that points to an unwritten sector, that sector may turn out to be unwritable.

The current root node must be chained to the next older version if historical data access is to be supported. Sequential access is obtained by linking all members of a given directory together.

Another algorithm of interest is to write directory structures to the optical disk in a heap fashion, building the access method during disk initialization. The directory records act as transaction records, recording all changes to the state of the optical disk. When the disk is loaded, the records are read and processed, creating an access structure based on any variety of methods such as B-tree or R-tree. This access structure is then stored on magnetic media.

The advantage of this method is minimal disk overhead and the ability to create or change the access method as needed. The disadvantage is that disk initialization can be lengthy and magnetic support is mandatory.

2.5.7 File Striping

File striping, or declustering (Livney *et al.*, 1987), is a high-performance algorithm based on the distribution of file data in a "stripe" over multiple optical drives. The SCSI interface allows up to eight controllers and 56 slave optical drives to be daisy-chained on a single bus. Instead of dumping a block of data to a single drive, the request is split, with each chunk being stored on a different drive, greatly increasing the effective transfer rates.

Reads are performed in the same fashion, with a single read request being broken into multiple requests, each serviced by a different drive. The directory is generally stored on a single disk, with provisions to extend it to another disk if necessary. All the disks of the stripe set must be initialized, and they become inseparable. New disks cannot be added to the set after initialization.

The directory must keep track of all volumes in the set and must not allow data access if all the set members are not on-line. Data pointers must include a reference to the volume to which they point.

The advantage of this algorithm is significant improvement in transfer rates, effectively transferring data in a multi-processor environment. The disadvantages are the increased complexity of the software coding, the added hardware costs, and the need to ensure that multiple disks are kept together. Figure 2.13 illustrates the concepts of file striping.

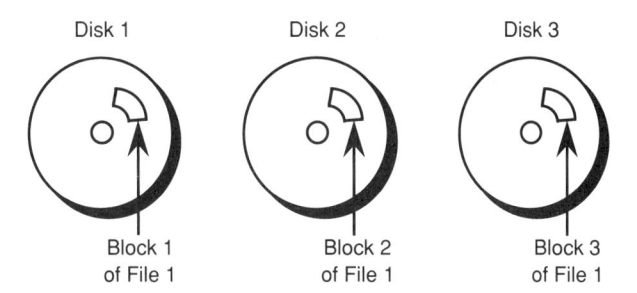

Figure 2.13 Example of file striping.

2.5.8 Multi-Volume Sets

Multi-volume sets treat multiple disks as a single logical, contiguous file system. This allows a given file system to grow virtually without limit. Data is written to disk 1 of the set until that disk is full, whereupon data is then automatically written to the next volume in the set, in effect treating all the disks as a single logical address space.

Multi-volume sets are generally implemented to be independent of each other. In other words, all members of the set do not need to be on-line. Volumes may be preallocated or added as needed. One of the big uses for this algorithm is with optical jukeboxes. Data is dumped continuously to the jukebox, and as each disk is filled up, the old one is swapped out and a new disk is loaded without stopping the data transfer. All disks in the jukebox are part of the same file system.

The advantage of this algorithm is the ability to create file systems up to several terabytes in size in a transparent manner. The disadvantage is added coding complexity for the management software. There are numerous boundary conditions, which must be accounted for when switching over to a new disk. These include preventing a file from spanning disks (this is necessary if each volume is to remain independent) and the implementation and updating of the master volume table.

2.5.9 Disk Software Format

All optical disk management software must incorporate an effective software format if high performance is to be achieved. Software format is the lowest building block from which other structures are built.

The first hundred or so sectors should be reserved for system information. This information includes a volume label, a unique indentifier to prevent disks with a different format from being mounted, and pointers to the start of the directory area and data area.

The directory area should come next and be allocated in blocks. When a given block is filled, the next block should be allocated and the prior block should point to the new one. Directory blocks allow the directory to be interleaved with the data blocks, helping to minimize seeks when accessing or updating information.

Data blocks must be written in ascending logical order to allow for large continuous transfers and lazy allocation. Drive controllers are not capable of writing data blocks in descending order. Even if they could, the spiral groove format prevents this from being efficient.

2.5.10 SCSI Performance

The manner in which the optical SCSI driver is implemented greatly affects the performance of the optical system. Using the best SCSI commands for a given job is vital for optimization.

Due to the overhead of issuing SCSI commands, data block sizes should be large. This indicates that the Group 1 Read/Write commands should be used when supported to allow for large block transfers. The Group 1 Write/Verify should be used, when supported, to eliminate the overhead of having a Write command followed by a separate Verify command.

Linked SCSI commands should always be used to process a queued list of requests. Linked commands allow an unlimited number of commands to be processed with a single Arbitration/Selection phase, reducing the overhead of separate, unlinked commands.

The drive controller should be instructed to disconnect when processing medium-to-large disk read/write requests. This frees the host CPU to process other requests in a more timely fashion.

Error retries, if overdone, can severely reduce performance. The controller should be instructed to retry a failing operation a maximum of three times. Care should be taken to eliminate any duplication of error handling between the driver and the file manager or kernel.

■ 2.6 OPTICAL FILE SYSTEM STRATEGIES

No operating system currently in use is capable of supporting WORM technology. Many cannot handle the capacities of optical media. The presumption by today's systems is that all storage devices are erasable with low to medium storage capacities. This problem has led to creation of file system strategies specifically for optical technology.

Development of these strategies has come chronologically in "waves." The first-wave strategy was the development of software that allowed WORM drives to emulate streaming tape drives. The second wave of optical management techniques were device drivers that allowed raw access to the optical drives or made the optical drive "appear" to be a Winchester drive.

The third wave saw the development of full-fledged optical file systems that were OS- (operating system) and hardware-dependent. The fourth wave has seen the development of general purpose optical file systems that are OS- and hardware-independent, allowing data disks to be interchangeable among different operating systems.

2.6.1 Tape Emulation: The First Wave

WORM technology was originally brought into the marketplace by many integrators to compete with streaming tape drive technologies. Control software was developed that made the WORM device appear to the host kernel as a streaming tape drive, allowing write-once media to be used by existing utilities for backing up or archiving all on-line data. Aquidneck Systems of North Kingstown, Rhode Island, provides this solution in a variety of different configurations.

The implementation of this algorithm is quite straightforward. The interface and format for magnetic tape is standardized and well documented, being the only storage technology that uniformly allows data to be transportable to different operating systems.

The general storage algorithms for tape are very conducive for implementation on WORM media. Data is sequentially written from the beginning of the tape to the end, allowing lazy allocation of data. Data is not randomly updated on tape, eliminating the need to update pointers. Data is dumped in large blocks, allowing excellent transfer rates without software optimization.

The software is generally combined with a SCSI host adapter board by burning the logic into a programmable read-only memory (PROM) set. The standard tape commands are emulated through this firmware. Advantages of this method are the ease of integration into multiple operating system environments, transparency to the host kernel, and high transfer rates. The major disadvantage of this technique is that it eliminates a major feature of WORM: random access. Access times to a given file are unbearable, due to the sequential nature of the tape interface.

2.6.2 Optical Device Drivers: The Second Wave

Many different approaches have been taken in developing device drivers for optical access management. One of the first methods developed was the "application-specific" device driver. In this method a magnetic database is created that contains pointers to data stored on the optical disk, effectively treating the optical media as an extension of main memory. The device driver is a simple SCSI driver that allows the application to read and write optical data blocks.

This method has the advantage of performance. The device driver can be tuned to the application for maximum data transfer rates unachievable by other strategies. The device driver is also extremely easy to implement.

The disadvantage is that the disk format is application-specific and the data is unusable outside the application. Furthermore, should the magnetic database be lost or corrupted, the data on the optical disk becomes inaccessible. Improvements have been made to this method, with such tactics as periodically dumping the database to optical or putting headers in front of the data blocks to allow for some type of disaster recovery.

This approach to optical storage software is never sold as a separate package but is instead buried within the given application package. The applications that have tended to do this in the past are generally document/image-processing systems. With the user demand for open architectures and nonproprietary systems, the optical device driver approach has fallen out of use.

The past two years have seen the development of sophisticated optical device drivers that make the write-once drive appear to the operating system kernel as a full read/write (erasable) drive. This strategy is known as "Winchester emulation."

2.6.2.1 Winchester Emulation

Winchester emulation allows the native file system to be implemented on the write-once media. This method involves the addition of an index structure below the file system. The purpose of the index structure is to maintain a set of indices to the most current version of a sector. The basic algorithm is as follows:

1. The first file is written to the new media.
2. The directory is updated and rewritten to the disk.

3. The file allocation table (FAT) (in the case of MS-DOS or OS/2) or the i-node (under UNIX), is updated and then rewritten to the new media.
4. The indices are updated and rewritten to correctly point to the new locations for the rewritten data.

The indices perform the logical-to-physical conversion of sector addresses. The indices are generally stored in a tree structure. The root or master table contains pointers to the first-level indirect index tables. Depending on the capacity of the optical disk, these first-level indirect tables will contain either physical sector addresses or pointers to second-level indirect index tables, which contain the current physical sector addresses. Two levels of indirection are all that is needed to address well over a terabyte (1024 gigabytes) of physical disk sectors.

The advantage of this method is that access to the optical drive, with few exceptions, is completely transparent. This allows standard application packages to access the optical drives using generic kernel calls. The device driver is also relatively easy to implement, with minimal effort.

The disadvantages of this method are clear. Media usage, especially with small files, can be very poor, with the index overhead consuming 50 to 75 percent of the disk. The disk is also not transportable. Only the operating system under which the data was written can understand the disk format.

A variation to this Winchester emulation technique involves the use of the Winchester hard drive as a caching vehicle for the indices and in some implementations, the data. The optical device driver works in conjunction with the Winchester driver in a manner transparent to the kernel.

When the optical medium is first loaded, the indices are dumped onto the magnetic drive. The indices are modified on the magnetic disk whenever sectors are updated.

When data is read from the optical disk, in some variations of this algorithm it is first stored in the magnetic cache and the indices are flagged to indicate that the data is now magnetic-resident. Subsequent accesses to the same data will be from the Winchester drive with its corresponding performance advantage.

The I/O algorithm for the data-caching model is as follows; When the kernel requests that a data block be read, the optical index is checked to see if the data is magnetic-resident. If so, the data is transferred directly from the magnetic drive. If the data is not in cache, the sectors are first transferred from optical to cache and then from the cache to the desired memory location. When the cache is full, data blocks are recycled using the least-recently-used (LRU) algorithm.

When the kernel writes data to the optical disk, it is routed to the magnetic cache instead. If the same data block is rewritten while still in the cache, the rewrite occurs on the magnetic disk and is never recorded on optical. When the cache is full, the driver will dump the oldest data (using the LRU algorithm) to optical, updating all affected indices.

When the disk is removed from the drive, the index tables and any residual cache data must be copied back to the optical disk. Failure to do this would result in loss of all data since the index tables were last stored.

The advantages of this method are improved transfer rates and greatly reduced disk overhead. The disadvantages are the need for larger and more complicated device drivers, required magnetic support, the loss of a complete "Audit Trail," and the additional operator commands required to flush the indexes and data to optical. More importantly, this method opens a window of undefined length in which the robust optical disk is susceptible to magnetic disk failure. If the hard drive fails, all data written after the last optical "unmount" will be inaccessible.

A variation on this algorithm implements asynchronous flushing of the index tables and data to the optical disk. The device driver periodically wakes up, via signals or hardware timer interrupts, and checks the state of the cache. If a user-defined period of time has gone by, the driver flushes the index tables and data to optical. The advantages of this algorithm are greatly improved data safety and frequent "history" snapshots of the disk, at the expense of higher disk overhead.

Corel Systems of Ottawa, Ontario, Canada, is the leading supplier of this type of software solution, having device drivers for MS-DOS, Macintosh, and Novell operating systems. Micro Design from Winter Park, Florida, has perhaps the most complete offering of device drivers, including MS-DOS, Novell, OS/2, Macintosh, and various flavors of UNIX.

One optical drive manufacturer, Laser Drive, has implemented Winchester emulation in the drive controller itself. The controller, via firmware, handles the index manipulation and logical-to-physical sector address conversion. The controller incorporates several megabytes of nonvolatile RAM to store the entire index in memory. The drive is hardware-switchable to use optical media in the write-once or Winchester emulation mode.

Advantages to this method are high continuous transfer rates and the ability to use standard operating system block device drivers. Disadvantages are the higher cost of the hardware, the lack of an accessible audit trail, high overhead, and the inability to read media between unlike operating systems.

2.6.3 Nontransportable Optical File System (Dedicated System): The Third Wave

The third wave saw the development of file systems designed specifically for WORM technology. These file systems allowed the capabilities of technology to be more fully used.

Third-wave file systems are based around a particular operating system and selected optical drives. They provide the same function and general structures as the host operating system. In the case of a third-wave file system based around MS-DOS, the optical file system would be based on the same filename conventions, attributes, file sizes, and so on.

The third-wave file systems generally fell into the trap of basing certain parts of their system around nonstandard or undocumented features of both the file system and the optical hardware, permanently tying them to that system. An example of this is that some optical drives allow you to rewrite a sector but most do not. Some third-wave file systems circumvented the implementation problems of write-once file systems by adding directory information and pointers to written sectors, implementing their own ECC.

The functionality of these systems varies. Some allow read/write capabilities but no update/append, some allow read/write/append but no update, and some offer full functionality. The algorithms used to create this type of system are almost limitless.

The advantages of the third-wave system are improved disk overhead, complete audit trails, improved performance, and relative ease of implementation. The drawbacks are dependencies on a given operating system and hardware platform, inability to read disks between unlike operating systems, lack of transparency (many off-the-shelf applications cannot correctly access the optical drive), and limited functionality.

2.6.4 General-Purpose Transportable Optical File Systems: The Fourth Wave

State of the art in the field of optical file management software is the emergence of the "fourth-wave" optical file systems. These file systems are both operating system- and device-independent. They offer functionality above and beyond the standard magnetic file systems of any current OS. Ideally third wave file systems should provide

- Extended file sizes (from 4 gigabytes to many terabytes)
- Superset functionality for any given operating system
- Low disk overhead
- Complete history and audit trail
- Extended directory structure/information
- High transfer rates
- Efficient support for multi-terabyte file systems

Fourth-wave file systems are generally referred to as Universal Optical File Systems (UOFS). The UOFS acts as an extension of the host operating system kernel. They are in fact a mini-operating system, more generally referred to as a file system kernel.

The UOFS makes the optical drive appear to be erasable at the logical interface level (open file, close file, and so on). The logic to perform all file system/disk system calls is contained within the optical kernel, bypassing the host kernel. The kernel implements the read/write algorithms, the caching algorithms, and the directory/disk structures and formats.

The UOFS generally consists of three layers. The top layer interfaces, or integrates, the optical file system into the host kernel. It is responsible for translating the host system calls into calls understood by the UOFS and vice versa. It must also reformat return information in a manner that makes sense to the host. This code layer is operating system–dependent.

The operating system interface under MS-DOS must revector interrupts 13h, 20h, 21h, 24h, 25h, and 26h. When one of these interrupts occurs, the interface must determine the destination of the call. If it is for the optical disk, the interface reformats the request and passes it down to the UOFS. If the request is not optical-bound, it is passed on to MS-DOS.

The undocumented DOS network redirector interface (2f11h) may also be used to interface with DOS. This method greatly improves the transparency and reduces the complexity of the operating system interface. There are fewer calls that must be supported under the redirector interface. Use of this interface requires expert knowledge of the MS-DOS internals, as Microsoft does not officially support this interface and the functionality of many of the calls is unknown.

Under OS/2, there are two methods for integrating the UOFS. An applications programming interface (API) can be developed and linked into the OS/2 API library, superseding the OS/2 API's. This layer then functions in a manner similar to the one just described.

The second method is to use the little-known foreign file system interface supported by OS/2. This interface allows the OS/2 kernel to directly support a foreign file system, relieving the optical interface module from having to process nonoptical requests. This interface is supported through the use of "file system drivers." The OS/2 kernel passes calls to the appropriate file system driver.

UNIX has a variety of options for interfacing the UOFS. All are based on the UNIX support for foreign file systems. Under SunOS, the UOFS may be attached through the Virtual File System (VFS) interface. This method causes the UOFS to run as a part of the kernel, requiring the UNIX kernel to be relinked.

The UOFS may also be attached as a remote file server via SUN's Network File System (NFS) using Remote Procedure Calls (RPC). The VFS method, running in the kernel mode, is harder to debug, and memory for caching is limited (kernel memory is not virtual), but it generally offers better performance. The NFS method, running in the user mode, offers unlimited virtual memory for caching; it offers remote user access; and it is easier to debug. The drawback of the NFS method is that it is based on the stateless machine concept—good for server/client crash recovery but poor for performance.

AT&T UNIX System 5.3 offers the Remote File System (RFS) interface, very similar in functionality to NFS. Various other flavors of UNIX offer what is known as a "File System Switch." The UNIX kernel maintains a table of file system managers, one entry for each file system present. The kernel determines which file system a given request is for and passes execution to the appropriate file manager. Under this method, the UOFS directly becomes an extension of the UNIX kernel.

The second layer is the UOFS proper. There are many different algorithms for implementing the UOFS. Some are implemented as a modified form of the UNIX file system, complete with a superblock and i-nodes. Many are proprietary implementations. High-performance implementations have developed unique directory structures that can efficiently handle access to millions of files.

The directory structures must, by necessity, contain a plenitude of information in order to support the functionality of different operation systems. In general the items needed to support the UOFS are the following:

- *Unique ID*: This ID identifies the sector as part of the directory structure and is used for crash/failure recovery.
- *Operating system*: This field identifies the operating system under which the file was created.
- *File name*: The file is from 20 to 256 bytes long, ASCII format, with very few naming conventions.

46 ▪ Optical Storage Technologies

- *Numeric values*: Numeric values must be recorded in both low-high (Intel) format and high-low (Motorola, others) format. This prevents the need to swap bytes every time a directory structure is read when changing from one processor to another.
- *Protection*: Fields must be included that allow for file ownership and rights, such as group ID, owner ID, and password.
- *Private data*: The private data field is used to support any variety of information needed for different operating systems, now and in the future. Its structure is undefined and is akin to BLOB data. This field is usually 256 bytes.

The bottom layer consists of the device driver. The driver is generally a simple SCSI device driver that allows the UOFS to communicate with the optical drive(s). The format of these drivers are operating system–specific and are generally written to conform to the OS standard format.

Figure 2.14 illustrates the structure of a fourth-wave file system. Pegasus Disk Technologies of Walnut Creek, California, is the leading supplier of fourth-wave optical storage software. It offers support for a variety of $5\frac{1}{4}''$ and $12''$ optical drives running

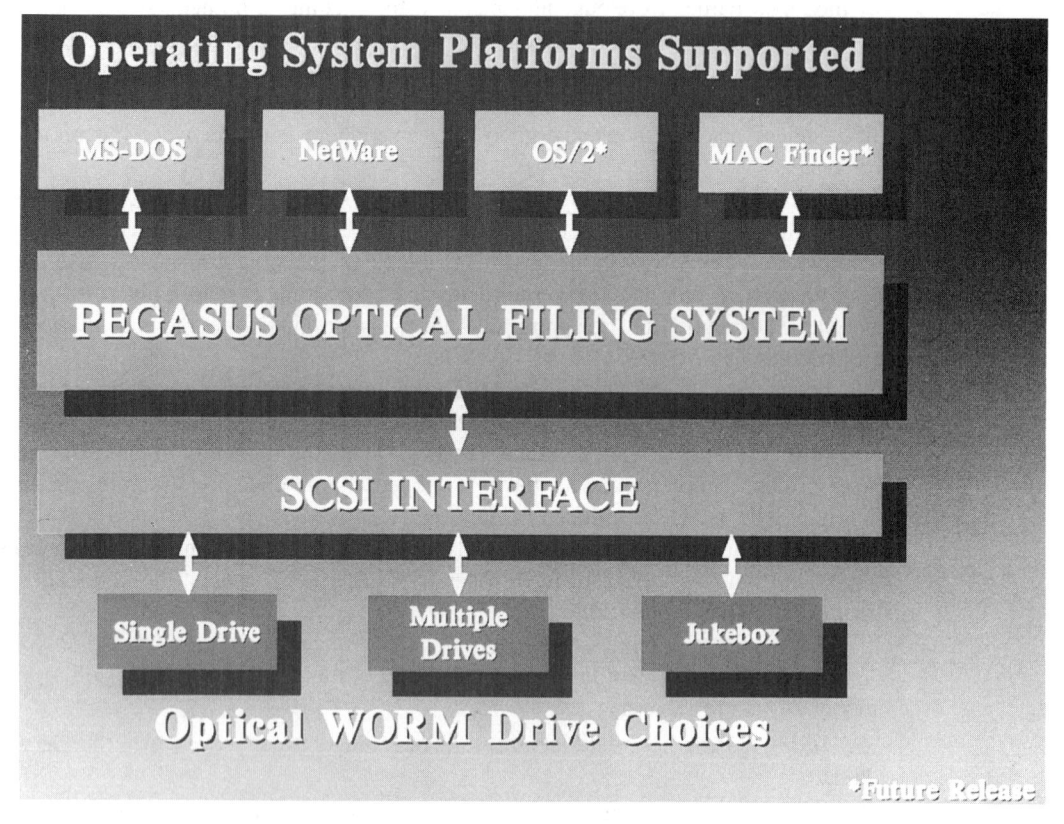

Figure 2.14 Structure of a fourth-wave optical system.

under MS-DOS, Novell, 3-COM, and Banyan operating systems. Pegasus also supports a variety of optical disk jukeboxes through the use of a sophisticated volume manager, which transparently maps all disks within one or more jukeboxes to a single hierarchical file system.

The advantages to the UOFS are many. Minimal disk overhead is achieved. The UOFS allows for the fastest transfer rates and fastest directory searches. The UOFS also offers full history functions and audit trails and greater functionality.

Perhaps the biggest advantage to the UOFS is that data disks may be transported to different operating systems. Huge databases may be created on a mainframe, and disks may then be distributed to micro- and minicomputers.

The disadvantages of the UOFS are not trivial. The UOFS is very complex to build and maintain. Development of a UOFS is labor-intensive and costly. Porting the UOFS to different operating systems is also costly, requiring both the operating system interface and device drivers to be completely rewritten. Adequate transparency is very hard to achieve and maintain, as the interface must correctly emulate all the features of a given operating system. New releases of the operating system often require changes to the interface software or drivers.

2.6.5 Future Optical File Systems: The Fifth Wave

The future will see a new breed of optical file systems to fill the need of the ever-expanding capabilities of storage systems. Fifth-wave file systems will be capable of managing both write-once and erasable disks (all storage devices in fact) natively. These file systems will be object-oriented. Data constructs, such as directories and files, will be seen as objects with inherent properties.

Fifth-wave systems will be capable of storing and retrieving vast file systems that are distributed over local area and wide area networks. These file systems will natively support multi-media types and full text retrieval of character-based documents.

No software is currently available which supports fifth-wave concepts. Pegasus Disk Technologies, mentioned in the previous section, is currently working on a fifth-wave implementation of their software.

2.7 OPTICAL JUKEBOXES

Removable media present a special set of circumstances when it comes to office automation. Removable media allow a single device to store and retrieve an unlimited amount of information by simply changing disks. The problem is, how does an end user access these disks in an automated fashion.

The optical jukebox is designed to solve just such a problem. The design of computer-based jukeboxes has its roots buried in the technology of the early Wurlitzer music jukeboxes. Many of the switches used in today's machines have changed very little over the years.

The major components of the jukebox are the import/export slot, the robotic arm(s), the storage shelves, the optical drives, and the jukebox controller. The import/export slot allows disks to be inserted or removed from the jukebox. The robotic arms are responsible for transporting the disks within the jukebox. The optical drives read and

48 ▪ Optical Storage Technologies

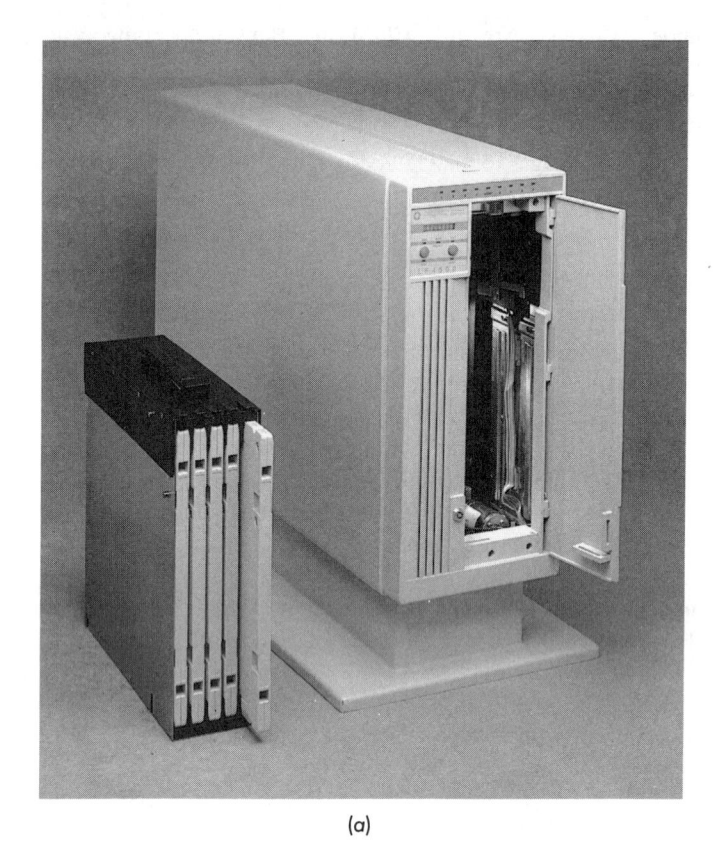

Figure 2.15 (a) An optical jukebox (courtesy Laser Magnetic Storage).

write data, while the jukebox controller is responsible for the overall operations of the jukebox. The storage shelves are as the name implies, a place to store the disks when they are not in use.

The storage capacity for jukeboxes ranges from 10 gigabytes, for the small IDE $5\frac{1}{4}''$ desktop model, up to several terabytes for the largest model, such as the DISC jukebox, which can house up to 114 drives and store several thousand disks.

Optical jukebox technology is playing an important role in the document storage field. The capacity needed by document systems is well met by jukebox devices. The nearly on-line access provided by jukeboxes allows disks to be swapped in and out of drives as needed. Figures 2.15*a* and 2.15*b* illustrate optical jukebox hardware.

▪ 2.8 FUTURE OPTICAL TECHNOLOGY

In terms of reacing its potential, optical technology is in its early infancy. The capabilities of optical storage will increase at exponential rates, reaching transfer rates and capacities yet undreamed of.

CD-ROM will see the release of WORM CDs. This technology will combine the mastered data of CD-ROM with unwritten, WORM-type data sectors left at the end of

2.8 Future Optical Technology ■ 49

(b)

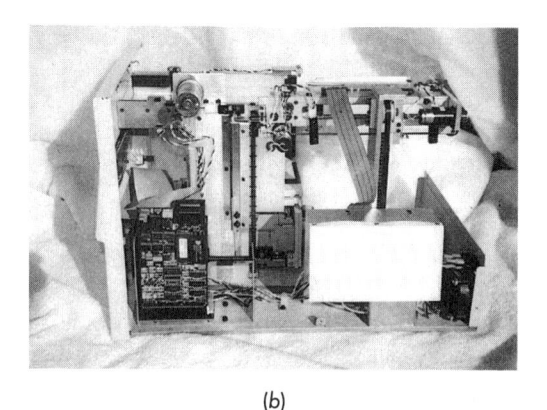

Figure 2.15 (cont) (b) An optical jukebox.

each track, allowing limited updates of the CD-ROM data. CD-ROM should eventually go to a block-based format, substantially increasing its performance.

WORM and erasable technologies will see the red light lasers replaced first by blue, then ultraviolet light lasers, greatly increasing disk capacities. A single side of an optical disk should, within five to six years, be capable of storing a terabyte of information (two terabytes per disk). A two-terabyte disk would be capable of storing the life history of every man, woman, and child on the face of the earth.

New methods of optical recording will also greatly increase capacities. One such technology, known as frequency domain recording, uses a recording film of organic or inorganic photon-gated compounds and two laser sources to record multiple data bits within the same focal diameter. A read/write laser is used to excite those molecules in the exposed area that are sensitive to that wavelength of light. A second beam provides additional energy to record a bit by bleaching an excited molecule. The presence and absence of such bleached molecules defines digital data.

With a slight variance in the frequency of the laser, other groups of molecules may also be bleached, allowing multiple thousands of bits to be recorded in the same exposed area. Technology advancements such as this will allow over 6.9 gigabits per square inch to be stored on optical disks within the next 10 years.

Optical head assemblies will continue to diminish in size, becoming comparable with Winchester technology. This will cause access times to drop and transfer rates to increase in quantum leaps. Access times of 5 to 15 milliseconds and data transfer rates of over 12 megabytes per second are achievable in the next five to seven years.

Optical drives will incorporate multi-platter disk systems, which use multiple disk arms, each containing multiple laser arrays. The end result will be the elimination of all physical movement of the optical head, resulting in access times and transfer rates that far exceed even the fastest Winchester drive. LMS has already released a dual-head optical drive system, which allows both sides of a disk to be read simultaneously.

Multi-function optical drives are just starting to be released. Multi-function drives will be capable of reading and writing both WORM and erasable media. This technology presents some interesting options and is seen by industry analysts as the manufacturers' attempt to cover all bases. From the early market indications, the multi-function drives are going to be quite popular.

A new type of optical medium technology, known as digital paper, is in the final stages of development. Digital paper has the advantages of regular paper (low cost, indelibility, and permanence), combined with the high recording density, long life, and laser characteristics associated with rigid optical disks.

Digital paper consists of a four-layer sandwich of thin films. The base substrate consists of a polyester base, such as Melinex, which provides the necessary strength to the entire structure. This substrate layer is from 25 to 75 microns thick, depending on the application.

A reflective layer of metal is deposited on to the substrate via sputtering. Over this metallic layer is the active layer, which is composed of a transparent polymer that contains an infrared-absorbent dye. The frequency at which the infrared light is absorbed is between 780 and 830 nanometers, wavelengths that correspond to today's most widely used solid-state lasers. The outer layer is a low-friction polymer, which seals the inner layers and allows the paper to slip smoothly, when coiled into reels of tape, or slip into a diskette cartridge.

Data is written by a pyroplastic deformation technique, which burns data pits into the active polymer. This pit diminishes that amount of polymer present to absorb the laser light, allowing a stronger reflection of the beam off the metal layer. The photodetector senses this as data. Both sides of the paper may be recorded.

The biggest advantages of digital paper are its low cost and its mechanical flexibility. This flexibility allows the paper to be produced and cut into a variety of formats, such as reels of tape or floppy disks.

Digital paper has heralded the creation of two new types of optical storage: optical tape and optical floppies.

The first optical tape drive to hit the market uses 12" optical tape, which can store 1 terabyte of data. This drive uses a novel recording technique in which 32 laser recording heads scan across the width of the tape from left to right and then from right to left in discrete chunks or frames. Each frame is 32 bits wide by 20,000 bits long, holding 80 kilobytes of data. The drive supports a sustained read/write rate of 3 megabytes per second. Average access time to any record is 28 seconds, and searching the entire terabyte of information requires a maximum of 60 seconds.

The optical floppy disk is based on the Bernoulli principle, which states that when fluid flows faster on one side of an object than on the other, the object feels a force towards the faster flow. It is this effect that allows an airplane to fly. The optical floppy incorporates a fixed circular plate, which contains the recording heads. As the disk spins, the plate channels and accelerates the air flow, drawn from perforations near the perimeter of the plate. This draws the floppy firmly towards the plate and the heads while still maintaining an extremely stable cushion of air. The disk is housed within a cartridge similar to that of $3\frac{1}{2}''$ magnetic floppies.

Both $5\frac{1}{4}''$ and $3\frac{1}{2}''$ disks and drives are being developed. The media are double-sided, and the drive will incorporate dual heads, allowing both sides of the media to be accessed on-line. Storage capacity will be 1.5 gigabytes per disk, with a cost of about two dollars per disk. Average access times will be less than 40 milliseconds, comparable to today's average PC Winchester. Sustained transfer rates will be in excess of 1.2 megabytes per second.

In the marketplace, look for WORM technology to completely replace microfilm, microfiche, and tape for archival storage. WORM will also make a significant dent in the use of paper for long-term storage. Given that 92 percent of the world's information is still stored on paper, the market for WORM technology will be very large indeed.

Look for erasable optical drives to completely replace all forms of magnetic storage—Winchester technology, in particular. Erasable drives will be faster, cheaper, and more stable. The media are removable, with far greater storage capacities, no head crashes, and far greater archival life.

The current and future state(s) of optical technology offer very significant benefits to database systems. The large capacities of optical allow new options in storage design. Storage software can afford to be more wasteful with storage consumption, thereby significantly improving the database performance. Today's database engines spend an inordinate amount of time conserving disk space with various techniques, such as software compression of data, at the expense of storage and retrieval times.

2.9 OPTICAL TECHNOLOGY IN INTELLIGENT OFFICES

Optical technology has expanded the boundaries of computer storage by orders of magnitude. The concept of intelligent offices would not be possible without the support of optical technology.

Optical technology provides the means to store and retrieve the multi-media office objects, as well as the mechanisms for archiving all static office objects. Mass distribution and replication of corporate data is also possible because of optical storage.

In the intelligent office, information often needs to be changed, with the old information saved at the same time for historical reasons. Write-once optical disks provide the best answer for historical access of information in intelligent offices. Not only do WORM disks provide the necessary storage capacity for the very data-intensive historical requirements, but they also physically prevent the erasure of irreplaceable historical data. The famous gap in the Watergate tapes would have never been possible had those tapes been WORM disks!

2.10 SUMMARY

Optical technology is playing a vital role in expanding the frontiers of software applications. The limitations of storage capacities have been eliminated, enabling new applications to be built and used. Document processing is one such example. The concepts of the intelligent office are brought to reality through optical technology.

From CD-ROMs to jukeboxes, optical storage is changing the way computers work, even though the technology has yet to reach even a small percentage of its potential. As optical technology gains in maturity, the possibilities that can be realized are tremendous.

The speed and capacity of optical technologies will continue to increase, eliminating the transfer rate bottleneck that hampers many of today's applications.

Optical technology is not a technology for the future. It is viable and useful today. The rapid growth of document processing proves that optical technology is now mainstream. The fact that industry giants such as IBM, WANG, DEC, and UNISYS are concentrating on their own imaging systems bears witness to this statement.

This chapter has presented the storage concepts, both hardware and software, that provide the foundation for storing vast quantities of office information. The next chapter will present the technology that allows office workers to share this information.

3

NETWORKING

■ 3.1 INTRODUCTION

The emergence of local area networks (LANs) during the latter half of the 1980s has brought about major changes in the way business computing is conducted. Business computing used to be the exclusive domain of centralized mainframes or minicomputers operated by a very expensive centralized MIS department. The advent of LANs, combined with phenomenal increases in personal computing horsepower, has brought about the decentralization of corporate information management.

What is a local area network? A LAN is a group of computers, connected together, that covers a limited geographical area. Each computer, or node, can communicate with any other node, and each node contains its own processor, requiring no central processor. A LAN allows a variety of independent devices to communicate with one another and share data. A LAN may be characterized as having the following features:

1. Its nodes are interconnected through a continuous medium such as cable.
2. It is privately owned, user-administered, and not subject to FCC regulations.
3. It supports both low- and high-speed communications channels.
4. It is commercially available in off-the-shelf packages. No custom programming required.
5. It allows dedicated nodes, which provide services to specific other nodes.

The growth rates predicted for local area networks are phenomenal. It is predicted that by 1992 there will be over 60 million PCs in use. Of those 60,000,000 PCs, more than half will be connected to a local area network. The trend of the Fortune 1000 companies is a continuation of the downsizing strategy by using PCs connected via LANs.

Local area networks have become one of the most important technologies of the 1990s. Networks are no longer an optional item, but one that each office must incorporate into the workplace if it is to remain competitive.

The most important fact about LANs is that without them the intelligent office could not exist. The ability for every person in the office to perform various tasks interactively

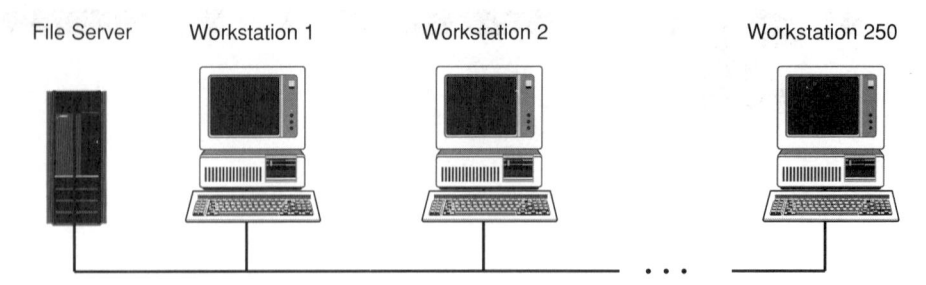

Figure 3.1 A typical LAN.

and to share information in real time is the architectural foundation of the intelligent office. The core of the intelligent office computing model is therefore based on and centered around the concepts of LANs. LANs are the "wheels" that move the intelligent office toward the productivity goals promised so long ago by computer technology but never achieved.

A LAN can typically connect from one to 250 workstations, as shown in Figure 3.1. However, through the use of bridges and gateways (described in Section 3.5.3), LANs can be internetworked, providing access to an almost unlimited number of nodes.

Chapter 2 presented the storage hardware and software technologies that provide for the safekeeping of information. This chapter discusses the communications technologies that tie all users in the intelligent office together regardless of their location.

3.1.1 Chapter Organization

This chapter begins by discussing, in Section 3.2, the hardware that provides the physical means of communicating information between remote users. The models and protocols of network operation are then presented, followed by the network model used by the intelligent office. The specialized operating systems that have been developed to provide the needed network services are presented in Section 3.3. The manner is which office users and information are managed and protected is discussed in Section 3.4. Finally, a description of the services provided by various type of network servers is presented in Section 3.5.

■ 3.2 NETWORKING TOPOLOGIES

A LAN may be configured and organized in a number of ways. Network configurations range from centralized, where a single network mainframe computer performs all the processing for users connected at a remote site, to fully distributed, where the processing is distributed among multiple remote sites. The LAN of the 90s typically uses a distributed topology.

The major network topologies are grouped into six types: star, point-to-point, multipoint, hierarchical, bus, and ring-based. The bus and ring configurations are most commonly used for LAN topologies. These six topologies are illustrated in Figure 3.2.

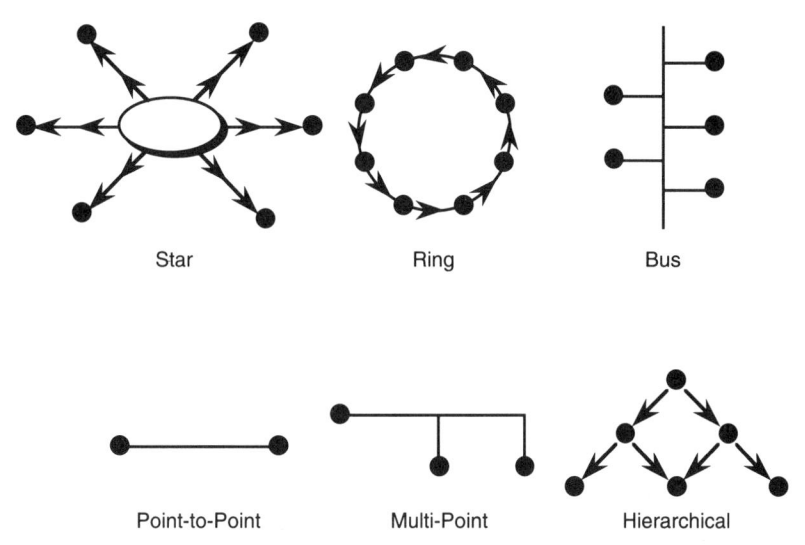

Figure 3.2 LAN topologies.

1. The star is an example of a centralized architecture. The main computing site acts as the hub of the network. Each remote site gains access to the main site via a single communications line.
2. Point-to-point networks are quite simple in design. A single remote terminal is attached to a single processing computer via a communication line. The terminal may be used in an on-line or a batch-processing mode.
3. Multi-point networks are an extension of the point-to-point configuration. Instead of a single remote terminal attached to the main computer, multiple remote terminals may be attached. Each terminal may be directly connected to the computer via its own communications line, or they may be multiplexed together via a single communications line.
4. Hierarchical networks are an example of a fully distributed topology. Hierarchical configurations use one or more mainframes at the top of the hierarchy. These have midrange computers tied into them, which in turn have mini- or microcomputers tied into them. Each node has its own processing power and may access the resources of those nodes higher or lower on the hierarchy.
5. The bus topology is also a distributed architecture that uses the concept of a central "backbone" communications line with arms or node connected off the backbone. As the signal traverses the backbone via a coaxial, fiber optic, or twisted-pair cable, each node on the system listens to the signal to determine if it is intended for that node. This topology is quite flexible, allowing nodes to attach into the network anywhere along the backbone. Ethernet is a fine example of bus structure topology.
6. Ring structure topologies are also distributed in nature and employ a closed loop, or ring. Each node in the ring is connected to the node on either side. The main

advantages of this topology are speed of transmission and simplicity of algorithms for avoiding and detecting data collision and garbling. Ring systems typically employ a token-passing algorithm for resolving which packet of data goes to which node. Obviously the often heard "Token Ring" is an example of this structure.

3.2.1 Network Cabling

Cabling is, in general, the physical medium that connects LAN nodes. The exceptions to this are the very few LANs that use wireless technology such as microwave, infrared, or satellite.

Three basic varieties of cables are available: twisted-pair, coaxial, and fiber optic. Twisted pairs and coaxial cables both use electrical currents in copper wires as the medium for signal transfer. Fiber optic cables transmit pulses of light that are generally made with a number of fine glass strands, but plastics are also employed. Figure 3.3 summarizes the different types of cabling.

Twisted-pair is the oldest cabling technology, but its main use has been for telephone connections. The first uses of twisted pairs for LAN connectivity suffered from slow performance, 1 million bits per second (Mbps) or less. Recent improvements in the technology are allowing transfer rates of up to 16 Mbps.

There are two major types of twisted pairs: shielded and unshielded. A shielded twisted pair has a layer of insulation wrapped around the two twisted wires. An unshielded twisted pair, which is an ordinary telephone cable, has no insulation. The shielded cable is more

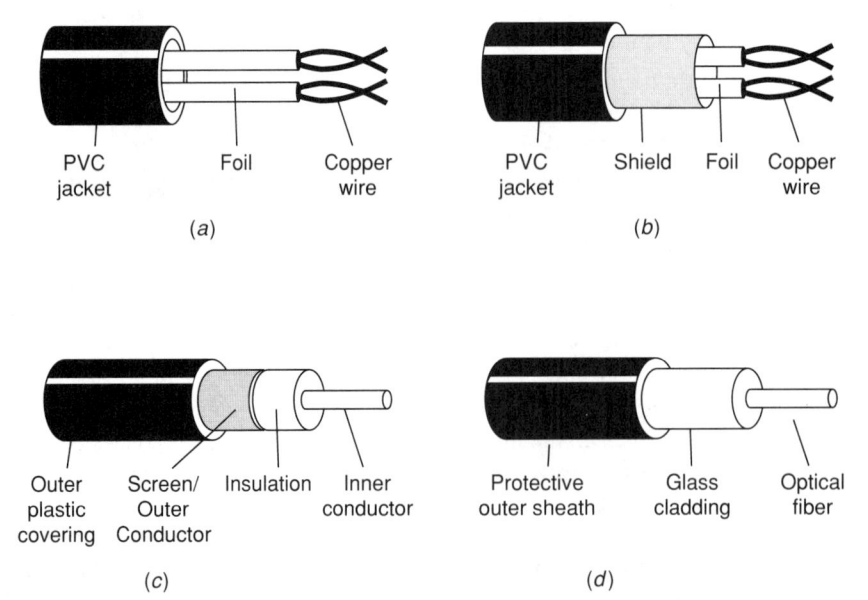

Figure 3.3 Cables used in LANs. (a) Unshielded twisted pair; (b) shielded twisted pair; (c) coaxial cable; (d) fiber optic cable.

resistant to interference, allowing for greater transmission speeds and distances between nodes. It is also more expensive.

Coaxial cable has long been used for cable television connections because of its ability to handle a large number of signals, or, in other words, different channels, simultaneously. Each channel runs at a different frequency and does not interfere with the other channels. Coaxial cable consists of four different pieces. A solid metal wire forms the core of the cable and is surrounded by insulation. A tubular piece of metal screen surrounds the insulation. An outer plastic coating completes the cable.

Coaxial cable is capable of very high bandwidths, making it an excellent choice for LANs that have a large amount of network traffic. Coaxial cable is also quite resistant to interference. Coaxial cable can also carry signals for a long distance, allowing nodes to be spread throughout an office.

Fiber optic cable is the most recent addition to the network cable family. It has unique characteristics, because it uses light pulses instead of electrical signals to carry the data. These characteristics include an immunity to electromagnetic interference, enormous bandwidths, and the ability to carry signals for a very long distance. Fiber optic cabling has been touted has the cure-all for the problems associated with wire cables.

Fiber optic cable consists of a core fiber enclosed in glass cladding. A protective outer coating surrounds the cladding. Light-emitting diodes (LEDs) are used to send the signal down the optical fiber. A photodetector is used to receive the signals and convert them into a digital computer format.

3.2.2 Ethernet

We expect Ethernet networks to be one of the most widely used types in the next generation of office environments. Platforms such as Unix are almost exclusively based on the Ethernet topology.

An Ethernet network connects multiple network stations at intervals to one long main cable. In other words, it has a bus topology. The main cable and the network nodes connected to make up a trunk segment. The main cable is called a trunk segment cable and is the backbone of the segment. The trunk segment cable is generally made up of a series of cable lengths attached together with connectors rather than one continuous piece of cabling.

The trunk segment is limited, having both a maximum length and a maximum number of workstations that can be attached. The network itself is not limited to one trunk segment. To extend the network beyond one trunk segment, a device called a network repeater is employed to attach trunk segments together. The repeater strengthens the network signal as well as being the connection point for a signal traveling between trunk segments. Figure 3.4 illustrates the various parts of an Ethernet network.

The network trunk cable is the sum of all the trunk segments. Just as the trunk segment cable is the backbone of the trunk segment, the network trunk cable becomes the backbone of the entire network. Figure 3.5 illustrates this concept of trunk cables and segments.

There are two types of cabling for Ethernet topologies. Thin Ethernet cabling is the least expensive choice for Ethernet cabling. Thick Ethernet cable is more expensive and harder to install. Both types of Ethernet use 50-ohm coaxial cabling. The difference

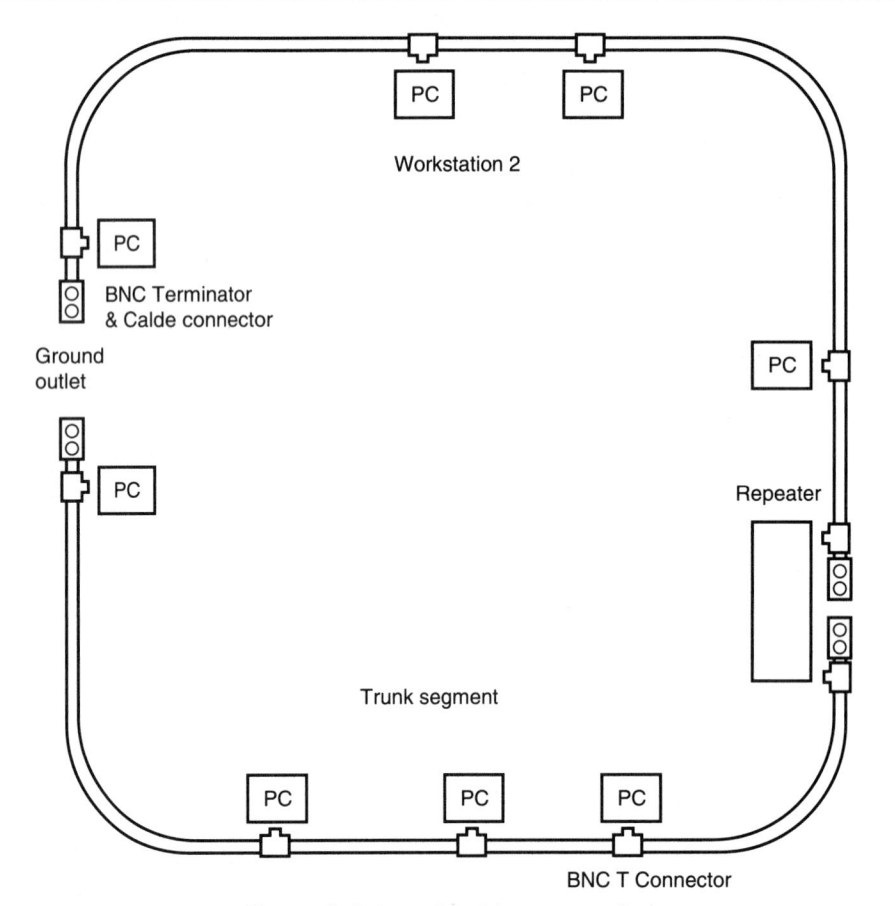

Figure 3.4 Parts of an Ethernet network.

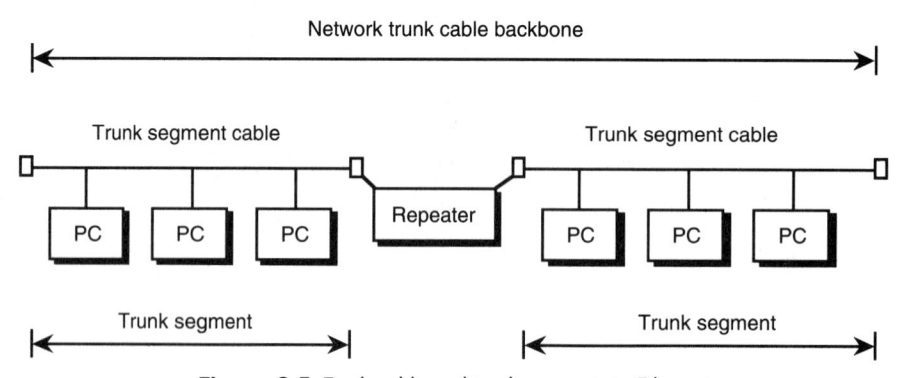

Figure 3.5 Trunk cable and trunk segments in Ethernet.

between the two is literally the thickness of the cable. Thin-Ethernet cable is 0.2-inch RG-58A/U cable, while the thick-Ethernet uses 0.4-inch cable.

Thin Ethernet cabling is a good choice if your network cabling requirements never exceed 3035 feet in length. You will need to take the following limitations and rules into consideration if you are thinking of using thin Ethernet cabling:

- The maximum number of trunk segments is 5.
- The maximum trunk segment length is 607 feet.
- The maximum network trunk cable length is 3035 feet.

The rules of thin Ethernet are as follows:

- A network signal terminator must be attached to each end of every trunk segment.
- One of the signal terminators must be grounded.
- Node connectors should be kept to a minimum.
- The fewer connectors, the more reliable the network communications will be.

Thick Ethernet cable will be required if your cabling requirements exceed 3035 feet or if, for security reasons, your network installation requirements dictate that the network signals must be shielded from the possibility of being monitored and deciphered by external equipment. The limitations of thick Ethernet cable are as follows:

- The maximum number of trunk segments is 5.
- The maximum trunk segment length is 1640 feet.
- The maximum network trunk cable length is 8200 feet.
- The maximum number of network stations per trunk segment is 100.

The rules of thick Ethernet are as follows:

- A network signal terminator must be attached to each end of every trunk segment.
- One of the signal terminators must be grounded.
- Node connectors should be kept to a minimum. The fewer connectors you have, the more reliable the network communications will be.
- It is best to use unspliced cable lengths between network nodes whenever possible.

3.2.3 Token Ring

The term "token ring" is an often-heard phrase in the networking community. Token ring is another methodology of passing data between workstation nodes on the network. A token ring consists of a group of network stations serially connected together via some type of communication cabling.

The transmission of data is performed sequentially, bit by bit, from one station to the next. As each station receives a bit, it also sends that bit down to the next node. Each station has the opportunity to read and interpret the information before sending it on to the next node. When the information has made the full trip around the ring, the node that originated the sending of the data removes it from the network.

The token ring is based on the network technology called token passing. A "token" on the network simply defines a device (a node) in a distributed polling list. Each device on the network must be polled. This polling is performed in a sequential fashion around the ring. As a device is polled or, in other words, receives the token, it has the opportunity to transmit data. The token is, in other words, the transmission security key of the network. Only the node that has received possession of the token may transmit information on the network. This implies that there can be no signal collisions using the token-passing scheme, in fact, token passing is a collision prevention scheme. The polling of devices does not need to be centralized, since each node can send the polling token on after it has performed any transmissions.

The token itself, in a token ring, is defined by a unique sequence of signals that are transmitted on the bus after each data transmission sequence. When a station detects the token, it may take "ownership" by modifying it. The station appends information to the token and then transmits the information. The station will remain in control until the information has completed the trip around the ring and is removed from the network by that station.

3.2.4 OSI/ISO and SNA Network Standard Models

In 1977, the International Standards Organization (ISO) organized a committee to investigate the compatibility between various pieces of network equipment. This committee led to the development of the Open Systems Interconnection Reference Model (OSI).

The OSI model defines seven layers of network functionality, whose purpose is to provide a concise network model, thereby allowing equipment from competing companies to coexist in the network. Figure 3.6 illustrates the OSI model.

The layers of OSI are the following:

- *The physical link (Layer 1).* Layer 1 is the hardware base of the network. This includes such items as cabling and network cards. While the other six layers are implemented via software, this layer is strictly hardware-based. This layer defines the mechanical and electrical behavior of the hardware. This layer is mandatory for conformance with the OSI model.
- *The data link (Layer 2).* Layer 2 defines the protocol for accessing and sharing the hardware of Layer 1. The concept of token passing and signal collision detection belong to this layer.
- *The network (Layer 3).* The network layer is defined for networks that require routing mechanisms to pass packets among the nodes. Many LANs do not require this layer if they broadcast the information to all nodes on the network.
- *The transport (Layer 4).* The transport layer provides the low-level connection functions for the network. This level is involved with the sending and receiving of packets, error detection and correction for packet transmissions, and packet flow control.

3.2 Networking Topologies ■ 61

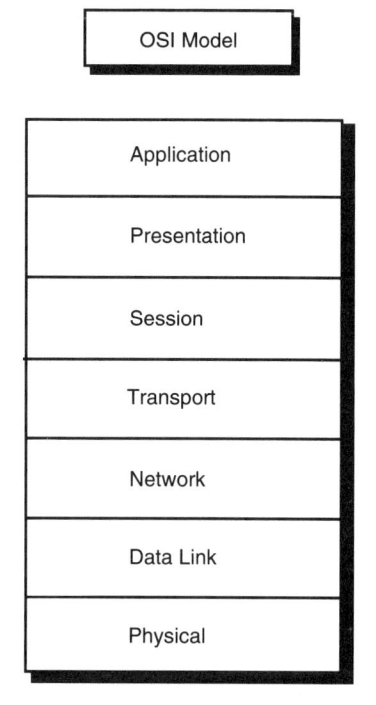

OSI Model

| Application |
| Presentation |
| Session |
| Transport |
| Network |
| Data Link |
| Physical |

Figure 3.6 The Open System Interconnection (OSI) Reference Model.

- *The session (Layer 5)*. The session layer provides for the establishment and termination of data stream connections between two or more nodes on the LAN. The main purpose of a LAN is to allow two or more nodes to connect together for communication purposes. This linking process is known as starting a session and is the purpose of this layer. Network address mapping to node connections is a function of the session layer.
- *The presentation (Layer 6)*. The presentation layer provides information translation services for the application layer. Data unpacking, character set conversion, protocol translation, encryption, and decryption are provided by this layer.
- *The application (Layer 7)*. The application layer provides network services to users of the LAN. This protocol layer is responsible for the initiation and reliability of data transfers. Items such as error recovery, handshaking, and network access are all part of this layer.

Another widely used network model that can be compared to OSI is one known as System Network Architecture or SNA. SNA was developed by IBM in 1974 to provide an overriding structure for the increasingly complex world of networks. Three years later, the OSI model was proposed by the ISO committee, and it is by and large similar to the approach of SNA.

62 ■ Networking

```
Open System              Systems Network
Interconnection          Architecture
```

OSI	SNA
	Data Streams
Application Layer	Transaction Services
Presentation Services	Presentation Services
Session Layer	Data Flow Control
	Transmission Control
Transport Layer	Path Control
Network Layer	
Link Layer	Data link Control
Physical Layer	Physical Control

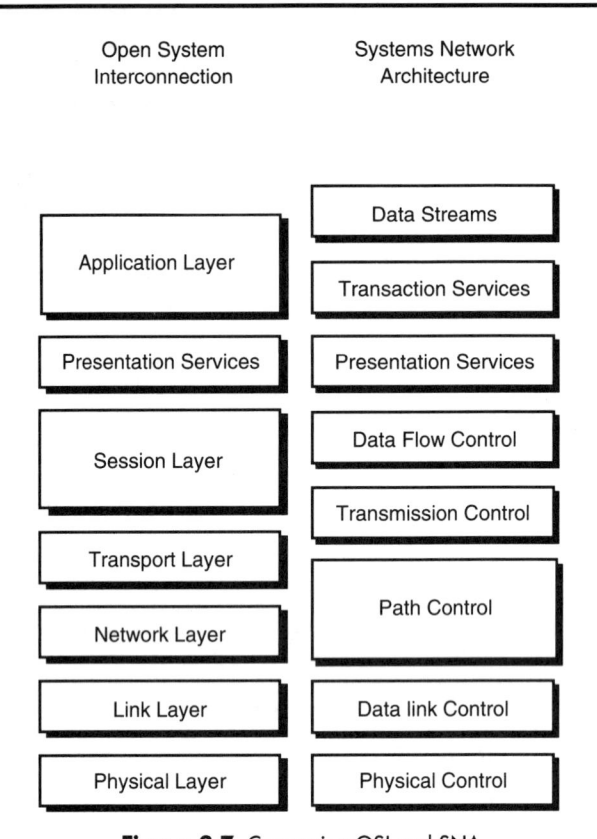

Figure 3.7 Comparing OSI and SNA.

Figure 3.7 compares these two models. At the lowest level, both protocols provide the hardware standards for the physical interconnection of devices. OSI and SNA both provide the next layer, which deals the control data needed to transmit data across a physical link.

At the next level, the two standards diverge. OSI distinguishes a network layer, which controls the routing of network traffic and a transport layer, which handles the data transmission and error recovery. SNA handles this with a single path control layer. At the following layer OSI defines a session layer, which defines the method that two programs use to coordinate the transfer of data. SNA divides this functionality into the transmission control and data flow layers.

Both protocols defines the next layer, the presentation services layer, which coordinates the translation of different data and coding formats between unlike computers. The OSI application services layer, which defines programs that directly communicate with the user, such as electronic mail, corresponds to the transaction services of SNA. Many of the items that are included by OSI in this layer are considered to be in the domain of the application by SNA and are not included in the transaction layer.

Finally, SNA defines a data stream layer, which defines a common message format between programs. OSI does not have a corresponding layer.

3.2.5 Data Transport Protocols

Finally, let us end our discussion of network models with a look at some of the higher-level protocols used for data transportation and where they fit into the network model. More specifically, we will look at the IPX, SPX, NETBIOS, APPC, and TCP/IP protocols. The purpose of the protocols is to provide a means of passing data from one network node to another.

1. Internetwork Packet Exchange (IPX) is the underlying protocol for Novell's network software. It is a close adaptation of the Xerox Network Standard (XNS) packet protocol.

    IPX supports only datagram-style messages (it is said to be "connectionless"). A datagram message is one that is never acknowledged by the receiver. This means that IPX guarantees neither the delivery of a packet nor that packets will be delivered in any particular sequence. IPX corresponds to the network layer of the OSI model.

2. The Sequenced Packet Exchange (SPX) is a session level, connection-oriented protocol. A session level protocol is a logical connection between two workstations in which delivery of a message is guaranteed. A connection must be established between two nodes before information may be exchanged. This protocol is part of the transport layer of the OSI model, one layer higher up than IPX. Both IPX and SPX were developed by Novell.

3. Network Basic Input/Output System (NETBIOS) was originally developed by IBM for its PC-LAN product. NETBIOS supports both datagram and session level connections. NETBIOS corresponds to the network layer, the transport layer, and the session layer of the ISO model. This is a higher-level protocol than either IPX or SPX.

4. Advanced Program to Program Communications (APPC) is also a session level protocol developed by IBM. APPC provides a high level mechanism for two programs to communicate with one another on a peer-to-peer basis. It is based on the use of IBM's Logical Unit 6.2, or LU6.2, which provides a mechanism for creating logical connections between workstations. APPC corresponds to the session level of the OSI model.

5. Transmission Control Protocol/Internet Protocol (TCP/IP) was designed by the U.S. Department of Defense (DoD) for their ARPANET wide area network. TCP/IP is a layer of protocols. TCP is similar to NETBIOS and APPC in that it provides point-to-point, guaranteed-delivery communications between workstations. The IP is a datagram-based protocol whose functionality is similiar to Novell's IPX. In regards to the OSI model, TCP/IP is entirely different. TCP/IP defines its own layers and is not compatible with the OSI model.

Figure 3.8 illustrates how the various communication protocols fit into the OSI model.

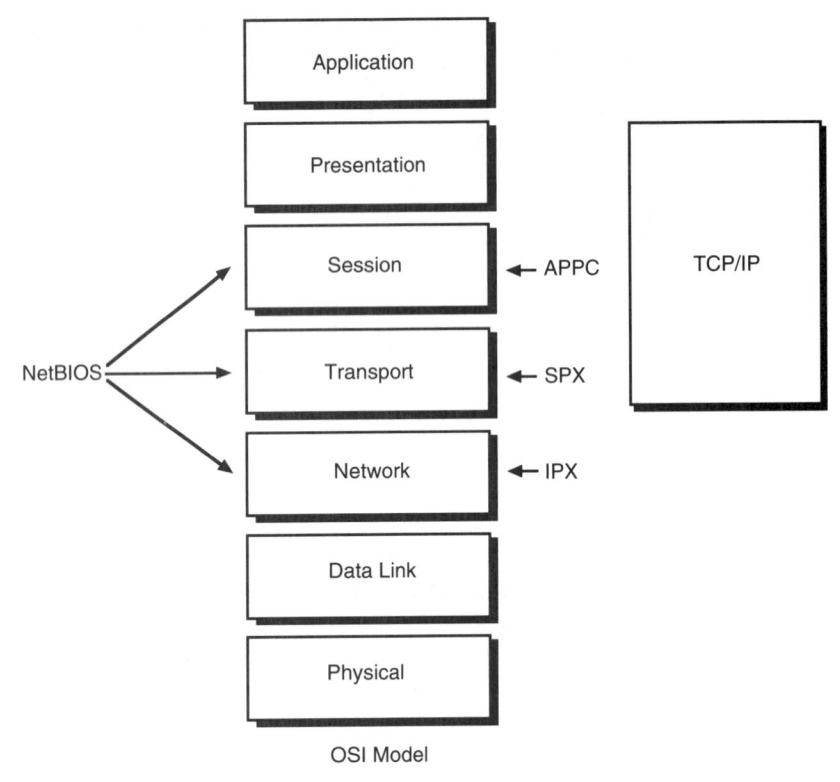

Figure 3.8 Correspondence of TCP/IP, Net BIOS, APPC, SPX, and IPX.

3.2.6 Client/Server and Peer-to-Peer Network Models in the Intelligent Office

There are two basic models of computing in the network environment. The first is the client/server model, and the second model is referred to as peer-to-peer. (Chapter 4 discusses the client/server model in detail.)

The client/server model dictates that one or more centralized servers are responsible for all the shared resources on the network. Individual workstations must acquire access to and use the shared resources via the appropriate central server. If the workstation wishes to share information with any other workstation, it must first upload that information so that others may use it. Any physical device that resides only on the workstation, such as printer, hard drive, or fax board, can never be shared or used by other workstations.

Client/server is the "authoritarian" model of network computing. The advantages of this model is that security and management of network resources can be centralized and tightly controlled. The centralized server is also dedicated and optimized for quickly and efficiently performing workstation requests.

The disadvantage is that a major portion of the resources that are connected to the network via the workstation are not accessible to the network and, therefore, underuti-

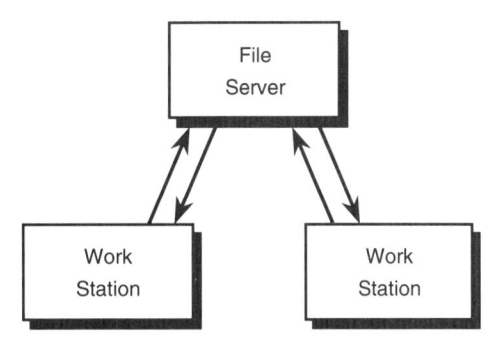

Figure 3.9 Basic client/server model.

lized. A great deal of replication and the expense associated with it are inherent in the client/server model. Figure 3.9 illustrates a typical client/server architecture.

The peer-to-peer model is the 180-degree opposite of the client/server model. The peer-to-peer model has no notion of a centralized server. Every workstation on the network is capable of acting as server to other workstations. Information stored on the workstation is directly accessible by other workstations. Sharing of both information and devices is easily accomplished in the peer-to-peer model.

Peer-to-peer is the "anarchistic" model of network computing. The advantages of this model are obvious. The utilization of resources on the network is far greater with the peer-to-peer model. The sharing of information is also an easier thing to accomplish. There is a great deal more flexibility in this model.

The disadvantage of such systems is that they are very hard to manage. Security is also a problem of concern, and performance cannot compete with the client/server model. Figure 3.10 illustrates a peer-to-peer architecture.

Office products of the past have exclusively used either client/server or peer-to-peer. This is not true of the intelligent office. The intelligent office incorporates both models within its computing paradigm, providing the advantages of both while eliminating the disadvantages. The intelligent office uses centralized servers to increase the performance, the security, and the manageability of the network, while at the same time providing peer-to-peer access to the objects located at the workstation for increased utilization of resources and improved shareability of information.

The central intelligent office server oversees the entire Intelligent Office. Expensive resources, such as jukeboxes or line printers, which need the computing horsepower that only the server can provide, are placed at the server, where they may best be utilized.

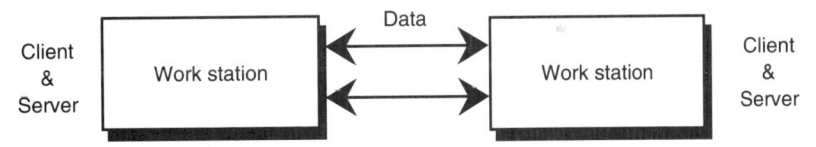

Figure 3.10 Peer-to-peer model.

The storage manager of the intelligent office server provides an advanced storage paradigm for the entire network. Information is stored in a hierarchical fashion, with the office objects most often accessed being stored in fast memory, such as RAM or high-speed Winchester drives. Less frequently accessed objects are archived to the nearly on-line storage provided by the optical jukeboxes. Objects that are no longer needed are stored off-line.

Information within the storage manager is contained within "libraries." The system administrator creates a library and assigns resources to the library, such as disk drives and jukeboxes. Disks are introduced to the library, and then objects are stored on the disks.

The management and security of the intelligent office is also a function of the server. This provides the centralization needed to administer the needs of the intelligent office effectively. To keep security levels high for the peer-to-peer access that is part of this paradigm, the server is responsible for granting outside access to objects that reside on the workstation. Once the server has provided the "key," the workstation may communicate directly, providing greater performance while relieving the server of any further burden.

The peer-to-peer aspect enables the intelligent office worker to communicate information directly to a fellow worker in a greater variety of ways. For example, Jane could send John a seminar registration form by sending the form to a fax machine at John's workstation. John then has an actual copy of the form to sign and send off. Bill could send a copy of John's daily itinerary directly to John's personal printer so that the itinerary could be printed at John's desk.

3.3 NETWORK OPERATING SYSTEMS

Network operating systems (NOS) are the software that operates the network, providing a host of services to the network user. File storage and retrieval, file sharing, network administration, user and resource security, name space resolution, resource accounting, and electronic mail are all functions of the NOS. Other advance features, such as transactions and location transparency, may also be part of NOS. The NOS should not be confused with such communications protocols as NETBIOS. An NOS provides functionality far beyond a NETBIOS and typically provides support for several different communications protocols.

Three methodologies are currently employed in the creation of network operating systems. Figure 3.11 illustrates these three approaches.

1. The first methodology relies on building the NOS from scratch, tailoring the NOS to the task at hand.
2. The second methodology retrofits an existing operating system with the required functionality so that it may act as an NOS.
3. The third method creates a separate software component that is responsible for the network functionality and is loosely tied to an underlying existing operating system, which provides the NOS layer with access to the resources of the machine.

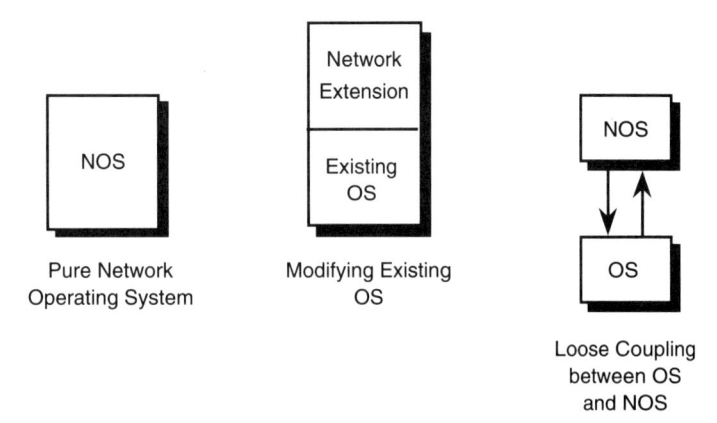

Figure 3.11 Network operating systems.

Each method has its advantages and disadvantages. The following sections examine the three most popular network operating systems and how they function in the context of the Network environment. These systems are Novell's NetWare 386, Microsoft's LAN Manager 2.0, and Banyan's Vines 4.0.

Each vendor claims the same benefits of high-performance, state-of-the-art features. Each claims to be the high-end computing platform of the future. All have reached such a degree of performance and technological advancement that they offer comparable features.

3.3.1 Novell NetWare

Novell NetWare, with 70 percent of the market share, is by far the most popular network operating system in the marketplace today. Novell has taken the first approach, building an NOS from scratch. Instead of a general operating system with networking capabilities, Novell has designed an operating system that is specific to the task of networking.

NetWare, the name of Novell's flagship product, is currently the only NOS that supports DOS, OS/2 and Macintosh clients. It also supports the largest number of peripherals.

Throughout the years, NetWare has maintained an edge with superior performance. This is undoubtedly due to Novell's having built a dedicated network operating system from scratch. Novell has been active in the NOS market for over 10 years and offers mature technology. Combining this with hardware independence has made Novell the industry leader.

Novell has paved the way for most key LAN technologies. Fault tolerance, file service, transaction tracking, and hardware independence are all key technologies that Novell has pioneered.

The large installed base supported by NetWare, along with its hardware independence, has attracted a large number of third-party developers to create a variety of applications and incorporate a large number of peripheral devices.

The latest version of Novell is a top performer. It is easy to install (unlike all previous versions!) and supports the widest variety of hardware. NetWare is now capable of au-

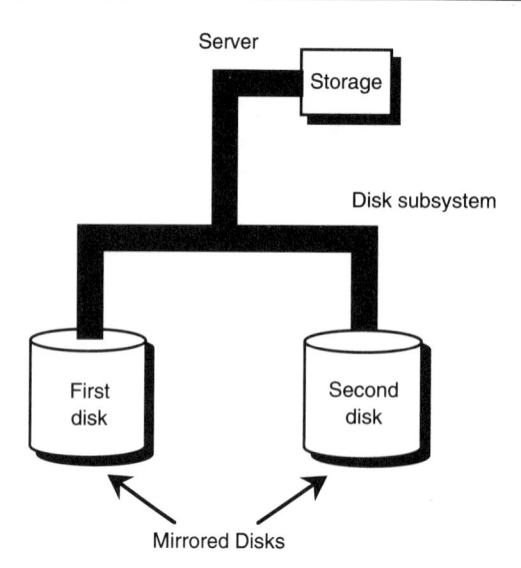

Figure 3.12 Disk mirroring.

tomatically optimizing the OS configuration parameters and memory usage on its own. This is a big boon to the network administrator.

NetWare has always been the front runner when it comes to robustness. The maturity of the software along with its disk mirroring, which is illustrated in Figure 3.12, and server mirroring make Novell quite reliable. One of the complaints about LANs has been that they are not reliable enough for many applications. NetWare is rapidly addressing this area of deficiency in the local area networking environment.

NetWare supports some notable new features such as remote console and the NetWare naming service, which help support the management of large, multi-server networks.

The advantages of netware are many. The performance is excellent. The ability for NetWare to automatically optimize its own performance eases the burden of the network administrator. The hardware support is good, as is the number of available applications. NetWare's system administration tools and capabilities are also satisfactory.

Some ongoing complaints about NetWare, including the lack of support for named pipes, the impossibility of installation, and the lack of a naming service, have been addressed in the latest version. The possible drawback of the proprietary nature of NetWare is no longer valid, because Novell owns 70 percent of the marketplace and supports a huge installed base.

Two areas where Novell does fall short is its lack of support for sharing local devices and hard drives, and the lack of a high-powered backup system that is incorporated into the NOS. NetWare also does not natively support a graphical user interface, an item which has become a necessity with respect to the user interfaces of the Nineties.

3.3.2 Microsoft LAN Manager

Microsoft LAN Manager was developed following the third methodology, that of creating a separate network layer which is loosely tied to the underlying operating system, which in this case is OS/2. LAN Manager acts as an extra layer to OS/2, handling all the network requests. LAN Manager's share of the marketplace is harder to determine, due to the many OEMs that sell LAN Manager, but it is estimated at perhaps 20 percent.

LANMAN, as LAN Manager is known, has suffered in the past from poor performance and a severe weakness in the security department. Microsoft has attempted to address these problems by completely revamping LANMAN in the 2.0 release of the product.

The first improvement in LANMAN 2.0 is the fact that the network volumes now use the OS/2 high-performance file system (HPFS). Microsoft has also beefed up the security and fault tolerance capabilities of LANMAN 2.0. They have combined the best of NetWare's fault tolerance and network administration features with Banyan's Vines' strengths in managing multiple servers.

LAN Manager offers a wide array of services from high-powered client/server features, such as the Sybase SQL Server, to simple resource sharing. Another benefit is the support of the high-powered graphical user interface inherent in OS/2, which makes using the various native utilities, such as Network Administration, easier.

Microsoft has addressed many of the past failures of LAN Manager, but LANMAN has yet to prove itself in the marketplace. A few other omissions, such as lack of support for Macintosh workstations and the lack of server-to-server bridging, need to be addressed. The performance tuning of LAN Manager is tedious at best, making it a difficult task to achieve a performance rating near Novell's.

3.3.3 Banyan Vines

Banyan has adopted the second methodology: using an existing operating system and retrofitting it with networking functionality. The Vines operating system is based on the UNIX operating system and therefore has the look and feel of UNIX. Despite many advanced features, Banyan has only managed to claim 4 to 6 percent of the market share.

Vines' emphasis is on enterprisewide networking with support for a very large number of nodes, geographically dispersed servers, and telecommunications. A typical Vines installation supports 500 to 1000 nodes with a dozen or more servers. Managing such a large system can be very problematic.

Banyan was the pioneer in the large network field, developing a protocol named Streettalk. Streettalk is a global naming service that translates logical names into physical network locations. This helps provide location transparency to the user. Resources can be moved around the network to balance the flow without having to overburden the user with knowledge of the location.

Vines is very strong in the wide area networking area. Vines has the built-in ability to connect to host mainframes and minicomputers, a very attractive feature to the large corporate user. Banyan is attempting to differentiate itself by building its "next generation" server platform based on symmetric multi-processing, providing the ability to distribute various tasks among multiple CPUs.

The drawbacks of Vines are several. First is a lack of workstation support. Vines currently supports DOS workstations only, though they have promised OS/2 and Macintosh within the year. Second, the performance of Vines is well below that of NetWare. Lastly, Banyan needs to revisit the area of user interfaces. Their user interface shows its primitive UNIX roots. In this day and age, the user interface is every bit as important as the underlying technology and functionality.

3.4 NETWORK ADMINISTRATION ISSUES

Network administration has become a very important aspect of networking. As networks continue to grow in size, resources, and complexity, the task of the network administrator has become increasingly difficult. Defining and managing users, security rights, and multiple, geographically dispersed servers is an overwhelming task.

There are some basic necessities to administering a network. First and foremost is the ability to define users, groups, and their access privileges. With the growing number of servers on the network, the administrator must also be able to define the "domains" to which the users and groups belong. A domain defines a set of servers and resources to which users and groups have automatic and transparent access.

The administrator must also be able to analyze the server performance and resource statistics. Are too many users being bottlenecked accessing one laser printer? Does the server need more RAM to have a better hit ratio for the disk cache? How many users are accessing a given server? Without easy access to this type of information the administrator cannot tune the performance of the network.

Troubleshooting is another area of concern for the administrator. The administrator must be able to monitor the network traffic, to identify problems after they occur, and more importantly, to spot potential trouble before it happens. Is server X running out of disk space? Does server Y have an unusual number of bad sectors on the drive? What happened when server M crashed? Is the network card at workstation XYZ losing information?

The intelligent office will alleviate these problems by automating many of these tasks. In particular, software can help to alleviate the administration nightmare.

3.4.1 Network Management Software and the Intelligent Office

One of the big problems of network management is to provide users access to resources in an efficient and easy-to-use way. In the world of multi-server networks, users can get hopelessly lost trying to determine exactly which subdirectory of which volume of which file server contains the information they are looking for. To make sense of this mire of information, network operating system vendors have developed management software known as a global naming service.

Banyan Vines's Streettalk, introduced earlier in this chapter, is an example of a global naming service. Under Streettalk everything on the network is assigned an item name, a group name, and an organization name. For example, suppose the user wishes to get the income statements from the accounting department at the San Francisco headquarters. The item might be called "IncomeStatements," the group might be called "Accounting," and the organization "SF." The name "IncomeStatements@Accounting@SF" would precisely define the location of the income statements in a straightforward manner.

Other NOS vendors, such as Novell and Microsoft, have recently provided global naming services.

Another essential capability is the ability to manage the network from remote terminals or workstations. With multiple servers residing on the LAN, it is no longer acceptable to be forced to control a server from the server's terminal.

A big problem with most existing management tools is that they are vendor-specific and proprietary. The emergence of enterprisewide networking dictates that the network

3.4 Network Administration Issues

will be a heterogeneous blend of network vendors. Proprietary tools that only work with a given vendor's software will not fill the need. Without a common management protocol, the administrator will have to use multiple workstations with different tools to manage the network.

Fortunately, the industry has heard the cries of dismay and has attempted to solve the problem by developing the Simple Network Management Protocol (SNMP), a standardized protocol that make it possible to maintain complex internetworks and reconfigure resources as the usage patterns change. SNMP was designed for the purpose of monitoring network performance, detecting and troubleshooting network faults, and configuring or reconfiguring network resources. SNMP performs various accounting tasks and provides for an assortment of fault detection capabilities.

SNMP is based on three major components: the SNMP protocol, the management information base (MIB), and the structure of management information (SMI). The SNMP is an application-layer protocol stack that defines a common method of communications among network devices. The MIB defines a common set of information variables and statistics that must be kept. The MIB defines an OSI-compliant registration hierarchy that groups logically related information into tables. For example, information relating to the error rates and addresses of communication interfaces would be placed in the interface table.

The SNMP software consists of agent software, which resides at the location of each resource being managed. The other element of the SNMP software is the network management station, which contains the master database of resources being managed.

Other attempts have been made to standardize management protocols, such as the Common Management Information Protocol (CMIP). While SNMP's goal is to keep everything simple, including the costs associated with network management, CMIP was intended to be a very in-depth comprehensive design for distributed, heterogeneous network and application management.

One of the key differences between CMIP and SNMP is the ability of CMIP to monitor applications as well as devices. This is due to the extensible nature of CMIP, which has the capability of dynamically adding new network objects to monitor.

We believe there is room for both protocols on the network, each one filling a need. The main point is that these protocols provide a means for third-party developers to create network management tools that are capable of managing the network of not only today, but also tomorrow.

The intelligent office environment goes beyond the SNMP and CMIP protocols. It concentrates on the administration and management of intelligent office objects, such as the following:

- Documents
- Folders
- Cabinets
- Office buildings and other fixtures
- Office workers
- Peripherals and devices
- Policies and procedures

An office worker's information and object domain will be managed by the intelligent office system. This system will take care of all aspects of heterogeneity, resource management, performance monitoring and tuning, and other administration tasks.

Note that this is an organization and management of office objects, not files and directories. Office objects may physically consist of files and directories, but the emphasis is on managing the object as a whole by the intelligent office system. Chapters 11 and 12 discuss the office objects in detail.

3.4.2 Security and Authorization

One of the drawbacks of new technologies is that they also have a tendency to create new problems. Before the era of LANs, security of information stored on personal computers was easy to accomplish. The emergence of LANs has opened up critical data to hundreds and thousands of users, making the task of security a monumental chore.

The basic need driving the growth of the local area network is the increase in productivity obtained by facilitating access to an ever-growing body of information. The ability of LAN to provide an ever-increasing user group with greater amounts of information with greater ease is what networking is about, but herein lies the great paradox of this paradigm. One goal is to provide easy access to vital information to a large user group, yet another goal is to prevent all unauthorized users from gaining access to any information.

Authorization defines the access rights of the users on the networks and determines what resources a user has access to and what operations that user may perform on those resources. Authorization and security go hand in hand.

Local area networks present a unique set of problems when it comes to security. First of all, the level of information distribution presents more avenues by which that information may be accessed. Any user sitting at a workstation may gain access to information, and unless that user's access is carefully monitored, he or she can gain unauthorized access to sensitive data. Compound this with the ability of remote terminals to gain dial-in access to the network; and it makes for a very tough security situation. The workstations themselves may contain sensitive information with little or no security to protect it.

Security and authorization start with the concepts of users and passwords. The network administrator defines every new user for the system, gives the user an account, and assigns to that user the rights to various network objects. To gain access to the system, users must log on to the system, specifying both their user names and their passwords.

There are various methods of improving password protection. The first of these is to require a password of minimum acceptable length. Another improvement is to make sure that all passwords are encrypted and are sent across the network only in encrypted form. Ensuring that all passwords in the system are unique helps to enhance security, as does enforcing the periodic changing of passwords.

In conventional network environments, files, directories and devices can be protected by a number of access rights. The user may be given privileges (such as read, write, update, delete, modify attributes, perform directory searches, execute, create, and supervisory) at the file or directory level. Files themselves may be further protected by attributes like read-only, which prevents the file from being modified.

Some systems support the notion of a security database, which is responsible for assigning and tracking the privileges of all objects on the network. All objects, such as users and files must be registered in the security database. This database then determines who is allowed to access what object. Novell supports this notion by using a database they call "the bindery," which binds network objects with a list of authorization rights.

All network operating systems support varying forms of security. Novell has always been the leader in the area of security, but the other NOS's are not far behind. Many people feel that the security of the NOS is sufficient. Others have added the use of third-party security software to enhance the level of security. Third-party packages add security measures such as enveloping the workstation in a protective shell or encrypting all information, including file names, on the network.

The problem of security comes down to those who use the LAN. The network is only as secure as you make it. If the security features of the NOS are partially used, ignored, or not enforced, then all the locks and guards in the world won't do any good.

For the intelligent office environment, the security and authorization of office objects are allocated to various individuals, offices, and groups in the intelligent office hierarchy. This is discussed in detail in Chapters 11 and 12. One paradigm used for defining the authorization of objects in offices is "locality."

The office cabinet provides a useful example. When the cabinet is located within an office, its contents are "owned" by the worker in that office. This worker defines who can see objects within the cabinet, and the cabinet is a private object. When the cabinet is located in a common area outside the office, then it becomes a shared object. The access rights to a shared object are defined by the office administrator. The intent of intelligent office security and authorization is to provide an intuitive paradigm that deals with the office objects.

3.4.3 Backup

The backing up of network data is a vital operation to prevent the catastrophic loss of data. The concept of backing up information has been greatly complicated by the LAN model—not only do multiple servers need to be backed up, but numerous workstations, all with local hard disk storage and all containing valuable information, must be protected from hardware failure as well.

There are two types of information backup. In the first, simply called "backup," the daily changes to the information base are temporarily stored to an alternate device in case the primary storage device(s) fail. The information on the alternate device is quickly overwritten by subsequent backups and is not saved for long periods of time.

The second type of backup, called "archiving," provides long-term off-line storage of critical data for historical and statistical processing. This type of information is never overwritten.

Backup is performed by a combination of hardware and software. The hardware for backing information up has come a long way from the time when tape drives were the only way to back up valuable information. The problem with tape drives is that they are hard to maintain, the tape breaks easily, and they cannot provide random access to the information that is saved.

Enter optical storage. Optical storage has changed the ability to back up information significantly by providing unsurpassed capacity, random access, and freedom from the failures of magnetic tape. Optical storage is also the only technology that can effectively handle both "backup" and "archiving." The erasable disks are used for the daily backup while WORM disks are used for archiving. (Optical storage was discussed in more detail in Chapter 2.)

The process of backup is, in principle, quite simple and uses three set of backup media. The first time a backup is performed, three duplicates of the backup set are made and then stored off site. After that, the sets are rotated in a round-robin fashion. The set of backup media that is the oldest (most out of date) is used to perform the backup. If the system should fail, either during normal use or the backup process, the most recent backup is used to restore the system. If that backup set should fail, the final set may be employed to prevent total data loss.

A standard backup is done on a set time basis, such as daily, weekly, or monthly. Its primary purpose is to prevent the catastrophic loss of information. Erasable optical drives are the medium of choice for this operation.

Archiving, on the other hand, is concerned with the long-term preservation of information. Archiving is performed whenever the current state of critical data must be saved. Write-once optical media are preferred for this operation.

Several choices of backup software are available. Most network operating systems provide some type backup software, but often this software is not up to the task and should not be used unless the LAN in question is quite simple and small. Third-party companies offer a number of choices that are worth investigating. The big void in network backup software, however, is the ability to automatically back up all nodes on the network. Novell made an attempt at providing this level of backup support with a product called Archive Server. Unfortunately, the project was canceled and the void remains to be filled.

The intelligent office provides the means to automate the backup and archive procedure. The office administrator and office workers input rules that describe how the backup or archive should proceed. Office objects may be saved based on a number of criteria, including their content, search attributes, when they were created, when they were last updated, owner, by location, type, size, etc. The time when the backup or archive should occur is also specified in the rule.

The devices used for the backup or archive are determined by the backup rules. The office administrator selects the default device(s) for backup and the default device(s) for archiving. These devices may be overriden based on the backup rule and the object being saved. For example, all folders that deal with employee records may be sent to a backup device located in the human resources department.

■ 3.5 NETWORK SERVERS

The concept of a server is basic to the network. Services on the local area network are provided by servers. The server, which contains the hardware and software needed to provide a particular service, offers a centralized and shared location for that service. The server sits at a location remote from the user, providing both multi-user and multi-tasking access to the shared network objects. (An overview of client/server architecture is provided earlier in this chapter and discussed in detail in Chapter 4.)

The types of resources placed on a server are complicated to set up and maintain, are expensive, and by definition require concurrent, multi-user access. An example of such a device is an optical jukebox. The jukebox, with a potential capacity of a terabyte or more, requires the dedicated hardware horsepower that only a server can provide. Given the fact that the price tag of a jukebox can reach six figures, it is not cost-effective to place the jukebox on a user's workstation.

Servers range in functionality from generalized servers such as file servers, which provide a variety of services, to specialized and dedicated servers, such as print servers, database servers, and asynchronous communication servers, which provide a very specific service. Let us take a look at some of these servers.

3.5.1 File Servers

The file server was the original enticement that brought about the LAN revolution. As more personal computers entered the office, the more the need to exchange information between those computers grew. The original method of transfer, employed even to this day, was known as "sneaker net": Barb needs a file that is on Jim's PC, so she runs over to Jim's desk, copies the file onto a floppy disk, runs back to her desk, and loads the file.

Disk servers were the first attempts at sharing storage device. Disk servers simply provided low-level disk access to multiple workstations. The operating system at the workstation was responsible for reading and writing the information. The disk server merely provided contention resolution when two operating systems simultaneously attempted to update the same disk block.

File servers were the next-generation design evolving from disk servers. File servers, as the name indicates, were designed to provide file services to multiple users. The file server can be dedicated or nondedicated. A dedicated file server takes over all the resources and can not be used as a workstation. The nondedicated file server functions as both a file server and a workstation, providing a cheaper LAN solution but also suffering in performance. With the ever-dropping prices of PCs, the nondedicated file server has fallen out of use in all but the smallest of offices.

As the complexity and the needs of the LAN have grown, so the responsibilities of the file server have increased. The file server provides a host of different services. The network operating system, with all its features, resides on the file server. Services such as electronic mail, message handling service (MHS), security and authorization, and some printing services are all the domain of the file server. (There are also dedicated print servers.)

The computers that house file servers have undergone significant change in recent years. The first computers to house file servers were simple PCs that were undifferentiated from the workstation. As the complexity of the network operating system and the number of users have grown, the need for specialized hardware has become evident.

Companies such as Compaq now make PCs designed to house file servers. These computers can house gigabytes of storage, contain multiple CPUs to increase the computing horsepower, and incorporate new bus architecture for improved disk performance. Other companies, like Netframe, have abandoned the PC architecture altogether and built entirely new architectures in machines classified as "Super Servers." These super servers have incredible performance and can be expanded whenever the network needs more power.

The super servers are generally based on Intel's 386 and 486 microprocessors. The basic variables that must be considered when looking at super servers are the bus type

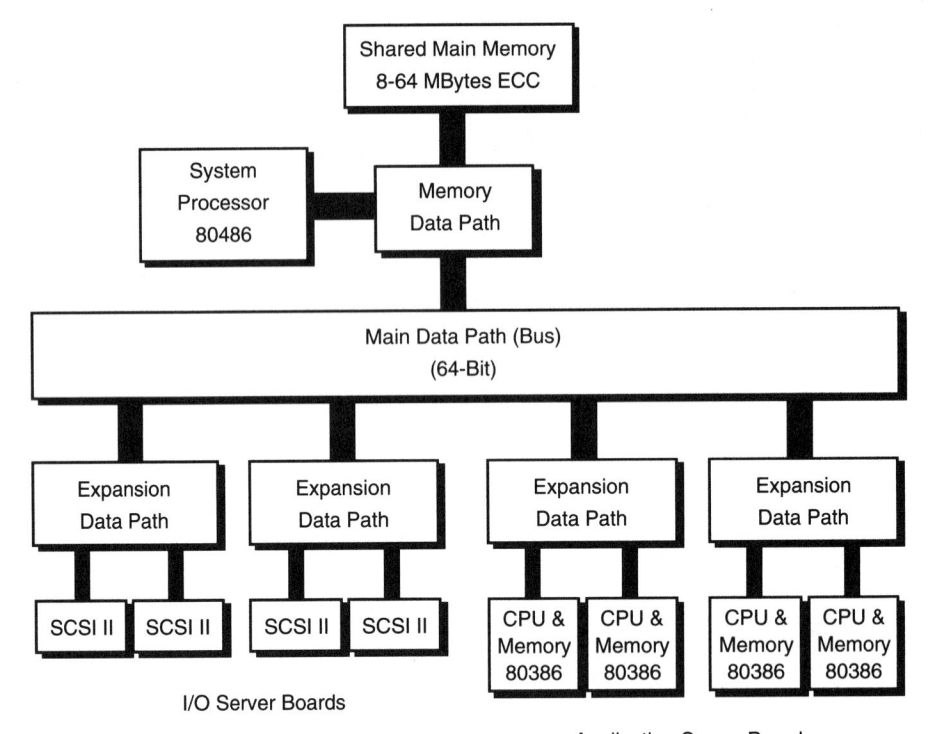

Figure 3.13 Netframe superserver architecture.

used, bus width and number, microprocessor speed and number, caching schemes, data redundancy, and error checking.

The bus architectures employed by these super servers are not the normal industry standard architecture (ISA) found on PCs. They range from IBM-enhanced Microchannel Architecture (MCA) and the new Extended Industry Standard Architecture (EISA) to proprietary bus architectures that borrow advanced bus features found on mainframes. Bus speeds must range in the 25 to 33 MHz range, while the bus width is 32 bits or greater. The transfer rates of the super servers range from 25 to 100 megabytes a second. Figure 3.13 illustrates an example of a super server architecture.

A specialized type of file server often used in imaging and document-processing applications is referred to as an optical file server. An optical file server is dedicated to the task of providing the mass archival storage to each workstation on the network.

Typically an optical server, using a dedicated PC with a large Winchester drive that is used for caching, will provide access to one or more daisy-chained jukeboxes and optical drives. Figure 3.14 illustrates a typical optical file server. (Chapter 2 gives a detailed description of optical hardware and software, and Chapter 6 discusses the imaging systems used in optical servers.)

3.5.2 Database Servers

With the growth of client/server computing, database servers have become an important part of the LAN environment. Database servers maintain the information base of the

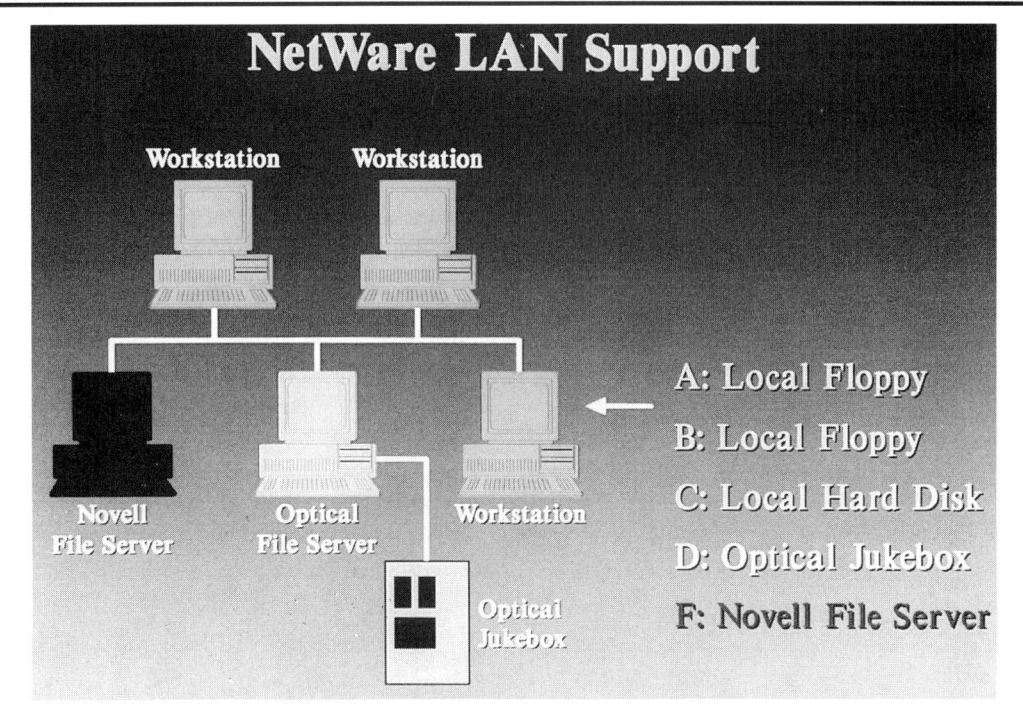

Figure 3.14 LAN with optical file server.

network, provide concurrent access to the information base, and maintain the consistency and validity of the data. Transaction control of database accesses is another key feature of the Database server. Database servers and database functionality are discussed in detail in Chapter 4 and briefly reviewed in this section.

Database servers come in two configurations. The first is a stand-alone configuration, where the database server sits on a dedicated workstation. In the second and newer configuration, the database server resides on the file server. In this situation the database server is dynamically linked into the network operating system. This tight integration of database engine and operating system has the advantages of improved security and efficiency.

With a database server, the client workstation passes a structured query language (SQL) request, in message form, to the server. The database server processes the request and then returns only the results. This saves a great deal of network traffic, since the code that processes the SQL request and the data both reside at the same location.

3.5.3 Communications Servers

Most LANs operate in the context of larger networks. A LAN that taps into a wide area network is common. Organizations often have several departmental LANs, which must communicate with one another. This communication is accomplished through the use of bridges and gateways.

A bridge is used to connect two similar networks together. Linking two Ethernet networks together would be an example of a bridge. Figure 3.15 illustrates a bridge.

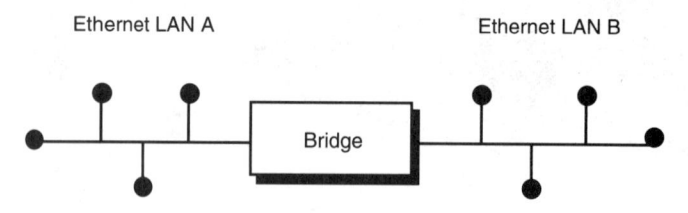

Figure 3.15 A bridge

A gateway, on the other hand, consists of both the software and hardware needed to connect two dissimilar networks. Connecting a token ring to an Ethernet would be an example of this. Figure 3.16 shows an example of a gateway. Typically a gateway is used to connect a LAN to a mainframe or a wide area network.

In simple cases, the bridge or gateway may exist in the file server. In the more complicated cases, the software and hardware reside on a dedicated server. This server then becomes responsible for maintaining and servicing the communications links between networks.

3.5.4 Network File Systems

One of the problems associated with file sharing on networks is that the underlying computer architectures can be very different. These differences range from the byte order of data to how the computer represents floating-point numbers and text. Clearly there must be some way for these workstations to share information.

Network file systems were created to alleviate this problem. The Network File System (NFS), perhaps the popular implementation in use, was developed by Sun Microsystems in 1984 to be machine-, operating system-, network-, and transport protocol-independent. NFS provides transparent remote use of shared file systems over local area networks.

NFS achieves this independence through the use of a two-layered protocol, remote procedure calls (RPC) and external data representation (XDR). RPC handles the exchanging of commands and data with a remote server. RPC allows procedures to be executed on a remote machine as if they were local to the calling software. The remote procedure call primitives are built on top of XDR, which provides a machine-independent method of representing data and eliminates such dependencies as byte ordering and floating-point format.

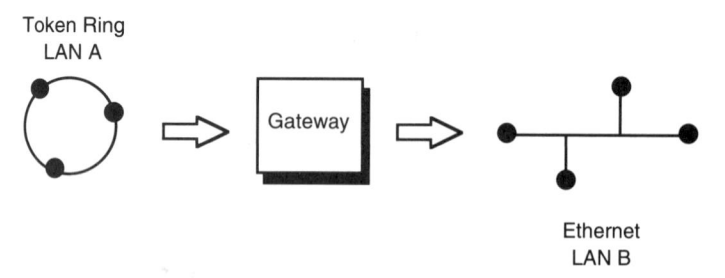

Figure 3.16 A gateway

```
┌─────────────┐
│ NFS Protocol│
├─────────────┤
│     RPC     │
├─────────────┤
│     XDR     │
├─────────────┤
│  Transport  │
└─────────────┘
```

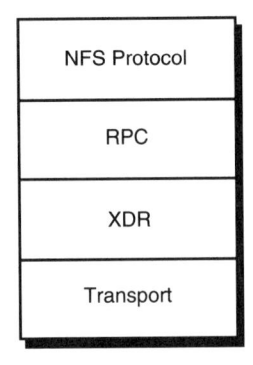

Figure 3.17 Layers of the Sun Network File System (NFS).

At the base level NFS perform two primary functions: It both exports and mounts file systems. One computer exports a file system by telling all other computers on the network that it has that particular file system available for use. The mount consists of attaching a file system to a specified place in the file tree. Figure 3.17 illustrates the structure of NFS.

There are other varieties of network file systems, such as AT&T's Remote File System (RFS). RFS, unlike NFS, is designed purely for UNIX file systems. The premise of RFS is that it should emulate local access completely. This means that all UNIX commands work normally, even though the file is remote.

Under RFS, a server advertises the availability of network resources (such as disk partitions), which are available for local mounting. Once the remote partition is locally mounted all accesses to that partition appear as if it were local. RFS has the advantage of NFS in a pure UNIX environment when it comes to transparency, but it does not address the needs of a heterogeneous network environment.

Additional file systems have been designed for massively distributed, wide area access. The Andrew File System (AFS), developed at the Carnegie-Mellon University and espoused by the Open Software Foundation, is one such example. AFS is tuned for much larger environments than NFS or RFS. AFS makes the entire network look like a single unified file tree for a large number of workstations. Each server contains named network volumes, which grow and shrink over time. Volumes can be moved from one machine to another, providing location transparency.

A number of emerging technologies and standards provide the user with distributed network file access. The trend, quite clearly, is to provide users with new file system methodologies that make sense for the LAN environment.

3.6 SUMMARY

Local area networks are a key platform for increased productivity in the 1990s and beyond, bringing users and information together. As the technology continues to grow, so will the potential for increased productivity.

Two major problems still hamper the productivity of LANs. The first is the ability to manage them. As LANs continue to grow in size and functionality, our ability to control the networks will be hampered. The present endeavors in the area of standard management protocols are beneficial, but work must continue in those arenas before the problem will be solved.

The lack of applications designed for the network is another area of concern. The amount of productivity that can be gained from LAN technology without good software to support it is limited.

The intelligent office is an attempt to solve this problem. By fully utilizing the abilities of the network to actively share information and ideas and by integrating existing applications into the LAN environment, the intelligent office can provide a framework within which we will use computers in the coming years.

This chapter has discussed network technology, which is the communications foundation of the intelligent office. The next chapter will discuss the database technologies that provide access to the information contained within the office.

4
DATABASE MANAGEMENT SYSTEMS

■ 4.1 INTRODUCTION

Database management systems, also called DBMS's, have been an integral part of medium- to large-scale applications since the mid-1960s. In essence, database management systems store and retrieve vast amounts of information. Any DBMS provides storage for a wide variety of data types, such as numerical (integer, floating-point, and decimal), binary, and textual.

Traditionally, DBMS systems have been used to keep track of corporate data, such as payroll and personnel information. With these types of applications, most DBMS's have been designed to provide storage and retrieval of highly structured data types, such as name, address, and gender. The recent interest in multimedia data, such as voice and images, has caused DBMS vendors to examine the storage and retrieval of multimedia data types.

The intelligent office environment will be supported in internetworked client/server architectures. This chapter describes the capabilities of database management systems in more detail. (Chapter 3 gave an overview of networking and server technologies.) In intelligent offices, databases will serve as the repository for all office objects (such as documents and folders) and allow them to be shared concurrently among various applications and office workers. More information about designing the intelligent office to use databases towards this goal is presented in Chapter 10.

4.1.1 Chapter Organization

Section 4.2 discusses the common capabilities provided by all DBMS's. Section 4.3 presents the evolution of databases from the network data model through the currently popular relational and object-oriented databases and the upcoming intelligent databases. Section 4.4 discusses relational databases in detail. Most of this chapter is dedicated to the relational data model, since the majority of applications requiring databases in the 1990s will be built on relational databases. The final section explores intelligent databases as the future direction of database management systems.

4.2 DATABASE CAPABILITIES

A DBMS is designed to store and retrieve vast amounts of information and to provide applications and office workers with concurrent access to the information stored in the database in the form of objects. A DBMS provides the following capabilities:

4.2.1 Persistent Storage

Information managed by a DBMS, such as payroll records or office documents, is stored on a long-term storage device such as magnetic disks. With the advent of multimedia data (such as voice and image), optical storage devices, such as CD-ROM, WORM, and rewritable optical drives, will soon play an important role in data storage. Chapter 9 discusses multimedia objects in more detail.

The main advantage of optical storage is the accessibility of huge and inexpensive secondary storage for large databases. Chapter 2 covers optical storage in detail. Imagine storing a picture of an employee with his or her personnel information. A picture of 100×100 pixels in size (assuming one byte per pixel) requires 10K bytes of storage. Thus, at least 100M bytes would be needed to permanently store the photographs of 10,000 employees.

In intelligent offices, most office objects will be persistent. For example, folders and documents within folders are persistent objects. Data about these objects and their relationship to other objects is managed by a database management system.

4.2.2 Transactions

A transaction (Eswaran *et al.*, 1976) is a program that is either executed entirely or not executed at all. This is called atomicity; transactions are atomic. If the user performs updates to the persistent database within a transaction, then either all of the updates must be visible to the outside world or none of the updates must be seen. In the former case, it is said that the transaction has been committed. In the latter case, we say that the transaction has been aborted. For example, in a database containing bank accounts, the act of transferring funds from one account to another requires two database operations: the removal of a fixed amount of money from one account and the deposit of the same amount into the second account. Since these two operations are treated as a single transaction, both or neither is recorded, thus maintaining the integrity of the database.

Most DBMS's support transactions with three primitives:

1. *Begin transaction*. This signals the starting point for any transaction. From this point until either of the following two transaction primitives occurs, all database statements are treated as an atomic operation.
2. *Commit transaction*. When a transaction is terminated with "commit transaction," all the database operations since the beginning of the transaction are executed and recorded in the database.
3. *Roll back transaction*. This primitive tells the database to discard all database operations that have occurred since the beginning of the transaction.

In intelligent offices, updates to persistent office objects will be done in the context of a transaction. For example, attributes of a document will be updated within a database transaction. When this transaction is committed, then all changes to the document attributes, such as its current status or new owner name, will be recorded in the database.

4.2.3 Concurrent Access

Database systems allow users to share the information stored in a database, and several users can concurrently access the database and retrieve or update information. To maintain the integrity of the data, the records that a user accesses within a transaction are locked. These locks are maintained until the end of the transaction.

In intelligent offices, the contents of a folder can be shared by one or more office workers. Several office workers can retrieve items concurrently within the same folder. When an office worker needs to update a document within this folder, that document is locked during the update operation to guarantee the integrity of its contents.

4.2.4 Query Languages

Database systems provide a language that allows the user to define and manipulate data. Most query languages fall into one of two categories:

1. A *data definition language* provides the database designer with the ability to define records, the types of each field within a record, and indexes for fast retrieval of data.
2. A *data manipulation language* provides the constructs for the insertion, deletion, modification, and (most importantly) retrieval of records in the database. SQL (discussed later in this chapter) is the standard query language for relational database systems.

In intelligent offices, office workers can retrieve office objects through the query language of the underlying DBMS engine. For example, an office worker may be interested in viewing all documents that have been updated within a certain period of time. Or an office worker may need to retrieve documents that are currently assigned to another individual.

4.2.5 Recovery

This mechanism restores the database back to a valid state after a failure (such as a system crash or media failure) occurs. For example, if the system crashes during a database operation, the recovery process may roll back all unfinished transactions in order to place the database in the sound state that existed before the failure occurred.

To ensure recovery after a media failure, a DBMS can be backed up and later restored from alternative media such as a tape drive. As a further safeguard, the database can coexist on two different drives. Thus, if one drive fails, the same database is available on another drive and can be accessed without any loss of time or data.

In intelligent offices, office objects stored in a database will be protected from mishaps, since the underlying DBMS engine keeps all these objects in a valid state.

4.2.6 Integrity and Security

Database systems provide an authorization mechanism to guard the data from spurious users. As part of the query language, the database designer can provide specific access rights to certain users. For example, in a payroll database, the designer may want to restrict the types of users who can examine or update an employee's salary.

4.2.7 Performance

Information in a DBMS can be retrieved efficiently. Using query languages, the database designer can define one or more indexes on fields that are accessed frequently. For example, since employee information is accessed periodically by the employee's name, employee records could be accessed faster by defining an index based on employee names.

Another performance enhancement provided by most DBMS systems is data caching, where frequently accessed data is stored in primary memory caches. Repeated access to the same data most often requires access to the data in the cache, thus minimizing access to the secondary storage.

■ 4.3 EVOLUTION OF DATABASE MANAGEMENT SYSTEMS

A DBMS defines data by organizing and interpreting it in a particular manner. Data modeling refers to the specific representation and interpretation of the data. Most database systems organize data into records and fields. Each record is a collection of fields, and each field contains a specific type of data. For example, an employee record is represented with name, address, age, and salary fields. In turn, each one of these fields has its own definition: the name and address fields are defined as strings of characters, the age field is defined as an integer number, and the salary field is defined as a fixed-point number.

The forerunners of database management systems were "generalized" file routines. In the 1950s and 1960s, data definition products were developed by large companies. This laid the foundation for network database management systems. The underlying data model of these databases presented the user with a network view of their databases. A network view (not to be confused with networked systems, discussed in Chapter 3) consists of record types and one-to-many relationships among the record types. The network model allows a record type to be involved in more than one relationship. A tree-structured hierarchical relationship among record types is a less general model. It is the basis of the hierarchical data model, which allows a record type to be involved in only one relationship as a parent and only one relationship as a child.

The Data Base Task Group (DBTG) of the Conference on Data Systems Languages (CODASYL) defined a comprehensive definition of network data models (CODASYL, 1971). A network data model is composed of record types and links (DBTG sets). A record type is a definition of a collection of records, and it is composed of zero or more data items. Each data item represents a field definition. For example, an employee's record type is composed of name, age, Social Security number, and salary data items. A link creates connections between record types. For example, given the "Office Worker" and "Department" record types, we can use a link called "Works for" to represent the concept of employees belonging to specific departments. Figure 4.1 represents the graphical

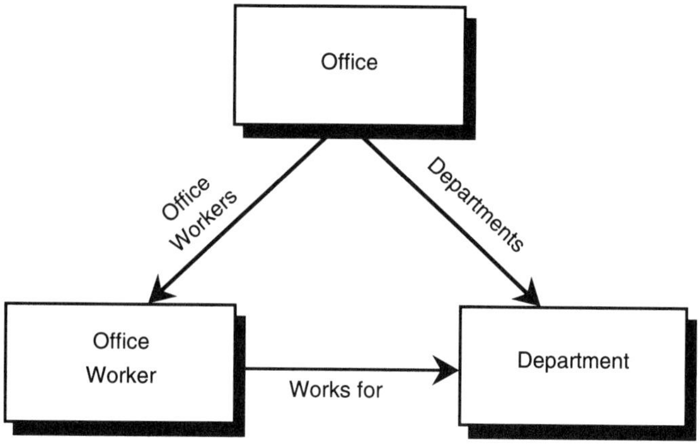

Figure 4.1 Network model for office workers.

representation of the network model for this example. Links or DBTG sets are limited to representing one-to-one or many-to-one relationships.

Hierarchical data models are a more restrictive form of network data models. In a hierarchical model, every node (except the root node) has a parent node. All links point from a parent node to a child node. The most popular hierarchical data model in use is IBM's Information Management Systems (IMS) (Lockwood, 1990). Most of the mainframe databases built in the 1970s were based on the IMS model.

Both the network and hierarchical data models were primarily navigational: The user started with a node and fetched a sequence of child or related nodes, effectively navigating through the physically stored database of nodes. Furthermore, the owner-member relationships (for the network model) or parent-child relationships (for the hierarchical model) were explicitly stored in the database records.

To provide more flexibility in organizing large databases and to alleviate some of the problems of the earlier models, Dr. E. F. Codd introduced the simple and elegant relational data model in the early 1970s. The underlying theory is based on the mathematically well-founded and well-understood concepts of relational algebra and first-order predicate calculus. Relational database management systems became increasingly popular in the 1980s, and their use and popularity are steadily increasing in the 1990s. Commercial relational systems and the propagation of relational databases stem from the success of the System/R (Astrahan et al., 1976) and INGRES (Stonebraker et al., 1976) relational database implementation efforts. System/R was an ambitious research project that paved the way for a number of commercial implementations from IBM including DB2, SQL/DS, and Extended Edition Database Manager. The relational data model is discussed in more detail in the next section.

In the late 1980s, almost all commercial database management systems were based on either a hierarchical, network, or relational model. Still, there were several alternative database-modeling proposals. One of the earliest alternative proposals was the semantic data model, which uses the node and link representation schema of semantic networks. Each node is an entity type. Similar to a data type in a programming language, an entity type represents a set of objects (entities), all having the same attributes. An attribute is a function that can apply to an entity in the entity type. The name of an entity type also identifies the extension (set of all instances) of the entity type. Entity types are analogous to classes, and entities are analogous to instances. Additionally, attributes are analogous to instance variables.

Semantic data models are primarily used as design tools for underlying relational or network databases. The forerunner of the semantic models was the famous entity-relationship model, introduced by Chen (1976). Other semantic data models closely related to the entity relationship model include the Semantic Data Model (Hammer and McLeod, 1981) and TAXIS (Mylopoulos *et al.*, 1980; Wong, 1983).

The entity-relationship data model (Chen, 1976) has been used widely as a database design tool. This model presents two major concepts: entities and relationships. An entity is the representation of an object, such as an employee, a department, or a sales account. A relationship is used to establish connections among entities. For example, the concept of an employee working for a department or an employee managing other employees is modeled as a relationship.

An entity-relationship model can describe several forms of relationships between entities, including one-to-one, one-to-many, or many-to-many. An example of a one-to-one relationship is the relationship between managers and departments, where each manager is in charge of one department. An employee and a department form a one-to-many relationship, because each employee works for one department, but each department has many employees. Students and courses have a many-to-many relationship, since each student is enrolled in one or more courses, and each course has one or more students.

Entity-relationship (ER) diagrams have been used to depict database designs. In an ER diagram, rectangular boxes represent entities, and diamond-shaped boxes represent relationships. In addition, circles or ovals indicate attributes of an entity. Figure 4.2 displays an example of an ER diagram that depicts the design of a small corporation. The entities modeled are "Office Workers," "Projects," and "Department." The relationships modeled are "Works For" and "Participate." The Letters N or M on the links of an ER diagram indicate many-to-many relationships. In this diagram, the "Works For" relationship has been defined as a one-to-one relationship, since each employee works for one department and each department has many employees. The "Participate" relationship is a many-to-many relationship, since each employee works on one project or many, and each project has one or many employees. Section 4.4.5 illustrates the usefulness of ER diagrams in designing relational databases.

A number of data models also attempted to incrementally extend the traditional relational data model to allow more flexibility while maintaining a solid theoretical foundation.

The object space in the relational model consists of a collection of flat tables. Each table is a set of rows (or tuples). The column values in each row (attributes of tuples) can only be instances of basic, atomic types, such as integers, floating-point numbers, or character strings. The flat-table representation is known as the first normal form.

Complex object models attempted to relax the first-normal-form restrictions (normalization is discussed in Section 4.4.5.1) while maintaining the strong theoretical foundation of the relational model. With nested and more general complex-object models, more

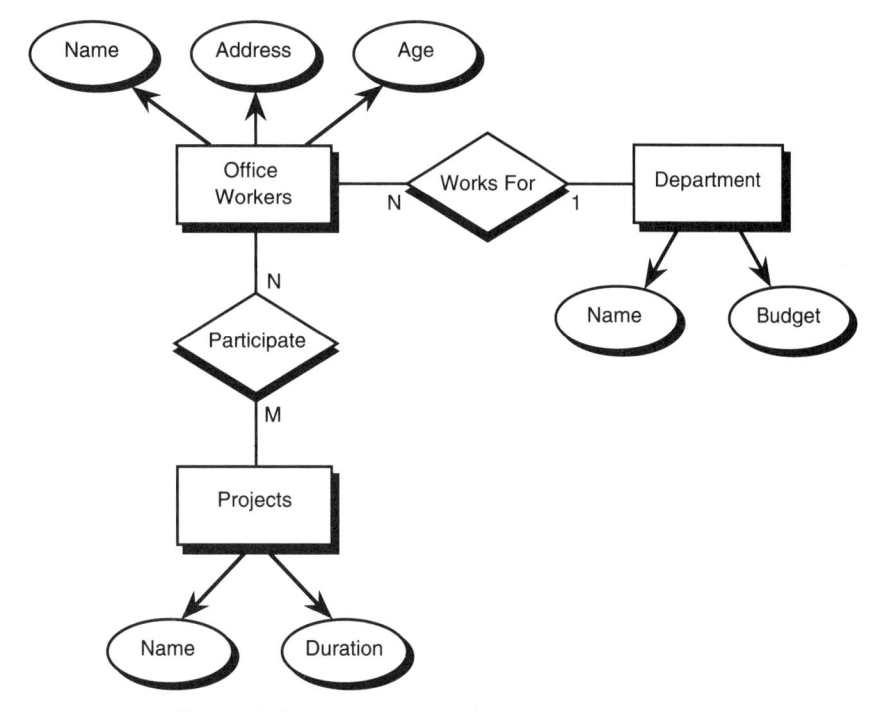

4.3 Evolution of Database Management Systems ■ 87

Figure 4.2 Entity-relationship diagram for office workers.

general object spaces can be constructed using set and tuple object constructors. The column values can thus be tuples, sets of base values, or sets of tuples (in other words, relations). If the model supports object identity, the sets and tuples could be referentially shared. Thus, users can construct arbitrary graph-structured object spaces and avoid the "unnatural" foreign key joins of the relational model. There have been a number of nested relational models, including VERSO (Bancilhon et al., 1983) and the nested relational model of Schek and Scholl (1986).

More general (nesting not only relations but arbitrary objects) complex-object models can be constructed by building object spaces on top of a collection of basic, atomic types, using two object constructors: sets and tuples. Bancilhon and Khoshafian (1986; 1989) and Khoshafian (1988) present more general complex objects using set and tuple object constructors.

The postrelational complex-object models mentioned so far only allow tree-structured object spaces. Although rich in conceptual foundation, these models did not allow the same object to be a subobject of multiple parents. They do not support graph-structured object spaces. To have this ability, object models need to support the object-oriented concept of object identity. One of the earlier object-oriented models that fully supported object identity was FAD (Bancilhon et al., 1987), which was implemented at the MCC Research Consortium in Austin, Texas. Objects in FAD were constructs from sets, tuples, and atomic objects. Each object has an identity independent of its type (set, tuple, or atomic) or value. Other object models that allow the construction of general graph-structured object spaces included GEM (Zaniolo, 1983) and LDM (Kuper and Vardi, 1984).

The semantic data models and the complex-object models were mostly research proposals, projects, or prototypes. The complex-object and semantic data models laid a strong foundation for the development of a number of object-oriented databases, both in research and in industry. Concepts such as complex objects, object identity, inheritance, and set- and tuple-valued attributes propagated into these powerful object-oriented database systems (Zdonick and Maier, 1990; Khoshafian, 1990; Cattell, 1991; Brown, 1991; Hughes, 1991). Each object-oriented database was influenced by one or more of the complex and semantic data-modeling alternatives. Perhaps through an eagerness to explore novel and emerging technologies, developers took quick notice of the opportunities and potential of the integration of object-oriented concepts with database capabilities (such as concurrency, persistence, access methods, and querying).

With the introduction of object-oriented database systems such as GemStone from ServioLogic, Gbase from Graphael, and Vbase from Ontologic, object-oriented database became commercially available in 1986–1987. The first object-oriented database workshop in Asilomar, California, during the summer of 1986, also demonstrated that great enthusiasm (similar to that in the object-oriented programming communities) was permeating the database community. The following years witnessed the development of several commercial object-oriented databases, including Statice from Symbolics (Symbolics, 1988), SIM from UNISYS, ObjectStore from Object Design, ITASCA, from Itasca Systems, Inc., Objectivity/DB from Objectivity, and many others.

Object-oriented databases remove the so-called semantic gap between an application domain and its representation in persistent storage. Since the real world is modeled as closely as possible, the links and relationships among entities in the complex real world are represented and manipulated directly. Object-oriented databases achieve their modeling capability through the object-oriented concepts of abstract data typing, inheritance, and object identity. Chapter 7 discusses object-oriented concepts in detail.

Object-oriented databases also alleviate the "impedance mismatch" between programming languages and database management systems. In complex applications, the data is retrieved from a database management system using a database query language (such as SQL) and then manipulated through routines written in a conventional programming language (such as C or PL/I). Conventional languages are procedural, whereas database query languages are higher-level and more declarative. Applications involving both languages mix these different programming paradigms. Furthermore, the data types in the different languages are not the same and have to be mapped onto one another.

Currently there are at least six approaches for the incorporation of object-oriented capabilities in databases:

1. Novel database data model/data language approach
2. Extending an existing database language with object-oriented capabilities
3. Extending an existing object-oriented programming language with database capabilities

4. Providing extendable object-oriented database management system (OODBS) libraries
5. Embedding object-oriented database language constructs in a host language
6. Application-specific products with underlying OODBS

For object-oriented languages and user interfaces, we are already witnessing the emergence of a number of standards: C++, Smalltalk-80, CLOS, and Ada for object-oriented languages and Microsoft's PM, HP's NewWave, and IBM's OfficeVision for user interfaces and environments.

In the area of databases, things are not so clear. Although there are some attempts, such as those pursued by the Object Management Group and various standardization task forces (including some from ANSI), standards are not emerging. The market share of object-oriented databases in the foreseeable future is negligible when compared to the relational, network, and hierarchical market shares. In fact, relational databases are just taking off, and they will continue to dominate in the 1990s. Yet relational database management systems are starting to incorporate object-oriented features. This falls under option 2 in the foregoing list. Many companies involved in the development of relational systems are incorporating object-oriented features in their products. Therefore, the dominant standard will be object-oriented extensions of SQL. Section 4.6 presents object-oriented extensions in future generations of SQL.

In the database community, there are two opposing views about the direction of object-oriented databases. On one side, object-oriented vendors argue in favor of brand new languages for OODBMS outside the current database languages. They claim that relational databases cannot be extended to encompass object-oriented technologies and that new object-oriented database languages are needed. They believe that the approach of extending the relational model is not a viable direction. Also, they claim that the current SQL language is already too complex. (The new SQL 2 language reference manual is over 500 pages.) Refer to the article by (Atkinson *et al.*, 1989) for more detail.

On the other side, relational database vendors are proposing to extend their products to encompass object-oriented technologies. The advantage of this approach is that during the last ten years most of the commercial world has invested heavily in relational database technology. A few research projects such as Intelligent SQL (Khoshafian, 1991a) and POSTGRES (Stonebraker, 1986) have demonstrated the technical viability of extending the relational model to encompass object-oriented concepts. We will discuss Intelligent SQL in Section 4.6.

The exact course of OODBS will be determined in the near future. The major impact of this technology will continue to be in the fields of computer-aided design (CAD), computer-aided manufacturing (CAM), and computer-aided software engineering (CASE).

A different but equally significant development in the evolution of databases was the incorporation of inferencing- and logic-based models in the early and mid-1980s. Through the launching of a number of fifth-generation projects (such as ICOT in Japan and MCC in the United States), Prolog became increasingly popular. Prolog provided an implementation of logic programming, and its programs consisted of collections of declarative rules. The interpretation of these rules utilized unification and SLD resolution. (SLD resolution stands for SL-resolution for Definite clauses, where SL stands for Linear resolution with Selection junction—Lloyd, 1984.) Prolog implementations were primarily in-RAM systems, with little or no capabilities to access bulk extensional databases.

Several scientists and researchers attempted to integrate Prolog and SQL. For example, PROSQL (Chang and Walker, 1986) attempted to incorporate SQL statements in the premises of Prolog rules. A more recent attempt was Intelligent SQL (Khoshafian, 1991; Khoshafian et al., 1991).

Other models, such as the Calculus of Complex Objects (CCO) by Bancilhon and Khoshafian (1986, 1989), the Logic-based Data Language (LDL) by Tsur and Zaniolo (1986) and the NAIL! project from Stanford (Ullman, 1988), attempted to provide complete conceptual models that incorporated deduction in a declarative rule-based database system. Unlike Prolog, which has backward-chaining left-to-right and top-down goal-directed execution semantics, these models provided more consistent and general logic-based semantics. More specifically, in the CCO, LDL, and NAIL! models the order of the rules and the order of the predicates that appear in the premises of the rules do not influence the behavior or the operational semantics of the logic programs. This enhances the expressibility and generality of logic-based database management systems. The generality and the ability to have consistent semantics of logically equivalent programs paved the way for a number of query optimization techniques, especially in the area of recursive queries (Bancilhon and Ramakrishnan, 1986).

The next evolutionary step after object-oriented and inferencing- and logic-based databases is toward intelligent databases. These databases integrate inferencing and object orientation. Object orientation models real-world persistent object spaces directly. Inferencing is important both as a declarative style of programming and as a base technology to perform inductive reasoning about databases. Object orientation, augmented with inferencing, provides a powerful model to support complex applications in the 1990s.

Intelligent databases also support multi-media data types such as text, images, and voice. The intelligent database user interface provides a high-level hypermedia programming environment to the user. Intelligent database tools enable users to automatically discover intricate relationships in their persistent object spaces. Section 4.6 presents extensions that can be made to SQL to incorporate intelligent database concepts.

4.4 RELATIONAL DATA MODEL

Relational databases are widely used in corporate environments. In the commercial world, SQL-based relational servers are just taking off. The virtue of the relational data model lies in its simplicity. A relational database is composed of a set of relations. Each relation can be viewed as a two-dimensional array or table, in which each column specifies an attribute of the relation. Each attribute has a specific type, called a domain. The domain of an attribute can range from a generic type definition (such as integer, floating-point, fixed-length character string, and varying-length character string) to a more constrained definition (for example, a sex attribute should only allow "F" and "M" character values). Each row of the table, called a tuple, consists of a collection of attribute values.

4.4 Relational Data Model

Office workers table

Emp#	Name	Age	Sex	Salary
01	Jack Kline	21	M	25000.00
02	Sue Smith	25	F	12000.00
03	Bob Adams	21	M	32000.00
04	Carol Krang	29	F	47000.00
05	Donald Smith	35	M	22000.00
06	Donna Avalon	38	F	19000.00

Figure 4.3 A relational table.

Figure 4.3 depicts the *OfficeWorker* relation. The attributes of this relation include *Emp#*, *Name*, *Sex*, *Age*, and *Salary*. Each of these attributes has a predefined domain: *Name* is a character string of length 32, *Sex* is a character string of length 1, *Age* is integer, and so on. The fifth tuple in this relation contains the employee data for (Emp#: 05, Name: Donald Smith, Age: 35, Sex: M, Salary: 22,000.00).

4.4.1 Data Independence

Relational database systems were first introduced by E. F. Codd in 1970 (Codd, 1970). In this paper, Codd defined the mathematical foundation for the relational data model. A central point in Codd's paper is the concept of data independence: A database application is immune from changes in the storage structure (called physical data independence) and from the schema definition (called logical data independence).

For example, in physical data independence, if new indexes are added or the database is reorganized to tune the performance of the system, applications should not have to be recompiled or modified to take advantage of these new changes. In previous data models (network and hierarchical), such physical storage tuning caused changes in the application programs. In logical data independence, for example, if new fields are added in a table definition, existing application programs should not be modified.

4.4.2 Entity and Referential Integrity

A relational data model represents each relation as a mathematical set. A mathematical set, by definition, does not contain duplicate elements, so each relation has a primary key to guarantee the uniqueness of tuples in a table. A primary key can be defined based on a set of attributes of that table. For example, the *Name* field in the *OfficeWorker* table could be defined as the primary key, which would then require the name of each employee to be unique. Attributes used in a primary key definition cannot accept null values. This property of relational database systems is called entity integrity.

In addition, relational database systems permit the definition of foreign keys. "In general, a foreign key is an attribute (or attribute combination) of one relation *R2* whose values are required to match those of the primary key of some relation *R1* (*R1* and *R2* not necessarily distinct)" [Date, 1986b]. Foreign keys provide referential integrity. For example, given a table representing employees and departments, we may define a foreign key to guarantee that as long as an employee works for a department, that department cannot be deleted.

4.4.3 Data Manipulation

One of the strengths of the relational model is a well-defined collection of powerful data manipulation operators. Since each relation in the relational database model is represented as a set, most data manipulation operators are derived from operations that can be performed on sets. The collection of these operators, along with their semantics, is known as relational algebra.

Some of the powerful relational algebra operators include selection, projection, join, product, union, intersection, and difference. The following subsections discuss these operators in detail.

Throughout these section, we will use the database in Figure 4.4 for illustration. This database represents a small corporation with a set of departments represented by the *Dept* table, a set of employees represented by the *OfficeWorker* table, and an *EmpDept* table representing the department of each employee.

4.4.3.1 Selection

This operator allows the selection of one or more tuples of a given table. To make the selection, a conditional expression (called a predicate) is applied to filter out the

Emp#	Name	Age	Sex	Salary
01	Jack Kline	21	M	25000.00
02	Sue Smith	25	F	12000.00
03	Bob Adams	21	M	32000.00
04	Carol Krang	29	F	47000.00
05	Donald Smith	35	M	22000.00
06	Donna Avalon	38	F	19000.00

(a)

Dept#	Name
01	Personnel
02	Engineering
03	Payroll
04	Accounting
05	Q&A

(b)

Emp#	Dept#
01	01
02	01
03	02
04	02
05	04
06	04

(c)

Figure 4.4 A relational database example. (a) Office worker table; (b) Dept table; (c) EmpDept table.

resultant tuples. For example, Figure 4.5a is the result of selecting female employees. The predicate in this selection is the expression "*OfficeWorker.Sex* is equal to 'F'."

Most relational data manipulation languages allow a wide range of operators in the predicate of a selection. In addition to equality, other comparative operators (greater, greater than or equal to, smaller, and so on) and string search operators, such as "Name field containing first name 'John'," are provided.

4.4.3.2 Projection

This operator allows the viewing of specific attributes of a table. In addition, if necessary, the redundant tuples in the result can be eliminated. Figure 4.5b displays the result of projecting the *Age* and *Sex* attributes of the employee table. Notice that we have eliminated the redundant tuples, since the employees with numbers 01 and 03 have the same *Age* and *Sex* attributes.

4.4.3.3 Product

This operator takes two tables and produces the Cartesian product as the result. Given two tables A and B, the Cartesian product is the result of concatenating each tuple of table A to each tuple of table B. Figure 4.5c displays the partial product result of the *OfficeWorker* and *EmpDept* tables. The product operator is used more often in conjunction with a join operator.

4.4.3.4 Join

This operator is one of the most popular relational operators. It allows the result of a query to be derived from data stored in two or more tables. This operator generates results by selecting matching attributes from the product of two or more tables.

For example, Figure 4.5d displays the result of joining *OfficeWorker* and *EmpDept* on the matching condition that *OfficeWorker.Emp#* is equal to *EmpDept.Emp#*. The result displays the department number of each employee.

Figure 4.5e displays the result of joining the three tables *OfficeWorker*, *EmpDept*, and *Dept* to display each employee name and his or her corresponding department name. To produce this result, *OfficeWorker* is joined with the *EmpDept* table, with the *OfficeWorker.Emp#* equal to the *EmpDept.Emp#*. This result is then joined with the *Dept* table, with the *EmpDept.Dept#* equal to *Dept.Dept#*.

4.4.3.5 Union

The union of two tables A and B is the set of all tuples belonging to either A or B. For example, assuming that a corporation has two divisions and that each division's employees are kept in a separate table, the union of these two tables produces the employees of the entire corporation.

In order to union two or more tables, the result from each table must be union-compatible. Union-compatibility is guaranteed when the number of columns derived from each table in the union matches the types of each resultant column within the union.

4.4.3.6 Intersection

The intersection of two tables is the set of tuples belonging to both tables. For example, Figure 4.5f displays the result of intersecting *EmpDept* and *Dept* to retrieve the departments that contain one or more employees. Again, the tables involved in an intersection operation must be union-compatible.

Emp#	Name	Age	Sex	Salary
02	Sue Smith	25	F	12000.00
04	Carol Krang	29	F	47000.00
06	Donna Avalon	38	F	19000.00

(a)

Age	Sex
21	M
25	F
29	F
35	M
38	F

(b)

Emp#	Name	Age	Sex	Salary	Dept#	Name
01	Jack Kline	21	M	25000.00	01	Personnel
01	Jack Kline	21	M	25000.00	02	Engineering
01	Jack Kline	21	M	25000.00	03	Payroll
01	Jack Kline	21	M	25000.00	04	Accounting
01	Jack Kline	21	M	25000.00	05	Q&A
02	Sue Smith	25	F	12000.00	01	Personnel
02	Sue Smith	25	F	12000.00	01	Personnel
.	...					
.	...					
.	...					

(c)

Emp#	Name	Age	Sex	Salary	Dept#
01	Jack Kline	21	M	25000.00	01
02	Sue Smith	25	F	12000.00	01
03	Bob Adams	21	M	32000.00	02
04	Carol Krang	29	F	47000.00	02
05	Donald Smith	35	M	22000.00	04
06	Donna Avalon	38	F	19000.00	04

(d)

Figure 4.5 Examples of relational operators. (a) Selection; (b) projection; (c) product; (d) join.

4.4.3.7 Difference

The difference of two tables is the set of tuples that belong to one table and not to the other. For example, Figure 4.5g displays the result of the difference between the *Dept* table and the *EmpDept* table to retrieve departments that have no employees. Again, the tables involved in a difference operation must be union-compatible.

Most relational DBMS systems provide a query language that supports relational algebra. Several relational query languages have been developed by different database

Emp#	Name	Age	Sex	Salary	Dept. Name
01	Jack Kline	21	M	25000.00	Personnel
02	Sue Smith	25	F	12000.00	Personnel
03	Bob Adams	21	M	32000.00	Engineering
04	Carol Krang	29	F	47000.00	Engineering
05	Donald Smith	35	M	22000.00	Accounting
06	Donna Avalon	38	F	19000.00	Accounting

(e)

Dept#	Name
01	Personnel
02	Engineering
04	Accounting

(f)

Dept#	Name
03	Payroll
05	Q&A

(g)

Figure 4.5 (cont) Examples of relational operators. (e) join; (f) intersection; (g) difference.

system and computer vendors. Examples of these vendor-specific query languages are QUEL for INGRES and Rdb for VAX Rdb.

SQL (Structured Query Language) has been accepted as the standard query language for all relational database systems. All relational database vendors support the SQL language with their own specialized extensions. SQL is discussed in more detail in Section 4.4.4.

4.4.4 SQL Language

Structured Query Language, called SQL (pronounced "sequel"), has been accepted by all database vendors as the standard interface to relational databases. All vendors provide a SQL interface that is compliant with the ANSI X3H2 SQL-89 standards. The SQL standard is currently going through another major revision, called SQL2. The SQL2 proposal is currently under consideration for approval and is generally expected to be adopted as the new standard soon.

One unique feature of the relational data model compared to the previously discussed data models is that all relational database vendors support SQL as the standard interface. In addition, almost all relational vendors' database engines provide their own extensions to this standard for their own special features. Section 4.5.7 presents Sybase's SQL Server, including some of the SQL extensions provided by this vendor.

The following discussion begins with data definition concepts and language constructs such as *CREATE TABLE* and *VIEW*s. Afterward, the data manipulation constructs, such as the *SELECT*, *INSERT*, and *DELETE* statements, are presented.

4.4.4.1 Data Definition

This section defines tables and fields and then examines some of the integrity constraint definitions such as primary and foreign keys. Following is a discussion of indexes and their definition in SQL. Next, we turn our attention to views, which are virtual tables that provide alternative presentations of stored data. The last part of this section discusses how SQL handles security and authorizations.

4.4.4.1.1 Tables and Data Types

In SQL, relations are defined by the *CREATE TABLE* statement. These relations are called base tables. This statement must identify the table name, the name and type of each field, and whether each field value is unique within this table. The following example illustrates the definitions of the *OfficeWorker*, *Dept* and the *EmpDept* relations:

```
CREATE TABLE OfficeWorker
    (Emp# integer UNIQUE, Name character(30), Age integer,
    Sex character(1) CHECK("M", "F"), Salary numeric(10,2))

CREATE TABLE Dept
    (Dept# integer UNIQUE, Name character(30))

CREATE TABLE EmpDept
    (Dept# integer, Emp# integer)
```

In this example, the *Name* field of the *OfficeWorker* table is defined as a character field of length 30. The *Age* field is defined as an integer, and the *Salary* field is defined as a numeric field, allowing storage of a monetary value (such as 20000.99). Also in this example, the *UNIQUE* constraint on the *Emp#* field was used to indicate that each employee number is unique within this table.

In addition, the *CHECK* option constrains the values that can be placed in the *Sex* fields to either "M" (for male) or "F" (for female). This option can be used to define more complex restrictions on the value of any field. For example, the following definition for the *Age* field is constrained to accept values ranging from 16 to 100, assuming that no one younger than 16 or older than 100 years old can work for this company:

```
Age integer CHECK (Age >= 16 AND Age <= 100)
```

Each table can have one primary key, composed of one or more field names and indicating the uniqueness of each tuple in the table (thus enforcing entity integrity). In order to establish relationships between tables in a relational data model, a database designer must incorporate fields in a table definition to reference tuples of another table definition.

In the corporate database, relationships were established between office workers and departments by defining the *EmpDept* table, which keeps track of which employees work for which department. The following example demonstrates the corporate database with the specified entity and referential integrity constraints.

4.4 Relational Data Model ■ 97

```
CREATE TABLE OfficeWorker
    (Emp# integer UNIQUE, Name character(30), Age integer,
    Sex character(1),
        Salary numeric(10,2))
    PRIMARY KEY (Emp#)

CREATE TABLE Dept
    (Dept# integer UNIQUE , Name character(20))
    PRIMARY KEY(Dept#)

CREATE TABLE EmpDept
    (Emp# integer, Dept# integer)
    FOREIGN KEY(Emp# IDENTIFIES OfficeWorker)
    FOREIGN KEY(Dept# IDENTIFIES Dept)
```

In this example, *Emp#* and the *Dept#* are guaranteed to be unique. When a tuple is inserted in the *OfficeWorker* table, the database checks for the uniqueness of *Emp#*. If the value of the *Emp#* is unique, the new tuple is accepted, if the value is not unique, the new tuple is rejected. The two *FOREIGN KEY*s defined on the *EmpDept* table also guarantee the validity of all references to the employee and department tables. Thus, for example, as long as the *EmpDept* table references an employee, that employee's number cannot be deleted or altered. A SQL table can be populated by using the *INSERT* statement, which is defined in Section 4.5.4.2.

4.4.4.1.2 Indexes

Without an index, a database scans a table sequentially and uses associative retrieval. Indexes can be defined on fields used commonly for searching and accessing, thus providing faster access to the information stored in a database. Indexes are defined on the values of one or more fields of a particular relation. For example, in the sample corporate database, employee and department names are often used as when searching through the employee and the department tables. The following indexes can be defined to optimize access to these tables:

CREATE INDEX EmpNameIndex ON OfficeWorker (Emp#)

CREATE INDEX DepNameIndex ON Dept (Dept#)

Indexes are named only during their creation with the *CREATE INDEX* statement and their destruction with the *DROP INDEX* statement. Indexes are not referenced by the user during any query operation. A relational DBMS contains a subcomponent known as the query optimizer. During any query operation, the database system's query optimizer analyzes the query and chooses the most efficient method to access any one table or group of tables.

4.4.4.1.3 View Definition

The base tables created by *CREATE TABLE* statements are real and physically stored on the secondary storage device. In addition to the base tables, the database designer can define virtual tables using the view mechanism. A virtual table, called a view in relational database terminology, offers several advantages. Views can be used to define a logical window of the database for special users. For example, to restrict access to employees' salary information, a view can be defined to provide access to all fields of the employee table except the salary field. This view is defined by the following example:

CREATE VIEW Restricted_OfficeWorkers (Emp#, Name, Age, Sex)
    AS SELECT Emp#, Name, Age, Sex
        FROM OfficeWorker

The *SELECT* statement, discussed in Section 4.5.4.2, retrieves the *Emp#*, *Name*, *Age*, and *Sex* fields of the *OfficeWorker* table.

The *Restricted_OfficeWorkers* view behaves and acts very much like any base table. Thus, it can be used like any table definition to access and retrieve information about the *Restricted_OfficeWorkers*. This view is updatable, so the user can update tuples into the *Restricted_OfficeWorkers*, which in turn updates the *OfficeWorker* table. Some views, such as the view in the following example, are not updatable.

CREATE VIEW NewRestricted_OfficeWorkers (Name, Age, Sex)
    AS SELECT Name, Age, Sex
        FROM OfficeWorker

The primary key for the *OfficeWorker* table is *Emp#*, which is not accessible by the *NewRestricted_OfficeWorkers*. As a result, no tuples can be added via this view definition. Since a primary key uniquely identifies an employee, each employee record must have an employee number. Any records inserted via this view definition would be rejected, since they would violate the primary key definition on the *OfficeWorker* table.

4.4.4.1.4 Security and Privilege

Relational databases protect their data from unauthorized access. As demonstrated in the previous section, views can be used to limit access to specific fields of a table. However, access to tables should also be restricted to certain groups of users. The view mechanism does not allow the definition of authorized users.

User authorization is defined by the *GRANT* and *REVOKE* statements. The *GRANT* statement permits the owner of a database object (such as a base table) to transfer specific access (such as the ability to retrieve or update specific fields) to other users or groups of users. Privileges that can be granted or revoked include select access to individual columns, update access to individual columns, insert or delete access into a table, and the transfer of the grant option to another user.

For example, the following *GRANT* statement grants select access to the employee salary field to any user in the *Payroll* group:

GRANT SELECT ON OfficeWorker(Salary) FROM Payroll

The next *GRANT* statement grants update access to the *Dept* table to any user in the *Personnel* group:

GRANT UPDATE ON OfficeWorker FROM Personnel

The following REVOKE statement forbids access to office workers' salary information to users in the ENGINEERING group:

REVOKE SELECT ON OfficeWorker (Salary) FROM Engineering

4.4.4.2 Data Manipulation

SQL provides the SELECT, INSERT, UPDATE, and DELETE statements to manipulate data stored in a database. The SELECT statement retrieves results from one or more tables. The INSERT statement populates a table, and the UPDATE statement modifies the values of any field of a table. Finally, the DELETE statement removes any tuple from a table.

4.4.4.2.1 SELECT Statement

This statement allows the retrieval of data from one or more tables in a SQL database. For example, the following query retrieves the name, age, and gender of all office workers:

SELECT Name, Age, Sex
FROM OfficeWorker

This query produces the following result:

Name	Age	Sex
Jack Kline	21	M
Sue Smith	25	F
Bob Adams	21	M
Carol Krang	29	F
Donald Smith	35	M
Donna Avalon	38	F

This query retrieves the Name and Age of each tuple in the OfficeWorker table. In order to restrict the result to a more specific set of tuples of the table (such as only female office workers), the previous SQL statement is modified with a WHERE clause.

SELECT Name, Age
 FROM OfficeWorker
 WHERE Sex = "F"

This new query produces the following result:

Name	Age
Sue Smith	25
Carol Krang	29
Donna Avalon	38

A WHERE clause defines an expression to filter out the selected tuples from one or more tables involved in the retrieval operation. SQL allows a wide range of operations in the WHERE clause. The operation may be a comparison, such as equality (=), inequality

(<>), less than (<), greater than (>), and others. In the previous example, the equality comparison was used for returning only female office workers.

The range comparison, or the *BETWEEN* operator, tests whether a value falls inside or outside of a given range. The next query returns the names of all office workers who have salaries ranging from $15000.00 to $30000.00:

SELECT *
FROM OfficeWorker
WHERE Salary BETWEEN 15000.00 AND 30000.00

The results of this query are the following:

Emp#	Name	Age	Sex	Salary
01	Jack Kline	21	M	25000.00
05	Donald Smith	35	M	22000.00
06	Donna Avalon	38	F	19000.00

Note that this example also demonstrates a new construct (*), which indicates to the database to return all columns from the selected table.

The *WHERE* clause can also perform set comparison using SQL's *IN* (set inclusion), *SOME*, *ANY*, *ALL*, and *EXIST* (set existence) operators. The following example returns the name of all office workers whose salary is either 47,000.00 or 22,000.00:

SELECT Name
FROM OfficeWorker
WHERE Salary IN (47000.00, 22000.00)

The following result is returned:

Name
Carol Krang
Donald Smith

(More examples of this operator are presented later during the discussion of the use of the *SELECT* statement with subqueries.)

SQL can perform the pattern-matching comparison using the *LIKE* operator, which allows the value of a character string field to be matched against a string pattern. For example, the following query returns the count of all office workers whose name begins with the letters "Do":

SELECT COUNT(*)
FROM OfficeWorker
WHERE Name LIKE 'Do%'

The answer returned to this query is 2, since two office workers ("Donald Smith" and "Donna Avalon") have names beginning with the letters "Do".

4.4.4.2.1.1 Support for Relational Algebra

The relational model is defined with a set of well-behaved operators, which were introduced in Section 4.4.3. The join operator is one of the most powerful and frequently used operators, and it retrieves data based on the combination of results from two or more tables. For example, the following join operation returns the department number of each office worker:

```
SELECT OfficeWorker.Name, EmpDept.Dept#
    FROM OfficeWorker, EmpDept
    WHERE OfficeWorker.Emp# = EmpDept.Emp#
```

This query yields the following information:

OfficeWorker.Name	EmpDept.Dept#
Jack Kline	01
Sue Smith	01
Bob Adams	02
Carol Krang	02
Donald Smith	04
Donna Avalon	04

In this example, the two tables *OfficeWorker* and *EmpDept* are joined based on the equality of the *OfficeWorker.Emp#* field against the *EmpDept.Emp#* field. The following query demonstrates the use of the join operator to return the name of each office worker with his or her department name.

```
SELECT OfficeWorker.Name, Dept.Name
    FROM Officeworker, Dept, EmpDept
    WHERE (OfficeWorker.Emp# = EmpDept.Emp# AND
        Dept.Dept# = EmpDept.Dept#)
```

The result is the following:

OfficeWorker.Name	Dept.Name
Jack Kline	Personnel
Sue Smith	Personnel
Bob Adams	Engineering
Carol Krang	Engineering
Donald Smith	Accounting
Donna Avalon	Accounting

This example retrieves the desired information by joining three tables: *OfficeWorker*, *Dept*, and *DeptEmp*.

4.4.4.2.1.2 Retrieval Using Subqueries

SQL contains set comparison operators, such as *IN*, *SOME*, *EXIST*, *ANY*, and *ALL*. The following query returns the name of any department that does not have any office worker:

```
SELECT Dept.Name
    FROM Dept
    WHERE Dept.Dept# NOT IN
        (SELECT Dept#
        FROM EmpDept)
```

This example also demonstrates SQL's support for the intersection operator.

4.4.4.2.2 INSERT Statement

This statement populates a SQL table with one or more new tuples. The following statement inserts a new tuple to the OfficeWorker table:

INSERT INTO OfficeWorker VALUES (07, "Vartan Manoogian", "M", 22, 27000.00)

This insertion can be viewed as the process of appending a new tuple to the end of the OfficeWorker table. Any indexes on this table are also updated to reflect this new tuple.

When a new tuple is added to a table, some columns may be left as unspecified. The following INSERT statement adds a new office worker without any initial salary information:

INSERT INTO OfficeWorker (Emp#, Name, Age)
  VALUES (07, "Vartan Manoogian", "M")

Because no salary information is provided, the Salary field will be filled with a default value (supplied by the CREATE TABLE statement) or else with the NULL value to indicate that the value is missing. If a default value does not exist for this table, the value of Salary will be returned as NULL when information is requested about this record.

4.4.4.2.3 UPDATE Statement

The UPDATE statement permits the modification of field values of existing tuples in a table. The following example gives a 10 percent raise to all office workers making less than $20,000.00:

UPDATE OfficeWorker
  SET Salary = Salary + Salary * .10
  WHERE Salary <= 20000.00

4.4.4.2.4 DELETE Statement

Finally, the DELETE statement permits the permanent deletion of one or more tuples in a table. The following example deletes all office workers earning salaries higher than $30,000:

DELETE FROM OfficeWorker WHERE Salary > 30000

The tuples selected in this operation are deleted only if they do not conflict with the integrity rules defined with the foreign keys. Given the foreign keys defined on the EmpDept table, the database system requires the following delete operation to precede the previous example:

DELETE FROM EmpDept
  WHERE EmpDept.Dept# IN
    (SELECT OfficeWorker WHERE Salary > 30000)

4.4.4.2.5 Cursor-Based Operations

All of the SQL examples illustrated up to this point perform an operation on a subset of selected results. In addition to set-oriented data manipulation, SQL also permits cursor-based data manipulation. In cursor-based operations, the user preselects the result and then can choose to perform a specific operation on any one of the previously selected results.

Cursor-based operations are always used when SQL is embedded in another language. Thus, the results can be retrieved a tuple at a time by the application. After the application analyzes the data in the individual tuple, it can update or delete the selection or move to the next tuple in the result.

The following actions initiate and perform cursor operations. First, a cursor is declared with a query that specifies the parameters of the desired results. Next, the cursor is opened by the *OPEN* statement, preparing the resultant stream of tuples for processing. Then, individual records are selected via a *FETCH* statement. (In embedded SQL, the *FETCH* statement permits the application to accept values of the result into application variables.) And finally, when the records have been processed, the cursor is terminated with the *CLOSE* statement.

The following example illustrates the *DECLARE* statement:

```
DECLARE EmpCurs CURSOR FOR
    SELECT Name, Age
    FROM OfficeWorker
    WHERE Salary > 20000.00
```

This example prepares a stream of office worker tuples, including *Name* and *Age*, corresponding to those workers whose salaries exceed $20,000.00. Before any tuple in this field can be processed, the following statements open the cursor and fetch the first record:

```
OPEN EmpCurs
FETCH EmpCurs
```

The tuples selected in a cursor can be updated or deleted individually. The following example changes the age of the next tuple in the result:

```
UPDATE OfficeWorker
    SET Age = 25
    WHERE CURRENT OF EmpCurs
```

In this example, *CURRENT OF EmpCurs* indicates that the update should only occur on the current row in the *EmpCurs* cursor.

The following statement deletes the next tuple in this cursor:

```
DELETE FROM OfficeWorker
    WHERE CURRENT OF EmpCurs
```

4.4.4.3 Embedded SQL

SQL is not a complete programming language. SQL constructs only allow the definition and manipulation of data stored in a relational database. SQL does not provide any constructs for generating reports or forms. In all database applications, SQL is embedded into another programming language, called the host language, such as C, COBOL, PL/I, or Ada. Embedded SQL statements can communicate with the application written in the host language by passing values in and out of the database through the application variables.

The following example illustrates a section of C code with embedded SQL:

```
int SearchSalary = 10000;
int EmpAge;
char EmpName(30);

EXEC SQL DECLARE EmpCurs CURSOR FOR
    SELECT Name, Age
    FROM OfficeWorker
    WHERE Salary > :SearchSalary;

EXEC SQL OPEN EmpCurs;
while (/* more data */)
{
    EXEC SQL FETCH EmpCurs INTO :EmpName, :EmpAge;
    printf("Name = %s, Age = %d", EmpName, EmpAge);
}
EXEC SQL EmpCurs;
```

In this example, the *DECLARE* statement accepts the minimum salary value from the application through the *SearchSalary* application variable. The results of the query are returned into *EmpName* and *EmpAge* application variables.

Notice that all embedded SQL statements are prefixed with *EXEC SQL*. In most cases a language compiler will not see these calls because a SQL precompiler converts the embedded SQL statements into routine calls from the appropriate database application programming interface. (Refer to Section 4.4.7.2 for an API example.)

4.4.5 Relational Database Design

The relational data model presents a simple but powerful modeling mechanism. This section describes the required design steps to map an application's persistent storage needs to a relational database.

The persistent information maintained by a database can be separated into three separate categories:

1. *Structural definitions*, such as tables, attributes, and indexes. Using these definitions, the application defines the tables necessary for tracking an application's different entities and the relationships between those entities. In the foregoing examples, office workers and departments are maintained in two separate tables, and the relationship of office workers to departments is stored in a separate table.

4.4 Relational Data Model ■ 105

Each table consists of a set of attributes that describe the required properties for that table, such as the name and age of each office worker. Indexes are used to optimize the performance of the process of accessing frequently referenced fields.

2. *The actual data stored in the database.* This data consists of the rows or tuples of all the tables in the database. In the corporate database, the tuples collectively stored in the *OfficeWorker*, *Dept*, and *EmpDept* tables represent the data stored for the given corporation.

3. *Integrity constraint definitions.* Integrity constraints guarantee that a database remains consistent and valid throughout its life. For example, all attributes of a given table will always have valid results. The gender of an office worker is always defined and is equal to either 'M' (male) or 'F' (female). (Refer back to Section 4.4.5.3 for more information about integrity constraint definitions.)

This section describes a commonly practiced technique for designing a relational database. Many other design strategies are available, and several alternatives are presented by Date (1986b) and Khoshafian *et al.* (1992). The design process discussed here involves the following steps:

1. Define the entity-relationship (ER) diagram(s) that models the necessary semantics of the application's persistent data. (Refer to Section 4.3 for a discussion of the entity-relationship data model and ER diagrams.)

Figure 4.6 depicts the ER diagram of a corporate office worker database. In this figure, we have modeled three entities: office workers, managers, and departments.

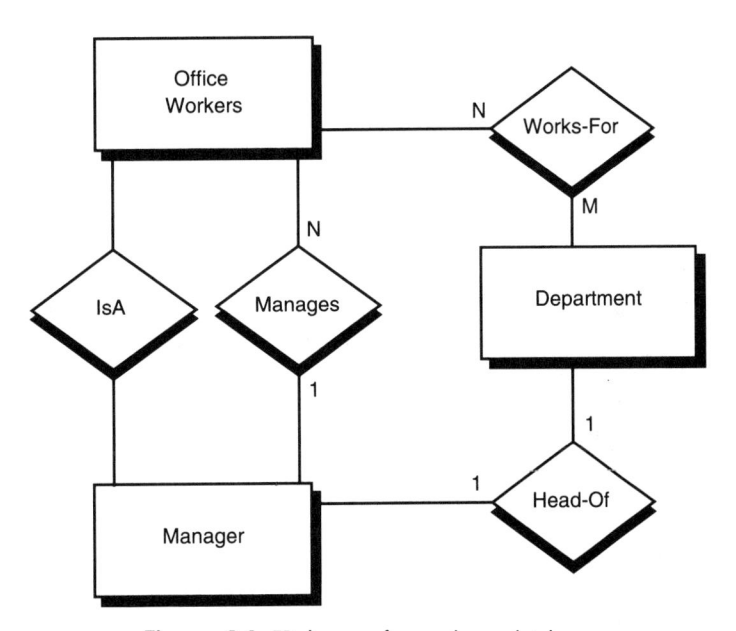

Figure 4.6 ER diagram for employee database.

The *Is-A* relationship indicates that all managers are office workers. The *Manages* relationship is a one-to-many relationship indicating that several office workers are managed by one manager. The *Head-Of* relationship is a one-to-one relationship, indicating that one manager is in charge of one department. The *Works-For* relationship indicates that an office worker is employed in one department but that one department has one or more office workers.

2. Decompose the ER diagram into a set of relational tables. Each table represents either an entity or a relationship among entities. The use of normalization as the commonly used decomposition strategy is discussed in Section 4.4.5.1. Briefly, the normalization process minimally guarantees that each column of a table is atomic and that data redundancy is minimized.

3. Define the integrity constraints. The integrity constraints define the necessary conditions for a consistent database. Section 4.4.5.2 describes the typical integrity constraints that should be considered with relational database design.

The integrity constraints and the relational database tables together represent the final relational database design. This design can be implemented by using a CASE tool that performs relational database design. Most CASE tools ask the user to define the ER diagram of a database design and the integrity constraints for the individual entities and relationships. Once given this information, the CASE tool can generate a group of SQL tables along with the necessary integrity constraints.

4.4.5.1 *Normalization*

Normalization defines a set of rules and guidelines for designing "well-formed" and high-performance relational databases. A "well-formed" relational database is designed to prevent inconsistencies, unnecessary data duplication, and anomalies. There are several types of normalization: first normal form (1NF), second normal form (2NF), on through the fifth normal form (5NF). Each one of these forms is more restrictive than the previous one. The ultimate goal of normalization is to get rid of all functional dependencies other than the dependency on the primary key.

The following discussion concentrates on the first three normal forms. For more detailed and analytical coverage of normalization refer to Khoshafian *et al*. (1992) and Ullman (1980).

The first normal form states that all fields in a table must be atomic. This restriction implies that no field in a table can be variable-length or multi-valued. This is the only form of normalization enforced by all relational database systems. (The other normal forms are enforced through the database designer.)

For example, an office worker can have one or more children. This is a typical example of a multi-value field. This is an example of a field that does not fit the first normal form. Figure 4.7 displays the 1NF tables corresponding to the entity-relationship diagram shown in Figure 4.6.

The second and third normal forms guarantee that a relation is in first normal form and, in addition, that every field is either part of the composite key or provides a nonrepeating fact about the whole key and nothing else. For example, in Figure 4.6, several

```
MANAGES(MGR#, EMP#)
OFFICEWORKERS(EMP#, Name, Address, Sex, Salary, Age)
DEPARTMENTS(DEPT#, Location, Budget)
WORKS-FOR(EMP#, DEPT#)
HEAD-OF(EMP#,DEPT#)
```

Figure 4.7 First normal form representation of employee database.

departments can be located in the same building. Instead of repeating building information with every department, this information can be grouped together in a table representing buildings. Figure 4.8 represents these transformations.

Another way to understand the normalization process is by using the notion of functional dependency (FD). "Field *B* of table *T* is said to be functionally dependent on field *A* of table *T* if and only if it is the case that, for each distinct value of field *T.A*, there is necessarily exactly one distinct value of *T.B* (at any given time)" (Date 1986b, p. 451). In Figure 4.8, *OfficeWorkers.Name* is functionally dependent on employee number if for each office worker id, a unique name exists for that office worker.

Each normalization process accepts a given set of tables as input and generates the same or additional tables as the result. The main goal is to present each fact in only one table of the database.

Even though normalization is a necessary process for relational database design, over-normalization can cause performance problems. Since each normalization step cuts a table definition into several smaller table definitions, more joins would be necessary to generate the same result that would have been the result before this last normalization step was introduced. Thus, the decision on what degree of normalization to use (4NF or 5NF) is left to the judgment of the individual designer or the CASE tool.

4.4.5.2 Integrity Constraints

In the previous section, we defined the structural description of each table. In the following step, the table definitions are augmented with constraints that represent the consistency and validity of the database during its existence. These constraints are called declarative constraints because they are defined through language extensions to the CREATE TABLE statement.

```
MANAGES(MGR#, EMP#)
OFFICEWORKERS(EMP#, Name, Address, Sex, Salary, Age)
DEPARTMENTS(DEPT#, Budget)
BUILDINGS(LOC#, BuildingName)
DEPT-LOC(DEPT#, LOC#)
WORKS-FOR(EMP#, DEPT#)
HEAD-OF(EMP#,DEPT#)
```

Figure 4.8 Third normal form representation of employee database.

The following declarative constraints could be placed on the corporate database:

- Each office worker and department must have an identifier.
- Each office worker's gender must be either 'M' or 'F'.
- If an office worker works for a manager, that manager's record must exist.
- One manager is head of only one department.
- Each office worker works for only one department.
- Age of each office worker is greater than 16 and less than 75.

Thus, many forms of integrity constraints must be enforced to guarantee database consistency. Declarative integrity constraints can be defined by several techniques:

1. *Primary key constraint.* The primary key constraint defines one or more fields in a table that uniquely identify a row. For example, in the OfficeWorker table Emp# uniquely identifies an office worker, so Emp# is the primary key. In the WORKS-FOR table, Emp# combined with the Dept# uniquely identifies a row in this table. Thus, these two fields combined should be used as the primary key for the WORKS-FOR table. In SQL, the PRIMARY KEY construct can be used to specify a primary key for table definitions.

2. *Foreign key constraint (referential integrity).* The foreign key constraint resolves the dangling reference problem. For example, in the HEAD-OF and WORKS-FOR tables no rows should reference a nonexistent Emp# or Dept#. In other words, at all times references to any worker or department number should point to an existing tuple in the office worker or department table. In SQL, the FOREIGN KEY construct can be used to specify foreign key constraints.

3. *Domain constraints.* The domain constraint allows field values to be restricted to a more meaningful result. For example, the Sex field of an office worker can be restricted to hold either 'F' (female) or 'M' (male) values. The Age field for an office worker can be restricted to permit values ranging from 16 to 75. In SQL, the CHECK constraint can be used to specify domain constraints.

4. *Non-null constraints.* In database systems, a null value represents a missing value. Because an office worker tuple will always have information in the Name field, that field can be restricted with a non-null constraint to guarantee that it will always contain a value during each update or insertion of information about new office workers. In SQL, any field of a table can be specified with NOT NULL to prohibit the missing value.

5. *Unique constraints.* A unique constraint guarantees the uniqueness of the combined value of one or more fields. In the office worker table, a unique constraint on Name guarantees that each name of an office worker will be unique.

6. *Trigger definition.* This is a general-purpose mechanism for specifying any type of integrity constraint. For example, in the employee database example, this allows the restriction that the budget of a department should always be larger than the combined salaries in all office workers in that department.

A trigger is a group of one or more SQL statements. Its execution is tied to certain generic database operations, such as SQL's *INSERT, UPDATE, DELETE,* and *SELECT* statements. A trigger definition has two major pieces: conditions and actions. The conditional component specifies a predicate describing the constraint condition. The action component describes one or more database operations, which are executed if the conditional component's predicate is satisfied. Each trigger can contain several conditions and actions.

A table can include several trigger definitions, which are each attached to a specific operation on the table. Any of the constraint definitions previously discussed can also be defined using triggers. (Refer to Figure 4.13).

Some database systems support integrity constraint only through trigger definitions. Declarative constraint definitions offer two major advantages. First, they are used often and are easier to define declaratively than by writing a trigger statement. Second, the database system can optimize declarative constraints more efficiently.

4.4.6 Client/Server Architecture

Most corporations today utilize distributed computing systems that may include IBM PCs and compatibles, Apple Macintoshes, UNIX workstations, and other computing resources. As a result, a major requirement of a corporation's database system is to provide users with access to data from one or more remote sites.

The client/server computing environment addresses this need. As the client/server environment in Figure 4.9 illustrates, the responsibility of data presentation and access is divided between the client and the server. A client workstation (generally a personal computer) focuses on the presentation of data to the user. The server machine, usually a powerful processor with vast storage capacity, concentrates on the storage and retrieval of the data.

When the user queries the database, the client machine presents a query to the server machine. The database system residing on the server machine accepts the query, compiles it, and selects the best optimization strategies (such as which indexes to use and the order in which joined tables should be processed). The DBMS then collects the result of the query and transfers the result to the client machine. Figure 4.10 displays these communications graphically.

Most database systems provide an application programming interface (API), which is used by client applications to access databases stored on a remote server. The typical protocol followed by a client machine and the database server providing the API is summarized in Figure 4.11. This protocol includes several actions:

1. *Establish a session.* Before any user on a client machine can formulate queries, he or she must establish himself or herself as an authorized user of the database. To establish a session with the server, a user specifies a user name and a password. The server checks the validity of both. If they are valid, the server establishes the session. From this point on, all communication between the client and the server is handled within the context of a session.

110 ■ Database Management Systems

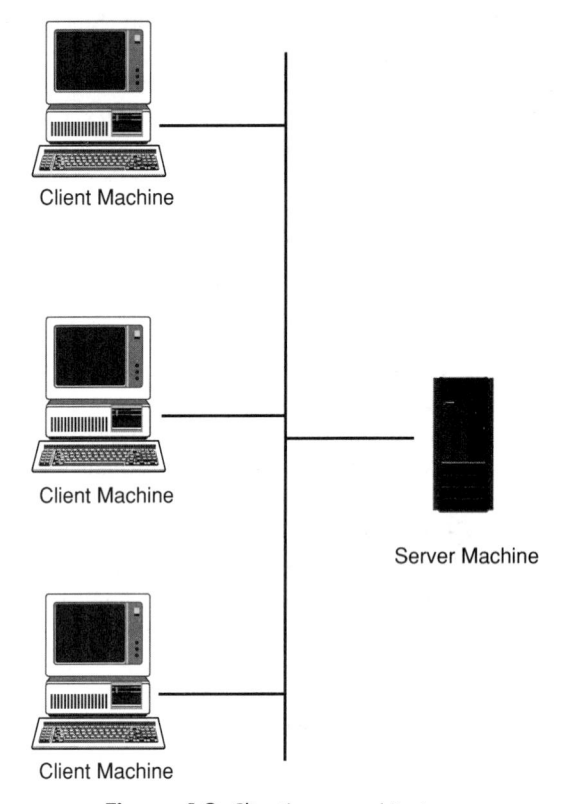

Figure 4.9 Client/server architecture.

2. *Prepare a query.* The client transfers a database request such as *SELECT*, *UPDATE*, or *DELETE* to the server. The database system on the server side performs the following steps:
   - Compile the request, checking whether all references to fields and tables are valid.
   - Optimize the compiled request to determine the fastest method for obtaining the results of the query. The optimization process takes advantage of indexes defined on tables within the database and reorders joins to minimize access to each table.

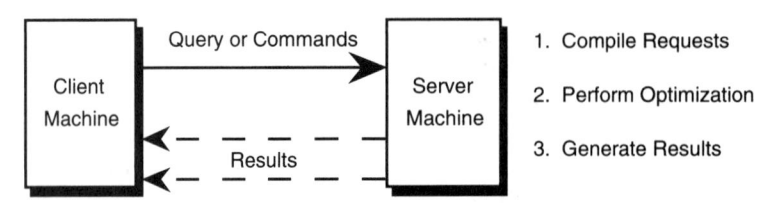

Figure 4.10 Client/server architecture protocol.

4.4 Relational Data Model ▪ 111

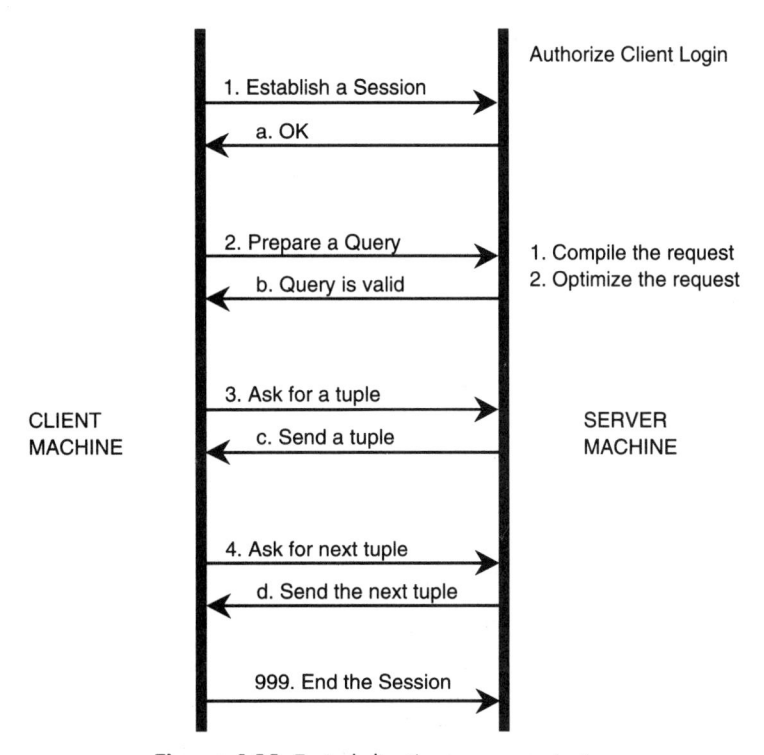

```
                1. Establish a Session  →    Authorize Client Login
                ←  a. OK

                2. Prepare a Query      →    1. Compile the request
                ←  b. Query is valid         2. Optimize the request

    CLIENT      3. Ask for a tuple      →    SERVER
    MACHINE     ←  c. Send a tuple           MACHINE

                4. Ask for next tuple   →
                ←  d. Send the next tuple

                999. End the Session    →
```

Figure 4.11 Typical client/server communication.

3. *Accept result and process*. If the query requires data retrieval, the client can ask for each tuple of the result, one at a time, from the database server. The client can accept each tuple one at a time and process them individually.

   Even though the client can request these tuples individually, the database server does not transfer each tuple across the wire individually. Instead, to avoid unnecessary network traffic, most client-server database systems provide a cache on the client side. When a query generates a stream of results, a chunk of these results is transmitted to the client machine in one batch across the network. When the client side cache is exhausted, the next batch of the results is transmitted across the network to the client.

4. *Terminate the session*. When the client has processed all of the requests from the database server, it terminates communication by ending the session.

4.4.7 SQL Server: A Case Study of a Client/Server Relational Database System

This section presents Sybase's SQL Server as an example of a relational database system supporting client/server architecture. This discussion of SQL Server is not comprehensive, but concentrates on its important features with respect to client/server computing. While other database systems (including IBM EE, Oracle, SQL Gupta, and VAX Rdb)

112 ■ Database Management Systems

support the concept of client/server computing, we chose SQL Server because it provides very good coverage of client/server architecture through the SQL language and programming interface extensions.

SQL Server is composed of the following components:

- *TRANSACT-SQL*, the SQL dialect supported by the SQL Server
- *dblibrary*, the SQL Server application programming interface
- *SAF* (System Administrator Facility), which permits the database administrator to define database, users and their passwords; to back up and restore databases, and to optimize the database's performance (Refer to Sybase (1990d) for more information about SAF).

4.4.7.1 TRANSACT-SQL

TRANSACT-SQL is the special SQL dialect of SQL Server (Sybase, 1990b and 1990c). In addition to performing the usual SQL statements described previously in this chapter, TRANSACT-SQL supports several important features:

1. *Control-of-flow language*. TRANSACT-SQL is a full-fledged programming language with the standard language elements, such as begin-end blocks, local variables, and looping and control constructs (WHILE, IF...ELSE, GO TO label)

2. *Stored procedures*. This is one of the major features of TRANSACT-SQL. A stored procedure is very much like a regular procedure in a programming language. It accepts a set of parameters as input and computes a set of tuples as the result. A stored procedure can contain any number and type of TRANSACT-SQL statements, such as control-of-flow statements.

    The main advantage of a stored procedure is that a group of commonly used SQL statements can be combined together and stored in a given server. A stored procedure can return results from one or more selected tables. In addition, a stored procedure can invoke other stored procedures. (Sybase does not support recursive stored procedure execution.)

    To access a stored procedure, an application calls that procedure and supplies the necessary parameters. When a stored procedure is accessed for the first time, the database system compiles the procedure and stores it in a special system-defined table. Subsequent execution of the same stored procedure by the same client application or other applications only causes the precompiled stored procedure to be executed.

    A stored procedure provides several benefits. First, it minimizes network traffic by storing commonly executed queries on the server. Second, it minimizes compilation and optimization by storing the precompiled results of stored procedures for subsequent access. Figure 4.12 displays a TRANSACT SQL stored procedure with some control-of-flow statements.

3. *Triggers*. As discussed previously, triggers provide a general mechanism for defining integrity constraints. A trigger is defined by specifying which data modification statement (such as UPDATE, DELETE, and INSERT) activates the trigger and which table is the trigger's target.

```
create procedure RichEmployees
as
    select Name, Age, Salary
    from Employees
    where Salary >= 10000.00
```
(a)

```
exec RichEmployees
```
(b)

Figure 4.12 Typical TRANSACT SQL stored procedure. (a) Definition; (b) execution.

SQL Server does not support the declarative form of the primary and foreign key definition. In order to define these keys, the trigger mechanism is applied. Figure 4.13 displays two trigger definitions for the OfficeWorker table to guarantee that all *Emp#* remain unique during any *INSERT* and *UPDATE* operations.

4.4.7.2 dblibrary

The dblibrary is the application programming interface between client applications and SQL Server (Sybase, 1990a). The dblibrary consists of a set of C routines and macros that provide the following types of operations:

1. *Initialization*. This category of dblibrary calls provides the necessary setup to establish a connection with a SQL Server or to access a particular database on a given server, since each server can manipulate several databases. Each database in SQL Server is a logical grouping of one or more tables and their corresponding tuples.

```
create trigger UniqueInsertEmp
on Employees
for insert
as if(select count(*)
        from Employees, inserted
        where Employees.Emp# = inserted.Emp#) > 1
    begin
        rollback transaction
        print "At least one employee exists with this employee number."
    end

create trigger UniqueUpdateEmp
on Employees
for update
as if update(Emp#)
begin
        rollback transaction
        print "Emp# can not be updated"
end
```

Figure 4.13 Typical Transact SQL trigger mechanism to support primary keys.

2. *Command processing.* Each connection to SQL Server has its own command buffer. A client application can place one or more TRANSACT-SQL statements in the command buffer. The set of statements in the command buffer is called the command batch. The client application can send the command batch to SQL Server as a single request. SQL Server compiles the command batch, checks for erroneous SQL syntax, and generates an optimized execution strategy if no errors are present in the command batch.

3. *Results processing.* The resultant tuples from the execution of the command batch are available to the client application. Each tuple can be requested individually. Each column of the result can be bound to a specific variable in the client's program. The client application can process each tuple individually until all the resultant tuples have been handled, or it can ignore the remaining result at any time.

   The dblibrary supports a separate row buffer for each connection. A client application can choose to set aside a row buffer to hold the results returned from the server. The results read in by the application are stored in a row buffer and are accessible to be read again. With a row result, an application can read a set of results and browse through the result.

4. *Information retrieval.* These API calls provide information about the state of the current connection and the state of the command and row buffers.

5. *Error and message handling.* These calls provide a mechanism for the client program to specify application routines to receive errors and messages generated by the dblibrary and SQL Server. Once an error message has been generated (such as an invalid table name), a user defined routine is invoked to handle the error condition.

Figure 4.14 displays an example of dblibrary calls from a C program. In this example, the name, age, and salary of all office workers earning more than $10,000.00 is requested.

■ 4.5 INTELLIGENT DATABASES

As stated earlier, intelligent databases represent the merging of a number of distinct paths of technological development. Until recently, these technologies were treated in near-isolation, with each technology being only weakly linked to others. For instance, expert systems have relied on little more than file-transfer protocols to gather data from databases. Due to the phenomenal growth in each field, the connections to the other fields did not have time to form. Now that these technologies have reached a stage of maturity, it is possible to define an overall unifying structure for viewing all these fields. Intelligent databases provide a common approach to the access and use of information for analysis and decision making. As stated in Section 4.3, intelligent databases integrate:

- Object orientation
- Deductive rules (expert systems and artificial intelligence)
- Information retrieval
- Multi-media

4.5 Intelligent Databases

```
#include <sqlfront.h>
#include <sqldb.h>

main ()
{
    DBPROCESS *dbproc; /* The connection with the SQL Server. */
    LOGINREC *login; /* The login information. */
    DBCHAR name[40];
    DBINT Age;
    DBMONEY Salary;

    /* Define user-supplied error and message handling routines. */
    dberhandle(error_handle);
    dbmsghandle(msg_handle);

    /* Get a LOGINREC */
    ligin = dblogin0;
    DBSETLUSER(login, "razmik");
    DBSETLPWD(login, "passwork");

    /* Get a DBPROCESS structure for communication with SQL Server. */
    dbproc = dbopen(login, "document_server");

    /* Retrieve name and age of all employees making more than $10,000.00 */
    dbcmd (dbproc, "select Name, Age, Salary from Employees");
    dbcmd (dbproc, "where Salary >= 10000.00");

    /* Send the command buffer to the server. */
    dbsqlexec(dbproc) == SUCCEED
    {
        /* Bind the result to program variables. */
        dbbind(dbproc, 1, STRINGBIND, (DBINT) 0, name);
        dbbind(dbproc, 2, INTBIND, (DBINT) 0, Age);
        dbbind(dbproc, 3, MONEYBIND, (DBMONEY) 0, Salary);

        /* Retrieve and print the results. */
        while (dbnextrow(dbproc)) != (NO_MORE_ROWS)
        {
            printf("Name = %s, Age = %d, Salary = %f", Name, Age, Salary);
        }
    }

    /* Close the connection to the SQL Server. */
    dbexit0;
}
```

Figure 4.14 Typical SQL Server dblibrary application program.

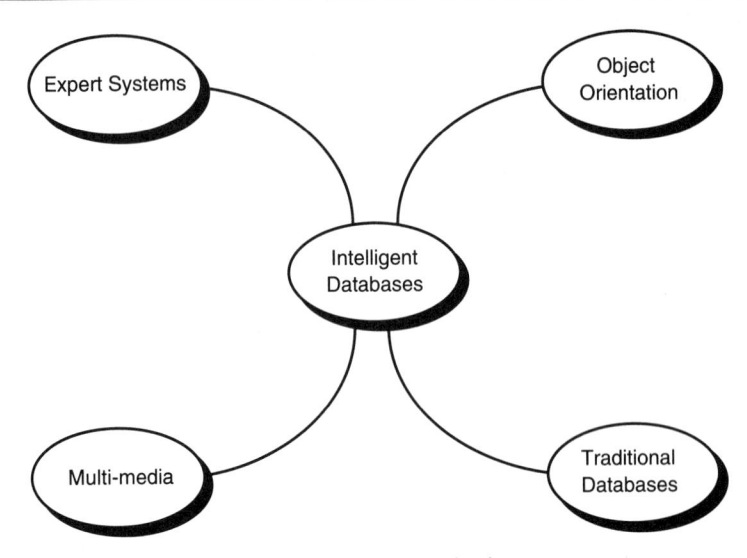

Figure 4.15 Intelligent databases.

Figure 4.15 illustrates these features. Most of these features are presented in the context of an SQL prototype called Intelligent SQL. Some of the elements of Intelligent SQL were presented in the Object-Oriented Data Base task group in May of 1990 (Khoshafian *et al.*, 1990; Khoshafian, 1991a). More detailed inheritance and generalization properties of Intelligent SQL are presented in Khoshafian *et al.* (1992) and Khoshafian *et al.* (1991). Additionally, features and architecture of intelligent database engines supporting intelligent SQL are presented in Khoshafian *et al.* (1990). Finally, deductive reasoning extensions to SQL systems are presented in Khoshafian and Thieme (1991). Some of these concepts are already part of the SQL3 proposal.

The top-level architecture of the intelligent database consists of three levels:

- High-level tools
- High-level user interface
- Intelligent database engine

As Figure 4.16 shows, this is a staircase-layered architecture. Users and developers may independently access different layers at different times. The details and functionality of each level is given in Parsaye *et al.* (1989).

The first of these levels is the high-level tools level. These tools provide the user with a number of facilities: intelligent search capabilities, data quality and integrity control, and automated discovery. These high-level tools represent an external library of powerful tools. Most of these tools may be broadly classified as information management techniques, similar to spreadsheets and graphic representation tools. They look and work much like their stand-alone equivalents, but they are modified to be compatible with the intelligent database model. They are object-oriented, and their basic structure mirrors the object representation methods of the intelligent database model.

4.5 Intelligent Databases

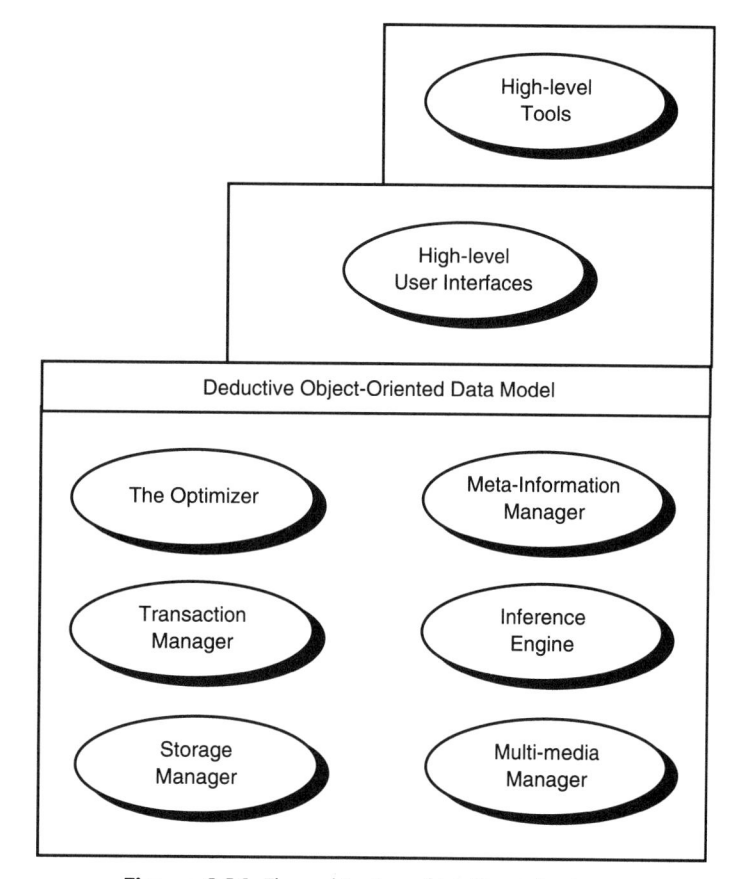

Figure 4.16 The architecture of intelligent databases.

The second level is the high-level user interface. Users directly interact with this level, which creates the model of the task and the database environment that users interact with. It deals as much with how the user wants to think about databases and information management as with how the database engine actually operates. Associated with this level is a set of representation tools that enhance the functionality of the intelligent database.

The user interface is presented in two aspects. First, a core model is presented to the user. This core model consists of the object-oriented representation of information along with a set of integrated tools for creating new object types, browsing among objects, searching, and asking questions. In addition, a set of high-level tools enhance the functionality of the intelligent database system for certain classes of users.

The base level of the system is the intelligent database engine and its data model. This model allows for deductive object-oriented representation of information, which can be expressed and operated on in a variety of ways. The engine includes backward- and forward-chaining inference procedures as well as optimizing compilers, drivers for the external media devices, and version handlers.

The intelligent database engine (Khoshafian et al., 1990), with its deductive object-oriented data (DOOD) model, is the underlying repository for integrated applications and products using the high-level tools and the high-level user interfaces. The engine is the core and the most important component of future systems, and it provides the functionality and performance for supporting integrated applications. In addition, access to other databases, distributed inferencing, and database management systems can be achieved through the intelligent database engine.

4.5.1 The Deductive Object-Oriented Data Model

The intelligent database strategy is to capture and represent deductive, object-oriented, and multi-media capabilities of intelligent databases. One option is to create an entirely new language with these capabilities. Another alternative is to extend an existing database language with these features. Recently emerging intelligent and object-oriented database products have chosen one of these two approaches. Some have introduced new languages, whereas others have extended the most popular relational language standard, namely, SQL. There are several advantages to extending SQL:

- It is the most popular relational language, endorsed by prominent vendors of relational database management systems.
- It is a declarative language with a clean underlying relational model.
- It is the only relational language that is standardized.
- It is the interface database language of the most popular relational database servers.

As discussed earlier, a number of the proposals in the next-generation (SQL3) standard incorporate inferencing and object-oriented extensions.

Similar to the visual and graphical interfaces to SQL engines, it is possible to have intelligent programming interfaces to SQL databases. These programming interfaces can be more general and higher-level than SQL. An extreme interface example is natural language interfaces. Less ambitious interfaces include declarative languages that support intensional and extensional databases, such as the Bancilhon-Khoshafian Calculus of Complex Objects (Bancilhon and Khoshafian, 1989) or LDL (Tsur and Zaniolo, 1986).

Intelligent database capabilities in DOOD primarily appear as an extension of SQL called Intelligent SQL. Intelligent SQL combines three main categories of extensions to SQL:

1. *Deductive rules* allow inferencing or proving of goals from within database queries.
2. *Object-oriented features* model the real world as closely as possible using abstract data typing, inheritance, and object identity.
3. *Multi-media data types* allow more direct access to multi-media objects through the database data manipulation language.

4.5.1.1 Deductive Rules and SQL

The integration of expert systems (rule-based systems) and databases is becoming increasingly important to a larger class of users and applications. Expert systems have proliferated diverse applications such as medicine, mathematics, business applications, and configuration of complex systems. Additional application areas include office automation, surveillance systems, manufacturing, oil refinery equipment, and battlefield management.

Inferencing rules, either as an extension of SQL or a higher-level interface on top of SQL-based databases, support powerful declarative constructs to perform complex computations on tables. As we mentioned earlier, to make SQL more computationally complete, some systems have extended SQL with only procedural constructs. SQL is a relational language, and the relational model has a clean underlying mathematical model (embodied in relational algebra). Providing only procedural extensions to the language to support more complex problems is a step in the wrong direction (Khoshafian and Thieme, 1991).

For languages, rules and inferencing are seamlessly integrated with SQL. The integration of rules with SQL will allow the user to have SQL *SELECT* statements in the premise of if-then rules and to have logical predicates in the *WHERE* clauses of SQL statements.

To illustrate the use of rules with SQL, consider the following schema:

```
CREATE TABLE OfficeWorker(
        Name      CHAR(20),
        Age       INTEGER,
        Address   CHAR(40),
        Rank      CHAR(1),
        Salary    INTEGER)

CREATE TABLE Manages(
        ManagerName        INTEGER,
        OfficeWorkerName   INTEGER
        Duration           INTEGER)
```

Three rules help find all direct and indirect subordinates of a manager in the above example. First, the *SubordinateOf* predicate is defined through two rules:

Rule 1: *OfficeWorker SubordinateOf Manager*
   IF
      OfficeWorker ReportsTo Manager
Rule 2: *OfficeWorker SubordinateOf Manager*
   IF
      OfficeWorker ReportsTo ImmediateManager
   AND
      ImmediateManager SubordinateOf Manager

The *ReportsTo* predicate is defined through a rule involving an SQL statement:

   OfficeWorker ReportsTo Manager
IF
   SELECT OfficeWorkerName AS OfficeWorker,
      ManagerName AS Manager
   FROM Manages

With these rules we can ask the intelligent database management system to tell us who the subordinates of John are, using the following syntax:

?X SubordinateOf John

In this statement, *?X* will bind *X* to the names of John's subordinates. Similarly, we can determine who are the supervisors of Mary, where *?S* will bind *S* to the names of supervisors of Mary:

Mary SubordinateOf ?S

Consider the following example, which finds the names and addresses of all young supervisors and the names and ranks of all office workers who report to them:

```
SELECT S.Name, S.Address, E.Name, E.Rank
   FROM OfficeWorkers S, OfficeWorkers E
   WHERE E.Name SubordinateOf S.Name
      AND S.Age <= 30
```

4.5.1.2   *The Object-Oriented Constructs in Intelligent SQL*

The three main concepts of object orientation are encapsulation, inheritance, and object identity (Khoshafian and Abnous, 1990). These concepts are discussed in Chapter 7. Here we discuss the concepts in the context of Intelligent SQL and intelligent database engines. All three concepts can be integrated in Intelligent SQL.

4.5.1.2.1   Abstract Data Types

As mentioned earlier, SQL3 incorporates user-defined abstract data typing. For abstract data typing, methods and operations can be associated with the following elements:

- User-defined data types, such as a stack
- Tuple types, such as an address (described later in this section)
- Tables, such as office workers and departments

The user-defined abstract data typing concept is an extension of another useful concept being supported by several commercial databases, namely user-defined functions. SQL systems typically come with a built-in collection of aggregate functions: *AVERAGE, MAX, MIN, COUNT, SUM,* and so on. Many systems allow users to define their own functions (and invoke these functions in SQL statements) using either a fourth-generation language (such as dBASE), a general-purpose programming language (such as C), or a procedural extension of SQL (such as Transact SQL). Abstract data typing extends this notion by allowing users to construct and use both types and operations in persistent SQL systems.

The operations or methods associated with table or tuple types are very similar to the operations or methods defined for classes. Consider the following simple example of the use of Intelligent SQL to support a generic *Stack* class with *Push* and *Pop* methods. The type parameter will allow creation of stacks of different types of objects.

```
CREATE CLASS Stack[T] (
    INSTANCE VARIABLES (
        ARRAY StArr[M] of T,
        Top INTEGER);
    METHODS (
        Push
        Stack X T -> Stack
        (St Stack, Value Integer
        St.Top = St.Top + 1 St.StArr[St.Top] = Value
        RETURN St);

        Pop
        Stack -> T
        (St Stack
        St.Top = St.Top - 1
            RETURN StArr[St.Top + 1]); ))
```

Once the data type *Stack* is defined, it can be used in Intelligent SQL tables as follows:

```
CREATE TABLE Account
        AccountNumber      INTEGER,
        Location           CHAR(20)
        Payables           Stack[DOLLAR])
```

Additionally, the data type *Stack* can be used in Intelligent SQL queries:

```
SELECT AccountNumber, Pop(Payables)
FROM Account
WHERE Location = "New York"
```

4.5.1.2.2 Inheritance

Inheritance is a very powerful object-oriented concept that can be used to organize the structure and instances of persistent tables. Inheritance achieves software reusability and software extensibility. Through inheritance, we can build new software modules or object spaces (such as tables) on top of existing hierarchies. New types, classes, and structures can inherit both the behavior (including operations and methods) and the representation (such as columns attributes) from existing types. Additionally, inheriting behavior enables code sharing (and hence reusability) among software modules. Inheriting representation enables structure sharing among data objects. The combination of these two types of inheritance provides a most powerful modeling and software development strategy.

The SQL3 next-generation standard supports inheritance through an *IS-A* construct. In the following examples, we use *SPECIALIZES* instead of *IS-A*. It is also possible to start from existing tables, to discover commonalities, and to *GENERALIZE* to supertables.

Specialization and generalization concepts in Intelligent SQL are discussed in Khoshafian et al. (1991) and Khoshafian (1991).

Consider the following example involving persons, office workers, and students:

```
CREATE TABLE Persons(
    Name      CHAR(20),
    Age       INTEGER,
    Address   CHAR(40))
CREATE TABLE OfficeWorkers
    SPECIALIZES Persons(
    Salary    FLOAT,
    Rank      INTEGER)
CREATE TABLE Students
    SPECIALIZES Persons(
    GPA FLOAT,
    Major     CHAR 10)

CREATE TABLE StudentOfficeWorkers
    SPECIALIZES OfficeWorkers, Students
```

Consider the following example to retrieve the age and address of all Office workers who earn more than $50,000.00:

```
SELECT Age, Address
FROM OfficeWorkers
WHERE Salary > 50000
```

Here is another example, which obtains the name, GPA, and salary of all student office workers who are more than 30 years old:

```
SELECT Name, Salary, GPA
FROM StudentOfficeWorkers
WHERE Age > 30
```

Since the definition of a table incorporates both the definition of a structure and an extension (the set of all rows of the table), table inheritance in Intelligent SQL has set inclusion semantics. For example, if a table T2 is a suitable of table T1, then the elements (rows) of T2 are also elements of T1. Consider the following query:

```
SELECT Name
FROM Persons
WHERE Age < 30
```

One important implication of the set inclusion semantics is that when we execute this query, we will retrieve the names of all student OfficeWorkers who are less than 30 years old; "plain" students (not OfficeWorkers) who are less than 30 years old; "plain" office workers (not students) who are less than 30 years old, and "plain" people (neither students nor office workers) who are less than 30 years old.

Additionally, another implication of this is that on any deletion or modification of a set of tuples in a supertable, the corresponding tuples are deleted or modified in all subtables. Consider the following example:

DELETE FROM Persons
WHERE Age >= 30

This operation will delete all student office workers, "plain" students, "plain" office workers, and other persons whose age is greater than 30.

4.5.1.2.3 Tuple-Valued Attributes

Tuples enable users to construct complex persistent object spaces and to retrieve complex structures without joins.

One serious problem with normalization (especially first normal form) is the fact that naturally occurring structures cannot be represented directly. Consider the example of a person's address. An address consists of a street number, street name, city, state, and ZIP code. This cannot be thought of as a set of atomic values; each piece has a different meaning. Still, there are several ways to store an address in the relational model. Minimally, the address can be stored as a long string of characters, but the structure of the address is lost. The user then has to worry about the different fields and attributes within the long field. Qualification on different fields of address becomes either difficult or impossible.

Another possibility is to capture the different fields of the address in the name of the attribute; that is, create different fields *AddressNumber*, *AddressName*, *AddressCity*, *AddressState*, and *AddressZipCode*. This option loses the logical aggregation of the address fields, however. The table definition looks strange, and the association of the different fields to the same logical object must be done by the user.

A third alternative is to store addresses in a separate table and to perform joins to retrieve the different fields of the address. Although this option avoids some of the pitfalls of the other two alternatives, it incurs the extra overhead of joins to retrieve the fields of a person's address. Moreover, the table of addresses is not an interesting grouping, since in most cases users retrieve addresses through a person's record.

The most natural representation for an address is to allow tuple-valued attributes. With this alternative, the address is a tuple and exists as a single logical entity instead of being spread across multiple fields or tables, yet the user can access and update each field separately. Consider the following example in Intelligent SQL:

CREATE TUPLE ADDRESS
    (Str #   *INTEGER,*
    StName   *CHAR(20),*
    City   *CHAR(20),*
    Zip   *INTEGER,*
    State   *CHAR(20))*

We can create the table *Persons* using the *Address* tuple type.

```
CREATE TABLE Persons
        (Name      CHAR(20),
        Dob        DATE,
        HomeAddr   ADDRESS)
```

An extended "dot" notation is used to retrieve different values of the tuple-valued attributes. For example, to retrieve the state where Jim lives, we have

```
SELECT HomeAddr.State
FROM Persons
WHERE Name = "Jim"
```

Similarly, we can retrieve the name and date of birth of all people who live in Concord:

```
SELECT Name, Dob
FROM Persons
WHERE HomeAddr.City = "Concord"
```

4.5.1.2.4 Object Identity

The tuple support discussed thus far does not allow tuples to be referentially shared (Khoshafian and Valduriez, 1987a). For instance, two people cannot reference the same address unless the addresses are either replicated or stored separately in another relation. As discussed in the previous section, both of these options have problems and do not provide a direct modeling and representation of the real world.

Since it is natural to share tuple values (such as addresses) and objects in general, Intelligent SQL also supports object identity for tuples. Object identity organizes the objects or instances of an application in arbitrary graph-structured object spaces. Identity is the property of an object that distinguishes the object from all other objects in the application (Khoshafian and Copeland, 1986; Khoshafian and Abnous, 1990). In programming languages, identity is realized through memory addresses. In relational SQL-based databases, identity is realized through primary keys. User-specified names are used in languages and databases to give unique names to objects. Each of these schemes compromises identity.

In a complete object-oriented system, each object is given an identity that is permanently associated with the object, regardless of the object's structural or state transitions. The identity of an object is also independent of the location or address of the object. With object identity, users can referentially share objects. Object identity provides the most natural modeling short of having the same object be a subobject of multiple parent objects. Object identity in Intelligent SQL practically removes the need for having referential integrity constraints.

Object identity can also be associated with atomic valued attributes (in other words, base types). This makes a lot of sense for fields that store multi-media data types. For example, in current database engines, if an image is shared, it must be normalized in a separate table and subsequently joined with the referencing table. With object identity, all the rows accessing the long field can have direct references to the object.

The REF or OBJECT constructs are used to indicate the referenced object. Consider the following example:

```
CREATE TABLE Departments    (
        CompanyName    CHAR(20)
        DeptName       CHAR(20),
        Budget         FLOAT,
        BldAddr        OBJECT ADDRESS
        BldPicture     OBJECT IMAGE)
```

Here, the building address is an object with an identity. Many departments can have the same address: the company's address. If the company moves and all its departments are relocated, the values of the street number, street name, city, state, and zip of the company address must be modified. Since the departments are referencing the same object, they will acquire these values automatically. The same is true of the building picture.

With object identity, rows of tables can be referenced as tuple objects. In the following example, the *Dept* attribute and a *Manager* attribute in an office worker table reference the corresponding table entry directly:

```
CREATE TABLE OfficeWorkers
    SPECIALIZES Persons(
        Salary     FLOAT,
        Dept       REF ROW Departments
        Manager    REF ROW OfficeWorkers)
```

To retrieve the salary, the manager's name, and the picture of the department building of office worker Joe's department we have the following query:

```
SELECT Salary, Manager.Name,Dept.Building.Picture
FROM OfficeWorkers
WHERE Name = "Joe"
```

4.5.1.3 Multi-Media Data Types

Multi-media data types (text, images, voice, video) are becoming increasingly popular. Some relational systems support arbitrarily large multi-media data types. For instance, SQL Server supports *TEXT* and *IMAGE* fields with up to two gigabytes in each row! Of course, long fields can be stored in operating system files. Storing them in the database allows the multi-media data to be concurrently shared by many users under transaction control. In most relational database systems that support long fields (called *BLOB*, *LONG VARCHAR*, *IMAGE*, *TEXT*, and so on), the functionality is primarily that of storing and accessing the fields, without much consideration of data typing (structure and operations).

Intelligent SQL provides special operators and predicates to query and retrieve multi-media objects. It extends the *BLOB* or long-data-field object support of some existing relational database management systems with more intelligent multi-media types. The "intelligence" in the multi-media type support is exhibited either through content searches of multi-media objects or through the association of attributes and different operations with multi-media object structures.

4.5.1.3.1 Text Data

Text documents constitute the most popular medium of storage in the office environment. However, in the typical automated office automation environment, full-text management and record management are completely independent. Users must interact with two independent and unrelated products to perform table searches and searches for long text fields within table rows. Thus, information management and database management are decoupled.

Intelligent databases integrate information and record and database management. There have been a number of proposals to integrate full-text querying capabilities into SQL. The SFQL proposal (AIA/ATA, 1990) is the most notable.

There is a simple Intelligent SQL approach that allows users to create, update, and retrieve text fields based on full-text Boolean expressions. The Intelligent SQL approach is similar to SFQL in many aspects, the most important of which is the provision of complex Boolean searches. The Boolean expressions can appear in SQL *WHERE* clauses in conjunction with the usual search expressions.

Suppose *T* is a text-valued field. An expression of the following form can appear as an SQL predicate:

```
["Term1" AND "Term2" ... AND "Termn"] IN T
```

This expression is true if and only if all of the terms *Term1* through *Termn* are in *T*. Of course, other kinds of Boolean expressions, such as those involving *OR* and *NOT*, are also allowed.

Consider the following example. To retrieve the author and publisher of all books published before 1986 that cover either "object orientation" and "databases" or "semantic data models," we have:

```
SELECT Author, Publisher
FROM Books
WHERE ["Object Orientation" AND "Databases" OR
       "Semantic data models"] IN BookText
       AND Year <= 1986
```

The schema of *Books* is:

```
CREATE TABLE Books (
        Author      CHAR(20),
        Publisher   CHAR(20),
        BookText    TEXT,
        Year        INTEGER)
```

Another important aspect of text retrieval is the *RANK* or *RELEVANCE* of the returned text. For instance, if we are searching for the occurrence of a particular term, and that term occurs 10 times in one record and 100 times in another, clearly the second record is more "relevant." Frequency of count is often used as a measure of relevance (Salton and McGill, 1983; Salton, 1990). Consider the following example in Intelligent SQL, used to return the rank or relevance:

```
SELECT Author, Publisher, RANK(BookText)
FROM Books
WHERE ["Object Orientation" AND "Databases" OR
    "Semantic data models"] IN BookText
        AND Year <= 1986
```

4.5.1.3.2 Image Data

Image data can correspond to graphs, charts, moving video images, two-dimensional bitmaps, or groups of shapes. Images can be generated by scanners or imported from external *.PCX*, *.TIFF*, or other image files. Images can also be used to represent spatial or geographic data.

Images can be represented and stored in vector format as groups of shapes at specific positions with specific sizes, shades, and colors. In general, the memory requirements using vector formats are less than those for bitmapped storage of the same image. However, vector formats are not as general as bitmaps.

Since each of these formats has relative advantages and functionalities, Intelligent SQL supports both raster images and a number of vector images such as points, rectangles, and polygons. The database engine supports grid files and other types of accelerators to enhance the retrieval and update of image data types.

Supporting tuple-valued attributes, as in the object-oriented extension of SQL, helps cluster the media-specific information with the multi-media field.

For spatial (vector image) data types, Intelligent SQL has built-in data types such as *RECTANGLE* and *POINT*. Each of these data types is a tuple type that can further be specialized by the user. More specifically, *RECTANGLE* is identified as follows:

```
CREATE TUPLE RECTANGLE(
        LOW-LEFT    XY-POINT,
        UP-RIGHT    XY-POINT,
        SCALE       FLOAT,
        ORIGIN      POINT,
        PICTURE     OBJECT IMAGE)
```

LOW-LEFT and *UP-RIGHT* indicate the lower left and upper right corners of a rectangle; the *SCALE* and *ORIGIN* provide the necessary information to place the rectangle on the *IMAGE*. The (optional) *IMAGE* field stores either the image contained in the rectangle or the image of the environment in which the rectangle is contained (for example, the rectangle contains a map and the *IMAGE* is the map of Madison, Wisconsin).

Similarly, *POINT* is a built-in data type identified as follows:

```
CREATE TUPLE POINT(
        POINT       XY-POINT
        SCALE       FLOAT,
        ORIGIN      FLOAT
        PICTURE     OBJECT IMAGE)
```

where SCALE, ORIGIN, and IMAGE are the same as those for RECTANGLE and XY-POINT is a tuple giving the X and Y coordinates of a point:

```
CREATE TUPLE XY-POINT (
         X-COORD    FLOAT,
         Y-COORD    FLOAT)
```

Following the PSQL (Pictorial SQL) (Roussopoulos et al., 1988) proposal, Intelligent SQL has a number of "built-in" operations, such as COVERED-BY, OVERLAPS, CLOSEST, PERIMETER, and AREA, associated with the "spatial" data types RECTANGLE and POINT.

Consider the following example to retrieve the city name, state, and population of all cities a unit distance from the point [4,9] that have a population greater than 1,000,000.

```
SELECT City, State, Population
FROM Cities
WHERE Location COVERED-BY (4 +/− 1, 9 +/− 1)
    AND Population > 1,000,000
```

The schema of Cities is as follows:

```
CREATE TABLE Cities (
         City       CHAR(20),
         State      CHAR(20),
         Location   POINT)
```

Intelligent SQL can also perform a juxtaposition query of dissimilar information stored in multiple spatial objects. Suppose REC1 and REC2 are rectangles. In SQL WHERE clauses, we can specify predicates such as the following:

```
REC1 OVERLAPS REC2
REC1 BORDERS REC2
REC1 COVERED-BY REC2
```

■ 4.6 SUMMARY

This chapter presented the major components of storage and retrieval of persistent data in any application. Major database concepts such as persistent storage, atomic operations, and recovery were discussed. In addition, these concepts were related to the intelligent office environment through examples.

Next, the evolution of database systems was examined. The early data models, such as network and hierarchical, were discussed, as were the currently popular relational and object-oriented databases.

The relational data model was examined in greater detail because a fair amount of database applications include relational databases. The SQL language was explored as the language of choice for accessing any relational database. Following this discussion, the process of designing relational databases was discussed at length. Client/server architecture was examined, with SQL Server presented as a typical example of a relational database systems supporting this type of architecture.

The last section presented intelligent databases as the future of database systems. Intelligent databases are a combination of the current generation of relational databases with object-oriented concepts (such as abstract data typing, inheritance, and object identity), rule-based inferencing capabilities, and support for multi-media data types. Extensions to SQL can be made to make most of these new concepts possible.

As will be shown in Chapter 10, database management systems, and especially relational databases, will be utilized as the object repository for the intelligent offices.

5

FULL-CONTENT RETRIEVAL

■ 5.1 INTRODUCTION

Full-content retrieval rests on the foundations of object orientation, database management systems, and multi-media objects. Object orientation can be used to structure the content of a document in such a way that very powerful search techniques can be used. Database management systems have pushed forward the technologies of index and search, which are extended in content-based retrieval. The introduction of multi-media objects has expanded the role of a document from simple text through pictures to combinations of these with sound and video.

The technology for storing information has raced ahead of that of retrieval. It is much easier to store a vast amount of information than it is to retrieve useful data on a particular topic. When the storage media for documents is paper or microfilm, their content is inaccessible by retrieval software, which relies on an on-line catalog of available information that lists the information's attributes. With information increasingly being stored on magnetic and optical media, the content of a document becomes accessible for searching for relevant data.

Documents exist in virtually every computer system in use. Up to now, most have been in text files, which are just streams of readable characters and positional information such as form feeds and tabs. The files are managed by the native file system, and users can type, print, and edit the files and perform similar operations on them. These files are on some storage medium that is also used for all the rest of the system's work. Standard storage media have now been augmented by other sources, dedicated to mass document storage. CD-ROMs are one such method. These are dedicated to mass storage of text, graphics and other information, and they differ from the more traditional storage media in both the amount of information available and the read-only method of access. In most cases, the amount of information available is at least an order of magnitude greater on a CD-ROM than on writable media of similar physical size.

Another newer source of raw text, and therefore of documents, is the increasingly common use of memos, or Binary Large OBjects (BLOBs), in relational data bases. Fields in a relational data base, since they fit into a tabular model, have a fixed length. Thus, a relational data base always has some intrinsic limit on the amount of information that a single text item can store. A memo field, on the other hand, uses a fixed-length part of a tuple in a relation only as a pointer to a large body of information with a virtually unlimited size. Thus, a memo field can be used to store a paragraph, a page, a book, or an entire encyclopedia, all using the same amount of space in the tuple.

The explosion of information available has overrun the capability of current database systems to manage it. The common forms of indexing used in relational databases depend on structures like B-trees, which are not suited to chunks of text of arbitrary size. There are existing inverted indexing systems, but they have historically been restricted to dedicated applications, and indexing text from external sources is difficult if not impossible. What is needed is a general-purpose indexing system that can handle documents from a variety of sources at the same time. The indexing system must be able to extract from the documents some meaningful knowledge about their contents, so that users don't have to read them to find things they need.

There are numerous ways to use document retrieval, either by itself or in the context of a database. There are many approaches to indexing documents and to performing queries against the indices. In order to remain flexible with respect to the applications encountered in the intelligent office, the main thrust is to have a simple basis for indexing and retrieval, but one upon which more complex structures can be built. This section will attempt to determine the scope of the problem, what part or parts will be addressed, and in what order.

One way that document retrieval is used is in a bibliographic mode. The documents are invariant over time, with the exception of newly added documents. This sort of document data base is most conducive to strategies like signatures, concept structures, and the like, because it is stable, and therefore more knowledge can be gained about it over time. In addition, these systems don't as a rule ever lose documents. More are added as time goes on, but none are ever taken away. Typical applications are in the legal area, where the law pertaining to a particular area does not change over time. Commentaries may be added, new court cases may cause new variations in interpretation, but the basic wording of the original law remains the same.

Another use of document retrieval is in the production and maintenance of documents such as those pertaining to policy or ongoing research. Here, there is a reasonably stable set of documents that have been developed over time and are not changed, and a second set of documents that are in the process of being produced. This type of environment has a combination of very stable documents and very unstable documents, with a lot of cutting and pasting going on. Here also, documents are typically removed when they have outlived their usefulness. These types of systems lend themselves more to inverted indices with the final documents (with the documents in progress not being indexed). When a document is complete, it is then indexed and becomes a more permanent feature. Since extraction of a document from an inverted index is typically a very time-consuming operation, it is done very seldom in such systems, and in fact it is usually more efficient to just reindex the whole set when one or more documents are to be deleted. It should be noted that over a long period of time, such systems may in fact start to gravitate toward the status of bibliographic systems, particularly if the documents are not weeded out as they age, and if the documents are about some body of knowledge that is conducive to the production of more complicated structures like concept indices and thesauri.

A third use of document retrieval can best be classed as anarchic. Here, documents come and go constantly. Existing documents are expanded and otherwise modified. Documents are added, deleted, and modified with such frequency that it is necessary to rebuild inverted indices, if they exist, on almost a daily basis. Also, since the document set is so volatile, it is not possible to create any sort of concept data base, since the concepts keep changing. This is the most difficult type of system to automate, but it does not occur very often, since anarchy is very hard to sustain. Given enough time, such systems will either cease to exist or settle down to a production-type system. Generally, the best strategy for such systems is to resort to scanning the documents, since any indices will usually be out of date.

There are obviously other uses of document retrieval, but the above examples illustrate a continuum that is fairly typical and that can be addressed within the context of a PC-based document database structure.

Given that there exists some document database in the above continuum, what do people expect to get from it? The most basic answer to that question is that people expect to find documents that contain information they need. The simplest question one could ask is for all pertinent documents that contain important words or phrases. The result of this sort of query in a system that scans the documents will be a list of documents that include the sought-for words, but no indication of how relevant the documents may be. It is up to the user to weed out the ones that have the sought-for words but are not of concern to the matter at hand. Inverted index systems return the same answer, but much more quickly. Again, the user has to decide which documents are really relevant, usually by reading them in whole or in part.

Document signature systems attempt to solve the problem in a more probabilistic way. They match the signature of the query against the signatures of the documents, all generated in the same manner, and thus attempt to retrieve those documents that are "closest" to the query. The match may not be exact, and in fact it seldom is exactly the same as an inverted index query, but there is the added ability to "grade" the resulting document set according to how closely they match the query. However, since statistics are involved, there is the possibility that relevant documents will not be found.

For both inverted indices and signature indices, we can develop methods that allow piecemeal additions to the indices without sacrificing query performance and with minimal impact on indexing performance. This means that the indices can grow over time without the necessity of reconstructing the entire index from scratch. For inverted indices, this is a fairly simple problem to solve. For signature indices, there may be additional complications, depending on the method employed. For example, if N-grams are used as the method of developing signatures, the N-gram space may increase, with a corresponding increase in the length of each document's signature vector. However, this still does not mean that the whole document set must be indexed, since the existing documents can still be indexed in smaller batches if necessary.

In contrast to the indexing systems just listed, concept-based systems depend on a deep knowledge of the vocabulary of the document set, the semantics of the language being used, and the subject matter at hand. Here the words in a document are weighted according to their relevance to each other across the whole document space, without any bearing on whether or not they appear together in any given individual document.

These systems depend on sets of rules, thesauri, equivalence and synonym lists, and the like to expand the words, terms, or vectors being sought in a query to include words, terms, or vectors that should be of equal interest. They also depend on some level of knowledge about the semantics of the documents, including their division into sentences, paragraphs, and other levels of structure.

A crude concept "index" may be built on top of an inverted or signature index. This will be referred to as "query-end concept indexing," since it is applied only to queries and has no effect on indexing. In this model, there is some tool that is used for building a "concept database" of connections between words in the dictionary developed by the other indexing methods. This set of connections is then used to "enhance" the normal text queries by adding terms or words that are determined to be relevant to those words or terms in the query. The relevance comes from examining the connections in the concept database. For text scanning or inverted indices, the concept-based system just expands the list of terms that is being searched for in the document set with those terms that are deemed to be relevant. In signature systems, the signature of the query is enhanced by combining its vector with vectors developed from the equivalent terms.

A better concept-indexing system will maintain its own set of indices determined by the concept database. This will be referred to as "index-end concept indexing," since a separate concept index independent of the other indices is created. Queries then are made against this index, rather than by enhancing a normal query against an inverted or signature index. In either case, the concept database must be set up and maintained. Historically, such systems have been labor-intensive. They are set up by people with a knowledge of the subject matter at hand, and they are typically done before anything is indexed. They are subject to human error and differences of interpretation, and they are almost never applicable to more than one area of subject matter.

All these approaches are elucidated in this chapter.

5.1.1 Chapter Organization

Chapter 4 described document searches that are based on a set of attributes attached to each document. Full-text retrieval takes this approach a stage further by enabling a search to be based on the textual contents of documents. Full-content retrieval generalizes this technique to encompass all document elements, including images and sounds.

This chapter begins by discussing the quality of information and how that quality enables full-content retrieval. Data refinement, which uses recognition and understanding to improve the quality of document content, and then the process of conducting a search are described. Full-text retrieval is described in detail, as this is a fairly mature technology that is widely available. The more common methods of organizing, indexing, and querying text are discussed. Finally, the importance of full-content retrieval in the intelligent office is explored.

5.2 QUALITY OF INFORMATION

If retrieval is to be based on the content of documents, then the nature of this content becomes important. Text can be searched using full-text retrieval, whereas an image of text cannot. With a vector drawing, access can be based on objects within the document, whereas this is not possible with bitmap images.

5.2.1 Data Refinement

Data refinement extracts meaningful information from raw data. A machine can manipulate the output more usefully than the input. For example, if a letter is scanned in, its textual content is inaccessible until it has been through OCR and proofreading processes. Once the text is accessible, then full-text retrieval is possible and searches can be based on key words.

Until the text has gone through a further process of semantic structuring, however, the search cannot be based on what the letter is about or who it is from. This restructuring brings the added benefit of refining the end product to a smaller size than the input data, thus requiring less storage space.

The following sections trace the refinement of text, graphics, and sound and the corresponding advantages for full-content retrieval.

5.2.1.1 Raw Data

Raw data is practically useless for a search based on content, because the information contained is rarely in a machine-readable format.

When text enters a computer system, it is usually scanned in as an image, though it may enter through a communications line as a character stream. The latter is true for E-mail, which is already in machine-readable format. Text in an image is inaccessible to a query, as it is just so many dots on the page (Rimmer, 1990). Figure 5.1 illustrates the "image" of textual information.

A graphical image might enter the computer from a scanner, a camera, or a video recorder. All of these generate a raster image, which records a picture by dividing it up into tiny picture elements (pixels) and digitizing the color, shade, and brightness for each. A raster image cannot be queried on the objects in the picture, as these are just different shades of color to the application.

Sound is sampled at regular intervals to produce a stream of amplitude readings in the computer. This process is described in Section 6.7.1. In this form, information such as the sex of a voice, or the tempo of a piece of music are unavailable to a full-content search.

5.2.1.2 Recognition

Recognition converts raw data into a more useful, machine-readable format. A recognition process applies knowledge about the elements from which the data is assumed to be composed in an attempt to match these elements to the data. After data has been through

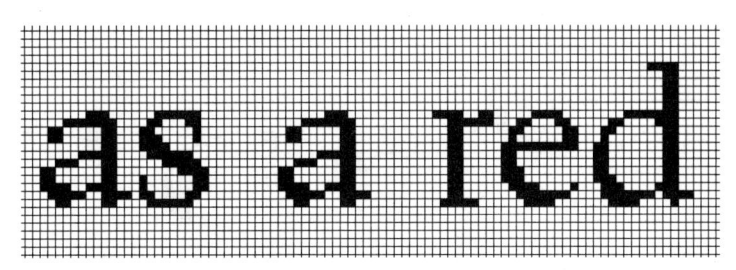

Figure 5.1 Image of text.

as a red

Figure 5.2 The text from the preceding figure recognized.

a recognition process, it becomes useful for full-content retrieval, because the searching application can apply queries to document contents.

Text recognition from an image is the familiar process of OCR, which is described in Section 6.5. Some form of proofreading is necessary to check the results of OCR; a simple automatic approach is to perform a spell check against a dictionary. Current full-text retrieval methods are incapable of coping with misspelt words (Salton, 1989). Figure 5.2 illustrates recognized textual information.

The technology for recognizing objects in a picture is not as abundant as for text recognition. The objects are composed of lines and shapes, as opposed to characters. The initial task of converting a picture to a shaded line drawing is called raster-to-vector (R-V) conversion. This conversion can be achieved by fitting curves to every shade or color interface on the picture.

A more sophisticated approach first attempts to find lines that are approximately straight. If more is known about the picture, such as in a production-line situation, then the line drawing can be compared to likely objects at various orientations to determine more about the content of the image.

Speech recognition is described in detail in Section 6.7.3, which describes how sound is broken down into a phonetic form. Music and other sounds can also be analyzed in terms of component frequencies, amplitudes, and durations. A frequency spectrum gives this information, which can be used to match against known instruments and noises.

5.2.1.3 Understanding

Text and speech are both parsed into sentence structures. This parsing involves identifying verbs, nouns, adjectives, and so on. With speech it also involves working out which words are present. The semantic net can be built up from the parsed sentence by identifying nouns as objects, which are described by adjectives and are related by verbs. Actually the process is far more complicated than this simplification suggests, and it is still an active area of research (Winston, 1984). Figure 5.3 illustrates "understood" text.

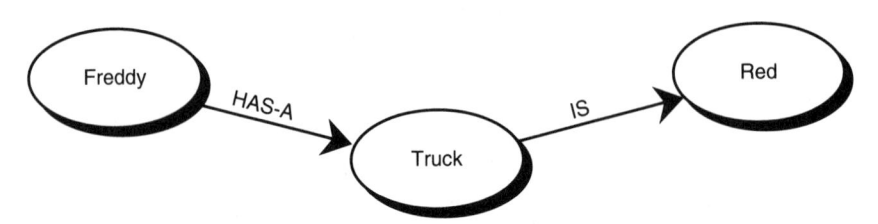

Figure 5.3 Text as it is 'understood.'

A picture can similarly be described in terms of objects and relationships. Image understanding is also largely at the research stage. One approach is to label edges, based on how they intersect one another, and from this derive surface direction. The combination of surfaces defines objects, and the arrangement of objects can be used to derive relationships between them.

5.2.1.4 *Intelligent Content Retrieval*

Once recognition has broken down raw data into a combination of elements, the way is open for calculating the relationships and structure of these components. There usually needs to be feedback from understanding to recognition to improve the latter. This feedback is particularly important in understanding speech, where there are many possible interpretations of the same phonetic sequence.

The result of understanding information is a semantic net. This represents information in terms of objects and relationships between pairs of objects. For example, the semantic net representing the sentence "Freddy has a red truck" will include the ownership relationship between the objects 'Freddy' and 'truck.' One way to implement semantic nets is through frames, to be discussed presently.

5.2.1.4.1 Knowledge Bases

When the semantic representation of document content is combined with a relevant knowledge base and inference engine, full-content retrieval becomes very powerful in performing abstract queries and searches.

One way to represent the network of interrelationships between the concepts of a full-text database is through frames. A frame corresponds to the notion of a class or object, as discussed in Chapter 7. Frames blur the distinctions between classes and instances and inherit directly from one another. Frames contain "slots" with "values," which may be applied to the dictionary of words from an inverted index to impose a thesaurus or synonym structure on the frame. For example, the frame structure could look like the following:

FRAME: Word
PARENT: Thing

FRAME: ampersand
PARENT: Word
SLOT: Synonym   VALUE: 'AND sign,' '&,' 'and'
SLOT: Broad Category   VALUE: 'special character'

In this very short example, the word "ampersand" can have an associated synonym list and a broader category to belong to, that of "special" characters. A thesaurus structure of broad, narrow, and related terms can thus be built with frames. A set of rules may also be applied to the resulting frame base to associate terms with each other for query and indexing purposes.

Concept indexing is a much better candidate for expression in terms of frames. There are actually a number of frame hierarchies in a concept database. One is the set of concepts. The concepts can be represented in a similar form to the foregoing short example:

FRAME: Concept
PARENT: Thing

FRAME: software
PARENT: Concept
SLOT: Related Term   VALUE: hardware, firmware, vaporware
SLOT: Synonym   VALUE: computer programs, code

FRAME: programming languages
PARENT: software

FRAME: Pascal
PARENT: programming languages
SLOT: Related Term   VALUE: block structure
SLOT: Synonym   VALUE: Wirth's language

FRAME: operating systems
PARENT: software

FRAME: UNIX
PARENT: operating systems

In this example, the concept of "software" includes "programming languages" and "operating systems." "Programming languages" include "Pascal," and "operating systems" include "UNIX." There is a clearly visible hierarchy leading from the root concept of "software" to the concepts "UNIX" and "Pascal." The broad-term and narrow-term relationships found in thesauri can be expressed as part of the structure. The children of a frame represent narrow expressions of the concept, and the parents of a frame represent broader expressions of the concept. Related terms and synonyms are still handled as lists of frames in the slots for each concept. This sort of structure can always be constructed by a human expert or by a committee. It can also be built through the interaction of a program and a resident expert. The program would attempt to fit new concepts into the structure depending on the context and some statistical information known to the program. If there is not enough information to make a decision, the expert is available for help. The expert can still manually adjust the concept hierarchy later, to repair any mistakes the program has made or to reflect new interpretations of the concepts in light of new knowledge or for particular uses and users of the data.

In addition to the concept frame hierarchy, there is a document frame hierarchy, which reflects the real world of information to which the concept data base is to be applied. These frames could look like the following:

```
FRAME:   document
PARENT:  thing
SLOT:    concepts    VALUE:
SLOT:    title       VALUE:
SLOT:    author      VALUE:
SLOT:    abstract    VALUE:

FRAME:   olds.man
PARENT:  document
SLOT:    concepts    VALUE:  auto repair,
                             auto maintenance
SLOT:    title       VALUE:  "Oldsmobile Owner's Manual"
SLOT:    author      VALUE:  Mr. Goodwrench
SLOT:    abstract    VALUE:  A short list of things to
                             look for and features of the
                             common Oldsmobile models
```

The slots in this frame can be filled in with information from a relational database structure, with the exception of the concepts slot. All the documents may appear in a single relation with titles, authors, abstracts, and information needed to extract the text, such as a memo field. The relational fields can then be plugged into the proper slots in the frame. Indexing the documents will result in finding a set of concepts from the concept database that are expressed in the document. A list of these concepts is placed in the concepts slot.

This example has only two levels of hierarchy. However, a set of documents can be subdivided into much finer detail. Among other things, a frame could be constructed for "owner's manuals," with children for owner's manuals for "cars," "appliances," "lawn mowers," and so on. Then, when a query is made against the concept index, the targets of the query can be restricted by placing rules on which parts of the document index are candidates for selection.

5.2.1.4.2 Rules

The processing of these frame hierarchies can best be done by using rules. The rules will fall into two categories. The first set of rules will be used when a user goes to choose some concept or concepts. The concept database can have certain access controls, governed by predicates associated with the frames in the concept database. Additionally, the concept database can be broken down into subsets by adding controlling information to slots in the frame. The next set of rules will use these slot values to trim the concept database down to a particular subset. This has nothing to do with access control; it just reduces the number of frames to be examined. Such a rule could be of the form:

```
if
    element-type of pollutant is gaseous
then
    term is relevant
```

This rule could be applied to a concept database to cause examination only of possible gaseous element pollution, thus restricting information retrieved to things like fluorine or chlorine and skipping over references to lead or arsenic.

Given an extensive concept database, its subdivision by such rules and the implied addition of slots such as "element-type" in the foregoing example, will be necessary to keep people from getting lost in the index.

The operation of the query engine against the concept database will be an iterative process. The user can pick one or more concepts or may browse among the concepts until something looks interesting. Rules that serve to restrict the user's access to the concept database come into play at this point. The interrogator (software that handles the user's requests) will invoke the rules as it goes along and present only those concepts that are the goal of the rules currently in force. The interrogator can not only restrict the concept space; it can also expand the concept space automatically, again based on rules pertinent to that user. For instance, the user may always wish to see synonyms. This would cause a synonym rule to be invoked whenever the user specifies a concept. The synonyms then appear as expansions of the concept space. The interrogator may also be able to infer what a user wants, based on previous queries that the user has made. Rules like:

> if
>   synonyms of concept is-not empty
> then
>   add synonyms to concept space

would cause the query to be enriched automatically.

Rules can also be applied at the query resolution end of the process. Once a user has refined or expanded the concept space to its desired shape, the set of document frames is searched for candidates pertinent to the query. Each concept may have any number of "pertinent" documents, but depending on the user and the application, "pertinent" may have different meanings. An example is a legal application. There may be many documents relating to pollution in a law database. Some may apply to criminal law, and some may apply to tort law. One way to handle queries that must be restricted to only criminal law would be to have two databases. This works fine until a user wants some overview of all pollution references. A better way is to add a slot to the document frame that refers to a broad subject, such as law, and one for narrower subjects under law. Then a few levels of hierarchy can be established among all the documents and rules, like:

> if
>   broad-subject of category of document is law
> and
>   narrow-subject of document is criminal
> then
>   document is relevant

can be used to restrict the search to the proper set of documents.

5.2.2 Refinement vs. Compression

A number of compression schemes, described in Chapters 6 and 9, are used to reduce the volume of data. They are particularly effective on raw data. This is partly due to these files being so much larger than processed information. However, the main reason is that much higher compression ratios can be achieved with the greater redundancy found in raw data. For example, an image of a letter is almost entirely white blank space, which the compression scheme takes advantage of. Another example is sound compression, where the scheme assumes (correctly) that the differences between amplitude measurements are small.

Refinement of data leaves behind most of the redundancy. The page of text now uses one byte, instead of a thousand bits, for each character, and those large spaces become tabs and carriage returns. An image of a business letter might occupy several hundred kilobytes. The same letter compresses to around twenty kilobytes. Once it has passed through recognition, it is down to only one or two kilobytes. (The assumptions made in these calculations are defined in the introduction to Chapter 6.) Compression of this text can still be useful (as described in Chapter 9) but the ratios are much lower than with the original image.

It is arguable whether the step from recognition to understanding decreases the size of the data. Whether it does depends largely on how the semantic net is stored and how closely it is integrated with the knowledge base.

Clearly, data refinement both reduces the volume of data to be stored and increases the power of full-content retrieval. Compression can be used after refinement, though it will not be as significant as with raw data and may impede a search or indexing method that accesses document content.

5.3 DOCUMENT COLLECTIONS

Before searching for relevant material among files, a user must specify a domain. For example, when one is looking for all documents that mention computers, the domain can probably be limited to word processor and text files in a few subdirectories on a hard disk. Another domain can be the collection of memo, or BLOB, fields in a relational table.

The specification of a domain saves time searching irrelevant areas and cuts down on spurious results. In a more elaborate general office application, documents are grouped into folders, file cabinets, and libraries, and the collection of documents to be searched can be defined in terms of these: "Search my personal folder called 'technology' and the MIS department filing cabinet."

The method of labeling areas where documents can be stored has many advantages. It can be assumed that an area called "library" will contain documents that are infrequently changed, whereas a "work in progress" folder will have frequent changes and updates. These assumptions will be used in Chapter 6 when levels of security and appropriate storage areas are discussed. When full-text retrieval is implemented, the method of indexing can be chosen for optimal performance based on these assumptions. Document areas are described in more detail in Chapter 10.

5.4 FULL-TEXT RETRIEVAL

Full-text retrieval is by far the most advanced of search methods that use document content. This section first describes how the word content of a document can be organized through filtering and grouping. Then some of the methods used to index and search the text are described.

5.4.1 Document Parsing

When a document is indexed, whether for an inverted index or to determine its signature, the document is scanned for its contents. This requires some rules of syntax and semantics. Inverted indexing will be treated first, followed by signature indexing.

In developing any text index, the document must first be broken down into its constituent parts, which in this case are words. What defines a word is not well defined. Among the variations are the following:

1. A string of letters. Example:

   cat

2. A string of letters and numbers, starting with a letter. Examples:

   cat

   H2O

3. A string of letters and numbers. Examples:

   1000

   cat

4. A string of nonblank characters, starting with a letter or number. Examples:

   S&L

   1,000,000.00

   cat

Similarly, the termination of semantic structures, such as sentences and paragraphs, is also open to interpretation. If sentences end with a period followed by a space, what does one do with abbreviations? Does a paragraph require indenting the first line or leaving a blank line?

The simplest approach to this problem is to choose some rules and leave it at that. Then word, sentence, and paragraph termination are fixed. A more complete solution allows the user some flexibility, either to choose among different definitions or to create new termination rules.

5.4.2 Organizing Words

When a database is used to organize documents, a fixed number of attributes are used to describe each entry. These might be name, creation date, subject, and description. Full-text retrieval goes further than this by allowing access of documents based on their content.

Basically, when all the common words in a document, such as "and" and "the" are removed, the remaining words are the attributes that describe the content of the document. The situation is more complicated than with a relational database, because a large and variable number of attributes are associated with each document.

5.4.2.1 Term Frequencies

One of the advantages of full-content retrieval is that indexing is automatic. The alternative for indexing text is for a human operator to read the text and assign key words. Apart from being slow, this method is inconsistent because two different librarians, or even the same person at different times, will choose different words to characterize the same document.

Automatic indexing for full-text retrieval must first choose the words that distinguish documents. Terms that are frequent in many documents are not useful to a full-text search. There is no point in including them in an index, as they are unlikely to be used in a query and would match on most of the document collection if they were.

The first step in indexing the contents of a document is to filter out the common words. This can be done by compiling a table of all the terms used in the document collection and counting the number of times each appears. This table is then arranged according to frequency, and the most common words can be removed. The least common terms can also be discarded, as they are unlikely to affect performance. The remaining, medium-frequency terms are then used to create the index.

Alternatively, if term frequencies are assumed to follow a standard pattern, words can be compared to a "stop list" or "negative dictionary," which contains all the words to be excluded from the index.

5.4.2.2 Stems

Once the common words have been removed, the remaining terms can be further organized by reducing them to their stems. The stem of a word is that which is left once information about gender, tense, and number, as well as elements that modify the word's use in a sentence, are removed. The following all have the same stem: "words," "wording," "wordy," "wordless," "wordiness." In this example, a process which simply takes the first four letters would correctly reduce these to "word." However, the stem is not always the first four letters; it may be shorter, longer, or even of variable length.

A more successful process uses a suffix and prefix list to work out the stem. The methods used make many mistakes, but the mistakes are consistent and will simply result in incorrect matches being returned along with the correct ones as the result of a search.

For example, only a sophisticated system will class "important" and "importing" as having different stems, but the result is that your search on "competitor imports" might include a summary of the last Olympic games ("important competitions"). This is called a "false drop" and can happen in a number of ways, depending on the indexing method used. To avoid this, some applications perform a text scan on the returned documents before presenting them to the user.

5.4.3 Indexing Methods

An indexing method is chosen on its search speed and how much overhead it introduces. Overheads include creation time, update time, and storage space. One extreme is to have no index at all and to perform a sequential scan of every document in the collection for each search. This method requires no overhead but is very slow.

There are many ways of indexing document contents, and each is appropriate to different situations. A document base usually falls into one of three categories: those that are unchanging, those with constant additions, and those with frequent changes, updates, and deletions.

1. The unchanging document base is characterized by a library: a large set of documents which are not changed or deleted. There may be regular additions, but these additions are finished documents and can be added in batches.
2. A document base with constant additions is characterized by a production system. There is a large body of documents that remain relatively untouched, though occasionally superseded. A smaller number of documents are subject to frequent alterations and updates while they are being worked on, and will eventually make their way into the larger body once completed. This is the most common situation in an office environment, and it is discussed in Chapter 6 in terms of libraries, filing cabinets, and folders.
3. The third category is where all documents are subject to frequent change, update, and deletion. In this sort of system there is little stability over time, so any index becomes out of date quickly or is continuously updated. An index is only beneficial if it saves time, so it is probably better simply to scan the entire document base for each search and to dispense with indexing entirely. This situation is unusual and is likely to settle into the second category over time as useful and relatively unchanging documents accumulate.

Various indexing methods have been designed to cope with full-text retrieval. The more popular ones are discussed next, and they are compared in terms of search speed and overhead.

5.4.3.1 *Inversion of Terms*

In a simple variation of this scheme, all the words that can be part of a search are sorted alphabetically. Each word has pointers to all of its occurrences in the document base. A query can then intersect these lists of pointers to find target documents. The scheme is optimized by using different structures to organize the list of words and their pointers. Figure 5.4 illustrates an inverted file.

This system requires a large overhead in terms of additional storage space, often requiring nearly as much storage for the index as for the original files. Update of the index can become slow as the document base grows. However, it is fast for searching, and relatively straightforward to implement. This method of indexing is currently the most common in full-text retrieval.

5.4.3.1.1 Inverted Indices

The inverted index is produced by a process that uses the parser to get all the words in the document and their locations. This information is sorted into a list by word and by the location of each word's occurrence in the document. This sorted list is used to extract statistical information about the words in the document, and is combined with statistics from indexing other documents to get overall statistics about the entire body of the data base.

Once all the documents are parsed into their words and the words' locations in the documents are known, a number of steps are taken to reduce the indexed information to something that will be meaningful. This is done by removing some words and by

5.4 Full-Text Retrieval ■ 145

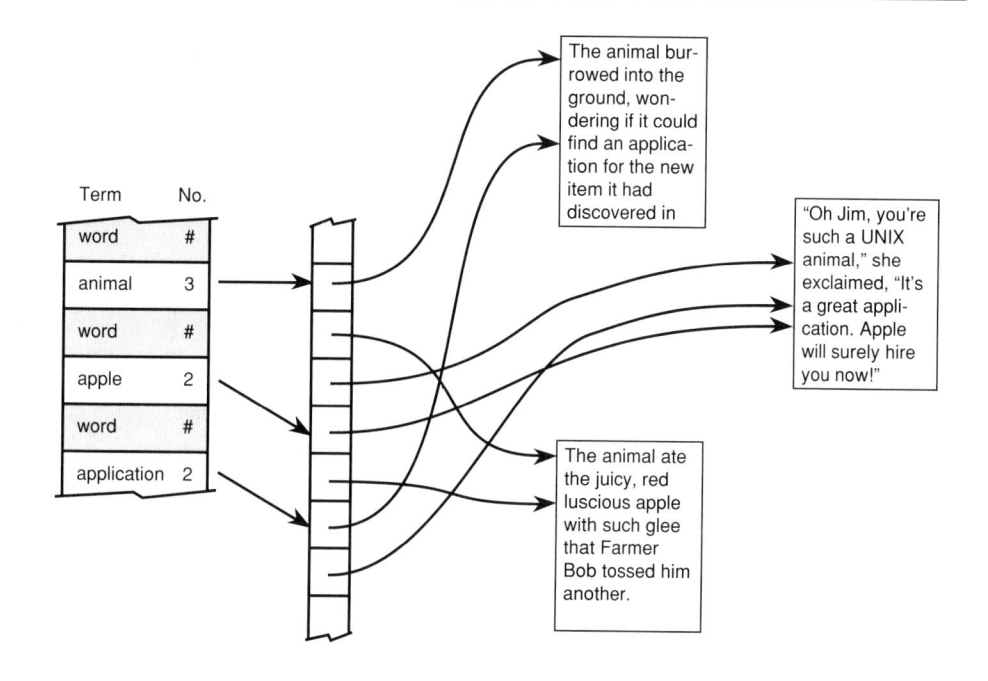

Figure 5.4 Inverted file.

adjusting the granularity of the information for the remaining words. In any document, there will be words that occur very often, such as "the," "a," and "in." These can be found in almost any document, regardless of its source. In addition, certain documents that pertain to a particular subject may have their own set of very common words. For example, the word "dosage" is ubiquitous in pharmacology. These are known as "noise" or "stop" words and should not be indexed. The reason is that selecting documents based on these words has a very high probability of choosing the entire document set. These words and all their location information are discarded after indexing.

Another group of words that may be candidates for removal are words that occur very seldom. There is not as good an argument for removing these words, since they may include such things as proper names, which may be very valuable in applications such as a review of court cases. Another problem with the automatic removal of such words is that if the document set is indexed piecemeal or incrementally, words that may at first appear insignificant may grow in significance as the document set grows. While many systems discard these words, a better implementation approach is to provide for the eventual storage of such indexing information in some off-line file. Then, if the system is later made capable of piecemeal additions to the index, the information may be placed back on-line and possibly used to add words that have increased in relevance over time.

In any sufficiently large body of documents, about half the words occur only once, and about half the remaining occurrences are for stop words. Thus, a good estimate of the actual number of occurrences to be remembered is 25 percent to 30 percent of the words in the document. Since the average word length of these words (at least in English) is about 6 characters, then using up to 12 bytes to remember each occurrence should still result in an overhead of 50 percent over the original text. Thus, inverted indexing schemes typically incur a 50 percent overhead.

The result of the inverted index will be a dictionary of words that are in the index (that is, words that were not discarded either because they appeared too often or too seldom). There is also a list of stop words, which will not be indexed. The on-line dictionary contains, in addition to the words, some statistics to indicate how often the words appear, both across the whole document set and on average for each document. It also contains some information that can be used to find the occurrence information. Query resolution consists of extracting the occurrences for the words being sought and determining if those occurrences are sufficiently close to select a document.

5.4.3.1.2 Inverted Index Creation

The inverted index is produced by indexing the members of a document set. The members of the set are identified by looking for document object columns in relations (or some other as yet unspecified source), taking each such object's value (which is in fact a structure), and using this value to perform the indexing function. As described previously, the document objects have in them some way to identify them as candidates for inverted indexing and some parameters to be used in that indexing process. Each document has its text pulled in through a common gateway. The text is divided by the parser into its constituent words. The indexer will pull out these words by calling the parser until there are no words left in the document. The words, along with some location information, will be sent to a sort stream. This sort stream will take all the occurrences for all the words in all the documents being indexed at one time. On the way to the sort stream, the words will be filtered according to the stop/go word lists available for each document. After all the documents have been processed, a sorted list will be extracted from the sort stream. The primary key will be the word, the next key will be the document ID, and the last key will be the word's location in the document. Thus, a typical result of the sort stream could look like the following:

Word	Document	Occurrence
after	doc_1	occurrence 1
after	doc_1	occurrence 2
after	doc_2	occurrence 1
⋮	⋮	⋮
zebra	doc_100	occurrence 2
zebra	doc_101	occurrence 1

Note that this list will contain no stop words for those documents that specified a stop word list, and will only contain go words for those documents that specified a go word list.

5.4 Full-Text Retrieval ■ 147

The next step in the indexing process is to process this sorted list and create a dictionary and inverted index from it. The process is best illustrated by the simplified logic:

```
while list not exhausted
   if this is a new word
      save statistics for previous word
      if word is too common
         discard indexing information
      else if word is too rare
         discard indexing information
      else
         add word to dictionary and index
      endif
      initialize statistics for new word
   endif
   if this is a new document
      save statistics for word for previous document
      initialize statistics for word for new document
   endif
   gather statistics for entry
   add entry to current word's index list
endwhile
```

This will produce a dictionary of those words that are considered by the automatic indexing parameters to be useful for indexing purposes. The indexing information can be further screened and reduced, depending on the level of indexing to be provided. If only Boolean logic is possible in the queries against the index, only a single occurrence of a word for a document needs to be maintained in the index. If more complex relationships between words are to be permitted, such as proximity operations, all the occurrences, along with their positioning information, must be maintained.

5.4.3.2 Signature Indexing

There are a number of ways of determining a signature for a document. One of the simplest is to take the first N (such as 40) characters and use those to determine if the document fits the query. In other words, if the query terms appear in the first N characters, the document is chosen as potentially relevant. This is obviously very crude, but it does illustrate the basic concept of signatures (Faloustos and Christodoulakis, 1984). What any signature system tries to do is to compress all the information in a document into a very small space. Obviously, much information will be lost, but the theory is that enough is retained to make some good judgements about relevance based on probability and statistics. Two common methods will be described here. The first is based on words, and the second on character strings.

Word-based signatures are created by looking for certain words in a document and then indicating whether or not the words are present, and occasionally, also how often they occur. The implementation involves choosing some method of changing a word into a number, usually by some hashing function, and then making a vector of the hashed numbers found in the document. Since the word is in the vector if it appears and not in the vector if it doesn't, each word can be reduced to a single bit. Of course, since there are a great many possible unique words, there may be many bits set for a document. Reducing this number is accomplished by means of stop words and compression schemes. One method is to choose only a certain fixed number of words, and setting bits if these words are found. This can also be easily related to existing thesaurus or concept structures, since they by definition include a fixed set of words. The bit patterns thus formed are kept in a database and are compared with bit patterns created from the query terms. Comparing the patterns not only identifies documents by how many hits they have, but by what words caused the hits to occur, and this can be related back to the word list in use to help assign relevance scores to the chosen documents.

If the average document is very large and the list of key words is reasonably small, more space than a single bit may be allocated to each word; this space (say a byte) may include how many times the word appeared in the document, and thus be an additional aid in determining relevance. Other approaches split the document into smaller parts, each with its own bit pattern, and thus serve not only to choose a document, but to isolate the part or parts in the document that are the most relevant.

Word signature systems may dispense with a fixed list of words and instead use a hashing scheme that spreads words out into a very large space. Here, each word is again represented by a single bit, but the bit vector is of almost arbitrary length. This vector is naturally very sparse, so it is compressed into a final signature, which is of comparable length to those acquired with fixed vocabularies. Again, it must be noted that this method is not as exact as inverted indexing, since relevance thresholds of the minimum number of common bits necessary to select a document may result in documents that include some of the query terms being omitted.

Character string signatures don't look at the words as such. They are more concerned with strings of two, three, four or sometimes five characters. The document is scanned and searched for these short pieces of words, and as each is found, a bit is set in a vector. This serves to identify the words in a document by the bits and pieces they are made of. For example, the word "vector" may trigger the setting of bits for the pieces "ve," "ec," "ct," "to," "or," "vec," "tor," and "vect." Of course, other words may cause some or all of these bits to be set also, but if a query contains the word "vector" and its bits are set in the query string, there is a good chance that the most of the documents selected as a result will include the word "vector."

Of course, with any signature system, the richer the query, the more information is available for comparison and the less subject the system is to error. Figure 5.5 illustrates a signature index.

5.4.3.2.1 Signature Index Creation

Creation of the signature index starts with the same steps as inverted indexing. The documents to be indexed are extracted from the database, and for each document, the parser extracts all its words. The signature indexer will take each word and scan it for the presence of signature elements. The signature elements in this implementation are referred to as *N*-grams. Briefly, an *N*-gram is a short string of characters,

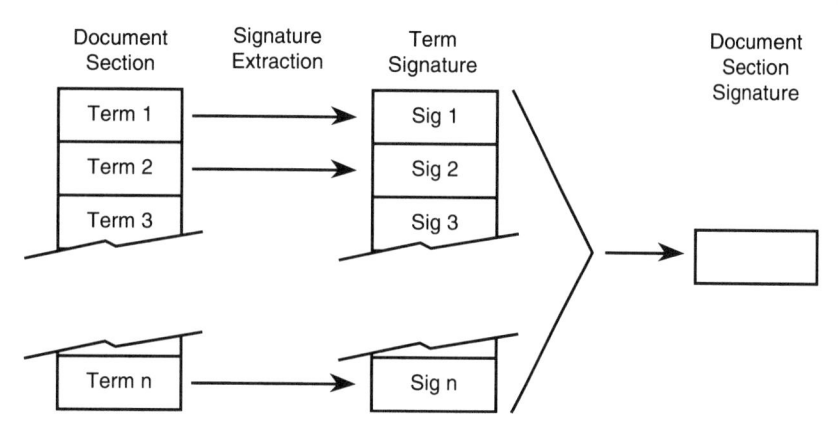

```
             Document      Signature       Term                    Document
             Section       Extraction      Signature                Section
                                                                   Signature
             ┌────────┐                  ┌────────┐
             │ Term 1 │     ────▶        │  Sig 1 │ ╲
             ├────────┤                  ├────────┤  ╲
             │ Term 2 │     ────▶        │  Sig 2 │   ╲
             ├────────┤                  ├────────┤    ╲
             │ Term 3 │     ────▶        │  Sig 3 │     ╲          ┌────────┐
             └────────┘                  └────────┘      ▶────▶    │        │
                                                        ╱          └────────┘
             ┌────────┐                  ┌────────┐    ╱
             │ Term n │     ────▶        │  Sig n │   ╱
             └────────┘                  └────────┘  ╱
```

Figure 5.5 Signature index.

like "gh," "tim," or "ng." A two-character string is called a 2-gram, a three-character string is called a 3-gram, and so on. The signature is developed by looking for all the N-grams in a document and creating a bit vector (the signature) with bits set for the N-grams that are present.

As each word is extracted and split into its N-grams, bits in a vector are set. In addition, a frequency vector is maintained for each document. Each time a particular N-gram is found, its entry in the frequency vector is incremented. This vector will be used for additional relevancy information at query time.

Once all the words have been extracted, the N-gram vector is stored in the signature file as a 512-byte (4096-bit) record. The frequency vector is added to the overall frequency vector for all the documents, and then it is processed by a similar method to that for the word lists of documents in inverted indexing. The most and least common N-grams are discarded and those remaining N-grams that are judged to be most meaningful are stored for the document.

The list of N-grams will begin with the possible 2-grams. After the initial indexing pass on the documents, the most common 2-grams will be chosen and expanded into 3-grams. The procedure is to pick the 200 or so most common 2-grams, which would include things like "in," and expand them to all the possible 3-grams; for "in," these would be "ina," "inb," through "inz." The next time the document set is indexed, these 3-grams will also be available. As long as there is room in the N-gram vector, the most common 3-grams can be expanded to 4-grams, those can be expanded to 5-grams, and so forth. The aim is to achieve finer- and finer-grain signatures of words. Also, the least common N-grams (those that never occur) can be weeded out over time. Thus, since the 2-gram "qk" never appears in English, it can be removed from the list.

The signature-indexing implementation will require an N-gram table, containing the N-gram, how many documents it appears in, how many times it appears across all the documents, and which bit in the N-gram vector it occupies. It also requires a signature file, which will contain the document ID of each indexed document and the bit vector for each document. In addition, each record in this file will include space for some number of the "most relevant" N-grams for that document, as determined at indexing time.

The parsing of words into N-grams is done by feeding them into a finite state automaton. Since the number of and content of all the N-grams does not change during indexing, the state tables can be set up at start-up.

5.4.3.3 Concept Indexing

A step beyond the more traditional indexing methods is concept indexing and retrieval. In a concept-based system, there is some mechanism for representing knowledge gained about the system. Some of the simpler concept development tools are dictionaries, synonyms, thesauri, and morphological analysis. These serve to expand the search targets by looking for equivalent terms in addition to those specified in a query. These features are available on many full-text retrieval systems and are typically applied to the query by adding more words or terms to the query target. Synonyms are not very intelligent. There is a simple replacement of one word or term for another. Thesauri are more complicated, since there are different levels of reference between terms. Both thesauri and synonyms are generated by "intelligent" users of the system and are a kind of "captured" intelligence, since the system has gained intelligence by the direct input of humans. Morphological analysis will automatically extract roots of words by stripping off prefixes, suffixes, plurals, and other changes to word morphology. It is typically based on sets of rules unique to the language being indexed, on lists of character strings that can be applied to word roots, and on rules for the construction and decomposition of compound words.

A dictionary, in this context, is a set of words. Often a dictionary is used to associate words, as in more comprehensive stem-finding systems. Dictionaries can also be used to spell-check a piece of text before it is indexed.

A thesaurus has many applications within full-text retrieval. It can be applied to terms in order to group them as concepts, and it can also be used for clustering documents.

Another mechanism for organizing concepts beyond the "linear" structure of synonyms and thesauri, Verity's "Topic" is a full-text retrieval system which allows the user to define concepts and then order them in a hierarchical structure. An example might be to define "Toyota," "Saab," and "Jaguar" as all being types of "Automobile." "Automobile" itself might be defined under "Transport." With this structure in place, the next time a search is initiated that includes "Transport" it will return documents that mention "Toyota" or "Automobile." Figure 5.6 illustrates a concept hierarchy.

The concept approach applies to both indexing and query specification. If the concept groupings are known before indexing, then they can be used to index terms that form part of the same concept, with the same index. A query can simply specify one or more concepts. Documents that contain any of the terms within those concepts will be returned, avoiding the need to search for each of the concept group members.

5.4.3.3.1 Concept-Indexing Techniques and Strategies

There are two approaches to concept access to documents. The first is concept queries, where a conceptual structure is built either on top of or beside an existing inverted or signature index, and concept indexing, where the indexing process is driven by the concept structures. In a concept query world, all indexing is done on individual words. The inverted and signature indices contain no real knowledge. When a query is made, the concept structure is scanned for words that appear in the query. If those words appear

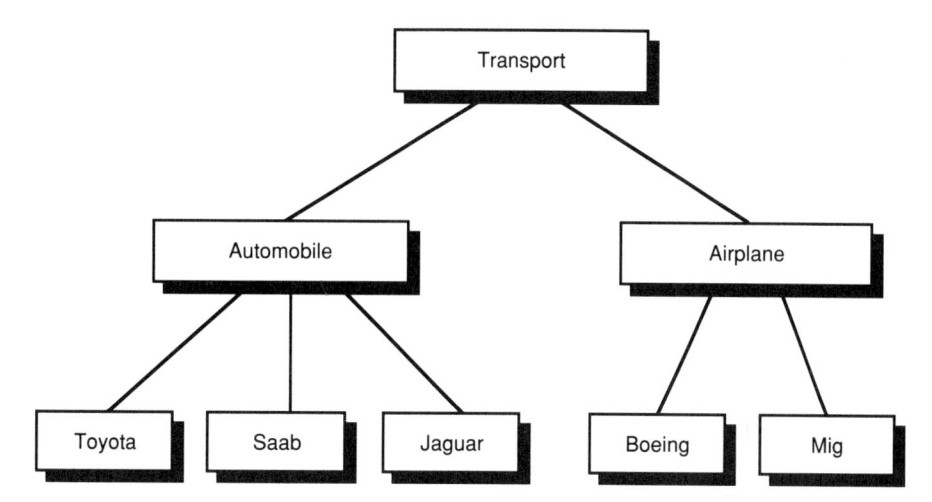

Figure 5.6 Concept hierarchy.

in the concept structure, that structure is used to enrich the query by adding alternate search terms. The resolution of the query still depends on the older, cruder indices. The advantages of this model are that the indexing models stay fairly simple and that there is a great deal of flexibility in the concept structures, since they can be of almost any form as long as their lowest levels consist of indexed words or terms. The major disadvantage of this model is that performance is degraded. If you know what the concept is and you have to extract it by going through additional levels of indexing, time will be lost. Also, since the crude indices have to pay attention to many more words, they are correspondingly much larger than they have to be to support concepts.

For the concept-indexing model, the concept structure is used to actually index the documents. For example, it may take a paragraph to describe a concept or make it intelligible to readers. Out of that paragraph, there may be only half a dozen words that are really meaningful to the recognition of the concept. In the concept-indexing model, these words, and in fact all the words in the paragraph, are never explicitly indexed. Only the fact that the concept was recognized is remembered. This model obviously saves a great deal of space and time, but its drawback is that it is very difficult to automate, since the written language is so fluid. However, as with most problems in software, there is a middle ground. What can be done is that words and phrases that can be classed as equivalent, or of some level of interest to each other, can cause multiple index entries for the same part of a document. For example, there can be a thesaurus that tells the indexing process that there is some relationship between the words "mammal" and "vertebrate," where "mammal" is a narrow term for "vertebrate." At indexing time, a path to occurrences of "mammal" can be constructed leading from "vertebrate," so that when a query is made against "vertebrate," and the user wishes to expand to include narrower terms, these occurrences are automatically included. This makes the index more complicated, but it will make it perform better, since what is happening is that some intelligence is working its way into the stored index data structures.

Using such concept-indexing strategies should in most cases allow more extraneous words to be removed from the inverted index. Also, driving the data base in this direction will in most cases serve to eliminate the need for semantic information storage in the inverted index. This further reduces the size of that index. It is not clear at this time what the exact tradeoff is, but it may be that the additional space needed for the more complex concept indices is made up for in reduced number of words and occurrence information in the inverted index.

5.4.3.3.2 Indexing Domain

Concept indexing is typically done against abstracts of documents, but it can, in fact, be performed on the entire document. The method to be used is that of attempting to fit documents into templates and to use those templates to create concept frames in a database. A template is a model containing a keyword and a slot. The list of keywords is chosen before indexing occurs and is determined by the documents being indexed. A keyword is a trigger to the indexing mechanism that the next word or phrase is to be interpreted as the filler for the template's slot. Keywords are typically prepositions or other semantic structures that serve to delineate phrases. For example, using the keywords "from" and "containing," the sentence

> There is danger from sardines from Sweden containing excess amounts of salt.

can be parsed, and among other things, be seen to include information about locations (*from* Sweden), products (*from* sardines) and dietary problems (*containing* excess amounts of salt). The templates for *from* and *containing*, when applied to this sentence, result in the identification of a location, a product, and a problem, and can be used to update and extend many associated data structures.

It is obvious that such a scheme works best on abstracts and indexed terms in documents, since these typically have much simpler syntax rules.

The information extracted from a document with the templates is used to create and update frames in the database. There are frames for the documents, frames for various categories, and frames for concepts. Each frame has a number of slots, the number and type depending on what kind of frame it is. Frames are connected together in hierarchies, where a frame has none, one, or more "parent" frames and none, one, or more "child" frames. The hierarchical links are through slots in the frames dedicated to those link functions. In addition, frames may have any number of other slots dedicated to whatever is needed for that frame. These other slots may in fact also be links to other frames. The resulting structure can potentially be an extremely complex network of frames. The complications can be controlled by putting some constraints on the possible links between frames.

Things like synonyms, thesauri and other conceptual links and relations can be represented by lists of frames. Accessing the frame database with the name of a concept or term then allows the extraction of the other related terms by following the appropriate path through the frame space.

5.4.3.4 *Clustering*

To complete our discussion on full-text search strategies, we present a brief overview of another technique called document clustering. This method groups similar documents together to form clusters. First of all, the text goes through the steps described in the previous section to produce a set of concepts. The set of concepts is used to generate a vector in "concept space," where each document is characterized by its vector and similar documents are close together. The "distance" between documents depends on the number of concepts that they share. The reasoning behind this approach is that similar documents are likely to be relevant to the same searches.

Definition of a search then generates a vector, and the result of the search is the set of documents within a certain distance of the search vector. Weighting can be assigned based on the distance between a document and this vector (Faloustos, 1985). Figure 5.7 illustrates a search vector.

5.4.4 Query Definition

The basis of information retrieval is a comparison of the user's request against the information within a collection of documents. A query is a representation of this request, and its success depends on the accuracy of this representation.

There is a range of ways to query the contents of documents. At one extreme the user has a clear idea of the target documents. In this situation a Boolean query is appropriate, where match criteria are logically combined. There is a clear distinction between documents that qualify and those which do not.

When the user is not so sure about the information to be found, a "fuzzy" query is needed. Groups of words and relevance to a subject are involved and must be incorporated into the query specification and response. The result of a query in this scenario would include a measure of how close the match is with each document.

Once the query specification and response have moved away from absolute precision, there has to be a way to measure the closeness of a match. A collection of documents that uses cluster indexing measures proximity in the vector space, as is described above. Concept indexing allows a user to specify concepts in the query, and the match might

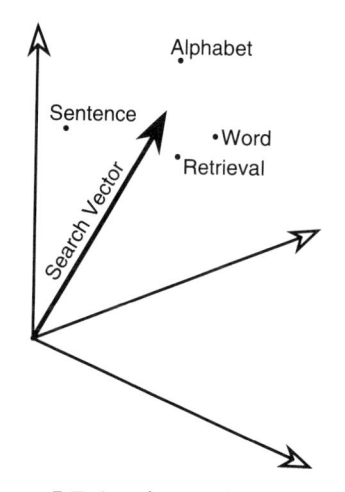

Figure 5.7 Search vector in concept space.

be judged by the number of references to a concept. Weighted Boolean querying where the weighting provides a relevance factor, is described in the next subsection.

5.4.4.1 Boolean

A Boolean query combines words and parts of words with logical operators such as *AND* and *OR*. An example might be

> ('computer' OR 'workstation') AND 'personal'

The result of such a search is a list of documents that matched the query. If a large number of documents are in the list of matches, the search must be further specialized.

A Boolean query is called "deterministic" because documents are retrieved only if they match the query precisely. The three main Boolean operators are *AND*, *OR*, and *NOT*. The user usually finds that a more complex query can be very difficult to formulate correctly, as it is easy to get bogged down in nested combinations of operators that are difficult to keep track of.

One approach to make the Boolean search less restrictive is to add weighting to the operators. Each operator is followed by a number that is a measure of its importance in the query.

5.4.4.2 Full-Text Query Language

There have been a number of approaches and proposals for a query language for full-content retrieval. One of the most notable of these was SFQL (AIA/ATA, 1990). SFQL is based on a subset of Structured Query Language (SQL) discussed in the previous chapter. It can impose a hierarchical structure on the text, dividing it into smaller components such as chapters, sections and paragraphs. Attributes are also distilled from the text, such as author, title, headings, and subheadings.

In order to illustrate how queries are formulated, we present a syntax for formulating full-text queries. Most full-text retrieval systems use similar constructs to formulate the Boolean expression over relevant query terms.

A text expression could be of the form

> <text item> CONTAINS <target>

where

> <text item> is some column name that is of document type.
>
> <target> is the term or terms for which the search is conducted.

The result of a *CONTAINS* operation will be that all records for which the document item includes the target will be selected.

The target is of the form

> (<text term> [* <text operator> <text term>])

where

<text term> is a word or phrase enclosed in single quotes or a parenthetical sub-expression.

<text operator> is AND, OR, NOT, WITHIN <number> WORDS, WITHIN <number> WORDS BEFORE, WITHIN <number> WORDS AFTER, or WITHIN <number> WORDS BEFORE <number> WORDS AFTER

Thus, the following are all legal text expressions:

TEXTITEM CONTAINS ('data' AND 'software' OR ('text' NOT 'index'))
TEXTITEM CONTAINS (('basis' OR 'basal'))
TEXTITEM CONTAINS ('gibberish')
TEXTITEM CONTAINS ('this' WITHIN 5 WORDS 'that')

The operators within the outermost set of parentheses are evaluated left to right, with parenthetical subexpressions being treated first—all in all pretty common syntax.

It is also possible to allow the specification of thesaurus or concept expansion in the query. This feature may be automatic, in which case all the query terms will be expanded by any available means by default, or it may be included in the syntax by some special character. For example, the # character may be used to indicate that a search term should be expanded, as in the following:

TEXTITEM CONTAINS ('#cement' or '#steel')

In this example, the # character would trigger the query expansion of "cement" to include "concrete," "prestressed concrete," and so on, while "steel" would be expanded to include "I-beams," "reinforcing rods" and the like.

For signature queries, Boolean operators and proximity operators don't make much sense. Instead, a typical query of such a system would be as follows:

TEXTITEM CONTAINS ('pertinent court cases concerning antitrust litigation in automotive manufacturing')

Note that there are a number of significant terms available for the development of a signature from this phrase. The signature will "or" all the words together and try to find documents that fit the pattern. Since the pattern match is not as exact, there is not usually any good reason to use any of the operators in the target, although the Boolean operators will still be available.

This syntax might not be appropriate for general end user usage. In other words, the end user will interact with one of the following:

- *A "natural" language tool:* The tool will extract words from the natural language query, look them up in the dictionary and in any existing concept data structures, and come up with a list of words and operations on those words, which must be extracted from the index. The intelligent tool will then formulate a query against either the inverted or the signature index, based on the syntax described here.

- *A graphical user interface window:* The user with such a tool might be offered a dialog of boxes and menu choices for predicates and connectors to construct the query.

5.5 DATABASE SUPPORT

The document objects are expected to exist in the context of some data base, probably a relational database server. The underlying assumption here is that the documents are stored on a database server and the full-text queries are submitted against this database to retrieve the qualifying document. In fact, often queries involve predicates both on the "content" and the attributes of a document. Predicates and queries on content were discussed in Chapter 4.

In order to process the full-content queries against the database server, a number of objects must be stored in the database. Some of these objects are discussed in the following subsections.

5.5.1 Dictionary

This is a list of all the words that appear in the document set and have been indexed (that is, contain entries in the inverted index or have been used in some signatures). This will not include any stop or noise words, nor any other words which have been for one reason or another discarded from the index. This list is accessed frequently—any time any document is indexed and any time a query is made. Lookup of individual words requires that they be a key into the list. The dictionary should be a database file with the word as a primary key, and it should include some statistical information about how often the word appears in indexed documents. For inverted indices, the entry for a word also needs to point to the location of the word's entries in the index. The expected appearance of this file is as follows:

Field	Type	Length	Key	Meaning
WORD	CHAR	1 to 40	Yes	the word itself
DOCS	BIN	32 bits	No	how many documents the word occurs at least once
OCCS	BIN	32 bits	No	how many times the word occurs in all indexed documents
WHERE	BIN	32 bits	No	where to find the word's data in an inverted index file

5.5.2 Stop (Noise) Word List

This is a list of all words which will not be indexed because they occur so frequently that they can convey no useful information. Again, the best way to store this list is as a database file containing one field, the word, and having that field be a key into the file.

5.5.3 Rare Word List

This is a list of words that appear very seldom in the indexed document and therefore are not expected to be useful in resolving queries. This list should ideally be a database file that can be kept remotely, since it is only useful during indexing operations. It can be kept on some removable medium and loaded back only when new documents are to be indexed.

5.5.4 Document Object Descriptors

There are two approaches to indexing documents in a database. The first consists of keeping a separate, databasewide document object database and having all document objects, regardless of where they appear in the database, be contained in the document object database file. For example, if there are two relations, each with a document field in it, the document fields would contain a pointer into the document object database file. There are some advantages to be gained from this approach, particularly if there is considerable partitioning and saving of sets of records, because then a single document object can be pointed to from any number of places and it only needs to be indexed once. The major disadvantage is that you always have to drag around the knowledge that all the documents are in one place. The other approach is to have each document column have its own database of document object descriptors. This means that each time a document object appears in a relation, there is an implicit set of associated files, including a dictionary, a stop word file, a unique word file, a document object descriptor file, and so on. This means more files, but since the index will typically be smaller, the indexing and query performance should be better. In either case, there should exist some structure to describe the document objects. This structure must include, at the least, the following:

Field	Type	Size	Key	Usage
INDEXED	BIN	48 bits	No	date/time last indexed
MODIFIED	BIN	48 bits	No	date/time last modified
SIZE	BIN	24 bits	No	length of text, in bytes
ID	BIN	24 bits	Yes	some unique, time-invariant identifier used to relate the inverted index to the column
WHERE	BIN	32 bits	No	where the text can be found

5.5.5 Document Storage

There must exist some place to store the documents. This should be accessible in fairly large pieces so that random access to the documents is available to a browser and editor tool to display and highlight text that has been found as a result of a query.

5.5.6 Index Storage

There must exist some place to store the index information. For signature files, this can be a normal database file with the signature as a key. For an inverted index, this is similar to the document storage file. The inverted index consists of many chunks of information that come in various sizes and have no fixed internal record structure.

5.5.7 Implementation Techniques Using Frames

In the following paragraphs we outline a number of implementation techniques that could be used to integrate inferencing and frame support in a full-content retrieval intelligent datatbase system.

5.5.7.1 Fixed Frame Support

The concept base depends on the existence and maintenance of a frame database. Each frame must have a name, one or more parents, and one or more slots. Each slot must have a name, a value, and optionally some verification predicates. While there will be some frame templates that are used over and over, in general each frame can be unique. A set of frames that all have the same structure can be represented as a relation with a name, a fixed number of parents, and a fixed number of slots. If the slots are complicated—they can include such things as lists—then the slot values can be in a separate relation that gets joined to the frame relation when needed. For those frames that have no fixed structure, all the parameters of the frame except its name will have to be in other relations that get joined to form the frames. For example, if the parents of a frame are needed, that frame's relation is joined to the parent relation and all the parents for that particular frame are extracted.

5.5.7.2 Amorphous Frame Support

The use of a relational database to store frames can obviously get to be quite inefficient for large concept bases, particularly if the frames don't have very much of a fixed structure. Therefore, a dedicated concept base can also be provided. This can be implemented using the BLOB or memo field capability provided by many databases. It can be based on a "normal" relation that contains a column for the frame name and a memo field for the frame's contents. This memo field can have the frame and all information needed to describe the frame contained in it. The first part of the memo field could be a common header, which could indicate how many parents there were, where the first parent started in the memo field, how many slots there were, where the first slot started, and similar information needed to access different parts of the frame.

5.5.7.3 Frame Compression Utility

A utility can be constructed to allow the creation of an amorphous frame file from fixed frames and related information and to make existing amorphous frames take up less space. As frames change over time and as frames from the relational database become more complicated, it will be necessary to put them into the dedicated concept base.

5.5.7.4 Rules and Goals

Using the concept and document frame hierarchies will require rules, as was described earlier. These rules will be used to prove goals using an inference engine. The rule sets can be stored in an ASCII file. There are two ways to deal with rules. The first is to maintain them in an ASCII file and provide users with a means to edit it, preferably in a structured manner. The second is to put the rules into a relational table and to modify or enhance the inference engine to take input from a relation for rule sets.

5.6 FULL-CONTENT RETRIEVAL IN THE INTELLIGENT OFFICE

One of the main strengths of the intelligent office is its ability to organize data and to assist the office worker in finding relevant information quickly and easily. The intelligent office deals not just with one or two types of file, such as text and image, but the full range of multi-media data types. Full-content retrieval expands the methods of full-text retrieval to include all document contents in combination.

Data refinement puts data in a more compact and useful form, which enables a search to be based on content as well as attributes. Full-content retrieval is particularly powerful when information is structured as a semantic net. In this form it is possible to use the techniques of inferencing to approach intelligence in the retrieval of documents.

Inferencing also relies on the amount of knowledge the system contains about the domain of the information which is being sought. For example, a search on "aerospace" will be more successful if the system knows that "shuttle" is a type of transport for reaching low Earth orbit. Knowledge-based full-content retrieval is a source of intelligence in the intelligent office.

5.7 SUMMARY

The power of full-content retrieval depends in part on the quality of document content. The more structured the data, the more meaningful the search that can be performed. The steps in data refinement are recognition and understanding. The former matches elements such as letters and sounds with the raw data in order to describe it in terms of these. The latter finds the objects and their relationships within the information to form a semantic net.

A query is applied to a collection of documents. Much can be gained by being able to define the search domain accurately. Document collections can be defined by source and by using office objects, such as "folder" and "filing cabinet."

Retrieval based on textual content serves as a detailed example of content-based search, as text has received the most attention in the industry. There are various methods for indexing and searching textual information. The appropriate method for indexing depends on how often the documents are changed, updated, or deleted. Choice of query definition is made depending on how much the user knows about the sought-after information.

Knowledge-based full-content retrieval is a powerful component of the intelligent office. It is dependent on the structure of the information and the complexity of knowledge about the information domain.

The chapters about graphical user interfaces and office objects discuss the techniques of hypertext and hypermedia, which complement and enhance the search and retrieval methods of this chapter and Chapter 4. Hypermedia techniques allow associative retrieval related to documents and their content.

6

IMAGING SYSTEMS

6.1 INTRODUCTION

This chapter discusses the evolution, purpose, components, and composition of imaging systems. Included are detailed descriptions of the systems' hardware components (scanners, compression boards, high-resolution display monitors, OCR systems, a variety of fax, voice, and video boards, and laser printers), and an in-depth exploration of how those components are combined in proprietary and stand-alone systems to perform document image management. Finally, several examples of real-world imaging system applications are presented.

Imaging systems (D'Alleyrand, 1989; Otten, 1987) first appeared in response to the urgent need to handle ever-increasing volumes of paper in certain mission-critical applications. These systems evolved in an environment where standards were not clearly defined and typical office computers were not powerful enough to cope with the task without additional hardware assistance. As a result, many early imaging systems were proprietary, closed systems that used their own formats, protocols, and custom hardware, and were dedicated to a specific task.

The price of selecting a closed, proprietary solution is higher than that of using an open, standard platform. In addition, the latter contains components available from many sources and is not restricted to a particular task. However, the higher cost of proprietary systems has not been a barrier to the early development of imaging systems, because this expense is easily recouped for the following reasons:

1. Storage of paper-based information is expensive, particularly if it is frequently accessed and needs to be located in the office. The lease on office space alone can pay for a system in a few months.
2. An electronic solution to document management is often considered in the situation where volumes of paper are increasing and the alternative is to either relocate the business or take on extra staff to handle the paperwork.
3. The imaging system can significantly reduce the need for human resources by sharply reducing the time needed for the retrieval and sorting of paper.

4. The loss of information can be very costly to an organization. The likelihood and severity of such a loss can be minimized by a well-designed imaging system.

The primary purpose of an imaging system is to scan in, index, and archive images. These images are then accessible for search, retrieval, and display. This is illustrtated in Figure 6.1.

Imaging systems have expanded from simply providing information-filing and retrieval capabilities to handling other aspects of the intelligent office. These aspects include the elements of work flow, the integration of fax, E-mail, host interaction, OCR, and text retrieval; and the ability to perform electronic document interchange (EDI).

Although a document-imaging system can help in the move toward a "paperless office," its role is to serve as a bridge from today's paper-based office to the technologies of the Intelligent Office. The system is designed to manage images stored on paper. In the future, when the information flowing into and out of an office is stored in electronic form, formats and methods of interaction will need to differ from those provided by an imaging system. For example, forms that enter the office are often computer-generated, so the need for an imaging system could be completely bypassed if given standards were accepted and levels of cooperation were achieved.

In the intelligent office, the method for inputting electronic information cannot be limited only to the keyboard and the mouse. The bulk of information in today's office environment, whether in the form of text or graphics, is stored on paper. Not only

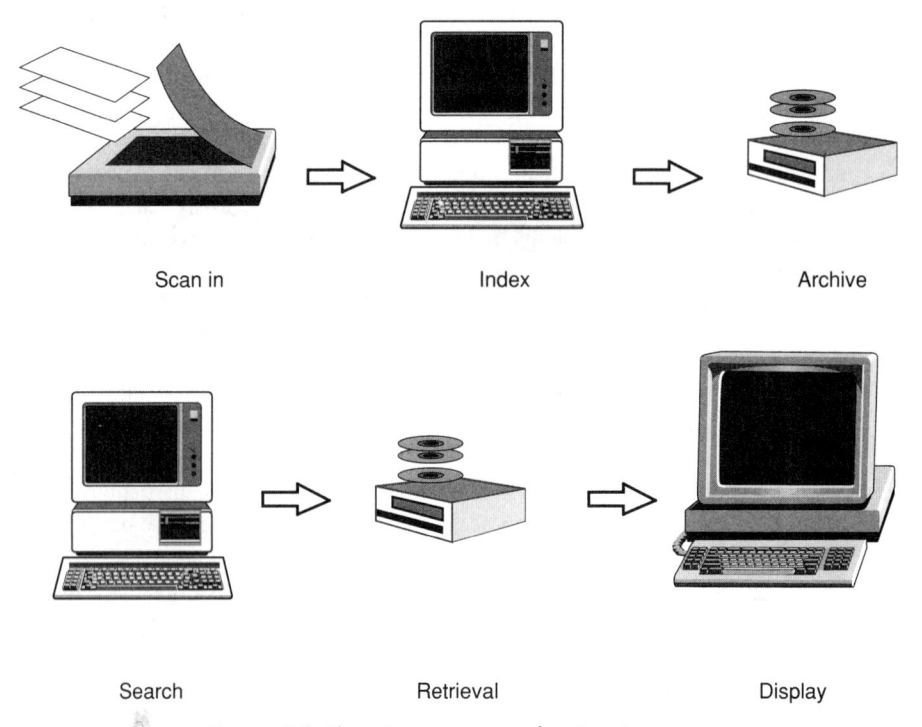

Figure 6.1 The primary purpose of an imaging system.

do we usually receive and transmit information using the paper medium, but most of the research information we gather (such as letters from customers and clippings from brochures) is usually stored on paper. None of this paper-based information originates in electronic form.

The trend will continue in that direction. The simplistic notion that the amount of information stored on paper will decrease because intelligent offices use more information in electronic form is fallacious. On the contrary, the amount of information stored in the paper medium continues to increase. It is contrary to human behavior to rid ourselves of all paper, and it will be a long time before we become a paperless society.

Clearly, the intelligent office needs to complement this trend, rather than change it. In other words, to make the office worker more productive, the electronic office needs to provide the means to transform nonelectronic information into electronic codes.

A standard office computer can be enhanced in many ways to serve the office worker better. Existing technology enables information stored on paper, transmitted as a facsimile, and transmitted as sound to be incorporated easily into its electronic equivalent. Scanners can convert just about anything on paper into an electronic file. Using fax boards, we can capture facsimile information into electronic image files. Voice boards allow sound to be readily input and output.

Because the boards that incorporate OCR and compression technology are hardware dedicated to a specific task, they can provide faster and more efficient service than the host processor. In addition, as computers become more powerful, more tasks are possible with the host processor. Consequently, there is a migration from dedicated hardware to software in functions such as compression, OCR, and voice and image processing.

6.1.1 Chapter Organization

Sections 6.2 to 6.9 describe the hardware components of imaging systems and how those components are tailored depending upon the need for different levels of capacity and throughput. An overview of each component's operation is provided, along with explanations of the parameters by which the manufacturers of each type of component define their products. These components are based upon technologies that are subject to rapid advancement, particularly with OCR, voice, and video, where the discussion covers current academic research that is likely to have an impact on the marketplace over the next few years.

Section 6.10 examines turnkey imaging systems, including single workstation and multi-workstation systems. The discussion covers different types of systems, including those designed for imaging and scanning, to act as the database server, and to provide storage, printing, and other services.

Section 6.11 deals with the interface to an imaging system in terms of forms software and the database interface. Section 6.12 presents the components used in the process of retrieving and manipulating images. Section 6.13 describes how imaging systems are currently used in some typical office applications, and Section 6.14 explores the evolution of imaging systems toward the intelligent office.

Throughout this chapter, estimates for gauging an imaging system's throughput and capacity are made in terms of the quantity of documents processed. These estimates are based on a storage requirement of twenty kilobytes for a letter-size, black-and-white image of typed text, printed at two hundred dots per inch resolution, compressed using the CCITT Group 3 two-dimensional compression scheme, and stored in the tag image file format (TIFF).

6.2 SCANNERS

All scanners are basically composed of a reading device, an interpretive software program, and an expansion board to interface with the CPU. Scanners fall into one of the four following designs. Each design, which is composed of the same three components and differs primarily in terms of the reading device, has its own merits (Glover, 1990).

6.2.1 The Four Scanner Designs

The flatbed scanner (sometimes called the full-page scanner) looks and works like most copy machines. The design provides the ability to scan anything that can be placed on the glass of the scanner, including books, heavy card stock, or paste-ups.

In contrast, the document-feed scanner can only handle single sheets and works very much like today's fax machines. Although this scanner can scan a full page, the original page must first be fed into a slot in the front of the machine. However, the obvious disadvantage of not being able to scan a book is overcome by the ability to handle multiple pages automatically. In fact, most middle- to high-end copiers contain both types of reading devices. As the market expands, most high-end scanners will incorporate both the flatbed and document-feed input methods. Figure 6.2 illustrates the Fujitsu scanner.

The third alternative is an overhead scanner, which is more expensive and usually best suited for a more specialized situation. This scanner's reading head is located above the scan bed, and the light source is reflected back from the page or object to be scanned. One great advantage offered by this technology is the ability to scan three-dimensional objects. Most commercial overhead scanners can handle up to a few inches of depth of

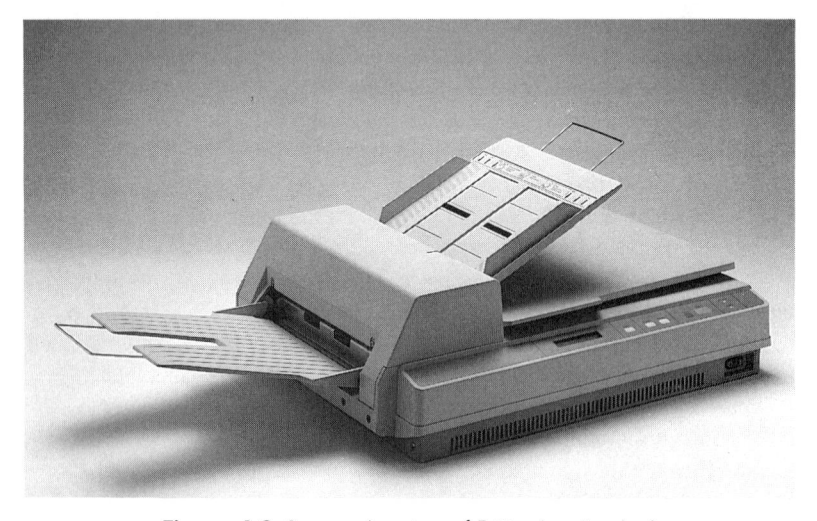

Figure 6.2 Scanner (courtesy of Fujitsu America, Inc.).

field. This approach is extremely useful for small item catalog publishing and scanning advertising copy drafts.

The fourth and most popular device is a hand-held scanner, sometimes called a half-page scanner. This type of scanner is available in many commercial brands and usually covers a four-inch wide stripe. When purchasing such a scanner, it is important to check the tracking device and test the scanner to see if it can easily roll in a straight line. The better manufacturers add a set of small tracking wheels to guide the user.

6.2.2 Optical Subsystem

A scanner contains a charge-coupled device (CCD) that reads the light reflected from the image. The resolution at which an image can be scanned depends on the number of these light sensors (CCDs) in the scanner. A 300-sensor-per-inch scanner provides a scan of 300 dots per inch (DPI).

When the scan is in progress, either the sensors move over the length of the scanned area, or the scanned area is passed over the sensors, at a fixed rate. Therefore, an $8\frac{1}{2}$ inch long scanning surface has 2550 sensors. The light source is usually a fluorescent lamp (red, green, or white). As these sensors are exposed to light, they generate an electrical voltage. The brighter the reflected light, the higher the voltage. Therefore, when a gray-scale scanner scans a gray-scale image, each CCD generates a charge related to each pixel's gray level.

With respect to handling a gray-scale image, scanners fall into three classes. The first class consists of non-gray-level scanners, which can only discriminate between black (on or 1) and white (off or 0). Therefore, all in-between gray levels are force-classified into black or white at the 50 percent level. With most scanners, the 50 percent threshold level can be adjusted, so the user can arbitrarily force the scanner to be more on the black side or the white side.

The second class contains gray-level scanners. In this type of scanner, the scanner's software goes beyond classifying the image as bright or dark and instead distinguishes the values of the image's brightness or gray level. The scanner's gray level is determined by the number of bits it allows per pixel. For example, if the scanner allows four bits per pixel, it is a 16-gray-level scanner. To calculate a scanner's gray level, use the following binary code combination.

If a scanner assigns eight bits per pixel, then each pixel can be one of the 256 gray levels of brightness. The more gray levels, the better the image's definition. However, a simple calculation will show that an $8\frac{1}{2} \times 12$ inch image at 300 dots per inch resolution and at 8 bits per pixel has a file size of almost one megabyte. To manipulate this amount of information would require a lot of RAM memory, a fast processor, and a large disk capacity.

The third class of scanners consists of color scanners. These scanners read each pixel of an image and convert the pixels to binary information in the same manner used by gray-level scanners. Thus, a four-bit color scanner will output only 16 colors, which is woefully inadequate for a photograph. To give a rendering of millions of colors, color scanners require at least 24 bits per pixel. However, because supporting hardware is needed to handle the throughput and processing for this type of scanner, it is considerably more expensive.

When scanning photographs, a few important points should be noted. Black-and-white photographs or continuous-tone art copy have gradients from black to white with little differentiation between the intermediate shades of gray. A monochrome printed copy of such a photograph from its scanned image is reproduced as a halftone, in which dots (dither patterns) of varying sizes simulate the shades of gray.

When a halftone picture is scanned and converted to the dither pattern of a monitor and printer, strange patterns result called Moiré fringes. These patterns result from the optical effects of overlaying dots and lines at different spacings and angles.

■ 6.3 COMPRESSION BOARDS

Lossless compression decreases the size of a file without losing useful information, and it is possible to recreate the original file exactly. All of the compression algorithms mentioned in this chapter are of this type, unless stated otherwise. The following example illustrates how a piece of data can be reduced in size without loss of information.

When a letter is scanned, it is converted into a bitmap of black and white dots. If you were to look at the list of ones and zeros, it would be apparent that it contains long strings of ones and shorter strings of zeros (in a black on white image, with white represented as one). The letter, which has large areas of white space and black letters in groups, is reduced to a fraction of its size if a string of ones (or a string of zeros) is replaced by a number representing a count of the digits in the string.

Three types of compression are commonly used on a file.

1. The first compression technique makes no assumptions about the data. This form of compression is based on the hypothesis that any file will contain some terms that are more frequent than others. When the file is being compressed, a table is made of the frequency of all terms in the file. In the case of text, the terms consist of letters or combinations of letters. When the file contains an image, the terms are the lengths of stretches of the same digit.

   Smaller identifying codes are assigned to the most frequent terms, and longer codes are assigned to the rarer terms. The file is then translated into these codes, thus shortening the file without losing information. In situations where different types of compression are combined, this type is used last, because it changes the assumptions made by the other two compression techniques.

2. The second compression technique relies on the characteristics of the data at hand. For example, if the numbers usually change slowly, then the differences between those numbers can be recorded rather than the digits themselves. The color values across a picture and the amplitudes along a sound wave share this characteristic. Information can be lost if such assumptions are made recklessly, but the loss may be imperceptible.

3. The third type of compression takes into account the significance of different aspects of the data in perception. Although this technique causes information to be discarded, that information is chosen so that it is minimally perceptible. For example, the human eye and brain are more sensitive to luminosity (brightness level) in a picture than to color information. Color information can therefore be stored in a coarser form (through "quantization") than data about luminosity.

The data must first be transformed into a form which makes it easier to select the data that can be discarded. In the case of a picture, the transformation splits brightness from color, so that each can be quantized separately. Sound can be transformed from a waveform into a frequency spectrum, and less audible frequencies can then be quantized in a coarser way than more audible frequencies.

There are two important reasons for using compression. It reduces the transmission time for a file, and it also decreases the file's storage requirements.

Compression boards are used primarily for compressing images, because those images are large and can be greatly reduced. An image can be compressed either at the scanner level or at the processor level. The preferred method is to compress the image inside the scanner through dedicated hardware, so that the data stream arriving from the scanner to the processor is already compressed. Various compression schemes are available, with names such as run-length, delta, and Huffman encoding. The most common encoding schemes are related to the facsimile standards, mainly CCITT Group 3 or Group 4 (described shortly in the fax board section).

A compression board plugs into the computer and can be used to display, scan, or print images. Earlier computers were not powerful enough to run software that could perform compression and decompression in a reasonable time. Today, however, it is common for decompression to take place in software, although hardware decompression is still used where a high throughput is needed (such as at a scan or print station). Compression boards (such as Kofax) also allow a daughter board to be added to control a particular type of scanner or printer.

Compression schemes for color and gray scale images are described in the video board section later in this chapter.

■ 6.4 HIGH-RESOLUTION DISPLAY MONITORS

At the time when imaging systems first appeared, a typical monitor in an office was insufficient for viewing images. A user who views many images every day would soon tire of having to zoom in and pan to read each one. An image of a letter at full size only becomes legible on the highest-resolution monitors available today. One of the reasons for the development of proprietary imaging systems is the requirement for the system to include a specialized screen attached to its accompanying hardware card. The components of a basic imaging system with a high-resolution monitor are illustrated in Figure 6.3*a*. Figure 6.3*b*, on the other hand, illustrates a document management system, which optically scans and stores large documents for printing and viewing on high-resolution monitors.

A monitor can be described by four sets of parameters:

1. The number of picture elements (pixels) measured across and down the screen quantifies how many dots make up the image display. When one uses this measurement, which is frequently (and incorrectly) referred to as resolution, the horizontal number is quoted first. This measurement usually ranges from 320 by 200 for a color graphics adaptor (CGA) up to 1280 by 1064 for a high-resolution monochrome monitor.

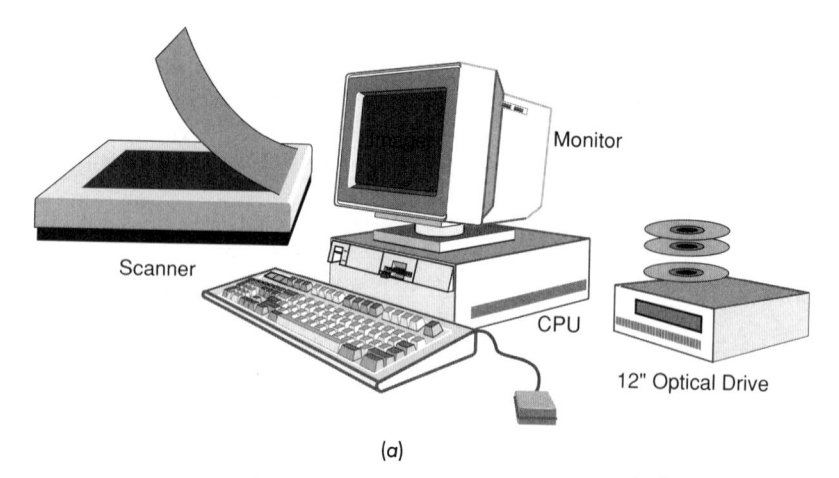

Figure 6.3 Imaging systems with high-resolution monitor. (a) Components of a basic imaging system.

2. The dimensions of the screen are normally quoted in inches. A single number gives the diagonal measurement; alternatively, the dimensions for the width and height can be given as a pair. A small monitor might be 12 inches diagonally, and larger monitors have up to twice this measurement. A doubling in the linear dimensions corresponds to a quadruple increase in screen area.

3. The resolution of a display is typically measured either in dots per inch (dpi) or as the width between the centers of adjacent dots (in millimeters). A coarse-looking monitor might use 30 dpi, whereas 120 dpi indicates a high-resolution monitor. When this is compared to the output from a laser printer with 300 dpi, it is easy to see why a printed page can be more easily read than a displayed image.

   When dot pitch is used to measure resolution, the lower the number, the higher the display's resolution. A VGA monitor is around the 0.3-mm mark.

4. The number of supported colors or shades is defined differently depending upon whether the monitor is analog or digital. An analog monitor receives a continuous signal, and the number of shades is a function both of the graphics card that drives it and the quality of its internal circuitry. A digital monitor receives a number of bits for each color displayed, and each color corresponds to a separate wire in the connecting cable. A color monitor with one wire (and therefore one bit) for each color (red, green, and blue) and one "brightness" line can display two levels of intensity for each, which combines to sixteen color/shades (Conrac, 1985).

■ 6.5 OCR SYSTEMS

In many offices, a large amount of useful information in magazines, books, and reports is not used because sifting through it would take too long. With optical character recognition (combined with scanning and full-text retrieval), this information becomes accessible. Once the relevant information is found, it can be cut and pasted directly into a report. OCR is a powerful technique that converts images created by a scanner or fax into machine-readable text. (This technique is not necessary with text, because text can be edited with a word processor or accessed using full-text retrieval.)

(b)

Figure 6.3 (cont) Imaging systems with high-resolution monitor. (b) Document managment system (courtesy of Litton Industrial Automation).

Earlier OCR packages required the user to teach them each new font by providing examples of the font and identifying letters as they were displayed. Teaching letters to a machine is a slow and tedious process.

The advancement of OCR and the availability of more powerful hardware have allowed the learning step to be avoided. The more recent OCR systems, called omnifont sys-

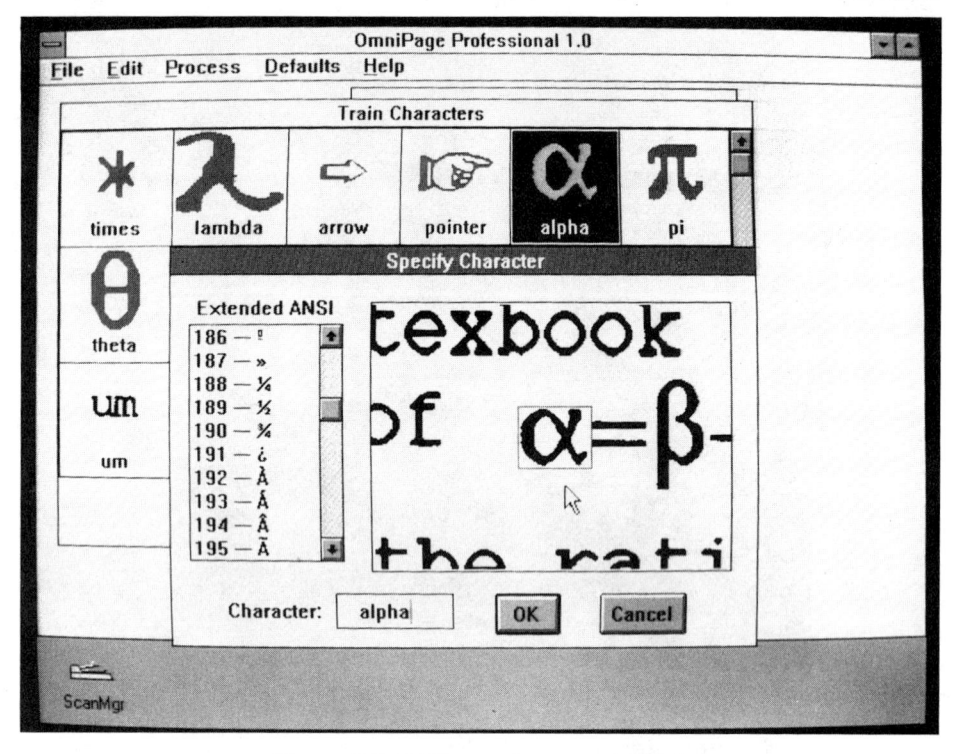

Figure 6.4 OCR system (courtesy of Caere).

tems, do not need to be taught and can recognize a variety of type fonts straight out of the box. An omnifont package will often have a learning mode for improved accuracy with an unusual typeface or unusual characters, as shown in Figure 6.4.

OCR is a processor-intensive function. Software implementations use the host machine processor and can work at satisfactory speeds only on the more powerful platforms, such as a SPARC-station, Macintosh II, or 386-20 or above PC compatibles. To achieve higher accuracy and speed, hardware boards or machines can be used, though these can be a very expensive solution.

6.5.1 Recognizing a Character

The first step in recognizing a character is to break the image down into individual character cells. Each cell is a bitmap containing a single symbol. The usual approach is to assume that a character is unbroken and surrounded by white space and that the members of a font are of similar size. A common error at this stage is for a single character to be split in two, particularly with a poor-quality image. Dot matrix print is especially difficult to process, because the characters are composed of dots, with each dot surrounded by space.

The second stage is to identify the character in the cell. There are a variety of ways to do this:

1. OCR packages that require teaching create an array of bitmaps associated with character codes. A character cell is compared to each bitmap, and the closest

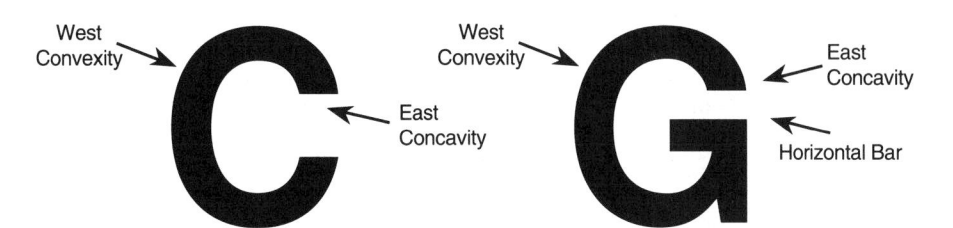

Figure 6.5 Character recognition by means of expert recognition of features.

match determines the character code. The process of comparison with this large array is time-consuming.

2. The technique of feature recognition is less dependent on font. Curves, lines and their relationships are derived from the character cell, and this combination of features is compared with a database to find the closest match.

3. The techniques of expert systems have been applied to character recognition. A number of experts are defined, and each responds to a specific feature (such as the "west concavity" of a C or a G). These are illustrated in Figure 6.5. Each expert provides a level of certainty, and a consensus is reached about the identity of the character. Redundancy among experts improves the tolerance to poor-quality print. The Kurzweil K5200 system is a high-level RISC-based hardware solution which uses this approach (Kurzweil, 1990).

4. The original OCR systems actually were optical systems. Light was shined through the image, casting a diffraction pattern onto an array of optical sensors. The pattern of light and dark regions identified the character. Optical computers might use the same system in the future.

5. The electronic equivalent of a diffraction pattern is a Fourier transform. The process of calculating the transform is slow, but it is very tolerant of noise and can identify the key features of a character while stripping out specific font details.

Accuracy in recognition is very important. Even a 99 percent success rate means that one word in this sentence would be read incorrectly. The context of a character can be used to improve accuracy. The most obvious way to do so is by spell-checking each word against a dictionary. This method can catch and correct most errors.

These five methods for character recognition are algorithmic in nature. Recently there have been advances in pattern recognition using neural networks. In the future, character recognition may be coupled with a better understanding of the way humans read text.

6.5.2 Preserving Format

A typical page of text uses various font types and sizes. It may be arranged in columns and include illustrations. Some OCR systems are able to preserve this information. They present the text output in the same fonts and layout and ignore illustrations, displaying them in the same place on the finished document. Recognizing a typeface is as complex as reading the characters, but size and arrangement information can be more easily preserved.

6.6 FAX BOARDS

A fax board attached to an imaging system provides remote scanning and printing from any location that has a fax machine. A fax board is a much cheaper alternative to a fax machine, because it cuts out the largely mechanical subsystems that handle the process of scanning and printing. Superior quality hard copies of incoming faxes can be produced on the network laser printer.

The inherent limitations on resolution, width, and transmission speed will remain until higher standards are adopted generally. These limitations can be improved depending upon the capabilities of both the sending and the receiving stations.

Fax boards incorporate a modem (modulator-demodulator) for transmitting and receiving information over a telephone line. More recent boards provide modem capabilities as well as fax, because most of the circuitry necessary is already present.

6.6.1 The Fax Process

A fax board performs several operations in hardware. The user, or system, provides it with a file name and a destination phone number. The file must be in one of the formats that the board supports. Text files are first converted to a bitmap image, either in software or on the board. (If a fax is being produced using a word processor whose native file format is not supported by the fax board, the file will need to be output in pure ASCII format.) Figure 6.6 illustrates the fax process.

In the first stage of the fax process, the image is compressed using a CCITT scheme. CCITT (International Telegraph and Telephone Consultative Committee) is an association that defines international telecommunication standards, including standards for facsimile apparatus and protocols.

The compression standards, called Group 3 (Recommendation T.4) and Group 4 (Recommendation T.6), are optimized for black-and-white typewritten text. Gray-scale and color are not currently included. CCITT Group 3 is usually used, though Group 4 is sometimes supported. Group 4 allows a higher compression ratio and therefore faster transmission.

The documents likely to be sent by fax between offices are also a good model for the documents to be archived in an imaging system. Therefore, image system designers

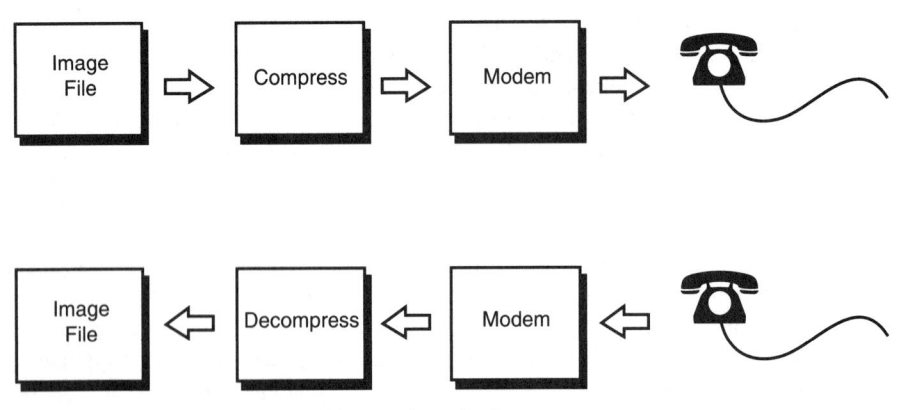

Figure 6.6 The fax process.

found a ready-made compression scheme in the CCITT recommendations. Documents being sent by fax from an imaging system may be already compressed and can go straight to the next stage.

The second stage of the fax process is handled by the modem. The modem encodes the stream of data (which is the compressed image) into a format for transmission over the public telephone system. This format is defined by the CCITT.

Next, the modem initiates the transmission by establishing the connection and exchanging information with the destination fax board or machine. It also provides synchronization signals and error checking during the transmission. Telephone systems are designed for transmission of speech, so the modem converts the encoded digital signal into audible frequencies by modulating tones.

The process of receiving a fax is the reverse of the process of sending one. The fax board answers an incoming call and receives the identity of the sending station. It then extracts the compressed image from the signal and stores it in a file.

6.6.2 Background Operation

So that the user does not have to interrupt work in progress in order to handle an incoming fax, fax boards are designed to run in background mode. They can be programmed to send a file at a later time or to retry regularly if the destination is engaged. They can also receive incoming faxes and store them in files for later review.

Background operation is controlled by a processor on the fax board itself. The processor can request and take over the computer bus, which it uses to transfer information to and from storage (usually the local hard disk). Control of the bus is then returned to the main processor. All of this happens without affecting any applications that the computer may be running.

■ 6.7 VOICE BOARDS

Typing speeds average 60 words per minute, whereas the typical rate of speech is much faster. For a computer to accept voice input/output, such as to a word processor, it must have both "external" peripherals to input the voice (such as a microphone) and output it (as through headphones). These are illustrated in Figure 6.7. Internally, the sound must be digitized, and then the computer must understand the meaning of the sound. The process of digitizing sound is trivial in comparison to the challenge of actually understanding speech.

Voice boards offer various levels of functionality. At the lowest level is the simple input or output of sound. This capability is built into some computers, such as the NeXT, Macintosh, or SPARC-station. PC compatibles include a loudspeaker that produces crude beeps, though it has been coaxed into almost intelligible speech by clever programmers. Sound digitization enables the voice annotation of documents without any additional functionality.

If the user wishes to talk with the computer or to use automatic dictation, then mere sound digitization is not enough. Speech synthesis can be performed by software or by using a chip designed for that purpose.

By far, the biggest challenge lies in understanding speech. The ultimate goal is speaker-independent, large-vocabulary, continuous speech recognition. The technology to achieve

174 ▪ **Imaging Systems**

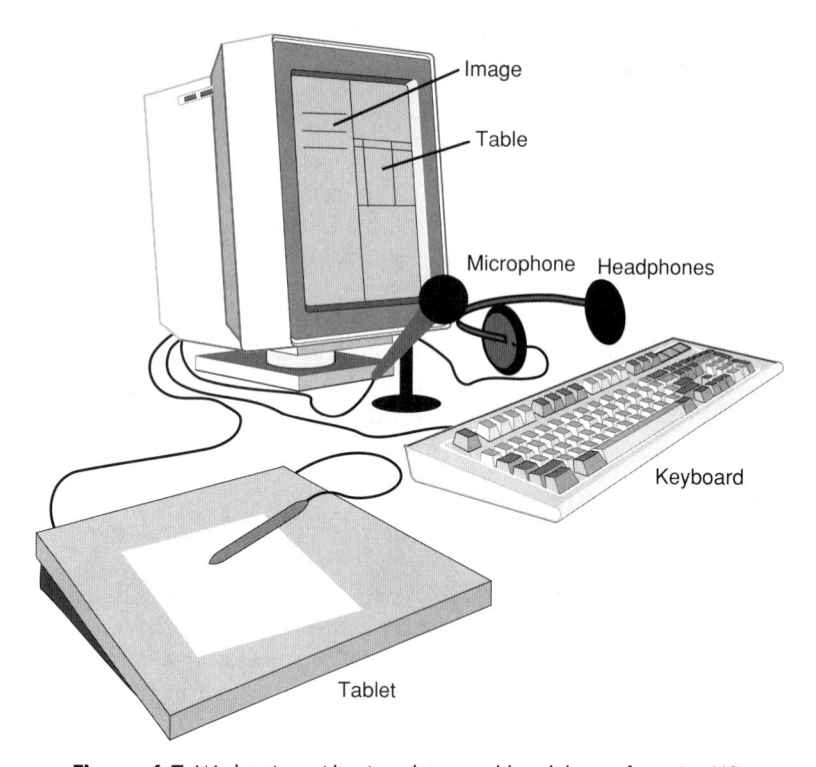

Figure 6.7 Workstation with microphone and headphones for voice I/O.

this goal is still in the research phase and requires quantities of expensive hardware. (See Chapter 9 for a discussion of voice in the intelligent office.)

6.7.1 Digitizing Sound

Before sound can be used in a computer, it must first be converted into digital form. The user speaks into a microphone which converts sounds into an electrical waveform. The microphone is connected to the voice board, where the waveform is "sampled" to convert it to digital information.

Sampling is the task of an analog-to-digital (A-D) converter, which measures the waveform at regular intervals, producing a stream of numbers. The sampling rate and accuracy are a simple tradeoff between the quality of sound reproduction and the volume of information to be stored.

The sample rate is measured in kilohertz (kHz), which translates to thousands of samples per second. The accuracy is measured by the number of binary digits (bits) required to store a single sample. For instance, eight bits can store 256 discrete values, and 12 bits can store 4096 discrete values. The higher the number of discrete values, the more closely the digital information can represent the original continuous signal. Figure 6.8 illustrates sound sampling.

The quality of sound recording and playback do not have to be very high for speech to be comprehensible. Contrast the quality of a telephone line to that of a compact disc

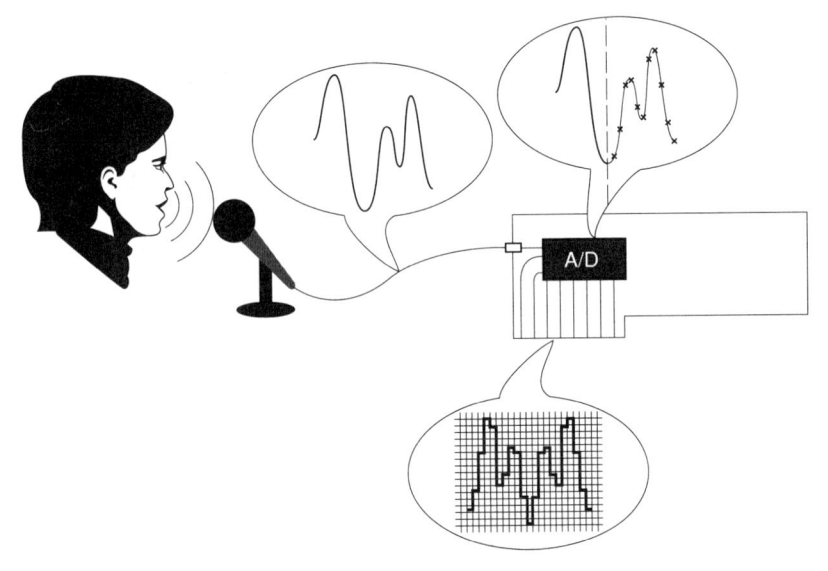

Figure 6.8 Sound sampling.

(CD) recording. The first can be matched at a sample rate of 8 kHz and 8-bit precision, whereas a CD has a sample rate of 44 kHz and 16-bit precision.

Using the values for a telephone line, 10 seconds of recorded speech can be stored in 80K bytes. The same period of CD-quality sound requires almost 1 Mbyte, over ten times larger. The first is practical for voice annotation of documents, while the second is not.

Storage requirements can be further reduced by compressing the data. Two common methods of sound compression are often provided on a voice card. The first is silence packing, which replaces periods of silence with a number defining the length of the silence. The second is to store the changes between samples, rather than the samples themselves.

A sound signal does not usually change much between one sample and the next, which means that the differences between samples are typically small numbers. Because a small number can be stored in less space, compression is achieved.

The playback of recorded speech is simply the reverse of the process just described. The sound file is sent to the voice board, which performs decompression and sends the stream of data to a digital-to-analog (D-A) converter. The converter produces a waveform, which can be sent to a loudspeaker.

6.7.2 Voice Synthesis

Just as the atomic unit of text is the letter (or symbol), so with speech the indivisible unit is the "allophone." The dictionary definition of a word usually starts with a phonetic representation to show how the word is pronounced. A voice synthesis board uses the same method to pronounce words.

The word to be output audibly is looked up in a dictionary and converted into a sequence of allophones. The sequences are assembled to produce a phonetic sentence, which is sent to a synthesis chip to be converted into digital sound. Finally, a D-A converter provides output to a loudspeaker. None of the steps are processor-intensive, and all can be performed in software, using a standard digital sound board for output.

The raw monotonic output of a sentence is flat and dull, and it sounds odd because there is no emphasis. To counter this, the output of voice synthesis can be modulated to emphasize the focus of a sentence. Modulation often defines the meaning of the sentence and can distinguish between a statement and a question.

6.7.3 Speech Recognition

In many ways, the development of speech recognition parallels that of character recognition (see Section 6.5.1). A simple speaker-dependent, small-vocabulary, discrete-speech system uses learning to compile a set of word or phrase templates. During the teaching stage, the user repeats phrases and associates them with text or a command. When a command is spoken, it is compared to the templates in the system, and if the best match is sufficiently close, then the associated command is sent to the current application. This sort of system is available in software or as a single voice board.

A more powerful solution breaks recognition into phonetic analysis and sentence parsing, with communication in both directions between them. Solutions of this nature are expensive and often require a large amount of dedicated hardware connected to the computer or network.

The process of phonetic analysis accepts digitized sound as input and outputs a stream of allophones. The digital sound is converted into a frequency spectrum using the Fourier transform. The spectrum is taken at a rate of around a hundred times a second, and gives amplitudes of the pure frequency elements which make up a complex sound.

Each allophone has a characteristic spectrum, which can be identified in the incoming sound. The stream of allophones produced is often accompanied by information about duration, relative volume, and a measure of certainty with possible alternatives.

The step of sentence parsing examines the allophone stream and attempts to recognize words. It is heavily dependent on context, because the same sequence may translate into a number of word combinations, words run into one another, and pronunciation changes with accent.

Chapter 9 provides definitions and uses of speech recognition capabilities.

6.8 VIDEO BOARDS

Various video boards are available for different tasks. Some allow live video to be displayed in a window on the computer screen, while others produce animation on a higher-resolution computer screen. Other video boards can output computer graphics to videotape or a television screen or enable video capture from camera or tape. A video board may provide a combination of the above functions.

Computers such as the Commodore Amiga, machines from Silicon Graphics, NeXT, and Macintosh, have video capabilities built in. There are various video boards available for PC compatibles, using specially designed chips such as Texas Instruments' graphics processors and INMOS's Transputers. Digital Video Interactive (DVI) boards now use Intel VLSI chips.

6.8 Video Boards ■ 177

6.8.1 Animation

A reasonable quality of animation is possible on a 386-33 PC compatible with VGA (or higher model) monitor. Video boards such as TARGA and VISTA from Truevision, and Hercules's color graphics cards, provide up to sixteen million colors at higher resolutions. Figure 6.9 illustrates an animation involving Planet Earth.

Animation can require substantial processing power with rendering time measured in hours, so graphics processing is usually provided on a board. The output from a high-resolution graphics display card is usually red, green, blue, and synchronization analog signals, which can drive a monitor directly. Some video boards provide video composite output, though additional hardware is usually necessary.

6.8.2 Video Capture and Overlay

A live-video card can, at a minimum, receive the signal from a TV or VCR and display it in a window on the screen. A more complex controller allows image capture to a file. Overlay is where computer-generated graphics and video signals are combined, as in the credits at the end of a TV show.

Any system that combines computer display with video signals has to coordinate precise synchronization. The standards used for television broadcast, such as NTSC and PAL, are composite analog signals which rely on accurate synchronization of luminance and color information. The device that combines encoded computer graphics and video signals is a "genlock," and a good one is complex and expensive.

Figure 6.9 Animation using Time Arts' "Lumina" Graphics product and Truevision Video Board animation of Earth Station One (Copyright 1989 National Geographic Society. Designed and produced by Exhibit Technology Inc. for Explorers Hall, National Geographic Society, Washington, D.C.).

6.8.3 Compression

Digital video requires large amounts of storage. A single color photograph can take up megabytes. Real-time video displays twenty or more frames per second, which adds up to vast storage requirements and high throughput of data (bandwidth).

Data compression cuts down the storage requirements to more manageable levels. Compression and decompression are performed in hardware on the video board. DVI includes a compression scheme described in Section 9.7.1. The Joint Photographic Experts Group (JPEG) is defining a scheme to be adopted by the International Standards Organization (ISO) and the CCITT. JPEG deals with still images and can be used to compress each frame.

The Motion Picture Experts Group (MPEG) is defining compression from full-motion video for ISO. The MPEG scheme takes advantage of the fact that the changes between one frame and the next are usually small. The most mature standard is Recommendation H261 from CCITT, which is designed to reduce the bandwidth necessary for video transmission, specifically for videophone and teleconferencing. A clear standard has not yet stood out but it will probably come from the JPEG and MPEG.

■ 6.9 LASER PRINTERS

Recent models of laser printers, such as the one shown in Figure 6.10, provide multiple fonts and PostScript capabilities. With text printing, information is sent as a stream of character codes, with which font and format information is sent as "escape" sequences

Figure 6.10 Laser printer (courtesy of Fujitsu America, Inc.).

(binary codes preceded by an escape character). The printer translates these into bitmaps on the page.

In order for a printer to print images, it must support graphics printing. Graphics printing handles the image as a bitmap, where each pixel is defined. Graphics mode involves much greater amounts of data than text mode. This is illustrated by the example of a typical letter, which has a few thousand characters but is composed of millions of pixels. Graphics printing is slow, and extra memory is necessary in order to add graphic printing capability to a laser printer.

Higher-speed graphic printing can be achieved in two ways. The first method is to use a faster protocol for the communication between the computer and the printer. An office laser printer typically uses a Centronics parallel or an RS-232C serial connection for this protocol. Some laser printers use SCSI to receive information at a higher rate.

The second alternative for increasing the speed of graphic printing is to plug a card directly into the video interface of the printer. This card is connected to a special board in the computer and allows fast transfer directly to the printing circuitry.

Most of the laser printers available (such as the HP Laserjet series) provide a letter ("A" or "A4")-size page at up to 300 dpi. Larger sizes such as "B" or "A3," are less common. Commercial printers and publishers use 1200 dpi or higher, but this extra resolution is unnecessary for most office needs.

■ 6.10 TURNKEY IMAGING SYSTEMS

All of the hardware components just described can be combined with optical storage technologies and network services in a turnkey imaging system to provide a solution for document image management (Otten, 1987).

A basic turnkey imaging system can scan in, display, index, archive, and retrieve images. It is closed, in that it does not communicate with other computer systems except perhaps with a host computer link. The system is dedicated to a particular task that involves large volumes of paper (D'Alleyrand, 1989).

6.10.1 Single-Workstation System

In a situation without high volume image processing or the need for multi-user access, a single workstation may be sufficient. The system will usually provide capabilities for the simple search and retrieval of images from an optical disk. In essence, this system is little more than a database integrated with driver and display software.

A single-workstation system will typically have a scanner, an optical disk subsystem, and a high resolution display. Often a printer will be attached for producing hard copy. Figure 6.3a illustrated a single workstation imaging system.

6.10.2 Multi-Component System

A multi-component system is required where higher volumes are involved or to provide concurrent access for a number of users. To cope with higher throughput, machines are dedicated to the tasks of scanning, indexing, archiving, and retrieving images.

A multi-component system contains a number of stations dedicated to specific tasks and connected through a local area network (LAN). At least one high-power machine is

180 ■ Imaging Systems

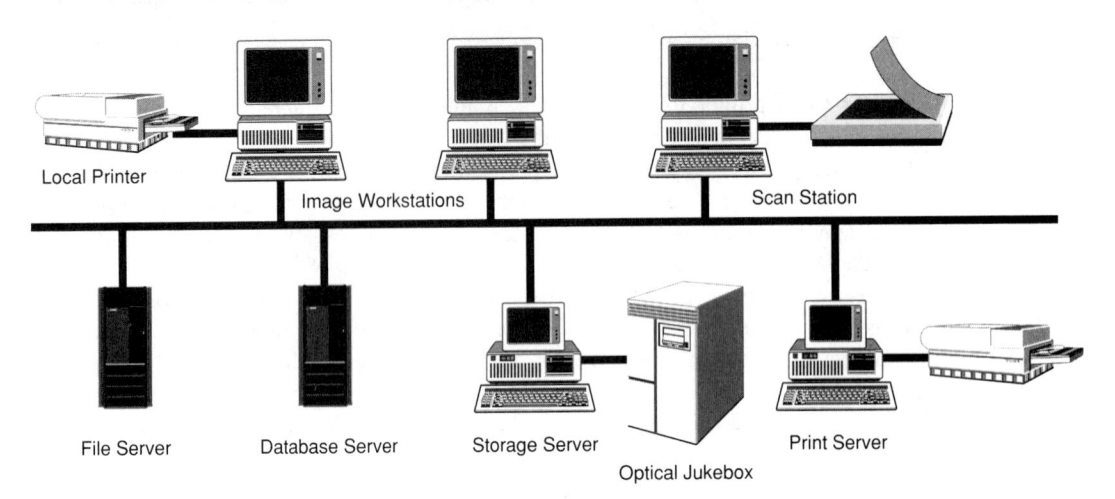

Figure 6.11 Multi-component imaging system.

needed to cope with the volume of processing and storage requirements, so the server for the network is likely to be a RISC machine running UNIX (or even proprietary hardware running a custom operating system).

Figure 6.11 illustrates a multi-component imaging system. The system is stand-alone in that it is not integrated with other computers or networks in an office.

6.10.3 Image Workstation

Once there are images in a system, an image workstation must have the ability to find, view, and manipulate them. The workstation includes a high-resolution monochrome monitor to display images as clearly as possible. (The ability to display a letter-size image requires this high resolution if the text is to be legible without zooming in.) If the workstation is sufficiently powerful, it can decompress images in software at a reasonable speed; otherwise, a hardware board is necessary for decompressing images. Figure 6.12 shows Wang's FreeStyle personal computing system.

It is more natural to interact with an imaging system through a graphical user interface (GUI) than to type text at a command line. The GUIs used in imaging systems were originally proprietary, because most platforms did not have a standard interface. Some vendors took the opportunity to integrate pointing devices (such as a mouse or a pen) to make the interface easier to use. The Wang system uses a pen and a tablet for adding handwritten annotations to images.

Another addition available with some imaging systems is sound capability. The hardware to do this includes a microphone and either headphones or a speaker connected to a board within the machine. This configuration allows the addition of voice annotation to images.

In order to find the documents in the system, a textual database interface is used. This function may use a second, low-resolution, monochrome monitor or the addition of a second window on the main monitor.

Figure 6.12 Image workstation (courtesy of Wang Imaging Systems).

6.10.4 Scan Station

Images are entered into the system at a scan station. (If a large number of documents on paper or microfilm already exist, they may be scanned and indexed by an outside bureau. The scan station is then used for new incoming documents.)

The nature of a scan station is dictated by the volume of paper that passes through the station and the size of the documents. The speed of scanning is limited by the nature of the document feed, the response of the light-sensitive device that converts a visual image into electronic form, and the power of the hardware used subsequently to process the electronic data. Processing often includes intensity adjustment, compression or dithering, and the generation of a file header.

1. A low-end scan station might comprise a flatbed scanner capable of one or two pages per minute, on-screen review of the resultant image, and rudimentary processing such as intensity adjustment and software compression. Indexing, clipping, rotation, and rescanning would all be done at this station.
2. A medium-range scan station is capable of 10 to 20 pages per minute. A document feeder moves documents from a hopper using rubber wheels to take the documents one at a time. Compression and manipulation of the data are accomplished either as a standard function of the scanner control card or through custom microcode on this board.

   Scanning is performed on batches of similar documents, and the steps of indexing and editing these documents are handled later, at another station.
3. A high-end scan station uses a high-speed scanner (often the size of a large photocopier and with similar functionality). To scan a large volume of paper, the document feed may employ a vacuum pump to hold each document as it travels through the scanner. The system may have the capability to scan double-sided images. The scan station may not have a screen, or it might use a low-resolution screen to show status and present options to the user. Indexing is performed at a separate station. This type of scan station is often located in a mail room (remote from the rest of the system), so that documents can be entered at their point of arrival.

6.10.5 Database Server

All of the documents in a document image management system are tracked and searched by a database, which may reside on the file server. Of all the system's components, the database usually requires the most processor power. There are a number of reasons for this.

Every archive or retrieval of a document requires at least one transaction with the database, so the database needs a high bandwidth connection to the network. In addition, database searches are also processor-intensive. Each document in the system, whether on- or off-line, requires one or more entries in the database. As a result, the database server has large, high-speed rewritable storage requirements, which increase in direct relation to an increase in the number of stored documents.

A database entry also must be maintained even if the actual image is archived to magnetic tape or off-line optical media. For these reasons, the database server will use more and more local storage that is separate from the media used for storing images, even if many of the database entries refer to rarely used documents archived off-site.

6.10.6 Storage

One of the main characteristics of a document image management system is a vast storage requirement. This stems from the nature of the data, where a single compressed letter-size image may occupy tens of kilobytes and an uncompressed color image may require megabytes of storage space.

Early document image management systems used microfilm or microfiche to store these data, and accessed them through a jukebox of film cartridges or fiche stacks. Photographic methods of storage have been almost entirely replaced by laser-read optical disk media. As with scan stations, the nature of the solution depends on the system's volume and speed requirements.

It would be natural to assume that storage management would be handled by the file server, which is the location for shared storage on a network. However, the file server is managed by the network operating system, which was not designed with write-once, read-only, jukebox, or slower media in mind.

Instead, document storage is usually handled by a separate machine. This approach also enables better management of the uniformly large files required for document storage. Different storage solutions are available for handling low and high volume requirements.

For low-volume storage ranging up to hundreds of megabytes (around 25,000 documents at 20K bytes per image, and 500-Mbyte storage), the installation of magnetic media on the file server or workstation will suffice. To provide the much larger capacity of up to a few gigabytes (a quarter of a million documents at 20K bytes per image, and 5-Gbyte storage), a twelve-inch write-once read-many (WORM) optical drive can be attached.

Note that the on-line storage capacity of an optical drive is equal to half the capacity of a single disk. This is because only one side of the disk is read by a single-head drive and the disk must be removed and reinserted in order for the drive to access the other side. On-line capacity can be increased by daisy-chaining drives and manually swapping disks. Off-line storage is limited by the capacity of the database to keep track of documents.

The distinction just made between on- and off-line storage is significant in terms of the retrieval time of a random document (and whether the user is prepared to continue swapping disks). The alternative is to use a jukebox, which is sometimes called "near-line" storage, because retrieval is faster than off-line and does not require the intervention of a human operator. The amount of on-line information still equals the number of drives multiplied by half the capacity of a single disk, but the delay in retrieving another disk is only a few seconds.

A jukebox can provide from tens up to hundreds of gigabytes (around ten million documents at 20K bytes per image and 200-Gbyte storage). It can range from a knee-height floor-standing system, containing a dozen $5\frac{1}{4}$ inch disks, up to a colossus holding fifty 12-inch disks. (If you plan to put the latter in your office, make sure you are insured for major structural damage to the building.)

A storage station that controls a jukebox should provide magnetic caching for the documents and will handle requests in such a way that disk swapping is minimized. Depending on throughput requirements, there may be one station per jukebox, or the jukeboxes may be daisy-chained. (Cinnamon, 1988).

6.10.7 Print Service

Despite claims about the "paperless office," the production of hard copy remains an essential requirement for a document image management system. The image must be decompressed and then printed as graphics (as opposed to text) on the printer. Before the image can be printed using a standard laser printer, a considerable amount of additional memory must be installed. Even so, the printer may take several minutes to print a single image.

Consequently, a print service is created either by dedicating a specialized graphics printer with a higher-speed SCSI port or by dedicating a standard laser printer that has been modified to write directly to the video interface. The combination of one of these alternatives with the use of hardware decompression in the print station can increase the printing speed up to the rate of a few pages per minute.

The print service is dedicated to outputting images and is independent of the network operating system. To create hard copies of other files, a separate printer and connection must be used.

The print service usually produces letter-size output. If larger sizes of output are required, the service can be modified by using laser printers that print those sizes.

6.10.8 Other Services

Other services sometimes added to document image management systems include host interface, fax service, optical character recognition (OCR), and image-processing services (Gonzalez, 1987).

- *Host access:* A company will often maintain mission-critical data on a mainframe. In order to access and update this information, the imaging system needs a host interface. This might be handled using an interface-specific card in a separate machine on the network or through a serial connection on the server.
- *Fax service:* A fax interface allows hard copy to be produced at a remote site. It also allows documents to be broadcast to different fax machines. A fax interface also allows remote input to the system by acting as a distant low-resolution scanner, which can cut down the load at the local scan station. In a document image management system, fax capability is provided on a separate server. This server contains a fax board connected to a phone socket and handles the queuing of incoming and outgoing faxes.
- *Optical character recognition:* Information is more useful and compact when it is in machine-readable form. This format allows semiautomatic indexing and enables the use of content-based searching methods. The use of OCR to convert from image to text is processor-intensive. Until recently, it was carried out exclusively in hardware, either on a dedicated board or else by using a custom machine on the network.

■ 6.11 FORMS

The previous section covered the hardware of an imaging system. This section and the following one cover the software of the system. This section deals with the interface for locating documents and extracting information. The following section covers image display and manipulation.

Forms provide a standard way to organize information (either on paper or in an electronic image) using an arrangement of named fields. A form can be filled out to specify a search or to assign attributes to a document. An image arranged as a standard form can enable the system to automate the extraction of information from it. Reports from the system are generated using forms.

6.11.1 Database Interface

An imaging system uses a database to organize the stored images. This database is usually a third-party relational database package integrated into the system from such vendors as Oracle, Sybase and Gupta Technologies.

The imaging system vendor may superimpose a custom interface on the database package's native interface, providing a more seamless link between the database's searching and indexing capabilities and the ability of the user to manipulate and view images. The proprietary user interface organizes all interaction between the user and the system. This hiding of the native database simplifies the use of the system, but it also compromises the power of the underlying system.

Imaging systems generally include some form of high-level organization of documents. The following describes the general scheme which they follow (note that naming conventions used by the particular system, and the extent to which this scheme is followed, differ between systems):

The user sees documents as belonging to one of a number of areas in the system. These areas are usually referred to as filing cabinets. The reason for defining areas is to assign differing levels of security and version control, and separate physical storage locations. These areas are administered by the database.

The most complex security and the tightest version control will be associated with the archive area, where documents are stored on optical media and will be infrequently changed. Other areas control personal documents and any documents still being processed. These are subject to more frequent update and access and contain fewer documents, so they are stored on magnetic media.

Within an area, there may be further separation into separate subjects, organized as folders. A folder is controlled by a single database table. The documents within a folder have attribute names in common, and searches can be applied to the folder.

When a system is first set up, it is very important to define folders and their attributes correctly. It is unusual to be able to search across folders, even though the underlying database may support joining of tables. (Otten, 1987).

Database Management systems were discussed in detail in Chapter 4.

6.11.2 Searching

The most simple search process occurs when the user knows all of the attributes for a single target document in the system. The user types these attributes into slots in a presented form, and the system retrieves and displays the document in an adjacent window or on a second high-resolution monitor. This situation requires no feedback about what is available in the system. Figure 6.13 shows a search specification (name starting with "Sm") and its result table for the items searched in the Insurance folder.

A more complex search scenario ensues when only partial information is known or where the target is a number of documents. Now the user needs to be able to specify ranges of attributes within which the target falls. The system provides the user with feedback about successful matches, usually as a list. This feedback can then be used to narrow the search until a manageable set of matches remains and documents can be selected directly from this set. Range specification is typically defined by using wild cards or a Boolean search, typed into the attribute slots of a form or table header. Once the target is selected from the set of matches, the associated document can be retrieved and displayed.

186 ■ Imaging Systems

6.11.3 Indexing

The technique of indexing allows a unique set of attributes to be defined and associated with a document for later search and retrieval.

Indexing is performed by presenting the user with an image and a blank form. The user then fills out the form with the attributes of the document and the association of image and attributes is made by the database. The documents may be simple and uniform, or they might be wide-ranging on disparate topics, requiring a skilled librarian to make decisions for each image. This labor-intensive process requires a person to type in attributes manually. However, some attributes can be added automatically, such as creation date and time, the name of the input station, and, with fax, the originator of the document.

Figure 6.14 illustrates indexing. The left-hand side is the application form scanned image. The right-hand side contains a form whose attribute values are entered by an office worker (data entry).

Even in the case of a scan station with a modest capacity, the rate of scanning clearly outstrips the speed of indexing. As a result, indexing becomes the bottleneck in an image-archiving environment. Indexing can be speeded up by running many indexing stations in parallel from a single scan station.

A number of other methods can also speed up indexing, including bar codes, OCR, machine–readable input, and standard forms. The first three methods are covered next, and the use of standard forms is discussed in the following section.

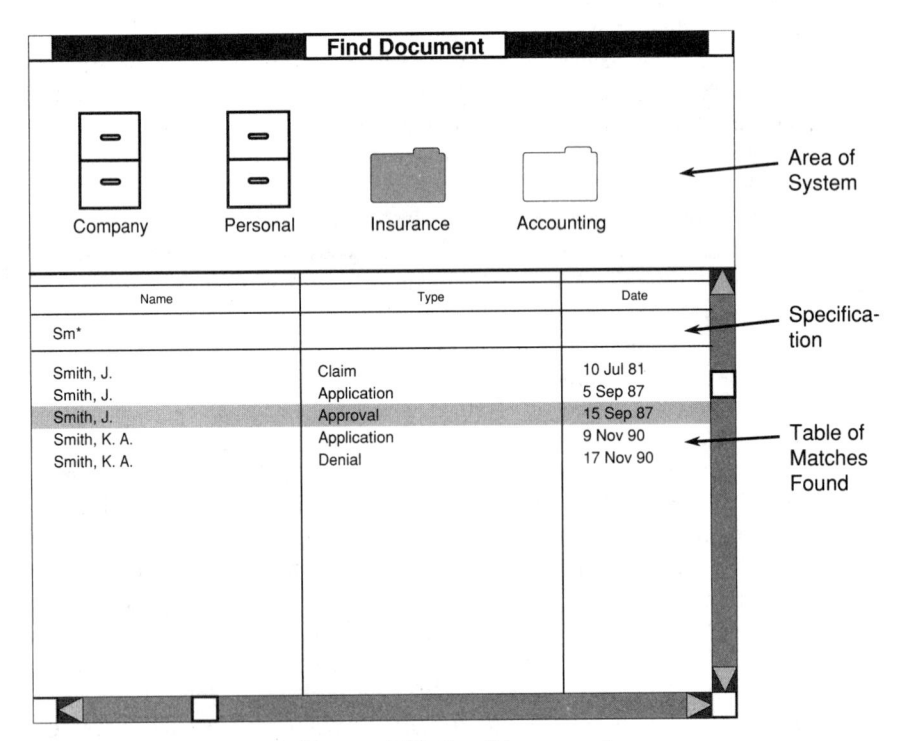

Figure 6.13 Specifying a search.

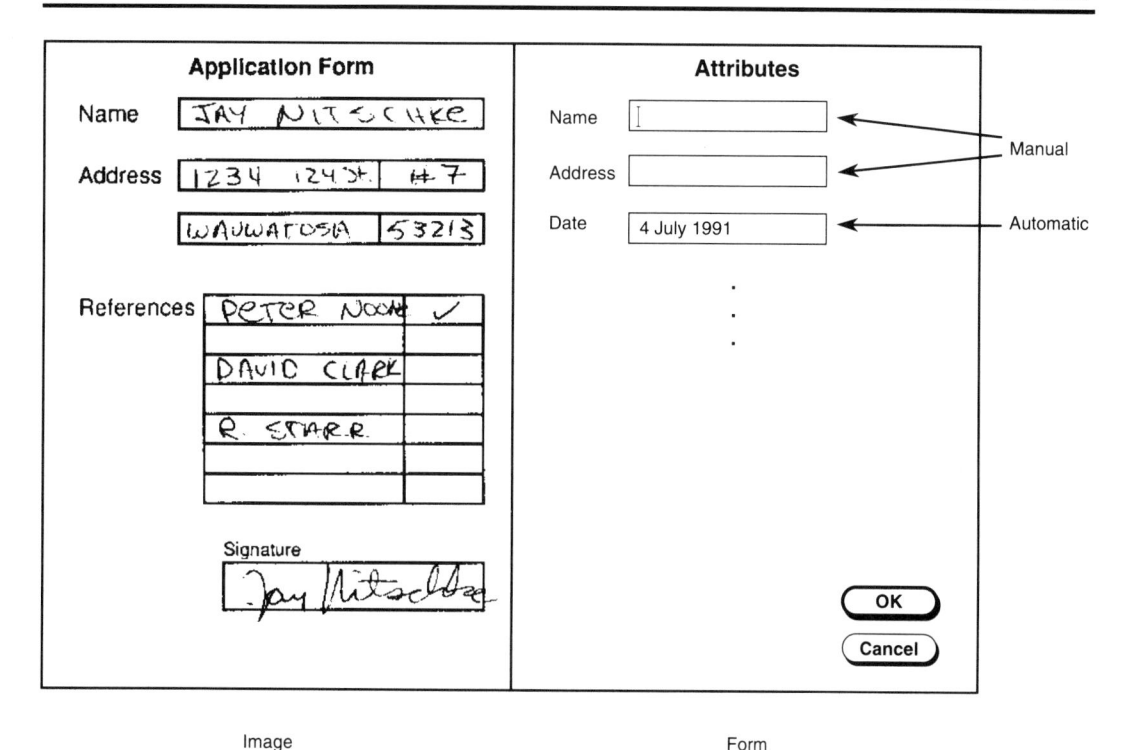

Figure 6.14 Indexing.

1. *Bar codes:* The process of indexing can be automated by incorporating bar codes in a standard form. Alternatively, paper documents can be sorted, classified, and then labeled with bar codes before they are scanned. The scan station then reads the bar code in hardware or software and associates attributes with the image accordingly.

   A variation on this scheme is used with checks, which are printed with characters which are legible as a magnetic bar code, using magnetic ink character recognition (MICR). Additional information (such as the amount of the check) are encoded in the same format when the check is used. When the check is scanned, the information is read off the bar code by hardware.

2. *OCR:* If an input image matches a known format, OCR technology can convert predefined zones to alphanumeric information. These data can then be assigned to attributes based on their zone position in the form.

   OCR has a higher success rate with typed text, but still introduces significant errors. A 95 percent success rate means that one letter in twenty will be wrong. If you are using a 10-digit number for indexing, then about half of those numbers will be misread! The success rate can be increased by using a known font.

   Error checking is also possible using a checksum. This method is adopted from communication theory, where redundant information is encoded in the data so that a simple calculation tests the validity of the data to a high degree of certainty. An error check will only test validity, however. The image will then need to be read by a human operator for correction.

3. *Machine-readable input*: Much of the information entering an imaging system is stored on computer–generated forms. If the data can be maintained in machine-readable form, then the need for scanning and OCR technology can be avoided (and many trees saved). Here, indexing is easily automated by reading the fields that have been defined within the data and then assigning them as attributes of the document. This scenario involves cooperation on the part of the information producer. The producer would have to supply data in a digital format, maybe on magnetic media or even via a communications line.

6.11.4 Input Format

The characteristics of the paper used for inputting information have a great impact on both the quality and legibility of the resultant scanned image and the ease with which indexing and later processing of the document are performed.

At the scan station, the quality, thickness, and size of the paper affect how the document feeder handles it. With a document feeder using rollers, paper that is too thin to be handled by the rollers will be methodically chewed up and jammed into the mechanism.

Also, scanners have a "drop-out color" to which the optical component does not respond. Any information printed on the original paper in this color will show up blank on the electronic image. (This can be an advantage for preprinted forms.)

If the document layout follows a standard form, then indexing can take advantage of knowledge about the location of different attributes. This knowledge can be used to automatically zoom to different portions of an image during indexing. It can also be used to define zones for an OCR process.

The operator of the imaging system often has control over the nature of the paper input. Such is the case with preprinted forms that are distributed, filled in, and returned (such as insurance forms).

Alternatively, the operator may be able to require information suppliers to conform to a standard format when submitting paper-based information (such as invoices). This format might specify paper quality and size, positioning of information, printing font and color, and bar coding. Figure 6.15 illustrates a paper form.

The ANSI standard X.12 takes standard forms a stage further. It addresses electronic data interchange (EDI), where an electronic form is transmitted between computer systems. EDI specifies a standard data format for forms, in terms of fields and attributes.

6.11.5 Reporting

In addition to viewing and making hard copy of images, the user of an imaging system needs to be able to generate reports based on attributes and volume of documents.

A reporting application interfaces to a database and allows a user to specify format and content of a report generated from attributes in the database, either once or on a regular basis. Image system vendors either use a reporting package native to the database or provide their own, integrated with the user interface. Frequently with the latter case, reporting ability is severely limited or nonexistent.

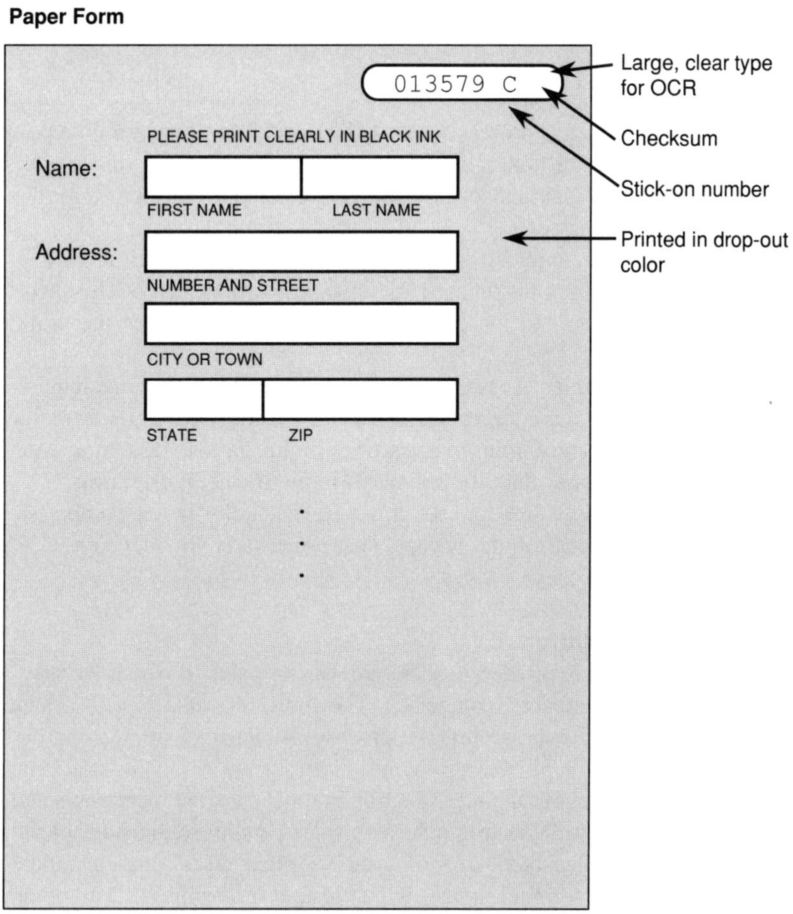

Paper Form

Figure 6.15 Paper form.

Reports typically cover profiles of system use, such as frequently requested images or daily scanning volume. They might also comprise form letters, which use sets of document attributes to fill in the blanks. Reporting facilities also cover the utilities familiar to network system administrators, such as setting up an audit trail and keeping track of security.

6.12 RETRIEVAL SOFTWARE

Retrieval software at its simplest will display a specified image. This involves reading a file from its archived state and decompressing it to the screen. A number of additional functions have become available to do more than simply display an image. The user may wish to alter or annotate the displayed image and perform a number of actions based on the information it contains. These actions might include update of a host computer and automatic flow of documents through an organization. Other functions which are useful are OCR of the image and sending and receiving of fax.

6.12.1 Image Decompression

With the increase in power of a typical workstation, it has become possible to decompress a black-and-white image in software at a reasonable viewing speed. A hardware board is still used at scan and print stations to maintain optimum throughput, often doubling as peripheral control.

Software decompression allows a standard workstation with a sufficiently high-resolution monitor to be used as an image workstation. This avoids the purchase of an expensive card for each viewing station and decreases the proprietary nature of an image system.

Compression is necessary because an uncompressed image requires a large amount of storage. An image compressed using the CCITT Group 3 scheme is typically 10 to 15 times smaller, and Group 4 gives even higher ratios. Decompression takes place at the workstation, rather than the server, to minimize network traffic.

Until recently, a standard for gray scale and color image compression was unavailable, and these images would occupy space measured in megabytes. Chapter 9 describes compression of these images.

6.12.2 Image Manipulation

Once an image is displayed, there are various ways in which we may want to manipulate it. These fall into two categories. The first are standard to a system and require little processing, while the second are processor–intensive, often using dedicated hardware in a batch mode.

The first category includes rotation in ninety-degree increments and clipping. Clipping is limited to defining a rectangle with sides parallel to the sides of the original rectangle.

More intensive processing is used for other tasks. Variable rotation can be used to remove the skew on an image, which results from imperfect alignment during scanning. Raster-to-vector conversion is used on images of line drawings, such as maps or blueprints, so that they can be manipulated with a computer-aided design (CAD) system. OCR is a form of image processing, discussed earlier. Thresholding and convolution can make an image clearer and can remove noise (as do raster-to-vector and OCR conversions).

Often the scanner or scan control hardware includes image-processing functions, such as alignment of the electronic image, automatic thresholding of intensity levels, and bar code interpretation.

6.12.3 Markup and Editing

A user viewing an image may wish to add comments or alter the document. Such additions include circling unusual items, adding typed notes or a signature, or forming a link to another document. Some systems allow voice annotations to be appended to a document. All of these are markups, in that they do not alter the actual document but add things onto it.

Editing involves a change to an image or markups associated with it. Editing of an image is not usually provided outside of the standard functions of rotation and clipping,

6.12 Retrieval Software

described in the previous section, or replacement with a newly scanned image. Sometimes a number of images can be grouped together as pages of a document or in a folder. Cutting and pasting of parts of an image may be available. These operations often only appear to alter the image, being implemented as markups that obscure or duplicate areas of the underlying image. Figure 6.16 illustrates some image annotations.

By allowing additions and changes to a document, we run into the matter of revisions and version control. These changes are outside the direct control of the database. An imaging system deals with this using a combination of restrictions on allowed changes and check-in/check-out mechanisms. The system is divided into sections, which are defined and associated with levels of version control, areas of storage, and security measures. They are named "library," "company (or personal) filing cabinet," "folder," and other titles used to distinguish between them.

6.12.4 Archiving Images

Once an image has been scanned and indexed, it is sent to an appropriate storage area. This has to be organized carefully, particularly on write-once and off-line media, so that images that are likely to be retrieved together or in close succession are grouped to minimize media swapping.

Images that are stored outside the control of the operating system, such as through an optical storage server or on top of the network operating system, will use the database

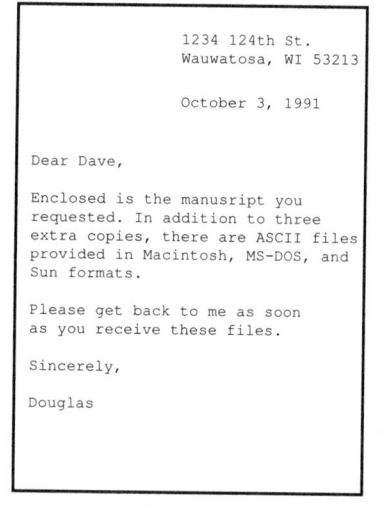

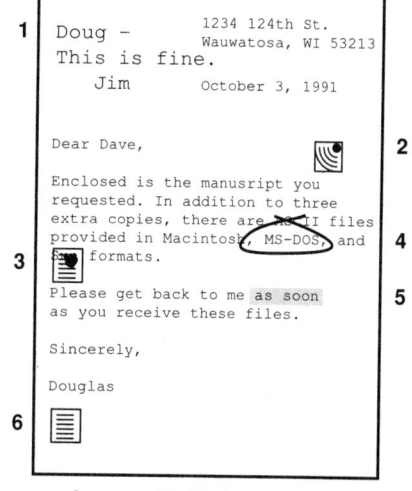

Image **Image with Markups**

1. Written
2. Voice
3. Document Link
4. Circling
5. Highlight
6. Note

Figure 6.16 Image annotation.

192 ■ **Imaging Systems**

to keep track of location. This means that although a user can send an optical disk to a remote site, the images on this disk are not accessible until a connection is established with the archive system's database. In other words, the media contents are not self-describing or self-contained.

6.12.5 Imitating Paper Flow

An imaging system is usually installed to replace a paper-based system that has involved a number of operations performed by various employees. The operations and their order are dictated by the content of the system's documents and related information from other documents or computer systems. It is therefore a natural progression to allow the imaging system to help with retrieval of related information and routing of documents through the system. An example paper flow is illustrated in Figure 6.17. Chapter 11 discusses work flow in more detail.

A wide range of functionality has been added to imaging systems by vendors. Simple routing allows documents to be passed between users defined within the system. A high priority is some kind of flow from scan station to indexing station to archive storage, providing aid with indexing along the way. Some systems, such as FileNet and Sigma Design, allow the flow of images to be defined based on attributes of documents. Another useful feature is to be able to access or update a host system as one of the operations.

6.12.6 Host Interface

Many companies maintain mission-critical information on a mainframe or minicomputer. When documents enter an office, one of the steps is to access related information and to update this host system. Consequently, imaging systems frequently include optional connection to a number of types of host computer. They then allow a user at an image

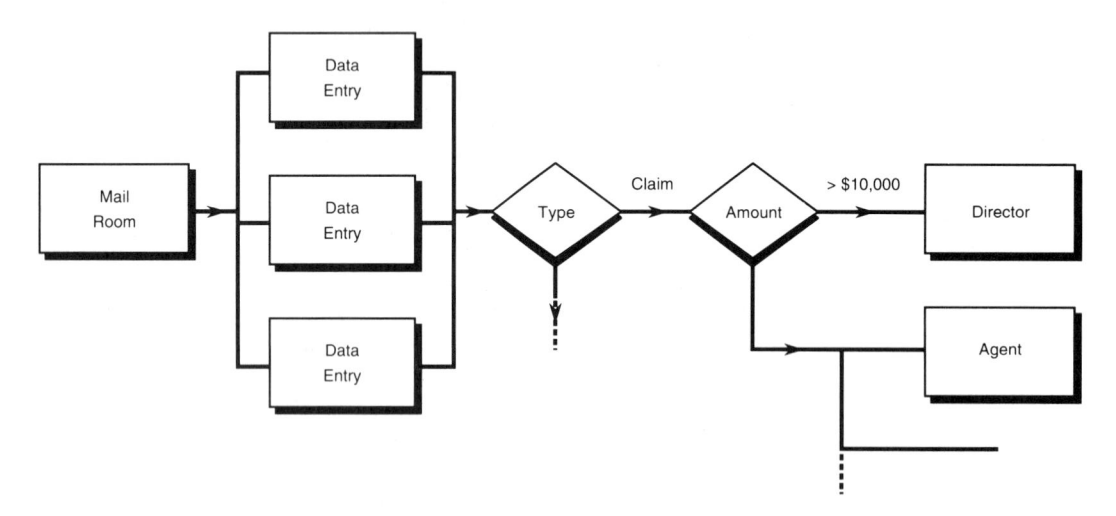

Figure 6.17 Example of paper flow.

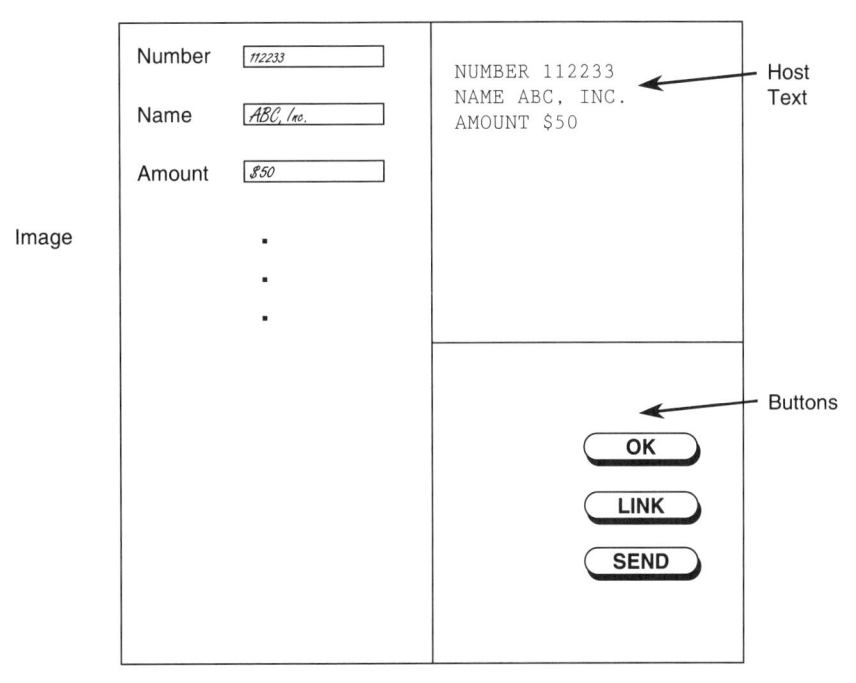

Figure 6.18 Host interface screen.

workstation to access the host system as they would at a terminal, or even provide mapping of document attributes to the host session. Figure 6.18 shows an image on the left-hand side of the workstation's screen, a host interface in the upper right-hand corner, and some control buttons.

Automation of the host interface is a complicated task. It involves both navigation through the host system and mapping of information to the screen. The minicomputer or mainframe usually runs custom software designed specifically for the customer's needs. Therefore, the automation needs to be tailored at each installation.

6.12.7 Other Capabilities

With OCR as part of an imaging system, it becomes possible to convert entire documents into machine-readable format. They can then be retrieved based on content rather than just assigned attributes. This is important in a system such as a news service. Documents entering the system are not structured like a form, and significant words that define the document could be anywhere on the page. (Full-text retrieval is discussed in Chapter 5.)

The addition of a fax service onto an imaging system presents many new possibilities, including remote entry and output and document flow to remote sites. This is used, for example, where a request for information is filled in on a standard form and sent by fax into the system. The system detects the presence or absence of marks on the page, or uses OCR, to decipher the request. It then responds by sending the resultant documents back to the remote fax.

■ 6.13 TYPICAL APPLICATIONS

An examination of some actual imaging systems applications will better illustrate the tasks performed by the systems' components and how those components work together to perform document image management.

Various factors affect the decision about whether a document-imaging system is applicable in a particular situation. Originally the need for a document-imaging system was indicated by the largest pile of paper in an office. With the advent of work flow capabilities, the focus has moved toward the volume of paper passing *through* a department, and other factors need to be considered (Lanford, 1991).

The process of scanning and indexing the existing mountain of paper, called back-file conversion, can easily cost more than the imaging system itself. The legal status of images archived on optical disk is also an important factor. Many countries now accept legal documents stored on media that cannot be overwritten, such as optical WORM. Another important cost factor is cost justification, which was discussed in the introduction to this chapter.

6.13.1 Insurance

Insurance is an obvious application for an imaging system, because it involves large volumes of paper forms. Considerable paperwork is handled during the entry and evaluation of applications and during claims processing.

In an imaging solution, an application form is filled out at an agent's office. The company has full control of the characteristics of this form and can organize it with the imaging system in mind. The application is sent by fax or by mail and then scanned in the mail room. The application indexes its information using a combination of bar code, manual entry, and (if the information is in typed form), OCR technology.

The application can then follow a flow within the system based on attributes such as document type and amount. It gathers references to other documents in the archive, such as previous applications and claims in the applicant's name. The amount of coverage may dictate whether approval is needed from an underwriter or a director of the company. The set of documents, together with denial notices or legal documents relating to approval, can be archived. Reporting might include automatic generation of a form letter when renewal is due.

A claim is submitted in a similar way. It can be combined in the system with the insured's file and presented to an employee for review.

6.13.2 Banking

Check processing can benefit from imaging technology, particularly in the case of signature verification.

A check includes a magnetic form of bar code when it is printed (described in Section 6.11.3). When a completed check is submitted, additional information is encoded in machine-readable form. The check is then sent to a central clearinghouse.

At the clearinghouse, imaging systems scan the check and use the encoded information for indexing. The signature card is retrieved from the archive on optical media and

Signature Verification

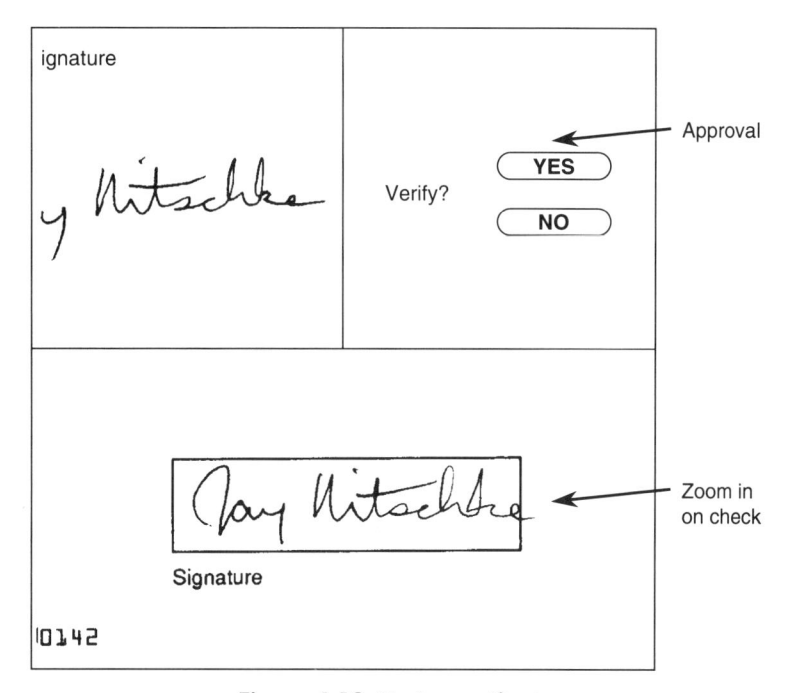

Figure 6.19 Signiture verification.

presented to the operator alongside the check for signature verification. Depending on volume, the threshold amount controlling the amount of checks that undergo signature verification can be raised or lowered.

A host connection then checks whether sufficient funds are available. If there are insufficient funds, or signatures do not match, then the customer's phone number is displayed. The operator advises the account holder about the situation while the information is still displayed on a screen. Figure 6.19 illustrates signature verification.

A check in the system can be found quickly through a database search, without the need to retrieve the original check from off-site storage.

6.13.3 Government

There are many applications for imaging systems within local and national government, where standard forms or a large document archive are involved.

An example is the system for processing and storing land title deeds. These deeds are surveys of individual properties within a region and are made available to building contractors and utility service providers. The deeds can be maintained on an optical jukebox and retrieved in response to a fax, mail, or personal request. Changes can be accommodated through markups to existing documents or by entering new documents as later versions of those on archive. Many documents can be hundreds of years old and

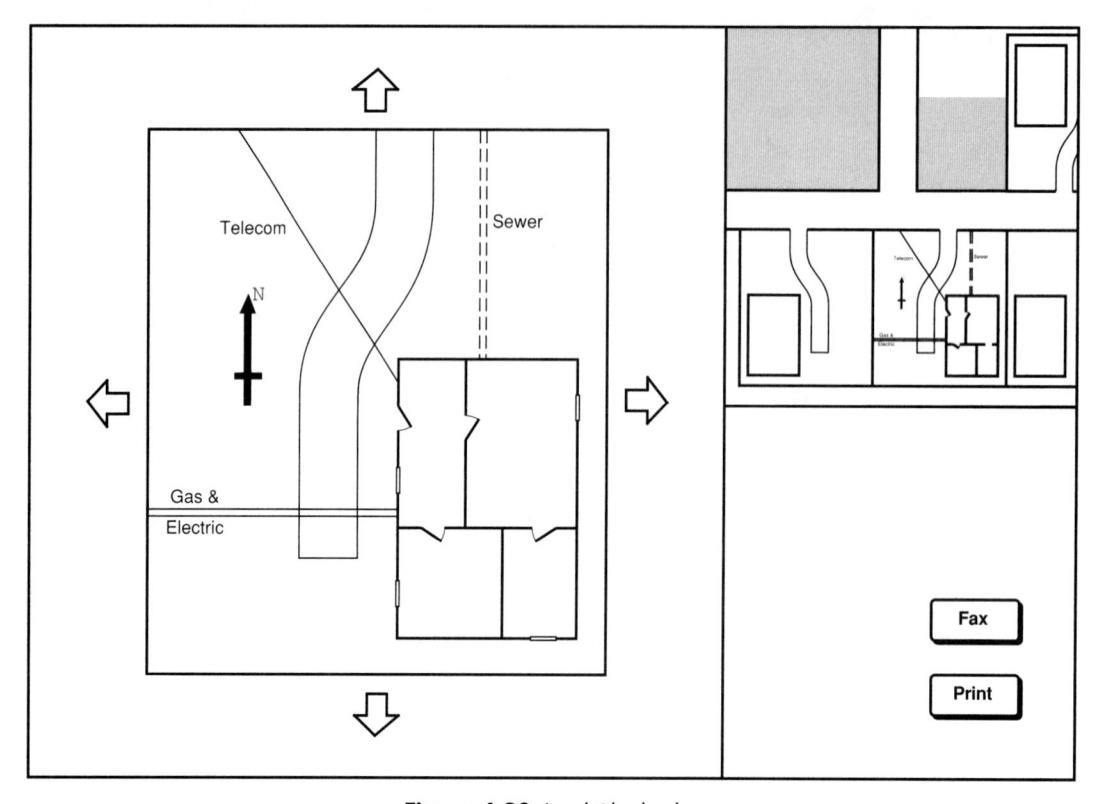

Figure 6.20 Land title deeds.

may require some form of image processing to regain legibility. Figure 6.20 illustrates a land title deed application screen.

Land title deeds and other geographical information are often arranged in a "spatial database." This allows navigation through the documents in a way that fits naturally with the characteristics of the data. A map of the region is presented, and the user can "zoom into" areas, switching to a more detailed map of the selected area. This form of navigation also allows lateral movement between adjacent maps.

6.13.4 Accounting

Accounting involves large numbers of forms. Imaging systems are often applied to accounts payable to manage purchase orders and invoices.

A purchase order enters the system, is routed for approval based on department and value, and is rejected or approved. If it is approved, a copy of the purchase order is sent to a supplier. Eventually an invoice arrives, maybe attached to the purchased item when it is delivered to the goods received area. The invoice is scanned in there or in the mail room. It is then matched up to the original purchase order by purchase order number. The combination of purchase order and invoice are sent to accounting to arrange payment.

The system will almost always involve an interface to accounting software on a host system. Ideally, the imaging system should automatically update this software to avoid the need for operators to enter the same information twice. The purchase order number might include a checksum. This number is common to related documents, and the error checking allows it to be read automatically. The purchase order and invoice can then be grouped together before they are presented to an operator.

6.13.5 Engineering

Imaging systems have been used in engineering where a team of engineers are working on a project. In the following example, the work flow capabilities of the system are more important than the longer-term archiving of large volumes of images.

In this scenario, the engineers create a design using CAD tools in a vector format. The design is converted into raster image projections. These projections are routed by the imaging system to various experts for review. The reviewers make comments and annotations on the images, which are returned to the authoring engineers for modification to the original.

Parts information can also be organized using imaging technology. A parts catalog is stored in image format on optical media. The catalog can be queried by part number and will respond with an image of the part or subassembly. The catalog can also be distributed to larger customers on optical media.

■ 6.14 IMAGING SYSTEMS AND THE INTELLIGENT OFFICE

With the rapid advance of computing technology, a typical office computer is now sufficiently powerful to perform image decompression without hardware assistance, though it may still require a higher-resolution monitor. Thus, a standard platform can be used in the intelligent office in place of proprietary imaging hardware. This platform should consist of a common graphical user interface, standard file and media formats, and standard communications protocols and platforms.

- A common graphical user interface reduces the learning curve for a new user to the system. It also enables diverse software applications to work together. The user is no longer limited to the functionality built in by the image system vendor and can take advantage of tools from various sources.

  A good example is word processing. Proprietary software might include limited text editing. In an open system, however, a complete word processor can be used alongside image retrieval software.

- When images are stored using standard file and media formats, they become accessible to other applications. This provides benefits in terms of image processing and manipulation, because the user is not limited to the functionality of the image system. Problems with version control can occur, however, if outside access is not carefully handled.

- Standard communications protocols and platforms allow imaging systems to take advantage of installed networks and to communicate with other systems. This permits wider access to a more useful system, for a lower investment.

Unlike the "closed" systems discussed in this chapter, the intelligent office environment provides "open," nonproprietary solutions for document management. The introduction of capabilities for work flow management into imaging systems is another way in which those systems are converging with the more general functionality of the intelligent office.

■ 6.15 SUMMARY

Imaging systems were originally designed to archive and retrieve large volumes of documents. They used dedicated hardware and specialized custom software to achieve this task. The systems are characterized by document feed scanner input, large amounts of storage, high-resolution monitors, and a central database to organize the images.

Emerging standards and new technologies have been adopted, and a significant trend towards work flow capabilities is also underway. There are many advantages to conforming to standards and running on currently installed platforms. These advantages are reflected by the evolution of imaging systems with respect to the intelligent office.

7

OBJECT-ORIENTED CONCEPTS

■ 7.1 INTRODUCTION

One of the most important characteristics of intelligent offices is their ease of use. This ease of use results from representing two key aspects of the office to the office worker as directly as possible: the items (objects) in the office, and the way in which a person interacts with other office workers and with those items. Direct representation is made possible by the concept of object orientation, which is the basis for software technologies in the intelligent office.

Object orientation permeates all aspects of the intelligent office environment. It allows office workers to interact with their environment in a more natural way: through sending messages to the protocol of office objects. The protocol of an object is the collection of operations that could be performed on the object (in other words, the messages to which an object can respond). This is very similar to the way office workers interact with one another or with other "physical" and nonelectronic office objects. The next few sections discuss the main object-oriented concepts and illustrate how these concepts are used in intelligent offices.

7.1.1 What Is Object Orientation?

Object orientation can be loosely defined as the software modeling and development (engineering) disciplines that make it easy to construct complex systems out of individual components. The intuitive appeal of object orientation is that it provides better concepts and tools for modeling and representing the real world. The advantages of this technique in terms of programming and data modeling are many.

Using conventional (procedural) programming techniques, code is generated to represent a real-world problem by encoding the problem and then transforming it into the terms of a von Neumann computer language (see Figure 7.1). Object-oriented techniques handle the transformation process automatically, minimizing the amount of code necessary for the transformation. As a result, the bulk of the code simply encodes the problem. The object-oriented programming discipline promises (and has delivered) significant benefits to each of the following three major groups of computer users:

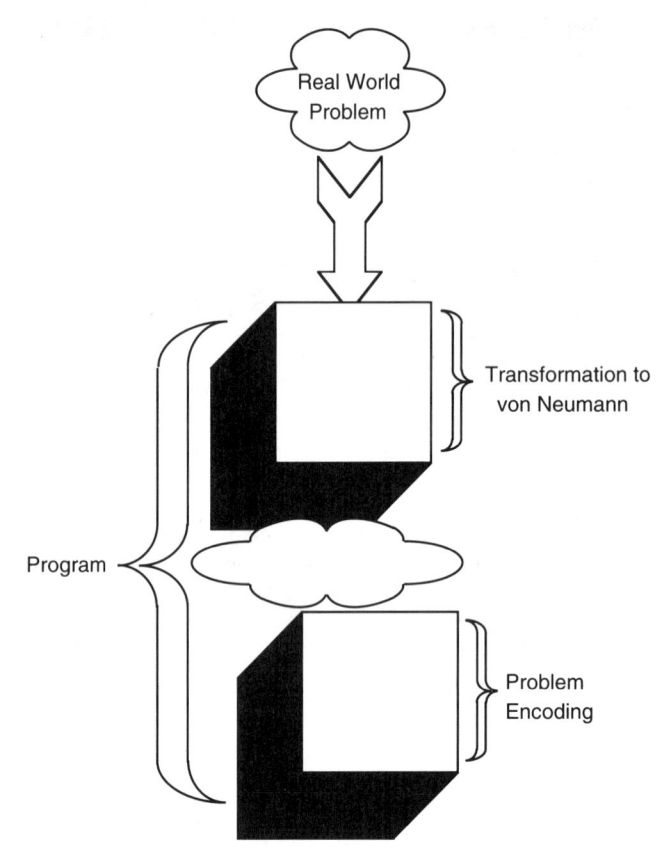

Figure 7.1 Conventional programming.

1. *Office workers,* including clerks, managers, secretaries, and executives. For this largest group of users, object orientation promises increasingly friendlier user interfaces. Object orientation will help integrate multi-media data types in the computing environment. Thus voice, image, and animation sequences as well as text data will be part of the computer's repertoire of stored and manipulated objects.
2. *Application developers,* including database designers and administrators, vertical application developers, and custom software developers. Object orientation promises to help the application developer by providing tools that are easier to use. Object-oriented hypermedia tools will help organize and link the multi-media nodes of an application. Object-oriented database design tools will help create the most natural abstractions of the end user's object space.
3. *System programmers,* including developers of spreadsheets, word processors, operating systems, and databases. These are the power users of computing systems. For these expert programmers, object orientation enhances the engineering and configuration management tools. Through specialization of existing software components, these programmers will be able to build complex systems more quickly.

Several different features of object orientation will satisfy the varying computational needs of these three user groups. The modeling and programming of user requirements have driven programming languages, databases, and user interfaces toward object orientation.

Chapter 4 presented an overview of the evolution of object orientation in database management systems. Chapter 8 will present an overview of the evolution of object orientation in graphical user interfaces. In the following section, we summarize the evolution of object orientation in programming languages.

7.1.2 The Evolution of Object Orientation in Programming Languages

Assemblers were the earliest computer "languages" that introduced symbolic representation of the underlying machine instructions. Some of the earliest assemblers include Soap for the IBM 650 (mid 1950s) and Sap for the IBM 704 (late 1950s). But the first milestone of "high-level" programming was undoubtedly the development of FORTRAN.

FORTRAN (mid 1950s) introduced several important programming language concepts including variables, arrays, and control structures such as iteration and conditional branching (Backus, 1978). FORTRAN is still one of the most popular programming languages. The language has an active ANSI standardization committee, which periodically releases substantive enhancements of and extensions to the language.

Yet in the late 1950s, one problem found when developing large FORTRAN programs was that variable names would conflict in different parts of a program. High-level programming languages that followed FORTRAN and found wide acceptance include PL/I, ALGOL, and COBOL (still a very popular language). COBOL and PL/I are still widely used in mainframe environments. ALGOL (and many of these earlier structural languages in office environments—especially for financial applications) provided barriers to separate variable names within program segments. This gave birth to *Begin...End* blocks in ALGOL 60 (Randell *et al.*, 1964). Since the variable names appearing within a block are known only to that block, their use will not conflict with the use of the same variable name in other blocks of the program. This was a first attempt at providing protection or encapsulation within a programming language. Encapsulation is an important object orientation concept. Block structures are now widely used in a variety of languages including C, Pascal, and Ada.

In the early 1960s, the designers of the language SIMULA 67 (Dahl and Nygaard, 1966; Dahl, Myhrhaug and Nygaard, 1970) took the block concept of ALGOL one step further and introduced the concept of an object. Although SIMULA's roots were in ALGOL, it was mainly intended as a simulation language. Thus, SIMULA objects had "an existence of their own" and could (in some sense) communicate with each other during a simulation. Conceptually, an object contained both data and the operations that manipulate its data. The operations were called methods. SIMULA also incorporated the notion of classes, which are used to describe the structure and behavior of a set of objects. Class inheritance was also supported by SIMULA. Inheritance organizes the classes in hierarchies, allowing the sharing of implementation and structure. SIMULA also distinguished between two types of equality: identical and shallow equal, reflecting the distinction between reference (identity)-based and value (content)-based interpretations of objects. Therefore, SIMULA laid the foundation of object-oriented languages and some of the object-oriented terminology. In addition to using object-oriented concepts, SIMULA was a strongly typed language. This means that the type of each variable is known at compile time; with strong typing, type errors will not be generated at run time but will be discovered when the program is compiled. In retrospect, if SIMULA implementations had had better marketing, SIMULA could have become a much more widespread language.

Another important milestone in the development of programming languages was the LISP (McCarthy *et al.*, 1965) functional programming language, which was introduced in the late 1950s and early 1960s. LISP was and remains one of the most elegant languages, using a few simple programming constructs (lists and function application) to perform complex computations. LISP remains the language of choice for many artificial intelligence applications. There are a number of companies that actively support LISP versions.

In the early 1970s, the concept of data abstraction was pursued by a number of language designers for the purpose of managing large programs (Parnas, 1972). There are two fundamental aspects of abstract data typing. One is to cluster the structure of the type with the operations defined on the type. For instance, with ALGOL or Pascal the language does not encourage the grouping of all the operations on a record type in the same module as the definition of the record type. SIMULA achieved clustering or grouping of structure and operations through classes.

The other aspect of abstract data typing is information hiding, where the details of implementation and representation of the objects are hidden and cannot be directly accessed through the users of the object. Languages such as Alphard (Wulf *et al.*, 1976) and CLU (Liskov *et al.*, 1977) introduced data abstraction. In CLU, for instance, abstract data types were implemented through clusters—an appropriate name. As these languages were developed, a good deal of the foundational and mathematical theory for abstract data types began to evolve. This helped establish the concept of abstract data types by providing a rigorous mathematical basis for using object orientation (Goguen *et al.*, 1975; Guttag, 1977; Burstall and Goguen, 1977). This theory was then developed further for application to specifications (Ehrig *et al.*, 1981).

One of the most important programming languages to support abstract data typing was Ada (Booch, 1986). The U.S. Department of Defense (DoD) commissioned the design of Ada to reduce and control cost of software development. The DoD intended Ada to be the language of choice for the development of new embedded systems. The language contains the usual control flow constructs (such as *if..then..else* and *while*) and ability to define types, functions, and subroutines. Object-oriented constructs in Ada include packets and packages. The DoD defined the requirements in a document called STEELMAN. Based on the requirements stated in STEELMAN, several language proposals were submitted, all based on the Pascal language. A large collection of people contributed to the design of the Ada language. Most of the language designers were from European nations; Jean Ichbiah from France was the primary language designer, and several other authors were from France, the United Kingdom, West Germany, and the United States.

It has been (and still continues to be) debated for a long time whether Ada is an object-oriented language. Ada supports several object-oriented concepts such as abstract data types, overloading of functions and operators, parametric polymorphism, and even specialization of user-defined types. Yet Ada does not support inheritance.

During the 1970s and 1980s, the object-oriented concepts from SIMULA and other earlier prototypes were embodied in one of the most influential object-oriented languages: Smalltalk (Goldberg and Robson, 1983), initially a research project at Xerox Palo Alto Research Center (PARC). During the 1970s, a group of researchers at Xerox PARC invented or solidified many technologies now recognized as object-oriented, in the realm of both languages and user interfaces. For languages, Smalltalk was developed at the PARC during this time. For user interfaces, both the Star workstation (also developed at the PARC) and its predecessor prototype, the Alto, influenced the design and look-and-feel of Apple's Macintosh, Aldus's PageMaker desktop publishing software, Microsoft's Windows, and Metaphor's DIS software environment.

In fact, Smalltalk was (and is) not just a language. It also incorporates a whole programming environment and a menu-based interactive user interface. The Smalltalk environment includes an extensive initial class hierarchy. Programming in Smalltalk entails opening a working window, browsing and extending the class hierarchy through another window, and so on. The programmer interacts with the system through dialogs and pop-up or pull-down windows, depending on the particular implementation of the environment.

Learning how to use the initial Smalltalk class hierarchy is a substantial but important investment in time. Programming in Smalltalk can be viewed as extending this class hierarchy.

There were several versions and dialects of Smalltalk: Smalltalk-72, Smalltalk-74, Smalltalk-76, Smalltalk-78, Smalltalk-80, and more recently Smalltalk/V from Digitalk. The most important and stable version remains Smalltalk-80. The computer scientists who were most influential in the development of the Smalltalk language include Alan Kay, Adele Goldberg, and Daniel Ingalls. The Goldberg and Robson book on Smalltalk-80 (1983) remains one of the most important and frequently referenced pieces of literature in object orientation.

The Smalltalk language incorporates many of the object-oriented features of SIMULA, including classes, inheritance, and support of object identity. However, information hiding is enforced more rigorously in Smalltalk than in SIMULA. Furthermore, Smalltalk is not a typed language. The types of the variables in Smalltalk are not specified at variable declaration time. The same variable can assume different types at different times in the same program. The type of a variable is the class of the object referenced by the variable. Classes are like factories that create instances from templates. Methods can be defined for class instances or can apply to the class itself.

Smalltalk is extremely rich in object-oriented concepts. In Smalltalk, everything is an object, including classes and base types (integers, floating-point numbers, and so on). This means, that throughout the entire Smalltalk environment, programming consists of sending messages to objects. A message can add a number to another number, it can create a new instance of a class, or it can introduce a new method in a given class.

Smalltalk will remain a powerful influence in object-oriented programming. Different variations and dialects of Smalltalk are continuously being designed, developed, and implemented on a host of different hardware platforms.

Besides Smalltalk, other influences and concepts swayed the amazing world of object orientation. Object orientation attempts to model the real world as closely as possible.

Another aspect of the real world is concurrency. For example, in an office environment, secretaries, managers, and other employees function simultaneously and independently. They communicate with each other through conversations, memos, electronic mail messages, and so on.

Although some object-oriented languages (most notably Smalltalk) introduced terms such as "messages" to describe the activation or invocation of a method by an object (thereby giving the illusion that objects are acting independently and concurrently), the underlying semantics and execution model of the language is purely sequential; the semantics of messages is nearly identical to the semantics of procedure calls. In order to support concurrency, Smalltalk employs another construct, namely, a process. Therefore, there are two concepts to concentrate on: objects and processes (Yokote and Tokoro, 1987).

To alleviate this problem, there have been some attempts to incorporate parallelism and to design concurrent object-oriented languages. The most notable and influential of these was Hewitt's actor model (Hewitt, 1977; Agha and Hewitt, 1987). Other concurrent object-oriented languages include Lieberman's Act 1 (Lieberman, 1981) and ABCL/1 (Shibayama and Yonezawa, 1987). Objects in ABCL/1 execute concurrently. An object is either dormant, waiting, or active. Objects get activated upon receiving messages. When an object has processed all its messages, it becomes dormant. The model represented by ABCL/1 and other concurrent object-oriented languages more directly captures the intuitive notion of objects sending and responding to messages. It is interesting to note that one of the most important applications of concurrent object-oriented languages is office automation. As discussed in a number of chapters throughout this book, office objects such as fax servers, printers, scanners, and so on can be modeled as independent concurrent objects (or "agents") providing services to various office workers or applications.

Throughout the 1980s and early 1990s, object-oriented concepts (abstract data types, inheritance, object identity, and concurrency), Smalltalk, SIMULA, and other languages began to merge and give birth to a number of object-oriented languages, extensions, and dialects. Next, we categorize the strategic direction of object-oriented programming language development.

7.1.2.1 Extensions, Dialects, and Versions of Smalltalk

There have been several proposals (and prototypes) to extend Smalltalk with typing (as we said earlier, variables in Smalltalk are not typed), multiple inheritance (original dialects of Smalltalk allowed a class to inherit from only one parent or superclass), or concurrent programming constructs (Yokote and Tokoro, 1987). These are primarily research projects or prototypes.

In terms of actual products, Xerox offers Smalltalk-80 on some of its machines. So does Tektronix. Another notable vendor of Smalltalk is ParcPlace systems, which supports Smalltalk-80 versions on a number of platforms. Digitalk offers Smalltalk/V for IBM-compatible personal computers and for Macintoshes.

7.1.2.2 Object-Oriented Extensions of Conventional Languages

One of the most popular object-oriented languages is C++. This language was designed by Bjarne Stroustrup at AT&T in the early 1980s (Stroustrup, 1986). The first implementation of the C++ language was released as a preprocessor to C compilers. C++ provides two constructs for class definitions. The first method is an extension of the *struct* construct, and the other method is through the new *class* construct. C++ allows hierarchies of classes and allows subclasses to access methods and instance variables from other classes in their hierarchy. The language permits ad hoc polymorphism by allowing overloading of function names and operators. But unlike Smalltalk, C++ does not come with a large collection of predefined classes. This task has been left to vendors supplying C++ libraries.

Another popular dialect of C is Objective-C (Cox, 1986). This language is a superset of C that incorporates object-oriented features from Smalltalk. It uses a modified version of Smalltalk syntax to add these features. Like Smalltalk, it comes with a large collection of predefined classes to ease the software development process. Objective-C supports abstract data types, single inheritance, and operator overloading. Unlike C++, however, Objective-C does not extend the definition of any existing C language constructs. It relies totally on the introduction of new constructs and operators to perform tasks such as class definition or message passing. When first released, the NeXT computer chose Objective-C as its primary development language.

For Pascal, popular object-oriented extensions include Object Pascal for the Macintosh, from Apple Computer, and Turbo Pascal from Borland for IBM Personal Computers. Object Pascal (Schumcker, 1986) was designed by Niklaus Wirth and a group of Apple Computer, Inc. engineers. It extends the Pascal language to support the notions of abstract data type, methods, and single inheritance. It extends the Pascal type and variable declaration statement to support the notion of object and class definition. MacApp is a large collection of class definitions developed mostly in this language.

7.1.2.3 Strongly Typed Object-Oriented Languages

We already mentioned the "father" of object-oriented languages, namely SIMULA. SIMULA was standardized in 1986, and a number of companies (mostly in Sweden—Lund Software and Simprog AB) offer SIMULA implementations on a host of platforms.

There have been some novel strongly typed object-oriented languages. A very interesting and commercially available language is Eiffel (Meyer, 1988), from Interactive Software Engineering, Inc. In addition to encapsulation and inheritance, Eiffel integrates a number of powerful object-oriented capabilities such as parametric types and pre- and postconditions for methods. Other strongly typed object-oriented languages include Trellis/Owl (Schaffert *et al.*, 1986), from DEC, and Ada (to the extent that Ada is truly object-oriented).

7.1.2.4 Object-Oriented Extensions of LISP

There have been several extensions of LISP. The most notable object-oriented extensions include Flavors (Moon, 1986), which is supported by Symbolics; CommonLoops from Xerox; Common Objects (Snyder, 1985); and the Common List Object System (CLOS). Common Objects is interesting because it attempts to resolve an apparent conflict between encapsulation and inheritance.

CLOS is significant since an ANSI committee (X3J13) is standardizing the language (Bobrow *et al.*, 1988). Both Xerox and Symbolics are involved in its development. CLOS introduces novel and interesting approaches to some of the object-oriented concepts, such as method combination for resolving method conflicts in multiple inheritance (see Section 7.3.4).

7.1.2.5 Object-Oriented Languages in the 1990s

Although most of the research work to develop object-oriented languages, interfaces, and databases was done in the 1970s and 1980s, the popularity and "mainstream" acceptance of object-oriented technologies is happening now (in the 1990s). The 1980s will probably be known as the decade that launched the object-oriented era of computation. 1986 saw the first major conference, OOPSLA (Object-Oriented Programming Systems and Languages), entirely dedicated to object orientation. 1988 brought the first journal entirely dedicated to object orientation, the *Journal of Object-Oriented Programming*. Other journals and publications dedicated to object orientation have started to appear *(C++ Report, Object* magazine, *Smalltalk* news letters, to name a few).

In the late 1980s and early 1990s, OOPSLA attendance steadily increased. Simultaneously, object-oriented languages such as C++ (Stroustrup, 1986), Objective-C (Cox, 1986), Smalltalk-80 (Goldberg and Robson, 1983), Eiffel (Meyer, 1988) and object-oriented extensions of LISP became commercially available. Several major computer companies such as AT&T, Sun, and Microsoft started pursuing object-oriented styles of programming for developing their own software. The 1990s also saw the emergence of several standardization efforts, the most notable of which was the Object Management Group (endorsed by major software vendors).

In intelligent office environments, office object orientation will be manifested in graphical user interfaces that provide object metaphors for all the office objects (information, peripherals, workers, processes, and procedures).

7.1.3 The Three Fundamental Concepts of Object Orientation

Object-oriented languages and tools are enabling technologies that allow real-world problems, such as complex office environments, to be expressed more easily and naturally by using modularized components. The three most fundamental concepts of the object-oriented paradigm are abstract data typing, inheritance, and object identity. Each of these concepts contributes to the representation and modeling properties of object-oriented systems. The next three sections explore these concepts using examples of intelligent office objects.

7.1.4 Chapter Organization

Section 7.2 discusses abstract data typing, explaining the object-message paradigm and the notion of classes to encapsulate object types. Section 7.3 discusses inheritance and shows how inheritance can be used to organize the classes of intelligent office objects. Section 7.4 concentrates on object identity, discussing how identity can be used to support the referential sharing of objects and to organize the instances of intelligent office object spaces.

7.2 OBJECT-MESSAGE PARADIGM

Object orientation is often described by the object-message paradigm. Objects make up the computational universe for this paradigm. Each object responds to a prescribed collection of messages that comprise that object's interface.

7.2 Object-Message Paradigm

In procedural models of computation, routines or functions call each other to return data values or update input data parameters. In the object-message model, every datum is an object capable of processing requests known as messages. These messages may do either of two things: ask the object to perform a computation and return a value, or modify the object's content, changing the state or the value of the object. Therefore, the data is the active computational entity in the object-message model of computation. An interaction within an object-oriented environment entails a number of objects sending messages to one another.

Figure 7.2 illustrates three objects sending messages to each other. Here, Object 1 received Message 1 and then sent Message 2 to Object 2. In turn, Object 2 sent Message 3 to Object 3. For example, Object 1 could be a fax server, which receives a fax (Message 1). It, in its turn, sends the fax to an OCR (Optical Character Recognition) processor to determine the destination of the fax. The OCR determines the recipient and sends it (as Message 3) to the destination object (an office worker).

7.2.1 Abstract Data Types

Underlying the object-message paradigm is the powerful discipline of abstract data typing. Abstract data types define encapsulated sets of similar objects with an associated collection of operations. Therefore, abstract data types specify both an object's structure (appearance) and behavior (which messages are applicable to the object). Abstract data

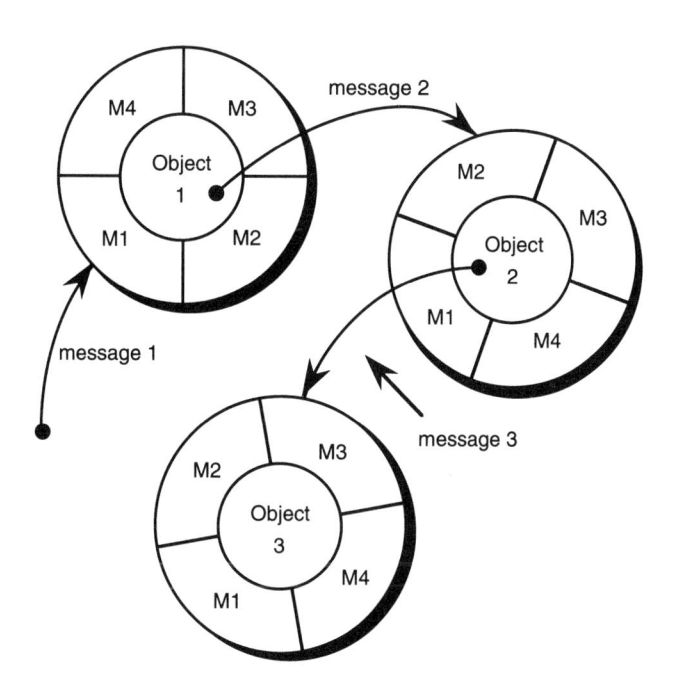

Objects send messages to each other

Figure 7.2 Objects (instances) and classes.

typing "hides" the internal representation of objects from the outside world and protects the internal algorithms that implement the objects' behavior from external meddling.

Languages supporting abstract data types provide constructs to directly define both data structures and the operations used to manipulate occurrences ("instances") of those data structures. In addition, all manipulations of instances of a data type are performed exclusively by operations associated with that data type.

Abstract data typing and the object-message computational model provide a more delegatory mode of computation: An object sends a message to another object, which determines how to respond to the message. In effect, the objects say to one another, "Tell me what you want me to accomplish. I'll do it in my own way."

7.2.2 Classes

A class is the language construct most commonly used to define abstract data types in object-oriented programming languages. A class incorporates the definition of the structure as well as the operations of the abstract data type. Elements belonging to the collection of objects described by a class are called instances of the class. A class definition (minimally) includes the following:

1. The name of the class
2. The external operations for manipulating the instances of the class, called the methods of the class (these operators typically have a target object and a number of arguments)
3. The internal representation, which captures the values of various states of the class instances (for instance, the set of documents contained in a folder or the salary of an office worker are internal instance variables for the corresponding objects)

As an example, Figure 7.3 depicts some methods of class SalesPerson. The interface operators (methods) of class SalesPerson include the following:

1. *Operator:* AddNewAccount
   Argument: The account to be allocated to the sales person
   Effect: Add and allocate a new account to the sales person.
2. *Operator:* RemoveOrder
   Argument: The order that is no longer active
   Effect: Remove the order from the set of pending orders allocated to the sales person.
3. *Operator:* TotalAccounts
   Effect: Return the total number of accounts allocated to the sales person.

A class definition must also include the code that implements the class's interface operators, plus descriptions of the internal representation of objects (object states) in that class.

7.2 Object-Message Paradigm ■ 209

```
AddNewAccount
GiveRaise
ChangeQuota
TotalAccounts

Class SalesPerson
The Methods
```

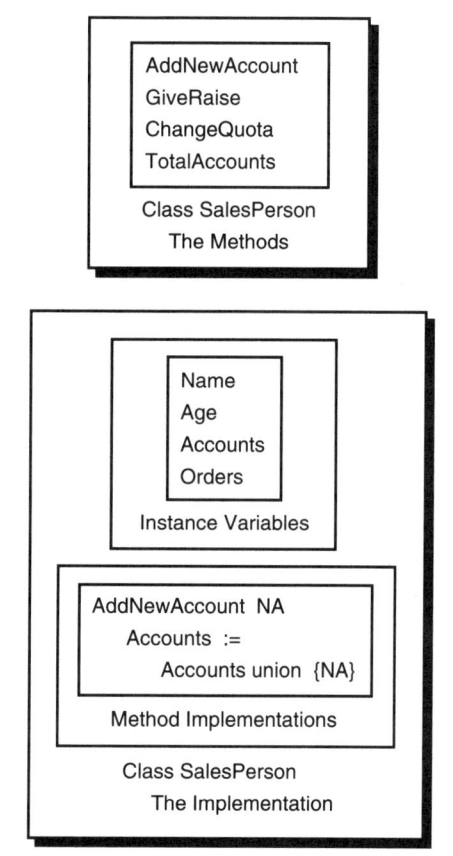

```
Name
Age
Accounts
Orders
Instance Variables

AddNewAccount  NA
   Accounts :=
      Accounts union {NA}
Method Implementations

Class SalesPerson
The Implementation
```

Figure 7.3 The class SalesPerson.

The values of the variables in the internal representation of the instances of the class pertain to individual objects. For instance, Joan's internal representation consists of her description (name, address, and so on) and the accounts and active orders she has handled. (Some of the values that describe Joan might also describe other objects: for example, Joan shares her office with her co-worker Jim, so the office is a shared value.) The aggregation of the full set of these values captures the state of Joan as an instance of SalesPerson.

Although the values of the variables in the internal representation vary for each instance of a class, all of the instances share the codes that implement the interface operators. Interface operators have a purpose similar to procedure calls in conventional programming languages.

Thus, a single code base implements such operators as AddNewAccount, ChangeQuota, and TotalAccounts. These operators are always invoked with a target object as argument. The object-oriented system knows how to apply the appropriate operations to the target objects without violating their internal states.

7.2.3 Containers and Class Extensions

Conceptually, a type or an abstract data type represents the set of all possible objects with the prescribed structure and behavior. Thus, *INTEGER* represents the infinite set of integers; *FLOAT* represents the infinite set of floating-point real numbers; *STRING OF CHARACTER* represents the infinite set of strings of characters, and so on.

By contrast, the extension, or extent, of a class corresponds to the actual instances of a class that have been created but not destroyed. It is comprised of the existing instances of a class. Thus, the extent of class SalesPerson corresponds to all the existing instances of SalesPerson: John, Mary, Suzan, Jim, and so on.

In object-oriented programming languages such as Smalltalk or C++, the user defines a class expressly as a template to generate objects. Although these object-oriented languages provide the primitives to create and (implicitly or explicitly) destroy objects, they do not support class extensions.

Why do we ever need to know or access the extension of a class? Actually, for some types such as *INTEGER* or *FLOAT*, the notion of an extension does not make sense. Indeed, in Smalltalk/V the class method *new* (which is used to create new instances of objects) generates an error for classes *Integer* and *Float*.

The most important use of class extensions is for the type of bulk information processing traditionally performed by database management systems. One of the main functions of a database management system is to process large numbers of objects of the same type. This leads to an interesting contrast between database management systems and programming languages with respect to use of types and classes.

In Chapter 4 we saw how SQL could be used to create tables. Actually, a table definition in SQL creates both a type and a handle to an extension. Thus, the statement

CREATE OFFICEWORKER

creates the "type" of an office worker (that is, the attributes and the type of each attribute) as well as a "handle" to the set of all existing office workers.

On the other hand, none of the most popular object-oriented languages (Smalltalk, C++, or Ada) support the notion of a type or class extent explicitly. However, through collection objects we can achieve the same goal. As with class extensions, we can create a collection that includes all instances of objects of the same class.

Most object-oriented languages support several built-in types or classes that are containers of other objects. The instances of these classes are actually collections of objects. In most cases, a collection object can be used instead of an extension to achieve the same functionality.

Collection objects may be sets, arrays, bags (sets that can have duplicate values), or other types of collections. Users can employ them in place of class extents as handles to collections of objects that are all instances of the same class.

Hence, there are two strategies to access and traverse the existing instances of a class:

1. Through the class extensions (if the language supports extents)
2. Through a collection object that contains the existing instances of the class (almost all object-oriented languages support collection objects)

Different applications will prefer to use one or the other of these choices. If the application incorporates only one interesting collection of objects, say sales people, the extent approach is preferable.

If, instead, object collections are naturally partitioned and accessed in different subsets, the collection object approach is better. For example, each library in a department will contain a set of objects: folders, documents, and so on. The application traverses and manipulates the set of objects in a library, but rarely or never the set of all objects in all libraries. In this case the Folder (or Document) class extension is useless. However, we may well use set objects to collect the folders within a particular library.

7.2.4 Overloading and Dynamic Binding

One of the most powerful concepts of object orientation is operation or method overloading. Overloading allows operations with the same name, but different semantics and implementations, to be invoked for objects of different types.

Overloading is neither new nor particular to object orientation. In conventional languages such as C or Pascal, programmers frequently use overloaded operations. Examples of overloading in object orientation include arithmetic operators, I/O operations, object creation functions, and value assignment operators. For instance, in the GUI environments of intelligent offices, the following operations will be overloaded:

> *CREATE*
>
> *CUT*
>
> *COPY*
>
> *PASTE*

A *CREATE* in an opened folder window creates a new document, whereas a *CREATE* in an opened cabinet window creates a drawer. Similarly, a *CREATE* method can be used to create new office workers, procedures, or policies.

Another concept closely associated with overloading is dynamic binding. Dynamic binding (also called late binding) is one of the most frequently cited advantages of the object-oriented style of programming. Dynamic binding means that the system binds message selectors to the methods that implement them at run time (instead of binding those message selectors at compile time). The particular methods used in binding depend upon the recipient object's class.

The run-time binding capability is needed for two reasons:

1. Object-oriented languages support operator overloading (as just described). For instance, consider the message "C + C2". To determine the method that needs to be executed for the message "+ C2", the system sends the message to the target object C. The target object checks whether the selector is in its protocol, and if yes, it executes the appropriate method. Therefore, the determination of the particular method to be executed for a message is performed dynamically at run time.
2. A variable's object class or type may not be known until run time. This is true of languages that do not type the variables, like Smalltalk. In these languages it

is very difficult or even impossible to determine at compile time the type of the object referenced by a variable.

To illustrate the advantages of dynamic binding, imagine a "Print" message applied to every element of a heterogeneous collection of office objects. Assume we have a stack that can contain any kind of object and we want to print every entry in the stack. Further, assume that different print methods are associated with each class. All these print methods rely on different implementations and are totally unrelated.

In the following statement, the stack is *St,* and is implemented as an array 1 to *Top* of objects. The Smalltalk/V code for printing every element of the stack is as follows:

```
for i := 1 to Top St[i] Print
```

Each object *St[i]* executes its appropriate print method, depending on the class to which it belongs. The object itself decides what piece of code to execute for the print message. Unlike procedure names in more conventional programming languages, the selector *Print* does not identify a unique piece of code. Instead, the actual code used is determined by the class of the target object to which the print message is sent. The object responds to the *Print* selector by using the printing method appropriate for its class.

If the language did not support overloading and dynamic binding, a large *case* statement would be needed. The appropriate print routine would then be invoked based on the selected object's type. Using a *case* construct, each entry in the stack would be a pair:

```
<object-type-class> <object>
```

A collection of print operators like *PrintDocument, PrintCabinet, PrintFolder,* and so on corresponds to the number of types. The process of *Printing* a cabinet or a folder entails printing all the documents in the cabinet or folder. Printing each element of the stack involves checking the type of the stack and calling the appropriate routine. Using a Pascal-like syntax, the code would be similar to the following:

```
for i := 1 to Top do
    case St[i].type
        Folder      PrintFolder(St[i].Object)
        Cabinet     PrintCabinet(St[i].Object)
        Document    PrintDocument(St[i].Object)
```

Note that if a new type *X* were added, the case statement would have to be extended with *PrintX*. This addition would force the recompilation of the entire routine that prints the elements of a stack.

In contrast, any number of new classes may be added to a system that uses overloading and dynamic binding. These extensions will never affect the method that prints all the elements of a stack. Nor will they force modification of any other previously defined method that uses generic selectors like *Print.*

Of course, the ability to manipulate collections of objects of different types (heterogeneous collections) implies that the language is not strongly typed. The previous example illustrated the power of overloading and dynamic binding. It also showed that this power is best utilized by typeless languages.

7.2.5 Constraints

Ideally, full support of abstract data typing requires the operations associated with an abstract data type (ADT) to be complete and correct. A real abstract data type represents a type of object, be it an information container such as a folder, a peripheral such as a scanner, or a data structure such as a stack. The full semantics of this abstract data type exist only in the mind of its creator. Therefore, realistically, the completeness or correctness of the ADT is only as good as the completeness or correctness of the code that captures its behavior.

To help the programmers better express the behavior of abstract data types, object-oriented programming languages need to provide constructs to indicate the constraints that test the correctness or completeness of the abstract data type.

There are two approaches to providing such language constructs:

1. *Constraints placed on objects and instance variables*. This approach places constraints on objects. Access and update constraint routines are executed when manipulating instances of the abstract data type. These constraint routines are incorporated in the definition of the class. They may be associated either with the object instance as a whole or with particular instance variables of the object. This is similar to the notion of integrity constraints in databases, which was discussed in Chapter 4. For example, the integrity constraint might specify that an office worker's salary should not exceed that of his or her manager. Every time the salary of an office worker is updated, the system checks the constraint. When the constraint is violated, there is an error. The system will reject the update.

    Attached predicates are a related concept used in some AI (artificial intelligence) systems. They could be used to restrict access, evaluate missing information, or enforce constraints on instance variables. An attached predicate can be an if-accessed or an if-updated predicate. An if-accessed predicate gets fired whenever the instance variable is accessed. An if-updated predicate gets fired whenever an instance variable is updated. Through these predicates, arbitrary conditions on the instance variable values could be checked to see if they are violated. For example, we can check if the number of accounts assigned to a sales person is at least 10 whenever we access the *Accounts* instance variable.

2. *Pre- and postconditions of methods*. The second approach associates preconditions and postconditions with the operations (methods) of the abstract data type rather than with the objects. Preconditions allow one to introduce certain constraints on the instance variables that must be satisfied before a particular method is executed. Postconditions allow articulation of other constraints that must be satisfied upon terminating the execution of the method.

    This is the approach taken in Eiffel (Meyer, 1988). For example, in Eiffel one can attach pre- and postconditions to the *Push* and *Pop* operations to guarantee the semantics of a *Stack*. A precondition for *Push* is the requirement that the stack instance must not be full. A precondition for *Pop* is the requirement that the stack instance must not be empty. Similarly a postcondition for *Pop* is the requirement that the stack instance is no longer empty and its total number of elements is increased by one.

The choice between object constraints and conditions on methods is mainly a matter of convenience and taste. The two approaches attempt to achieve the same effect. Both help the programmer express the semantics of the abstract data type as directly as possible. However, there is no magic in constraints and conditions on either objects or operators. The completeness or correctness of the abstract data type is still only as good as the completeness or correctness of the code used to capture its behavior. It remains the programmer's responsibility to use these constructs to express the semantics of the abstract data type explicitly.

7.2.6 Advantages of Abstract Data Typing

The advantages of abstract data typing can be summarized as follows:

1. It allows better conceptualization and modeling of the real world; enhances representation and understandability; and categorizes objects based on common structure and behavior.
2. It enhances the robustness of the system. If the underlying language allows the specification of the types for each variable, abstract data typing allows type checking to avoid run-time type errors. Furthermore, integrity checks on data and operations greatly enhance the correctness of programs.
3. It enhances performance. For typed systems, knowing the types of objects allows compile-time optimization. It also permits better clustering strategies for the persistent objects.
4. It better captures the semantics of the type. Abstract data typing clusters or localizes the operations and the representation of attributes.
5. It separates the implementation from the specification. Allows the modification or enhancement of the implementation without affecting the public interface of the abstract data type.
6. It allows extensibility of the system. Reusable software components are easier to create and maintain.

7.3 INHERITANCE

In addition to modeling real-world applications as closely as possible, object orientation also attempts to achieve software reusability and software extensibility. The powerful object-oriented concept that provides all these capabilities is inheritance.

Inheritance enables the construction of new object types and software modules (such as classes) on top of an existing hierarchy of modules. This avoids the need to redesign and

7.3 Inheritance

recode from scratch. New classes can inherit both the behavior (operations and methods) and the representation (instance variables and attributes) from existing classes.

Inheriting behavior enables code sharing (and hence reusability) among software modules. Inheriting representation enables structure sharing among data objects. The combination of these two types of inheritance provides a most powerful modeling and software development strategy.

Inheritance also provides a very natural mechanism for organizing information. It "taxonomizes" objects into well-defined inheritance hierarchies.

Inheritance has its roots in "common sense" knowledge representation paradigms used in artificial intelligence. One example is Ross Quillian's (1968) psychological model of associative memory. The "node-and-link" model introduced by Quillian is one of the earliest semantic network knowledge representation models.

Semantic networks consist of nodes representing concepts (objects) and links representing relationships. In semantic network representations, nodes and links have labels. The most powerful label representing inheritance relationships is the *Is-a* link.

Figure 7.4 illustrates a semantic network for sales people, where a sales person *Is-a* office worker. Similarly, a sales manager *Is-a* sales person, and a district manager *Is-a* sales manager. A sales person has *Account* and *Order* attributes, and a sales person works in a department.

Inheritance is also incorporated in object-oriented languages through class inheritance. As discussed earlier, classes can implement encapsulated sets of objects that exhibit the same behavior (in other words, abstract data types). The earliest object-oriented programming language, SIMULA, allowed classes to inherit from one another. In the most common object-oriented languages such as SIMULA, Smalltalk, Eiffel, and C++, classes can inherit both methods (behavior) and instance variables (structure) from superclasses.

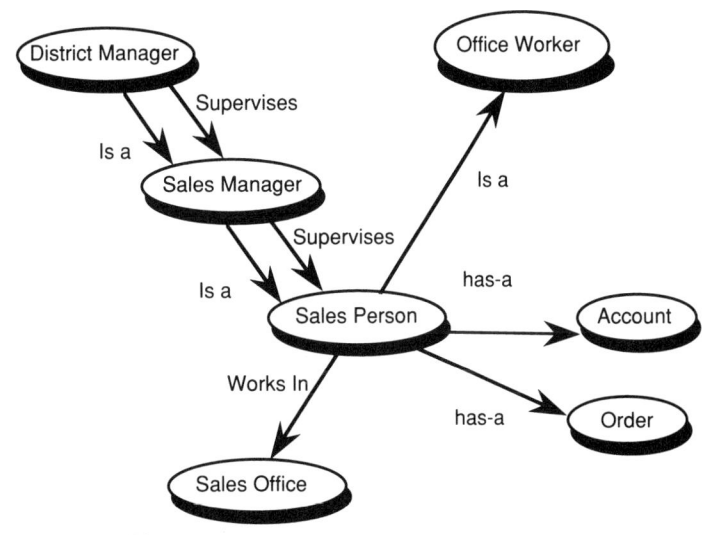

Figure 7.4 A semantic network for SalesPerson.

216 ■ Object-Oriented Concepts

Besides providing a powerful tool for organizing information, the most important contribution of inheritance is code sharing or code reusability.

To illustrate code reusability and the appropriateness of class inheritance in object-oriented systems, the classes rooted at *Person* can be further "specialized." Figure 7.5 shows the additional classes and the inheritance hierarchy: Secretaries and sales persons are office workers; sales managers further specialize sales people; and district managers specialize sales managers.

The classes Secretary and SalesPerson are subclasses of OfficeWorker. The class OfficeWorker is a superclass of Secretary and SalesPerson. The subclass and superclass relations are transitive. Thus, if X is a subclass of Y and Y is a subclass of Z, then X is also a subclass of Z. For example, since DistrictManager is a subclass of SalesManager, it is also, by transitivity, a subclass of SalesPerson and OfficeWorker.

If the class OfficeWorker implements the following methods, then subclasses of OfficeWorker such as SalesPerson, SalesManager, and DistrictManager can inherit these methods without having to reimplement them.

> EvaluateBonus
>
> GiveRaise
>
> ChangeDepartment

In fact, the class SalesPerson can have its own additional methods, such as:

> TotalOrders (returns the total number of orders)
>
> TotalAccounts (returns the total number of accounts)

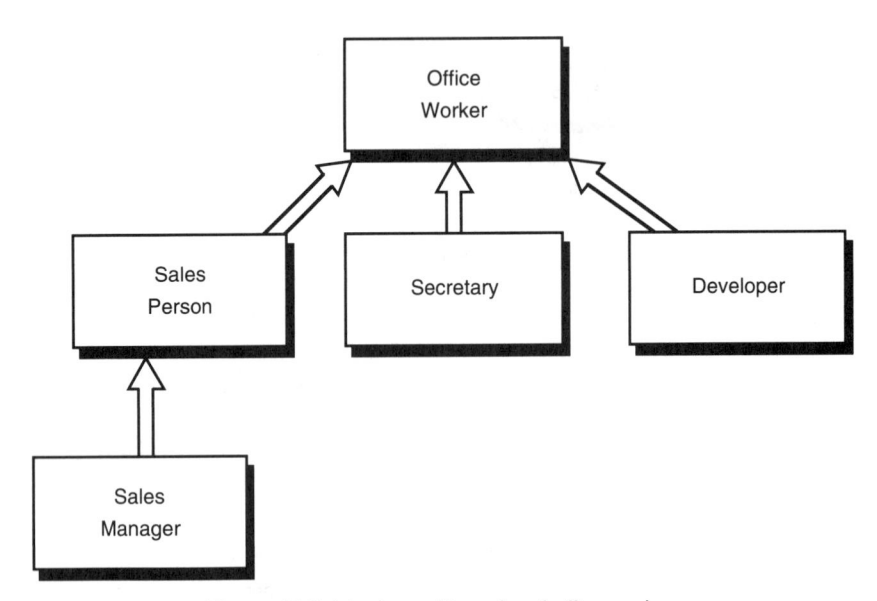

Figure 7.5 Inheritance hierarchy of office workers.

In turn, these methods would be inherited by SalesPerson's subclasses SalesManager and DistrictManager.

The class inheritance hierarchy of object-oriented languages provides an excellent means of organizing complex code bases. Some object-oriented languages, such as Smalltalk, come with a comprehensive initial class hierarchy. The users of the language can specialize some classes in the initial class hierarchies to create classes for their applications. Smalltalk programmers spend a substantial amount of time familiarizing themselves with the workings of the initial class hierarchy of the Smalltalk programming environment.

In summary, class inheritance has two main aspects:

- *Structural:* Instances of a class such as SalesPerson, which is a subclass of OfficeWorker, have values for instance variables inherited from OfficeWorker such as Name, Address, or Salary. Note that the instance variables Name and Address are actually inherited (transitively) from class OfficeWorker.
- *Behavioral:* A class has methods such as AccumulatedVacationLeave, GiveRaise, or ChangeAddress, which are inherited by its subclasses, such as SalesPerson and Secretary. As a result, a message can be sent with selector GiveRaise to an instance Margaret of Secretary, in order to execute the method GiveRaise in OfficeWorker with Margaret as the target object.

7.3.1 Inheriting Instance Variables

The class of an object describes its structure by specifying the object's instance variables. In all object-oriented languages, instances of a subclass must retain the same type of information as instances of their superclass.

One way to achieve this is to inherit the instance variables of the superclass directly and allow methods in the subclass to access and manipulate the instance variables of its superclass(es) without any constraints. This is the strategy in Smalltalk.

In this scheme, each subclass declares the additional instance variables that it introduces (as specialization or extension). Thus, if class C_1 declares

Class C_1
  Instance Variables: X_1,
                     X_2,
                     X_3

and class C_2 is a subclass of C_1, then C_2 declares just the following additional instance variables that it introduces:

Class C_2 subclass of C_1
  Instance Variables: X_4,
                     X_5,
                     X_6

The state of each instance of C_1 is stored in variables X_1, X_2, and X_3. The state of each instance of C_2 is stored in variables X_1, X_2, X_3, X_4, X_5, and X_6. This is illustrated in

Figure 7.6, which also demonstrates the state of OfficeWorkers. In general, the instance variables of a class is the union of the instance variables of all its superclasses.

7.3.2 Inheriting Methods

As indicated earlier, a class defines both the structure and the behavior of a collection of objects. The behavior is specified in the methods associated with the instances of the class. Methods are operations that can either retrieve or update the state of an object, and the object's state is stored in its instance variables.

In an inheritance hierarchy, a method defined for a class is inherited by its subclasses. Thus, the inherited methods are part of the interface manipulating the instances of the subclass.

For example, a TextDocument and an ImageDocument both inherit from the Document class. The "generic" (or abstract) Document class has several methods, such as

OPEN
CLOSE
SAVE
SAVE AS

which are inherited by both TextDocument and ImageDocument.

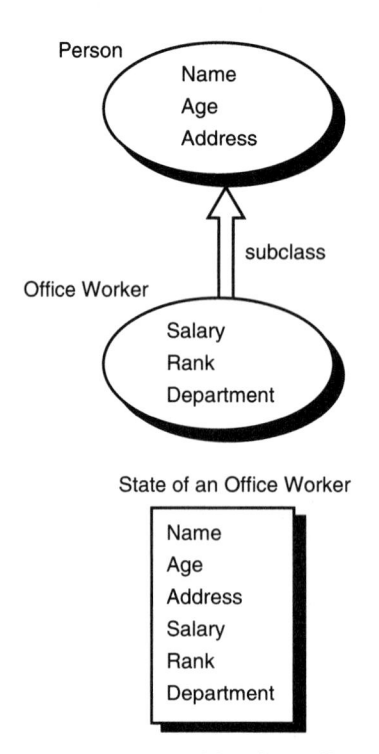

Figure 7.6 Instance variables of an OfficeWorker.

In the TextDocument subclass, more specialized methods for editing and modifying font, character size, and so on for text strings are defined. These methods are not (or not necessarily) defined for just any document. They are applicable to (primarily) text documents. Similarly, ImageDocument has specific methods such as zooming and rotating, which are applicable to image documents.

Similar to instance variable definitions, the collection of methods applicable to an instance of a class is the union of all the methods defined for the ancestors of the class plus the methods defined in the class definition.

7.3.3 Method Overriding

A subclass can also override an inherited method. In other words, a method called M in class C can be overridden by a method also called M in a subclass C' of C. Thus, when a message with selector M is sent to an object O, the underlying system binds M to the method with the same name in the most specialized class of O.

For example, consider the hierarchy of OfficeWorkers, with SalesPerson a subclass of OfficeWorker and SalesManager a subclass of SalesPerson. Assume that the formula for evaluating the end-of-year bonus for sales people is completely different from that of regular employees. In particular, the evaluation of the bonus of a regular employee is a function of the employee's manager's ranking (a number between 1 and 5) and the number of years the employee has worked for the firm:

EvaluateBonus code in class OfficeWorker:

Bonus := Rank*1000 + NumberOfYears*100

The formula to evaluate the bonus of sales people is a function of the total sales and the number of years the sales person has worked for the firm:

EvaluateBonus code in class SalesPerson:

Bonus := TotalSalesAmount*0.01 + Rank*1000 + NumberOfYears*100

Finally, the formula to evaluate the bonus of a sales manager is a function of the following:

1. The total sales of all sales people under the sales manager's supervision
2. The total amount of direct sales made by the sales manager
3. The number of years the sales manager has worked for the firm

The following statements reflect these factors:

EvaluateBonus code in class SalesManager:

Bonus := TotalSalesForceSales*0.005 + TotalDirectSalesAmount*0.01 + Rank*1000 + NumberOfYears*100

Now, when the method EvaluateBonus is invoked, which piece of code is used? For example, assume:

>Mary is an instance of SalesManager
>John is an instance of SalesPerson

Note that in addition to her position as a sales manager, Mary is a member of the abstract set of SalesPerson and, by transitivity, also an OfficeWorker. Similarly John is a SalesPerson and an OfficeWorker. However, Mary is created as an instance of SalesManager. If the message "What is your class?" is sent to Mary, the answer is "SalesManager."

When the following message is sent, the search for a method called EvaluateBonus starts at the class SalesManager:

>*Mary EvaluateBonus*

Since such a method is found in the declaration of this class (the class SalesManager), the search stops there: the appropriate method has been found and can be executed.

7.3.4 Multiple Inheritance

So far all the inheritance examples have used single inheritance: Each subclass had one and only one immediate superclass. The class inheritance hierarchy with single inheritance is a tree, with the most general class (typically the class Object) at the root of the tree. In many situations, though, it is very convenient to allow a subclass to inherit from more than one immediate superclass. In the Person class hierarchy, for example, there can be people who are both office workers and students. With single inheritance it is impossible to express this multiple-parent relationship directly. There are numerous such real-life examples of multiple inheritance. For example, Figure 7.7 illustrates a BorderedTextWindow, which allows editing of text in a bordered window inheriting from both TextWindow and BorderedWindow.

The mechanism that allows a class to inherit from more than one immediate parent is called multiple inheritance. With multiple inheritance, we can combine several existing

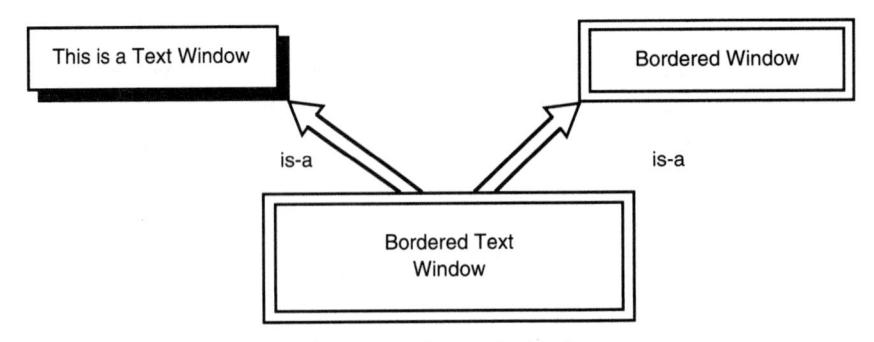

Figure 7.7 Example of multiple inheritance.

classes to produce combination classes that utilize each of their multiple superclasses in a variety of usages and functionalities. Then the class inheritance hierarchy becomes a directed acyclic graph (DAG), since a class can have more than one immediate predecessor.

We saw earlier that the set of instance variables for the subclass is the union of the instance variables of its immediate superclass and the additional instance variables defined in the subclass. Similarly, the set of methods for the subclass is also the union of the methods of its immediate superclass and the additional methods defined in the subclass. Of course, methods in the subclass can override methods in the superclass.

With multiple inheritance these strategies are extended to the union of all immediate parents. More specifically,

$$\text{Instance variables of } C = \text{Local } C \text{ instance variables} \cup C_i \text{ instance variables}$$

where each C_i is an immediate predecessor of C.

Similarly, the methods of C are defined by

$$\text{Methods of } C = \text{Local } C \text{ methods} \cup C_i \text{ methods}$$

Suppose a Rectangle has two instance variables, LowerLeft and UpperRight, representing the coordinates of the lower left corner and upper right corner. A ColoredRegion also has two instance variables: Color and Brightness. A ColoredRectangle, therefore, will have

UpperRight
LowerLeft
Color
Brightness

Unfortunately, combining instance variables or methods of immediate predecessors is not that simple. The problem is that predecessors could have instance variables or methods with the same name, but with totally unrelated semantics. For example, a TechnicalConsultant and a Manager can have values for Skill that are totally unrelated. For the technical person, Skill reflects the technical abilities and experience in a particular technical domain. For a manager, it reflects people management skills, knowledge of project management techniques, and so on. Therefore, the "units" and domains of the values of Skill in these two classes are unrelated. Now what happens when a class such as TechnicalManager inherits from both? In other words, what happens when there is a conflict? By "conflict" we mean that different methods or instance variables with the same name are defined in a totally unrelated way by two or more superclasses.

The bulk of the problems of multiple inheritance deal with conflict resolution strategies. There are many such strategies, and each object-oriented language supporting multiple inheritance provides a slight variation of a basic strategy in its implementation. For more details, see Khoshafian and Abnous (1990), pp. 133–141.

7.3.5 Inheriting the Interface

Inheritance is used to specialize. Sales people are more specialized office workers who are involved in selling items; sales managers are sales persons who manage the quotas and other attributes of sales people; and so on. Nevertheless, characterizing inheritance as specialization has caused some confusion. A class C_1 inherits from class C_2, but the interface of C_1 (the subclass) is a superset of the interface of C_2!

This is illustrated in Figure 7.8. Viewing class types as sets of objects with the same structure and behavior, the set of OfficeWorkers is a subset of the set of Persons. Similarly, the set of SalesPersons is a subset of the set OfficeWorkers. The set of Secretaries is also a subset of the set of OfficeWorkers. The set of sales managers is a subset of the set of sales persons and the set of district managers is a subset of the set of sales managers.

With respect to interfaces and the representation, the inclusion hierarchies are reversed. For example, the set of attributes of SalesPersons includes all the attributes of OfficeWorkers as well as additional attributes, such as Accounts and Orders. The interface of SalesPerson is also a superset of the interface of OfficeWorkers and includes additional methods, like AddNewOrders and TotalAccounts.

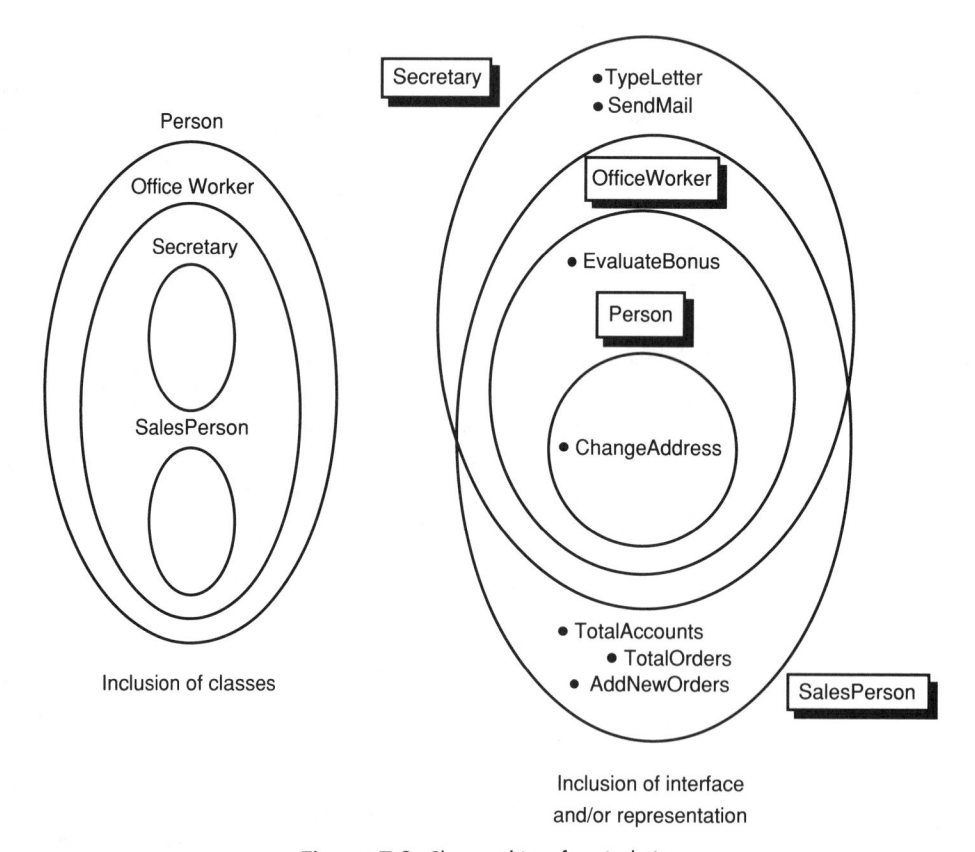

Figure 7.8 Class and interface inclusions.

Thus, in addition to providing specialization, inheritance can also be viewed as an extension: When a class C_1 inherits from a class C_2, it provides additional interface routines (methods) and attributes to the external environment. For example, if the end-user license for a commercial software program is viewed as a contract between the designer of a class (the software) and its "clients" (the software users who create instances of the class), inheritance extends the contract with additional "terms" and "clauses" of execution. These contractual addenda can be viewed as restrictions (specialization) or additional capabilities (extension).

7.3.6 Advantages of Inheritance

Inheritance provides several advantages for modeling intelligent offices:

1. It offers a natural model for organizing information. For instance, inheritance directly captures the fact that sales managers are also sales people.
2. It allows the sharing of code and representation, reducing the overhead of intelligent office systems.
3. It allows new classes and objects to be defined on top of existing hierarchies rather than from scratch. This increases the flexibility and extensibility of the intelligent office class hierarchies.

7.4 OBJECT IDENTITY

While abstract data types and inheritance model and organize the types or classes of objects, object identity organizes the objects in the object space manipulated by an object-oriented program.

Object identity is that property of an object that distinguishes the object from all others. The most commonly used technique for identifying objects in programming languages, databases, and operating systems is user-defined names of objects.

Using object identity, objects can contain or refer to other objects. This eliminates the need to use variable names without the support of object identity, which introduces practical limitations. One limitation is that a single object may be accessed in different ways; it may be bound to different variables. The system must find a way to find out if they refer to the same object (Saltzer, 1978).

For example, a sales person identified by the name $P1$ may be characterized as the employee of the sales manager John Smith who had the best sales in June of 1991. The same sales person bound to a different name $P2$ may be characterized as the sales person who made three overseas trips during 1991. Assuming $P1$ and $P2$ can only be bound to objects (in other words, not to pointers), many conventional languages do not provide predicates to directly correlate such identical objects.

In contrast, object-oriented languages provide a simple identity test with the expression $X==Y$, which is different from the equality test $X=Y$. The identity test checks whether two objects are the same. (The equality test checks whether the contents of two objects are the same.)

7.4.1 Path Names in Operating Systems

In operating systems, names are used to identify files and sub-directories within a directory. Both UNIX and DOS have hierarchical directory structures, where each directory

224 ■ Object-Oriented Concepts

contains a collection of files and possibly other directories. The name of a file must be unique within a directory. Each file is accessible through a directory path, which is basically a concatenation of directory names.

For example, assume an office has organized its computer inventory in Software (Soft) and Hardware (Hard) directories. This is illustrated in Figure 7.9. All the files describing HP laser printers will be accessible through the path

Items/Computer/Hard/Print/HP

Paths and "where things are stored" cause considerable headaches to both novice and advanced users of operating systems. Resolving ambiguous file references is one of the most frequently occurring problems for users of operating systems. Often the office worker (the user) remembers the "name" or attributes but not the location (the "path") of the file.

Another problem with concatenated names is that the object (file) space is often a tree. To store or access the same file within multiple directories, the user must make multiple copies of the file. Besides replicating storage, copying requires user interaction to maintain consistency. For example, if the information pertaining to a particular printer is updated in the Print subdirectory, then all files referencing the printer must be explicitly updated by the user.

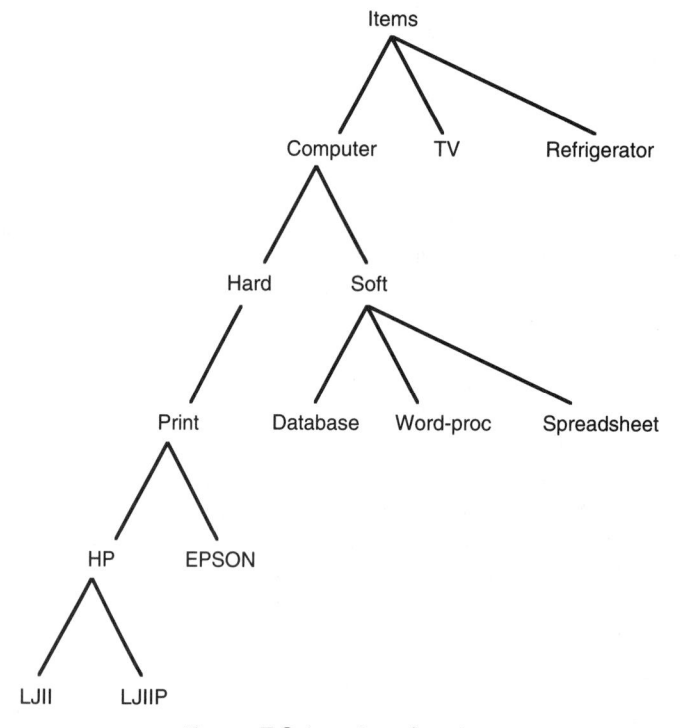

Figure 7.9 Items in an inventory.

One way around this problem is through "linking" from one directory to another file in another directory. As we shall see, this is similar to "referential sharing" with object-oriented systems supporting object identity. Although it provides some level of support for more general object spaces (more general than trees), the file linking is not as general and powerful as full support of object identity.

7.4.2 Identity Through Identifier Keys

Another method for identifying objects is unique keys (also called identifier keys). This mechanism is commonly used in database management systems. For example, for the database table storing OfficeWorker, the key would be a person's name (last name, first name); for the database table storing items, the identifier key would be the item number. Database management systems were discussed extensively in Chapter 4.

In the relational model a relation is a set of records (tuples, rows) of the same type or structure. A relation can be viewed as a two-dimensional table of rows and columns, where all the elements in a column have the same base type (integer, character string, floating-point number, and so on). Each row is a tuple or a record. The column values of a row are its attributes. An identifier key is some subset of the attributes of an object that is unique for all objects in the relation. Figure 7.10 presents the Person table, where the key is indicated as the concatenation of the last name and first name attributes of a person.

Using identifier keys for object identity confuses identity and data values (or object state). There are three main problems with this approach:

1. *Modifying identifier keys*. One problem is that identifier keys cannot (or should not) be allowed to change, even though they are user-defined descriptive data. For example, a sales manager's name may be used as the identifier key for the sales manager and replicated in sales person objects to indicate for whom the employee works. But the sales manager's name may need to change, due to a change in marital status or because the locals find the foreign name of the manager too hard to pronounce or spell. This would cause a discontinuity in the identity for the sales manager object.

Last Name	First Name	Age	Address
Adams	Tim	23	"12 Sutton..."
Brown	Jim	32	"43 Doloney..."
Ripper	Jack	70	"1 London..."
Silverman	Leo	34	"55 H Street..."
Smith	John	32	"1212 Main..."
Smith	Mary	32	"1212 Main..."

(identifier Key = Last Name + First Name)

Figure 7.10 The Person table.

2. *Nonuniformity.* The main source of nonuniformity is that identifier keys in different tables have different types (integer, character string, floating-point) or different combinations of attributes. For example, the identifier key for the Item table is the ItemNumber, an integer; for OfficeWorker, it is (LastName, FirstName), a string of characters. Dealing with different collections or types of attributes for identification is inconsistent and gives added difficulty when working with several tables.

   A second, more serious problem is that the attribute(s) to use for an identifier key may need to change. For example, RCA may use employee numbers to identify employees, while General Electric may use Social Security numbers for the same purpose. A merger of these two companies would require one of these keys to change, causing a discontinuity in identity for the employees of one of the companies.

3. *"Unnatural" joins.* A third problem is that the use of identifier keys causes joins to be used in retrievals instead of simpler and more direct object retrievals, as in GEM (Zaniolo, 1983), FAD (Bancilhon *et al.*, 1987), and OPAL (Maier and Stein, 1986).

For example, suppose we have an employee relation

OfficeWorker(Name, Age, Address, Salary, DeptName)

and a department relation

Department(Name, Budget, Location, ...)

and the *DeptName* attribute establishes a relationship between an employee and a department. Using identifier keys, *DeptName* would have as its value the identifier key of the department. A retrieval involving both tuples would require a join between the two tuples.

Thus, in SQL, to retrieve for all employees, the employee name and the location the employee works in, we would use

SELECT OfficeWorker.Name, Department.Location
FROM OfficeWorker, Department
WHERE OfficeWorker.DeptName = Department.Name

This is unnatural; in most cases what the user really wants instead of the *DeptName* is the actual department tuple. Tables in relational systems are in first normal form; they are normalized or flattened. With normalization, the user is restricted to a fixed collection of base types and is not allowed to assign and manipulate tuples, relations, or other complex object types of the attributes. Hence, normalization loses the semantic connectives among the objects in the database. In fact, relational languages such as SQL incorporate additional capabilities, such as foreign key constraints to recapture the lost semantics. In Chapter 10, we describe several complex object and semantic data models that allow a more direct and intuitive representation of object spaces.

7.4.3 The Type-State-Identity Trichotomy

A class implements a type, which describes both the structure and the behavior of its instances. The structure is captured in the instance variables, and the behavior is captured in the methods that are applicable to the instances. An object O can respond to the following message by returning the name of its class:

O class

The values of the instance variables of an object constitute the state of an object. Each instance variable value is also an object. Assume that each OfficeWorker has the instance variables (Name, Age, Address, Salary, Rank, Office, Department, Manager) with the following types (where Name, Integer, Dollar, Office, Address, Department, and Manager are also names of classes):

Instance Variable	Class
Name	Name
Age	Integer
Address	Address
Salary	Dollar
Rank	Integer
Office	Office
Department	Department

The class Name contains the following instance variables:

| LastName | String of Characters |
| FirstName | String Of Characters |

Similarly, the class Department contains the following:

Name	String of Characters
Budget	Dollar
Location	Address
Manager	OfficeWorker

Therefore, each instance of Employee contains several instances:

One instance of Name (the value of Name)

Two instances of Integer (the values of Age and Rank)

One instance of Address (the value of Address)

One instance of Dollar (the value of Salary)

One instance of Office (the value of Office)

One instance of Department (the value of Department)

Hence, the following is true about each object:

1. The object is the instance of a class (its type).
2. The object has a state, which consists of the values of its instance variables.

In addition, each object has a built-in identity, which is independent of its class or state. The identity of an object is generated when the object is created. The state of an object (the values of its instance variables) can change arbitrarily (for example, an office worker's address can change), but the identity remains the same. Object-oriented systems supporting strong built-in identity also allow the object to undergo structural modifications (such as changing its class) without any changes in its identity.

As discussed earlier, identity formalizes the notion of pointers used in more conventional languages. Without identity, or another means of referencing objects independent of their state, it is impossible for the same object to be the value of the instance variable of more than one object.

This can be demonstrated by two examples:

1. *Same address:* Assume that the employee Mary Smith is John's wife and lives at the same address. If we do not have a mechanism whereby the instance variable values of Address in both objects have as values the same address object, then it will be very hard, if not outright impossible, to maintain consistency across all occurrences of this same address value. Here, the value of an instance variable is overridden by another object.
2. *Same department:* In some cases, the state of the object that is the value of an instance variable can be modified. For instance, assume that Jim Brown works in the same hardware department as John Smith. If the budget of John's department is changed, all copies of the budget of the hardware department instance occurring everywhere need to be updated consistently. Object identity makes this unnecessary, because the system contains only one copy of the hardware department instance.

An object's state is constructed from base values, such as integers, character strings, and floating-point numbers. Using just base values of instance variables (such as integer, character strings, floats) without identity or object references, objects can be shared using two possible solutions:

1. Object replication is illustrated in Figure 7.11. The instance John Smith and the instance Mary Smith each replicate the address information. In addition to wasting storage space, the main problem with replication is consistency. The following statement changes the value of the Address instance variable to NewAddress:

    JohnSmith ChangeAddress NewAddress

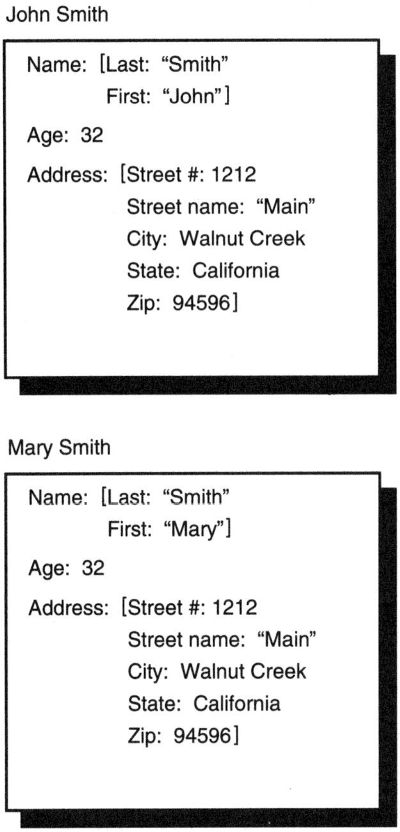

John Smith

Name: [Last: "Smith"
          First: "John"]
Age: 32
Address: [Street #: 1212
              Street name: "Main"
              City: Walnut Creek
              State: California
              Zip: 94596]

Mary Smith

Name: [Last: "Smith"
          First: "Mary"]
Age: 32
Address: [Street #: 1212
              Street name: "Main"
              City: Walnut Creek
              State: California
              Zip: 94596]

Figure 7.11 Replicating the same address.

Whenever an instance variable is updated, the user has to make sure all addresses that must be the same as John's address are updated accordingly. The user is forced to create and maintain auxiliary structures in order to preserve the semantic consistency of two people having the same address.

The same is true when the following statement changes the budget of John Smith's department:

JohnSmith ChangeBudget NewBudget

In this scenario, the user must access and update the budgets of all employees who work in the hardware department.

2. In "identifier key" systems, like relational databases, tables containing all addresses or all departments are constructed. A table must have an identifier key, such that each object has a unique key value. The key value is then stored in the referencing object. For instance, we can use the department name as the key value of a

Departments table and store the same key value (that is, the department name) in both John Smith's and Jim Brown's instances.

This solution poses several problems. First of all, the Department instance variable is not storing an instance of class Department, but rather a string of characters (the name of the department).

Second, in order to retrieve or update any information for John's department, a join operation must be performed to match the name of the department stored in John's Department instance variable with a key value in the Departments collection or table. In other words, this scheme needs a declarative database query/retrieval sublanguage. This is exactly what happens in relational systems, where the model imposes normalization constraints that force the retrieval of objects through matching key values in different tables.

Object identity does not require the overhead of replication and identifier key solutions. The use of identity causes a logical identifier (pointer) to be associated with each and every object in the system. The advantages of identity and the direct representation of complex object spaces through object identity are discussed in the next section.

7.4.4 Object Spaces with Identity

Object spaces are built on top of base objects. The most common base object type or class is the Integer. Other base types include Floating-point numbers, Characters, and Booleans. Objects that are instances of these classes usually do not have instance variables. Instead, these classes are built-in object types by the underlying system. In most cases, they map onto object types directly supported by the underlying hardware.

Many object-oriented systems do not assign identities to base objects. For example, Smalltalk does not accept two different objects with the integer value of 5—only one integer 5 object can exist! Smalltalk supports two equality predicates:

== to check for identical objects

= to check for equality of object states

However, the following are both true:

5 == 5
5 = 5

Furthermore, both of the next two messages generate errors:

Integer new
Float new

The *new* message typically generates an identifier and associates it with the newly created object. But base objects don't have an identifier; their value is their identifier.

7.4 Object Identity ■ 231

Conceptually, an infinite pool of identifiers exists such that:

1. An identifier is associated with every nonbase object.
2. The identifier is associated with the object at object creation time and remains associated with the object irrespective of any state or type modifications undergone by the object.
3. Each identifier can be associated with one and only one object. Furthermore, if there is an identifier in the system, it must be associated with an object. In other words, an object and its identifiers are "indistinguishable": The identifier uniquely identifies the object, and the object remains associated with an identifier throughout its lifetime.

A number of alternative graphical representations clarify this conceptual model of object spaces. In Figure 7.12, identifiers are associated with nonbase objects. Each object is framed in a rectangular box. Note that the Department instance variable value for John Smith is a nonbase object. The identifier value of the Department instance variable for Jim Brown is the same! In other words, Jim and John share the same department.

Figure 7.13 provides an alternative graphical representation of objects, following the representation of set-and-tuple models, as in Bancilhon *et al.* (1987), Bancilhon and Khoshafian (1989), or Khoshafian (1989). Here each object is labeled by an identifier. Furthermore, for each instance variable (attribute in set-and-tuple models), there is a labeled and directed arc from the object to the value of the object. The label is the name of the instance variable, and the target is the value of the instance variable. As clearly illustrated in the figure, the values of the Department instance variables of John and Jim are the same object.

The object space illustrated in Figure 7.13 is a directed acyclic graph. Actually, it is just as easy to represent arbitrary graph-structured object spaces with cycles. For instance, assume that each person has an additional instance variable Spouse. Then an office worker can reference his or her spouse and be referenced back without any constraints. In Figure 7.14, John and Mary also share their Address and Children.

As mentioned earlier, programming languages use virtual address pointers to achieve this object-referencing ability and allow variables to "point" to the same object from multiple sources. In fact, pointers (or virtual memory addresses) can be used to implement object identity.

The fundamental difference between object identity and virtual addresses or pointers is that identity is a semantic concept associated with objects. Addresses represent memory locations of an underlying von Neumann machine.

7.4.5 Advantages of Object Identity

Object identity, then, offers several advantages:

1. Object identity allows the direct representation of graph-structured object spaces.
2. With object identity, users do not need to maintain referential integrity.
3. By the same token, all memory or database dangling reference problems are resolved.

232 ■ Object-Oriented Concepts

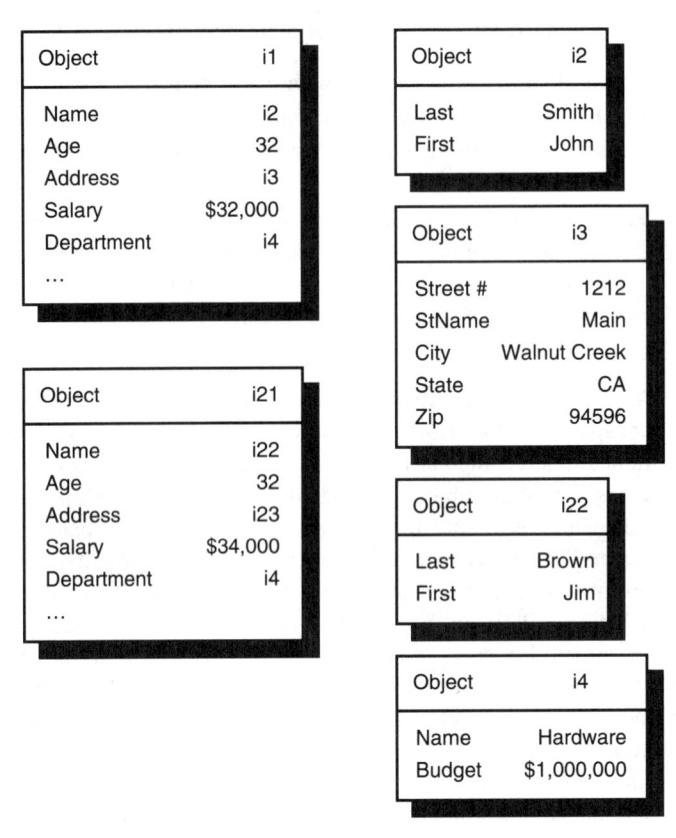

Object	i1
Name	i2
Age	32
Address	i3
Salary	$32,000
Department	i4
...	

Object	i2
Last	Smith
First	John

Object	i3
Street #	1212
StName	Main
City	Walnut Creek
State	CA
Zip	94596

Object	i21
Name	i22
Age	32
Address	i23
Salary	$34,000
Department	i4
...	

Object	i22
Last	Brown
First	Jim

Object	i4
Name	Hardware
Budget	$1,000,000

Figure 7.12 Objects represented as rectangular boxes.

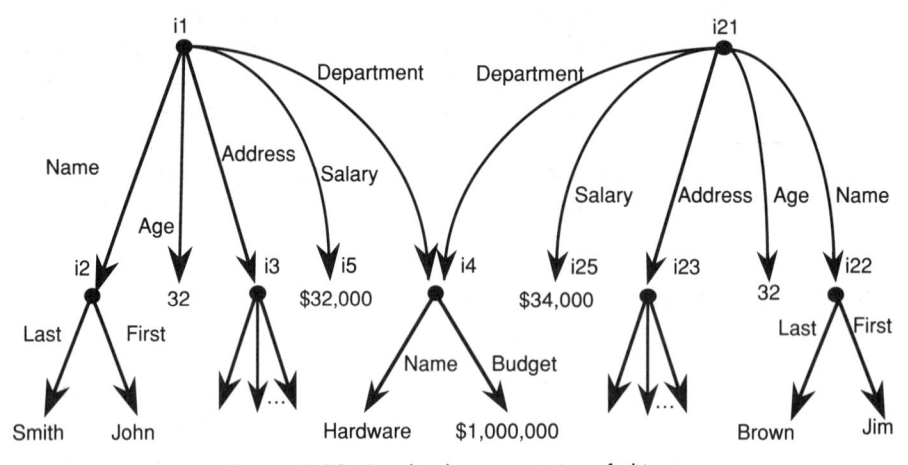

Figure 7.13 Graphical representation of objects.

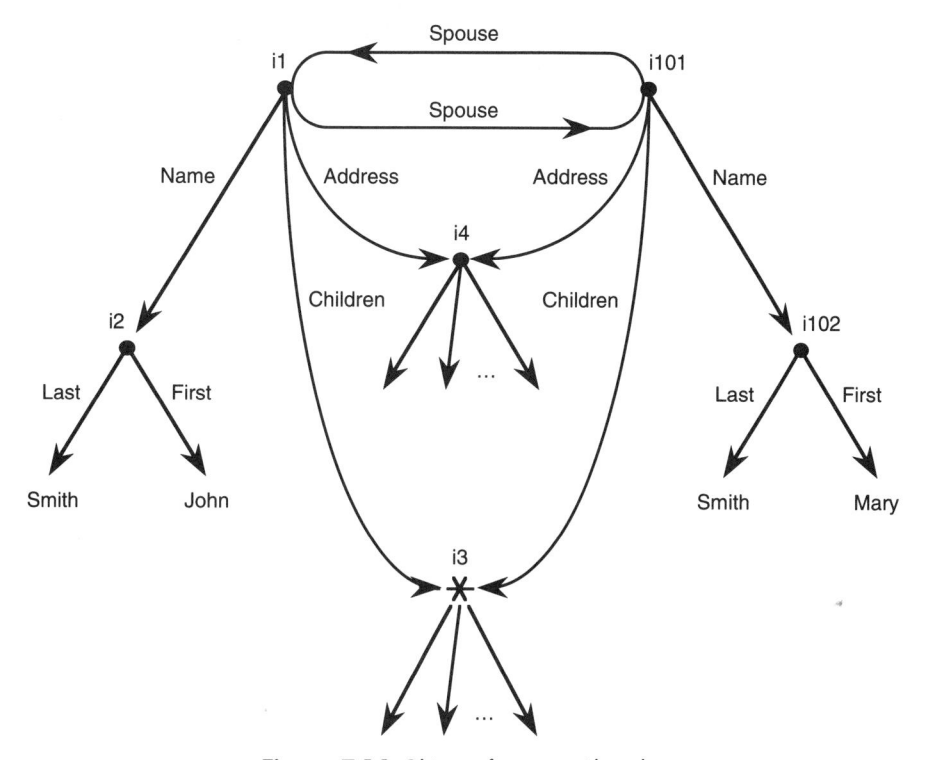

Figure 7.14 Object references with cycles.

4. The various operations (predicates, copying, and so on) associated with object identity provide powerful object manipulation functionalities for intelligent office objects.

■ 7.5 SUMMARY

The preceding sections described the main concepts of object orientation and their applicability to intelligent offices. Object orientation is defined as:

Object orientation = Abstract data typing + Inheritance + Object identity

Each of these concepts provides various advantages to the modeling and implementation of intelligent office environments.

Abstract data typing models various classes of intelligent office objects, where each class instance has a protocol: a set of messages to which it can respond. Thus, there are classes for office worker, office peripherals, folders, documents, and so on. These will be discussed in more detail in Chapter 10.

Inheritance organizes the classes of intelligent office objects in inheritance class hierarchies. It models the hierarchies of office workers, peripherals, folders, and other objects and allows representation, protocol, and implementation to be inherited from superclass to subclass. Inheritance also organizes the classes of the intelligent office environment.

Object identity organizes the instances of intelligent office classes (that is, the objects) in graph-structured object spaces. It allows objects to be referentially shared, and it supports the construction of complex and compound object spaces. These object spaces are most natural and direct in intelligent office environments.

Further chapters will show how the combination of these three paradigms provides an easy to use, intuitive environment for intelligent offices.

8

GRAPHICAL USER INTERFACES

■ 8.1 INTRODUCTION

This chapter turns to the impact of graphical user interfaces on intelligent office environments. The modern user interfaces are revolutionizing the application of computers by users with diverse needs and backgrounds. The popularity of the Macintosh, the "computer for the rest of us," is due to its intuitive interface, which allows the user to perform complex tasks with little knowledge of operating systems, programs, or memorized commands.

The mouse as a pointing device allows users to perform activities, such as invoking procedures and moving data, without memorizing commands. The desktop metaphor makes computers usable by the general population of computer novices and nonprogrammers, for whom the personal computer was invented.

One of the main goals of graphical user interfaces is to simplify the commands used for performing tasks on the computer. For example, systems like Xerox Star or Apple Macintosh provide generic commands such as cut, paste, and delete, which apply to different types of objects. The user selects a word, paragraph, or whole sections of a document or graph and then invokes the menu option once to use that option on the entire selection.

In recent years, computer giants such as IBM, Microsoft, Digital, and Hewlett-Packard (HP) have placed greater emphasis in migrating toward more friendly user interfaces. Command-driven user interfaces are being replaced by windows, menu bars, pull-down menus, and dialog boxes. The mouse remains the primary pointing device to select menu choices.

IBM has directed its efforts toward building a common user interface throughout its architectures, based on System Application Architecture (SAA). Large independent software vendors such as Lotus, Microsoft, and Computer Associate are also adapting their tools to be compatible with SAA.

8.1.1 Chapter Organization

This chapter first examines the historical evolution of user interfaces from the early days of timesharing systems to the modern graphical user interfaces. Section 8.3 presents the common user interface terms used in this industry. Section 8.4 discusses two popular PC-based graphical user interfaces: Microsoft Windows and the Macintosh Toolbox. Section 8.5 explores some of the popular object-oriented user interfaces such as Actor, MacApp, and NextStep. Section 8.6 presents ToolBook as an hypermedia presentation tool, and then Section 8.7 concludes by examining HP NewWave.

8.2 HISTORY

Until recently, the primary means of communication with computers have been through command-based interfaces. In command-based interfaces, users have to learn a large set of commands to get their job done. In early computer systems, paper tapes, cards, and batch jobs were the primary means of communicating these commands to the computers. Later, timesharing systems allowed the use of CRT terminals to communicate and interact with the computer. These early systems were heavily burdened by users trying to share precious computer resources, such as the CPU and peripherals.

Batch systems and timesharing led to command-based user interfaces. Users had to memorize commands and options or consult a large set of user manuals. In some systems, meaningful terms were substituted for command names to help the end-user. In other systems, the end-user had to memorize arcane sequences of keystrokes to accomplish certain tasks. Early computer users were engineers and "expert users," who were very interested in learning about the computer systems and the technology. Command-based interfaces were acceptable or tolerated by the majority of these users.

In the 1970s, computers were introduced to a new class of non-technical users, such as secretaries and managers. These new users were less interested in learning computer technology and more interested in getting their jobs done through the machine. The command-based interfaces caused many of these new users to develop computer phobia. (Imagine memorizing lengthy commands such as "Control-Shift-D" to delete a word or "Control-Escape-D" to undelete a word.)

To make life easier for the end user, many devices have been invented to control, monitor, and display information. The early (and still widely used) peripherals are the keyboard and the video terminal. But user interfaces did not change dramatically until the mouse was introduced commercially in the late 1970s.

The mouse was in use before the 1970s, but only in research groups. In the 1960s, projects at SRI International, MIT, and other universities led to the invention of pointing devices and windowing systems (Perry and Voelcker, 1989). The mouse and joystick were among the pointing devices invented in this period. These research pioneers also invented the notions of splitting the screen, to allow the display of multiple windows, and the direct manipulation of objects.

In the 1970s, researchers at Xerox Palo Alto Research Center (PARC) designed powerful new workstations armed with graphical user interfaces. Their experiments concentrated on applying the associative memory of the end user combined with direct manipulation capabilities (Johnson *et al.*, 1989). The basic assumption of these new workstations was that one user could have a powerful desktop computer totally dedicated to his or her task. Thus, in addition to performing the user task, the computer could also provide a much more intuitive and easy-to-use environment.

To apply the user's associative memory, menus and dialog boxes are used for interacting with the user. Instead of memorizing commands for each stage, the user selects a command from a menu bar displaying a list of available commands.

For example, Figure 8.1 shows the menu bar from the Microsoft Write utility. This menu bar displays a list of available commands, such as File, Edit, and Search. When the mouse is clicked on any of these commands, the appropriate action is taken. Pull-down and pop-up menus display options (commands) available for each selection. Figure 8.2 shows the pull-down menu displayed when the "Character" menu item is selected. The user can then select from different character styles.

Dialog boxes allow more complex interaction between the user and the computer. They employ a large collection of control objects, such as dials, buttons, scroll bars, and editable boxes. Figure 8.3 shows how a dialog box is used to open a file. This dialog box contains two buttons (Open and Cancel), an edit box that allows the file name to be entered, and a scroll region allowing navigation through the list of files and directories available on the disk. Clicking on the Open button causes the file to be opened.

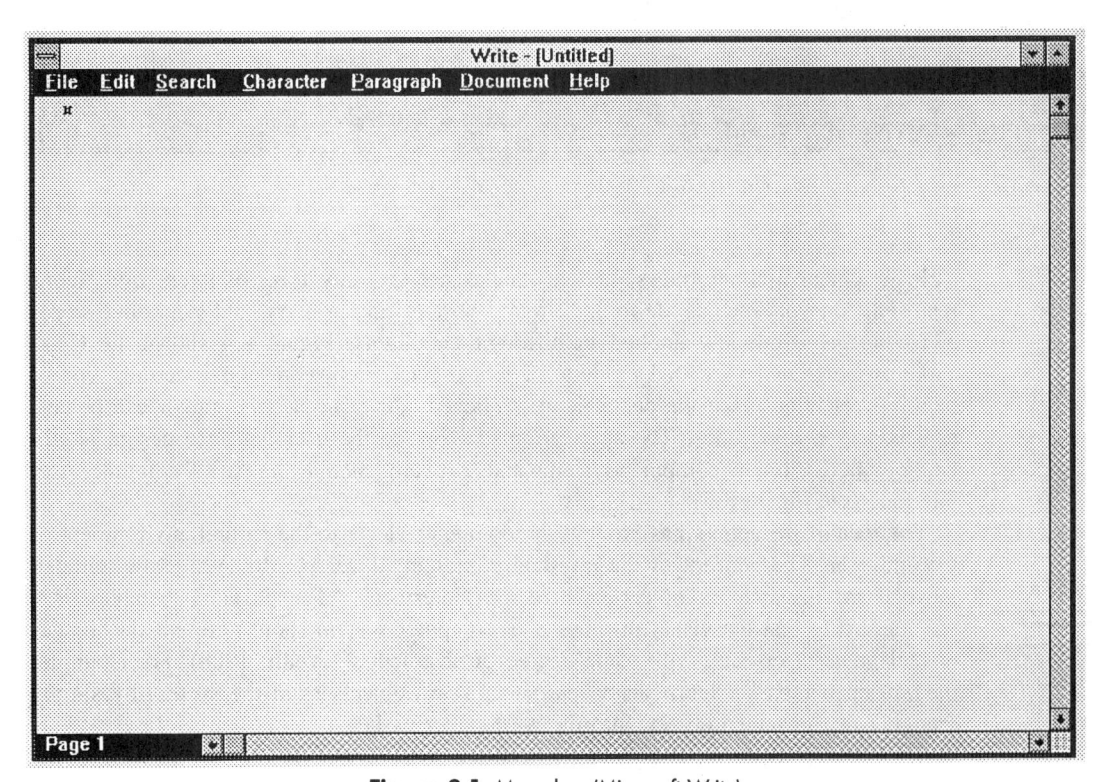

Figure 8.1 Menu bar (Microsoft Write).

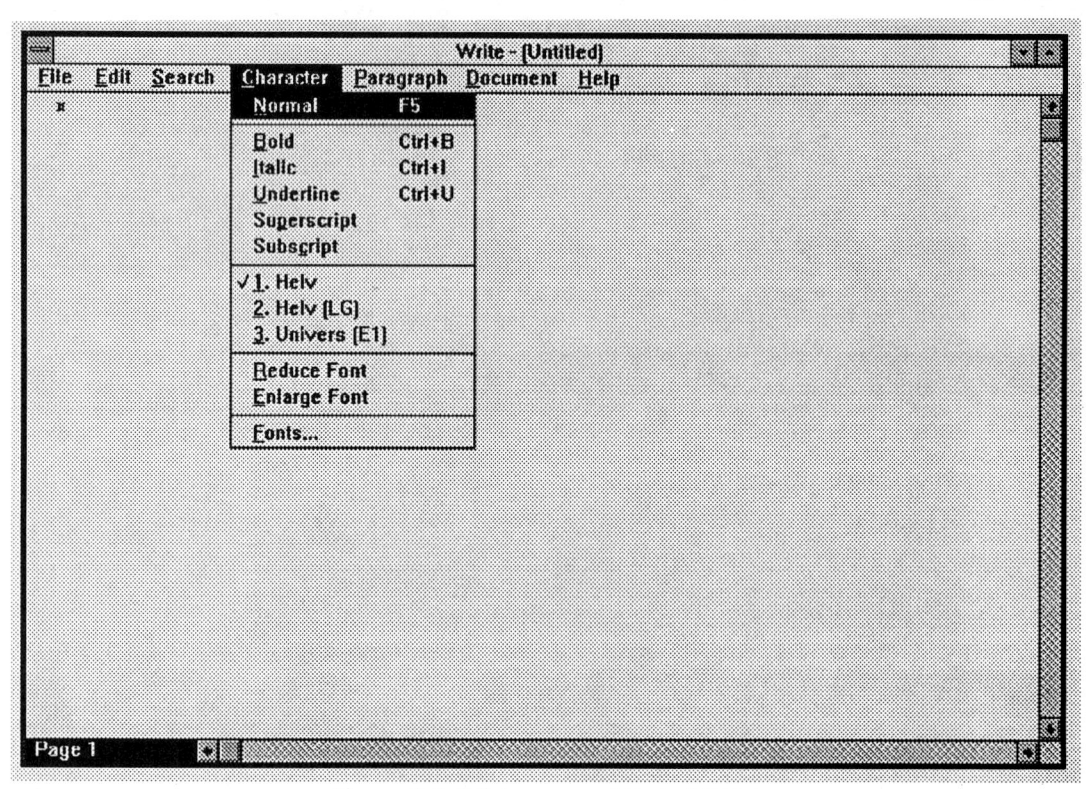

Figure 8.2 Pull-down menu (Microsoft Write).

In graphical user interfaces, textual data is not the only form of interaction. Icons represent concepts such as file folders, waste baskets, and printers, and symbolize words and concepts commonly applied in different paradigms. Figure 8.4 shows the Corel Systems CorelDRAW! with its palette of icons. Each icon represents a certain type of painting behavior. Once the pencil icon is clicked, for example, the cursor can behave as a pencil to draw lines. The application of icons to the user interface design is still being explored in new computer systems and software, such as the NeXT computer user interface (see Figure 8.5).

The idea of metaphors has brought the computer closer to the natural environment of the end user. The concept of the physical paradigm, developed by Alan Kay, initiated most of the research for object-oriented user interfaces. "The physical metaphor is a way of saying that the visual displays of a computer system should present the images of real physical objects, with some degree of abstraction" (Veith, 1988). For example, the wastepaper basket icon can be used to discard objects from the system by simply dragging the unwanted objects into the wastepaper basket.

The desktop metaphor has probably been the most famous paradigm. Because of the large set of potential office users, this metaphor can have the most dramatic effect. In

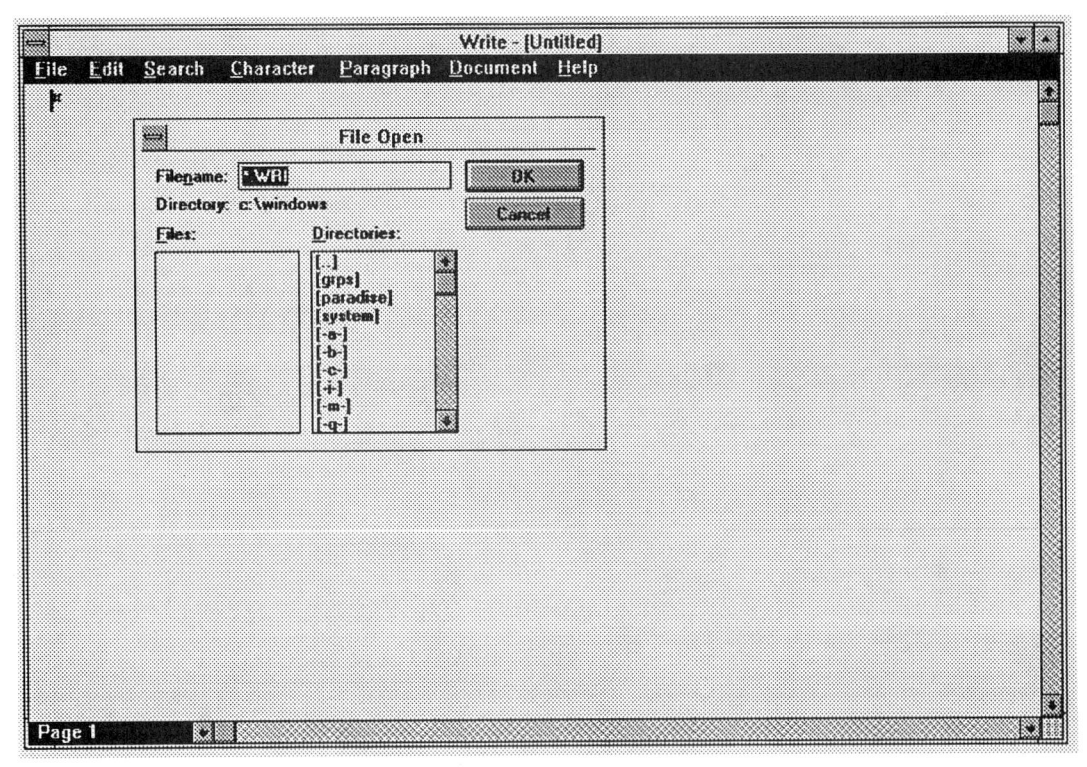

Figure 8.3 Dialog box (Microsoft Write).

this paradigm, the computer presents information and objects as they would appear and behave in an office, using icons for folders, in-basket, out-basket, and calendars.

OfficeVision from IBM relies heavily on the desktop metaphor in its graphic user interfaces. It provides an environment for secretaries and executives to represent and manipulate office objects such as files, folders, and even the telephone.

In systems employing the desktop metaphor and direct manipulation, end user data and the application are not separate entities. The object representing the end user information encapsulates the data as well as the procedure required to modify it. In HP's NewWave, for example, an icon representing a report contains data plus information about the word processor used to create the report. When the mouse is clicked on this icon, the processor is invoked and loaded with the report data (see Figure 8.6a).

Object orientation (via physical metaphor) allows novice users to create new applications and compound documents. In Metaphor's DIS, an end user can create ad hoc applications graphically by connecting icons representing tools such as database management systems, spreadsheets and graphics (see Figure 8.6b). Furthermore, the user can graphically direct individual icons to produce certain results. For example, the database management utility can be visually programmed to produce the result of an SQL query

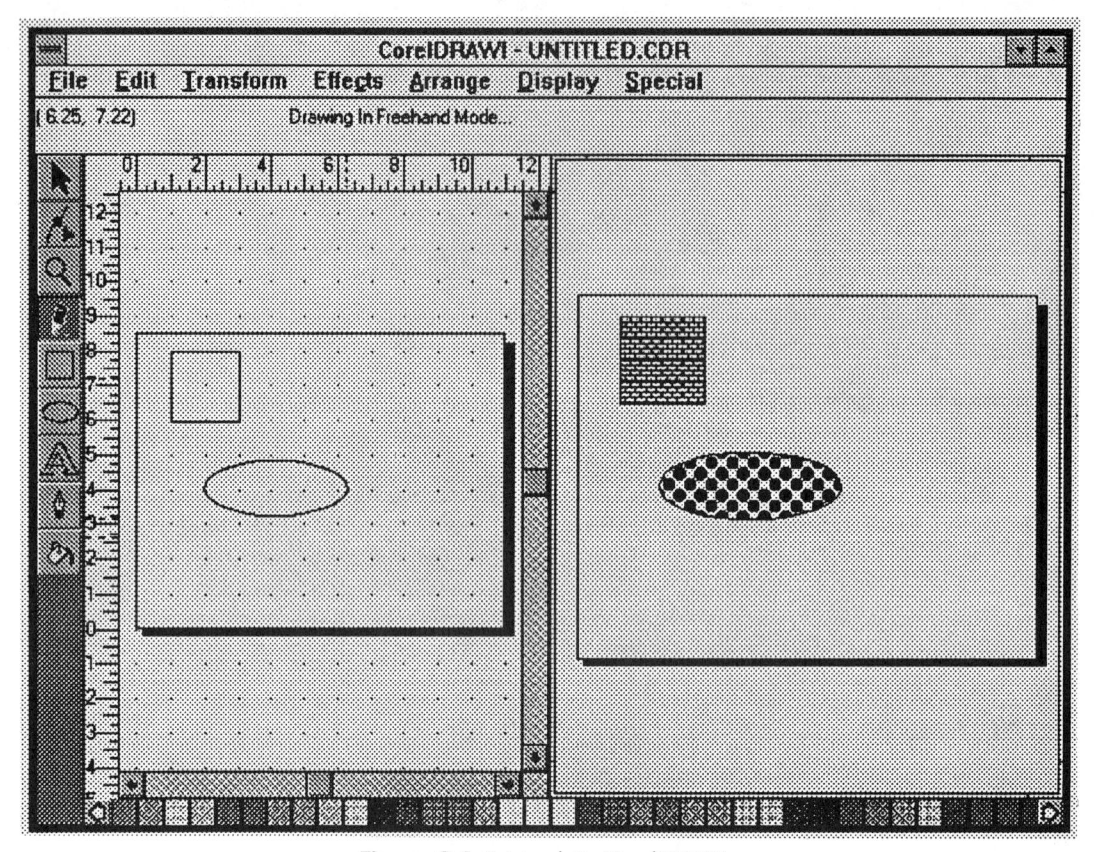

Figure 8.4 Paint palette (CorelDRAW!).

from a corporate database. Users can create documents composed of different objects such as text, graphics, and images.

Object orientation also comes to the rescue of the software engineer by lightening the burden of user interface development. New user interface concepts require the development of complex software to display screen objects and handle their events. Simple tasks, such as displaying a featureless window, require several pages of code in a high-level language such as C.

To streamline this work, user interface development environments such as MacApp and Actor provide libraries composed of object hierarchies. Each class within the hierarchy defines the attributes necessary for its objects and inherits features from its superclasses. Each object within the hierarchy communicates with other objects in the system by transmitting messages (see Chapter 7). User interface designers can further extend the class hierarchy by adding their own screen object designs. These new screen objects can inherit properties from existing classes. In addition, they can refine old properties or define new properties as needed.

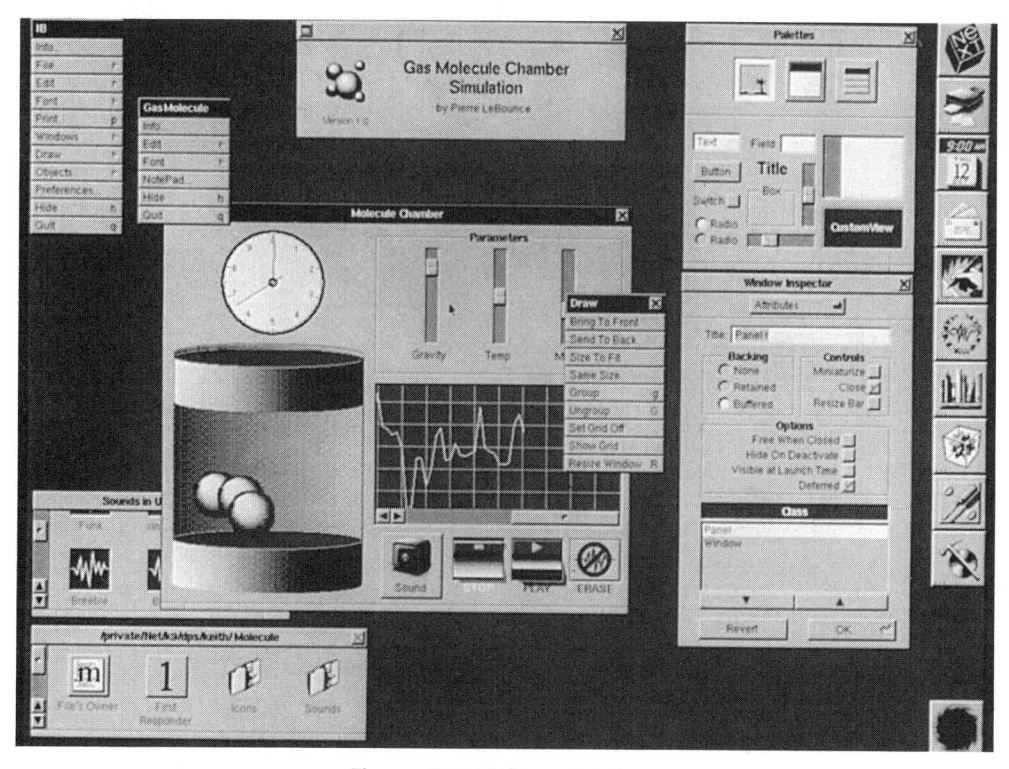

Figure 8.5 NeXT user interface.

The most recent advances in user interface design come from NeXT Corporation. Using the NeXTStep Interface Builder, a designer can quickly develop a user interface graphically by selecting, placing and resizing user interface objects (Webster, 1989). Figure 8.5 depicts the NeXTStep Interface Builder.

■ 8.3 COMMON USER INTERFACE TERMS

This section presents a list of terms commonly used with graphical user interfaces (GUIs). For a more in-depth discussion of GUIs, refer to Johnson *et al.* (1989); Pertzold (1988); Perry *et al.* (1989); Pfaff (1985); and Schneiderman (1987).

1. *Pointing devices*: Pointing devices allow users to point to different parts of the screen. Pointing devices can be used to invoke a command from a list of commands presented in a menu. They can be used to manipulate objects on the screen by selecting objects on the screen, moving objects around the screen, and merging several objects into another object.

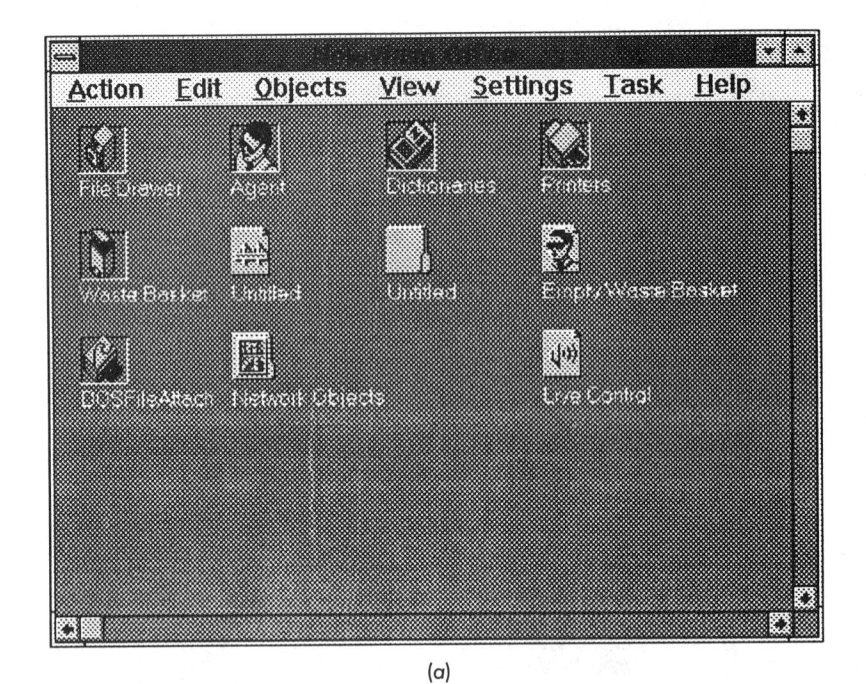

Figure 8.6 Use of icons. (a) HP's NewWave; (b) Metaphor's DIS.

Since the 1960s, a diverse set of tools have been used as pointing devices. These include the light pen, joystick, touch-sensitive screen, and mouse. The popularity of the mouse is due to optimal coordination of hand and eye and easier tracking of the cursor on the screen.

2. *Bit-mapped displays*: As memory chips get denser and cheaper, bit-mapped displays are replacing character based display screens. Bit-mapped displays have several advantages over character displays. Bit-mapped displays are made up of tiny dots (called pixels), and so have much finer resolution than character displays. Bit-mapped displays have graphic manipulation capabilities for vector and raster graphics, which allow presentation of information as appears in the final form on the paper.

3. *Windows*: When a screen is split into several independent regions, each region is called a window. Several applications can display results simultaneously in different windows. Figure 8.7a presents a screen with two windows, one from Microsoft Manager and the other from Corel Systems CorelDRAW!. The end-user can switch from one application to another or share data between applications. Windowing systems can display windows either tiled or overlapped, as shown in Figure 8.7b. Users can organize the screen by resizing the windows, moving related windows closer, or changing windows into icons.

4. *Menus*: A menu displays a list of commands available within an application. Figure 8.8a presents Microsoft Word for Windows with its menu bar. The menu bar contains a list of words or icons, called menu items, that represent a command or a function. Menu items are invoked by moving the cursor onto the menu item and clicking the mouse to select it.

When a menu item is invoked, it may cause other menus, called pull-down menus, to appear. Pull-down menus present a group of related commands or options for a menu item. Figure 8.8b presents the File pulldown menu for Microsoft Word for Windows. The end user can select file operations, such as opening a file or saving the existing file.

5. *Dialog boxes*: Dialog boxes are used to interact with the user. For example, when the user chooses to print a file, in Microsoft Word for Windows the dialog box shown in Figure 8.9a is displayed to get additional information, including the number of copies and the page numbers to be printed.

Alert boxes are dialog boxes that indicate actual or potential error conditions. In Figure 8.9b, an alert box gives the end user one more chance to save the changes before exiting from Microsoft Word for Windows.

Dialog boxes use a wide range of screen control elements to communicate with the user. Figure 8.10 displays some of these control elements. For example, an edit box is used to specify the magnification, radio buttons permit selection of an item such as print quality from a list of choices.

6. *Icons*: Icons provide a symbolic representation of any user-defined object, such as a file or an address book. Different types of objects are represented by specific types

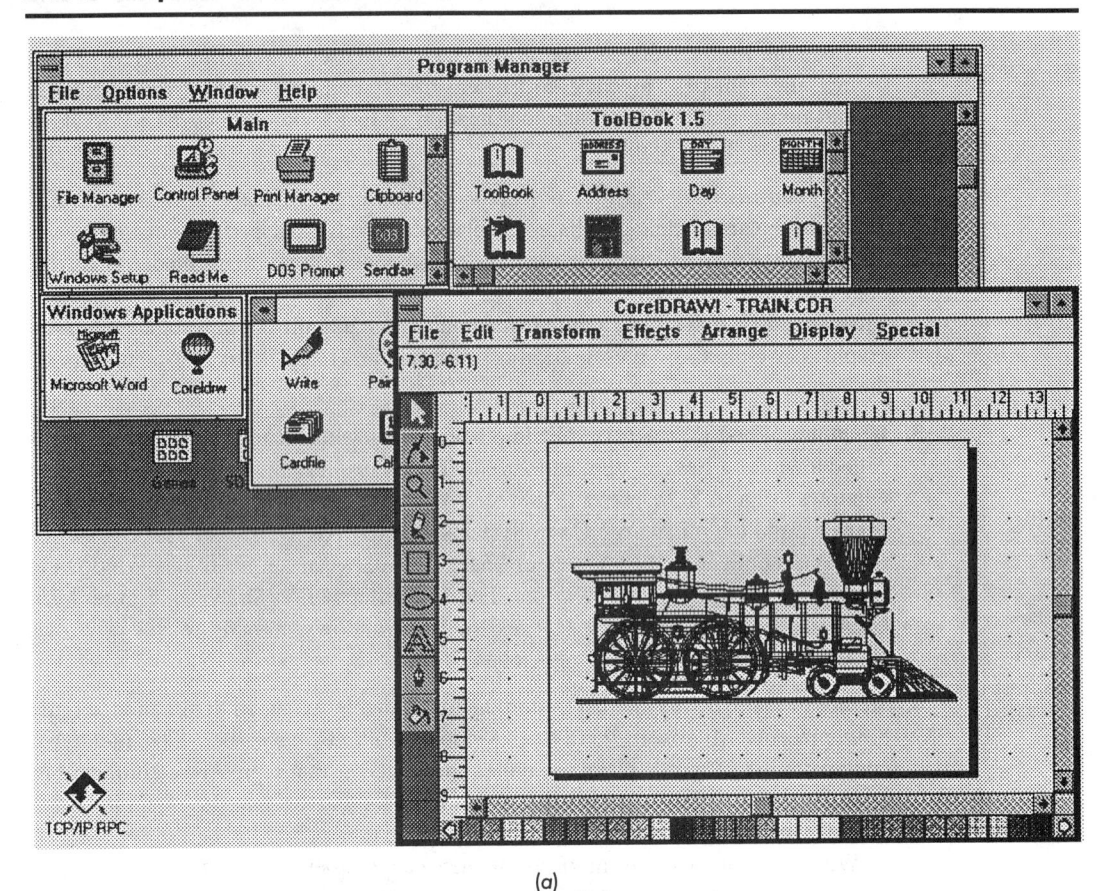

Figure 8.7 Use of windows. (a) Microsoft Windows, Program Manager and CorelDRAW!

of icons. On a Macintosh, documents representing folders are symbolized by a folder icon (see Figure 8.11). A folder icon contains a group of files or other folder icons. Clicking on the folder icon causes a window to be opened displaying a list of file and folder icons representing the folder's contents. To delete a folder, simply drag its icon into the garbage can icon.

7. *Direct manipulation*: In today's computers, most applications provide a large set of commands, allowing the user to manipulate the application. Direct manipulation simplifies the interface greatly by allowing object manipulation without the need to memorize commands. For example, on a Macintosh, when a display of icons, symbolizing a group of files, is presented, users can manipulate the files by manipulating the icons directly. To move one or more files, the user simply drags the file icons from one folder to another.

8. *Desktop metaphor*: In the desktop metaphor, users are not aware of programs or applications. Users deal with icons of objects that might appear in an office on a

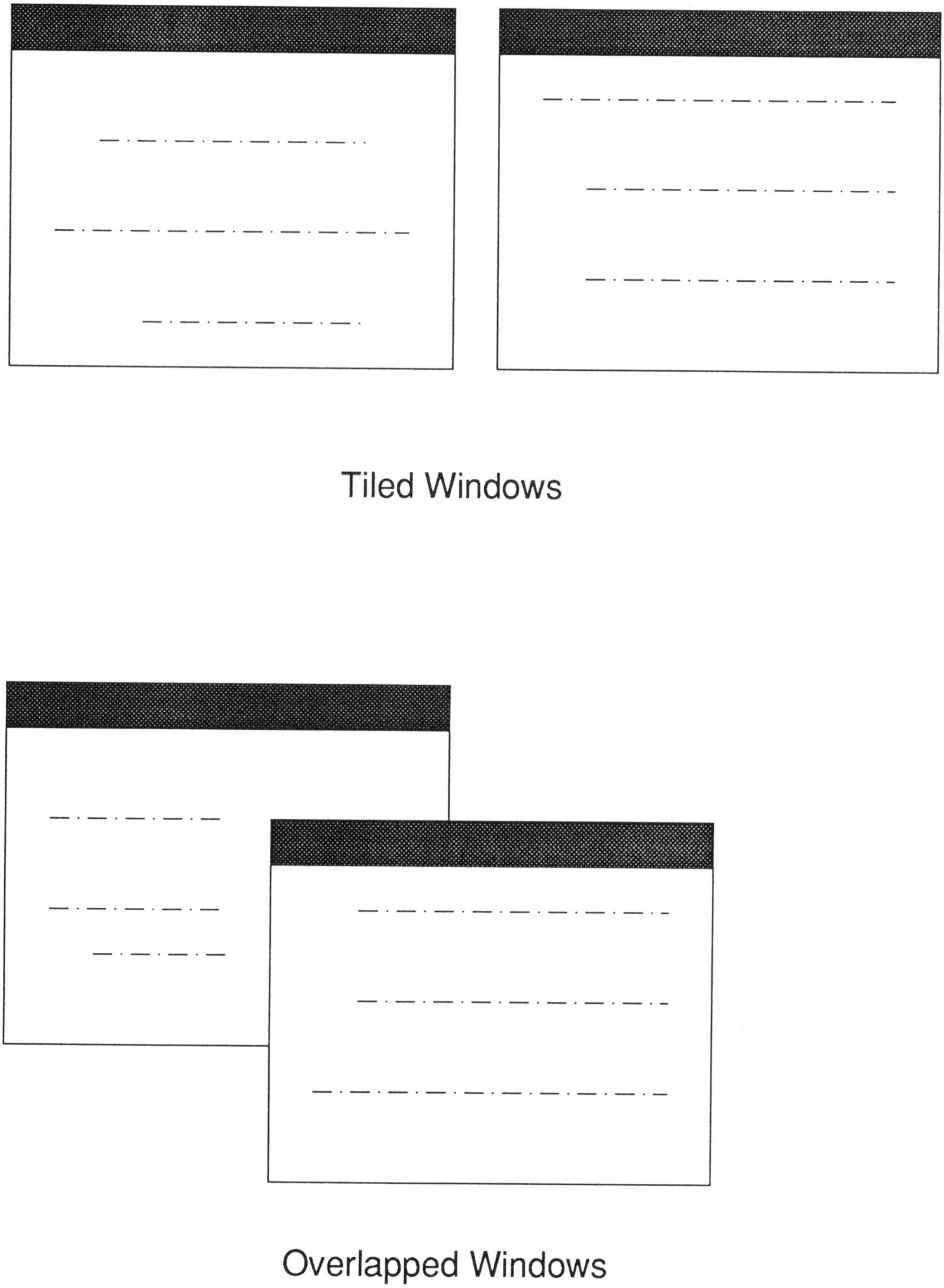

8.3 Common User Interface Terms ■ 245

Tiled Windows

Overlapped Windows

(b)

Figure 8.7 (cont) Use of windows. (b) tiled and overlapped windows.

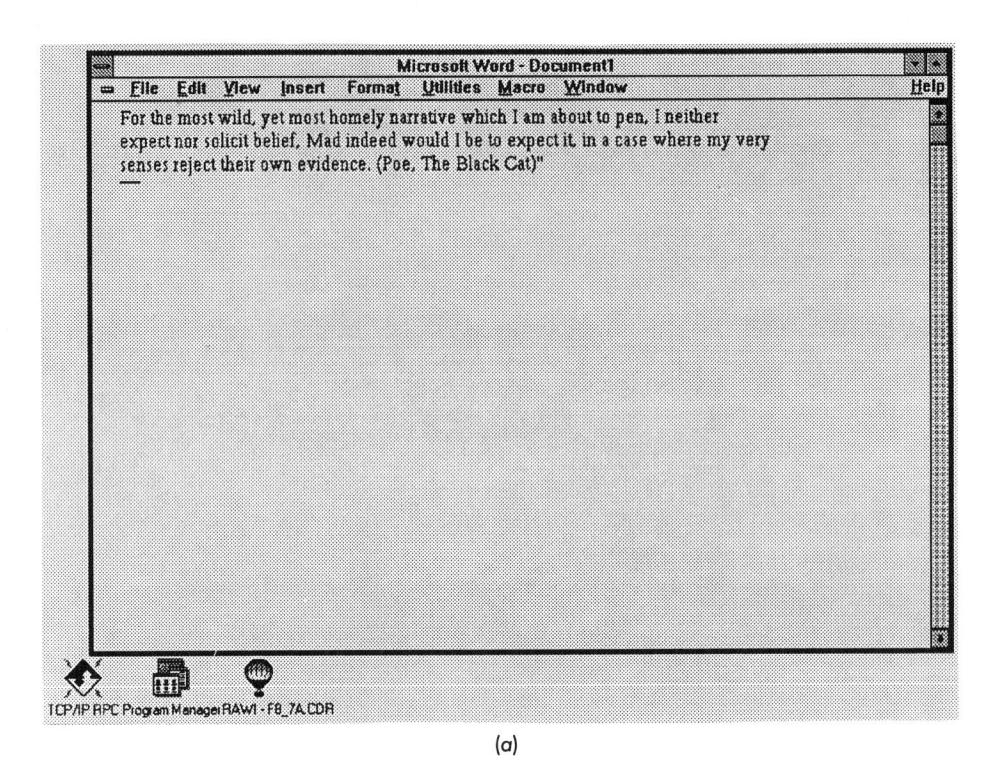

Figure 8.8 Use of menus (Microsoft Word for Windows). (a) menu bar; (b) pull-down menu invoked by clicking the menu bar option.

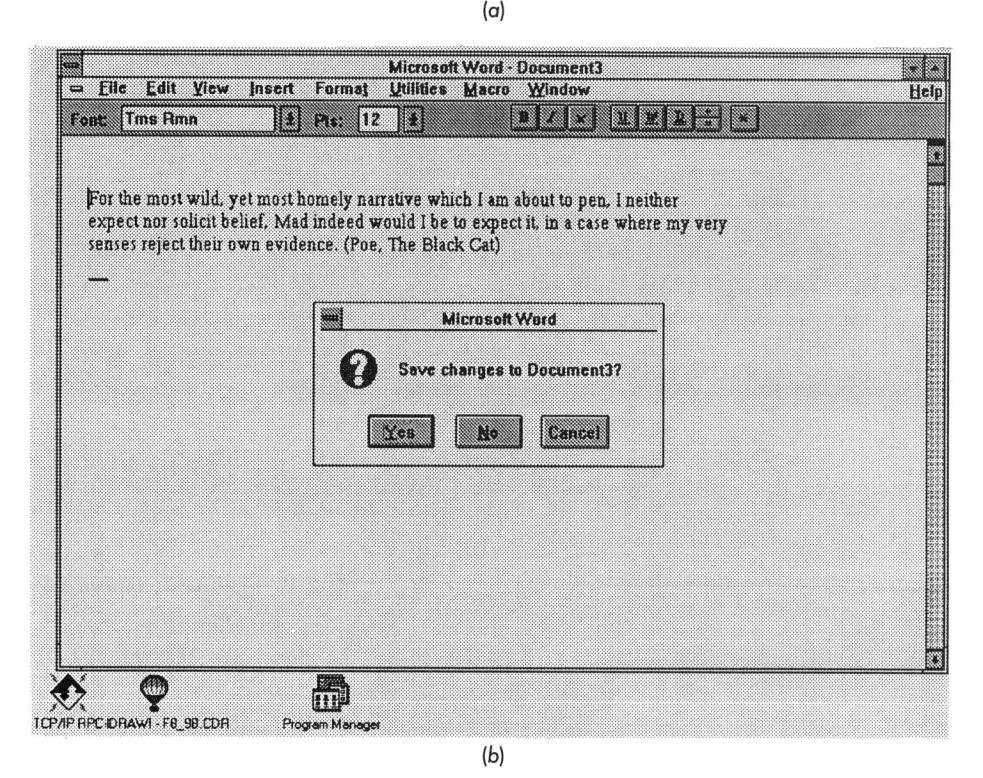

Figure 8.9 Dialog boxes (Microsoft Word for Windows). (a) print specification dialog; (b) alert box.

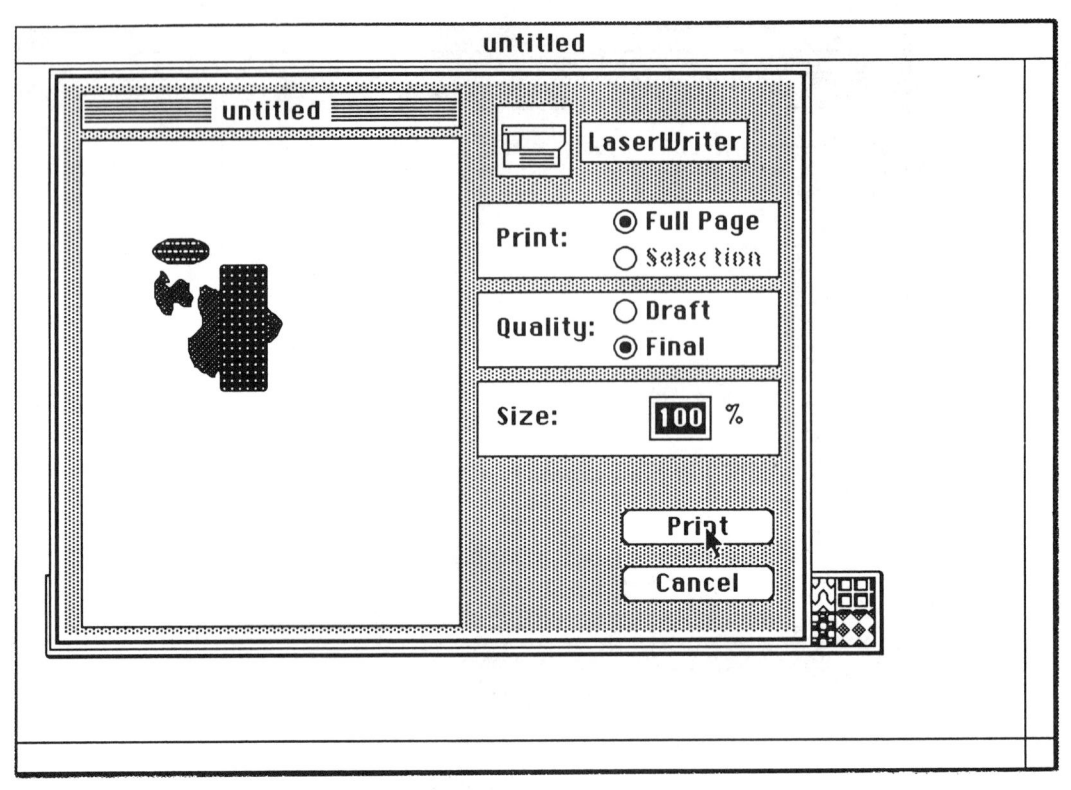

Figure 8.10 Control elements in a dialog box (Ashton-Tate Full Paint).

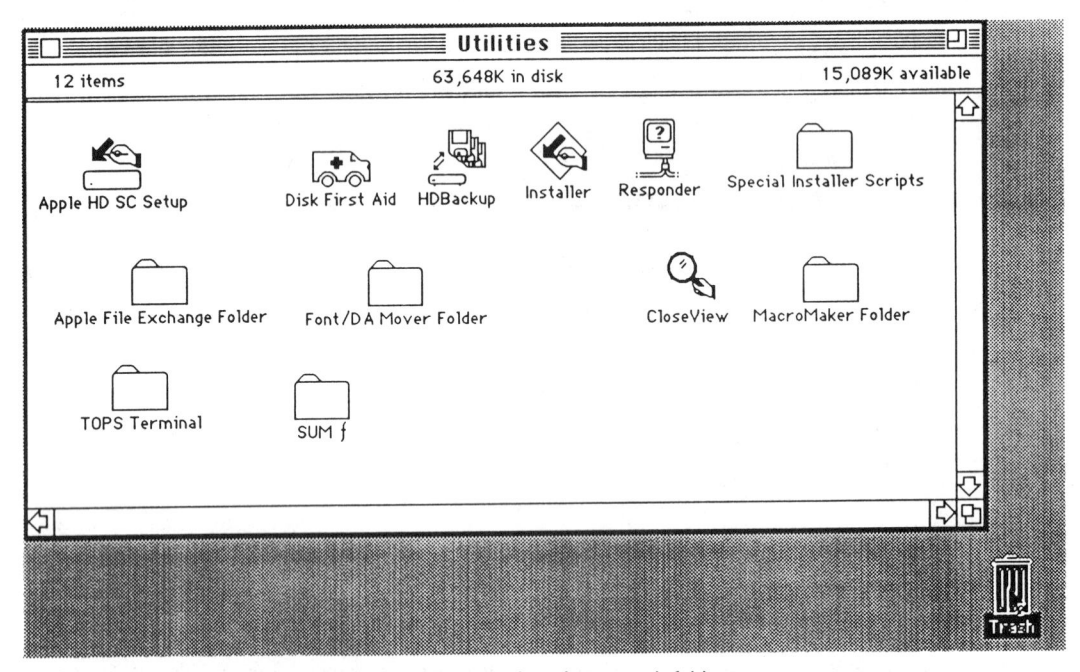

Figure 8.11 Examples of Macintosh folder icons.

desktop, such as files, folders, drawers, a clipboard, an in-box, and an out-box. Instead of typing commands to start the word processor and load a report file, users merely click the mouse on an icon representing the report. The word processor is invoked and loads the report file implicitly. The Xerox Star was one of the first systems that introduced this concept (Johnson *et al.*, 1989). Today, other computing environments, such as the Macintosh, Metaphor DIS, and HP NewWave, provide this capability.

9. *Graphical User Interfaces*: GUIs are systems that allow creation and manipulation of user interfaces employing windows, menus, icons, dialog boxes, mouse, and keyboard event handling. Smalltalk MVC, the Macintosh Toolbox, Microsoft Windows, and X Windows are some examples of GUIs. Sections 8.4.1 and 8.4.2 cover Microsoft Windows and the Macintosh Toolbox in more depth.

■ 8.4 GUI ON PCs

This section presents graphical user interfaces (GUIs) available on personal computers. Two popular GUIs, Microsoft Windows and the Macintosh Toolbox, will be covered to provide a broad picture of the subject. A great many popular GUIs now exist, including X Windows, Smalltalk MVC, NeXT NextStep, and more (see Section 8.5.3 for the NeXT machine). Several books and many articles are completely dedicated to this topic. Some of these include Brown and Cunningham (1989); Hayes and Baran (1989); Pfaff (1985); and Schneiderman (1987).

The GUIs provide an application programming interface (API) that allow users to do the following:

1. Create screen objects
2. Draw screen objects
3. Monitor mouse activates
4. Report screen events to the user

Most GUIs use an object-oriented approach to deal with screen object manipulation. For example, a template (class definition) is used to introduce a new type of windows or icons. To display a screen object, an object is first instantiated and then drawn on the screen. Communication about the state of screen objects is accomplished through messages sent between the application and the user interface engine. For example, when a mouse is clicked on a menu bar, a message is sent to the event handler responsible for the menu bar.

8.4.1 Microsoft Windows

Windows is the most popular GUI for IBM Personal Computers. Windows was announced November 1983 and released November 1985. According to Microsoft, over two million copies of Windows have been sold as of 1989 (Seymour, 1989b).

The next several sections examine Microsoft Windows in more detail, including its functionality, object-oriented features, windows, resources, and Graphics Device Interface.

8.4.1.1 Feature Overview

Windows provides an environment that enhances DOS in many ways. The major benefits of Windows are the following:

1. *Common look and feel across applications*: Windows presents a common look and feel across all applications. A user who is familiar with one or two Windows applications, can easily learn another one.
2. *Device independence*: Windows presents a device-independent interface to applications. Unlike most of today's DOS applications, a Windows application is not bound to the underlying hardware (such as a mouse, keyboard or display). Windows shields the application from this responsibility. The application deals with the Windows API to manipulate any underlying devices.
3. *Multitasking*: Windows provides nonpreemptive multitasking support. Users can have several applications in progress at the same time. Each application can be active in a separate window.
4. *Memory management*: Windows also provides memory management to break the 640Kbyte limitation of MS-DOS. An application can use extended memory, share data segments with other applications, and swap unwanted segments to disk.
5. *Support for existing DOS applications*: Windows allows most of the standard MS-DOS applications to run under it directly. Any application that does not directly control the PC's hardware or use the PC BIOS or MS-DOS software interrupts can run in its own window.
6. *Data sharing*: Windows allows data transfer between applications using the Clipboard. Any type of data can be transferred from one window to another with the Clipboard. The Dynamic Data Exchange (DDE) protocol defines how two applications can share information, including bitmap, metafile, character strings, and other data formats.

8.4.1.2 Creation and Manipulation of a Window

MS Windows presents a predefined style for user-defined windows. This section presents the structure of a window, followed by a discussion of window creation and manipulation.

8.4.1.2.1 Structure of a Window

Figure 8.12 displays possible screen elements for a Microsoft window. The caption bar (or title bar) displays the name of application within the window. The system menu box contains names of commands available in all applications, such as minimize, maximize, revise, and close. The minimize box, clicked once, reduces the window to an icon, and the maximize box enlarges the window.

The menu bar contains a list of commands used in the application. The client area is the area inside the window which is under the application control.

Scroll bars can be used to control vertical and horizontal scrolling. Scrolling is achieved by clicking on the arrows or dragging the scroll thumb.

8.4.1.2.2 Creating Windows

MS Windows is object-oriented to some extent. To create a window, defines a class specifying the properties desired. Each window created on the screen is a member of

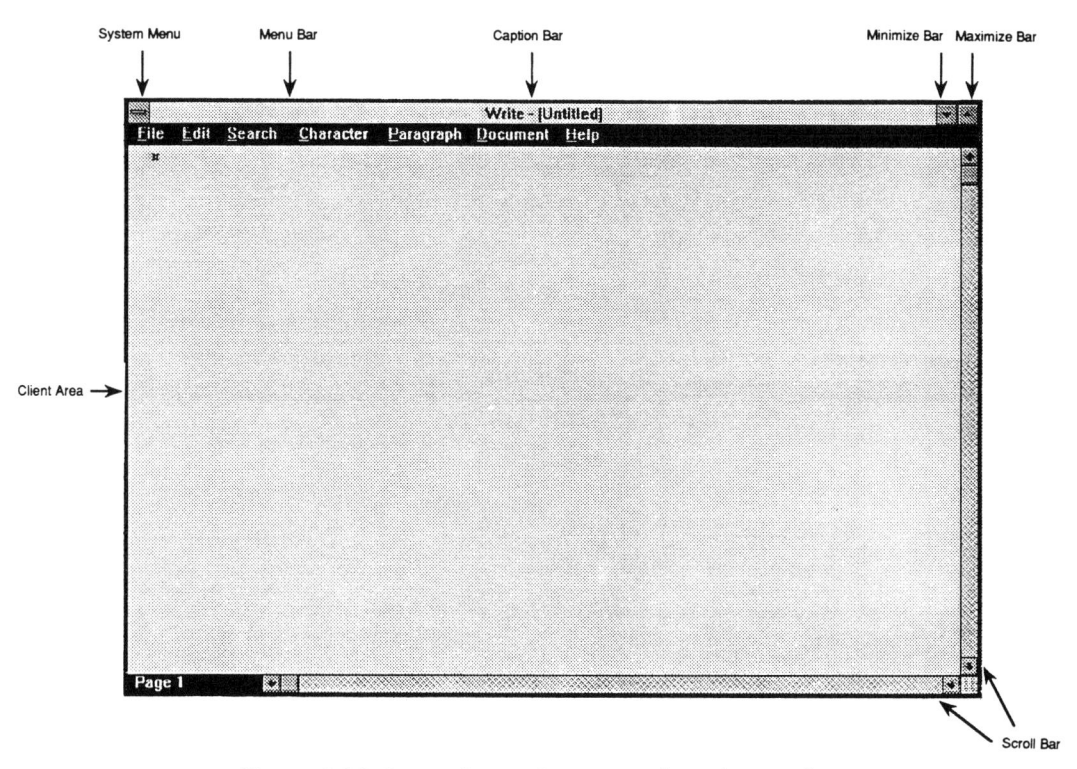

Figure 8.12 Screen elements for a Microsoft Windows window.

some user-defined window class. Window classes are created by application programs. Several window classes can be active simultaneously. Each window class in turn can have several instances active at the same time. There are no predefined generic window classes that comes with MS windows.

To create a window, the following steps must be taken:

1. Set up a window class structure, which defines the attributes of the window class. Attributes that can be defined include the following:
   - The window function, which handles all messages for this class
   - The icon and the cursor used for this class of windows
   - The background color of the client area
   - The window class menu
   - The redrawing function used when resizing horizontally or vertically
2. Define the window class. MS Windows refers to this process as registering the window class. Once a window class is registered, it is accessible to all Windows applications.

252 ▪ Graphical User Interfaces

3. Create instances. After a window class is registered, then several instances can be generated by one or more applications.

Once a window has been created, an application can choose to display the window, resize the window, display additional information in the client area, and so on. As stated previously, most of these actions are taken by sending messages from the application to the Windows run-time system.

8.4.1.3 Pop-up and Child Windows

Pop-up and child windows are special types of windows that communicate information between the application and the end user.

Pop-up windows are used to communicate information such as help, warning, and error messages from the application to the user. They remain on the screen for a short period of time. Figure 8.13 displays an example of a pop-up window. In this example, the pop-up window displays information about a given file, such as date and time of

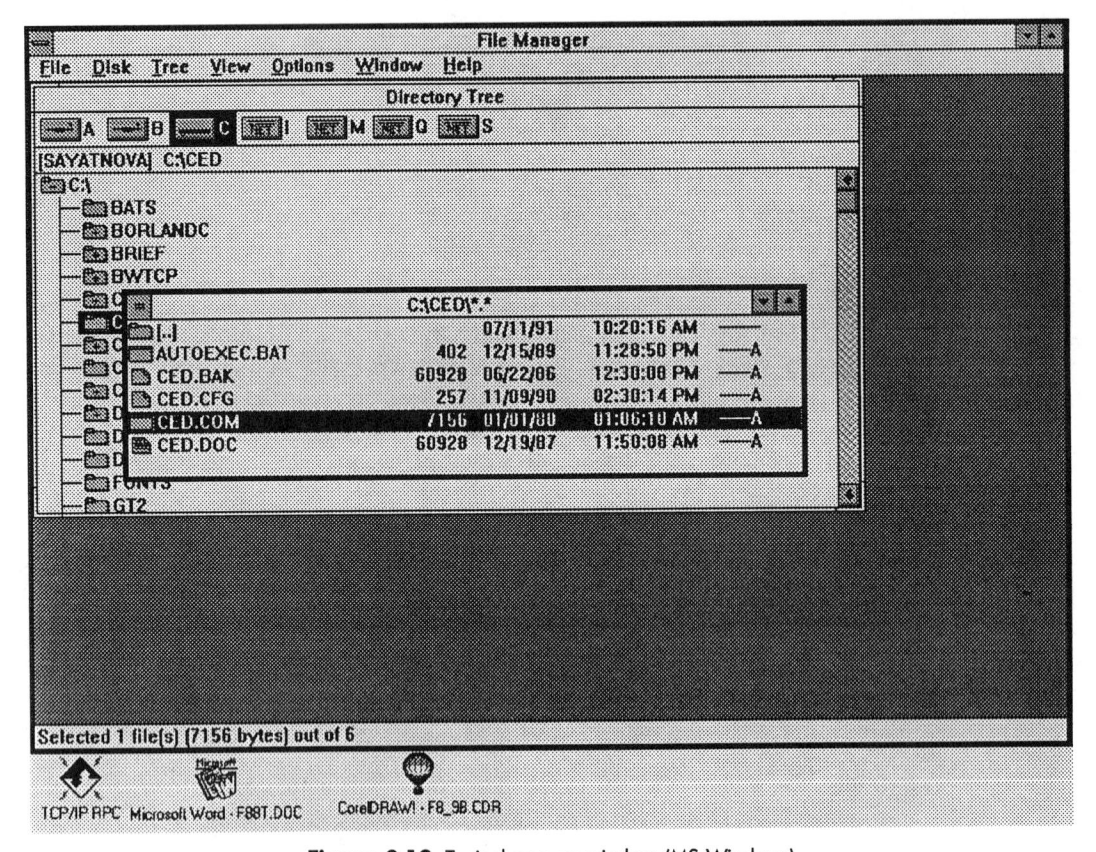

Figure 8.13 Typical pop-up window (MS Windows).

creation and the file's size. Dialog boxes, a more sophisticated form of pop-up windows, are described later in this section.

Child windows, as the name implies, are siblings of another window. They are commonly used as part of a dialog box. Most often, child windows are used to allow the end user to control the application and input data to the application. For example, buttons and scroll bars within a dialog box are represented via child windows.

A child window is defined as a separate window class by itself. It has its own window function to handle messages from Windows. For example, a mouse event within the boundaries of a child window causes Windows to send a message to the child's window function for processing.

A child window can communicate with its parent window by transmitting messages back and forth. Through messages, the parent window can change the state of the child window or the child window can inform the parent window about its current state. A developer can define child windows that can be controlled by any user-defined operation. For example, Figure 8.14 shows the Microsoft Windows File Manager. The drives "A" and "C" are examples of user-defined child windows. When the user clicks on the drive "A" icon, the File Manager displays the directory hierarchy on this drive.

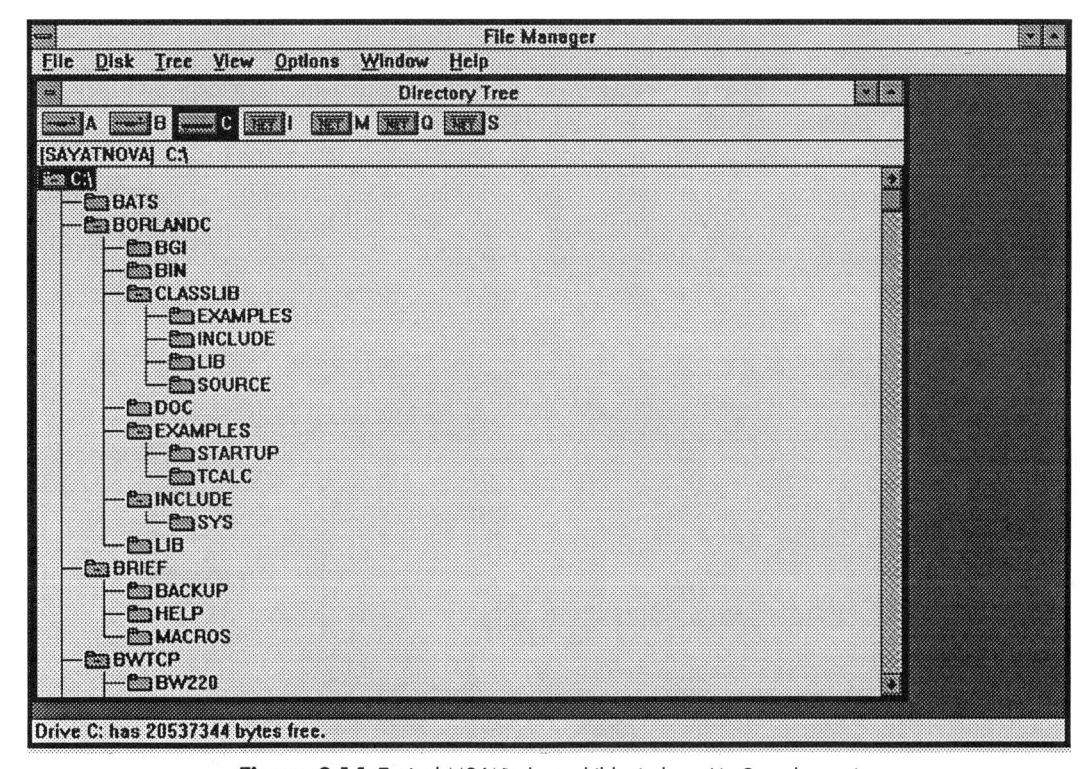

Figure 8.14 Typical MS Windows child windows (A, C, and so on).

MS Windows provides a collection of predefined controls, shown in Figure 8.15, which are the most common usage of child windows. Windows provides the following predefined classes:

1. *Buttons:* Windows provides eleven styles of predefined buttons. Once a button is clicked, it tells its parent window about its current status. A user-defined text string can be associated with each button to provide a description of the functionality provided (for example, "OK" and "Cancel" buttons, or time zone buttons with text "PDT" and "EDT").

   Some of the more popular styles of buttons, depicted in Figure 8.15a, are the following:
   - A push button is used to initiate an action such as canceling a command or computing results. The text identifying the push button appears inside the button and represents the action taken when the button is clicked.
   - A radio button behaves very much like the buttons for preset stations on a car radio. Once clicked, it stays pressed, indicating that it is "on." A set of radio buttons can be used to represent a set of mutually exclusive conditions. For example, three radio buttons can be used to represent parity information: even, odd, and none.
   - Check boxes are used as binary switches. Clicking the box turns the switch on if it was off and off if it was on. While the switch is on, an × appears in the box. Turning the switch off causes the × to disappear.
   - Three-state buttons are very much like checkbox buttons, except that they can represent a three-state switch (on, off, disabled).
   - A group box is used to encapsulate other buttons into a group.

2. *Scroll bars:* Windows provides horizontal and vertical scroll bars, shown in Figure 8.15b. This type of control is useful for showing data that is not displayed in its entirety because it is too large to fit on the screen.

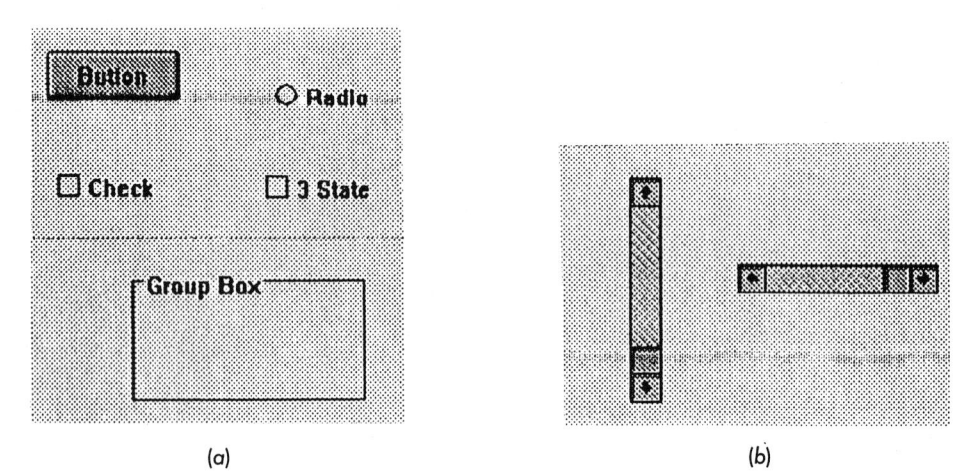

Figure 8.15 Microsoft Windows controls. (a) buttons; (b) scroll bars.

3. *Edit boxes:* These allow textual information to be entered. For example, an edit box can be used to retrieve a new file name, as shown in Figure 8.15c. The text in edit control can be left- or right-justified or centered and can have multiple line input. A scrolling option is provided to scroll left, right, up, and down the edit window. Cut, copy, or paste operations using the mouse are also supported.
4. *Static boxes:* This class of items displays a box with associated text. This class of child windows does not handle any message from the mouse or keyboard. They are most often used to contain a group of other child windows. Figure 8.15d displays a static control object containing a group of radio buttons.
5. *List boxes:* This class allows a list of strings to be displayed and one or more of these strings selected. For example, a list box can be used to display a list of file names and allow one or more of these files to be selected, as shown in Figure 8.15e.
6. *Combo Boxes:* This class is a combination of the edit class and list box class. Often, only the edit box of an combo box is displayed. The user can enter a new selection by typing the selection in the edit box or click on the down arrow and pick an item from the list box, as shown in Figure 8.15f.

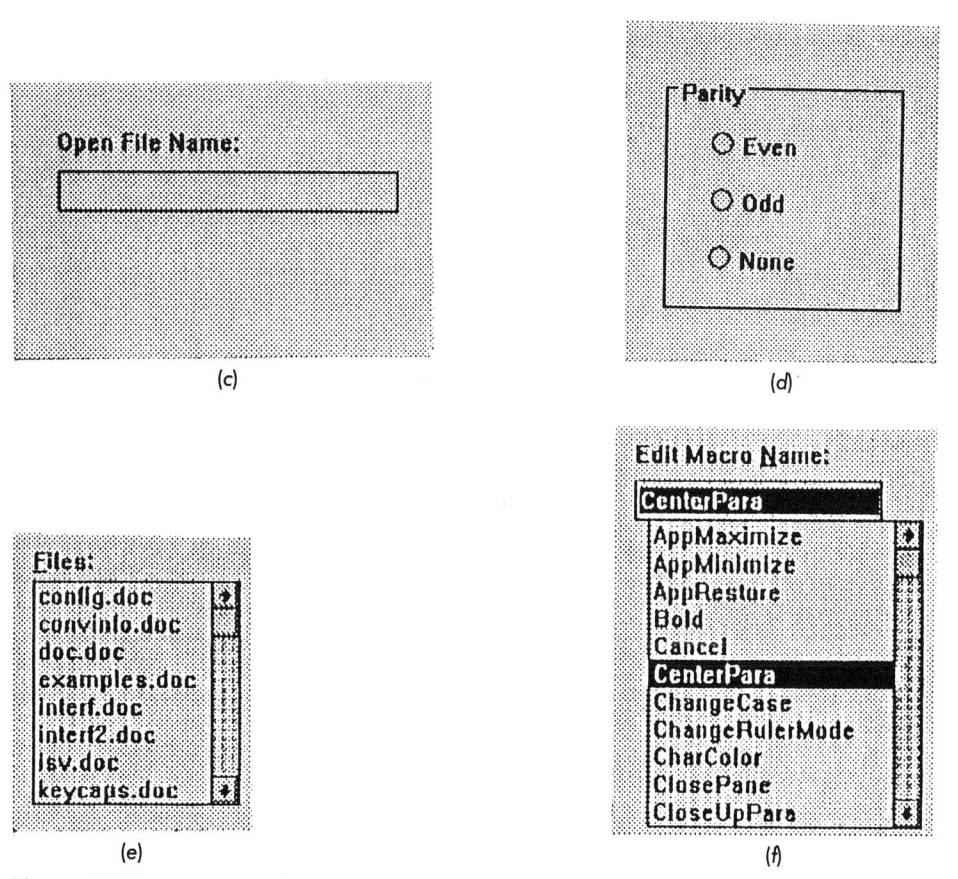

Figure 8.15 (cont) Microsoft Windows controls. (c) edit box; (d) static box; (e) list box; (f) combo box.

8.4.1.4 Resources

Resources are used to manage windows and user-defined objects. MS Windows provides nine kinds of resources to application developers: icons, cursors, menus, dialog boxes, fonts, bitmaps, char strings, user-defined resources, and keyboard accelerators.

1. *Icons and cursors:* Windows defines a few types of icons and cursors. An icon or a cursor is essentially a bitmap region that symbolizes a window or a cursor. A developer can also define their own icon or cursor using the IconEdit utility.
2. *Menus:* Each window can have its own menu bar. A menu item can be a character string or a bitmap. Each item of a menu bar can in turn have a pop-up menu presenting a list of options. Currently, Windows does not support nesting of pop-up menus within other pop-up menus, but a pop-up menu can invoke a dialog box. When a menu item is selected, Windows sends one or more messages to the window function of the window containing the menu bar. These messages can be interpreted to perform the function corresponding to that menu item.
3. *Dialog boxes:* These provide another way to obtain information from the end user. Dialog boxes are much more flexible than menu bars or pop-up menus. The end user can type in a string as input to a dialog box option. Dialog boxes usually contain a group of child windows, such as buttons, scroll bars, and edit boxes. Like windows, dialog boxes have a function for processing messages received from the user on selection of options.

    Generally, dialog boxes appear as a pop-up window. After the user selects the option from the dialog box, the dialog box disappears. Figure 8.16 depicts an example of a dialog box that contains an edit box, two list boxes, and OK and CANCEL buttons. The end user can specify the name of a file either by selecting from the list box or by typing the name of the file in the edit box. When the user clicks on the Open button, the application will open the selected file.
4. *Fonts:* Windows provides a few families of fonts with different sizes and shapes: Modern, Swiss, Roman, Helvetica, and Script. Applications such as word processors and desktop publishing can define additional fonts as needed.
5. *Bitmaps:* These are used to represent icons or cursors or to draw pictures on the screen. Both monochrome and color bitmaps can be defined.
6. *Character strings:* Character strings are handled as resources mainly to provide a manageable solution to internationalization of a window application. Instead of including a character string as part of the code, it can be placed in a resource file and handled as a resource. Once in a resource file, different versions of the same character string resource file can exist for different languages. This separation of the character strings from the code makes internationalizing and maintaining the application much easier.
7. *User-Defined Resources:* This type can be used for any purpose and will support any user-defined data type. Any arbitrary data can be managed as a user-defined resource.
8. *Keyboard Accelerators:* A keyboard accelerator is a combination of keys that can generate a Windows message. These key combinations can represent a menu item or any action chosen by the application.

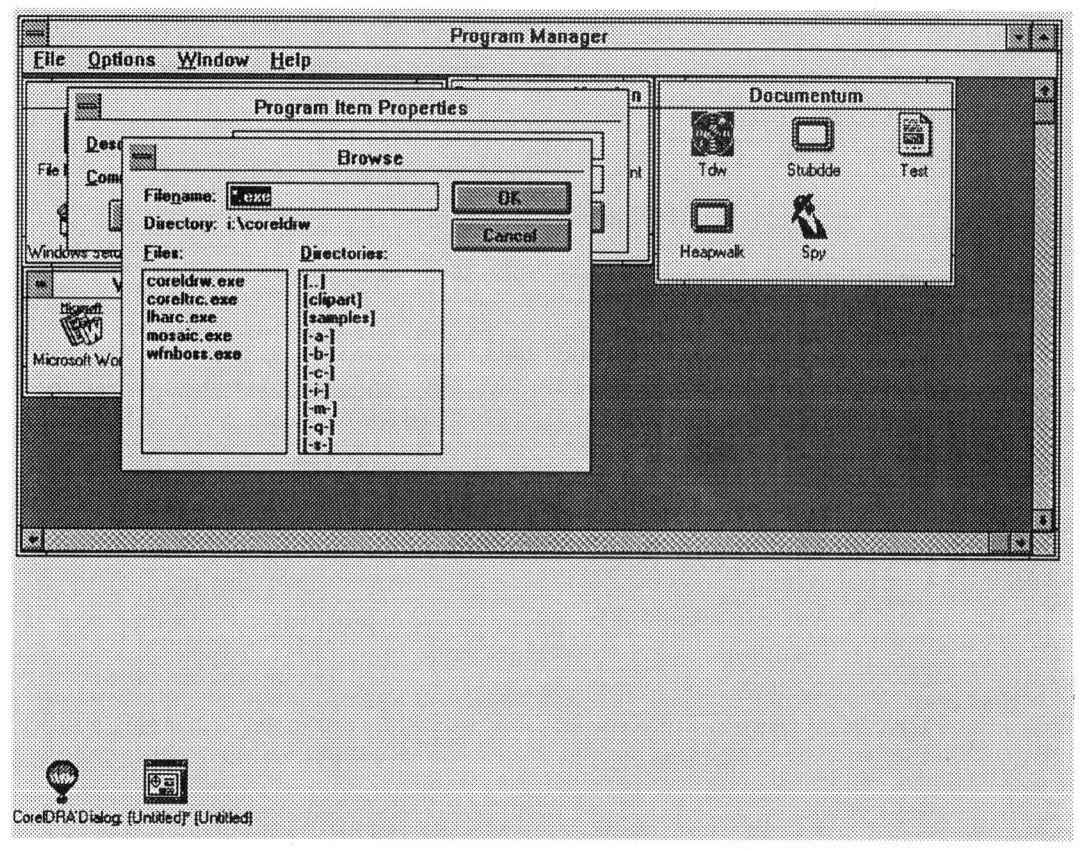

Figure 8.16 Typical dialog box (MS Windows) with an edit box, a list box, and push buttons.

Resources are defined in a text file called a resource script. They are compiled through a utility called the Resource Compiler and linked with the Windows application. Resources are read-only data. Once a resource script is compiled, it can be shared with other window applications.

8.4.1.5 Graphics Device Interface

Graphics in Windows are handled by the Graphics Device Interface (GDI). Both vector and raster color graphics are supported by GDI, but it supports only two-dimensional graphics. Vector graphics are supported by a set of vector-drawing functions such as a line, a point, a polygon, an arc, or a pie chart.

Raster graphics are supported by pixel manipulation, and they can be stored or manipulated either as a bitmap or a metafile. A bitmap representation of the graph can be manipulated using utilities such as BitBlt, PatBlt, and StretchBlt. A metafile provides binary encoding of GDI functions such as "draw vectors" and "fill a region with a bitmap." Metafiles take up less disk space than a bitmap representation, since they do not represent each pixel directly on disk. When metafiles are played, they execute the functions encoded and perform the necessary graphics operations to display the graphics output.

8.4.2 Macintosh Toolbox

The tremendous success of the Macintosh computer popularized the window-style, menu-driven user interface. The Macintosh originated from technology introduced by Apple's Lisa, which in turn drew upon ideas developed by the Xerox PARC effort in the 70s with the Star and Smalltalk environments.

The Macintosh GUI, called the Toolbox, is discussed in the following sections.

8.4.2.1 *Functional Overview*

The Toolbox provides a collection of utilities to access and manipulate the Macintosh's hardware and software resources. It provides a set of utilities to manipulate user interface components such as windows, the menu bar, and dialog boxes. Some of the utilities provided the following:

1. The Font Manager allows manipulation of system and user-defined fonts.
2. The Event Manager provides monitoring of events generated by keyboard, mouse, and keypad.
3. The Desk Manager provides access to desk utilities such as the Calculator.
4. TextEdit provides simple text-editing capabilities, such as display, insert, delete, cut and paste.
5. The Memory Manager provides a set of routines to manipulate dynamic memory.
6. The File Manager provides a set of routines to manipulate files and transfer data between files and applications.
7. The Sound Driver provides access to sound and music capabilities.
8. The Toolbox Utilities are a set of general routines to manipulate icons, patterns, strings, fixed-point arithmetic, and so on.

The Toolbox can be manipulated either from assembly language or from any Macintosh Programmer's Workshop (MPW) language (Pascal, C, C++, Smalltalk). One of the major features of the Toolbox is that most of the Toolbox routines reside in ROM. This provides a very responsive user interface. The original Macintosh had a 64K-byte ROM, and the newer Mac II and SE have a 256K-byte ROM (Brown and Cunningham, 1989).

A large portion of Toolbox application code is dedicated to detecting and handling events. MacApp, presented in Section 8.5, presents a simpler approach to developing Macintosh applications.

For a more complete description of the Toolbox, refer to Apple Computer (1985–87) and Seymour (1989a). From this point on, the discussion concentrates on the user interface components of the Macintosh Toolbox.

8.4.2.2 *The Window Manager*

The Window Manager allows the application developer to manipulate windows on the screen. It handles such actions as overlapping and resizing windows, moving windows around the screen, or changing a window from a front to a background window.

Developers can create and manipulate predefined Toolbox windows or define their own windows. Macintosh allows the developer to create windows with any desired shape and form, such as a circular or hexagonal window.

Toolbox comes with a series of predefined windows. The most popular of these windows is the document window, shown in Figure 8.17. The document window has the following regions: title bar, close box, scroll bar(s), size box, and content region. The title bar contains the title of the window. By clicking and holding the mouse within this region, the user can drag the window to a different part of the screen. Clicking inside the close box causes the window to disappear. The size box is used to resize the window. The horizontal or vertical scroll bars (which the developer must specify separately) can be used to scroll the contents of the window. The content region is the area controlled by the application.

In creating a document window, any one of the components just described can be omitted. For example, any one of the scroll bars can be absent from the document window. New types of windows can be created using either the Window Manager or the Resource Manager. The Resource Editor can be used to create a window template, which defines a class of windows that can be instantiated by an application. For each class of windows defined by the system or the user, there exists a function called the window definition function. This function is used to handle the behavior and appearance of the window. When a window needs to be drawn or resized, a message is sent to the window definition function to perform the appropriate action for that type of window.

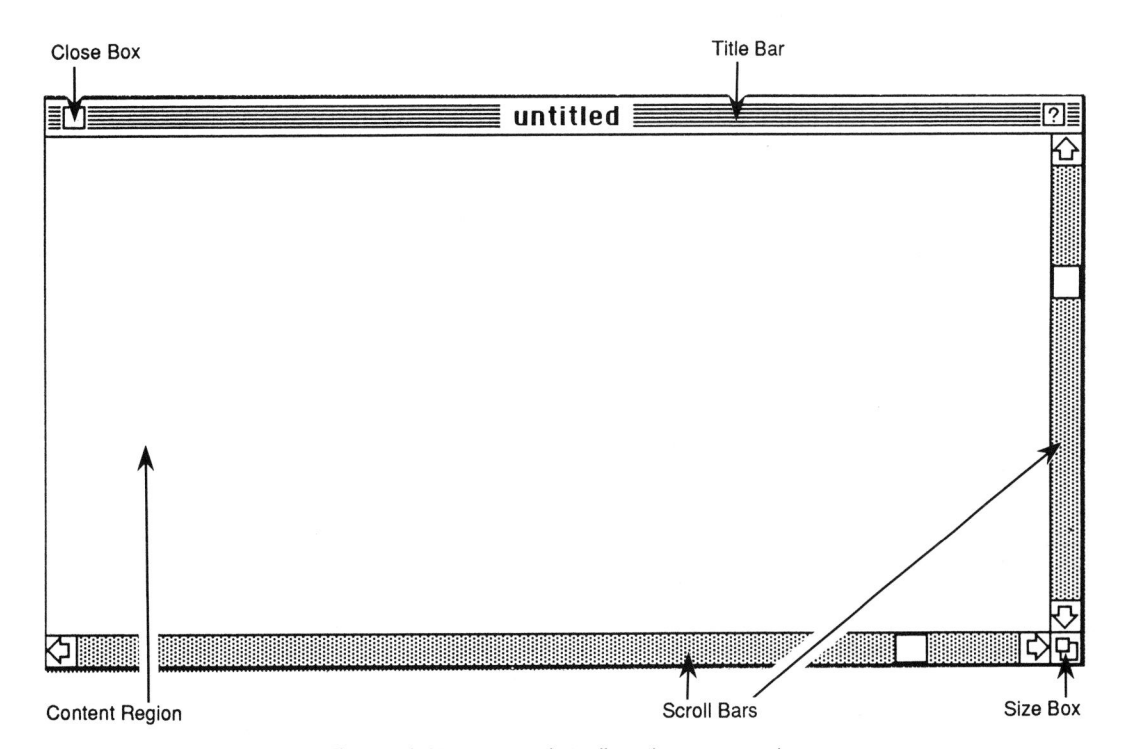

Figure 8.17 Macintosh Toolbox document window.

The Window Manager provides a large collection of routines to create, display, resize, hide, activate and deactivate windows on the screen. The protocol used to draw a window on the screen is as follows:

1. *Create the window:* An application can create either a system-defined window or a user-defined window. This step returns a window pointer, which later can be used to resize, hide, deactivate, or close the window.
2. *Manipulate the window:* The Toolbox Event Manager reports all events, including mouse and keyboard activities. For example, clicking the mouse inside the horizontal scroll bar causes the Event Manager to report a mouse event. The application code then calls the appropriate Window Manager routines to decide what region of window should handle the event. Finally, the appropriate action for the scroll bar is taken; that is, the window is scrolled horizontally.
3. *Close the window:* When a window is no longer needed, it can be closed by calling the CloseWindow function.

8.4.2.3 The Resource Manager

The Resource Manager provides access to various resources such as icons, menus, windows, and fonts. A user-defined resource, such as a window, is defined using the Resource Editor. The template of the window and the window definition function are stored in a file called the resource file. A unique resource identifier is used to access a predefined resource. A resource identifier can be used to recognize the type of the resource and the actual resource file to be read.

8.4.2.4 The Menu Manager

The Menu Manager provides a set of routines to create and manipulate menus. A menu bar, depicted in Figure 8.18, can contain a list of one or more menu items. Each menu

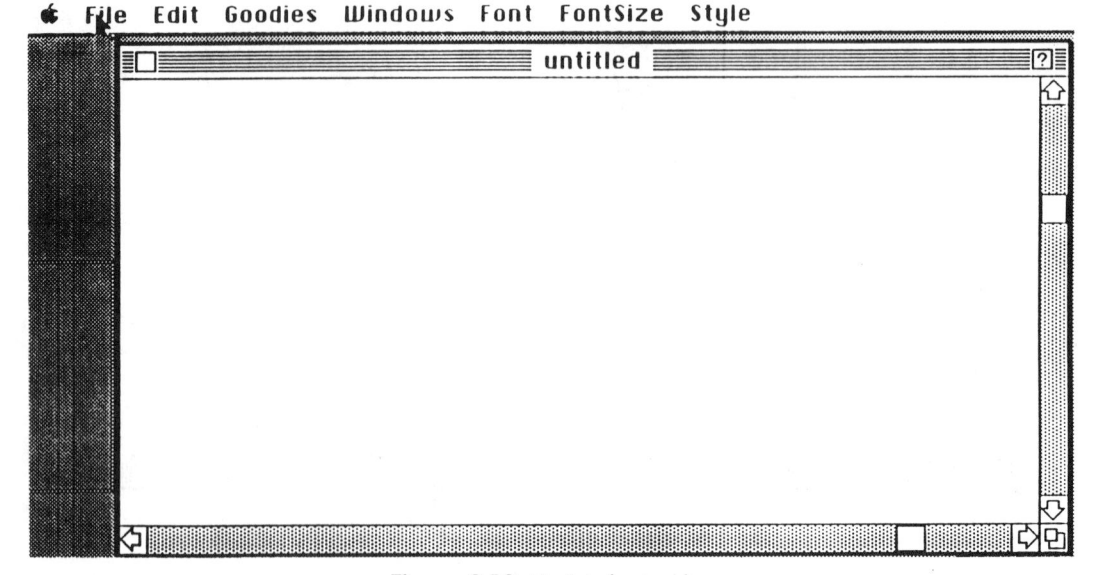

Figure 8.18 Macintosh menu bar.

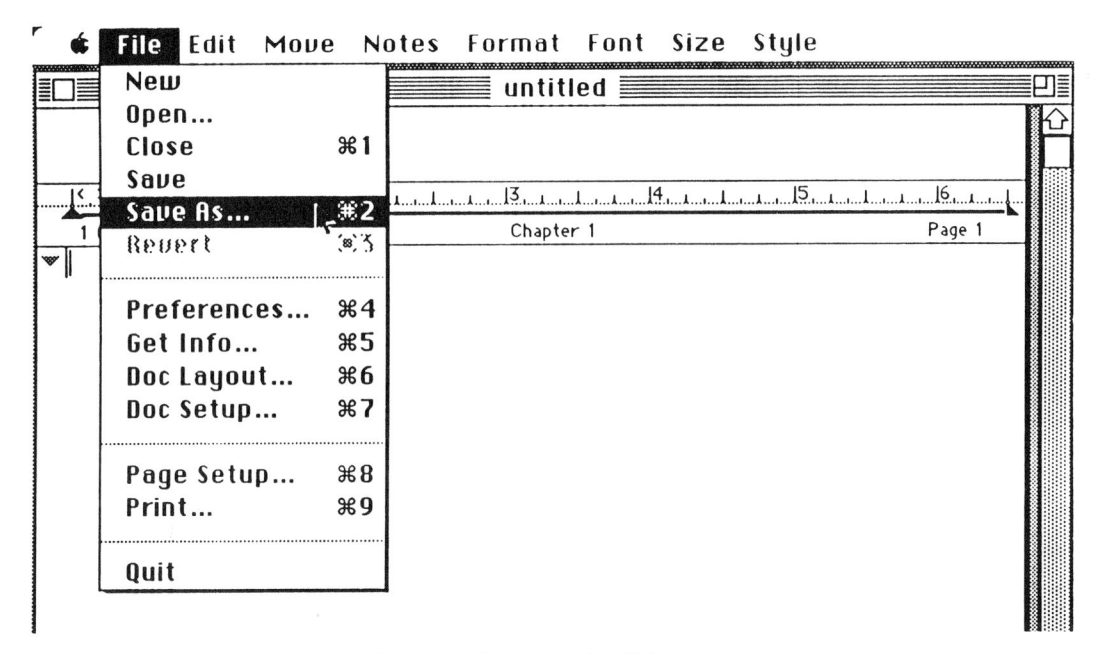

Figure 8.19 Macintosh pull-down menu.

item highlights itself when clicked with the mouse; this indicates the item is selected. The developer can define a menu using the standard Apple menu bar or define a menu of any shape or form using QuickDraw. Menus can be stored as a resource and managed by the Resource Manager. Once the menu is given to the Resource Manager, a unique identifier is used to reference the menu.

A menu item can invoke a pull-down menu, which can be used to set attributes or choose additional selections, as shown in Figure 8.19. A menu item in a pull-down menu can then invoke a dialog or an alert box. A menu item can be a textual item or any icon. Unlike those of MS Windows, menus on Macintosh cannot be part of a window definition. Menus are only used to define the menu bar associated with one Macintosh screen.

8.4.2.5 The Control Manager

The Control Manager provides a set of routines to define and manipulate control objects such as buttons, check boxes, and scroll bars. Controls are usually defined within a window. For example, the scroll bars can be defined as part of a document window. Most often, controls are defined as part of a dialog or alert box. The Toolbox defines a set of controls, depicted in Figure 8.20:

1. *Buttons:* These cause an action to take place once the mouse is clicked inside the region of the button.
2. *Check box:* This control indicates a binary option. A mouse click inside the check box is used to set or reset the check box. An × appears inside the box to indicate that the check box is set.

262 ■ **Graphical User Interfaces**

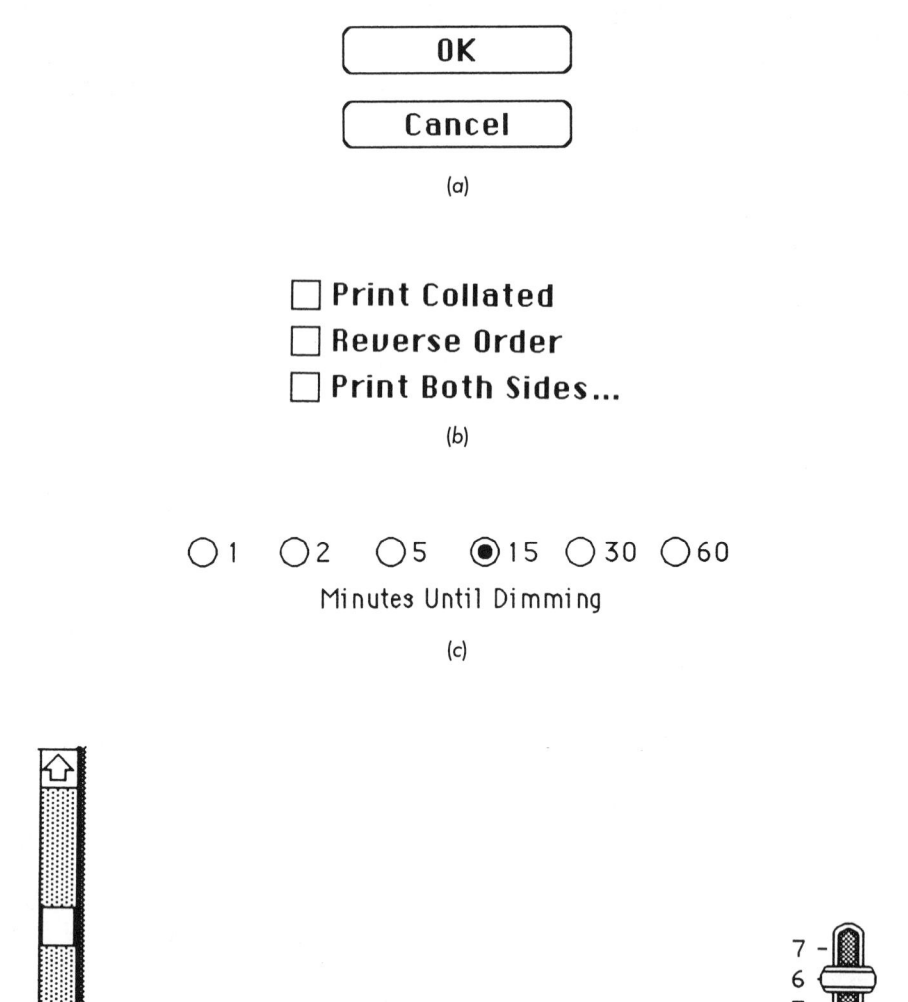

Figure 8.20 Macintosh Toolbox controls. (a) buttons; (b) check boxes; (c) radio buttons; (d) dials.

3. *Radio buttons:* Like check boxes, they are used for binary or on-off decision. Normally, a group of radio buttons is used, only one of which can be on at a time. They are similar to MS Windows radio buttons.
4. *Dials:* These controls display a quantitative setting or value, typically in some pseudoanalog form such as the position of a sliding switch, the reading of on a thermometer scale, or the angle of a needle on a gauge; the setting may be displayed digitally as well." (Apple Computer, 1987–1989) The scroll bar is the only standard dial control object defined by the Control Manager. Both horizontal and vertical scroll bars can be defined.

An application can define its own control objects. For example, user-defined dials can be defined to represent a thermometer or a three-way check box. To define a control type, a developer uses the QuickDraw utility to build the graphic representation. The control object is managed by the Resource Manager.

The behavior of a user-defined control is defined by the application developer via the control definition function. This function performs all necessary actions on the control. For example, in a user-defined control representing a thermometer, a mouse click inside the thermometer can be used to change the temperature setting.

8.4.2.6 The Dialog Manager

The Dialog Manager provides a set of routines and data structures to manipulate dialog and alert boxes. Dialog boxes obtain additional information from the end user of an application. An alert box provides information, such as a warning or a cautionary message. Figure 8.21 displays an example of each.

A dialog box or an alert box is a kind of window, and actions performed on windows, such as moving or resizing, can sometimes be performed on dialog boxes. A dialog box can contain all control types, such as dials, scroll bars, and check boxes. It can even contain one or more textual regions where the user can provide a response by typing in characters. Icons can be placed in a dialog box and used as controls.

A dialog or alert box can be defined with the Resource Editor. The template for the dialog or the alert box is stored in a resource file. To create a dialog box, the resource identifier is used to access the dialog template stored in the resource file.

8.4.2.7 The Scrap Manager

The Scrap Manager allows the user to move data from one application to another. A portion of one window can be cut from one window, placed in the Scrap Manager, and then pasted into another window. Once a portion of a window is cut, it is placed in the Clipboard. The user can then paste the contents of the Clipboard into another window.

8.4.2.8 QuickDraw

QuickDraw provides capabilities to draw and manipulate a large collection of graphics shapes, such as lines, rectangles, oval shapes, wedges, arbitrary regions, and text. The graphic objects can be defined with different shapes and forms. The text can be drawn in different fonts and sizes. QuickDraw also handles cursors and patterns.

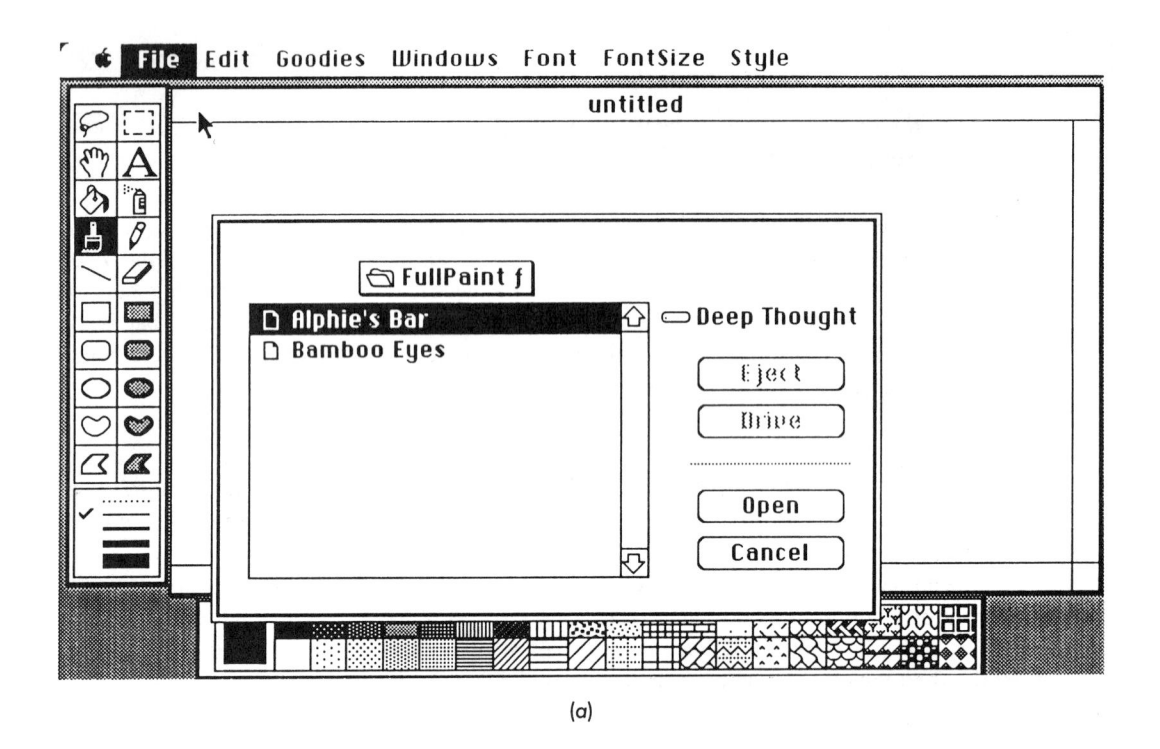

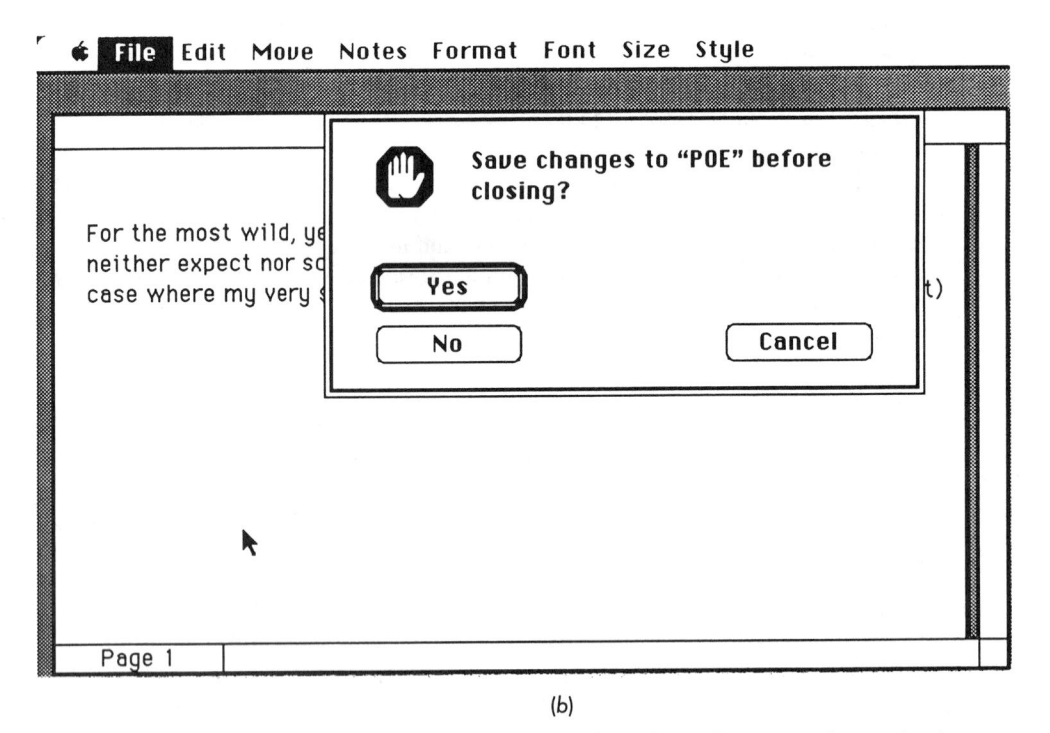

Figure 8.21 Macintosh dialog boxes. (a) Modal dialog (Ashton-Tate FullPaint); (b) alert.

8.5 OBJECT-ORIENTED USER INTERFACES

8.5.1 Actor

Actor, by Whitewater Group, is a complete object-oriented language specifically designed for developing Microsoft Windows applications. It provides a library containing a collection of classes to perform a wide variety of functions. Most of these classes deal with Windows objects such as windows, menus, dialog boxes, and graphics. Actor currently runs on MS-DOS and MS Windows. Future versions of Actor are expected to run on OS/2, UNIX, and other platforms. The following sections discuss Actor in detail.

8.5.1.1 Overview

Actor is an object-oriented environment tailored for designing MS Windows application (Whitewater Group, 1989a). The major components of the Actor environment are the Actor language, its development environment, and the class hierarchy.

The Actor language, like Smalltalk, is a novel object-orientated language. The language supports abstract data typing, data hiding, single inheritance, and polymorphism (overriding of methods within the hierarchy). The language comes with a predefined hierarchy of classes, which is discussed in Section 8.5.1.2. Everything in Actor is an object—numbers, windows, even a class. Like instances of a class, a class object has instance variables and methods.

The language is a procedural language like C or Pascal. Some of the language constructs and features are the *if...then...else*, *case* statement, *while* loop, and calling outside the Actor.

The language supports automatic garbage collection and incremental compilation. Even though Actor seems like a simple language at first, its power becomes quite apparent after a few trials with the system. Whitewater Group recently announced a product entirely built in Actor called the Whitewater Resource Toolkit (Whitewater Group, 1989b). This product provides an interactive environment to build Windows resources, such as cursors, dialog boxes, icons, and menus.

In addition to the language, Actor comes with a powerful development environment:

1. The Inspector lets the user examine the contents of an object. It also allows the user to change the state of any attributes of this object. Figure 8.22 displays the Inspector window.

2. The Browser allows the developer to view and edit the Actor system and the class hierarchy. Figure 8.23 displays the Browser window. The developer can extend the class hierarchy with the Browser. Methods and instance variables attached to a class definition can be examined and modified. The class hierarchy can be traversed and new subclasses can be added very easily.

   The developer can add or remove a method or an instance variable to a class definition. Methods for both classes and objects of a particular class can be examined. The Browser is also a powerful file editor, and the user can cut and paste code from one method to another.

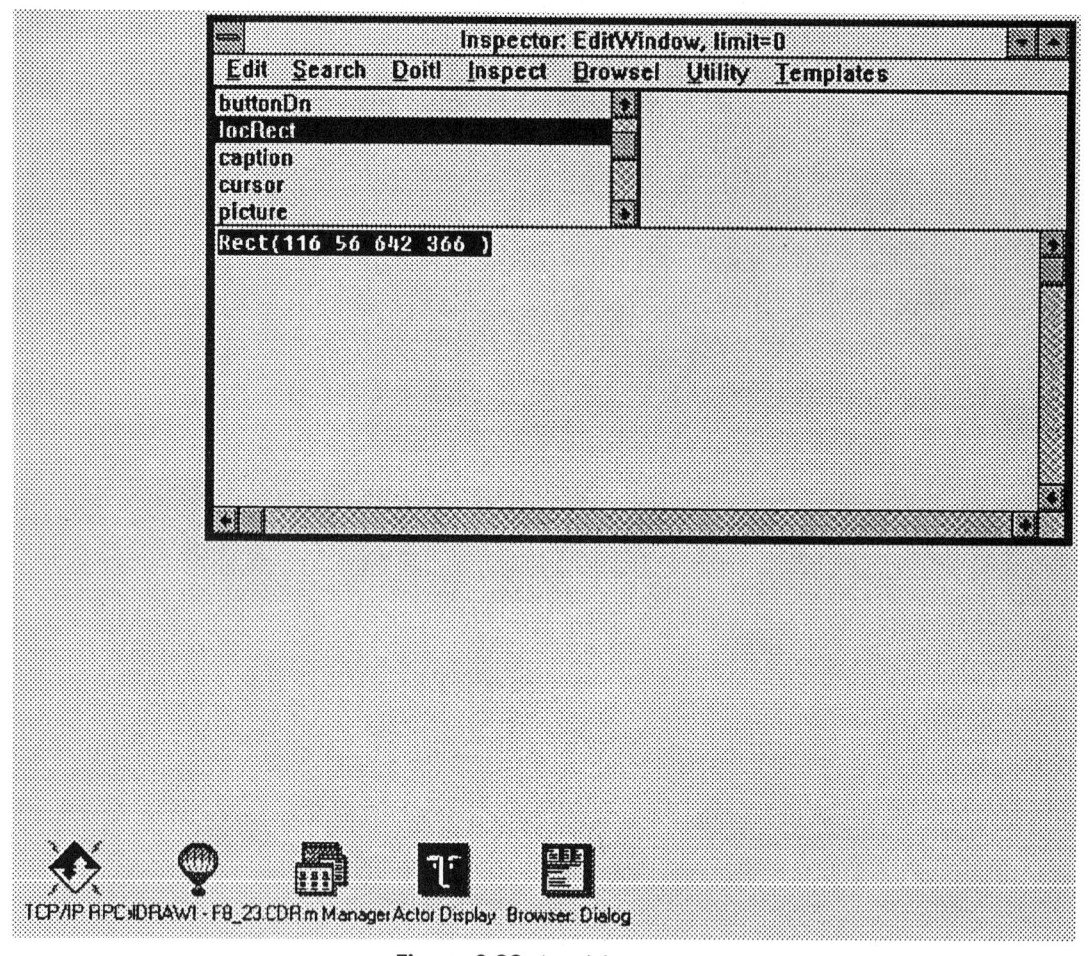

Figure 8.22 Actor's Inspector.

3. The Debugger is a combination of the Browser and the Inspector. Figure 8.24 displays the Debugger window. A Debug Dialog is produced when an error is encountered. It can be used to enter the Debugger window to change the value either of an attribute, such as a method, or an instance variable.

Actor also provides an extensive library of class definitions. Some of the functions supported with this library are easy manipulation of MS Windows, set and collection objects, file I/O, parsing, and string handling. The next section concentrates on the user interface capabilities of the class hierarchy. In addition, the class hierarchy can be extended to support any user-defined object.

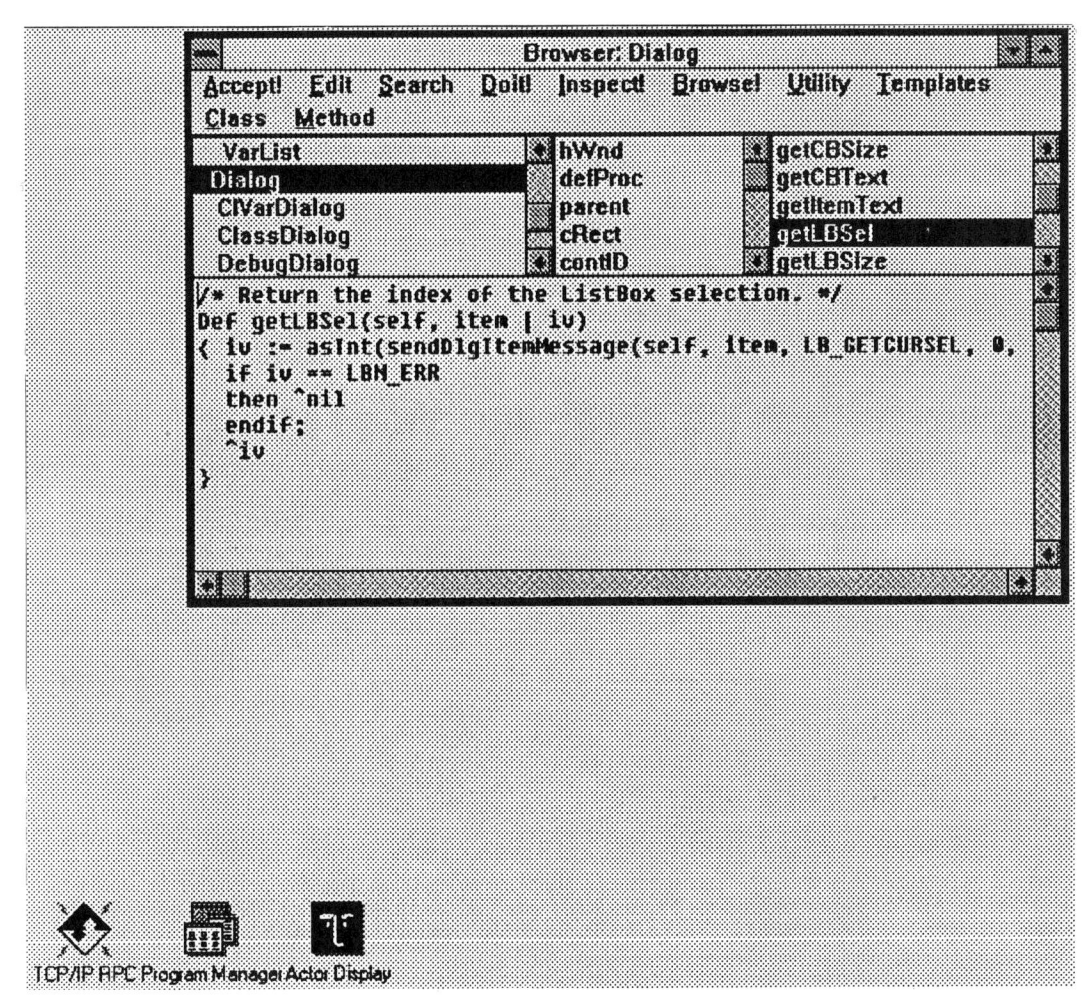

Figure 8.23 Actor's Browser.

8.5.1.2 Class Hierarchy

Most of the power of Actor resides in functionality provided by the class library. Figure 8.25 displays the entire class hierarchy of the Actor 2.0 library. In this section, only classes related to user interface development are discussed.

Actor makes Windows application creation quite easy. Methods provided and inherited by the Windows object hierarchy automatically deal with mouse actions such as dragging and clicking, keyboard actions, and more. Invoking a method causes a message to be transmitted between Actor and MS Windows. These messages initiate actions such as resizing, closing, overlapping, and dealing with control objects such as scroll bars and buttons. For example, if the radio dial is turned off, a message is sent from MS Windows

268 ■ **Graphical User Interfaces**

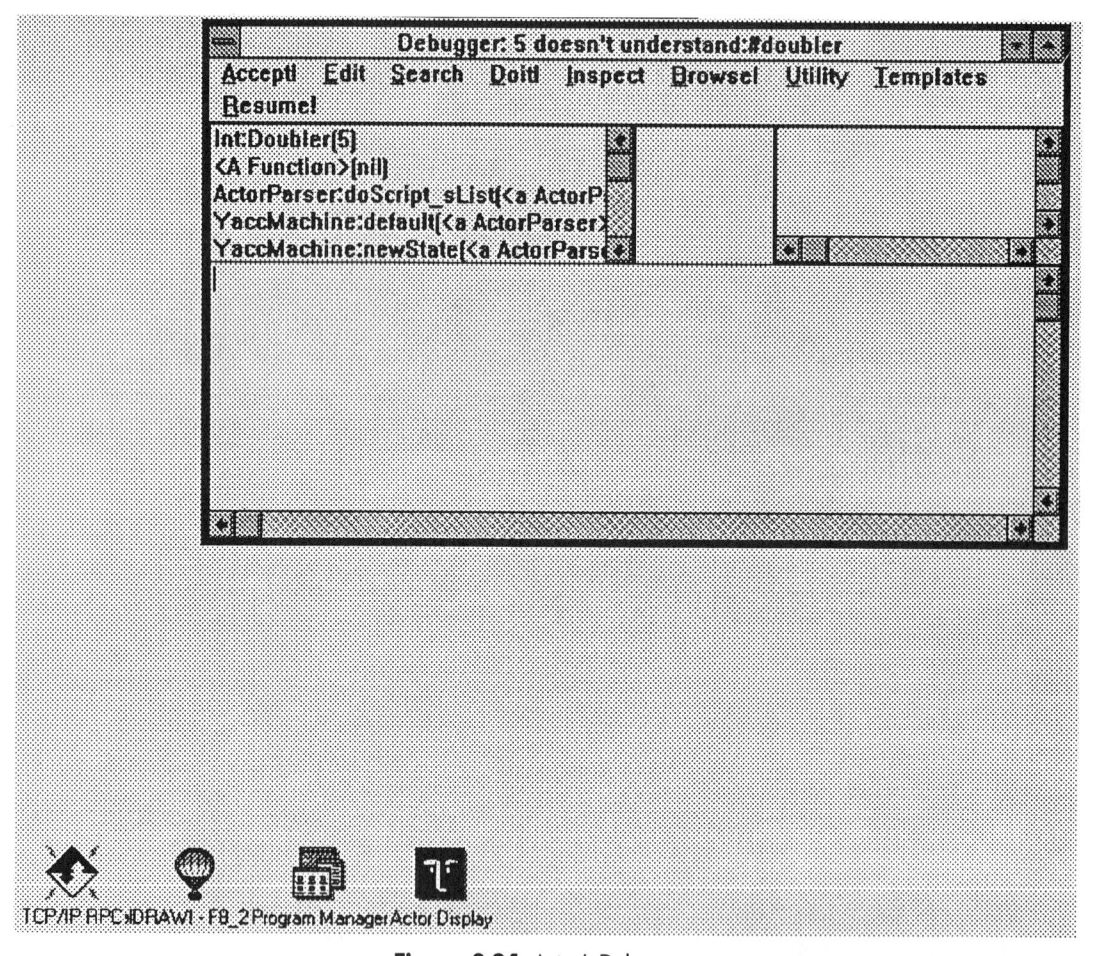

Figure 8.24 Actor's Debugger.

to the control object. Or to close a window, Actor sends a message to MS Windows to perform this action.

The user can add a new class definition to the hierarchy with more specialized Windows features. If this new class definition requires a special treatment of events, such as different mouse handling, then the existing mouse handling methods can be overridden or extended.

To create an editable window, as in Figure 8.26, all the code required in Actor is as follows:

```
Wind :=
    new(EditWindow, ThePort, "editmenu", "Easy Edit", nil);
show(Wind, 1);
```

8.5 Object-Oriented User Interfaces

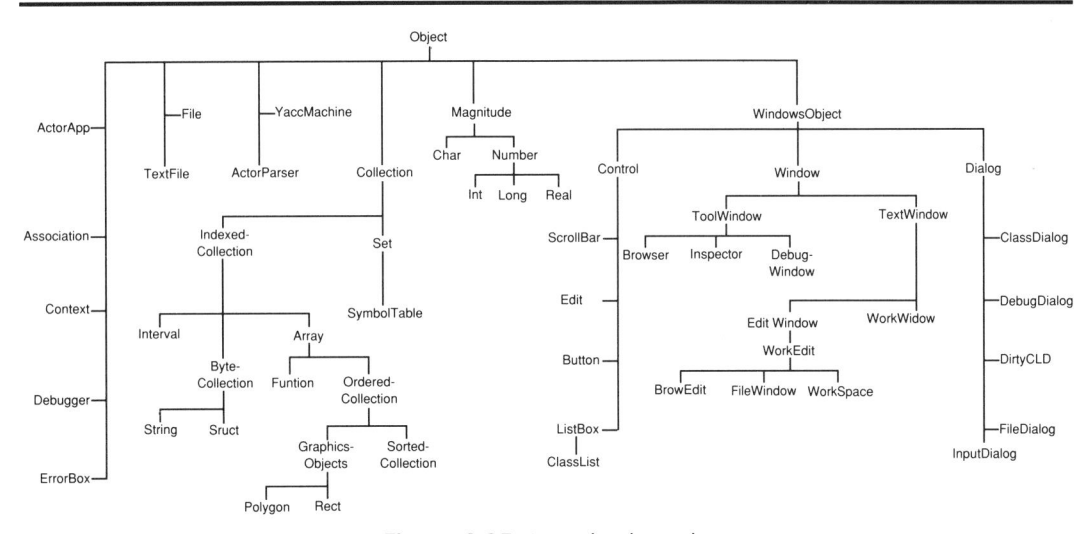

Figure 8.25 Actor class hierarchy.

The equivalent code in Microsoft Windows is few pages long. This simple program provides all the capabilities required in an editable window, such as cut, paste, and backspace deleting.

The foregoing code works as follows. The method *new* instantiates an object called *Wind* as member of an *EditWindow* class. Then the *show* message sent to the *Wind* object causes the new window object to appear on the screen.

Besides instantiating a new object, the message *new* specifies additional parameters for the object. For each class definition, the *new* method is overloaded with a different set of parameters specific to that class. For example, the parameters specified for the *new* method of *EditWindow* in this example are as follows:

1. Parent of the new object: *ThePort*, containing the window object that has the current input focus,
2. Title of the new window: "*Easy Edit*"
3. Window style used: "*editmenu*"

The rest of this section presents the major user interface classes, which include the *Window*, *Control*, and *Dialog* classes. Figure 8.27 displays the Actor 2.0 WindowsObject class hierarchy.

8.5.1.2.1 Window Classes

To create an instance of a window class, the user specifies the type of window (for example, whether it is editable), the parent window, the menu used, the window title, and the location. All the events affecting that window are handled by the methods defined for the windows. Events handled include mouse, keyboard, and screen events.

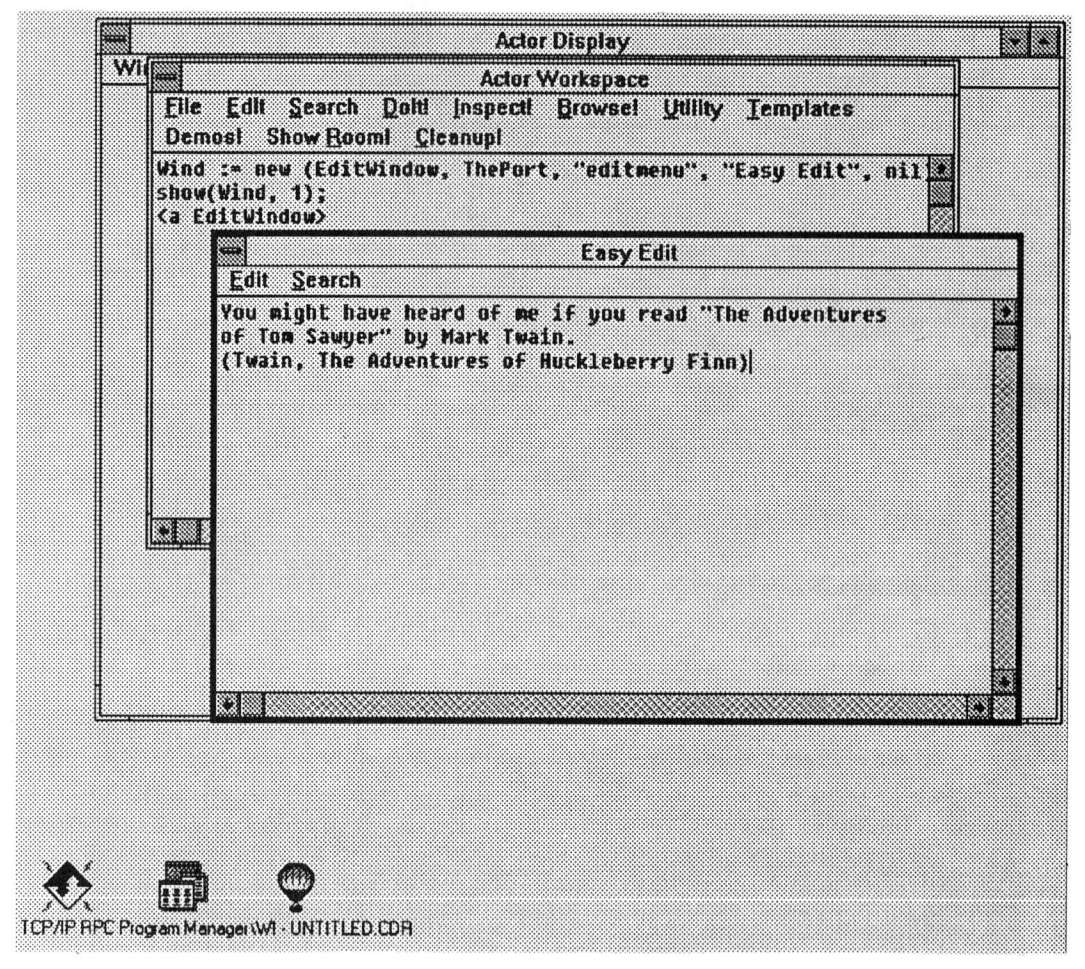

Figure 8.26 EditWindow example in Actor.

A window's menu can be either defined with a resource file or created dynamically. Menus created dynamically can be easily manipulated with methods attached to Window classes. These methods are used to append a new item or to remove or change an existing one. Menus stored in a resource file are preferred over dynamic windows, as they are more efficient and shareable by several applications.

One of the most useful Window subclasses is the EditWindow. It allows windows to be created with built-in text editing capabilities such as cut, paste, and backspace. Objects of this class are defined with the "*editmenu*" option, which supplies a pulldown menu. This option allows cutting, copying, and pasting of textual data inside the window region.

In a sense, the window content appears as a simple text editor. Text scrolling, both horizontal and vertical, is also supported. The vertical and horizontal scroll bars are active and fully controlled by the methods attached to this class. All complicated MS Windows events are handled automatically, even editing capabilities.

8.5 Object-Oriented User Interfaces ■ 271

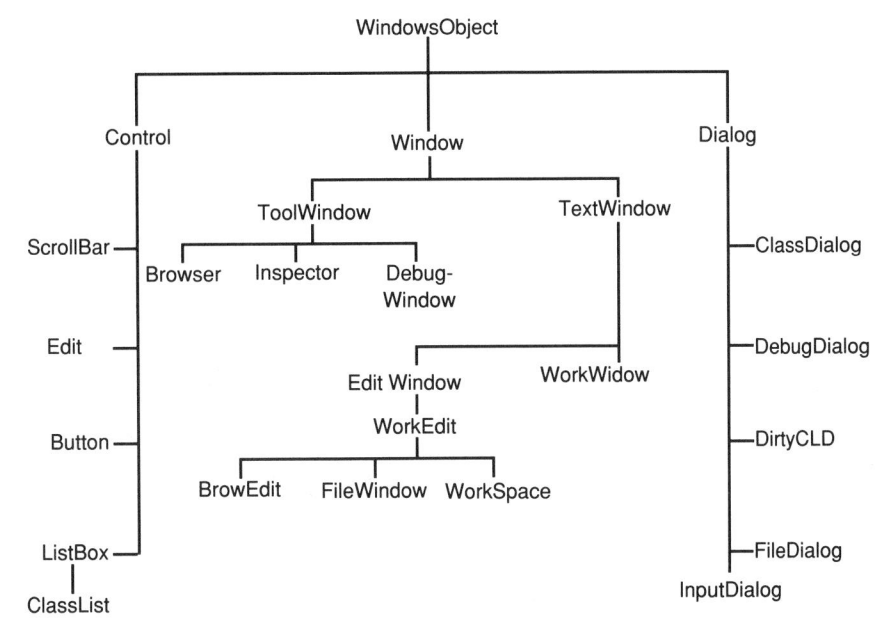

Figure 8.27 Actor WindowsObject class hierarchy.

8.5.1.2.2 Control Classes

One branch of the tree in Figure 8.27 depicts the class hierarchy used for control objects such as buttons, scroll bars, edit string boxes, and list boxes. All control windows are child windows of the window containing them. This means that events such as moving and closing the parent window are also carried to child windows. Most of the time the control objects are created as part of a dialog window, which is discussed in the next subsection.

A special subclass of control objects is *ListBox*, which allows the user to select an option, identified by a screen, from a list. To use it, an instance of *ListBox* is created and then the *insertString* method is called to add strings as items. Other methods defined for list boxes handle moving the scroll bar through the list and highlighting the selected item. When a selection is made the actual text of the selection can be returned with the *getSelString* method.

8.5.1.2.3 Dialog Classes

These classes allow creation of both modal and modeless dialog boxes. A modal dialog box appears when user input is required. All user input (as from the keyboard) is directed to the dialog box until the box is closed. The modeless dialog boxes, on the other hand, do not take control of user input and behave more like a pop-up window.

To program a dialog in Actor, one must first create a *Dialog* object and then display it on the screen. A dialog object, like any object, is created with the *new* method:

D1 :== new(Dialog);

Then the dialog must be displayed and initiated with either the *runModal* or the *runModeless* method. These two methods have the following definition:

runModal(dialogObject, resourceID, parentObject);
runModeless(dialogObject, resourceID, parentObject);

The first parameter is the dialog object that receives this message. The second parameter is a constant identifying the resource used for this dialog. This resource ID is used by MS Windows to find the dialog resource file on disk. Most likely, a given type of dialog class will have several dialog styles (resources) associated with the dialog definition. The last parameter is the parent object that the dialog belongs to. If the parent object is ever closed, a message is sent to the dialog box causing it to be closed too.

Methods attached to the dialog classes handle a variety of events for dialog objects. Until the dialog box or window is terminated, Actor and MS Windows communicate with each other through messages. Actor sends messages to change the input focus from one control to another or to change the current value of a control. Windows sends messages back to Actor to communicate information such as the current state of a button. Some of the events handled are creating the controls within the dialog box, changing focus among control objects, and terminating the dialog box.

The developer does not have to create the controls within the dialog window. This is done automatically by the methods attached to the dialog's class definition. When the dialog is initialized, the developer can direct MS Windows to change the screen focus from one control to another. By default, the first control object has the screen focus. In addition, default values for all the controls can be defined by messages sent when the dialog object is created. For example, if a control is present to display a list of file names in a file list box, then a method is used to load the list of files in this control.

A dialog can be ended by the state of a button, such as an "OK" or "Cancel" button, or by pressing the carriage return key. This activity is handled by MS Windows sending a message to the dialog object to close the window. In turn, the corresponding object recognizes the message and terminates the dialog box.

8.5.1.2.4 Existing Dialog Class Hierarchy

Actor provides some predefined classes for dialog boxes. Figure 8.27 displays the class hierarchy for the dialogs. Even though there are few dialog classes, they provide the general mechanism to handle dialog box events between Microsoft and Actor for all predefined and user defined dialog classes. Among the classes provided are *Dialog*, *ErrorBox*, *InputDialog*, and *FileDialog*:

1. *Dialog* is the center focus of all dialog classes defined either by the system or by the user. The methods attached to this class allow the user to perform a wide range of functions. Some of these functions include:
   - Sending a message to a specific dialog item
   - Changing focus from one item to another
   - Retrieving an item from a list
   - Retrieving or specifying the text from an edit box

8.5 Object-Oriented User Interfaces ■ 273

2. *ErrorBox* is used to display an error message on the screen in an error (alert) box and wait for the user acknowledgment by clicking the "OK" button or hitting the carriage return key. The *ErrorBox* is not a direct descendant of the *Dialog* class hierarchy; it is a descendant of the *Object* class.

The developer can choose to display several styles of error messages and icons within an ErrorBox object. For example, to create the error window displayed in Figure 8.28, with the hand icon and "OK" and "Cancel" buttons the following message is sent:

new(ErrorBox, ThePort,
  "Do you really want to override READ.ME?",
  "Save As", MB_OKCANCEL + MB_ICONQUESTION);

The parameters to this method specify the class name (*ErrorBox*), the parent object (*ThePort*), strings representing the error message and the title, style of the but-

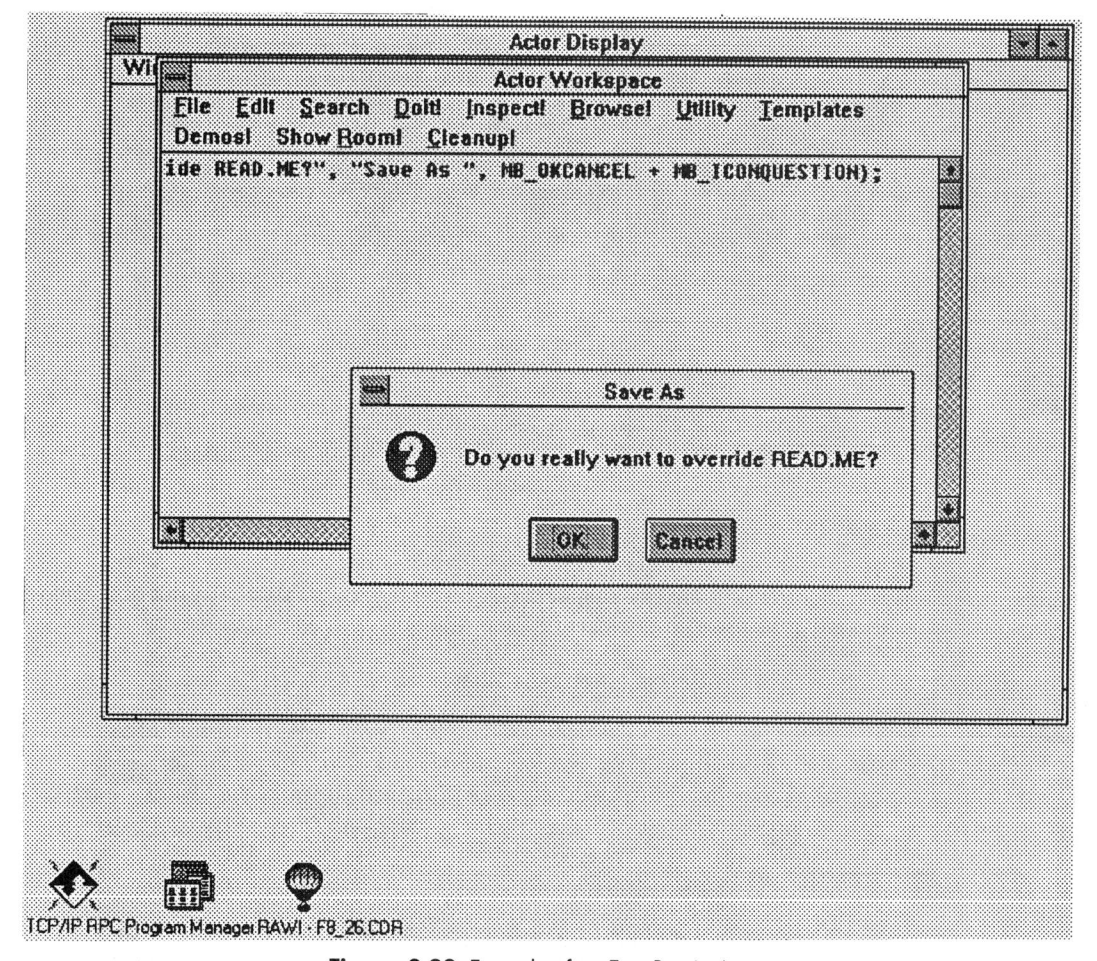

Figure 8.28 Example of an ErrorBox in Actor.

274 ■ Graphical User Interfaces

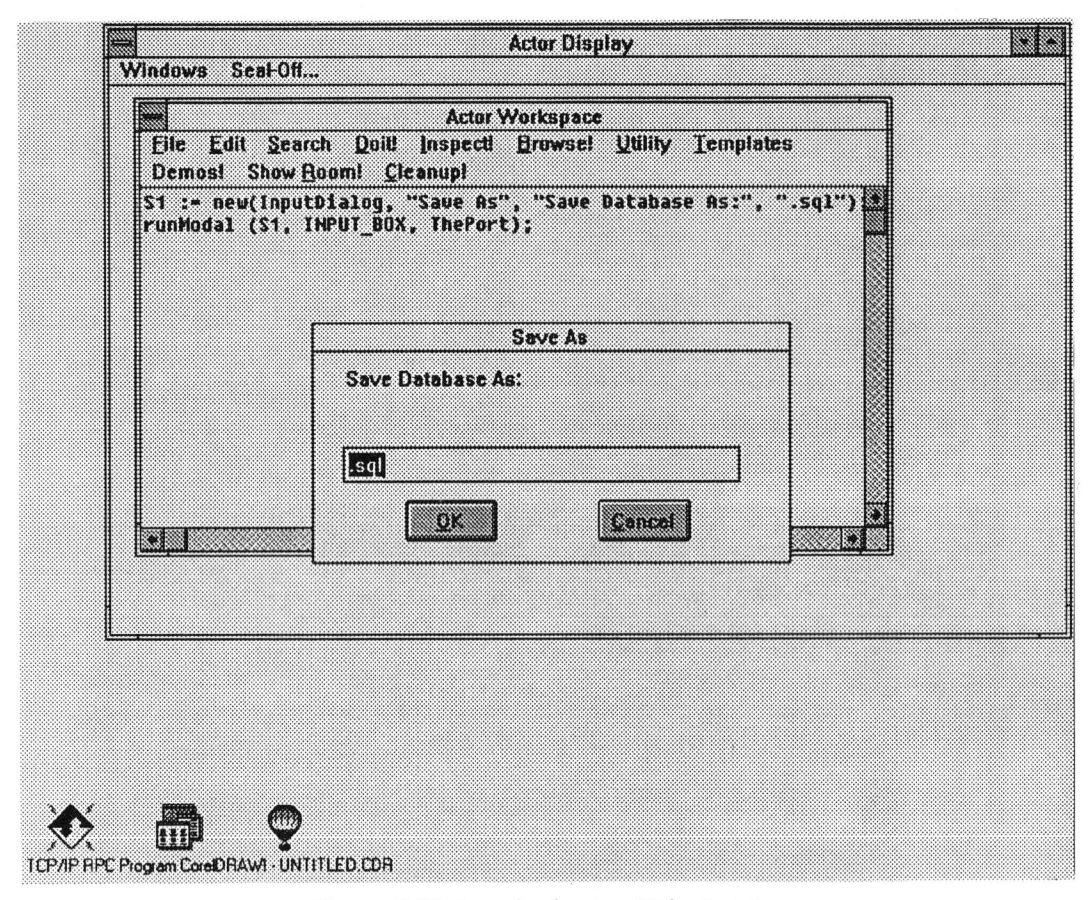

Figure 8.29 Example of an InputDialog in Actor.

ton and the icon. Objects of type ErrorBox are automatically displayed during creation.

3. *InputDialog* provides a class definition with one editable text control box, plus "OK" and "Cancel" buttons. The input dialog box in Figure 8.29 is the result of a request to save a database. It is created by the following *new* message:

S1 := new(InputDialog, "Save As", "Save Database As:", ".sql");

The parameters specify the name of the class (*InputDialog*), the title of the dialog box, the message inside the box, and the default string displayed in the edit box.

The dialog box *S1* just created can be displayed either as a modal or a modeless box. To display it as modal, the following message is sent to the *S1* object:

runModal(S1, INPUT_BOX, ThePort);

which causes Figure 8.29 to be displayed. At this point the input is focused on the edit control box *INPUT_BOX*. The end user can type in the name of the file in the edit control box and click on the "OK" or the "Cancel" button to terminate the dialog box.

If the "OK" button is clicked, the developer can access the text by invoking the following method:

fileName := getText(S1)

which returns the text. If the "Cancel" button is clicked or the ESC key is pressed, then the *getText* message returns the previous value of the edit control box before the user typed in the new value.

InputDialog objects can be used repeatedly once they are created. When used again, the object remembers the last value of the input control box. For example, if the user makes a mistake by typing PAYROL.RPT instead of PAYROLL.RPT, the first string is displayed again and can be corrected.

4. *FileDialog* is used to load a file from a list of file names. This class is by far the most complex dialog class definition provided. For example, to load a database from a list of databases, the dialog depicted in Figure 8.30 can be used. The edit

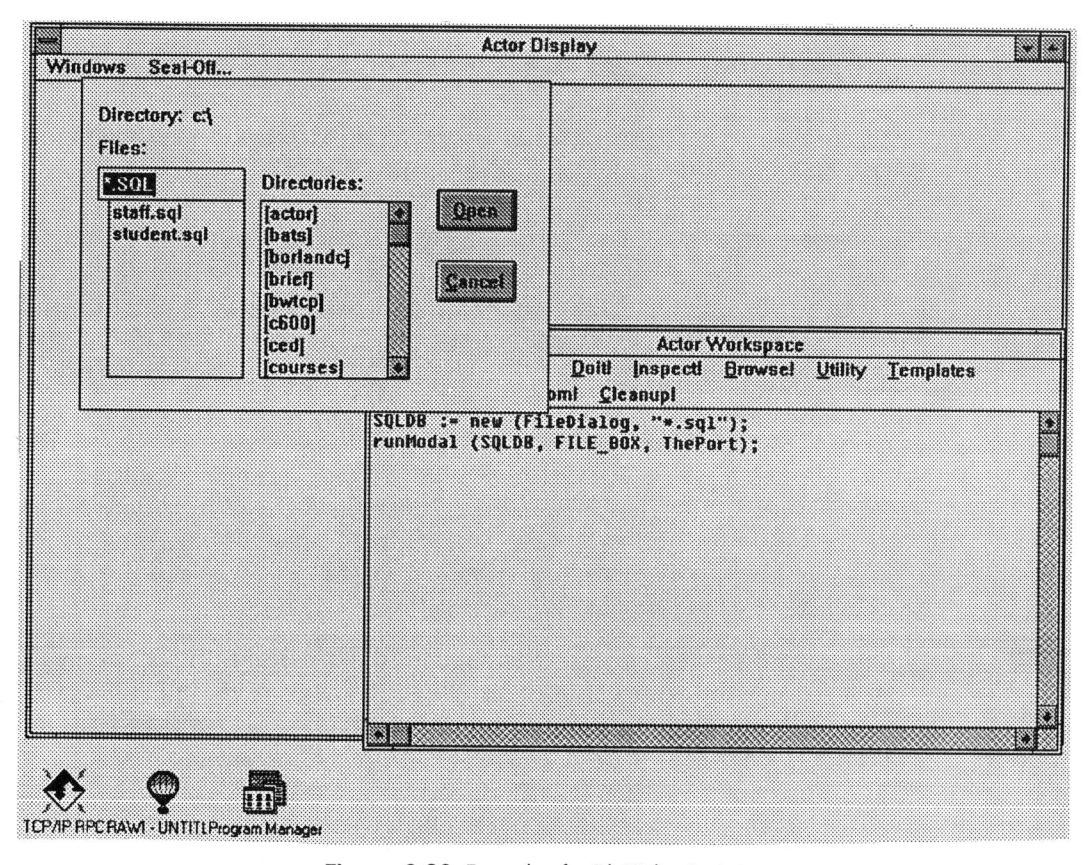

Figure 8.30 Example of a FileDialog in Actor.

area of the file name combo box can specify a wildcard file name; for example, *.SQL will display the list of all files with extension .SQL. You can also provide a directory specification instead of the directory used as the default. When the dialog window is displayed, the end user can type in a new search pattern in this box or type in any existing file name.

The file combo box displays a list of file names that satisfy the search pattern in the file edit box. Double clicking on a file will cause that file to be selected. Double clicking on a directory entry in the directory list box causes the current directory, or even the disk, to be changed. "Open" and "Cancel" buttons can be used to terminate the dialog box.

To create an object of this class, the following message can be sent:

SQLDB :== new(FileDialog, ".sql");*

which defines the SQLDB object and specifies the search pattern used for the file name edit box.

Then, to display the dialog box as modal, the following message is sent to the SQLDB object:

runModal(SQLDB, FILE_BOX, ThePort);

When a file is selected and the dialog box is terminated, the developer can retrieve the file name by invoking the following message:

getFile(SQLDB);

This method returns a string representing the current file name, if opened or double clicked, or the last file name, if Canceled.

8.5.1.3 Extending the Class Hierarchy

Users can extend the class hierarchy by defining new subclasses. The user interface hierarchy can be extended to support additional styles of windows and dialogs. The developer can define a new window class definition with specialized attributes. For example, to create a new class of windows without resize boxes, a subclass can be added to the *Window* class hierarchy with the resize box disabled.

The *Window* hierarchy is most often extended to support new types of dialog boxes. Creating a new dialog box requires two major steps:

1. Define the dialog box resource. This resource specifies features of the dialog box, such as the types of controls used and their position inside the dialog box. This task can be accomplished by writing resource script in Windows or by using the Dialog Editor that comes with the Windows Software Development Kit.

2. Define the new dialog subclass. Create the class definition using the Actor language. This class is created as a subclass of Actor's *Dialog* class, thereby inheriting the methods attached to the *Dialog* class definition. In addition, the designer can

override existing methods or attach new methods to handle messages for the new features of the subclass.

8.5.2 MacApp

MacApp is an object-oriented layer on top of the Macintosh Toolbox. MacApp is a library providing a large collection of classes defined using Object Pascal and MPW Assembly Language. (Object Pascal is an object oriented extension of standard Pascal (Apple Computer, 1987)). This large collection of classes provides services for creating windows and handling file I/O, icons, cursors, and control components such as buttons, dials, and scroll bars.

Without MacApp, programming a Macintosh application requires the ghastly task of writing code directly in the Toolbox utilities. The simple task of creating a window with a simple resize box requires a great amount of code to handle the events from the mouse, and to control the display window and the scroll bars.

The next section concentrates only on the user interface capabilities of MacApp. Other components will not be discussed here. To get more information, reference Apple Computer (1988) and Schmucker (1986).

8.5.2.1 Overview of MacApp Capabilities

A developer who programs directly in the Toolbox will need to write a large body of code just to manipulate user interface objects. One function of MacApp is to provide prebuilt class definitions that simplify creation and manipulation of user interfaces for the Macintosh. Some of the operations automatically handled by these predefined classes are as follows:

- Managing windows, menus, and mouse
- Handling errors
- Editing text within windows
- Filing documents

Besides managing screen objects, event handling for each class definition is a major feature of MacApp. For example, in Figure 8.31, when the mouse is clicked in the scroll bar region, MacApp's predefined event handlers perform the necessary action to deal with the scroll bar. These event handlers can also be directed to invoke an application—specific event handler before returning control.

MacApp also provides powerful debugging tools:

1. Inspector window, used to view instance variables of any object present in the system
2. Interactive debugger, used to debug methods attached to a class; execution can be interrupted at the beginning or the end of a method
3. Debug menu, which can appear in the menu bar during application development; this allows examination of objects or data from your application

MacApp can be used from any MPW language. If the user chooses to extend the class definition, then the new class definition must be defined in an object-oriented language.

278 ■ Graphical User Interfaces

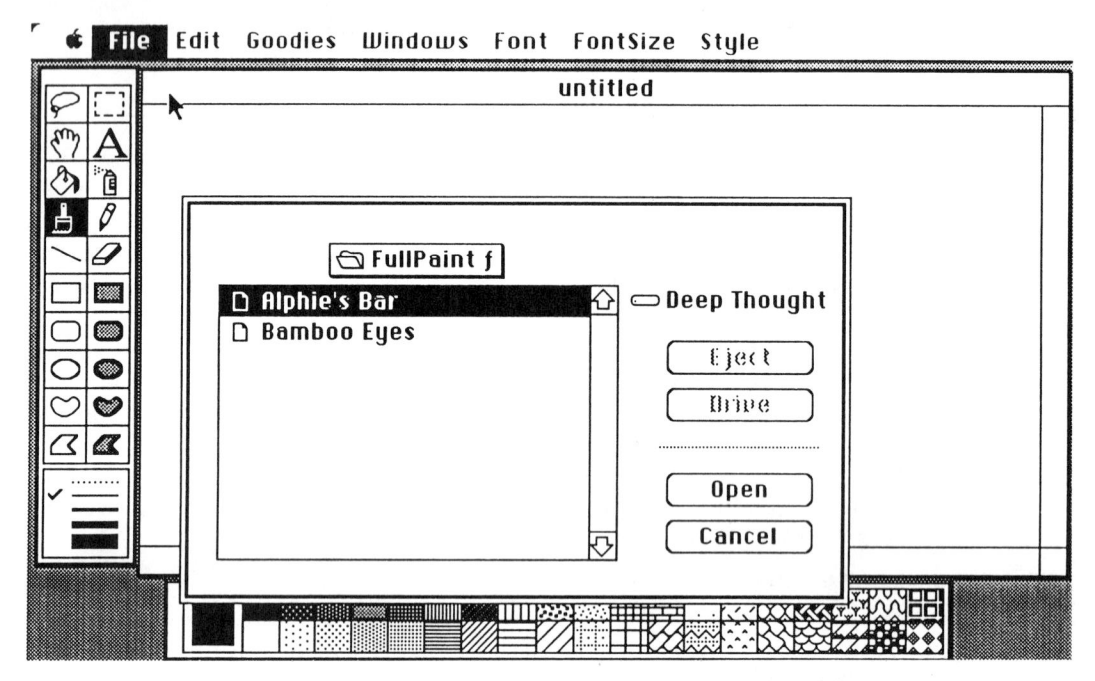

Figure 8.31 An example of Macintosh dialog box (Ashton-Tate Full Paint).

Among the MPW languages, Object Pascal or C++ can be used to define new MacApp subclasses.

8.5.2.2 User Interface Class Hierarchy

Figure 8.32 displays the entire class hierarchy for MacApp. The behavior and functionality provided by the classes *TApplication*, *TDocument*, *TCommand*, *TList*, and *TView* is as follows:

8.5.2.2.1 TApplication
This class opens and closes an application. When the user chooses an application by double clicking on the application icon, the application is opened and its menu bar is displayed.

8.5.2.2.2 TDocument
This class manages application files, including opening, saving, or specifying the I/O format. View objects, to be discussed, can be used to display objects of *TDocument* class.

8.5.2.2.3 TView
A view is a rectangular display object with a given size and position. Every screen object, such as a window, a scroll bar, or a control, is an instance belonging to one of the *TView* subclasses. The *TView* class definition itself is usually not instantiated directly. It provides an abstraction used by all subclasses, including methods for event handling.

8.5 Object-Oriented User Interfaces ■ 279

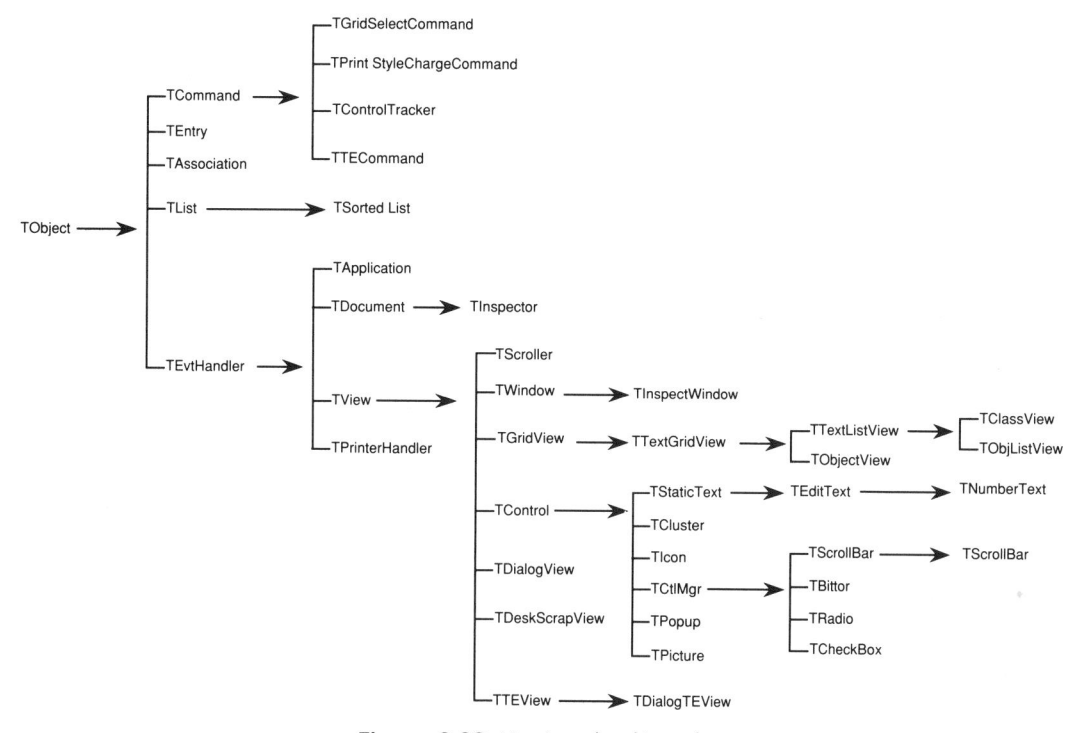

Figure 8.32 MacApp class hierarchy.

Figure 8.33 displays the subclasses of *TView*. Some of the important subclasses of *TView* are *TWindow*, *TControl*, *TDialogView*, *TTEView*, and *TScroller*.

- *TWindow*: Toolbox-predefined windows are created by instantiating objects of this class. MacApp-predefined methods handle events such as closing, resizing, and moving the window around the screen.

    When creating a window, the developer does little work except to instantiate a *TWindow* object and specify regions required. For example, the developer can instantiate a *TWindow* object and request only a size box and a zoom box for the window. The developer does not need to write code for window event manipulation, such as close and resize boxes. All the developer has to do is to manipulate the contents of the window.

- *TControl*: Objects of this class are used to manipulate Toolbox—defined controls such as the scroll bar, push buttons, editable text items, simple pop-up menus, and user-defined controls. Certain attributes, such as whether the control is dimmed or highlighted, can be set or reset by sending a message.

    Controls are usually grouped together in a dialog or an alert box. *TControl* subclasses also provide a mechanism to create a grouping of control boxes.

- *TDialogView*: Objects of this class are used to manipulate dialog box windows. The developer can create both modal and modeless dialog boxes. A modal dialog box

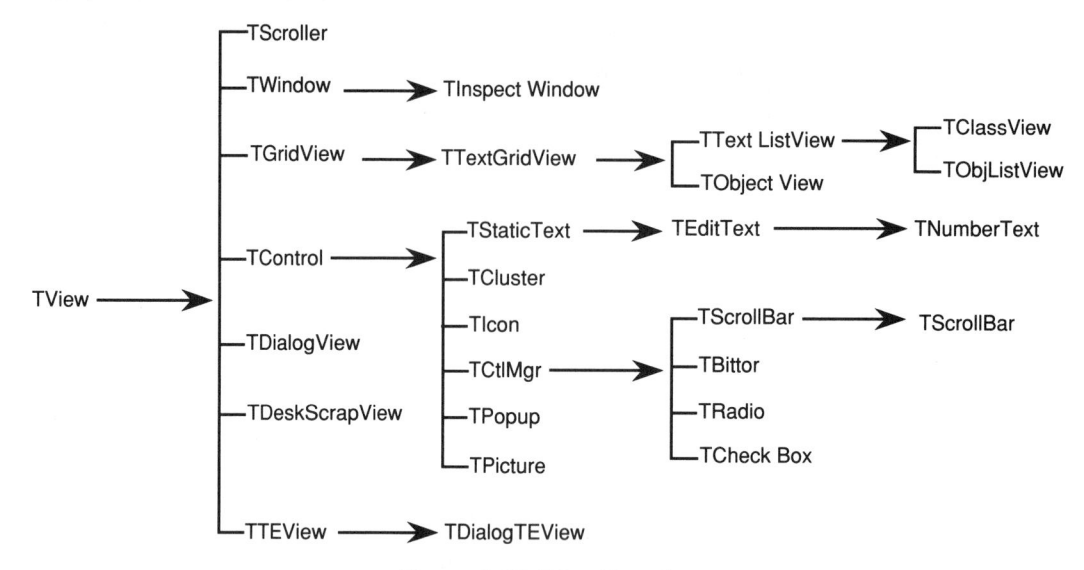

Figure 8.33 TView hierarchy.

requests input from the user before the application can continue. A modeless dialog does not interrupt the execution of the application.

- *TTEView*: Objects of this class provide text views with the ability to handle the mouse for cut and paste editing and for inserting and modifying textual data via the keyboard.
- *TScroller*: This class of object is used to manage any scrollable collection of views. *TScroller* objects automatically take care of all the scrolling tasks, such as translating coordinates with the scroll bar movements.

One common feature of all view objects is that instances of view subclasses can be nested. Each view instance can be a superview of another view, and each view object can contain one or more subviews. This hierarchy of views can be displayed as either tiled or layered views. Tiled views are used to subdivide a window into several sections. Layered views are used to make one view act as the background for one or more other views.

Any view can serve as a background for another view. Figure 8.34 depicts an example of both tiled and layered views. In this figure, we layered an object of *TScroller* and *TEView* and tiled these layers with two *TScrollBar* objects. Figure 8.35 depicts the superview/subview hierarchy relationship of these view objects.

The nested view mechanism is extremely handy when designing a dialog box. Every dialog view is made of a list of *TControl* subviews. These subviews use a *TDialogView* instance as their superview. When the mouse is clicked inside one of these subviews, the subview will handle the appropriate action.

During the display of a hierarchy of views, a view draws itself and then requests each of its subviews to draw themselves. Then each Subview draws itself and request its subviews to draw themselves. This process continues till there are no more views in the hierarchy to be drawn.

Similarly, event handling is handled from the top layer down to the leaf views.

8.5 Object-Oriented User Interfaces ■ 281

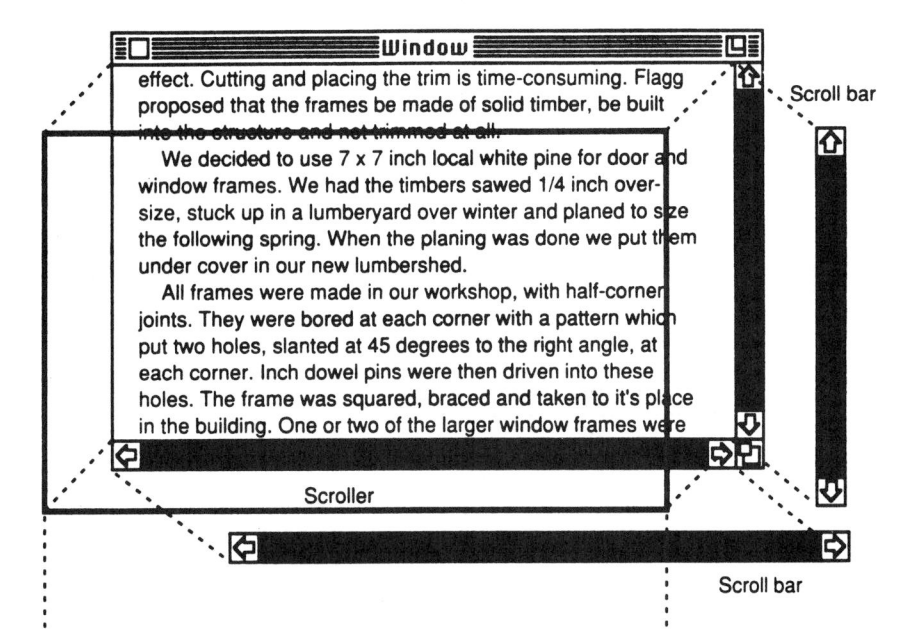

Window

effect. Cutting and placing the trim is time-consuming. Flagg proposed that the frames be made of solid timber, be built into the structure and not trimmed at all.

We decided to use 7 x 7 inch local white pine for door and window frames. We had the timbers sawed 1/4 inch oversize, stuck up in a lumberyard over winter and planed to size the following spring. When the planing was done we put them under cover in our new lumbershed.

All frames were made in our workshop, with half-corner joints. They were bored at each corner with a pattern which put two holes, slanted at 45 degrees to the right angle, at each corner. Inch dowel pins were then driven into these holes. The frame was squared, braced and taken to it's place in the building. One or two of the larger window frames were

Scroll bar

Scroller

Scroll bar

Regular door and window frames (unless they are metal) are made of 2 x 3 or 2 x 4 inch material, which in it's turn, is covered by trim. In practice, the trim is beveled, beaded and otherwise varied and decorated, giving a fussy, over-dressed effect. Cutting and placing the trim is time-consuming. Flagg proposed that the frames be made of solid timber, be built into the structure and not trimmed at all.

We decided to use 7 x 7 inch local white pine for door and window frames. We had the timbers sawed 1/4 inch oversize, stuck up in a lumberyard over winter and planed to size the following spring. When the planing was done we put them under cover in our new lumbershed.

All frames were made in our workshop, with half-corner joints. They were bored at each corner with a pattern which put two holes, slanted at 45 degrees to the right angle, at each corner. Inch dowel pins were then driven into these holes. The frame was squared, braced and taken to it's place in the building. One or two of the larger window frames were too heavy to handle in one piece. They were built in the shop, assembled, tested for square, taken apart and reaasembled on the job.

Figure 8.34 Example of tiled and layered views.

282 ■ Graphical User Interfaces

Window

Horizontal Scroll bar

Scroller

Vertical Scroll bar

We decided to use 7 x 7 inch local white pine for door and window frames. We had the timbers sawed 1/4 inch over-size, stuck up in a lumberyard over winter and planed to size the following spring. When the planing was done we put them under cover in our new lumbershed.
    All frames were made in our workshop, with half-corner joints. They were bored at each corner with a pattern which put two holes, slanted at 45 degrees

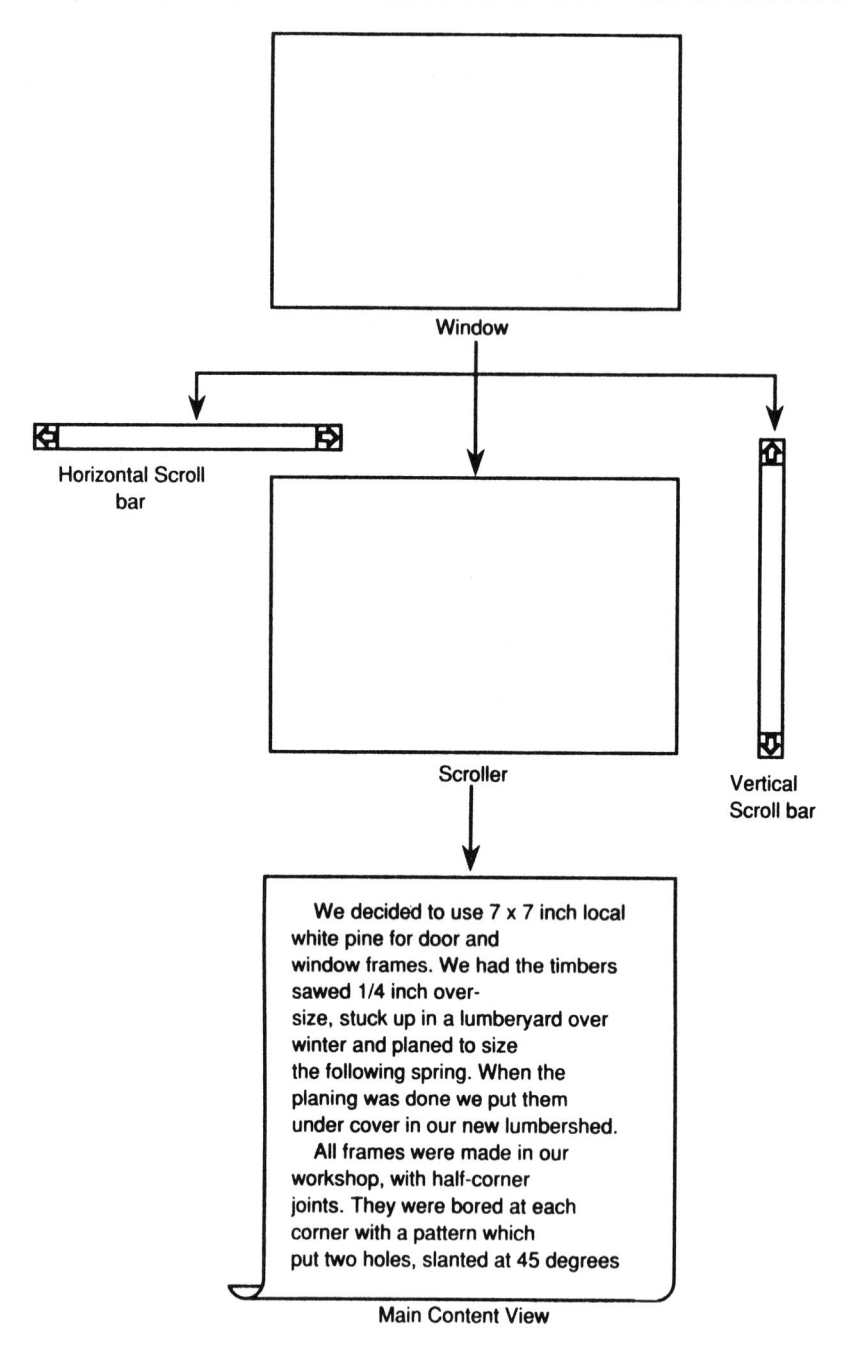

Main Content View

Figure 8.35 Hierarchy of tiled and layered views.

8.5.2.2.4 TCommand

Menu, mouse, and keyboard commands are handled by objects of this class. If desired, a developer can define a subclass of *TCommand* and override the definition of its methods, such as *DoIt*, *UnDoIt*, *ReDoIt*, and *Commit*. When the menu item is chosen, the *DoIt* method will be invoked to perform the appropriate action. If the user chooses to "Undo" and selects that item from the menu bar, the *UnDoIt* method will be called.

8.5.2.2.5 TList

Objects instantiated by this class definition are used to form a list of objects. For example, a *TList* object can be used to keep a list of direct subviews of a view object.

8.5.2.3 *Extensibility*

Users can add any new subclass to the MacApp class hierarchy, provided that they write the extensions using an object-oriented language such as Object Pascal. The MacApp class hierarchy can be extended to define a brand new class definition or a more specialized subclass definition.

To create a brand new class, the user must add a class definition to the hierarchy. For example, a class called *TPalette* can be added to support palettes. Each palette is a table of icons where each icon enables certain types of features. The palette displayed in Figure 8.36 is used in a graphics editor. When the mouse in clicked inside one of the items, such as the pencil icon, the cursor shape and behavior changes. The *TPalette* class definition can be added as a subclass of *TView*, since it is a display object. The developer must define appropriate methods and instance variables to fully implement palettes.

A developer can specialize a class by creating a new subclass definition. For example, a class definition can be added to support windows with built-in horizontal and vertical

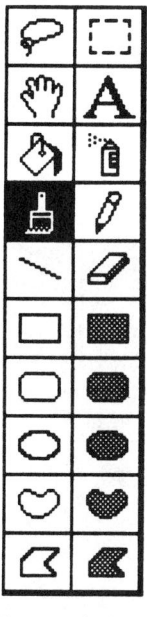

Figure 8.36 Typical Macintosh's palette.

scroll bars. The new subclass definition will be added to the hierarchy as a subclass of *TWindow* with horizontal and vertical scroll bars built in to the subclass.

8.5.3 NeXT

The NeXT computer, introduced in 1988, has grabbed the attention of the computer industry because of its three-dimensional look and feel. The machine has been hailed as the most innovative computer invented in recent times (see Figure 8.37). The computer was initially intended for educational market, but the NeXT Corporation decided to widen the market for its machine to the commercial arena. The success of this machine depends on whether its technical innovations are applied to build new applications.

A brief overview of the NeXT software tools and capabilities follows, along with a discussion of the capabilities of the user interface design. For additional information, refer to Webster (1989) and Knor (1990).

8.5.3.1 *Overview of NeXT Software*

The NeXT computer is designed for use by a wide range of users, from nontechnical to power users. The nontechnical users can take advantage of the graphic user interface to perform tasks by manipulating menus, icons, and dialog boxes. The power user can directly interact with the machine's Mach operating system.

The NeXT system software is comprised of three major pieces: the Mach operating system, applications, and the NeXT user interface. The Mach operating system, devel-

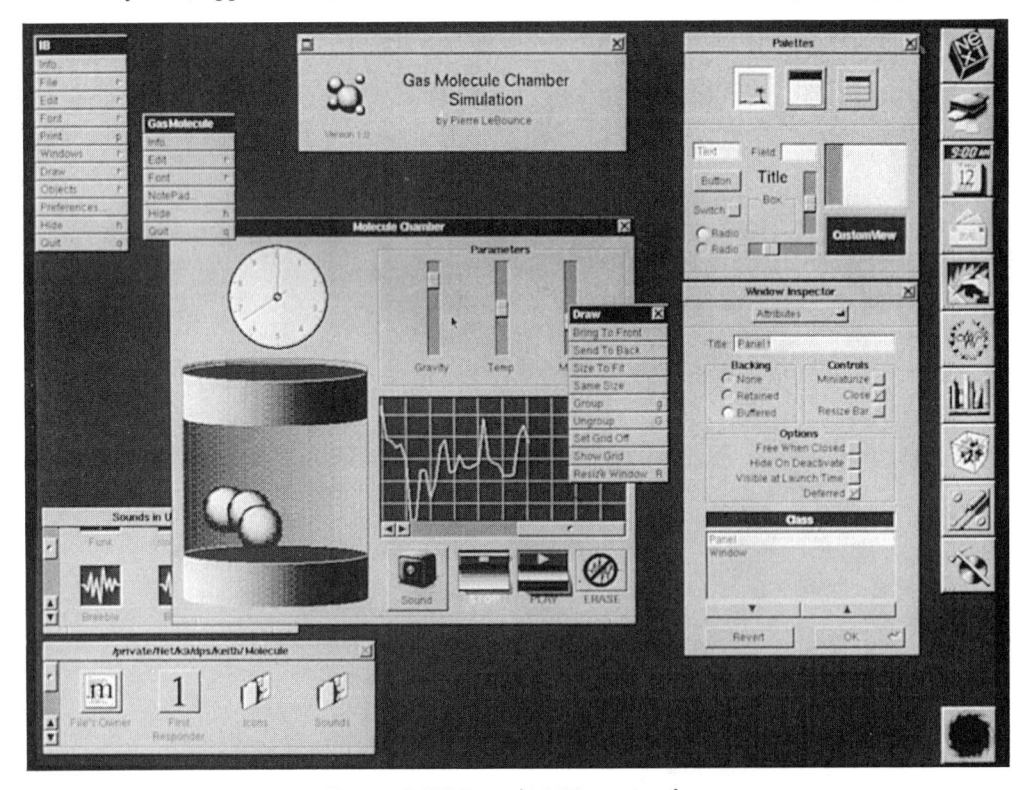

Figure 8.37 Typical NeXT user interface.

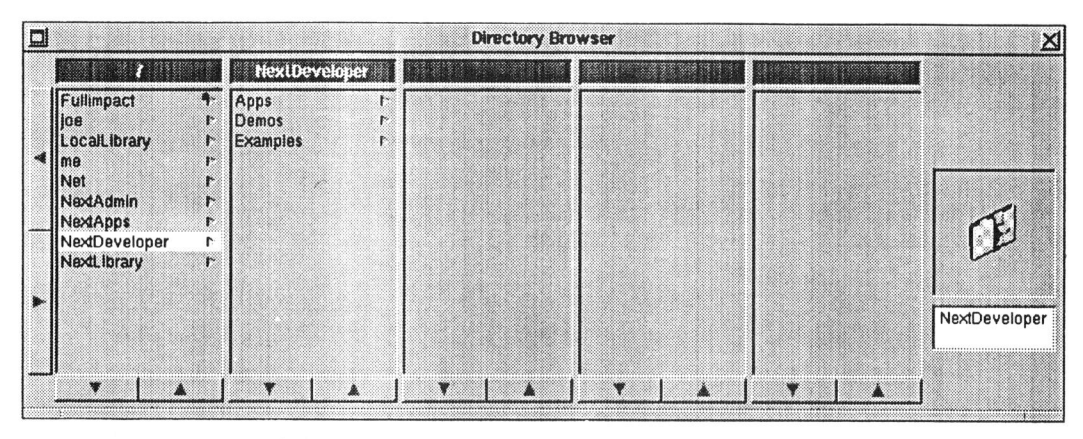

Figure 8.38 NeXT Workspace Manager Directory Browser.

oped at Carnegie Mellon University, is a redesigned UNIX. Mach redesigns the UNIX kernel to reduce the size.

NeXT also comes with a set of bundled applications. Currently, new applications are being developed to take advantage of NeXT hardware and software capabilities. Some of the applications supported on NeXT are NeXT SQL Database Server, Mathematica (symbolic mathematic package), and "what you see is what you get" (WYSIWYG) editors and word processors.

8.5.3.2 NeXT User Interface

The third and last component, the NeXT user interface, is the most impressive piece of NeXT technology. The NeXT user interface draws heavily on direct manipulation and modern graphic user interfaces. The interface has four components: Workspace Manager, Interface Builder, Application Kit, and NeXT Window Server.

The Workspace Manager allows the user to manage files and directories and to execute programs. When a user logs into a NeXT machine, the Workspace Manager is invoked, as shown in Figure 8.38. The Directory Browser window is used to navigate through the files on disk.

The Interface Builder lets the user create interfaces on the screen without writing a single line of code. Users simply select the menu, control, and screen objects from a palette, then move the controls to the desired location. They can also resize the controls to the desired dimension (discussed in more detail shortly).

The Application Kit is a library of user interface objects, used in conjunction with the Interface Builder to design user interfaces. The Application Kit is discussed in the next section.

The Window Server manages all screen activities, such as drawing windows and handling mouse clicks. The Window Server itself does not perform the drawing and screen I/O commands. Display PostScript, designed by Adobe and NeXT, handles all such activities. Up to now, PostScript has been used only as a language for printer engines. With the advent of Display PostScript, both screen and printer share the same protocol. Therefore, one drawing method is used to display objects on the screen and the printer.

8.5.3.3 Application Kit

The Application Kit provides an extensive library of predefined classes. The hierarchy of classes is shown in Figure 8.39. These classes provide functionality to define user interfaces composed of menus, windows, buttons, slide bars, and sound. Each class within the hierarchy defines the behavior of its objects. For example, a menu knows how to handle mouse events, when the user clicks on a menu item.

The Application Kit can be extended by adding new subclasses to the hierarchy. To add a new subclass, the class definition is written using the Objective-C language. Each NeXT machine comes with a copy of Objective-C.

Objective-C is an object-oriented extension of C language (Cox, 1986). The language is a superset of C that uses a modified version of Smalltalk syntax to add object-oriented features. Like Smalltalk, it comes with a large collection of predefined classes to simplify the software development task. The language supports abstract data types, single inheritance, and operator overloading. Unlike C++, Objective-C does not extend definition of any existing C language constructs. It relies totally on the introduction of new constructs and operators to perform tasks such as class definition and message passing.

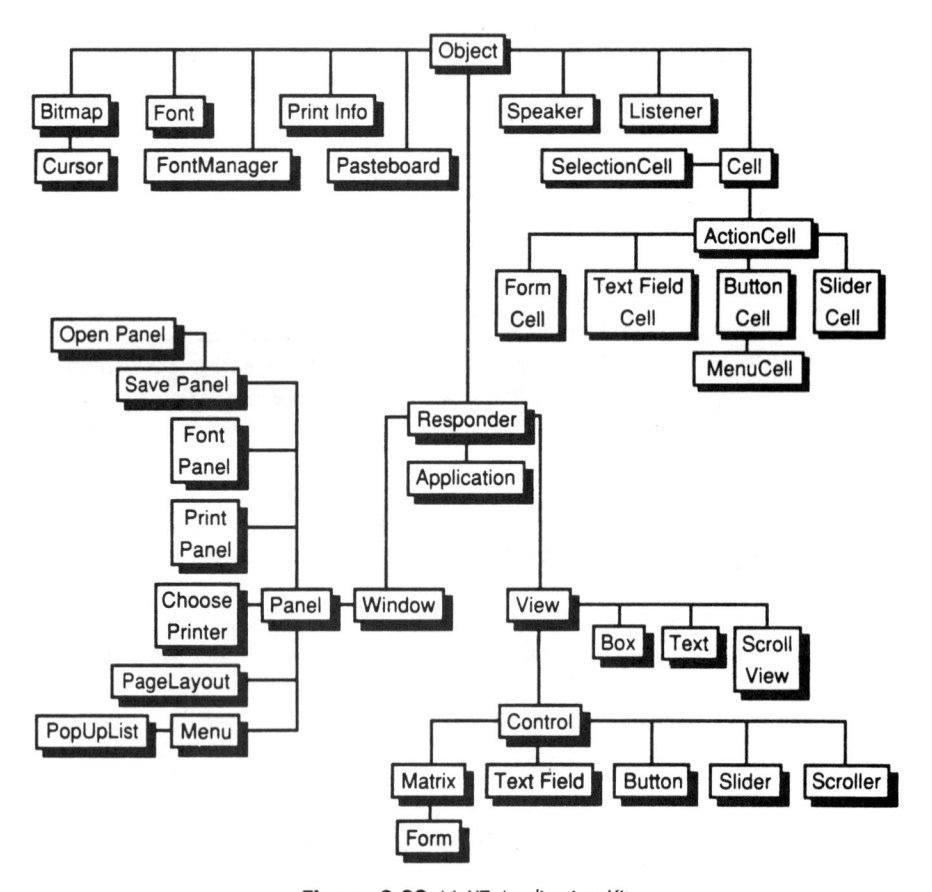

Figure 8.39 NeXT Application Kit.

To develop user interfaces, designers can use Application Kit from Objective-C directly. (This would be very much like developing an application using MacApp.) They can create instances of objects from the Application Kit hierarchy and modify the attributes by calling the methods attached to the class definition. But the other method of defining a user interface, using the Interface Builder, is much easier than coding it entirely in Objective-C.

8.5.3.4 Designing User Interfaces with Interface Builder

The Interface Builder provides a utility for designing a user interface by simply using the mouse and the screen. The Interface Builder is similar to an icon editor or screen painter (see Figure 8.40). Designers can define the screen layout by selecting the screen objects from the Interface Builder palettes. The Interface Builder also helps to define the user-defined class and make connections between objects. However, it doesn't perform all of the work of coding, and the Application Kit and the Objective-C language are also needed.

Defining a user interface using the Interface Builder requires the following steps:

1. *Define layout of screen*. The interface designer defines a user interface by simply selecting screen objects from the Interface Builder palettes, shown in Figure 8.40.

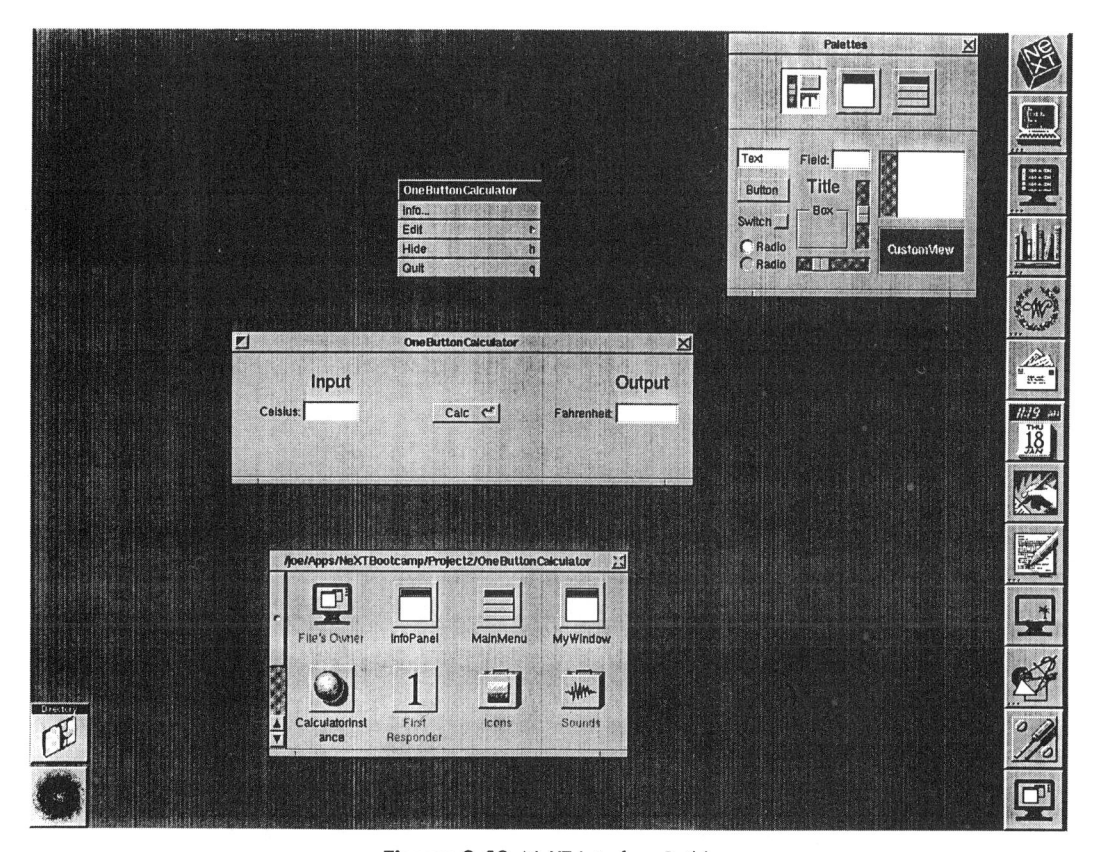

Figure 8.40 NeXT Interface Builder.

Once picked from a palette with the mouse, the object can be dragged into the destination window and resized as desired. The Interface Builder Palettes include objects such as windows, menus, buttons, fields, and radio buttons.

At the top of the palette's window, three buttons allow the interface developer to select a wide array of user interface objects. Clicking the left button displays the view objects such as radio buttons, switches, text fields, horizontal, and vertical scroll bars (see Figure 8.41a). The middle button displays the window palette, which allows the user to define new windows and panels (see Figure 8.41b).

(a)

(b)

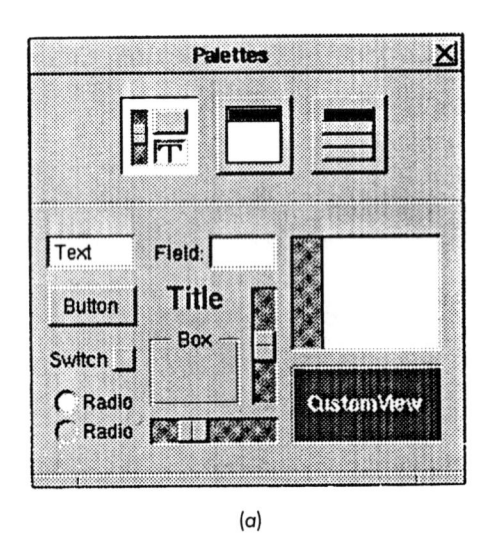

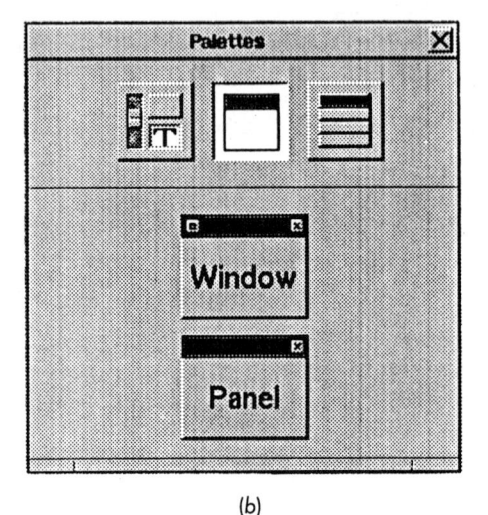

Figure 8.41 NeXT Interface Builder palettes. (a) control palette; (b) window palette.

Clicking the rightmost button (see Figure 8.41c), displays the palette for menus. Application menus can be defined by selecting menu objects from this palette.

Attributes of objects such as the title or text associated with a button are specified using Interface Builder Inspector. For example, the developer can select a window object and drag it to a new area on the screen. Using the Inspector, the developer defines the title of the window and can enable or disable any controls (such as "Miniaturize" or "close" options) by simply clicking on the controls' buttons.

2. *Define the user-defined classes.* The developer defines a new class definition using the Classes Window. The Classes Window allows the developer to extend the Application Kit class hierarchy. The developer navigates through the class hierarchy and creates a new subclass within the hierarchy. Methods and outlets (see below) are defined for this new class definition. When a class is defined this way, only the template of the class is created. The actual implementation of each method is defined later by writing the code in Objective-C.

3. *Make connections.* The previous steps defined the layout of the user interface. At this step, the developer needs to make connections among application objects. For example, when a scroller's slide bar is moved, a message is sent to an application object to perform certain actions such as shifting the text. Again, the Inspector is used to connect user interface objects with methods of classes within the application.

The other form of interconnection is via outlets. An object's outlet contains the object identity of another application object. Thus, an object can send messages to the object connected by its outlets. An object can have many outlets, allowing connections to several objects simultaneously.

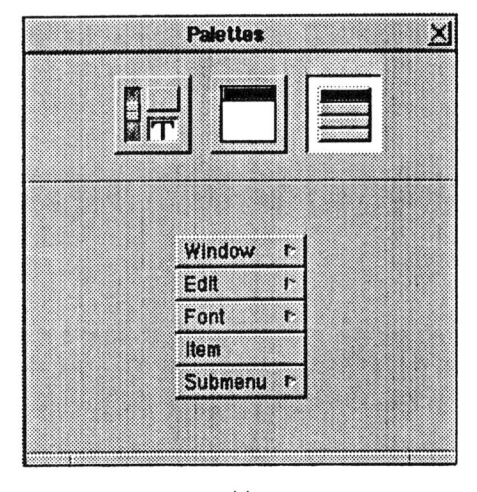

(c)

Figure 8.41 (cont) NeXT Interface Builder palettes. (c) menu palette.

4. *Write actual application code*. The previous steps are handled by Interface Builder directly. The last step is accomplished by writing the application code in Objective-C. When the developer is done with the first two steps, the Interface Builder defines the source files necessary to build the application. These files contain templates for the class definitions and the connections made among objects. At this stage, the developer needs to extend these source files. Extensions are made to specify the logic of the program and the code for method definitions.

8.6 TOOLBOOK: A HYPERMEDIA GUI APPLICATION

After the success of HyperCard on the Macintosh, a long series of hypermedia developments appeared on the IBM PC-compatible personal computers. One of the most successful hypermedia development environments is Asymetrix's ToolBook. ToolBook is an object-oriented hypermedia application development environment for Microsoft Windows.

ToolBook and similar hypermedia development environments provide a complete Windows application development. The next section examines the overall functionality of the ToolBook, then provides an overview of different types of system-defined objects and their properties before examining the ToolBook scripting language. For a more complete coverage of Toolbox, refer to Asymetrix (1989 and 1990).

8.6.1 Overview

Windows applications in ToolBook are called books. Each book contains one or more pages. Pages can contain any combination of text, graphics, and Windows control elements such as radio buttons, check boxes, or edit boxes. Pages can be connected together with links, which are attached to objects on a page (such as buttons). These concepts are illustrated in Figure 8.42. When the user presses the "Next" button, the next page in the series of pages will appear on the screen.

ToolBook supports two types of users: readers and authors. Readers can flip through pages of a book, add pages, edit text in fields, and print results. At author level, new books can be designed. Pages of a book can be designed at this level with the ToolBook authoring tools. (See Figure 8.43). Graphics, buttons, and text can be placed anywhere on the screen. Linkages between pages can be defined; they either identify a page as the destination or attach a script with the screen object to compute a corresponding destination page.

ToolBook application can communicate with other Windows and non-Windows applications through Windows dynamic data exchange (DDE) and dynamic link libraries (DLL). With access to Windows DDE, Windows applications can communicate with each other and share data. ToolBook applications can communicate with other Windows applications. The OpenScript language provides the necessary constructs to transmit messages and data through Windows DDE.

ToolBook also provides access to Windows dynamic link libraries (DLL). Thus, it can invoke both Windows and non-Windows applications and procedures. The OpenScript language also provides constructs to access Windows DLL.

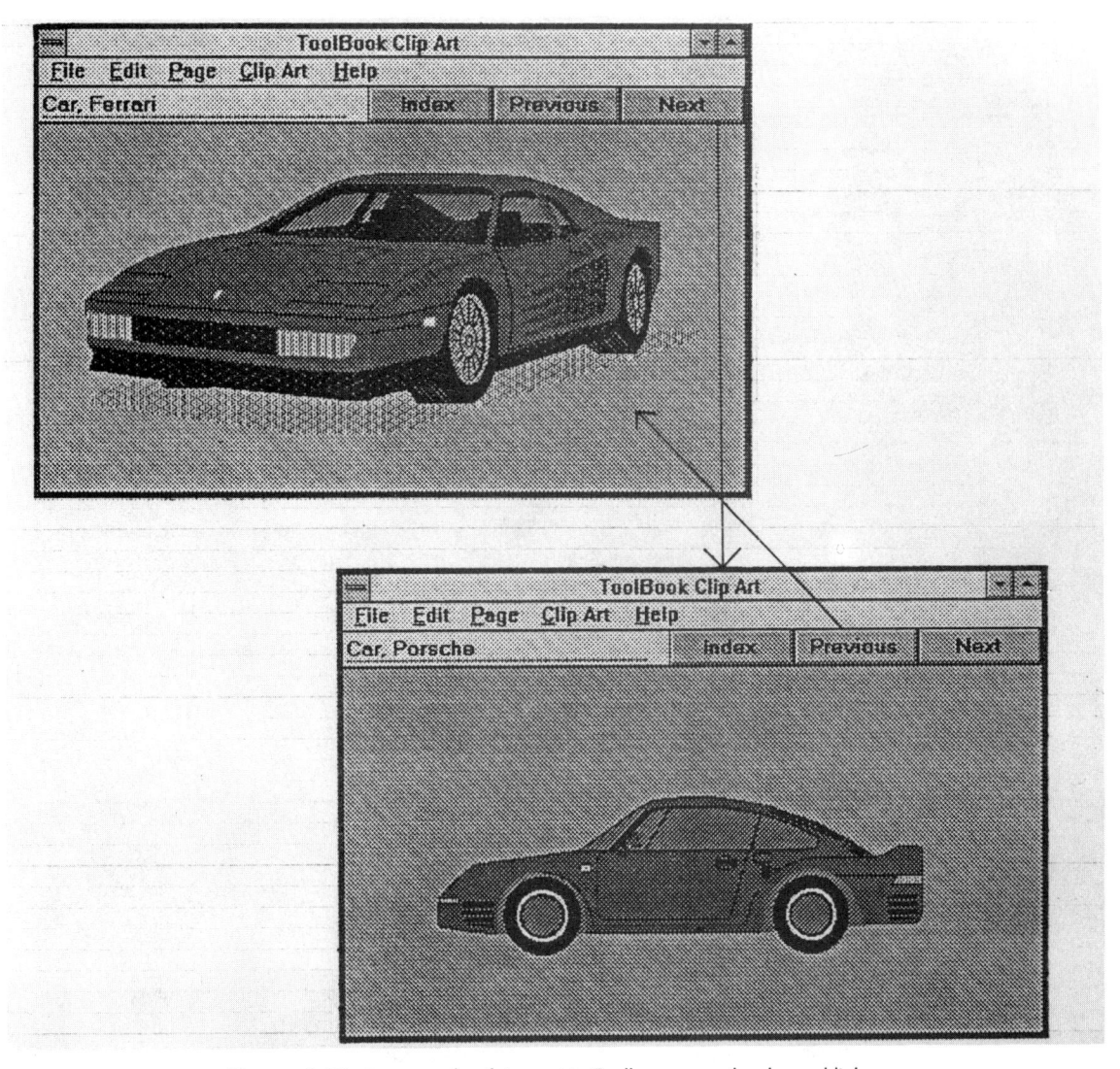

Figure 8.42 An example of Asymetrix Toolbox pages, books, and links.

8.6.2 ToolBook Objects

ToolBook is an object-oriented environment. Each of the ToolBook components (books, pages, buttons, and so on) is considered an object. Each object has a set of properties that can be modified at author level.

Properties are further divided into identifiers and visual style properties. Identifiers specify the type of the object (button, field, graphs, and so on), its name, its unique ID, and information about its relationship to a given page, such as whether it's part of the foreground or background of a page. Visual style properties include the object's border and fill color, text formats for a button or a field, the pattern and line style for graphics,

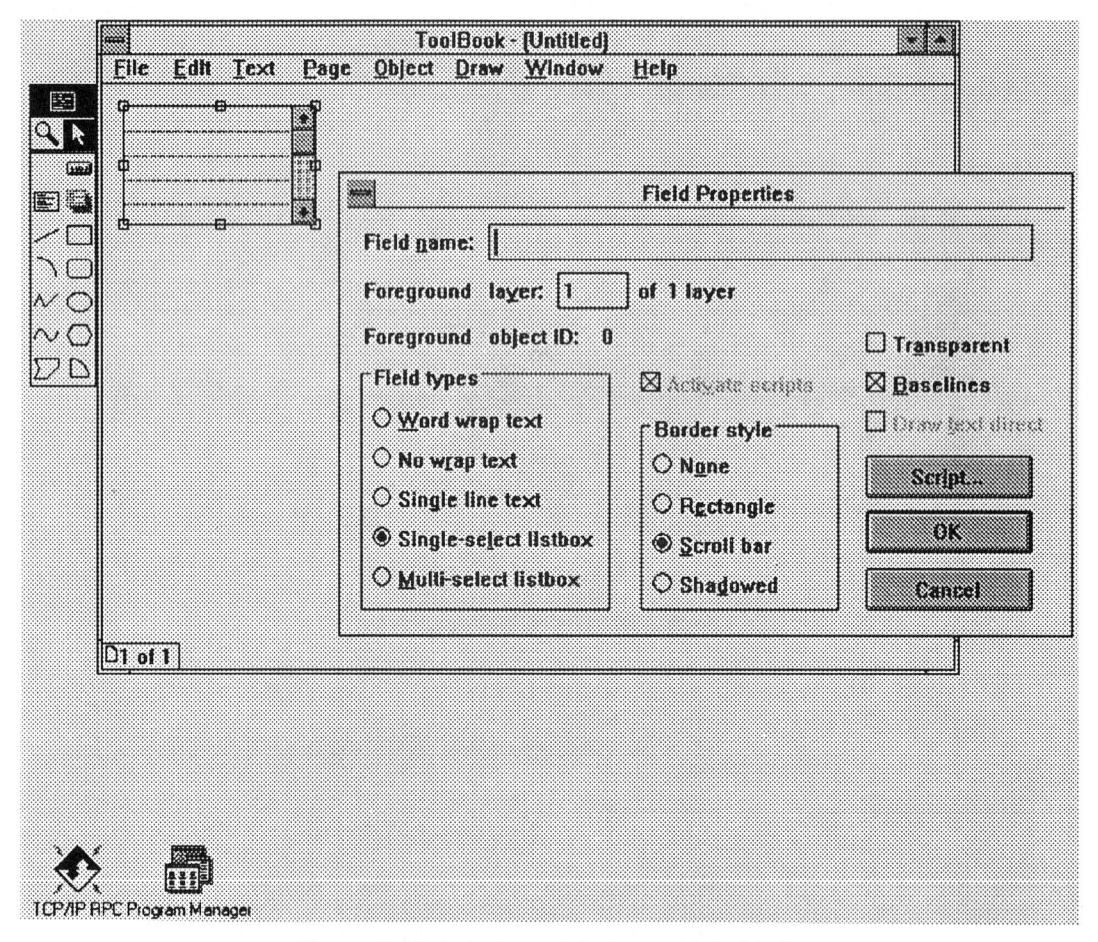

Figure 8.43 Authoring tools in Asymetrix's ToolBook.

a button's or field's visual appearance, and whether an object is transparent or opaque. Figure 8.43 illustrates properties that are attached to field objects.

In addition, each object has a script, which is a program written in ToolBook's OpenScript programming language (discussed shortly). A script, attached to an object, handles the messages sent by the user or an application to that object. For example, a script attached to the "Next" button on the display in Figure 8.44 causes the next page to get displayed on the screen, whereas the script attached to the "Search" button causes the application to search for software with a given title or subject provided by the end user.

The following subsections describe each of the ToolBook objects and their properties with more detail.

8.6.2.1 Books

Books are composed of one or more pages. At any given time, a single page of a book is displayed on the screen. Book properties include a caption, which can appear on the title bar; page size and orientation (vertical or horizontal); and passwords, which provide protection for accessing a book either as a reader or an author. In addition, an author can attach scripts to a book. Book scripts are used to handle messages sent to a book or messages that have not been handled by the objects on the current page.

8.6.2.2 *Pages*

A page is the basic unit of viewing information on a screen. Each page is composed of several layers, including background and foreground layers. Each object on a page dwells on a single layer. Backgrounds are shared by several pages of a book and convey information common in those pages. Each book can have those backgrounds. Each background is also treated as an object. Background properties include name, fill pattern, background color, and number of objects on the background.

Foreground layers convey information that is unique to each page. For example, in Figure 8.44, information about the current software item will be on the foreground layers, and the buttons at the bottom of the page ("Next," "Search," and so on) that are commonly used will be part of the background layer.

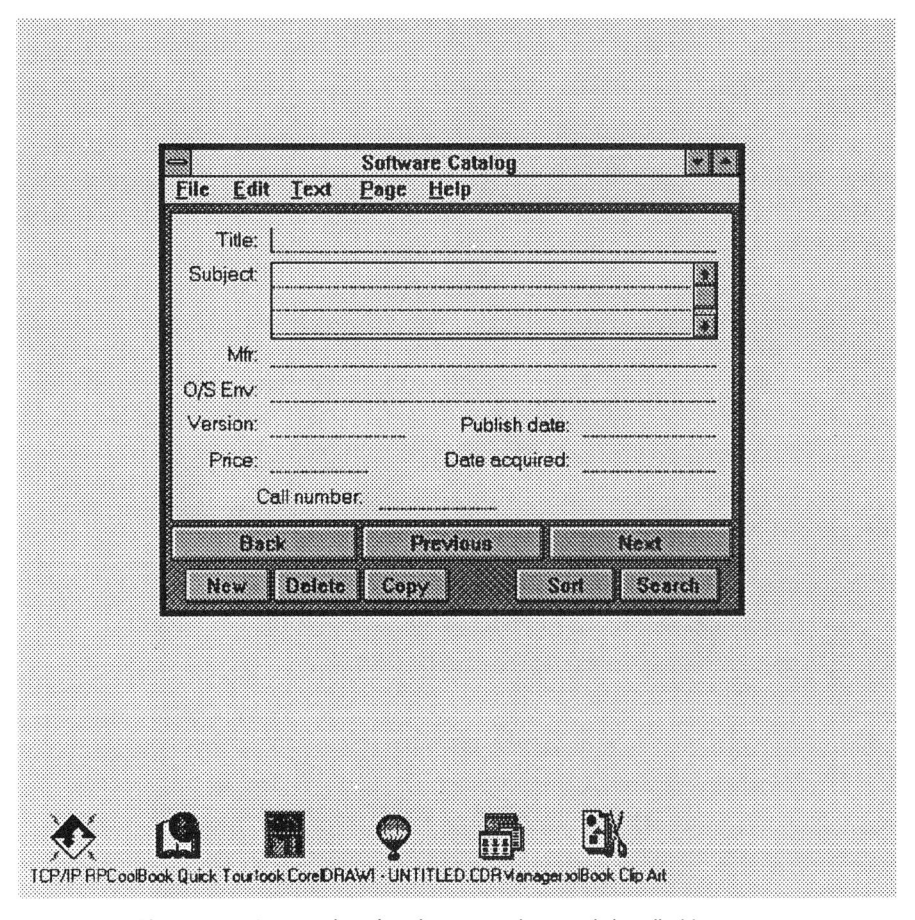

Figure 8.44 Typical ToolBook page, with controls handled by scripts.

8.6.2.3 Fields

Fields provide objects where the user and the application can read, display, edit, and format text on a page. Field objects can be defined with a variety of visual styles, such as single-line vs. multiple-line and support for scroll bar. Field properties include name, layer number, ID, border style (shadowed, none, rectangle, scroll bar), single-line, transparent, and baseline (dotted lines to show the line spacing).

Text appearing in a field object can be entered by both readers and authors. In addition, an author can decide to designate the contents of a field as read-only; such fields are called locked fields and are used to display informational messages.

An author can attach scripts to parts of one or more words, called hotwords, in a field. When the user clicks on a hotword, the appropriate script is executed, causing another page to appear on the screen, hidden fields to display, or other operations to be performed.

8.6.2.4 Buttons

Buttons are popular control elements in GUI applications. ToolBook provides several styles of buttons, including checkbox, radio, and several rectangular styles such as invisible border, rounded edges, and shadowed border. Button properties include name, label appearing on the button, border style, layer number, ID, transparent or opaque appearance, and a script attached to the button.

Buttons are commonly used to link pages of a book together. An author can modify the script of a button to go to a specific page of the current book or any other book.

8.6.2.5 Graphics

ToolBook provides tools to design detailed graphics objects. Each graphic on the screen is treated as a single object with its own properties such as script, ID, and shape type (circle, rectangle, fill pattern, and so on).

ToolBook supports two types of graphics: draw objects and paint objects. Draw objects include lines, arcs, rectangles, polygons, ellipses, and pie wedges. ToolBook provides tools to draw these shapes and to modify their properties, such as pen color, shape, and fill pattern. Paint objects are essentially any monochrome or color bitmap. Any bitmap can be pasted from the Windows Clipboard, placed on a page, and resized to the appropriate proportions.

8.6.3 OpenScript Language

Scripts are used to define the behavior of objects such as a page, button, or hotword. OpenScript is an object-oriented programming language that defines the behavior of any ToolBook object. To communicate with an object using OpenScript, a message is sent to the object. For example, in order to display a hidden button, a show message is sent to a named button object.

OpenScript is a full-fledged programming language with a wide range of operators such as arithmetic, logical, and string concatenation. It supports local and systemwide variables and treats all variables as string variables. It also supports control constructs such as *if...then...else*, *while* and *do...until* loops, and conditions...*when...else* (*switch* or *case* statement). In addition, OpenScript provides a long list of built-in functions to support arithmetic functions (such as trig functions, min, max, random number generation, and so on); string functions such as case conversions, word and character count; and others.

```
              to handle buttonup
                 - - - - -
                 - - - - -
                 - - - - -
              end
              to handle buttonDoubleClick
                 - - - - -
                 - - - - -
              end
```

Figure 8.45 Typical ToolBook message handlers.

OpenScript programs are usually written in small pieces. Each piece, called a script, is defined as part of an object definition. Each object's script specifies messages handled by this object and is composed of one or more message handlers. Each message handler is a group of OpenScript statements that manages a particular message. For example, Figure 8.45 displays a script attached to a button. This script handles two messages: button up and button double click.

Messages can be built-in or user-defined. Built-in messages indicate ToolBook events such as menu activities (choosing an item from a menu), mouse or keyboard activities (mouse up, down, double click, or typing a character in a field), object creation or destruction, mouse focus activity (mouse leaving or entering an object region), or no activity (idle event). Built-in messages are generated by the system, are caused by a user action, or are the result of another script sending a message to an object.

User-defined messages handle menu commands and any user-specified messages that are usually sent from one script to another script. For example, the developer could choose to display different information on a page based on the user's level of expertise with a book (novice or advanced). To do so, two messages could be defined, called *Novice* and *Expert*. When each message is sent to a book, different options and buttons will appear on each page.

When a message is generated by an event, such as a mouse button being released (*buttonUp*), the message is sent to the object located under the pointer when that event occurred. That object may choose to handle this event. If it does not handle the event, the message will travel through the ToolBook object hierarchy, which is shown in Figure 8.46. For example, if the pointer happens to be placed on a button at the time of release and that button's script does not handle this activity, then the group object containing this button is examined, the page object's script is examined, and so on.

All built-in messages have default handlers. There are no default handlers for user-defined messages and ToolBook will generate an error message.

8.7 NewWave

Hewlett-Packard introduced NewWave into the market in 1989. NewWave provides a layer on top of Microsoft Windows that enhances and extends the capabilities provided by Windows with respect to communication, abstraction, ease of use, control, and other issues. In the future, it is expected that the NewWave environment will be offered on top of UNIX and OS/2 machines.

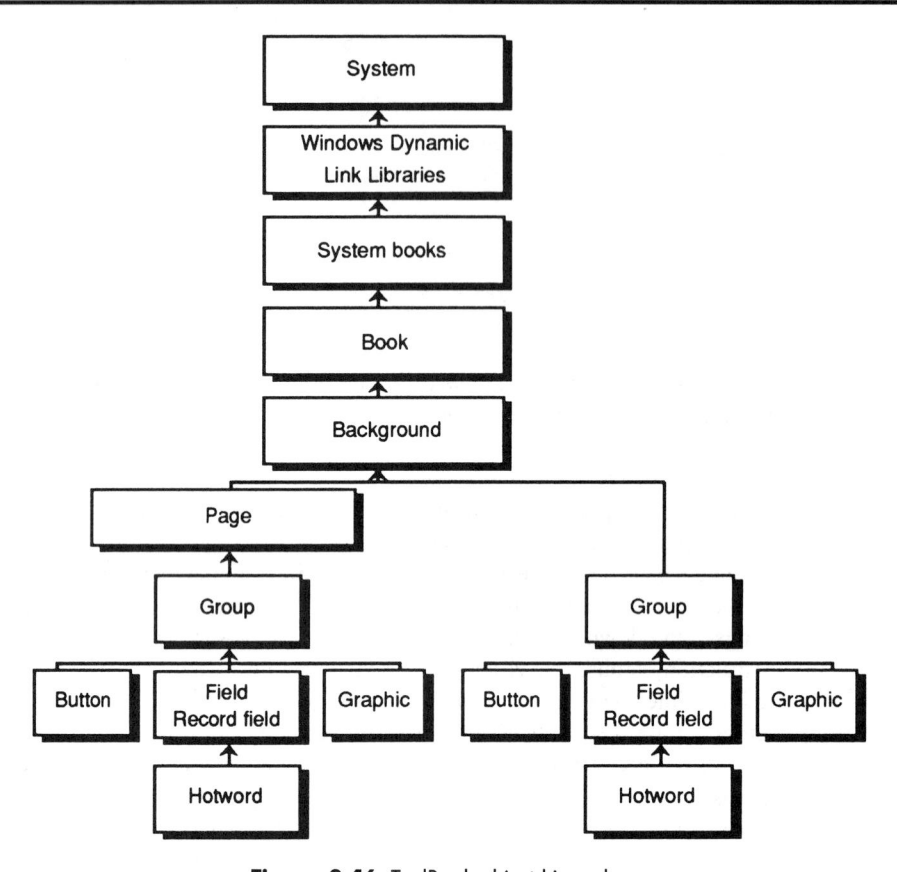

Figure 8.46 ToolBook object hierarchy.

8.7.1 Overview of NewWave Software

NewWave comes with a set of utilities including the NewWave Office (Hewlett-Packard, 1988). NewWave applies the desktop metaphor and object orientation throughout its environment, and it allows end users to create compound documents composed of text, graphics, images and voice. NewWave (and its tools such as NewWave Office) provide an end user environment that is easier to use than DOS. Existing tools such as Lotus 1-2-3 or dBASE can run within the environment with no change.

To take full advantage of NewWave, however, the application must be retrofitted to work within the NewWave environment. Several software companies such as Microsoft, Adobe, Gupta Technologies, Neuron Data, and Samna have committed to writing new applications for use with NewWave or to rewriting existing applications.

When NewWave is invoked, the NewWave Office window displays on the screen, as depicted in Figure 8.47. NewWave Office provides a desktop metaphor environment for office end users. It includes tools such as a Printer icon, an electronic mail utility (Mail), and a WYSIWYG word processor (Write) supporting the full capabilities of the NewWave environment.

In terms of ease of use, one of the advantages of NewWave is that it provides a desktop metaphor for DOS machines. NewWave Office displays every tool, utility, end user file and document as icons on a desk. The end user manipulates the system by manipulating these icons.

NewWave views everything as an object. For example, spreadsheet data is treated as an object. When the user clicks on the spreadsheet icon, NewWave automatically loads the spreadsheet tool with the end user data in that object. One of the strengths of NewWave is that it allows the user to create compound documents composed of varied types of data. The end user can also share an object among several compound documents or provide a limited portion of an object within another compound object. For example, a section from a spreadsheet, or even a bar chart representation of the spreadsheet, can be included within a compound document.

8.7.2 NewWave Architecture

The architecture underlying the NewWave utilities is composed of two major components: the Object Management Facility (OMF) and the Application Programming Interface (API). Figure 8.48 displays the relationship of these components to Microsoft Windows and the end user.

The Object Management Facility (OMF) manages the interrelationship of objects created in NewWave. An object can be any type of data or application—a spreadsheet utility, a database tool, an image, or a text file.

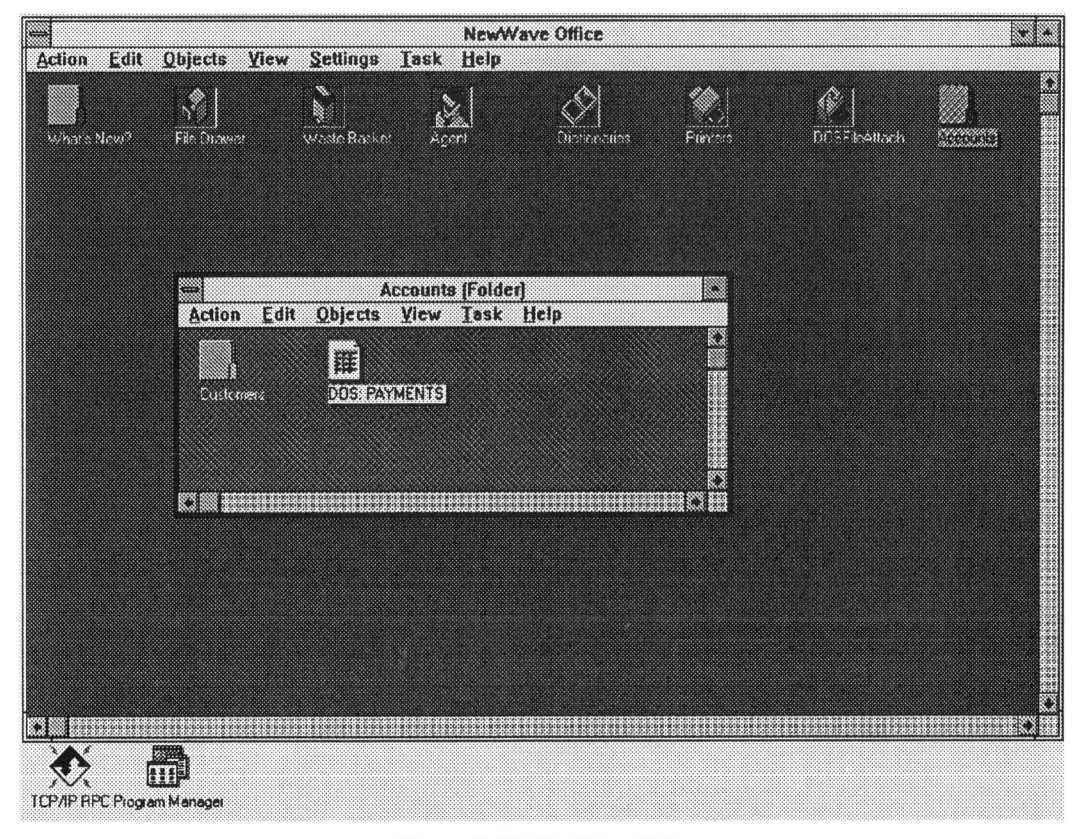

Figure 8.47 NewWave Office.

298 ■ **Graphical User Interfaces**

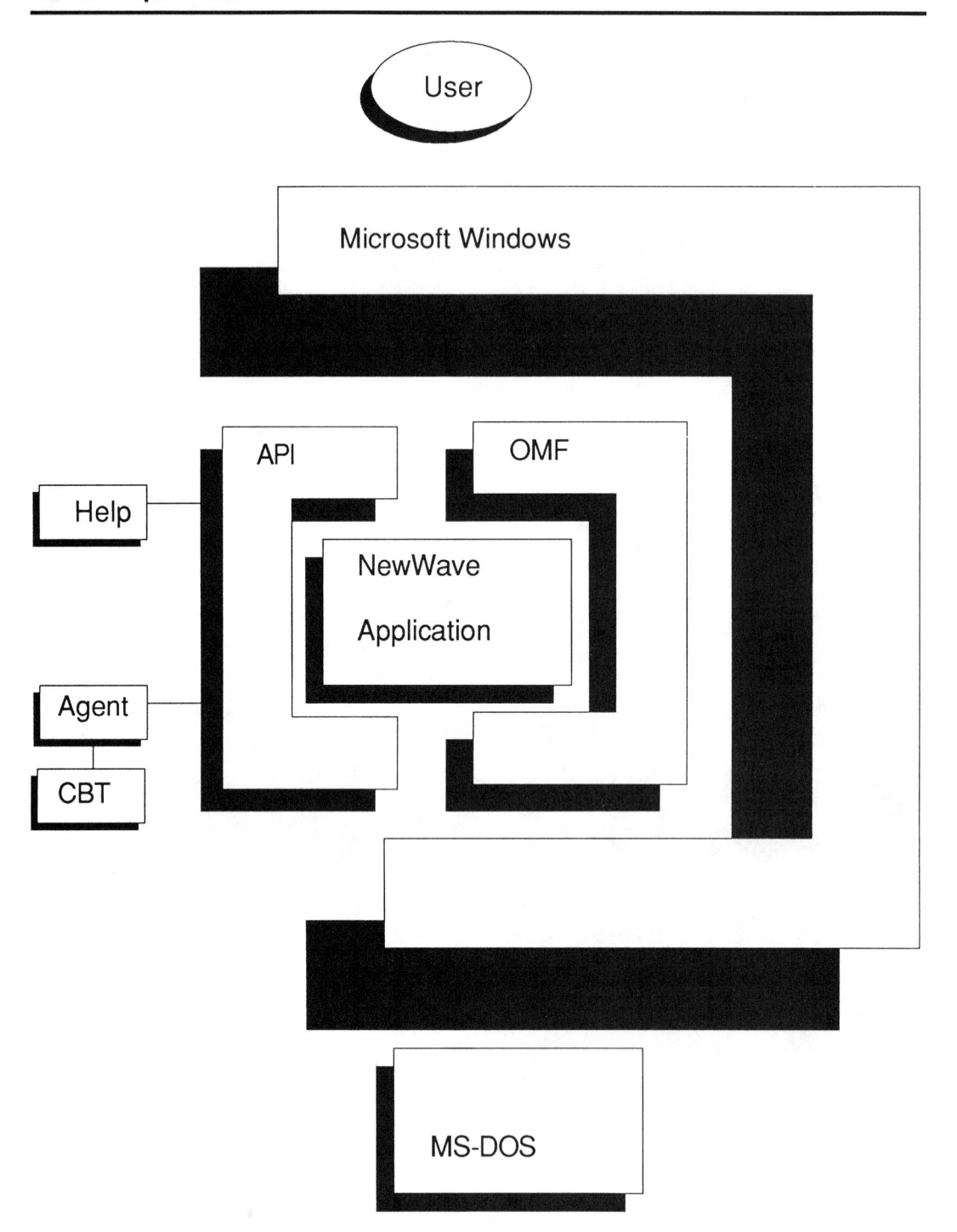

Figure 8.48 The NewWave architecture.

The OMF allows data created by different applications to be combined to form a compound document. Each application remains responsible for maintaining its own piece of data. The OMF allows these pieces of data to be treated as objects. It keeps track of links created from one data object to another one. The OMF allows the user to create different types of links between objects. (OMF objects and links are covered in more detail in a section to come.)

A financial report is an example of a compound document. A report usually contains diverse types of data, such as the pie chart, text, and bitmapped image shown in Figure 8.49. Each data type can be created and maintained by a separate tool, and the entire compound document (representing the financial report and all of its components) is seen as an object by the OMF. When the report is printed or updated, each of the data objects is printed or updated by the corresponding utility that understands it.

The Application Programming Interface provides a set of system-wide services, such as Agent Facility, Computer-Based Training (CBT), and context-sensitive help.

The Agent Facility provides a batch facility for Windows applications. Users can record, save, and play back a set of Windows activities. The playback can be activated either at a specified time or by user demand.

The NewWave CBT facility, which is an application of the Agent facility, allows the user to develop on-line tutorials for new tools. Developers can create lessons to teach different features of their NewWave tool. CBT authors can easily monitor, record, play back,

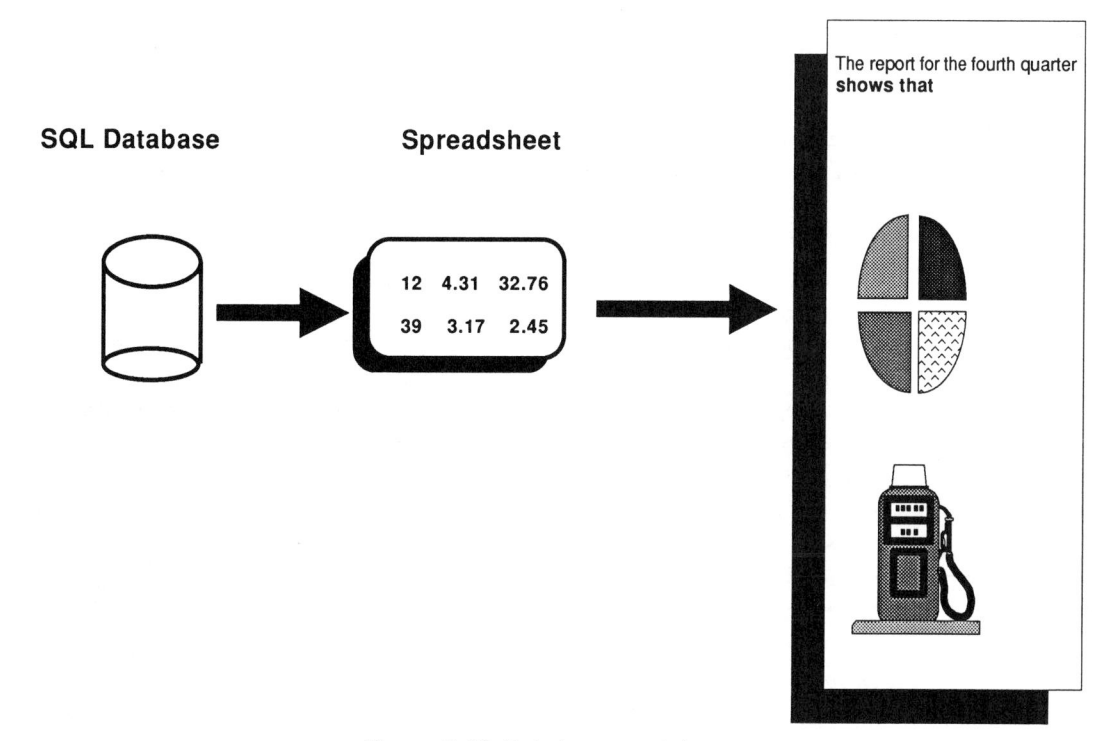

Figure 8.49 Typical compound document.

and get responses from their student users. The CBT facility allows an author to create on-line tutorials without extensive knowledge of NewWave or Windows programming.

A NewWave application developer applies the context-sensitive help facility to catalog and link help messages to the application commands. The help subsystem for the NewWave application can be developed in parallel with the development of the application.

8.7.3 Object Management Facility

In addition to managing objects created by the system and the end user, NewWave OMF also manages the relationship of objects with each other. The following section discusses different types of objects and links that can be created in OMF.

The Object Management Facility provides an object-based file system and manages all relationships between user data and applications. Different types of information, ranging from user data to applications, are treated as objects. Users can create links among several types of objects. These links can contain several objects into a folder object or link an application and data together as a single object that can be manipulated as a single entity. Even though an application may be part of a compound object, the user can still double click on the application object, bring up the application, and manipulate the original data file. For example, an icon representing a spreadsheet can be dragged into a report document. Though the icon is inside the report document, clicking on the spreadsheet icon loads only the spreadsheet, not the report.

In addition, objects can communicate to each other using messages. For example, when an entire compound document is displayed, a message is sent to each child object to display its own view of the data.

8.7.3.1 Objects

As stated previously, objects can be created by the user or the system. Figure 8.50, used throughout this section, demonstrates different types of objects managed by OMF. The different types of objects permitted include user objects, office tools and systems objects, container objects, and compound objects.

1. *User objects* are created by the user to manage data such as databases, spreadsheets, charts, images, and voice. User objects are linked to their applications. For example, double clicking on the Payroll icon automatically starts the database application and loads the user data corresponding to the payroll database.

   User objects can easily be moved, copied, and destroyed by the user. To destroy a user object, for example, the user drags the object icon on top of the Waste Basket icon.

2. *Office tools and system objects:* NewWave treats all tools and system services as objects.

3. *Container objects* hold one or more objects. A file folder, or the Waste Basket, is a perfect example of a container object. When a file folder is opened, it displays icons or titles representing list of objects it contains.

4. *Compound objects* provide the ability to handle objects that are composed of simple objects or other compound objects. Compound objects can be printed, copied, and moved as a single object. Compound objects communicate with containing objects via messages. For example, to print a business report composed of graphics,

Office Tool

A File Drawer

Container Object

A Folder

Compound Object

A Technical Report

Simple Object

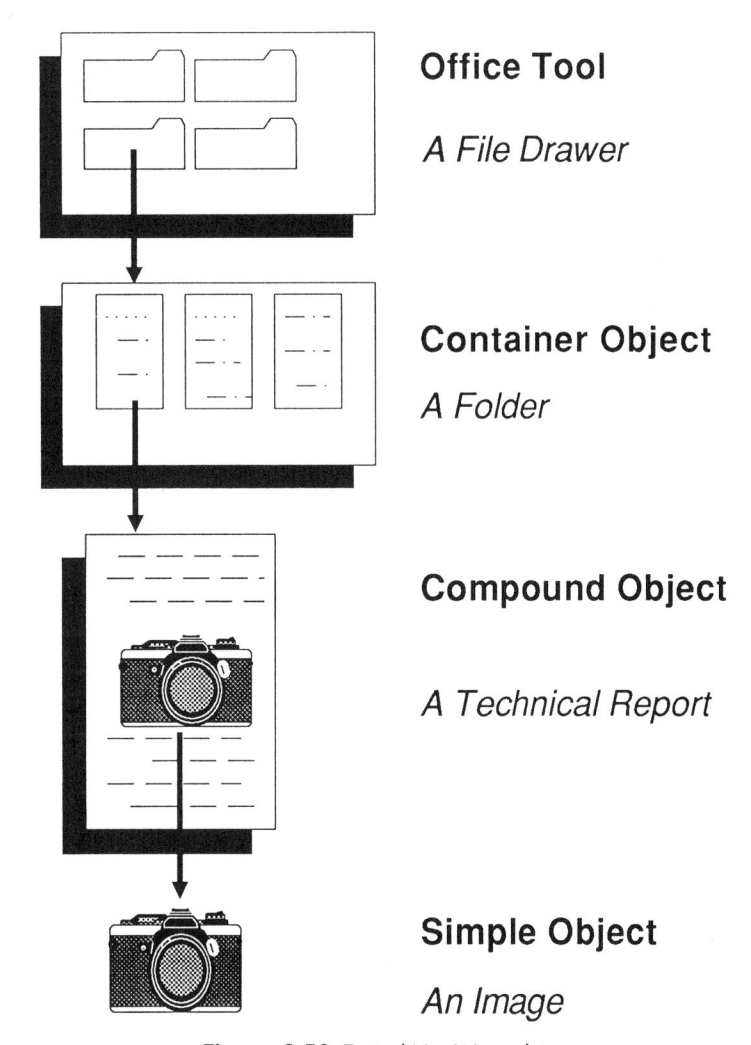

An Image

Figure 8.50 Typical NewWave objects.

spreadsheet, and text objects, the compound object sends messages to the individual objects to print themselves. Thus, the graphic tool is invoked to print the graphics.

8.7.3.2 Links and Views

Links and views allow connections between OMF objects. The links in OMF form a directed acyclic graph. This means that any object can have multiple parents and children. An object can be included in one or more compound documents, as depicted in Figure 8.51.

Objects can share and pass information through links. For example, multiple links to a single object allow an object to be shared by several compound objects. Suppose an object is shared among several other objects. If the source object is modified, OMF automatically notifies the destination objects and updates the compound objects.

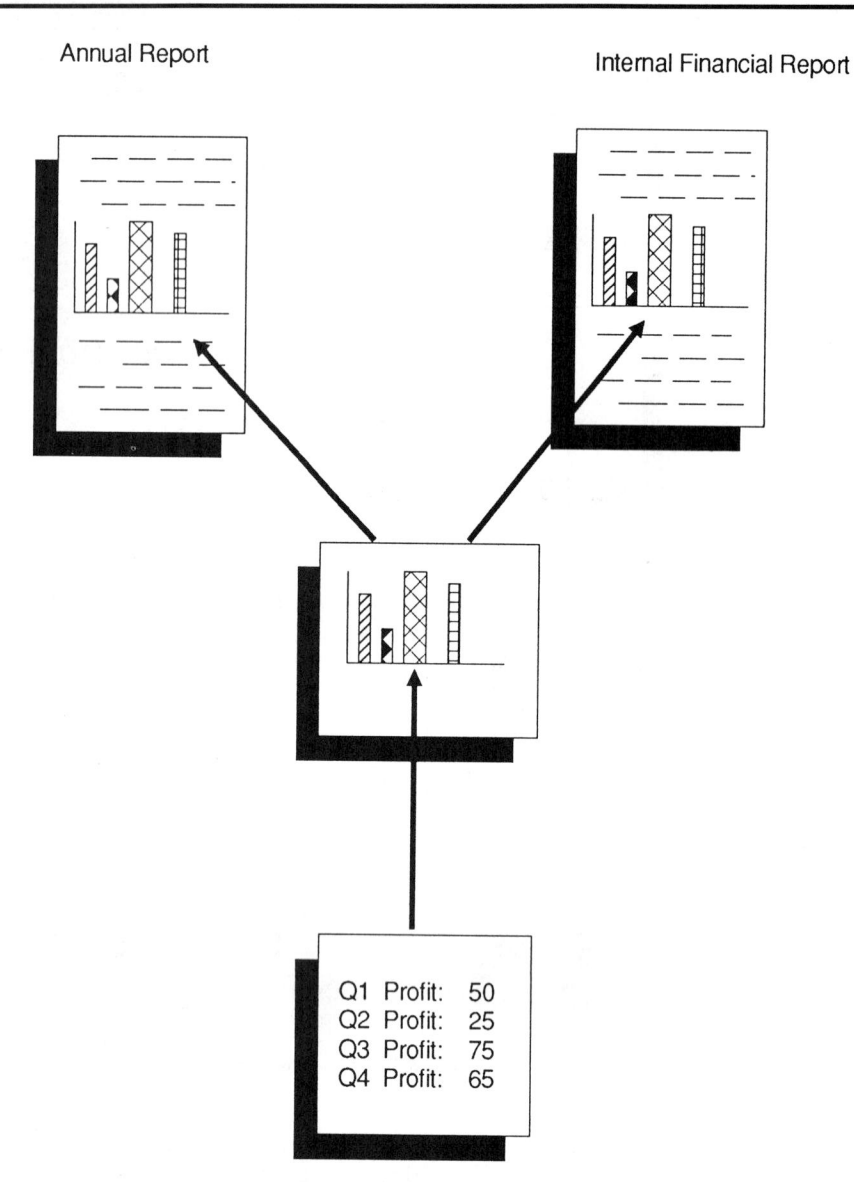

Figure 8.51 Typical NewWave object sharing.

All links are persistent and dynamic. For example, an object is part of several compound objects. A user updates the object by accessing the application directly. The new changes affect all references of the child object in the compound documents.

Figure 8.52 displays an example of different types of OMF links. Three types of links are allowed:

1. *Simple links* are used mainly by container objects to connect to other objects. For example, a file folder is connected with its individual files using simple links.

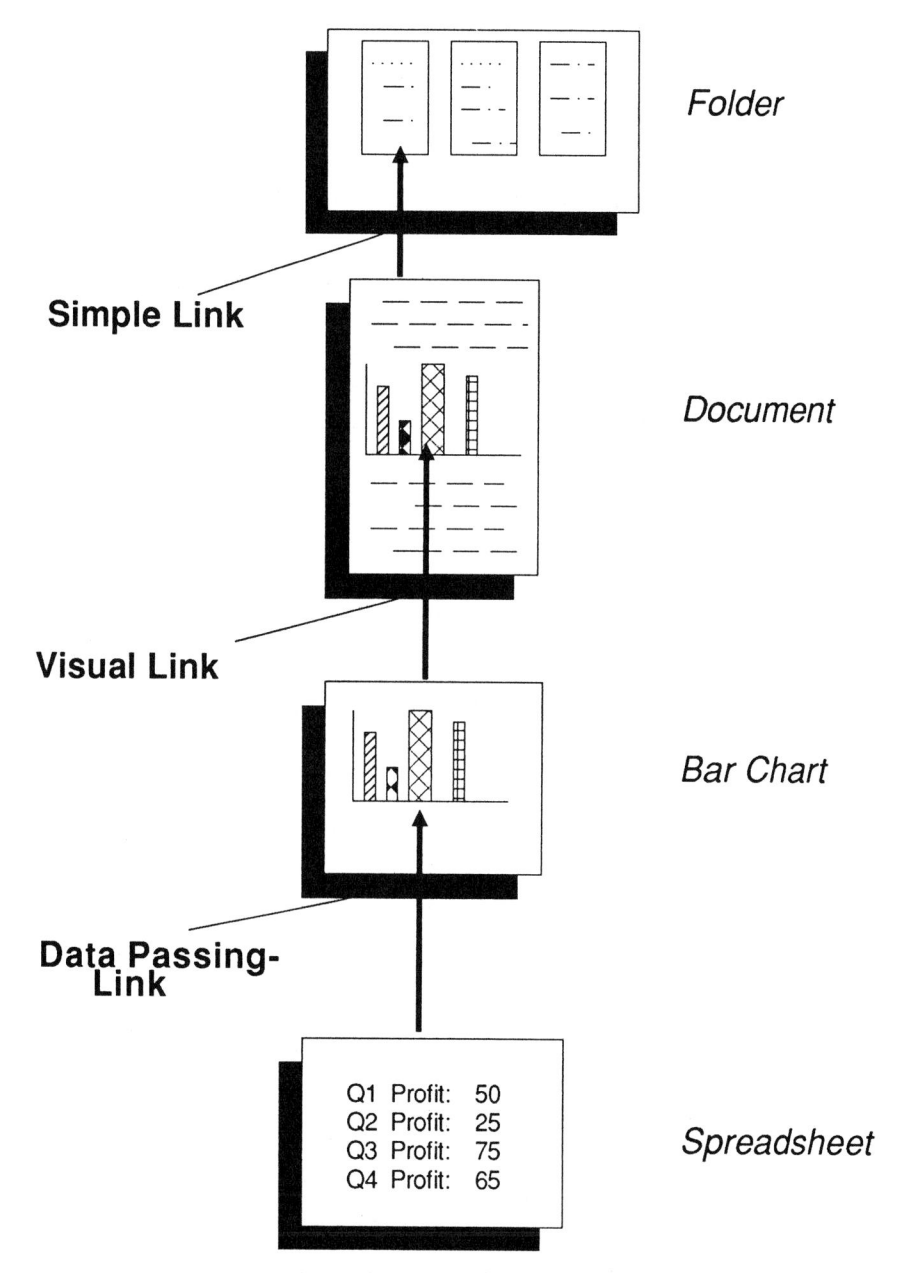

Figure 8.52 Typical NewWave links.

2. *Visual links* allow one object to be projected inside another object. For example, a pie chart graph is included in the financial report using a visual link.
3. *Data-passing links* allow data to be passed from one object to another one, thus allowing interpretation of the data by the destination object. For example, a portion of a spreadsheet's cells can be passed into a graphic tool to draw a pie chart representing the spreadsheet data.

8.8 SUMMARY

As demonstrated in this chapter, the utilization of graphical user interfaces is widespread among different users within an office. The graphical user interfaces enable users at any level of expertise, ranging from the novice to the computer expert, to apply computers with a greater ease of use. With a simple click of a mouse button or the simple operation of dragging an object from one folder to another folder, office objects can be manipulated.

This chapter presented the basic concepts of graphical user interfaces such as menus, dialogs, and icons. We also discussed concepts such as direct manipulation and physical metaphor. We demonstrated the utility of these concepts in providing a computing environment that fits seamlessly within the working environment of an office worker. We also presented two popular PC-based GUI systems: MS Windows and Apple's Macintosh. We believe that these systems will be the major front-end platforms for the intelligent office environments. In addition, we discussed some of the development tools available on these platforms: MacApp for Macintosh and Actor and ToolBook for MS Windows.

Chapter 10 demonstrates the utility of the graphical user interfaces in intelligent offices and typical office objects such as documents and folders.

9
MULTI-MEDIA OBJECTS IN THE OFFICE

■ 9.1 INTRODUCTION

Earlier chapters discussed the devices and peripherals that manipulate multi-media data and the imaging systems that utilize those data. This chapter concentrates on the structure and use of multi-media objects in the office.

The advent of multi-media technology has made the concept of the intelligent office possible. No longer is the office worker limited to using simple computer data types for the expression of information. Multi-media provides the foundation for a new paradigm in information processing.

This chapter attempts to define the multi-media objects that provide the foundation for data processing in the intelligent office. The multi-media model is explained in detail, showing how the model's flexibility and extensibility allow the intelligent office to evolve in a variety of different directions.

What is multi-media? There is no single definition for this term. The question needs to be answered, not only with respect to the concept of multi-media as perceived by such leaders in the field as Commodore, Apple, and more recently Microsoft, but also in terms of how multi-media will be defined in the context of the intelligent office environment.

The basic concept of multi-media is the marriage of voice, text, image, and video data types within an application to enhance the output. Multi-media combines traditional data processing with graphics, speech, animation, audio, video and synthesis. The standard emphasis of multi-media is to enhance presentation software for corporate users. Figure 9.1 illustrates a typical multi-media presentation system.

The concept of multi-media under the intelligent office is a much broader and more useful paradigm. The goal of multi-media in the intelligent office is to enhance the productivity of the user by improving traditional office data-processing techniques through expanding both the types of data processed and the methods used for processing the data. Intelligent offices combine the typical multi-media types of text, image, video, and sound with full-text, hypertext, and pattern recognition processing methods to provide a phenomenal improvement in the usefulness and quality of corporate data.

The intelligent office's multi-media capabilities are based on an object-oriented paradigm. This approach increases the ability of the intelligent office to model real-

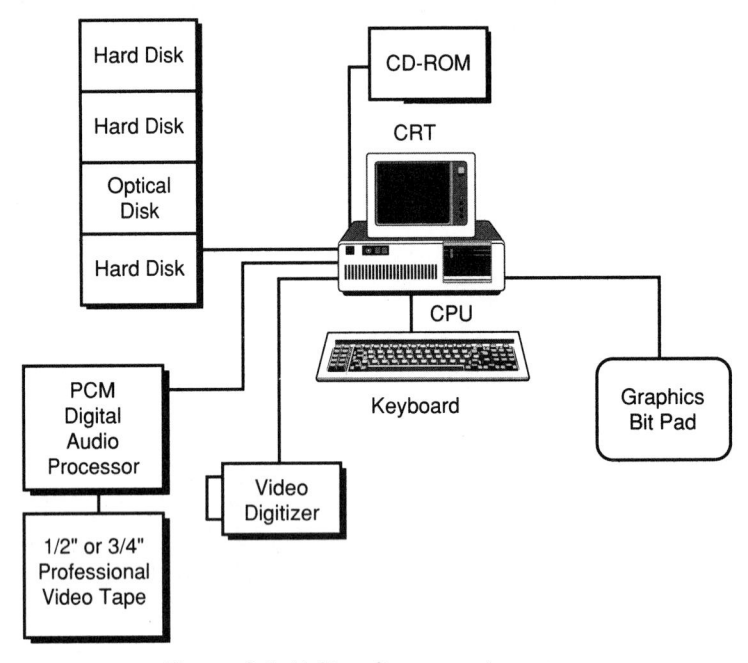

Figure 9.1 Multi-media presentation system.

world office environments correctly (for example, each multi-media data type or peripheral can be defined as an instance of a class). The combination of multi-media types with advanced object methods, such as inferencing, allows the term "multi-media" to be redefined, bringing it out of the realm of the computer enthusiast and into the office. The term "multi-media information processing" (MMIP) is perhaps a more useful description of the functionality of the intelligent office multi-media environment.

Only recently has the underlying technology been in place to allow multi-media to become a viable part of the intelligent office. The availability of mass storage on optical media has been particularly critical in the development of multi-media information systems. The storage demands of multi-media information are exacerbated when that information is linked into hypermedia systems that may include versioning (retention of the previous history of the database); see Copeland and Khoshafian (1987). Fortunately, the availability of mass storage has kept pace with the demand, largely due to the impact of optical storage (discussed in Chapter 2).

The basic reason for introducing multi-media data types into the intelligent office is productivity. The rich set of data types provided by multi-media contain more information, and are far more expressive, than the simple numeric and ASCII data types provided by the typical MIS application.

The ability of multi-media to provide more information through the combination of data types such as image, text, voice, and video allows the office worker to be more productive by obtaining more information in a shorter period of time. In effect, multi-media "compresses" the information into a more manageable or understandable format by using voice annotation, video clips, text, animation, and so on. The incorporation of multi-media into the office will change forever the way we interact with computers.

9.1.1 Chapter Organization

Multi-media objects are presented in Section 9.2, and Section 9.3 discusses multi-media data types. Sections 9.4, 9.5, 9.6, and 9.7 discuss text, image, voice, and animation data types, respectively, and their peripherals.

■ 9.2 MULTI-MEDIA OBJECTS

Multi-media objects can be divided into three major categories: classes, data types (an extended set of types including audio and visual data), and peripherals (processes and devices). In the intelligent office environment, multi-media objects fit well into the framework of the client/server model (discussed in Chapters 3 and 4). Figure 9.2 depicts multi-media client/server architecture in the intelligent office environment.

Multi-media processes handle the conversion of multi-media data types (for example, converting a magazine article into computer-represented text by using a scanner and OCR technology), and may use hardware assist depending upon how processor-intensive they are. Multi-media devices handle the storage or projection of multi-media data types and, by very definition, involve hardware equipment.

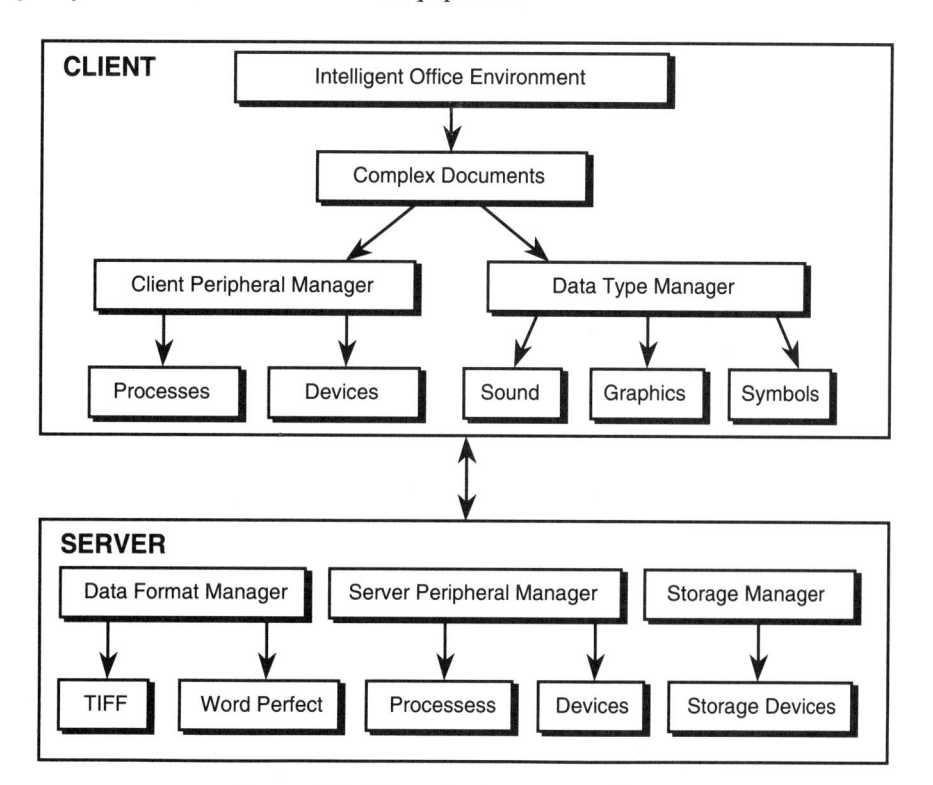

Figure 9.2 Multi-media client/server architecture.

308 ■ Multi-Media Objects in the Office

The intelligent office places the rich set of data types (such as pictures created by a scanner), along with a subset of multi-media processes and devices, on the client-side workstation. For the purpose of increasing network efficiency, client processes perform compression and decompression locally. Client devices (such as scanners, which must be hand-fed) are used by the workstation and are not meaningful at the server.

The multi-media server contains objects whose services need to be centralized. Storage devices and the manager that acts upon those devices are located at the server. Processes for indexing and retrieving document sets also belong on the server. Other server-based objects, such as OCR, make intensive use of the storage manager. A third category of objects, such as printers and fax machines, may reside either on the client or the server.

The client side consists of two major object branches: data types and peripherals (processes and devices). The data types on the client side are much richer than those of the server. For example, image and voice are meaningless to the server, because only the office worker at the workstation can meaningfully process those data types.

All processes and devices on the client workstation side are used locally. For example, sound boards must be at the workstation to be useful to the application and the user.

Figure 9.3 includes devices and processes that may reside on the client side of the intelligent office. Most of the devices and processes in the list can be identified with a physical device. Those that are not related to a physical device, such as a software-implemented compression algorithm, benefit from the same metaphor. Note, however, that although software implementations are presented as a coherent entity, they may be implemented through distributed processing.

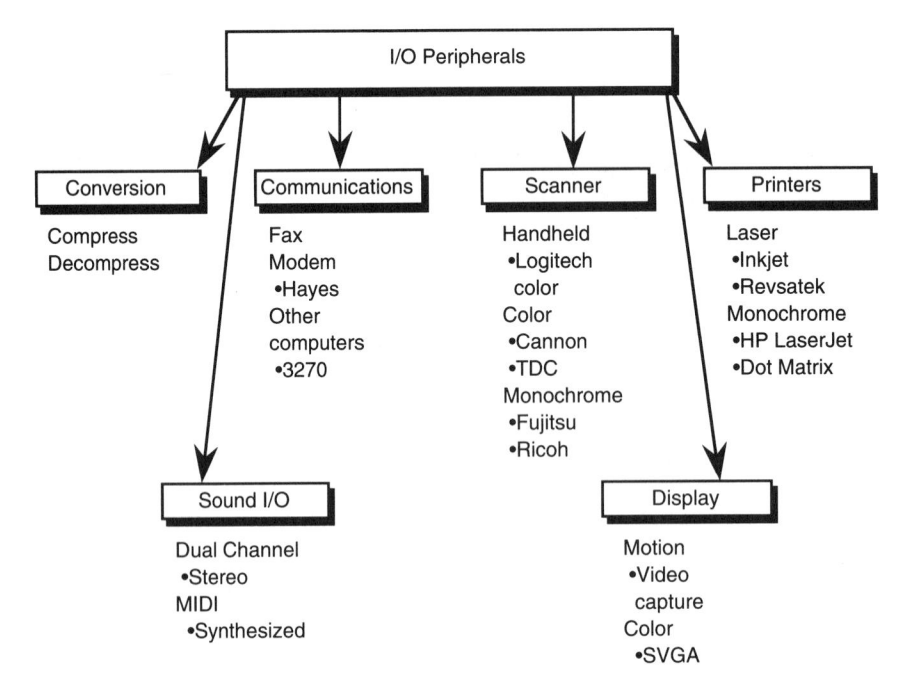

Figure 9.3 Devices and processes on client side.

9.2 Multi-Media Objects ■ 309

On the server side, five major object types provide some of the basic functionality of the multi-media system:

1. BLOB
2. Processes/Devices
3. Storage devices
4. Document sets (collections)
5. Boolean, full-text, queries

BLOB (see Section 5.1) are the basic multi-media storage type and include a set of files that contain multi-media bits. "Processes" include OCR, optional compression or decompression routines, and "devices" are such items as faxes and scanners.

"Storage devices" are the peripherals that store multi-media data types, and are managed by the storage manager. "Document sets" are the objects that make up the full-content retrieval engine, and "Boolean queries" perform searches of "document set" objects.

The server processes use the storage manager extensively and so, for performance reasons, must be located on the server. For example, the OCR process located on the server can convert a large number of images stored at the server.

Compression and decompression routines are useful for managing data generated at the server (such as incoming faxes received by the server), or for performing compute-intensive compression (for example, when generating color images) that can be performed in the background during idle times.

The process of creating indices based on the content of textual documents, called full-text indexing, is also a function of the multi-media server. After the office worker creates document collections, an index is developed based on all words contained within the documents. The user can use the index to retrieve a document according to words in that document. Since these documents are stored at the server site, the server is the logical place for this process to occur.

Server devices are those devices shared in the office, such as printers, internal fax boards, and storage devices (jukeboxes and disk drives).

9.2.1 Structure and Interactions of Multi-Media Objects

This section explores the application of object orientation to multi-media. Figure 9.4 illustrates the breakdown of the basic multi-media objects. Because all of the data types

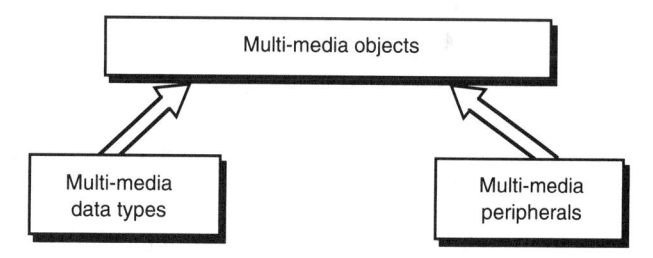

Figure 9.4 Breakdown of basic multi-media objects.

310 ■ **Multi-Media Objects in the Office**

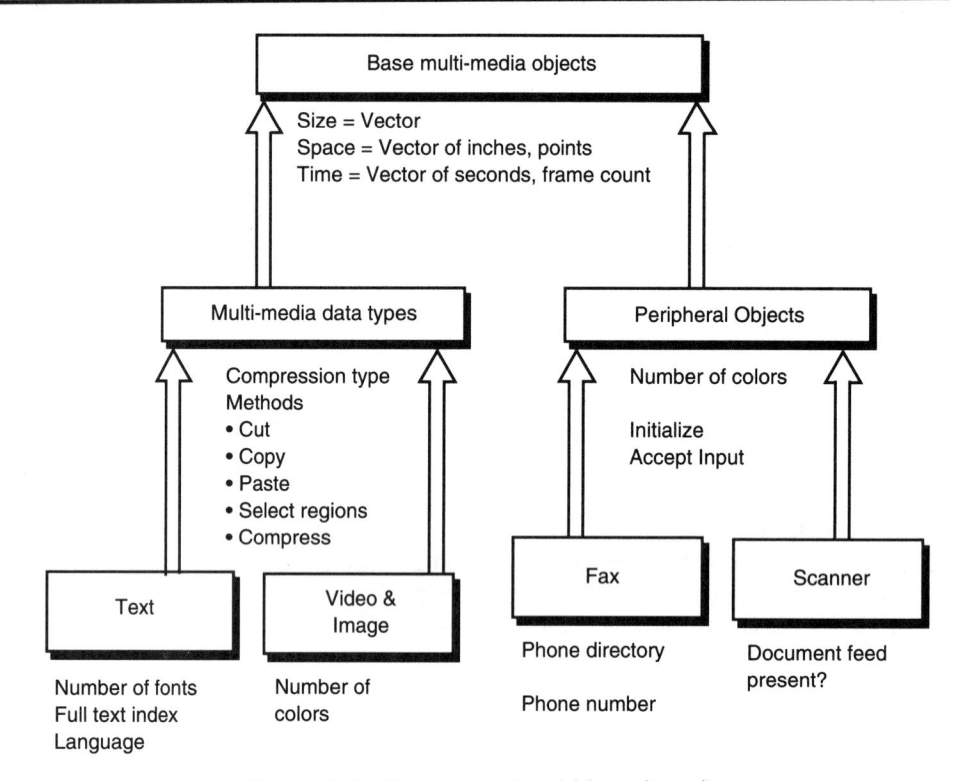

```
                    ┌─────────────────────────────┐
                    │   Base multi-media objects  │
                    └─────────────────────────────┘
                        △                      △
                        │  Size = Vector        │
                        │  Space = Vector of inches, points
                        │  Time = Vector of seconds, frame count
         ┌──────────────┴──────┐         ┌──────┴───────────┐
         │ Multi-media data types│       │ Peripheral Objects│
         └───────────────────────┘       └───────────────────┘
            △              △                △            △
            │  Compression type│              │ Number of colors
            │  Methods         │              │
            │   • Cut          │              │ Initialize
            │   • Copy         │              │ Accept Input
            │   • Paste        │              │
            │   • Select regions│             │
            │   • Compress     │              │
       ┌────┴───┐      ┌──────┴──┐       ┌────┴──┐    ┌────┴────┐
       │  Text  │      │ Video & │       │  Fax  │    │ Scanner │
       │        │      │  Image  │       │       │    │         │
       └────────┘      └─────────┘       └───────┘    └─────────┘
    Number of fonts   Number of        Phone directory   Document feed
    Full text index   colors                             present?
    Language                           Phone number
```

Figure 9.5 Object-oriented model for multi-media.

and peripherals in the intelligent office are objects, they are defined by their attributes and methods. Attributes include values for resolution and image size, while methods enable data types to display themselves and enable peripherals to be activated.

Figure 9.5 provides an example of an object-oriented structure for multi-media. It begins with the class of all multi-media objects and then specializes those objects into data types, peripherals, and ultimately specific types of objects. A vector denotes a list of values which apply to different dimensions. For instance, a vector of two numbers can define the width and height of an image, and a vector of three dimensions defines a video clip by adding the component of time.

■ 9.3 MULTI-MEDIA DATA TYPES

Multi-media data types provide the means for conveying ideas and vital corporate data in the intelligent office. Pictures, drawings, writing, sound, and video clips are all data types, the clay from which presentation of information is formed.

The client side of the intelligent office multi-media manager supports a rich set of data types, which enhance the functionality of the office. The three main types of data on the client side are symbols, graphics, and sound.

Symbols are characterized by text data types but are more global in nature, as opposed to being tied to any particular culture or language. International icons are a good example

9.3 Multi-Media Data Types

of global symbols. They include such types as kanji character sets. Graphics include a variety of types such as images (raster and vector) and video. Sound includes such types as voice, stereo, and musical instrument digital interface (MIDI). The data types on the client side are illustrated in Figure 9.6.

All of the data types shown in Figure 9.6 can be thought of as objects. These objects must know how to display themselves and how to interact with any one of the peripherals listed in following sections. For instance, a CCITT compressed image, when confronted with a LaserJet printer must present data, which must be decompressed, to the printer object, which then sends this information to its print buffer.

All data types have to respond to a set of common methods, with a few additions for some (such as the method of "Play" for a piece of music).

Because they are objects, data types must be able to respond to a request to display themselves, even if the response is simply the reply that they are unable to display themselves in the current environment, or an offer to invoke the application that created them. (They need not, however, be directly responsible for display.) They must also be able to respond to device interactions, such as fax and print requests. A collage of different data type instances (such as text and picture combined into a compound document) should have all of these capablities.

The server side does not need the rich set of data types provided at the client workstation in the intelligent office environment. Server side data types consist entirely of BLOB, or Binary Large Objects, which provide a more generic method of storing information. BLOB are the basic object used to store and retrieve multi-media data. They provide the ability to open, create, close, read, write, insert, delete, append, and destroy multi-media data.

Client Side

Multi-Media Data Type

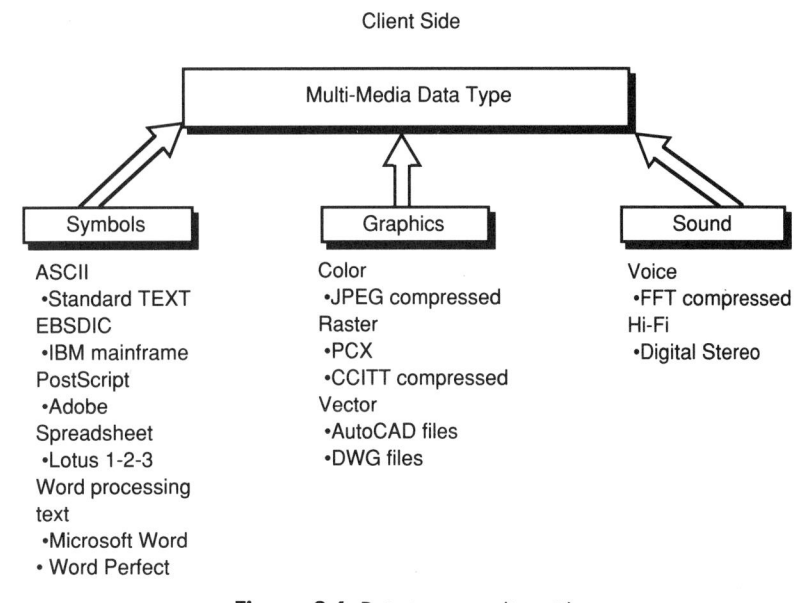

Symbols
ASCII
•Standard TEXT
EBSDIC
•IBM mainframe
PostScript
•Adobe
Spreadsheet
•Lotus 1-2-3
Word processing text
•Microsoft Word
• Word Perfect

Graphics
Color
•JPEG compressed
Raster
•PCX
•CCITT compressed
Vector
•AutoCAD files
•DWG files

Sound
Voice
•FFT compressed
Hi-Fi
•Digital Stereo

Figure 9.6 Data types on client side.

312 ▪ **Multi-Media Objects in the Office**

Because a BLOB consists of a set of files, it can span volumes, disk drives, and file systems. The BLOB interacts with the storage manager to retrieve and store the component files. Alternatively, BLOBs may also reside as special fields within a database, allowing all the concurrency and safety implicit within a database management system. Various database managers, such as Informix, Sybase, and Interbase, provide the ability to store BLOBs (see Chapter 4).

BLOBs are specialized into different formats (both text and image), so that a variety of different text files' may be retrieved based on their contents. Image formats must be known at the server so that images may be converted from one format to another.

▪ 9.4 TEXT DATA

A generic term that embodies all types of text data is "symbols," which can denote any item used as a written representation of any language. Symbols are incorporated as a data type in the intelligent office to create a software environment that is not only internationalizable (portable to different languages), but international in scope as well.

Software can no longer be unilingual in its ability to handle text. With the advent of wide area networks, applications must be able to simultaneously handle different symbols.

The concept of symbols has had a profound effect on the way software is written. Full-text retrieval technology in the intelligent office must be able to index and retrieve different symbol sets, providing information to users having different native languages. (This presents an interesting challenge, because not all ideas are translatable and many subtle meanings are lost during the process of translation.)

Figure 9.7 illustrates the attributes of the text data type.

Text data comes in a variety of different formats. Word processors change standard text to include a variety of fonts and sizes, each with a different and nonstandard file format. Text data must also take into account the process of internationalization. Each written language on the face of the earth represents text data that contains valuable information.

Computer representations of text also vary considerably. The American Standard Code for Information Interchange (ASCII) use a seven-bit representation for alphanumeric text data. Numbers and lower case and upper case letters are represented by different bit

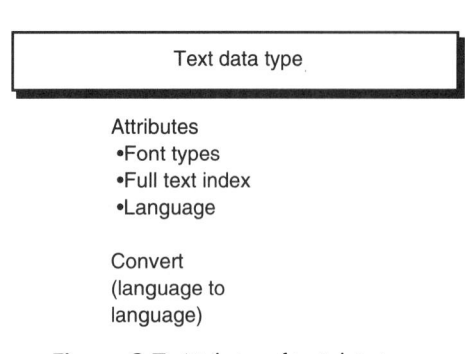

```
               Text data type

       Attributes
       •Font types
       •Full text index
       •Language

       Convert
       (language to
       language)
```

Figure 9.7 Attributes of text data type.

values. ASCII, the most commonly used text representation in the computing environment, was developed and agreed upon by the American National Standards Institute (ANSI).

Certain sections of the IBM world use a text representation known as the Extended Binary Coded Decimal Interchange Code (EBSDIC), which utilizes an eight-bit representation that has nothing in common with ASCII. In the international arena, characters in the Japanese character set (kanji) must be represented by two bytes of computer information each.

All of these varieties of text representation can be successfully managed in the intelligent office environment through the use of symbols.

■ 9.5 IMAGE DATA TYPES: ATTRIBUTES AND ORGANIZATION

Two basic types of images can be used in the intelligent office environment: raster or bitmapped images, and vector. Bitmapped graphics associate information about the pixels of a display screen or printer. An image is broken down and described in terms of pixels. The term "bitmap" means that each pixel used to describe the image has bits associated with it that describe its color, intensity, and whether that pixel is on or off. The term "raster" comes from the horizontal scan line of video terminals.

Vector images are described by individually describing the component geometric shapes of the image. Vector images are typically used for CAD/CAM applications, where the objects are composed of various shaped lines. The term "line art" is often used to describe these images.

A bitmapped image can be anything displayable in the graphics mode of the video display card.

9.5.1 Image File Formats

A number of different file formats can be used to create and store images, ranging from application-specific formats to general, industry standard formats. Some of the most popular formats are MacPaint, PCX, TIFF, GIF, and IMG.

MacPaint originated with the Apple Macintosh. There are literally gigabytes of MacPaint files available in the public domain and available for download from bulletin boards.

The benefits of this format are the ease of decoding and efficient compression. The MacPaint format, however, is less flexible than the others discussed in this chapter. This format is inherently black and white, and unlike all other image formats, has a fixed size of 576 pixels across by 720 pixels deep. It also uses an excessive amount of overhead. These factors make the MacPaint format of limited use as a standard.

The PCX format is an example of an image format that was originally specific to an application but has come to be widely used. The PCX format was developed by the Zsoft corporation to be used with their PC Paintbrush program. The PCX format supports color images, but, due to a lack of design foresight, it only supports 16 colors (a very small number in today's world of super VGA). Support for 256 colors has been hacked into the format but is neither clean nor widely supported. PCX is probably the most widely used in the PC arena.

The IMG format has garnered support in the desktop publishing community but has not gained widespread use elsewhere. The IMG format is most widely known for its use with Digital Research's GEM windowing software and in Ventura Publishing's desktop publishing software. IMG contains the same benefits as MacPaint (good compression and easy decoding), supports an image of any size, and contains very little overhead. This format does not support color images, however.

TIFF is widely used for document imaging systems. The name TIFF stands for Tagged Image File Format, but it is actually not so much a format as it is a suggestion on how the image might be physically stored in the file. TIFF is the most flexible of the formats described in this chapter, because it is an attempt at standardization. It is both operating system– and display device–independent, allowing the images to be ported across systems.

TIFF can support any size image, as well as black and white, gray-scale, and 24-bit color images. Its drawbacks are the level of programming complexity needed to manipulate TIFF image and a loss of utility due to the extreme flexibility. Figure 9.8 illustrates a TIFF image.

The GIF format, developed for the CompuServe dial-in modem service, is perhaps the most complex and most interesting of those just described. The acronym GIF, pronounced "jif," stands for the Graphics Interchange Format. GIF can support up to 256 colors and was intended for today's top-of-the-line VGA technology. The GIF format is wholly in the public domain and was never devised for any particular software package. Countless images are available for download from CompuServe and elsewhere.

9.5.2 Image Compression

Images are quite disk- and memory-intensive. Even a small image can consume a quarter of a megabyte of storage space. In light of this, the compression of image data has become de rigueur. Hundreds of algorithms and methods exist for compressing and

Figure 9.8 A TIFF image.

9.5 Image Data Types: Attributes and Organization ▪ 315

decompressing data. Basic compression theory states that any data which exhibits some form of predictability and repeatability can be reduced in size by using tokens to represent those patterns.

One of the more popular algorithms for images is known as LZW (which stands for Lempel-Ziv and Welch, the originators of this technique). LZW is the most recent and most sophisticated entry in the compression algorithm field. LZW works especially well with unknown bit streams, whereas other compression techniques are quite particular to the type of data they're compressing. LZW also can create on the fly the tokens that represent patterns. In other words, the algorithm doesn't need to scan the dataset first before building the tokens.

The basic theory of LZW is to break down an image into a series of tokens, which are smaller in size than the original file. This process can go awry, however, creating a resulting file larger than the original.

Another method of compression, called Huffman encoding, can also be used for arbitrary data. The Huffman method first analyzes the data set to build a list of frequency counts of predictable strings of data. From this list of frequency counts, Huffman codes are assigned to replace the strings, with the shortest (in bytes) codes assigned to the bit strings with the highest frequency counts. This Huffman tree must then be stored with the data itself.

Because of this fact, generic Huffman is rarely used. Instead, the code that performs the Huffman compression and decompression is designed for a specific type of data by building a fixed Huffman tree for that dataset. This is known as modified Huffman. Terms such as "CCITT Group 3" or "Group 4 compression" refer to a modified Huffman code for a particular type of image. Figure 9.9 shows a Huffman tree.

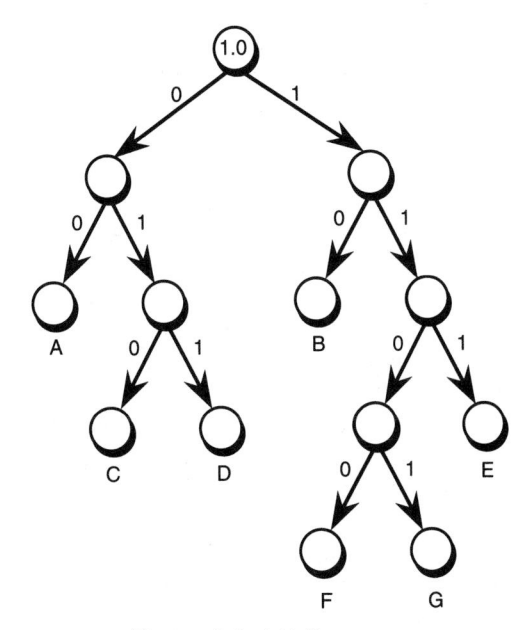

Figure 9.9 A Huffman tree.

Other common terms for types of compression include MPEG, which is used to compress and decompress motion video, and JPEG, which is designed for still-frame video. In addition, there is a host of others.

9.5.3 Dithering

If color images are going to be printed using a non-color printer, they must be converted from their normal representation to the world of black and white. This problem also holds true in displaying a color image on a monochrome terminal.

Any color image can be turned into a gray-scaled image with a simple conversion formula. The gray-scale produced from this process must then be retouched to improve the contrast.

Dithering is a process that transforms the contrast of color images that have been converted to gray-scale images. Dithering can be performed in numerous ways. A simple method of creating a black-and-white image is to assign an arbitrary threshold level above which a pixel is considered white and below which a pixel is considered black. The results of this method are extremely high contrast and an image which is not too recognizable.

One of the earliest methods of dithering is known as Bayer dithering. This method produces up to 64 levels of grey using a fixed matrix pattern. Pixels that are out of the range of this matrix are changed to white or black. The fixed patterns present problems, however, and can create very poor-quality images. Other dithering algorithms have been developed to replace the Bayer dither, such as the Floyd-Steinberg dither, the Burkes dither, and the Stucki dither.

9.5.4 Images in the Intelligent Office

Images and graphics are basic data types in the intelligent office. They are used in compound documents to more fully express the information contained within the document. Figure 9.10 illustrates a compound, multi-media document.

The attributes associated with an image must be sufficient to allow navigation through the intelligent office. Attributes must include the general type of the image (such as "a human"), to more specific attributes (such as the image is a man, the man is a president of the United States, the man's name is George Bush).

The image must also keep track of which documents refer to it. This allows an image to be retrieved, which in turn allows the office worker to scroll through each document that refers to the image.

Images must also retain hypermedia-links to any images that are related to or "like" them. Users may then browse through a series of related images, as well as through the hypermedia compound documents which refer to those images.

Images are organized using two different methodologies. The first organizes images based on their concepts, using a variation of concept indexing. (Concept indexing in relation to full-text retrieval is discussed in Chapter 5.) The second method organizes images according to the complex documents that contain them, using the document/folder/cabinet paradigm described in Chapter 10.

The concept method indexes images based on a hierarchy of concepts, from the most general to the most specific. Users may query the image base using concepts and ideas

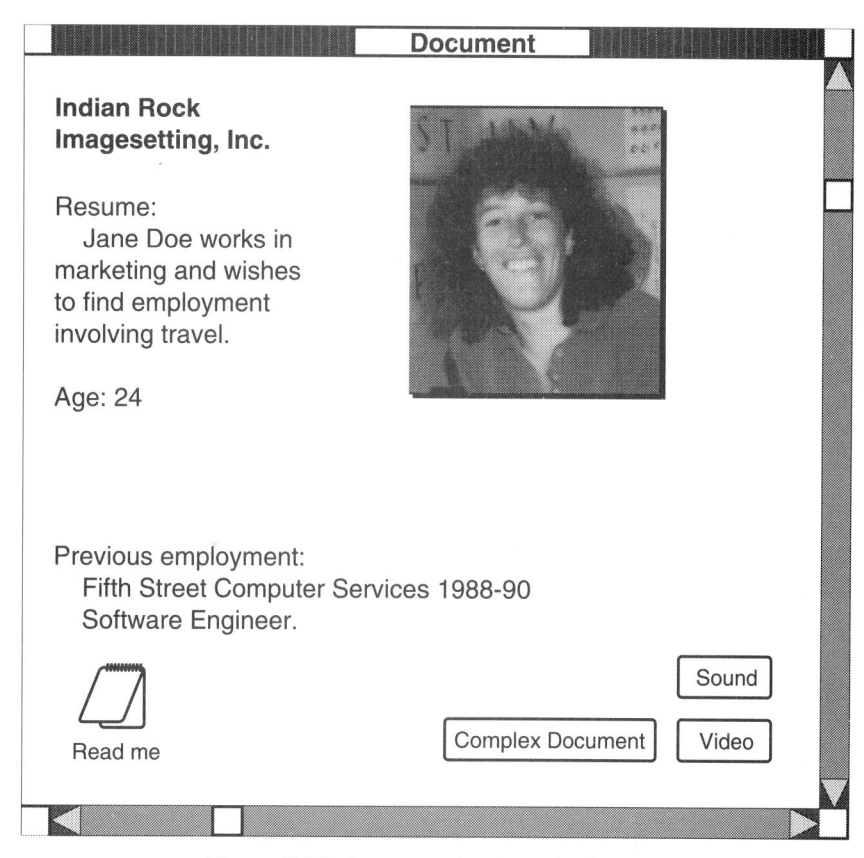

Figure 9.10 A compound multi-media document.

as the key, to retrieve both the images and the documents which reference them. Figure 9.11 illustrates concept indexing.

9.5.5 Optical Image Recognition and Neural Network Technology

The concept of optical image recognition, a term that does not yet exist in the computer world, describes the potential ability of a computer to recognize, categorize, and index an image based on its "content." For example, if a user scans a picture of a cow, the OIR software would not only recognize that the image is a cow, but potentially what kind of cow it is.

One technology that has the capability of making OIR a reality is that of neural networks. This technology is an attempt to mimic the manner in which the human brain processes information, thereby gaining the brain's versatility, its flexibility, and its ability to learn, remember, and infer facts from incomplete information.

Neural networks move away from the inefficient digital processing of information to offer a different approach. A neural network is composed of many interconnected

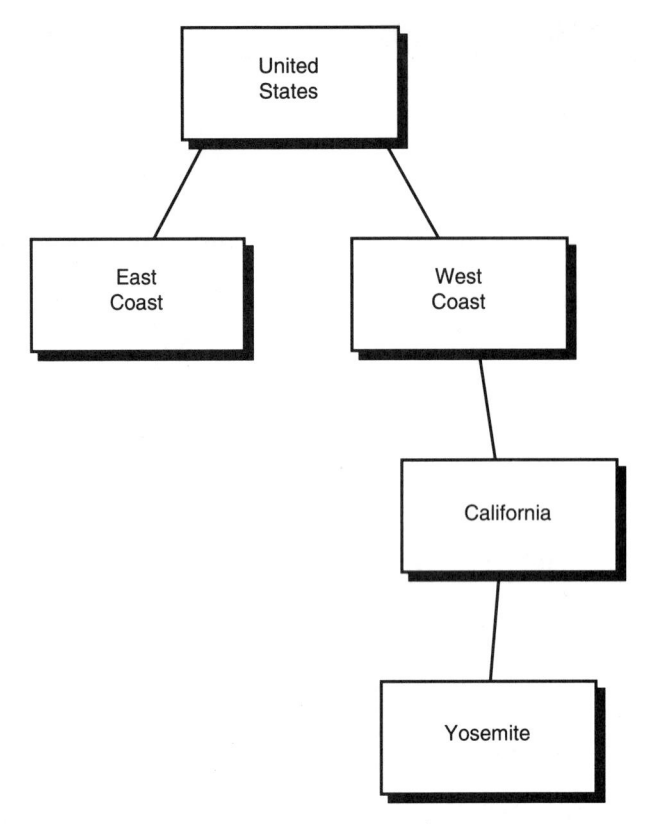

Figure 9.11 Concept indexing.

processing elements that operate in parallel. Instead of programming the network, the developer "teaches" it. Figure 9.12 illustrates the concepts of a neural network.

A neural network is taught by inputting known sets of information, assigning weight values to the various connections, and running the network until the desired level of accuracy (in terms of results or output) is achieved.

Neural networks attempt to emulate the biological structure of the brain. The processing element of a neural network is akin to a neuron of the human brain. A biological neuron consists of axons, dendrites, and synapses. Artificial neurons emulate the axons and dendrites with wires and emulate the synapses with resistors containing weighted values.

Neural networks are quite good at recognition. They are currently used for both optical character recognition and speech recognition. As the technology matures, optical image recognition will also become a viable application.

■ 9.6 VOICE IN THE INTELLIGENT OFFICE

Just as images bring documents to life in the intelligent office, voice adds depth. Imagine viewing a résumé of an applicant for a position as public relations director. First, the résumé displays on the computer screen with a picture of the applicant. Next, after the

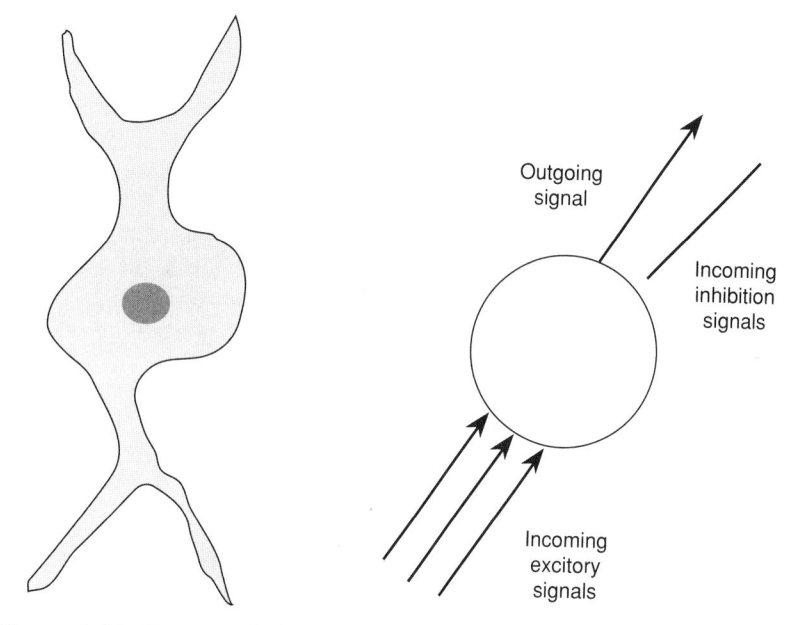

Figure 9.12 Illustration of a human neuron and a computer representation of a neuron.

viewer clicks the mouse, the applicant begins "speaking" about his or her qualifications. In the space of a few minutes, the viewer can obtain a great deal of information about the applicant.

Voice, as a data type and a means of information transfer, is already used in the office place today. Most companies employ voice mail to improve communications. Computers often used synthesized sounds to communicate error messages. Some computer companies have started incorporating voice data into the digital environment. NeXT computers have incorporated the ability to record and play voice messages, and even allow a user to send voice data across the network and then play it at another user's workstation. The NeXTStep graphical user interface comes standard with application software for recording and editing voice and other sounds. The new NeXT machine contains a digital signal processor for improved performance when handling this type of data.

Microsoft has also incorporated voice into the Windows environment through the multi-media extensions to Windows. Multi-media Windows has many of the same features as the NeXT computer. These extensions greatly enhance the usability of the Windows platform.

Although the PC is not natively a multi-media machine, add-on boards for voice, midi, and video extend its boundaries. However, only a machine with at least a 33-Mhz 386 and 8 megabytes of RAM will be able to perform adequately.

9.6.1 Speech Recognition

Speech recognition hardware and software attempt to understand the meaning of spoken words and translate the words into computer actions. The intent of speech recognition is to enable users to interact with the computer by talking.

Intel has dedicated extensive resources toward the development of speech recognition hardware and has been working on a speech workstation product that uses Intel's Speech Transaction Manager and Generator firmware. The firmware is responsible for word recognition, dialog management, speech reference pattern maintenance, and communications with an external speech synthesizer. This workstation allows the user to perform work by speaking to the workstation. Editing and data entry can all be done through the use of speech.

Speech recognition holds the potential to remove the communications barrier between people and computers. Besides ease of communications, the spoken word is faster: Most individuals can speak at over 200 words a minute.

The features of speech recognition can be broken down into the following issues:

- *Speech understanding vs. speech recognition*: The technique of "speech understanding" attempts to interpret what the speaker means, as opposed to what the speaker says. In contrast, the technique of "speech recognition" attempts to recognize a string of words, and is more accurate than speech understanding.
- *Speaker dependence vs. speaker independence*: A speaker-dependent device can only recognize one individual's voice. A speaker-independent device can recognize anyone's voice, but provides less accuracy.
- *Discrete vs. continuous word recognition*: Discrete word recognition systems require the user to pause after each spoken word. Continuous recognition systems allow the user to speak in a normal fashion, but they provide less accuracy.

A recognition system can also be classified according to its vocabulary size (the number of words the system can recognize) and grammar complexity. Since accuracy is an obvious goal, the usability and the accuracy of any word recognition system are a trade-off.

Speech processing and recognition consist of converting the analog-based voice signal into a compressed and digitized format. This digital voice waveform is processed, to remove the redundancies in the waveform and to enhance meaningful differences, and is then converted to a series of floating-point arrays. To recognize the speech, these floating-point arrays are compared against prestored speech patterns (all speech recognition systems must first be "trained").

Laptop and notebook manufacturers are also looking at voice technologies to provide an alternative to keyboard computing. This type of technology requires an extreme amount of horsepower, however, with 200 to 300 million instructions per second (MIPS) of computing power being a minimum. The problem lies with the brute-force method of pattern matching for voice recognition. Current research in digital signal processing and neural network may reduce the computing requirements of voice recognition, but commercially available products are five to ten years away.

9.6.2 Potential Uses of Speech

Current uses of speech in computing barely scratch the surface of the potential. The application of voice in the concept of the intelligent office is far more comprehensive and uses voice as an alternative to text for conveying information. The annotation of compound documents (a verbal Post-It note) is one of the primary uses for speech in the intelligent office. Productive use of the speech data type must not wait for speech recognition technologies to become viable—speech in the intelligent office is useful in the here and now.

For example, spoken electronic mail in the intelligent office can send and receive speech data in place of textual data, giving users the ability to "talk" to one another across the network. Interactive speech windows provide users with the ability to perform cooperative work tasks in real time. Two office workers can both be editing the same document while conversing, removing the need for interoffice telephones and sneaker-net communications.

9.7 VIDEO AND ANIMATION

Research and development activity with respect to enhancing information retrieval systems using video has been underway for a long time. Only recently have the relevant technologies (such as videodisc) become affordable and sufficiently available to make an impact on the intelligent office.

Video can be differentiated into two varieties: full-motion (including animation) and still-frame. The nightly TV broadcast or VCR tapes are an example of full-motion video. Animation, shown in Figure 9.13, is a familiar technique that can be used in the intelligent office. In contrast, still-frame video compares to pictures taken by camera.

The basic difference between full-motion video (animation) and images is the concept of motion and change. Full-motion video and animation move through sequences, referred

Figure 9.13 A frame in an animation (created by Neil & Darlynne Colmer of Motion Pixel, RR #1, Box 38, Pickering, Ontario, Canada).

to as frames, which change both the form and location of the objects contained within the frame. This brings about the feeling to the user that what they are seeing is "live." Still-frame video differs from standard graphics types because it looks "real" to the user as opposed to being a computer-generated shape.

Full-motion video and animation are similar to other graphics types in that they are stored as information with a document.

It is often assumed that video is always the object of a search and retrieval operation. The user searches for a document on San Francisco, finds it, hits the video annotation button, and a video clip of San Francisco is displayed.

This is not the case, however. Video can actually improve the search operation. Video can provide spatial information when navigating an information base. For example, to find information on the Civil War battle at Gettysburg, the user could watch video clips of various scenes and click on selected items for detailed information.

Traditional video technology produces video information in the form of analog signals. Electrons horizontally scan the light-sensitive surface of the video camera, producing a readable signal. The strength of the signal continually varies, making peaks and valleys, with the peaks indicating the bright portions of the horizontally sliced scene.

This analog technology is fine for the world of television, but presents a problem for computers. Analog signals make it extremely difficult for a computer to determine the contents of a given frame or even to find a video frame at all.

Digital video, on the other hand, can be manipulated by image-processing techniques. Through the use of new technologies such as neural networks, the computer can recognize and identify shapes within video sequences. This type of technology is already used by industrial robots to "see," identify, and move objects.

Existing hardware can already convert analog video images to a digital format, which can be edited, compressed, and stored for use. Figure 9.14 illustrates the process of converting an analog video signal to digital format.

The question of analog vs. digital has not yet been resolved. The only method of obtaining live full-motion video is through the use of analog signals, as a digital video frame can be significantly larger than its analog counterpart. The real-time full-motion requirement of 30 frames a second cannot be met. Digital video, on the other hand, is the only way to fully use video within the context of a computer.

Video computing is in its infancy, and its full potential will not be realized for a long time to come. New video concepts, such as holography (which can provide pictures that move and have depth and dimension), have yet to leave the cradle. The addition of a third dimension to the computing environment would be interesting indeed.

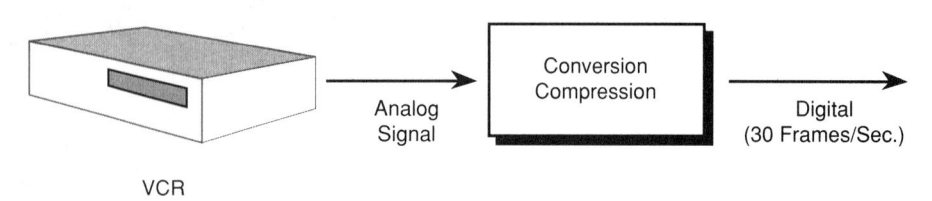

Figure 9.14 Analog-to-digital video conversion.

9.7.1 Digital Video Interactive

As was just mentioned, video information must be digitized into data that can be used by the computer system and added to the information base. This digitization process presents problems with respect to the display of full-motion video, restricting many multi-media systems to partial-screen video or still-frame images. Even "video-aware" computers, such as the Amiga, do not handle full-motion video on the screen as digital information. In fact, their limit is to overlay graphics on top of a full-motion video segment that is in analog form.

The problem lies in the megabytes of information which digital video represents. An 800-megabyte optical disk can store about two minutes of full-motion video in its normal form, thus making it impossible to retrieve the video information at the required 30 frames a second.

There are two ways to solve this problem: to speed up the hardware so that the required frame rate can be achieved (but I/O rates of this caliber are years away), or to compress the video information into a small enough size and then provide real-time decompression that can meet the frame rate required for full-motion video.

Enter Digital Video Interactive (DVI), shown in Figure 9.15. Invented by General Electric and RCA, DVI promises to provide the second solution. The DVI technology, currently owned by Intel, is a combination of hardware chips and software that bring full-motion digital video to the computer.

DVI consists of a pair of microprocessors known as the i750 chip set. The pixel processor, running at 12.5 MIPS, is a complete parallel processing architecture that includes RAM. The other chip is a display processor that handles the actual real-time display of full-motion video.

The DVI system compresses digital video down to 1 percent of its normal size, allowing one hour of video to be stored on a standard CD-ROM. DVI can combine motion video, multi-track audio, and computer graphics in a single integrated environment.

This technology promises to enhance the computing environment of the future. Although the images are currently not at broadcast TV quality, this problem will soon be conquered. Another problem with this technology so far is that Intel's DVI chip set is too pricey to allow it to be widely used.

9.7.2 Video, Animation, and the Intelligent Office

Video and animation provide the intelligent office with new means of expressing information. Both will be used to bring icons to life, allowing the meaning of the icon to become more apparent to the user.

Video and animation also provide excellent spatial feedback to the user. Spatial orientation is of utmost importance in the intelligent office, where users can organize terabytes of information from the individual desktop up to the corporate level. Traversing this large information base requires visual spatial information about the user's current location within this information base, and also about where the user has been. (Most implementations of the hypertext paradigm have failed because the users become hopelessly lost with respect to where they are, where they have been, and what got them there in the first place.)

(a)

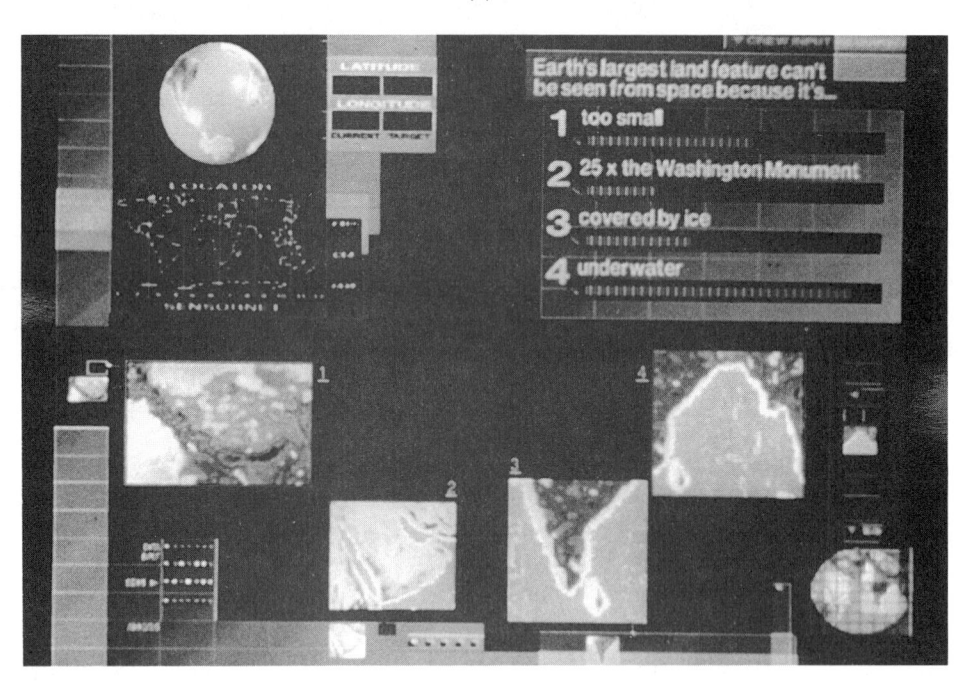

(b)

Figure 9.15 DVI examples: (a) DVI Point of Purchase display (Designed and produced by John Kalb of Exhibit Technology Inc., 31 E. 28th Street, New York, NY) (b) Interactive Theater (Copyright 1989, National Geographic Society; Designed and produced by Exhibit Technology Inc., for Explorer Hall, National Geographic Society, Washington, DC).

Video conferencing is another use of video technology. Opening a window and having a real time audiovisual conversation with someone else on the network is both meaningful and useful.

Video annotation of complex documents can provide enhanced meaning to the document. Going back to the earlier résumé scenario, imagine how a video clip of the applicant would enhance the viewer's knowledge about that person. A video annotation of a speech would add depth to a document that cannot be achieved using words or still images.

Adding the human factor to computers is one of the most important goals that video and animation can achieve. One of the great tragedies of the computer revolution was the depersonalization of the work environment and society in general. Technology such as video can help regain some of what was lost.

9.8 SUMMARY

Multi-media has enhanced our ability to express information. The limitations of the data types of the past have been removed. Multi-media marries new data types such as voice, text, image, video, and animation to provide a new method of information representation.

The intelligent office makes maximum use of multi-media to enhance the productivity and "humanness" of the office environment. The usefulness of information is only as good as our ability to understand that information. Multi-media provides the means to bring users, information and computers closer together.

10
OFFICE OBJECTS AND THE OFFICE OBJECT REPOSITORY

■ 10.1 INTRODUCTION

The intelligent office environment offers numerous types of objects that are manipulated by the office worker. This chapter concentrates first on the organization of these objects in various "containers" and hierarchies and then demonstrates the storage and retrieval of these office objects using underlying database systems.

Some office objects represent the various types of information that are used, accessed, and updated by office workers. Other objects correspond to peripherals attached to the intelligent office worker's workstation. Still other objects correspond to office policies and procedures for interaction between workers. Office workers themselves can be represented as office objects that can be queried, given privileges of access to other objects, assigned to various office object categories, and interact with protocols. All of these object categories can be stored and retrieved using database systems.

Although many features of object-oriented databases make those databases suitable for storing intelligent office objects (and most of the following discussion applies to object-oriented databases as well), this chapter focuses on relational and SQL-based databases for several reasons:

1. The installed base of commercial object-oriented databases, now and in the foreseeable future, is negligible compared to those of relational (SQL) systems and multi-media file servers.
2. A number of technical problems with object-oriented databases still remain unresolved. The most important problem is the need for an agreed-upon calculus and algebra of objects.
3. Although some standardization efforts have been made, there are still no agreed-upon standards or major endorsements of object-oriented database systems.

This chapter provides a very simple discussion showing how an object repository can be used in a client/server environment to store, update, and access intelligent office objects. To do so, the chapter explores the process of performing queries, updates, and check-out/check-in on a few simple object types (folders and simple documents). The same concepts apply to other object types of the intelligent office environment that are shared through a common area or libraries.

10.1.1 Chapter Organization

This chapter starts with a discussion on the intelligent office environment. Section 10.2 summarizes the various features and characteristics of intelligent office objects. Then Sections 10.3, 10.4, 10.5, and 10.6 discuss the attributes and methods of buildings, departments, offices, and containers (cabinets, folders, documents), respectively. Section 10.7 illustrates some of the attributes of office workers. Section 10.8 shows how intelligent office object-oriented modeling can be used to manage information in paper form. Section 10.9 concentrates on the repository of the persistent office objects, using a relational database management system. Section 10.10 summarizes versioning and change management in intelligent offices. Section 10.11 presents the overall check-out/check-in algorithm for accessing office objects in client/server architectures.

■ 10.2 THE INTELLIGENT OFFICE ENVIRONMENT

The intelligent office environment attempts to capture the natural and expected behavior of office workers. It provides a direct mapping of the worker's environment that includes all of the objects with which the office worker interacts (the people, policies, and procedures of the office).

As described in Chapter 1, one way to understand and capture the office worker's "universe" is by analyzing the characteristics of the "nonelectronic" (or "noncomputerized") office. The various physical objects in the office (as illustrated in Figure 10.1) can be grouped into the following categories:

- Objects to prepare documents (such as a typewriter)
- Objects for performing calculations (such as a calculator)
- Objects to collect and organize paper documents, illustrations, tapes, and so on (such as folders or cabinets)
- Objects to communicate information (such as a whiteboard or a telephone with an answering machine)
- Objects to organize flow of the information (such as an in-out bin)
- Objects to organize various office processes (such as a calendar or notepads)

Figure 10.1 also illustrates an office with a common area where several offices share a space. Each "locality" in this figure pertains to either an office worker or a role of an office worker. That is, office workers might have different offices, each pertaining to a particular function or role.

The concept of "localities" is neither original nor unique to intelligent office models. Many systems have used "physical metaphors" to represent actual objects in graphical user interfaces. The GUI environments concentrated on personal desktops, where the "folder" was the main collector of documents. Some systems went beyond that level to

10.2 The Intelligent Office Environment ■ 329

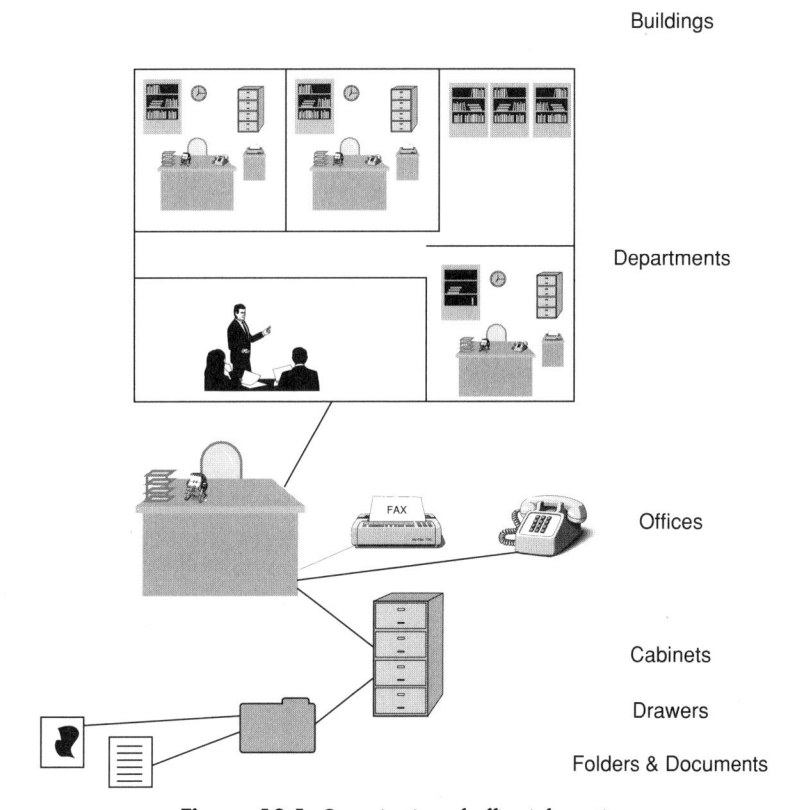

Figure 10.1 Organization of office information.

provide icons representing "higher-level" container objects, such as offices, rooms, and halls.

One of the earliest and best known systems that provided metaphors for offices was the Rooms windows manager developed at Xerox PARC (Henderson and Card, 1986). Rooms allowed the user to divide his or her workspace into several "virtual" workspaces and then organize tasks in separate rooms. Each room contained the tools and documents necessary to perform a particular task. For instance, the user could designate a room for Correspondence (containing all the letters, electronic mail, memos, and word processors). However, Rooms emphasized the organization of an individual office worker's object space.

Another interesting system that provided direct support for metaphors such as "Entering a Room" and visual representations of objects in a room such as Whiteboard, Shelves, and an Exit door was MILAN (Multimedia Interactive LAN), described in Hämmäinen and Condon (1991) and Condon (1990).

The depiction of localities in the intelligent office introduces an important organizational concept: the office aggregates different objects into a single compound object. Offices collect information, peripherals, and processes for particular tasks and domains. For instance, the Marketing VP's office contains documents about marketing analysis, product introduction plans, and so on. The office might also contain a scanner and printer used only by the marketing department. The office "aggregates" all these objects into a single compound object, to which the marketing VP is granted access privileges.

10.2.1 Issues to Resolve

An overall analysis of the intelligent office uncovers the following features and issues, all of which must be resolved in order to create an efficiently functioning work environment.

10.2.1.1 Office Workers and Office Objects

Office workers have individual privileges and are subdivided into groups and subgroups. A typical enterprise includes an administrative department, a personnel department, a purchasing department, a marketing department, and so on. Each of these departments uses documents, spreadsheets, databases, and other common information bases.

Each of these departments also owns and manages various office resources. Furthermore, the departments are subdivided into groups for particular tasks. For instance, an overseas operation department can be divided according to continents, and responsibilities for each continent can further be divided according to countries. Each of these subdivisions also maintains information bases and office resources.

Departments have department heads or managers and are divided into offices. Each office is owned by an office worker. Office workers have various titles and access privileges.

The office environment is thus organized as a partitioning of information and office objects, where office workers have specific privileges to operate on either the information (data) or other office objects. These privileges are given to those office workers who have special titles (ranks) or roles.

10.2.1.2 Heterogeneous Information

The information and information types managed by the departments, and the organization of the information, are varied and heterogeneous. For example, documents include text, forms, receipts, pie-chart diagrams, tape recordings, and other types. There are many types of peripherals, such as fax machines and scanners.

The information objects and peripheral objects must be categorized and grouped together. Some information can be represented using tables, while other information is represented graphically in diagrams and illustrations. Other objects are stored in various "collection" objects, such as folders and cabinets. An office worker or a department can use different folders, drawers, and file cabinets to organize the information.

Often different companies use different organizational methodologies for their information bases. For instance, one company might require that departments maintain a copy of all memos and meeting minutes, and then analyze and summarize them at the end of each month in a "Progress Report" folder. Another company might give more freedom to its individual departments to manage their data as they like. The type of information storage and representation might differ as well. One company might store all information in microfiche, and another might store it in paper form.

10.2.1.3 Concurrent Sharing

Many office objects need to be shared concurrently. This extremely important factor requires the use of client/server architectures and database management systems software over local area networks to allow multi-media objects, peripherals, and different collections of these objects to be shared concurrently by multiple office workers and applications. For instance, several departments and office workers might need to examine the same information at the same time.

In addition to the concurrent sharing of information, another type of information sharing—where the same information must be placed and maintained consistently in different folders and documents—is very common in intelligent office environments. This referential sharing is made possible by the support of object identity in the underlying system. (Object identity and referential sharing were discussed in Chapter 7.)

For instance, a purchase order might be replicated within purchasing as well as by the department that issued the order. The status of the order must be maintained consistently by both departments.

10.2.1.4 Procedures and Policies

The handling and management of information follows certain procedures and policies. In this respect, a policy refers to a set of rules pertaining to a prescribed corporate strategy, such as the rules and conditions dictating the possible amount of salary increase available to an office worker. A procedure refers to an algorithm or a flowchart showing the corporate processing involved in performing a particular task. For example, once it is decided that an office worker can and should get a salary raise, the paperwork and the various approvals to put the raise into effect follow certain procedures.

Each company (and, possibly, each department within a company) has its own policies and procedures prescribing rules, integrity constraints, the information that must be maintained, how the information is maintained, and who has the responsibilities and privileges for creating the information, organizing it, maintaining it, or accessing it.

These policies roughly correspond to business rules and integrity constraints. They can be implemented in the intelligent office environment through integrity constraint specifications in the database (as discussed in Chapter 4).

Procedures, on the other hand, deal with algorithms for the flow of information. They can be implemented through the work-flow systems introduced in this chapter and discussed further in the next chapter.

10.2.1.5 Collaborative Work

The office must induce a collaborative group work environment. This point cannot be overemphasized. Although a computerized and internetworked corporation typically does provide for the concurrent sharing of information through file or database servers, an intelligent office environment must enhance the communication and collaborative work of office workers. In addition to work flow, an automated and computerized office environment must also support electronic meetings, collaborative editing, and multi-media information exchange as well as other primitives to coordinate and integrate office tasks. This is discussed in more detail in Chapter 11.

10.2.2 The Object Categories

The intelligent office environment contains at least four categories of objects:

1. *Information:* First and foremost is information from different sources, stored in different formats. Chapter 9 presented an overview of the multi-media information types in intelligent offices. Information is almost always persistent and should be under versioning and transaction control. Any concurrently shared information

should also be under the transaction-based concurrency control provided by an underlying database management system. In an intelligent office environment, the multimedia, textual, tabular, and object-oriented databases are concurrently shared in dynamic client/server architectures.

2. *Office workers:* Office workers hold certain relationships to other workers and to other office objects. Two fundamental relationships exist with respect to other workers: the inheritance relationship (a Sales Manager is also a Sales Person; a Sales Person is also an Office Worker), and the organizational relationship (The VPs report to the president; the president reports to the CEO). Office workers also have various ownership and access privileges for other office objects (such as documents and peripherals).

3. *Office tools, resources, devices, and peripherals:* The office environment includes tools (such as an electronic mail system), resources (such as storage space), devices, and peripherals, all of which are objects. This chapter discusses the container object aggregates, such as offices, folders, and cabinets, that are constructed using the multi-media data types and peripherals presented in Chapters 6 and 9.

4. *Policies and procedures:* Intelligent offices also include policy and procedure objects, which could be instantiated and executed in the office environment. A policy or procedure is an object in the sense that it has attributes (instance variables) which can be read, searched, or updated. Policies and procedures also have operations (methods) associated with them that can be used to activate the procedure or policy.

Each of these object categories and their relationships are explored in more detail in the following sections.

10.2.3 Organizing the Office Environment

The intelligent office environment incorporates policies and models for organizing office information with the ability to set information access privileges that reflect the information access privileges used in the "nonelectronic" office. Thus, information typically locked in an office worker's office can be electronically designated as available only to that person.

This discussion revolves around two interrelated characteristics of the information or objects in the office: locality (importance) and privilege. The most frequently accessed information is usually placed very close to the worker or department. The most private information has lock privileges.

Intelligent office objects are organized in an overall office environment involving buildings, floors, offices, desktops, peripherals, and other office objects. The office workers are assigned to various departments and groups, and the departments are assigned to various office floors. Each worker is assigned to one or more offices and is the primary owner with privileges in that office. The objects within an office are under the control of the worker who owns the office. Since the intelligent office environment supports referential sharing, the object representing the worker can contain references to objects that are shared or owned by other workers. This corresponds to the natural behavior of "borrowing" a document from a library or another worker. The borrowed or checked out object must eventually be checked back in. Also, unless explicitly given the right by the owner of the object, the borrower does not have the privilege to modify or destroy the object.

Thus, besides the organization of an individual's object space or tasks, the main emphasis in intelligent office environments is the organization of the information, tasks, processes, and procedures of the entire corporation ("enterprise"). The goal of an intelligent office model is to provide a common model environment for the enterprise as a whole (similar to IBM's AD/CYCLE and the Enterprise Model of the Repository Manager).

The intelligent office model office enables workers and corporations to organize the following:

- The object spaces (information, peripherals, processes, and procedures) of individual office workers, providing various levels of privileges and supporting the notion of localities for combining objects with the same privileges and ownerships in the same "office"
- The object spaces of the entire corporation, with shared libraries and common areas represented iconically and visually, allowing office workers access (check-out/check-in) and interaction with various objects in these shared environments using familiar metaphors
- The office worker hierarchies (inheritance and organizational), with the allotment of various privileges and relationships to other workers or other office objects

To conduct on-line cooperative tasks, the intelligent office environment also incorporates conference rooms, as shown in Figure 10.2. The conference rooms themselves contain whiteboards, through which users can exchange information and interact. The office environment also includes peripherals, devices, and resources that either are private, and pertain to an office, or are shared between different office workers. The shared resources are in common areas (corridors or libraries).

Note that the office environment can (but does not have to) replicate the actual physical layout of the office. Since the organization of the office is through software, the office workers have more flexibility in "arranging" the office environment. Thus, the electronic office environment actually complements and extends the physical office environment. The next sections describe each of the "container" types in intelligent offices.

10.3 BUILDINGS AND CORPORATIONS

At the very top level, the intelligence office environment contains a building, representing the corporation as a whole. One Building/Corporation object serves as the root of all the objects in the corporation. The following attributes of a building are also the attributes of the corporation:

Name: Building/Corporation name
Address: Building/Corporation address
Businesses: Building/Corporation businesses

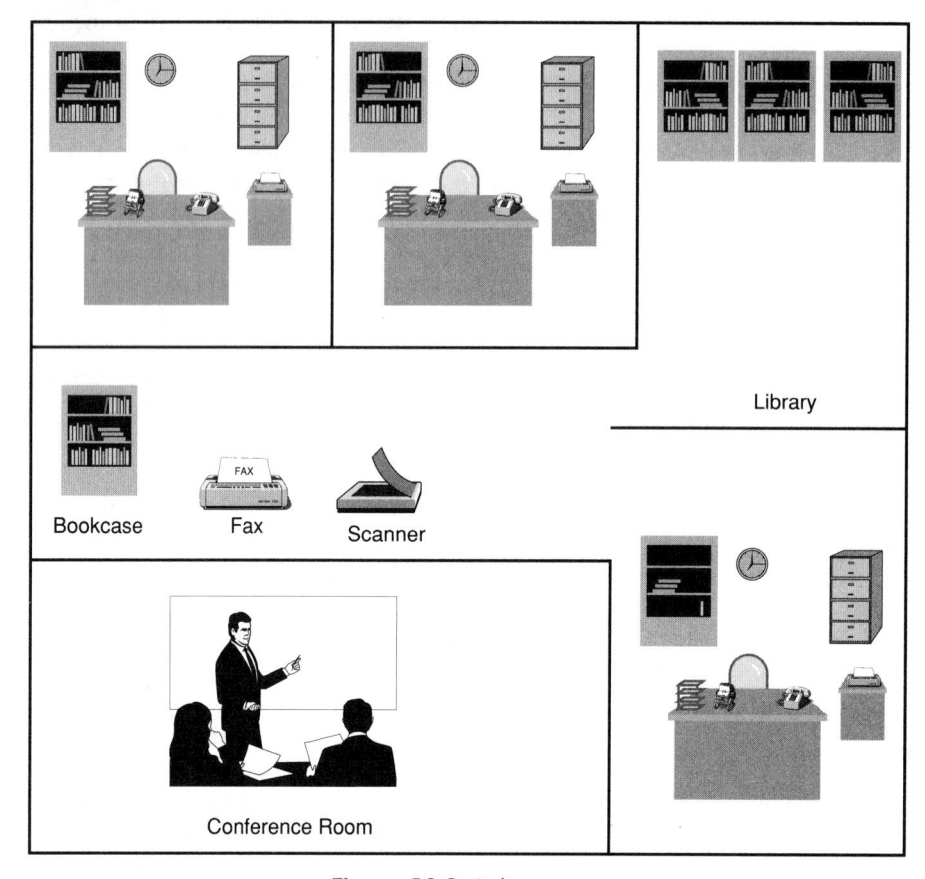

334 ■ Office Objects and the Office Object Repository

Figure 10.2 A department.

Organization: Building/Corporation executive organization

Corporate resources: The corporate databases, libraries, and information bases of the Building/Corporation

Departments: The Departments contained in the Building/Corporation

Policies/procedures: The Building/Corporation policies and procedures

Since each building is an object, operations (methods) are also applicable to corporation objects. The two most commonly used operation types are the following:

Accessor/update methods: These are used to access and update the various instance variables (state) of the Building/Corporation object. When the attributes are contained in sets (Businesses, Policies) the methods can insert or delete individual objects (for example, add a new department or delete a policy).

Aggregation methods: Other methods gather aggregate information about the object: The Number Of Departments, the Number Of Employees, and various averages and summaries are all examples of methods which summarize or aggregate information from the corporation state.

10.3.1 Security and Resilience

One of the most serious problems with respect to the Business/Corporation's aggregate information is the protection of that information. Some security schemes allow officials of the corporation to hold keys and/or security passes providing access to corporate information subspaces. In this situation, the most simple approach is to map various privileges directly to an individual's rank or title. More elaborate schemes can provide "keys" constructed through the concatenation of various subkeys granted to different office workers.

It is beyond the scope of this book to discuss the various schemes and ramifications for security. They are very similar to those used with corporate databases. The complexity and heterogeneous nature of the information stored in an intelligent office system accentuates the need for security and resilience. However, two fundamental techniques for security are applicable here and are discussed next.

10.3.2 Corporation Policies and Procedures

In each corporation, a number of policies and procedures apply to the enterprise as a whole (such as sick leave policies and hiring procedures set by the human resources department). The "text" or description of a corporate policy or procedure is just like any other document. When expressed in the proper form, these procedures and policies can be executed electronically.

In other words, a policy or procedure can be represented as an intelligent office environment program that shares the following attributes with computer programs:

1. Script language to express the policy and procedure (in intelligent offices, a rule-based object-oriented language that manipulates the intelligent office objects)
2. An environment or a virtual machine that interprets and executes the policy/procedure "language"
3. A document that describes and illustrates department procedure or policy
4. Descriptive attributes, such as the author, date the policy was issued, place the policy was issued, or the category of the policy

10.3.2.1 Procedures and Policies as Objects

Procedures and policies are objects, which have attributes (instance variables) and operations (methods). Based on the discussion in the previous paragraphs, some of the attributes of policy and procedure objects include the following:

> *Name:* The name of the policy/procedure
>
> *Description:* The description of the policy/procedure, indicating why we have such a policy/procedure and when it will be activated
>
> *Author:* The department/office or office worker who created the policy/procedure

> *Rule Base:* The set of rules that captures the semantics of the policy or procedure

The most important categories of operations (methods) are the following:

> *Accessor/Update* methods to access or update the instance variables of the policies and procedures
>
> *Activate* methods to "run" a procedure or enforce a policy

Policies are usually activated to enforce integrities in office environments when an event updating the state of office objects occurs.

Consider the following example policy, which gets activated when a new office worker is hired within a corporation:

> Name: Hiring Policy
> Description: This policy is enforced when a new office worker is hired
>
> Rule Base:
> IF Worker IS-NOT Citizen OR Resident
> AND Worker DOES NOT HAVE Valid Work Permit
> THEN Reject Hire
>
> IF Worker HAS Expertise X
> THEN Insert X IN Worker Expertise List
>
> IF Worker Requests 401K
> THEN Activate 401K Plan For Worker

While the rules of this example policy are trivial, such a policy should be "enforced" and triggered every time a new employee is hired.

To trigger the activation of the policy, the following predicate should be attached to the collection object which contains the office workers:

> if-inserted: Hiring <- Activate

(The if-inserted predicate is an extension of the if-updated predicate, which was discussed briefly in Chapter 7.) In other words, if AllWorkers is a set containing all the office workers in the corporation, the predicate if-inserted should be attached to the set object such that every time a new employee's name is inserted into this set, the Activate method of the policy called Hiring is run. This is similar to a "business rule" that enforces integrity.

10.3.2.2 Policy and Procedure Hierarchies

The corporation's organizational structure creates a constrained hierarchy of policies and procedures. Every object at a lower level of the hierarchy can do the following:

> 1. *Extend or specialize the policies and/or procedures at a higher level of the hierarchy.* (Particular departments could extend or specialize hiring policies of the

corporation.) However, the extensions must be semantically consistent with the policies and/or procedures of the parents. Thus, a department cannot give arbitrary raises to its employees, and it must follow corporate guidelines.

2. *Introduce new policies and procedures.* Departments, offices, and other objects at the lower levels of the organization can introduce new policies and procedures that should not conflict with policies and procedures at the higher levels.

Figure 10.3 illustrates inheritance hierarchies for both corporate policies and procedures. Office policies and procedures both inherit from and create specialized department policies and procedures. Similarly, department policies and procedures inherit from and create specialized corporate policies and procedures. The specialization and extensions must follow the two points just listed. Departmental policies and procedures are either extensions (specializations) of corporate policies and procedures, or additional policies and procedures that pertain only to the department.

Any extensions made by a department to corporate policies and procedures must be consistent with their corporate counterparts. In other words, a department can add additional policies to restrict existing corporate rules, but it cannot relax or omit the corporate policies. This notion is very similar to inheritance through constraints as discussed by Khoshafian and Abnous (1990).

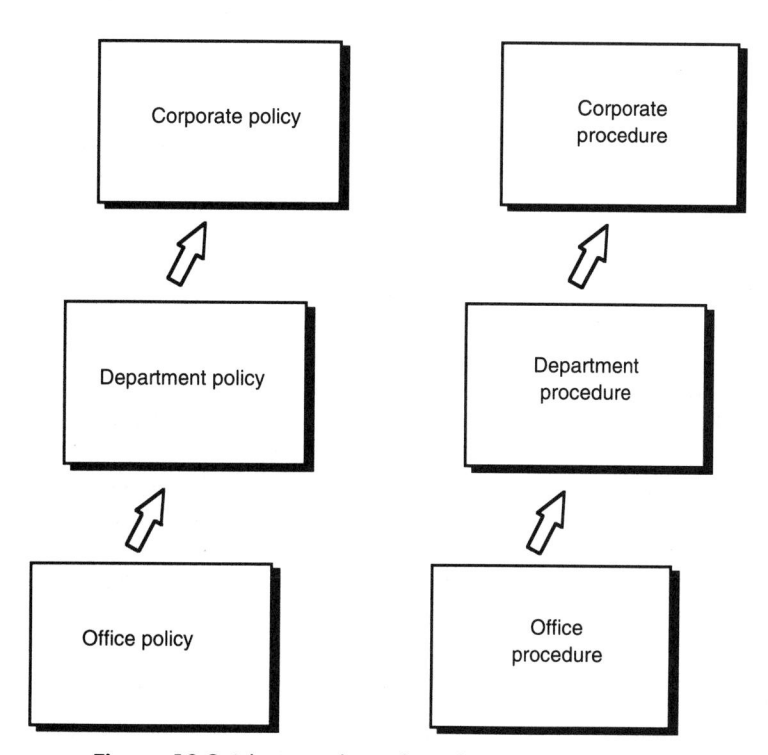

Figure 10.3 Inheritance hierarchies of policies and procedures.

10.4 THE FLOOR/DEPARTMENT

The intelligent office environment captures the office model and automates it through interconnected computer networks.

As shown in Figure 10.2, a floor depicts a number of offices, libraries, and a common area. The floor represents a department. In a floor, each office is iconized and has one of the following states:

> *Open:* Other office workers can come in and check out objects from the office.
> *Closed:* None of the objects in the office are accessible to other office workers.

The common area ("corridor") can contain a number of objects available to all office workers in the department. Some of the object types in common areas are:

1. Cabinets (discussed in the following section)
2. Peripherals (such as printers and scanners)
3. Repositories or servers storing "logical" databases

A floor also contains two other room types:

1. *Libraries* contain information which can be shared by all office workers. Libraries can contain cabinets, which are owned by a Library Administrator. The door of the library can sometimes be closed. (This implies the administrator is, most probably, reorganizing the information therein.)
2. *Conference rooms,* unlike other offices, are created and destroyed dynamically. In order to maintain the information stored in a conference room, the users must export the information into a shared document and store the document in a cabinet (probably in the common area).

When a worker has the appropriate privileges to objects, the worker can "shuffle" them around through "point-and-click" interfaces. For instance, the office worker can move an object to a common shared area, or move a shared object into the worker's own office. Notice that moving a shared object into a worker's office is different from checking out the object, because moving the object changes its ownership. The object remains in the office until the worker returns it to the common area.

There is a fundamental difference in the check-in/check-out model between objects in an office worker's office and the objects in the common area. For the former, a checked-out object can be reclaimed by the office worker: The owner has higher priority. By contrast, objects in the shared common area are accessed with equal priority by the different office workers.

10.5 CABINETS, DRAWERS, FOLDERS, AND DOCUMENTS

Some graphical user interface environments pursue an "anything can go in anything" strategy and allow users to store any type of object in a container object (such as a folder

10.5 Cabinets, Drawers, Folders, and Documents ■ 339

or a cabinet). Although this gives more flexibility to users, it can also cause confusion. A more constrained environment restricts the type of objects that a container object can hold.

Figure 10.4 illustrates the organizational constraints on container objects. Each object at a lower level can be contained in an object that is its immediate predecessor. Thus, a document contains a collection of multi-media objects or application files; a folder contains a collection of documents or other folders; and so on.

Objects can be referentially shared, with the same object contained in multiple container objects. For instance, the same document can exist in multiple folders; the same folder in many drawers; and so on.

Each object consists of

- A collection of <attribute> <value> pairs
- A collection of subobjects that are contained in the object (an object can contain subobjects of a lower level in the containment hierarchy)

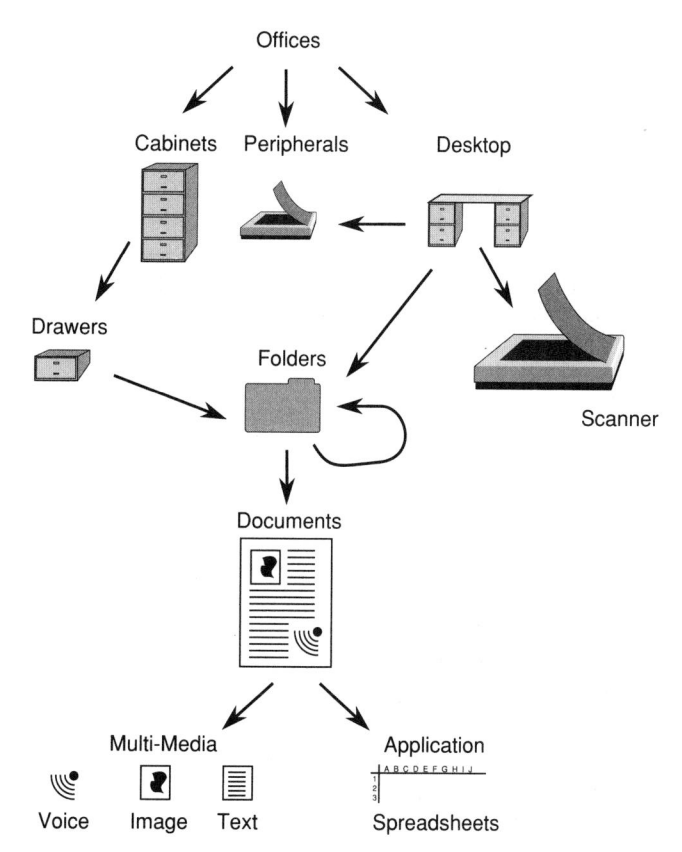

Figure 10.4 Containment relationships for office objects.

Object attributes, such as the following, are also common to all object types:

- The Name of the object
- The Date the object was created
- The Label of the object (which appears under the object's icon)
- The Owner of the object, which identifies who owns the object (this attribute is more complex than Name or Label, which are character strings; an Owner has many attributes itself, such as name, picture, title, and position)
- Voice Annotation for the object, which can describe the purpose of the object
- The Lock State of the object, which indicates whether the object is locked, in what mode, and by whom

The following paragraphs briefly describe each of the object types in the containment hierarchy, starting with cabinets.

10.5.1 Cabinets

In addition to common attributes, each cabinet contains drawers. When the office worker opens a cabinet, he or she will be presented with a sequence of labeled drawers. The cabinet object can respond to search requests to locate objects contained within it. These objects can be drawers, folders, or other documents. Figure 10.5 depicts a window showing the contents of the cabinet.

A cabinet also holds indexes containing an organized "table of contents" for all objects in the cabinet. Indexes can be organized by subject, date, category, owner, or any other user-specified attribute.

Some of the operations applicable to drawers and other cabinet objects are create, delete, and reorganize.

10.5.2 Drawers

Along with the attributes for its label, owner, and description, a drawer can contain various types of folders. The following operations (methods) can be performed upon the folders:

1. Create a folder
2. Delete a folder
3. Reorganize the folders in the drawer
4. Check-out/check-in a folder
5. Modify the folder's attributes

The check-out/check-in protocol for folders enables office workers to perform update operations on folders or objects in their desktops. In other words, to create, insert, or delete documents within a folder, or to manipulate the documents within the folder, the office worker must first check out the folder to his or her desktop, perform the manipulations, and then check it back in.

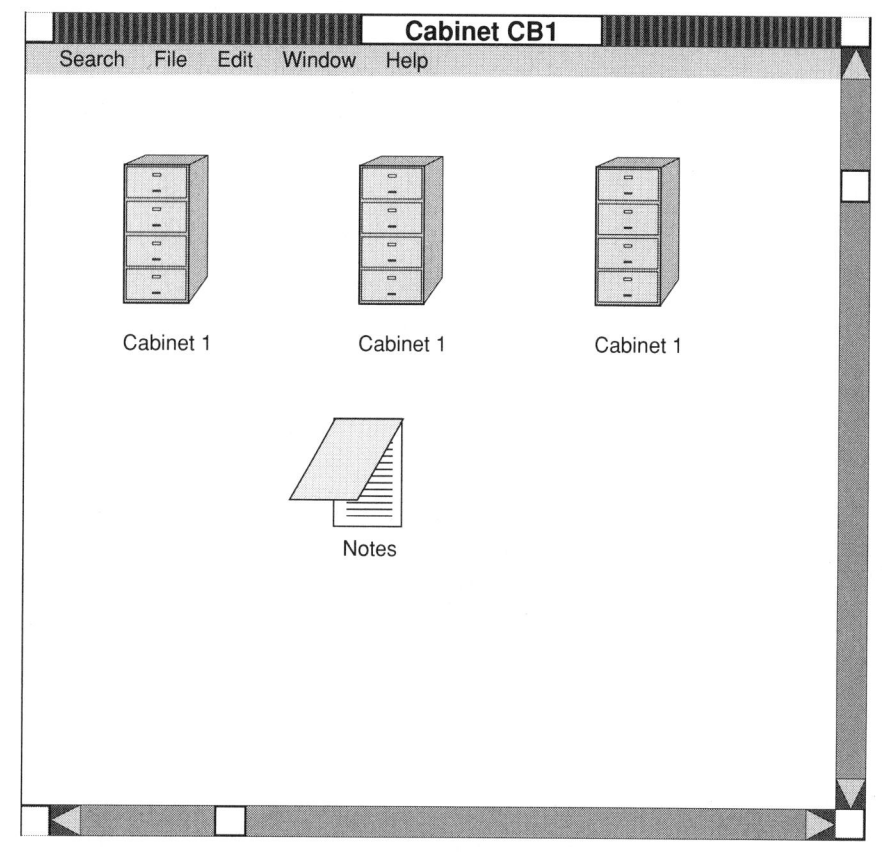

10.5 Cabinets, Drawers, Folders, and Documents ■ 341

Figure 10.8: A cabinet. **Figure 10.5** A cabinet.

10.5.3 Folders

Folders are contained in drawers or desktops. The folders on a desktop are the active folders the intelligent office worker is currently manipulating. To access and manipulate the documents stored in a folder, the office worker must follow several steps:

1. Access the cabinet and the drawer containing the folder.
2. Check-out the folder to his or her desktop.
3. Work on the documents in the folder.
4. Check the document back in, creating a different version of the document.

The following actions can be performed upon documents:

1. Create
2. Delete
3. Reorganize documents in the folder
4. Modify documents in the folder

10.5.4 Documents

The "lowest" level of the containment hierarchy holds compound hypermedia documents. Hypermedia documents are built through associative structures. A normal document is linear and read from beginning to end. In contrast, the process of reading hypermedia is open-ended—the reader can jump from idea to idea, depending on his or her interests.

A simple paper-based example of hypermedia is a thesaurus, which has no single beginning or end. Each time the thesaurus is consulted, it is entered at a different location, based on the word used to initiate the search. Hypermedia can be thought of as an enriched thesaurus where links exist between documents and text fragments instead of between words.

The prefix "hyper-" is used a great deal in this industry. In the context of this chapter, hypertext and hypermedia refer to individual elements of a document that are linked to further related information. This might be a word or picture that, when invoked (usually by a mouse-click), responds with a definition, a description, or another document. The word "hyperlink" describes any link between one document and another.

Hypermedia provides an associative way to browse through a set of documents. It complements the method of search and retrieval, where the nature of target documents is specified and then a set of matches is returned. Hypermedia allows a user to find related information without initiating further searches, and to form new links between documents.

Hypermedia systems are more flexible than traditional information structuring methods, because they allow information in a variety of forms (media) to be attached to nodes. Thus, a node in hypermedia may consist of a sound or picture, as well as text. Nodes in hypertext (hypermedia) can include icons, anchors, or buttons that provide links (send messages) to other nodes.

Figure 10.6 illustrates a "page" of a hypermedia document with various multi-media nodes. The node types in hypermedia documents correspond to the various multi-media data types discussed in Chapters 6 and 9. A hypermedia document management system also deals with the viewing and display of the multi-media information in graphical user interface environments (Chapter 8).

Here is a brief description of the node types in hypermedia documents:

1. *Text nodes*. These consist of alphanumeric text fragments. A hypermedia link can be made from an entire text fragment or a portion of the text fragment.

    The existence of hypermedia links can be indicated using several techniques: highlighting (using reverse video) a portion of text, placing a graphical anchor near the text, or changing the shape of the cursor when it passes over text that has hypermedia links. All these alternatives are illustrated in Figure 10.7.

    Various anchors, annotations, or cursor shapes can be used to indicate different types of links. For instance, changing the shape of the cursor to a "?" when passing on a term in a text fragment can indicate that help is available on that term.

2. *Image nodes*. The image (and various other multi-media) data types were discussed extensively in Chapter 9. There are various formats of image data types (TIFF, GIF, PCX, and so on). The user can edit an image node through editing commands such as Cut, Paste, Copy, Zoom, and Rotate.

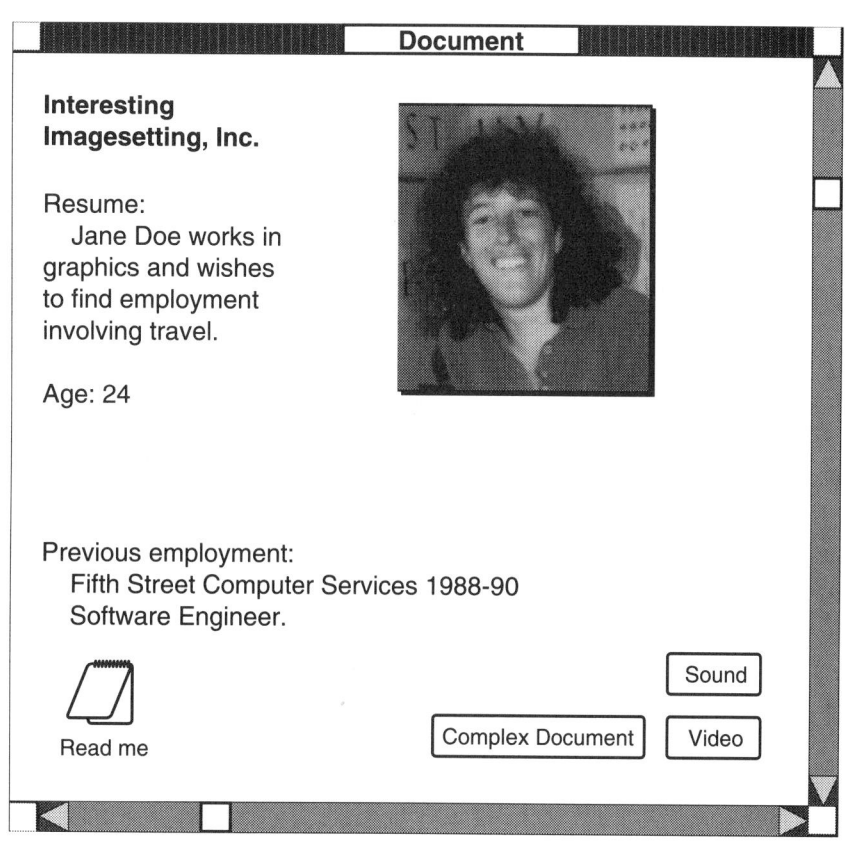

10.5 Cabinets, Drawers, Folders, and Documents ■ 343

Figure 10.6 Hypermedia "page."

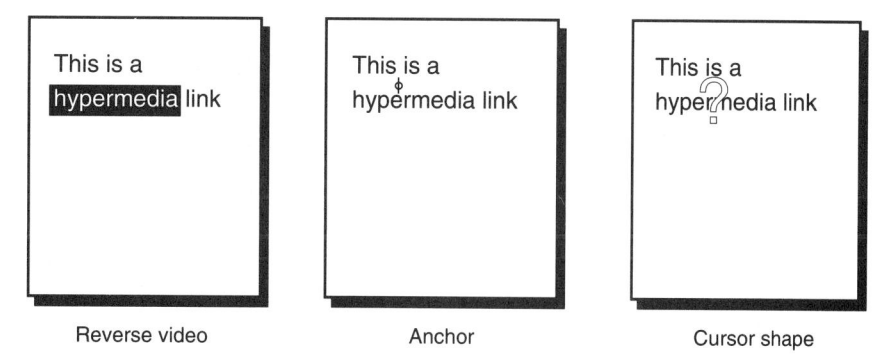

Figure 10.7 Hypermedia link alternatives.

3. *Sound nodes*. Like graphics, sounds may be embedded within text or exist as nodes in their own right. Sounds may be treated in similar fashion to pictures, although they are less likely to be zoomed. Sounds, too, represent uninterpreted information. Since sound nodes cannot be represented graphically, a visual representation, such as an icon, represents the underlying audio data. Unlike text or image information, sound nodes are leaf nodes: with current technology we cannot have links to other node types from within sound nodes. Sound nodes can only be played back.
4. *Application nodes*. In the intelligent office desktop manager, application objects (such as graphics, spreadsheets, or word processor data) can be incorporated in hypermedia documents. For instance, a fragment of a spreadsheet can be designed as a hypermedia node and appear (or be "embedded") in, say, a word processor document. This is exactly what happens with Microsoft's OLE.
5. *Buttons*. Many objects in the graphical representation of hypermedia document behave like "buttons" (Chapter 8). For instance, an icon can act as the "button" for playing back sound data. In hypermedia documents of intelligent offices, buttons can be used to invoke different programs. It is difficult to distinguish between buttons and links, and in a sense, buttons are a generalization of links. Within hypermedia documents, button objects can act both as nodes and as links.

These text and multimedia nodes can be manipulated (edited) by applications (graphics packages, word processors, and so on). Each displayed text fragment, multi-media image, or voice data is associated with an application program, which can be used to manipulate the multimedia information.

As illustrated in Figure 10.8, a hypermedia document has the following general structure:

- Nodes with associated "applications" or editors, which allow the information in the node to be updated, created, and so on
- Annotations on the multi-media information, which represent the links (discussed in the next section) to other (perhaps hypermedia) documents

In intelligent offices, hypermedia document nodes are objects. Each node has a number of attributes, each has a set of well-defined operations to which it responds (these are the operations of the application associated with the node), and each node type has supertypes or superclasses from which it inherits structure and behavior.

10.5.5 Links

Links between nodes are also objects that define the structure of the hypermedia document and provide the capability for browsing and exploring the nodes. Many different categories of links can be defined, including navigational links and links that are organizational in nature. A link can be one-directional from a source to a destination, such as a one-directional link from a multi-media document containing a voice annotation to the voice annotation itself (the link is represented by an icon). A link can also be bidirectional between two nodes, allowing the user to treat either node as a source or a destination.

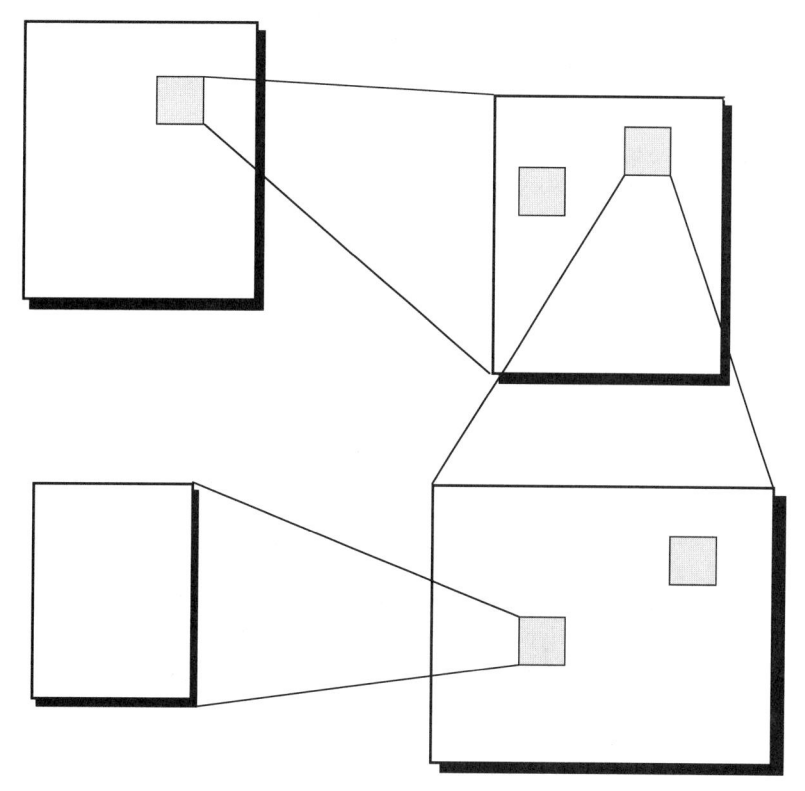

10.5 Cabinets, Drawers, Folders, and Documents ■ 345

Figure 10.8 Hypermedia links between objects.

The model presents four main types of navigational links. The intuitive meaning of these links can be grasped by analogy to the operation of a video camera. Links as navigational entities correspond to changing perspectives on a display in roughly the same way that the operation of a video camera changes the appearance of a visual scene. The user can simply move the camera back and forth (move-to link). The user can zoom in on a particular portion of the scene (zoom link) and then pan back out to the larger picture (pan link). Finally, while different filters can be used on a camera to highlight different aspects of the scene, hypertext provides view links, which are conditional on particular sets of contextual constraints.

The four types of navigational links are described as follows (Parsaye *et al.*, 1989):

1. *Move-to links*. These links simply move to a related node, allowing the user to move around or navigate through the hypermedia document.
2. *Zoom links*. These links expand the current node into a more detailed account of the information.
3. *Pan links*. These links return to a higher-level view of the hypertext (particularly useful in browsing facilities). Pan links are normally the inverse of zoom links, so that every zoom link has a corresponding pan link and vice versa.

4. *View links*. The availability or activation of these links is conditional upon the stated purposes of the user, and may also be used for security purposes. View links are hidden unless they are of interest or a user has access to them.

Views provide the fundamental mechanism for customizing hypertext to the needs and interests of different users. They also help prevent hypertext from becoming unnecessarily complex and bombarding users with information not relevant to their needs.

Different strategies can be used for linking objects in compound hypermedia documents:

1. *Relationship links:* Links at the document level can implement relationships between the documents. Examples of relationships include inheritance (is-a), ownership (has-a), and adjacency (is-above, is-to-the-right-of). Adjacent links can be used to implement a spatial database and are often used in cartography (mapping) systems. In these systems, a map is displayed on the screen, and the user can use hyperlinks to move to adjacent maps to the left or right, above or below.
2. *Linking document regions:* A region of a document can be assigned a hyperlink. The region is defined (usually as a rectangle) by document coordinates. This method is used in HyperCard on the Macintosh to assign actions to areas of a card. A mouseclick in a particular region will run the code associated with that hyperlink. The regions are often invisible to the user.
3. *Linking documents and actions:* A document element, such as an icon or piece of text, can be linked to another document or to an action. Invoking an icon of a notepad might display a piece of text related to the original document, such as a description or a part number.
4. *Glossary:* A glossary is a table of words with associated links. The link is applicable to all occurrences of the same word or word stem within a document. This system is used to implement a help index or to provide a set of definitions. If a dictionary is used as the glossary for a word processor document, then any word can be queried for its definition by invoking its hyperlink.

10.5.6 Design for Extensibility

Up to this point, we have only used system-supplied attributes for both documents and folders. In most cases, the end user may want to add attributes to a certain document. For example, in a lawyer's office we may want to keep track of accounting information, such as how long a document was used by an individual lawyer or legal assistant. Thus, the system must be extensible to facilitate such needs.

The system could provide extensibility by permitting the user to add an attribute to each object at any given time. A more structured mechanism would be that the user or a system administrator will predefine the requested attributes for a given firm. Here object orientation can be used for extensibility. We discussed class hierarchies in Chapter 7. To provide extensibility, the system can permit document type hierarchies, as depicted in Figure 10.9. Each node in the hierarchy, from top to bottom, defines its

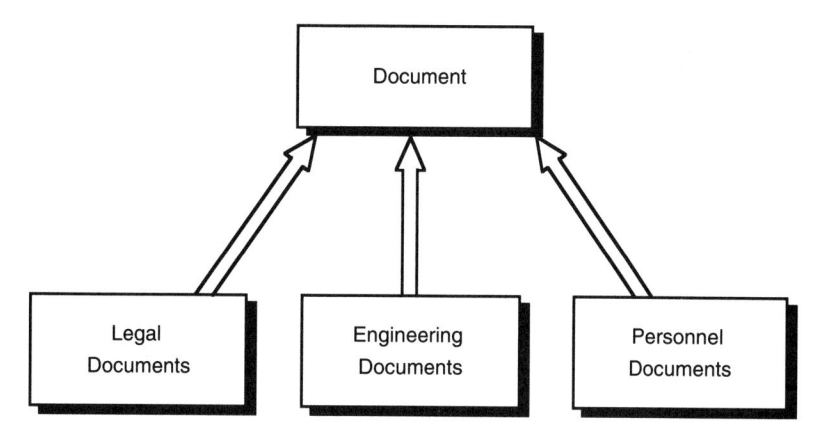

Figure 10.9 Document type hierarchies.

own document attributes and, in addition, inherits attributes from its parent node. For example, the Legal Document can have its own specialized attributes, such as case name, client, court date, and others.

■ 10.6 THE OFFICE

In the intelligent office environment, offices are objects owned by office workers. Like all other objects, they have attributes and operations. The most important operations for offices are those used to search and navigate the content of the office.

As shown in Figures 10.4 and 10.10, each office can contain several items:

- *A desktop:* The intelligent office desktop is a specialized hierarchy of object types representing the most commonly used objects in the office. The intelligent desktop categorizes each of the object types and their relationships. The desktop provides the environment where the user performs editing, update, and management work.
- Zero or more *cabinets*
- Zero or more *peripherals*
- *A door:* The office window shows the icon of a door. When the user clicks on this door, he or she is offered the option of "going-to" another office, a library, or the common area or to view the entire floor.

From the floor, the office worker can zoom into his or her office, making the office the active window. The office worker can further zoom into the desktop, a cabinet, or the whiteboard.

The same office worker, depending on his or her roles and tasks, can actually have multiple offices. The various offices can be used by the office worker to organize his or her tasks and workspaces.

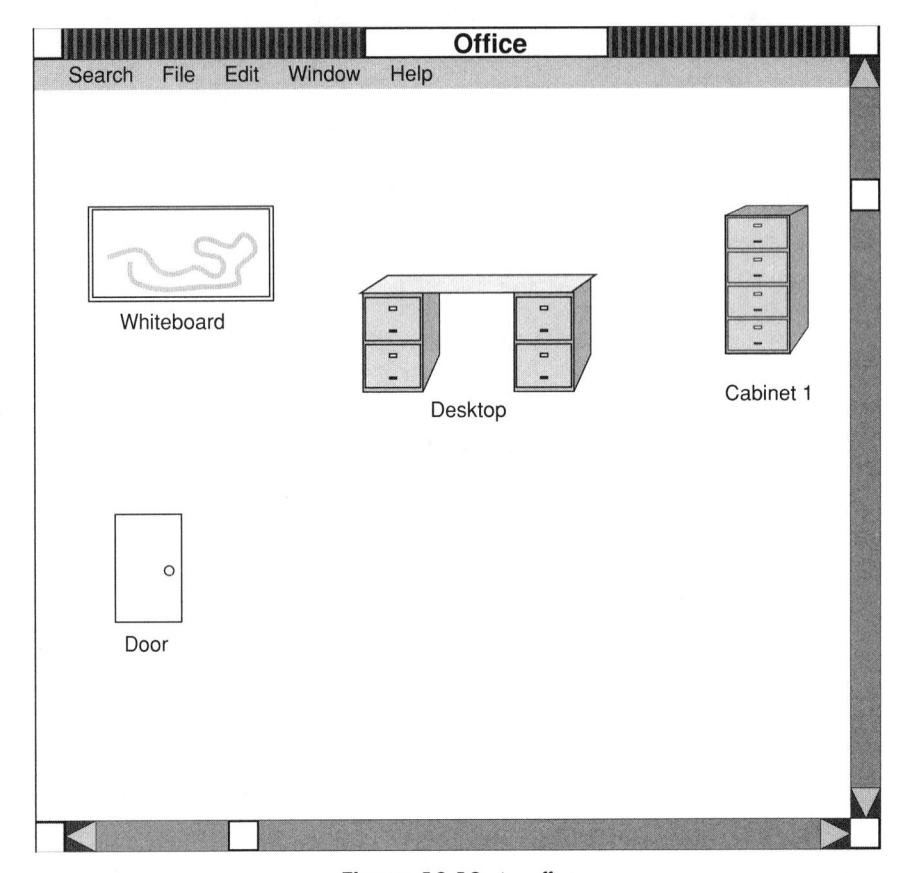

Figure 10.10 An office.

■ 10.7 ORGANIZING THE OFFICE WORKERS

The office environment is organized by partitioning information and office objects, with privileges for manipulating the information or other objects assigned to different office workers as appropriate.

For example, consider the hierarchy of office workers illustrated in Figure 10.11. The figure illustrates two types of relationships:

1. *Organizational relationships:* Workers report to Managers; Managers report to VPs; VPs report to Presidents; and Presidents report to CEOs.
2. *Inheritance hierarchies:* CEOs have the privileges and attributes of Presidents; Presidents have the privileges and attributes of VPs; and so on. Everyone has the attributes of Workers: Name, Address, Office, and so on.

In terms of privileges, office workers are assigned to various offices. An "office" thus represents the collection of all objects belonging to a worker within the corporation.

10.7 Organizing the Office Workers ■ 349

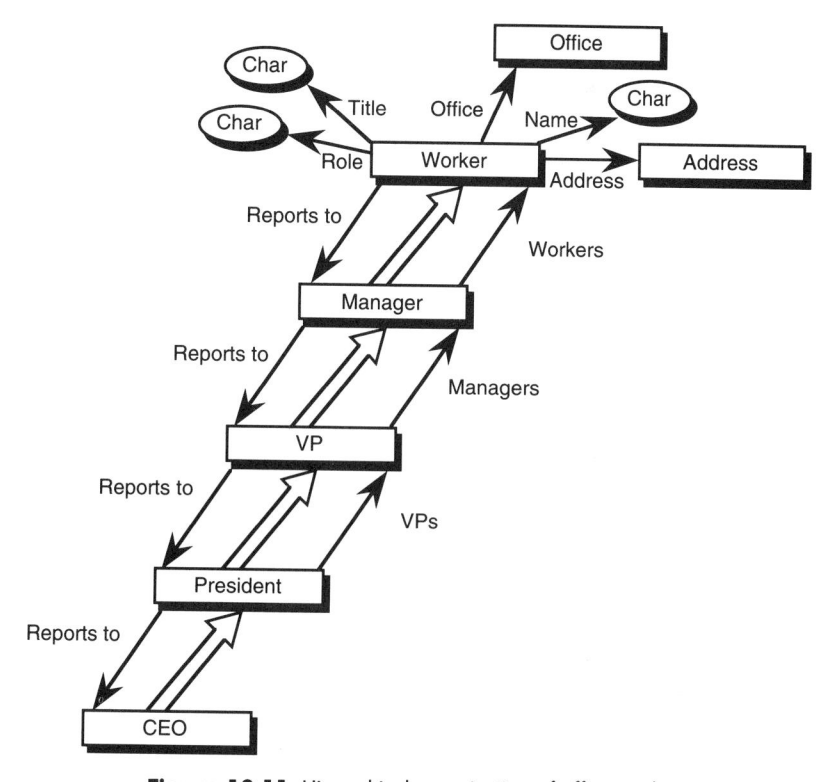

Figure 10.11 Hierarchical organization of office workers.

Note that the same office worker can belong to different departments and thus have different offices. Figure 10.12 illustrates the assignment of office workers to various offices and departments.

Because organization hierarchies are much more elaborate than "who reports to whom," the intelligent office environment also incorporates the notion of a group. Groups, which are also objects, have three important attributes:

1. *Charter:* the objectives and responsibilities of the group
2. *Privileges:* Usually groups share their common information bases in libraries, as illustrated in Figure 10.12. Individual group members will have access to these libraries and can check information out.
3. *Members:* the office workers who belong to the groups, and their respective roles

Each worker can belong to one or more groups in one or more departments. Groups may also cross department boundaries. As a result, each office worker has several characteristics (attributes):

- Descriptive attributes (name, address, and so on)
- Departments

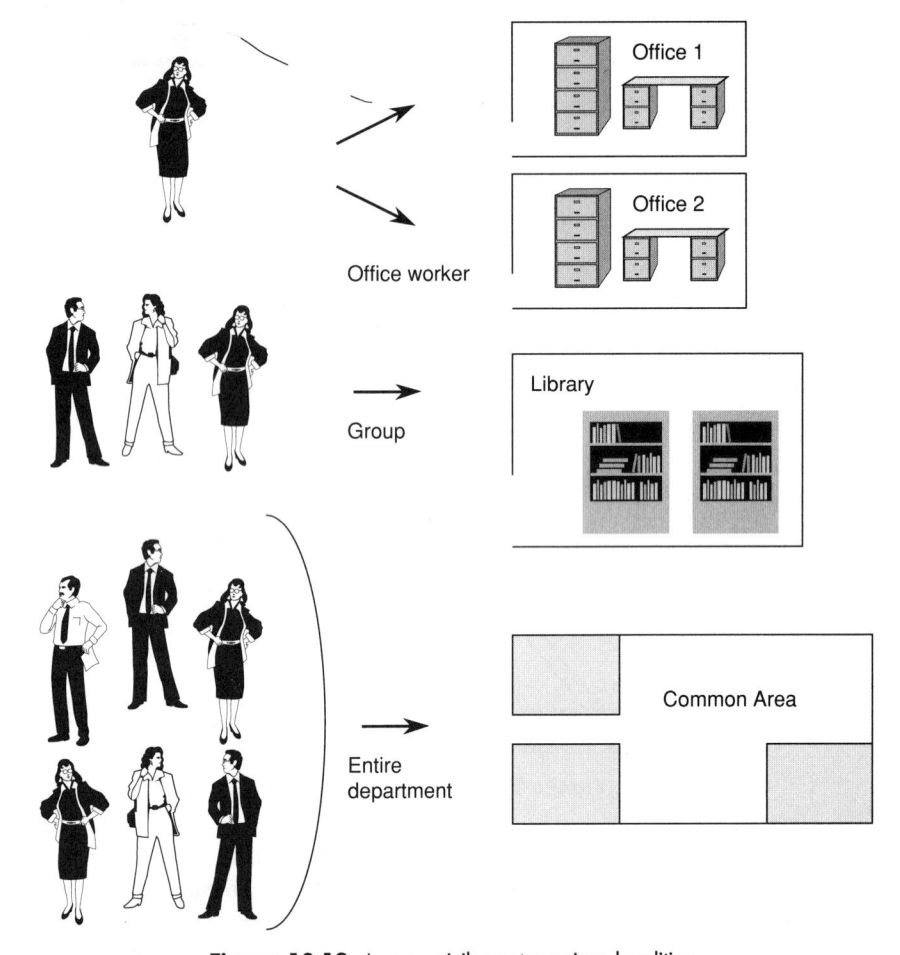

Figure 10.12 Access privileges to various localities.

- Groups
- Titles and roles (a person with the title of Administrative Assistant to the CEO may also play the role of the Corporate Information Coordinator of the CEO, and in that role have more privileges than even the president and the VPs in accessing and updating information pertaining to the CEO)
- Subordinates
- Immediate supervisor (in each group or department)
- Responsibilities (policies or interface) for various tasks (these correspond to the "protocol" or interface of the office worker as an object: For instance, the protocol of an administrative assistant includes tasks such as "mail package," "make reservations," "control calendar," and so on)
- Privileges to access or update office objects

Office workers are also organized in inheritance hierarchies with respect to characteristics, protocols, and policies. These inheritance hierarchies reflect the structural and information sharing among the workers.

All office workers inherit from the root (generic) class of Office Worker. The Office Worker root incorporates a number of attributes (including those just listed) that are common to all office workers. In addition, specializations provide more specific attributes (structure) and policies (behavior) for various workers in a corporation.

10.8 MANAGING PAPER INFORMATION

The current trend is to replace paper shuffling incrementally through electronic information exchange. However, besides the scanning and representation of information in electronic images, the intelligent office environment also offers the constructs to manage paper.

Paper management in intelligent offices is achieved through two ways:

1. Support of an object-oriented data model to represent any type of object, including electronic information, peripherals, and nonelectronic "objects" such as office workers and paper documents
2. Procedures (work flow) that can specify how any type of "object" in an office environment must be organized and "manipulated" (this also can apply to nonelectronic objects, including office workers and paper documents)

Figure 10.13 illustrates how an object-oriented intelligent office environment can be used to manage paper information. Here the design captures information about the book, the book's owner, and the book's status (who checked it out and when), plus the location of each book. Note that the books themselves exist in paper format.

Through such organizations (and provided that the office environment enforces the discipline of updating the organization library and keeping it current), paper information bases can be managed by the system. Of course, the books should be indexed on various attributes and content to enable them to be searched.

The check-out/check-in policy of paper documents within the office would need to be enforced by the following:

- The paper document information must be modeled and stored in the intelligent office environment.
- The policy or procedure for accessing the paper documents must be stored in a shared information base. For instance, regulations such as "A document cannot be checked out more than 2 weeks" can be expressed through rules and stored in the knowledge base.
- Since the access is to paper (and not electronic) documents, the office workers must either discipline themselves to record their actions (such as checking out a paper document) or be supervised so that their actions are entered into the office information base.

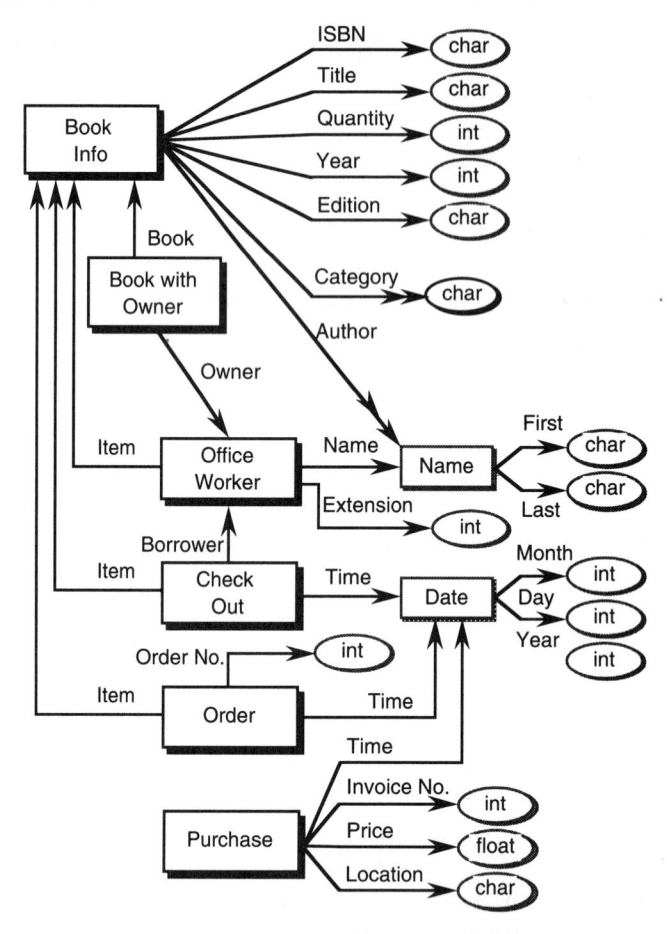

Figure 10.13 Organizing a library.

The last requirement would be probably the hardest to enforce. Office environments managed with a "Big Brother Watching Over You" philosophy are neither productive nor desirable. On the other hand, a completely loose office philosophy can cause loss of information and chaos in locating paper documents. Hence, a disciplined balance must be achieved, respecting individual freedom yet protecting the corporation's assets and information. Since human beings enforce this discipline, intelligent office environments will inevitably encounter problems and difficulties with managing paper information.

■ 10.9 OBJECT REPOSITORY FOR OFFICE OBJECTS

The previous section clearly illustrates that the persistent object spaces manipulated in intelligent offices are graph-structured. This means that objects (such as folders, cabinets, or offices) contain or reference other collection of objects (such as documents). Furthermore, as the discussion in the previous section illustrated, each of the object types is a class: It contains a number of well-defined collections of operations. These intelligent office classes are organized in inheritance hierarchies (such as inheritance of folders or document types). Therefore, an object-oriented database (OODB) appears to provide the best model and repository of the intelligent office objects. However, here we present an object repository solution for relational databases. There are several reasons for this approach:

1. OODBs are still in their infancy, although there are commercial products such as Object/Store and GemStone. Standards for an OODB model are still to emerge. There are some promising signs, such as efforts by Object Management Group and ANSI OODB Task Group.
2. The SQL3 standard and the emergence of a number of RDBMS with object-oriented capabilities clearly illustrate that relational databases will soon integrate object-oriented features such as abstract data typing, inheritance, and object identity, as discussed in Chapter 4.
3. The relational DBMS have penetrated commercial markets, whereas OODBMS currently are found in specialized markets such as CAD/CAM/CASE. In fact, it is estimated that 17 percent of relational database systems are used for document management.
4. Since SQL systems are easily available to our readers, the relational design presented in this section could be useful for building prototypes.

This section applies the relational database model to the storage and retrieval of office objects. The database design for the most commonly used office objects (documents and folders) is presented. (Other office objects, such as cabinets, are similar in their representation to folders and will not be presented.)

The document object has the following attributes:

- Name, which must be unique among all documents stored in a given folder
- Owner, indicating the original creator of the document
- Creation date, representing the date that the document was created
- Current user, indicating the individual currently modifying (or who recently modified) the document
- Last-modified date, which is updated every time a document is modified by the end user
- Status, indicating whether a document is Opened by a user or Closed (and thus available to be opened)
- Server file location, indicating the location of the file on the server
- Type, specifying the format of the document (such as Microsoft Word, WordPerfect, Scanned Image, Text, or a more general compound hypermedia document)

The folder object has the following attributes:

- Name, which must be unique among all folders stored within another folder
- Owner

- Creation date, representing the date the folder was created
- Last-modified date, indicating the last time a folder entry was added or removed
- Contents, representing the set of documents and folders contained within this folder

10.9.1 Relational Database Design

This section presents the relational database design for folder and document objects. Chapter 4 discussed one popular approach to designing a relational database. The approach discussed was to model the database using an entity-relationship diagram first and then decompose the entities and relationships in this diagram into relational tables.

Figure 10.14 shows the entity-relationship (ER) diagram used to design the database containing the document and folder objects just described. Notice that this ER diagram uses a diamond representing the Containment relationship. On one side, the Containment relationship is depicted by two lines, one leading to Document entity and the other to the Folder entity. This indicates that a folder object can contain either one or more document objects or one or more folder objects.

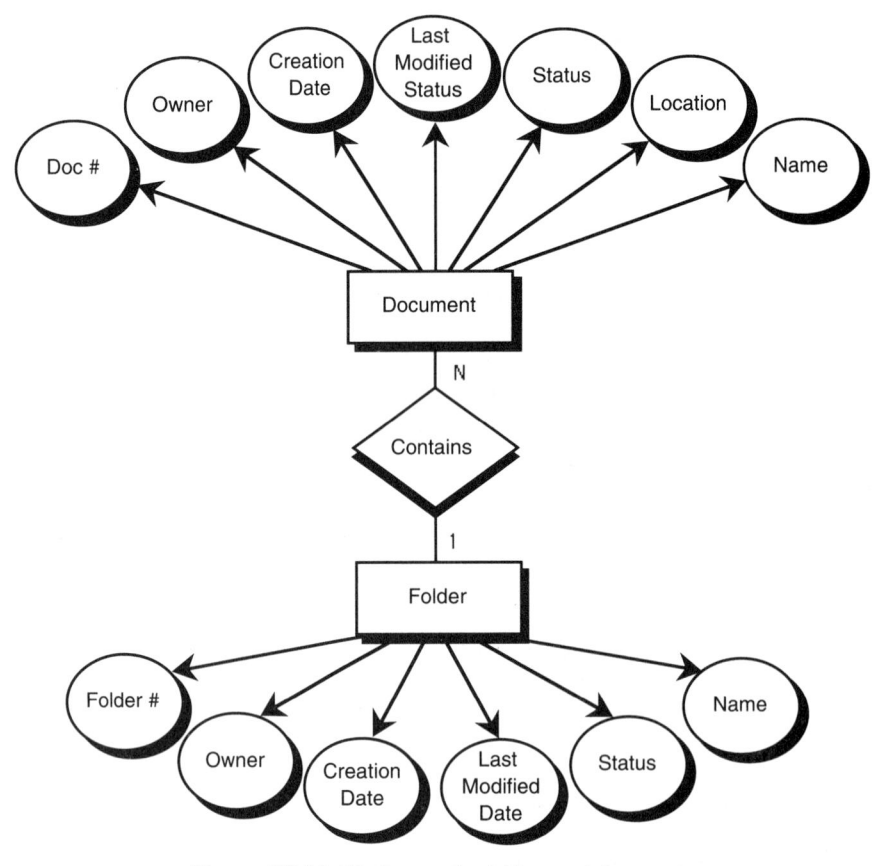

Figure 10.14 ER diagram for folders and documents.

Document Table
Doc#
Owner
CreationDate
CurrentUser
LastModDate
Status
Location
Name

Folder
Folder#
Owner
CreationDate
LastModDate
Status
Name

Containment
Folder#
Obj#
ObjType

HighestObject#
Obj#

FreeObject#
Obj#

Figure 10.15 Relational tables for office objects.

The relational schema design of the documents and folders is represented by the five tables shown in Figure 10.15. Notice that the document and folder tables each have an additional field called *Doc#* and *Folder#*. These fields uniquely identify a folder or a document.

When an object is created (whether a folder or a document), the system assigns a unique identifier for the object. In order to maintain the object numbers, the system takes advantages of two tables: *HighestObject#* and *FreeObject#*. The first is a table of one entry that tracks the next object number available for assignment if the *FreeObject#* table is empty. The latter table recycles the object numbers. When an object is destroyed, its object identifier is inserted into this table for later reuse. (After all, this is the age of recycling, and object numbers can be recycled forever!)

As part of the initialization process, the *HighestObject#* table will contain one entry with the value of 1, indicating the next object number available. Initially, because no recycled object numbers will be available, *FreeObject#* will at first be empty.

10.9.1.1 Maintaining Object Numbers

First we will examine the simple case, without recycling in mind, and then we will incorporate recycled object numbers. The following statement assigns a new office number and returns the current object number:

select Obj# in NewObject# from HighestObject#

The next available object number is computed using the following statement:

update HighestObject#
set Obj# = Obj# + 1

With recycling in mind, the next step is to examine the contents of the *FreeObject#* table before accessing the *HighestObject#* table. If the first table contains any entries, then the first tuple is deleted from it. If the following statement returns zero, then the previous two statements generate the next object number:

select count(*) from FreeObject#

If the result is other than zero, then the following two statements compute the next available object number.

select Obj# in NewObject# from FreeObject#
delete from FreeObject# where Obj# = NewObject#

10.9.1.2 Populating the Database

Given the object numbers just discussed, we can now create documents and folders. Each document or folder is contained by another folder. When creating either object, the home folder object number is required. The following set of SQL statements creates a new folder. In these statements, *Today* holds the date value and *NewObj#* represents the newly assigned object number to this folder.

insert into folder values
 (NewObj#, "Main", "John", Today, "John", Today, "Closed")

Since the root folder is not contained in any folder, the following statement sets *HomeFolder#* equal to zero:

insert into Containment values
 (HomeFolder#, NewObj#, 2)

The following two SQL statements create a new document:

insert into document values
 (NewObj#, "Test.Doc", "John", Today, "John", Today, "Closed", "s:test.doc")
insert into Containment values
 (HomeFolder#, NewObj#, 1)

10.9.2 Query Forms

Now that the relational database has been designed and the document and folder objects have been stored in the database, the database can be queried to access any one of these objects. The following discussion examines object queries in the following categories: navigating throughout the folder hierarchy, querying objects in the current folder, and querying objects within a document database.

10.9.2.1 Folder Navigation

The basic commands for navigating through the folder hierarchy involve the process of moving down to a child folder or moving up to a folder's parent. At any given time, a user is in the context of a given folder. Each folder has an *Obj#*, and the current folder number is stored in *CurrFolder#*. Before navigating downwards in a folder, we must access the folder's containing objects. The following query generates a list of documents and folder within the current folder:

> select * from Containment
>   where Folder# = CurrFolder#

When the query requests all objects within the main folder, the following list is generated:

Folder#	Obj#	ObjType
1	2	1
1	3	2
1	4	1
1	8	2
1	9	2

To change the current folder to the second folder in the list with the *Obj#* equal to 5, simply assign the value 5 to *CurrFolder#*.

The process of moving up the hierarchy is simple, because each containing object keeps track of its parent folder. To move up, simply assign *CurrFolder#* to be the parent folder.

To increase efficiency and minimize disk access, cache some of the traversed hierarchy. For example, a last-in last-out cache can be implemented to retain the last N number of folders in memory, eliminating the need to access the database for that information. When a memory cache is used, it is important to keep the cache information up to date, since a folder can be accessed by several concurrent users.

10.9.2.2 Accessing Objects in the Current Folder

Once a folder is opened, a user may submit certain queries against the containing objects of this folder. For each contained object, the system provides access to its identifier and type. Given these two pieces of information, either the folder or the document table can be queried to retrieve attributes of any contained object. For example, if the current folder contains a document with the *Obj#* equal to 4, the following query retrieves the attributes of this document:

select * from Document
  where Obj# = 4

As another example, the following query returns the attributes of the list of documents modified on October 5, 1991:

select * from Document
  where LastModDate = "10/05/91"
  and Obj# IN (select ChildObj#
    from Containment
    where ParentObj# = CurrFolder#)

The following query finds all documents in the current folder that are authored by *"John"*:

select * from Document
  where Owner = "John"
  and Obj# IN (select ChildObj#
    from Containment
    where ParentObj# = CurrFolder#)

The next query retrieves an alphabetical listing of all entries in the current folder:

select Obj#, Name from Document
  where Obj# IN (select ChildObj#
    from Containment
    where ParentObj# = CurrFolder#)
union
select Obj#, Name from Folder
  where Obj# IN (select ChildObj#
    from Containment
    where ParentObj# = CurrFolder#)
ordered by Name

10.9.2.3 Accessing Objects in the Document Database

In addition to accessing objects in the current folder, the user may pose queries about objects within the current document database. For example, the following query locates all documents authored by *"John"*:

select * from Document
  where Owner = "John"

Queries of this form are much simpler than those discussed in the previous section. A query of the current folder is more complex, because a subquery is necessary in order to get information about the current folder as a subset of the entire document database.

10.9.2.4 Updating Objects

A document or folder tuple is updated when the corresponding document or folder is manipulated by the end user. For example, when a user modifies a document, the document date must be changed to reflect the modification. The following SQL statement indicates a new modified date for a given document:

update Document
  set LastModDate = '05/01/91'
  set CurrentUser = 'Barbara'
  where Obj# = 12

The process of adding new entries in a folder requires two operations: adding one tuple in the *Containment* table and adding another tuple in the *Folder* table. The following example adds a new folder, with the identifier equal to 21, to the parent folder, with the identifier equal to 10:

insert into Containment values (10, 21, 2)

and

insert into Folder values
  (21, "NewBook", "Bob", "05/19/92", "05/19/92")

The process of removing objects from the database requires more care. To remove a document, we must ensure that no other user is currently updating it. Thus, the status must be *Closed*. Second, the document's *Obj#* must be added to the *FreeObject#* table. For example, following SQL queries delete the document with the *Obj#* equal to 12:

delete from Document
  where Obj# = 12 and Status = "Closed"

When the foregoing query is successful, the following query removes the document from the containing folder:

delete from Containment
  where Child# = 12

The following query recycles the deleted document's object number:

insert into FreeObject# values (12)

Before one removes a document, several issues should be considered. First, if the folder contains other folders, should all containing folders be deleted? This operation is more drastic and also expensive. To eliminate this scenario, a folder must contain no folders during removal. The following sequence of folders enforces this condition for the folder with *Obj#* equal to 21. First, the following query ensures that the folder does not contain any folders:

```
select count(*)
    from Containment
    where Parent# = 21 and ObjType = 2
```

If the foregoing query returns zero, then the next step is to remove all containing documents, as explained earlier. Then the empty folder can be deleted by the following calls:

```
delete from Folder
    where Obj# = 21
```

The deleted folder's number is then added to the recycling bin:

```
insert into FreeObject# values (21)
```

10.9.3 Locking Shared Objects

Because office objects are used by several users concurrently, it is important to guarantee that a given document is updated by a single person. To do so, a document is locked (or checked-out) when the user is modifying its contents; when the user is finished making changes, he or she releases the lock (or checks it in). The following protocol accesses a document:

1. *Lock(Document#, UserName)* attempts to lock a given document for a specified user.
2. *Unlock (Document#, UserName)* releases the *Open* lock held on the given document for the specified user.

The process of locking a document (or any object) is more complex. Essentially, granting a lock is a simple operation. If no other user currently has the document locked, then it is locked for the requester. The following query presents the SQL equivalent of the *Lock* protocol.

```
update Document
    set Status = 'Opened'
    set CurrentUser = 'Jack'
    where Obj# = 13 and Status = 'Closed'
        or Status = 'Opened' and CurrentUser = 'Jack'
```

This query locks the document that has the object number 13. This statement then grants the lock to the current user if either the document is locked by this user already, or no other user is currently modifying this document.

If the prior query fails, the document is already locked by another user, and one of several scenerios may occur. First, the current user should be placed on a queue until the document becomes available, or else the user should be notified that the document is unavailable.

Since a document may be locked by one individual for a long period of time, additional information can be tracked in order to handle locks more thoroughly. This information may include the name of the user, the exact time when the lock was granted, and the lock's electronic address.

This information makes different courses of action possible. First, if several users request a locked document during a period which the system may consider as "long" (such as a few days), the person holding the lock can be notified via electronic mail that other users need the document. Eventually the system may also decide to release the lock, if the lock is held for an extensive period of time.

The *Lock* table can also store the length of time requested by the user for locking the document for his or her use. This information provides the basis for determining whether the duration is too long for the system. Alternately, the system may function like a library and grant locks to an individual for a fixed period of time. In this case, if no other user requires the document, the current user can extend the duration of the locking period. Otherwise, the document is returned to the system by releasing the lock.

The process of unlocking a document simply requires that the document *Status* be changed to *Closed*, as in the following SQL statement:

```
update Document
  set Status = 'Closed'
  LastModDate = '07/23/91'
  where Obj# = 13 and Status = 'Closed'
    or Status = 'Opened' and CurrentUser = 'Jack'
```

■ 10.10 CHANGE MANAGEMENT

In most corporations, the changes made to a document are important, and the evolution of the document needs to be tracked. One way to do so is to store the previous versions of a document and the newly updated version. Thus, if a document has been modified several times, the system contains a set of documents representing each release of the document, as depicted in Figure 10.16.

The end user typically wants to access the most recent version of a document and is provided that version by the system. When the user finishes updating the document, the updated document becomes the most recent version. This structure allows users to access any individual version of a document by naming a specific version as "v1," "v2," "v3," and so on, or by requesting a version, using parameters such as the date of modification.

Each document may consume large amounts of disk space, and tracking all versions of all documents would be very expensive. Several strategies alleviate this situation. First, the system may provide a purge operation, where older or selected versions of a document can be deleted. Alternately, older versions can be archived on a WORM or tape drive. Still another strategy is to store the incremental changes from one version to another. When a specific version is requested, the system extracts the relevant portion of the document for that version.

When several versions of a document exist in a system, the system must be able to determine the differences between two versions of a document. Version management can provide this functionality.

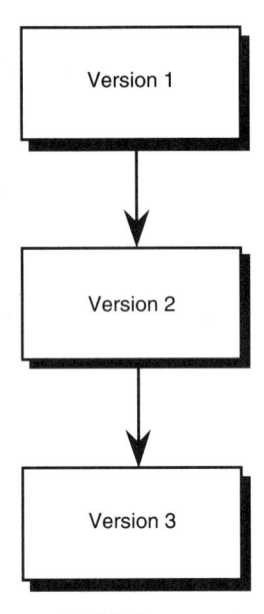

362 ■ Office Objects and the Office Object Repository

Figure 10.16 Linear version set.

If concurrent access to one document must be provided, a more sophisticated version management system is required. Up to this point, change management has been discussed with respect to documents deriving from one another linearly, as in Figure 10.16.

To permit concurrent access to a document through change management, a more hierarchical version management (as shown in Figure 10.17) is necessary. In this scenario,

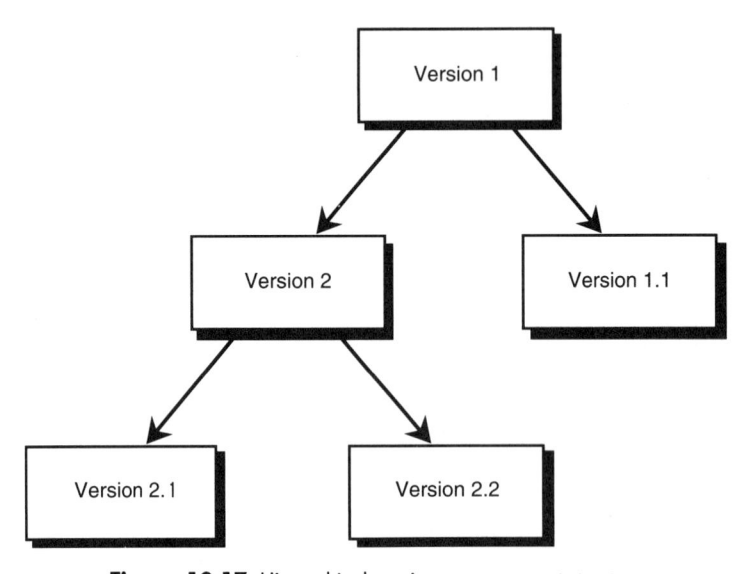

Figure 10.17 Hierarchical version management structure.

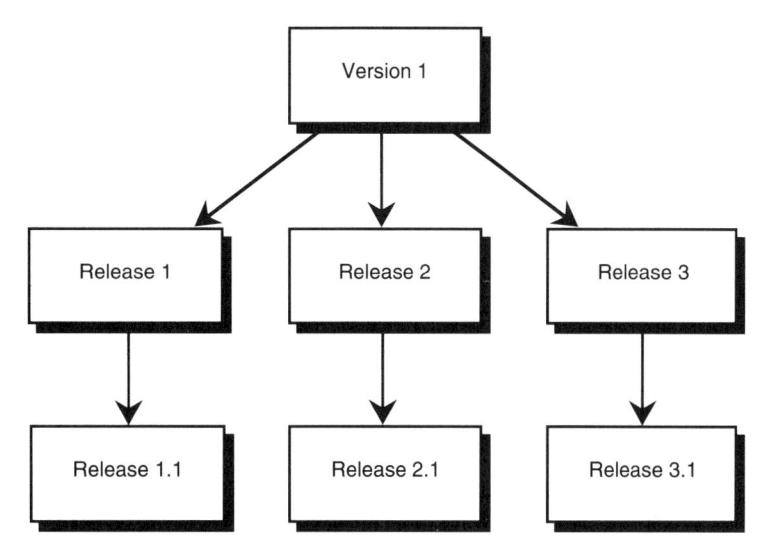

Figure 10.18 Version tree for a software product supported in three releases.

each concurrent user creates his or her own branch of the tree. If only one user accesses a document, then only one branch is required. If another concurrent user requests a lock on a document, a new branch in the version management tree is created to track the changes made by the second user.

Once several parallel branches have been created by different users, their efforts should be combined by merging the work done on the same document. This requires a mechanism for merging two separate versions of a document and recording a new version that includes all changes. During the process of merging, the software can decide how to handle changes made by the authors that do not conflict with each other. When any changes conflict, the end user should decide the result of the merge operation for that section of the document.

A hierarchical version management system provides a much richer mechanism for change management. For example, if a document provides information about a product, then information about each version of the product can be managed through a hierarchical version management system. Figure 10.18 presents a version management tree for a product containing three versions.

Each version of a document may require minor changes. The change history of each version can have its own sub branch, and the end user can choose to merge the earlier changes into the most recent release of the document.

■ 10.11 CHECK-OUT/CHECK-IN OF OFFICE OBJECTS

The previous sections discussed the processes of querying, updating, locking, and versioning functionalities for shared persistent objects in the repository. As explained earlier, concurrently shared objects must be first checked out from common areas or libraries, operated upon, and then checked in. The overall algorithm for accessing objects concurrently in client/server architectures is as follows:

1. Begin transaction.
2. Navigate to or locate the object(s) to be manipulated.
3. Check out the objects with either Read or Write Lock, depending upon intent.
4. Manipulate the object(s), possibly updating it.
5. Check in the object(s) back to common area (repository), possibly creating a new version.
6. Commit transaction.

If the process goes smoothly and the object is updated, a new version of the object is created. If anything goes wrong (because of transaction, system, or user conflicts) the transaction can be aborted, the locks released, and any updates on the checked-out objects undone.

Figure 10.19 illustrates how client/server architecture corresponds with an object repository and the office worker's workspace.

Objects can be checked out by the following two techniques:

- Providing its unique identifier (its *Obj#* or key value)
- Providing various selection criteria

The first strategy is obvious: The office worker simply checks out the object using a "handle." The second strategy involves performing searches and then checking out an object according to its attribute values or its relationship with other objects. For instance,

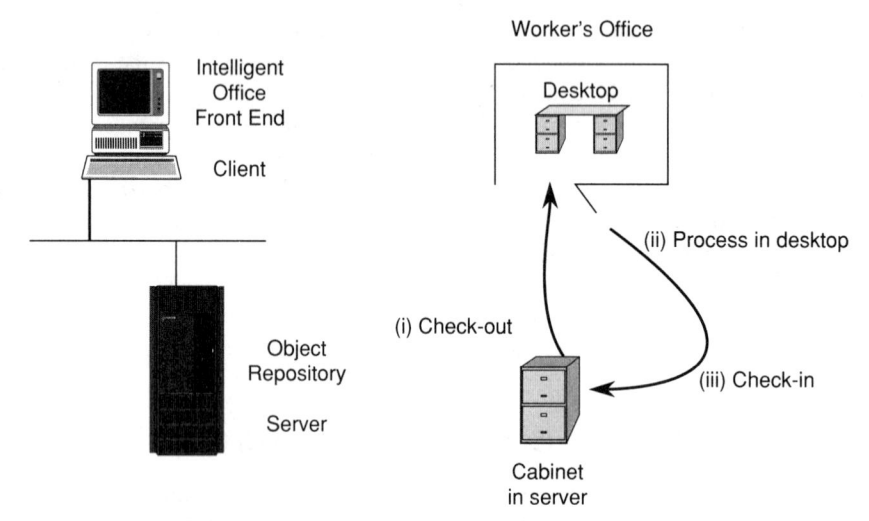

Figure 10.19 The check-out and check-in of objects from the repository.

documents in a folder whose type is WordPerfect can be checked out using the following pseudocode:

```
Check-Out Documents D In Folder F1
    WHERE D.Type = "WordPerfect"
```

Another important issue with respect to object check-out/check-in is the granularity and levels of the objects. For example, when a folder is checked out, what objects have been checked out? When the office worker checks out folder *F1*, is he or she checking out all objects contained in *F1*? When a compound hypermedia document is checked out, are all the documents linked to the hypermedia document also checked out?

It can easily be seen that the process of checking out a document can imply a substantial amount of locking. Of course, in client/server architectures locking large objects reduces the concurrency and has an adverse effect on the throughput of the system. On the other hand, the process of checking in or checking out objects with a finer granularity can incur a substantial overhead in locks and could even prohibit the office worker from accessing all the documents he or she needs.

Therefore, since the office worker has the most knowledge about what he or she needs to access, the office repository can provide the following alternatives:

- Given an object handle O, check out only O. Other office workers or applications cannot access or update the attributes of O, and if O contains other objects, they cannot insert or delete objects in O. However, they can access or even check out objects contained in O or reachable from O.
- Given an object handle O, check out O and all its immediate children. For instance, if O is a folder, this option will check out O and all documents or folders immediately contained in O. The advantage here is that the office worker has access to all the objects contained in the folder without locking the entire "universe" reachable from the folder.
- Check out all objects that are directly or transitively linked or reachable from the object handle. This option can be very useful for accessing self-contained hypermedia documents.

10.12 SUMMARY

The intelligent office environment is an object-oriented environment, where the office worker interacts with object classes representing other office workers, buildings, policies, and so on. The documents in intelligent office environments are compound hypermedia documents. In fact, the entire intelligent office environment can be regarded as a hypermedia environment, allowing users to navigate from one node to another through hypermedia links.

This chapter illustrated the various intelligent office environment "objects." Each instance in these intelligent office classes has attributes. These attributes can be searched to identify qualifying intelligent office objects.

The objects in an intelligent office environment can be in a common area (that is, shared by multiple office workers). In the underlying system, these objects will be stored in concurrently shared databases.

This chapter also demonstrated how the objects are stored in database servers and shared by multiple office workers concurrently. We have discussed how documents and folders are represented in the database. We presented how the relational database is applied to represent these objects. We used numerous SQL examples to illustrate documents and folders manipulation. In addition, we discussed how documents are shared by several users. We discussed a simple locking mechanism to guarantee that a document is updated by only one user. Later on, we presented change management and how it can be used to keep track of several concurrent versions of a document. In addition, we presented how change management can be used to permit several concurrent users to update several different versions of a document and later on merge their changes into a later version of a document. Next, we discussed how the check-out/check-in paradigm is used to access persistent office objects in common areas or libraries and create new versions of them. We listed various options for checking out objects and various issues dealing with the granularity of the objects being checked out.

11

COLLABORATIVE WORK AND WORK FLOW IN INTELLIGENT OFFICES

■ 11.1 INTRODUCTION

Local area networks are permeating the workplace like never before. The growth of connectivity greatly expands the opportunities for office workers to cooperate and work together. As pointed out by Winograd and Flores (1991), "In most work environments the coordination of action is of central importance." Many tools and products have been developed to address the very important issue of collaboration through computer networks over local and wide area networks. This trend is expected to continue well into the 1990s.

Internetworked LANs allow information exchange, message exchange, and improved information flow throughout a corporation. These LANs can span buildings, departments, cities, and even continents. (LAN technologies and internetworked LANs were discussed in detail in Chapter 3.) Figure 11.1 illustrates the architecture of interconnected LANs in a corporation. Each department has a LAN, which is internetworked with the other departmental LANs through bridges. The "wires" and "vines" carry the information that enables cooperative work in the intelligent office environment.

The most important application of LANs in next-generation intelligent office environments will be intelligent systems that support cooperative exchange, coordination, and sharing of information between office workers. This technology has been called computer-supported cooperative work (CSCW) (Greif, 1988) and (Wilson, 1991).

At a very rudimentary level, cooperative work within an intelligent office environment depends upon two systems: an electronic mail, or messaging, system and intelligent database repositories.

Electronic mail or messaging systems allow office workers to send and receive information (documents or messages) electronically. Other services provided by electronic mail systems include the abilities to store, retrieve, archive and prioritize messages and to "cut and paste" the contents of messages to and from applications in the worker's environment.

More sophisticated systems allow information in various formats (such as spreadsheet and word processing files) to be transmitted through electronic mail. Other advanced features include computer on-line conferencing and information flow control. In fact, the trend of electronic mail products is to incorporate increasingly more sophisticated groupware and work-flow utilities.

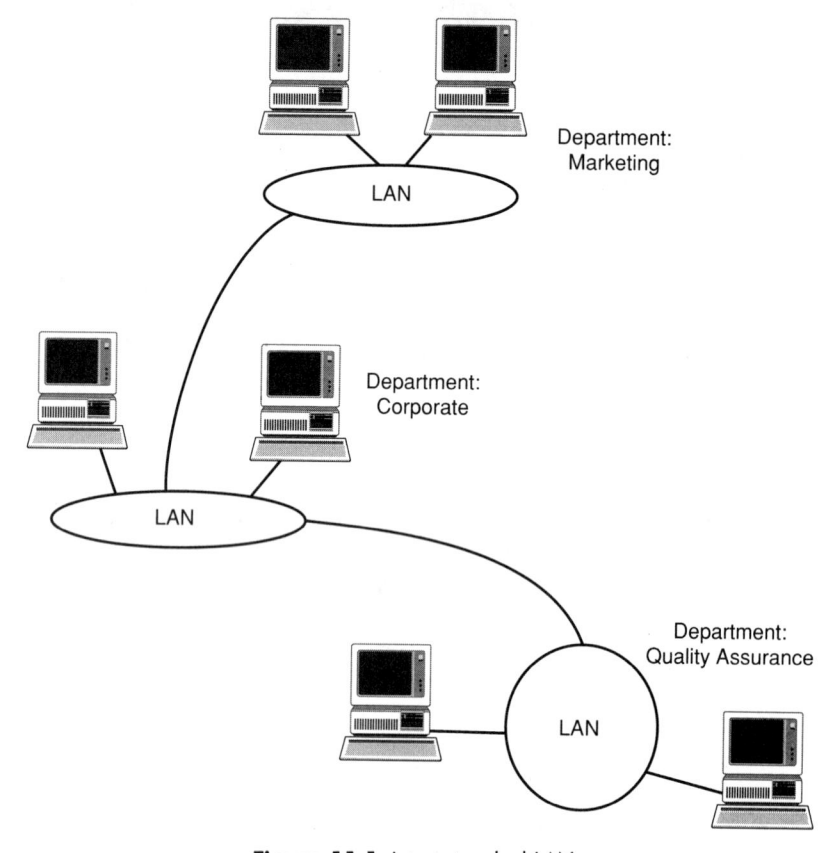

Figure 11.1 Internetworked LANs.

The second system that enables cooperative work in the intelligent office environment is the intelligent database repository. While the electronic messaging or information flow utilities provide a paradigm for directly exchanging information between office workers, an alternative paradigm has also been used extensively since the dawn of the computer age: the "centralized database" (or repository) model.

As discussed in the previous chapter, office workers who collaborate on a document must check out the document from the central repository, work on it, and check it back in. The repository model requires a client/server architecture (Khoshafian et al., 1992) where the clients (office workers) request access services from file or database servers over a local area network.

These two systems actually capture two models of collaboration in an intelligent office environment:

- A peer-to-peer direct exchange model between office workers or groups in the intelligent office
- An indirect client/server "check-out/check-in" model of exchange and collaboration between office workers or groups

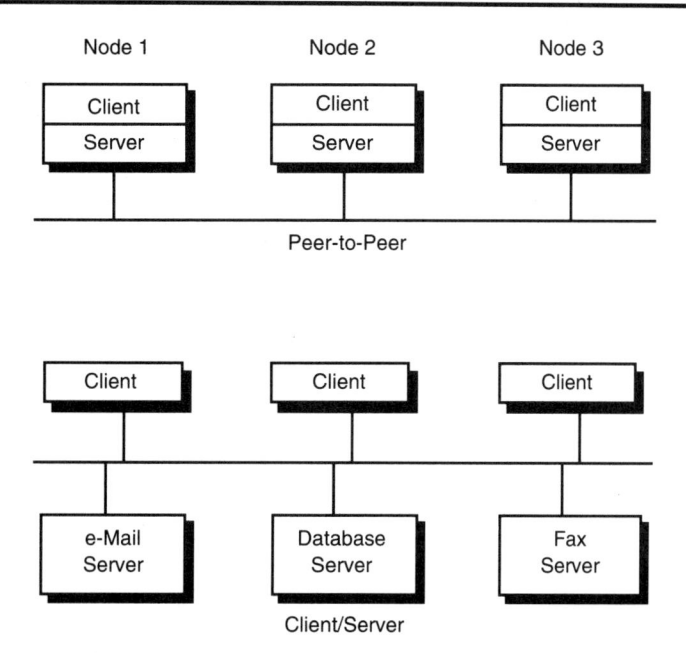

Figure 11.2 Peer-to-peer and client/server architectures.

These two models are illustrated in Figure 11.2. The collaborative work and work-flow utilities in intelligent offices use and build upon these two paradigms. We believe that in an intelligent office environment, both paradigms are necessary for collaborative work. In fact, in most sophisticated intelligent office applications users will be using both models at different stages of accomplishing a task.

In the cooperative/collaborative work arena, the past decade has witnessed the emergence of a number of technologies, with sometimes confusing scopes and definitions. In addition to electronic mail and server technologies, two other prominent terms have emerged in this area: groupware and work flow.

Both of these technologies utilize the underlying local area networks to exchange information. Although electronic messaging is more prominent in groupware, both technologies employ it for collaborative work. Also, although the use of database servers to store and retrieve shared information is more prominent in work flow systems, both technologies can use database servers.

11.1.1 Groupware: An Overview

As discussed throughout this book, intelligent offices attempt to solve the information overflow problem through organizing the information bases and the communication of information in collaborative environments. Computer-supported collaborative work (CSCW), as its name suggests, attempts to organize and regulate the sharing or exchange of information in intelligent office environments. This could entail real-time conferencing to collaborate on a problem, coordinated activities to develop a document, or "asynchronous" accesses to centralized servers by collaborating clients. CSCW is a new and emerging interdisciplinary field that integrates a number of technologies, including electronic messaging, social psychology, natural language systems, and behavioral psychology. The book of readings on CSCW edited by Irene Greif (1988) provides a comprehensive introduction to the literature of this emerging field. A more recent work summarizes some of the CSCW research activities (Wilson, 1991).

Groupware is the hardware/software systems which enables computer-supported collaborative work. In a sense (and based on the perception of many researchers in this area), groupware can be defined as an all-encompassing term for all systems that support collaborative work.

By this definition all local area network software, all client/server systems, all work-flow software, all electronic information exchange systems, and all project management systems fall under the umbrella of groupware. However, the past few years have witnessed the emergence of a number of local area network application products with specific collaborative work features for office environments, which came to be known (and sold) as groupware products. This does not mean that, for example, client/server or work-flow systems are not groupware. These products have the following characteristics:

- They are primarily LAN application products. Most groupware products operate as applications on top of a local area network.
- They exhibit common characteristics or provide certain common features: there have been a number of attempts to categorize the groupware discipline. These have ranged from simple augmentations to electronic messaging (E-mail) systems to elaborate "intelligent" electronic meeting systems. The former have appeared as PC LAN products and the latter as advanced research work in universities.
- They are known primarily as groupware products. Any type of product that facilitates communication and collaborative work between workers can be labeled as "groupware."

Typically, groupware software provides one or more of the following features:

1. Electronic mail, supporting the notion of users and groups with various electronic mail features. Typically, these mail messages are semi-structured, which means they have particular fields indicating sender, receiver, subject, date, and so on. In more elaborate electronic mail systems the electronic message types are organized in inheritance hierarchies, as discussed in Section 11.2.
2. Appointment Schedulers and Calendars, allowing groups of intelligent office workers to schedule nonconflicting meetings and activities. Groupware products such as Right Hand Man typically provide support for appointments, group scheduling, and group calendars.
3. Electronic audiovisual meetings and real-time document editing, allowing groups of office workers to exchange messages and even collaborate on a document or a project on-line with a group.

These are by no means the only features provided by groupware products. Other features include integration with the telephone system, management of telephone messages, project management, and the tracking of editorial comments on documents. Some of these features are discussed in the context of intelligent offices in subsequent sections of this chapter.

The key point to remember about groupware is that it is more than just the automation of the group activities between the various office workers. Groupware is the conglomeration of all the technologies in the office environment that help and enhance the collaborative effort and synergy of the group.

11.1.1.1 Groupware Research

Any discipline that involves human behavior is fascinating. By the very nature of the "beast" (no pun intended), such disciplines usually end up having an inertia of their own, creating and solving more problems as they mature. (Do disciplines that deal with human nature ever mature?)

CSCW and the groupware system do touch upon interaction between humans more than any other discipline in computer science. Not surprisingly, ever since the propagation of workstations and local area networks, a number of interesting research projects have concentrated on collaborative work (or groupware research) developing innovative software and hardware systems. Here we summarize some of these projects. Other examples can be found in Greif (1988) and Wilson (1991).

> *Colab* from Xerox PARC (Stefik *et al.*, 1988). The Colab system is a meeting room that incorporates several workstations, a large screen, and a whiteboard. It attempts to facilitate the generation, integration, and documentation of ideas through face-to-face interactions between workers, collaborating through a WYSISWIS (what you see is what I see) interface. With this discipline, participating workers see exactly the same screens in collaborative idea exchanges. The organization of ideas progresses through proposals, arguments, and evaluations.
>
> *NLS/AUGMENT* (On-Line System), developed at Stanford Research Institute (Englebart and Lehtman, 1988). The development of this system started in the mid-1960s and concentrated on collaborative work between geographically distributed workers. The project developed novel and innovative devices and systems and allowed users to collaborate in text documents. It provided mechanisms for workers to have group authorship of documents.
>
> *Object Lens*, developed at MIT (Lai *et al.*, 1988). This system integrated object-oriented "databases" with electronic messaging and rule base agents to facilitate collaborative work applications in the office. One of the interesting features of this system was rule-based filtering of electronic mail messages through user-defined rules.
>
> *Electronic Messaging Systems* (EMS) (Nunamaker *et al.*, 1991), developed at the University of Arizona, attempts to address various configurations of group work: small groups, large groups, groups at a single site, and groups dispersed in different sites. A software product called GroupSystems, used at EMS facilities (there are about 100 EMS facilities throughout the country), helps the group select an agenda, generate ideas, organize the ideas, and prioritize. Some GroupSystems sessions take place in networked meeting

rooms with a workstation per user and a large-screen video display. Similar meeting rooms have been adopted by GroupSystems sites at IBM.

Action, developed by Terry Winograd (1987). Action coordination systems utilize language theory to coordinate requests, promises, questions, and other conversation demanding responses and actions between users. Action Technologies has actually a product called Coordinator, which is based on this concept.

Besides these, there are many other projects concentrating on groupware. Some of these utilize expert system and inferencing technologies to assist workers (provide "expertise") integrate in groups and coordinate with others. COKES (Carleton Office Knowledge System) is one such system, developed at Carleton University (Kaye and Karam, 1987). Others also attempt to integrate "knowledge" or intelligence in the office environments.

In the following sections, we shall illustrate how some of these concepts could be integrated in intelligent office environments.

11.1.2 Work Flow: An Overview

As mentioned earlier, some office automation specialists consider work flow as one of the components of an overall groupware system. Be that as it may, we separate the overview on work flow because historically it evolved from a different type of technology rather than local area networks.

Work flow became popular primarily through document-imaging system products, such as FileNet and Wang's imaging system. There is a simple reason for this: The types of activities and applications in document imaging require the organization and control of the imaging documents. Corporations that purchase a document imaging system often have a serious paperwork bottleneck. Existing paper documents and the increasing additional flow of paper documents, which constantly arrive via fax, courier, and mail from branch offices and customers, can easily translate into inefficient usage of office workers' time.

In fact, the more successful a corporation becomes, the greater its paper overload will be. It is estimated that, on the average, the on-line information in corporations is only 1 percent of the corporation's data. 4 percent are in archived (electronic or microfiche) format, and the other 95 percent are stored on paper (WANG, 1989).

Once the necessary components of a document-imaging system are installed, the next task is to model and "program" the process of converting paper documents into organized electronic cabinets. For instance, the corporation might install a high-speed scanner in the mail room and volume-scan some of the incoming paper mail. The pipeline of scanned images then can go to an indexing and data entry node. Each processed image can then be stored on an optical disk. In some cases, scanned textual information can be OCRed to allow the subsequent full-text retrieval of the document. Figure 11.3 illustrates this work flow.

Although popularized by document-imaging systems, work flow is by no means limited to imaging. Other office or desktop products, although not emphasizing imag-

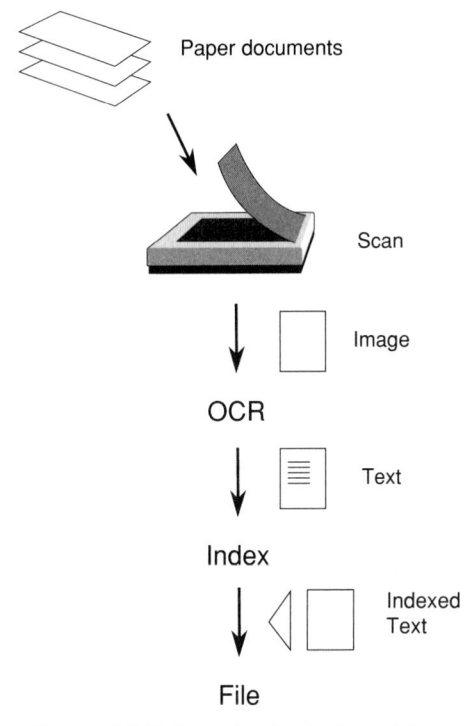

Figure 11.3 Example of a single work flow.

ing as such, also support work-flow models. For example, IBM's OfficeVision (Martin *et al.*, 1990) incorporates an In Basket and Out Basket for work which needs immediate processing by the office workers. Similarly, Metaphor's DIS allows users to construct data flow diagrams between application (spreadsheet, word processor, database) nodes, controlling the flow of the information from one node to the other.

A work-flow product, therefore, concentrates primarily on the control of the flow of information between various objects in the intelligent office. These objects could be office workers, application files, database servers, peripherals (such as scanners), to name a few.

Typically, work-flow products allow the office worker to construct a node-and-link diagram by linking nodes representing the intelligent office objects involved in the work flow. In a graphical user interface environment, the nodes are icons providing a visual metaphor for the underlying object.

The links between various nodes of a work-flow control the flow of the information. Links can perform filtering or direct the flow of the information conditionally, depending on the content (values) of the information they carry.

Work-flow systems can involve more sophisticated features such as schedulers, notifiers, advanced project management, and dynamic work flow. Most of these features will be discussed in the context of intelligent offices in Section 11.5.

11.1.3 Intelligent Collaboration

Collaborative work control and work flow in intelligent offices goes beyond these first-generation functionalities and incorporates true intelligence in the collaborative office environment. Intelligent offices provide additional features to support collaboration, in the following ways:

1. They go beyond simple electronic messages and allow intelligent searching, filtering, and abstracting of the electronic information being exchanged. The searches can be indicated through declarative rules.
2. They go beyond mere access of a group calendar to allow the intelligent optimization of group activities and calendars. Again, the "expert system" that indicates how to optimize the schedules, productivity, and synergy within a group is expressed through rules.
3. They step past mere file and relational database access to provide intelligent database support and true distributed database access. The office worker is freed from location or distribution considerations and collaborates with fellow workers at a much higher level, capturing the more natural interaction between humans.
4. They expand beyond mere support of electronic exchange of alphanumeric documents to allow real-time interaction in voice, video, and multi-media documents. In electronic meetings, office workers can exchange any type of multi-media information.
5. They go past simple in and out baskets and work-flow diagramming tools, allowing a much richer set of flow constructs and agents. This provides a uniform object-oriented model of work flow, where nodes and links are objects with attributes and behavior, organized in inheritance hierarchies. The work-flow system in intelligent offices allows office workers to construct work-flow procedures both statically through node-and-link diagramming tools and dynamically through a work-flow script language, specifying in rule bases the conditions of flow of information.
6. They go beyond control of editorial comments on documents or on-line editing of documents, and support intelligent merges, multiple versions, and multiple views of documents.

The following sections discuss the most important components of collaborative work support in intelligent offices.

■ 11.2 ELECTRONIC MESSAGING AND MAIL SYSTEMS

Electronic messaging or mail systems have often been identified with electronic mailboxes. Thus, E-mail has become synonymous with the ability to send and receive electronic mail over local and wide area networks, given the address of the individual or group.

However, in its broadest definition, electronic messaging includes any messaging system that incorporates the electronic exchange of information. With this definition,

11.2 Electronic Messaging and Mail Systems

other electronic information exchange systems, such as fax stations and electronic fund transfer (EFT) systems, are also electronic messaging systems.

In fact, as illustrated in the following sections, the intelligent office environment integrates the exchange of a rich set of document and information types. This chapter, however, will concentrate primarily on the exchange of messages through mailboxes.

Electronic mailboxes, such as those in UNIX networks and PC LAN–based systems, are becoming increasingly popular. A mail system is designed to enable communication between individual users, groups of users, and special users or groups (such as administration).

Mail is initiated by commands similar to the following:

Mail John
Mail Marketing

These commands invoke the mail application, which then allow users to type in the mail message, include a file containing a message that the user would like to send, or both. Figure 11.4 illustrates a mail messaging window. Users can "carbon copy" a mail message to other users or groups of users. Once a message is sent, the receiver of the message can chose to reply to the message. In fact, users can keep on sending messages and replies to one another discussing a particular issue or topic. These messages and replies are organized as conversations in Action Technologies' Coordinator product.

Electronic mail messages could be interchanged over both types of networks:

- Local area networks (this primarily applies to messages which deal with issues concerning a particular enterprise, company, or department)
- Wide area networks (electronic messages can span states, countries, and continents)

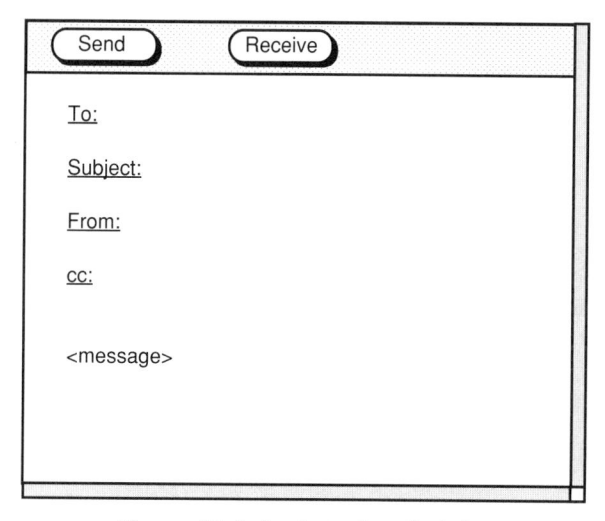

Figure 11.4 An electronic mail window.

The electronic mail addresses of groups or individuals over wide area networks are structures identifying the user, the institution, the type of the institution, and so on, as in the following:

<Name>@<Institution Name>.<commercial, gov. or educational>

11.2.1 Electronic Messaging in Intelligent Offices

The electronic messaging system in an intelligent office integrates with existing electronic mail systems and recognizes existing electronic mail box addresses. However, it enhances and extends electronic messaging systems through these fundamental features:

1. It allows intelligent office addresses to be identified through their attributes or relationships. For instance, messages can be forwarded to office workers based on interests, expertise, background, reports-to relationship, works-with relationship, and other criteria.
2. It allows messages to be filtered through rules. For instance, the office worker can specify through declarative rules the messages he or she would like to see, how messages based on content must be forwarded to different users, and what folders messages should be placed in.
3. It supports full-blown multi-media information exchange with multi-media content or attachments.
4. It supports a rich collection of message types and, in fact, an inheritance hierarchy of messages. Like most objects in the intelligent office environment, many types (classes) of messages are organized in an inheritance hierarchy. Figure 11.5 illustrates an inheritance hierarchy of message types.

Each message type (as an object) has

- A number of characteristic attributes, which reflect the format of the message

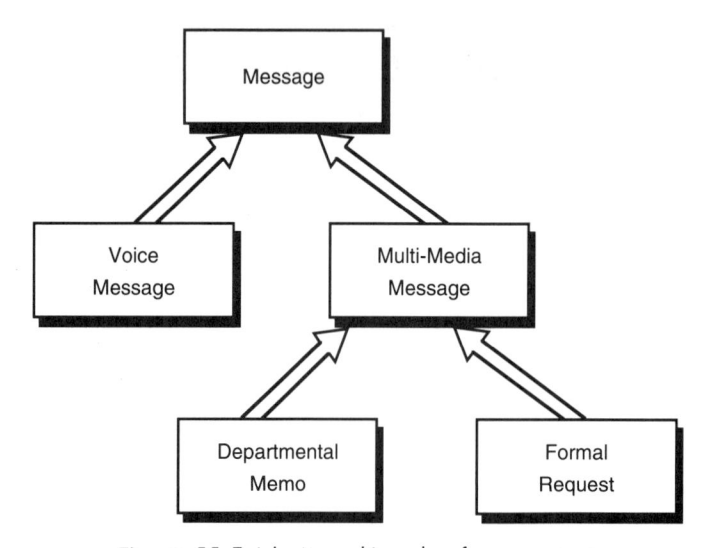

Figure 11.5 Inheritance hierarchy of message types.

- Operations, which reflect what can be done with the message or how the message/messaging system can be manipulated

Figure 11.6 illustrates the following attributes of a message class:

Sender
Receiver
Subject
Date
Response Request
Content and Attachments

The content and attachments of the message could be hypermedia documents, other messages, or references to another office.

The difference between the content and attachment of an electronic message is fundamental. The content of the message is sent to the addressee, and it is a full-blown copy of the information, which will be completely owned and accessed by the addressee. If the message is broadcast to several office workers, each one of them will have a copy of the content.

The attachments, on the other hand, are references to other office objects

- Objects in the sender's office
- Objects in the common area
- Objects in libraries
- Objects in corporate databases

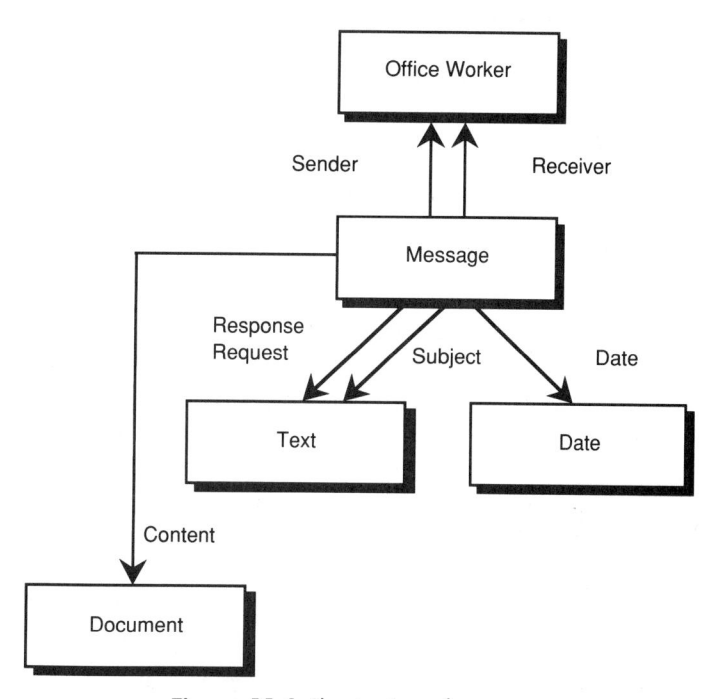

Figure 11.6 The structure of a message.

Since the messages contain references to the objects, the receiver will access the object under transaction and configuration control, as discussed in the previous chapter.

11.2.2 Launchers, Viewers, and Object Linking

Since the attachment to an electronic mail message can be an application file (such as a spreadsheet or a word processor file) or a hypermedia document, the receiver of the message should somehow have the ability to "read" or view the message. Typically, application program files are read only by the system that created them. Some systems can "import" different file formats (for example one can import MultiMate files in Microsoft Word). When an attachment of a particular application is received, and if the system which created the application is available on the recipient's desktop, the mail system launches the application to manipulate the attachment.

In case the application is not available on the receivers workstation, another alternative for the mail system is to provide *viewers* for various types of attachments. Viewers allow the receiver to look at the attachment without actually launching an application (which can actually edit the attachment).

More recent systems, such as Microsoft's OLE (Object Linking and Embedding), are attempting to eliminate the need for viewers and launchers and provide a much more integrated environment for compound documents. With OLE, "attachments" will actually be embedded objects within the mail message. As long as the mail system is an OLE-compliant application, the spreadsheet, image, or voice annotation in the message can be launched by the receiver by simply clicking on the fragment of the attachment appearing in the message. The difference between OLE and launchers is that the Microsoft Windows environment takes care of the embedding: the mail system developer must just comply to it. Launchers, on the other hand, have to be developed by the messaging system. Of course, in both cases the application must be available on the receiver's workstation.

11.2.3 Rules and Messages

In messaging systems in the intelligent office environment, rules can be used both for messages and for routing the messages to the appropriate office workers. These options are discussed in more detail next.

11.2.3.1 Message Filters

The filtering of the message will depend on various search criteria on the sender, subject, length, or date of the message. Consider the following "rule base" for message filtering:

IF Message Subject Is "Chit Chat"
THEN Ignore Message

IF Message Subject Contains "Marketing"
THEN Copy Message Into Marketing Account Folder

IF Message Subject Contains "Production" AND ("Problems OR "Observation")
THEN Keep in Mailbox AND Alert Me Tomorrow Morning

The rules specify what must be done with various messages:

- Messages containing chit-chat between office workers on an ongoing topic are automatically deleted, even if the office worker is a recipient.
- Messages about marketing announcements are also deleted, but they are first copied into a Marketing Announcements folder.
- Messages about production problems or observation are kept in the worker's mailbox. However, the worker has also asked to be alerted when such messages arrive.

The filtering of messages can go well beyond the mere partitioning of messages into various "bins." Through accesses to various newsgroups and information services, office workers can filter and even obtain summaries of information available on electronic bulletin boards. In fact, the filtering of these messages can take the form of complex pattern-matching and full-text retrieval capabilities, retrieving relevant information or forwarding relevant messages to the user.

11.2.3.2 Message Forwarding

Using rules to specify certain criteria, office workers can forward messages to other workers or other groups. The forwarding can be for messages originated by the office worker or for messages that have arrived in the worker's mailbox. In either case, messages can be selected for forwarding according to their subject, date, length, or other attributes, as well as the name of the sender and characteristics of the recipient.

Here are some rules for forwarding messages:

IF Message Subject Is "Auto Insurance"
THEN Forward Message to Legal Department handling Auto Insurance

IF Message Sender is a Customer
AND Customer Is Delayed In Payment
THEN Forward Message TO Finance

Assume that the office is an insurance firm. Here the office worker has indicated the following procedures:

- If the topic of the message is auto insurance, always forward the message to all the lawyers handling auto insurance cases.
- If a message arrives from a customer complaining about delays in payments, always forward the message to the Finance department handling insurance claims.

Note that in a sense, the messaging system is allowing the intelligent office environment to organize some "work" (or rather information) flow between workers or objects. In other words, workers are performing work-flow operations through the messaging system!

This should not come as a surprise, since intelligent offices provide a fully integrated environment for the organization and flow of information. The concentration of the intelligent office workers is not on what they are doing (for example, messaging versus work flow) but rather on getting the job done! Thus, we shall see a lot of the same mechanisms of messaging in work flow management.

11.3 SCHEDULERS AND CALENDARS

Many windowing systems come with individual schedule organizers and calendars. These are excellent visual electronic tools, which replace the need for "paper" calendars.

However, most of these tools are personalized and not shared concurrently or coordinated by the multiple users who use the calendars, so they suffer from the same coordination problems as "paper" calendars. For example, John and Terry take an appointment at 3:00 P.M. Tuesday in the library. Terry is on time, but John is late. "I had you on my calendar," says Terry. "Sorry, I forgot to put our appointment on my calendar," responds John. Sounds familiar? The problem is that it is very easy for the parties involved to forget the placement of the appointment on the calendar, since each person's recording media or environment is separate from the others'.

Through the intelligent office environment, office workers can access calendars in the offices of their fellow workers in order to schedule appointments. (Of course, to schedule an appointment, as is the case when updating any other object in the intelligent office environment, an office worker must have the appropriate access privilege.) Figure 11.7 illustrates a calendar on the desktop of an employee in an intelligent office. This is very similar to most PC desktop systems that support calendars, but the fundamental difference is that a calendar in the intelligent office environment can be accessed (via the network) by others.

Like most other objects in the intelligent office, the office worker can associate rules with his or her calendar. These rules can be changed dynamically, depending on the worker's policies or preferences. The most obvious rule is the "lax" time between

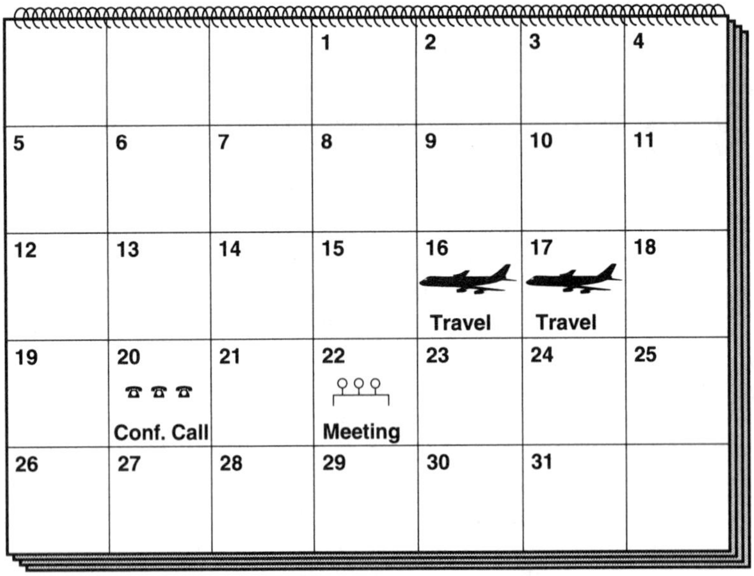

			1	2	3	4
5	6	7	8	9	10	11
12	13	14	15	16 Travel	17 Travel	18
19	20 Conf. Call	21	22 Meeting	23	24	25
26	27	28	29	30	31	

Figure 11.7 A calendar.

appointments. Another rule is the frequency of arranging appointments with certain other workers: "I want to meet John once a week, but not more than three times within a week."

11.4 CONFERENCES AND MEETINGS

One office type discussed earlier in this book is the conference room. Each conference room has a whiteboard, through which the office workers in the conference communicate and interchange messages, graphs, and ideas. Because conference rooms are created and destroyed dynamically, the information on the whiteboard must be exported into a shared document, to be saved after the conference is over and then stored in a cabinet (probably in the common area).

In the intelligent office, workers can import a document to a conference room to work on it on-line concurrently. The document edited by the office workers in a conference room pertains to the group and, in most cases, must be checked out from a cabinet accessible by members of the group. Thus, in the intelligent office environment, electronic meetings in conference rooms are held for two purposes:

- To hold "informal" chats and perform brainstorming through a common information exchange platform: the whiteboard
- To work on a common document collaboratively and on-line

In the intelligent office, a conference can be arranged in the following manner:

1. A group leader creates a meeting room, arranges a time for a meeting by accessing the calendars of the group workers, and sends a message to all the team members to attend the meeting.
2. The group leader has a meeting agenda and places the agenda on the whiteboard. One of the items on the agenda is to work on a Financing Proposal document.
3. At the prescribed time, all the members arrive and the leader conducts the meeting following the agenda. When the group is ready to work on the document, the group leader checks it out and brings it to the conference room.
4. Once the meeting is over and the work on the Financing Proposal document is concluded, the group leader checks the document back in to the library with all the comments and updates generated during the meeting.

Electronically, the conference or meeting room con be activated through either of the following:

- An actual physical room is set up for group discussion and information interchange, with an interconnected network of workstations, where each workstation is allocated to an office worker involved in the meeting. This is the strategy used in IBM's Decision Support Center (Nunamaker *et al.*, 1991).

- A meeting is scheduled and "attended" directly through an office worker's desktop (without physically being located in the same room as other members of the group). This is sometimes known as *desktop conferencing*. Possibilities here range from simple "talk" systems to elaborate windows reflecting office worker whiteboards, common compound hypermedia documents, and so on.

Since electronic meetings deal with interaction between humans, numerous behavioral issues need to be resolved in order to increase productivity in the collaborative environments. Some of these issues are anonymity; group size; group organization hierarchy; proximity of the workers; allotment of time and resources.

11.5 WORK FLOW IN DOCUMENT MANAGEMENT SYSTEMS

Work flow is used in document management systems in order to organize and control flow around the components of the system. A document management system is typically installed in a situation where large amounts of paper are involved, and it is primarily perceived as an archive and retrieval tool. The documents arrive by fax or through scanning and must be indexed, archived, and made available to the office workers. As volume increases, it becomes clear that the system must provide some sort of automatic organization and control of the documents.

Work flow typically exerts its control over the documents in a system in one of two ways; either document-based or event-driven.

- A document-based system attaches routing information to a document. An example might be a routing slip, which holds a list of workers to whom the document is routed in turn. Each worker who receives the document would look at it, maybe perform some annotations, and then forward it. The forward command would then trigger the work flow to route the document to the next worker in the list. Decisions can be incorporated through rules which are fired at the time of forwarding to decide where the document should go next.
- An event-driven system routes documents when they fulfill specific criteria. An event could be the arrival of a fax, which would be routed to a specific worker based on the phone number of the sending party. Decisions are made automatically, once the event has fired, to determine where the document should go next.

Both methods of work flow can be used to achieve the same task in different ways. A common route for a document is from scanner to OCR process to full-text retrieval indexing, then to a worker based on the textual content. An event-driven system implements this by attaching rules to the completion events for each process. A document that has been scanned in is sent to the OCR process if it is of a certain type, and so on through OCR and full-text index with a filter at the output of indexing to determine which worker should receive the document. A document-based system lists the route from scan to OCR to index to a decision box and finally to the appropriate worker. At the completion of each step, the document is checked to see if a work flow is attached, and if so, it is run to determine the next step in the flow.

Various document management systems now incorporate work flow capabilities, which are integrated with the more traditional roles of index, archive, and retrieval. Here are some examples:

- *FileNet* customers are able to create scripts, which define custom work flow. This definition can combine integration of data from mainframe and other applications with automatic prioritization, storage management, printing, processing, and retrieval of images.
- *Odesta's Document Management Systems* (ODMS) includes work flow organized by a central database as projects. A project is created by defining the steps of which it is comprised. These steps are created or modified from standard work flows by filling out a form for each.
- *Sigma Imaging Systems* include a RouteBuilder within their OmniDesk product which allows the worker to design and modify a work flow graphically. The work flow is displayed as iconic nodes, which represent processes, devices, people; and links between these.

Many other document management systems also include work-flow capabilities, and the trend seems to be toward putting the power to create a custom work flow in the hands of the office worker, away from lengthy projects involving programmers and system integrators. Specification of the flow is through forms, graphical nodes and links, scripts, and combinations of these. Typically, the system will allow communication with other applications, either on the same platform or on a host computer. Work-flow specification links devices, such as a printer and scanner, together with processes, such as OCR, and with workers and workstations.

11.6 WORK FLOW IN INTELLIGENT OFFICES

As indicated earlier, the concept of work flow concentrates on the control of the flow of information between various objects in the intelligent office. Work flow diagrams are constructed by linking nodes that represent objects involved in the work flow. The links between nodes control the flow of the information. Links can perform filtering or direct the flow of the information conditionally, depending on the content (values) of the information they carry. Also, a queue of objects could be processed at the target node of each link.

Figure 11.8 illustrates a sample work flow diagram with a source node connected to two destination nodes. In this example, a scanned image is forwarded to both the Legal and Purchasing departments. After processing and completing their tasks, these departments forward the document to a decision-making node. The diamond indicates that a choice exists. The routing of the image is "intelligent" in the sense that the selection of a route depends on the content of the information. (In the example, it is based on the form of the scanned image.) In other situations, the routing could depend on values of particular fields or on matching of terms of documents.

Work-flow models are similar to "assembly line" processing of large amounts of information. Each node processes a queue of requests. As illustrated in Figure 11.9, a queue of papers needs to be scanned, and the queue is associated with the input link

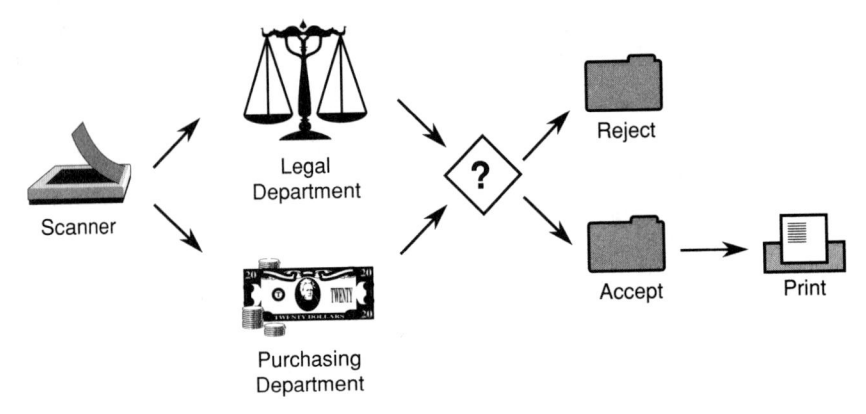

Figure 11.8 A work flow involving peripherals, workers, and folders.

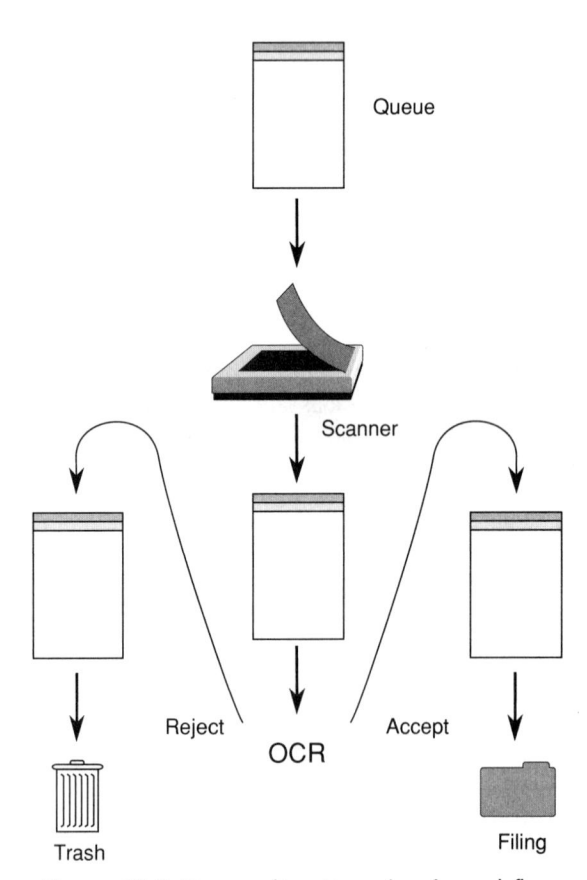

Figure 11.9 Queues of input to nodes of a work flow.

to the scanner. Similarly, a queue of scanned images is waiting to undergo OCR and is associated with the input of the OCR process.

The work flow in intelligent offices is object-oriented in the following senses:

- The nodes, links, and queues in a work flow are all objects, with attributes, state (values of attributes), identity, and an interface. In addition, tasks are performed at each node, link, or even queues of a work flow. For nodes, these tasks correspond to the operation performed on the incoming objects of the queues: scanning paper documents, OCRing image data, forwarding incoming messages, and so on.
- The work-flow template is itself a "class" object from which instances of work flow can be created. An instance of a work-flow class contains attributes indicating the type, description, initiator, and various statistics about the work flow.
- The work-flow templates can be specialized, and one work-flow class will inherit from another work-flow class. Given a work-flow class, office workers can specialize and create other work-flow classes that extend existing classes. For instance, given a work-flow class for hiring new employees at a corporate level, a particular department can introduce additional nodes or rules to extend and specialize the departmental hiring work-flow procedure. This is illustrated in Figure 11.10.

The nodes of the work flow can correspond to any of the following:

1. *Office Workers*: The office worker is assigned a particular task or tasks to perform on the incoming objects of the given work flow. For instance, a Secretary node can be assigned the task of analyzing, making attachments to, and forwarding

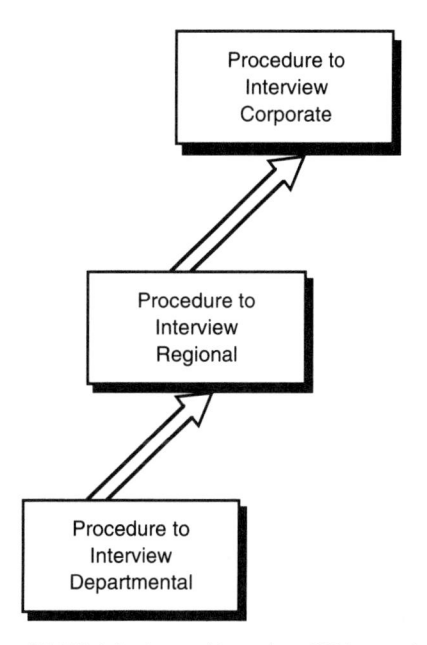

Figure 11.10 Inheritance hierarchy of hiring work flows.

each incoming message. The task performed on the objects actually corresponds to methods executed by the office worker (or part of the office worker's "protocol").

2. *Devices and peripherals*: These correspond to input and output devices (such as scanners, printers, and display devices) that operate on information queues. These devices can correspond to actual physical devices or be "virtual" devices. Scanners are examples of the former, and software compression "devices" are examples of the latter.

3. *Application programs*: Another type of node consists of application programs (viewed as objects), which "process" the incoming information. OCR, word processors, spreadsheets and databases can be viewed as application programs. For instance, a word processor node can modify fonts or identify spelling errors for each incoming document in a work-flow queue. Similarly, a spreadsheet process node can perform calculations on each document of its queue.

11.6.1 Intelligent Work Flow

In intelligent offices, there are two basic mechanisms for creating or specifying work flow:

1. *Static work-flow diagrams*: The discussion up to this point has focused on static work flow. Most work-flow systems in the market today are static and correspond to mostly static node-and-link diagrams that encapsulate the work-flow process. As indicated earlier, there is some freedom to add dynamic work flow and decision making based on the content of a document. However, all the possible target nodes must be known ahead of time.

2. *Dynamic work flow*: The other alternative is dynamic work flow, where the flow of the documents or messages is specified entirely in terms of rules. The firing of the rules creates the work flow, which is determined entirely at run time. Typically, dynamic work-flow documents or messages are more "intelligent," in the sense that they decide where to route themselves based on values of their attributes, their content, or their relationships to other objects.

Consider the following set of rules specifying dynamic work flow:

IF Paper Document Arrives
AND Scanner Operational
THEN Scan Document
AND Place Document on OCR Queue

IF Document In OCR Queue
THEN Analyze Document

IF Document Analyzed
AND Document Contains More than 50 percent Error
THEN Place Document In Reject Folder

IF Document Analyzed
AND Document Contains Less than 50 percent Error
THEN Index Document

The rules have forward-chaining event-driven semantics. When all the premises of a rule are satisfied, the rule fires, making assertions that satisfy premises of other rules. Note that these rules provide the same Scan-OCR-Recognize-File work flow of Figure 11.9, now encoded with rules. This illustrates that dynamic work flow (besides being more intelligent) is more flexible than static. In fact, dynamic work flow exists every time messages or documents are forwarded based on the satisfaction of certain premises. Therefore, besides explicit work-flow objects, dynamic work-flow activities can exist through the following:

1. Rules and predicate attachments associated with objects or object attributes. For instance, a predicate can be attached to a folder, saying

   IF NumberOfElements > 100
   THEN Send Message to Owner: "Folder Contains Too Many Elements."

   Note that this simple work flow is captured through a rule attached to the attribute value *NumberOfElements* of folder objects.

2. Rules and predicate attachments associated with methods (operations), processes, or applications, as in the rule

   IF Message arrives
   AND Priority HIGH
   THEN Forward to Immediate Supervisor.

The forwarding of messages can also be thought of as a simple dynamic work flow. Here the execution of an operation (sending a message) activates the work flow. This is in contrast to the state of an object activating the work flow.

11.6.2 Components of Work Flow In Intelligent Offices

The work-flow software in intelligent offices incorporates the following:

1. A diagramming tool to construct static work-flow templates using nodes consisting of icons, sources, sinks, and destinations, by constructing links between the nodes of an object
2. The ability to indicate attributes or object types of the nodes, links, queues, arrows, sources, sinks, or destinations (that is, any of the objects) in the work flow. In other words, the mechanism for the object-oriented design of classes for work-flow node, link, and queue objects
3. The ability to design dynamic work flow through the specification of rules, which indicate how the documents and messages need to be forwarded (note that, like static work flow, dynamic work flow can be constructed as classes with their attributes, especially status attributes; furthermore, other dynamic work flow classes can be constructed through specialization)
4. The ability to associate processing time or even executable scripts with the nodes of work flow (through association of time and ordering dependencies, a work-flow system can be used as a project management tool)

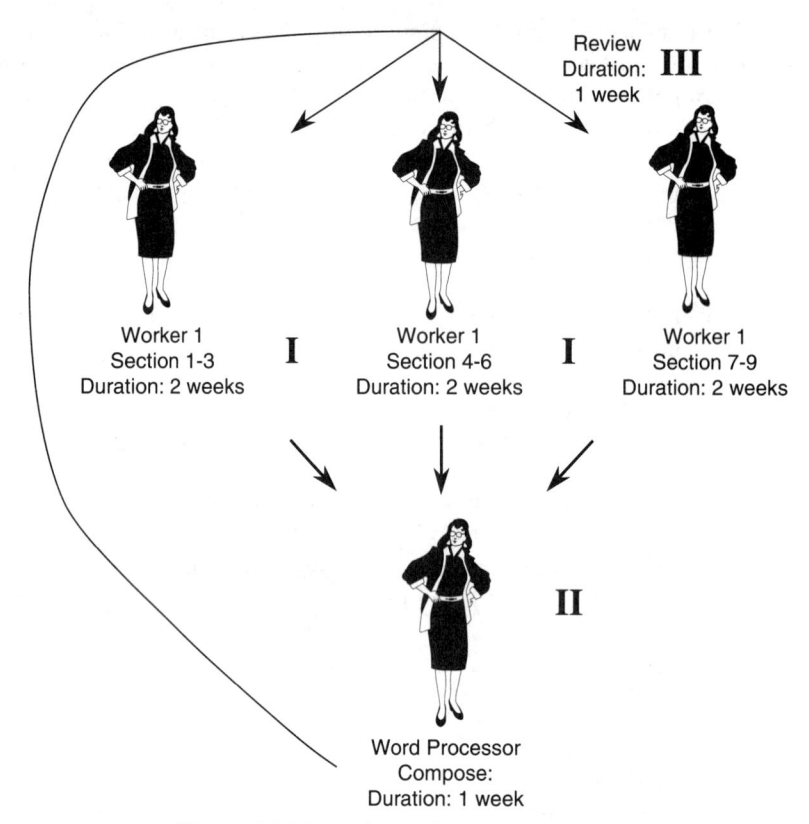

Figure 11.11 Workers with project management.

This is illustrated in Figure 11.11, which shows the work flow of the composition of a document. There are time constraints at each node. When an office worker does not process his or her portion of the document, a reminder message is sent. If three reminder messages get sent, the document gets revoked from the worker. The duration of the task and reminder messages is indicated in the work flow.

5. The ability to query different aspects of a work flow object which has been activated (since work flows are actually persistent objects stored in the underlying intelligent database, various office workers can query about the status of the work flow)

■ 11.7 SUMMARY

This chapter introduced work flow and groupware models in intelligent offices. Groupware touches upon all aspects of software that deal with collaborative work in local area networked office environments. Work flow concentrates primarily on the control of the flow of information between various intelligent office objects.

In terms of groupware, intelligent office environments support calendars, schedules, and meetings. Meetings are scheduled and held in meeting rooms, which may be physical or electronic facilities.

Work flow in intelligent offices can be either static or dynamic. With dynamic work flow, the routing of the information or documents is specified through declarative rules.

12

SUMMARY

We have submerged ourselves in the information age. Whether on a personal, family, or corporate level, we are generating and (unsuccessfully) attempting to digest unsurmountable mountains of information. In the corporate world, information access and management problems are plaguing the office environments of the 1990s. There is just too much information and not enough time to search, organize, and communicate. Intelligent offices attempt to solve the information glut problem through integrating a number of mature, enabling technologies. Like intelligent document systems and intelligent databases, intelligent offices provide a model for organizing and accessing large, complex, and heterogeneous information bases.

Advances in telecommunication, mass storage, and multi-media technologies are in fact adding to the woes of the office executive: More inexpensive "real-life" information is becoming readily available, but who has the time to search, access, analyze, and organize this information? Who has the means to readily sort the information and communicate to colleagues? Who has the time to filter and extract knowledge from these vast information storehouses?

The amount and heterogeneity of information bombarding the average worker is just incredible. Consider some of the sources of data that are available to office workers:

- Paper information (magazines, memos, reports, documents)
- On-line data from corporate database
- Electronic application files, such as word processor files and spreadsheets
- CD-ROM, containing encyclopedic information
- Voice mail and voice data

In this assortment of information types, paper documents constitute a considerable percentage: about 95 percent of information is still in paper form. Intelligent offices provide document management solutions—the ability to automate:

- The scanning of paper documents
- Performing OCR (optical character recognition) or data entry on scanned documents

- The storage of scanned documents on optical disk servers
- The subsequent access and retrieval of these documents

Like document management systems, intelligent offices also provide a number of groupware and work-flow solutions: the ability to intelligently route the heterogeneous information. However, intelligent offices integrate other capabilities, such as direct models for office workers, corporate policies, and procedures as well as accesses to heterogeneous databases. These augment and complement the document management functionalities to provide a more complete solution for the information-processing needs of corporations. The intention is to provide these through the integration of "off-the-shelf," affordable components.

The preceding 11 chapters described the main features of intelligent offices. The intelligent office environments integrated a number of technologies:

- Optical storage technologies
- Client/server networked architectures
- Database management systems and intelligent databases
- Full-content retrieval
- Imaging systems
- Object orientation
- Graphical user interfaces
- Multi-media data types and peripherals

The first eight chapters of the book concentrated on the enabling technologies for intelligent offices. Thus, the optical storage technologies and networking chapters presented the lower-level storage and trafficking media used in intelligent offices. The database management systems and full-content retrieval chapters illustrated the more "intelligent" concurrent access and retrieval strategies of the concurrently and referentially shared information stored in servers. The imaging chapter concentrated on the hardware and software technologies used to digitize, convert, index, and access paper information. The chapters on object orientation and graphical user interfaces provided an overview of the real-world end user interaction model of intelligent offices.

■ 12.1 OPTICAL STORAGE TECHNOLOGIES

Converting information that is in paper form into electronic on-line information requires a substantial amount of storage space. Even with the most advanced compression strategies, the digitized image of an $8\frac{1}{2}$" $\times$ 11" paper document requires at least an order of magnitude more storage space than the ASCII form of the same information. Hence, the ability to store, archive, and retrieve large amounts of information through relatively inexpensive media is critical for intelligent office environments. Optical disks provide ideal storage media for intelligent offices, since they offer the following advantages:

1. *Removability and transportability:* Although some magnetic media, such as floppy disks and magnetic tapes, share these characteristics, optical disks are more rugged and can be transported without fear of data loss.
2. *Higher storage densities:* Compared to magnetic technologies, optical disks are much denser. Magnetic bit densities, measured in bits per square inch (bpsi), are about 4×10^7 bpsi. Optical (write-once) bit densities are two orders of magnitude greater, at better than 10^9 bpsi.
3. *Lower Cost:* One of the results of the higher density of optical disks is their lower storage costs. Optical disks are orders of magnitude cheaper in bit-per-dollar terms than magnetic disks. This ratio will continue to improve in favor of optical disks in the future.
4. *Longer archival life:* Archival life of magnetic media is about 2 to 3 years. In comparison, the archival life of optical media is from 30 to 100 years.

Optical disks come in many forms and shapes. The most popular of these are CD-ROMs, WORMs, and erasable optical disks.

12.1.1 CD-ROMs

CD-ROM will play an important role in the intelligent office by meeting the vital need for the ability to mass-replicate static information cheaply. CD-ROM allows information to be widely distributed and replicated, thereby improving the accessibility of that information.

Entire libraries of books and information can be placed on-line at each office. These on-line libraries, combined with the ability to perform full-text searches, greatly enhance the office workers ability to glean useful information.

12.1.2 WORMs

WORM (write-once read many) technology differs from CD-ROM in that the data is not prestamped but written during run time. Due to their high densities, longer archival life and the fact that once information is stored, it cannot be erased, WORD devices are ideal for archiving in intelligent office environments. The storage hierarchy of the intelligent office allows for infrequently used office objects, such as documents and folders, to be archived onto optical storage. The archived data may be stored in a jukebox, if more frequent access is needed, or it may be stored off-line and be brought back on-line if the need ever arises.

12.1.3 Erasable

The newest arrival on the optical technology scene is erasable optical drives. Erasable optical drives offer the same rewrite capabilities currently offered by magnetic media. This breakthrough allows optical technology to enter new marketplaces and fill the requirements of new applications. Magneto-optics, the only commercially available erasable technology, combines the principles of WORM technology with that of magnetics.

Optical technology is not a technology for the future. It is viable and useful today. The rapid growth of document processing proves that optical technology is now mainstream. The fact that industry giants such as IBM, Wang, DEC, and UNISYS are concentrating on their own imaging systems bears witness to this statement.

394 ■ Summary

■ 12.2 NETWORKING AND CLIENT/SERVER ARCHITECTURES

In intelligent office environments, office workers access and share information concurrently. They communicate with each other through electronic mail and share resources through various "servers" available on local area networks (LANs).

Therefore, local area networks are a key platform for increased productivity in the 1990s and beyond, bringing users and information together. As the technology continues to grow, so will the potential for increased productivity.

A LAN is a group of computers, connected together, which cover a limited geographical area. Each computer, or node, can communicate with any other node, and each node contains its own processor, requiring no central processor. A LAN allows a variety of independent devices to communicate with one another and share data. A LAN may be characterized by the following features:

1. It consists of nodes, which are interconnected through a continuous medium such as cable.
2. It is privately owned, user-administered, and not subject to FCC regulations.
3. It supports both low- and high-speed communications channels.
4. It is commercially available in off-the-shelf packages. No custom programming required.
5. It allows dedicated nodes, which provide services to other nodes.

Two major problems still hamper the productivity of LANs. The first is the ability to manage them. As LANs continue to grow in size and functionality, our ability to control the networks will be hampered. The endeavors in the area of standard management protocols are beneficial, but work must continue in those areas before the problem will be solved.

The lack of applications designed for the network is another area of concern. The amount of productivity that can be gained from LAN technology without good software to support it is limited.

The intelligent office is an attempt to solve this problem. By fully utilizing the abilities of the network to actively share information and ideas, and by integrating existing applications into the LAN environment, the intelligent office can provide a framework by which we will use computers in the coming years.

■ 12.3 DATABASE MANAGEMENT SYSTEMS

Database management systems (DBMSs) have been an integral part of most medium- to large-scale applications since the mid-1960s. They store and retrieve vast amount of information. In intelligent offices, databases will serve as the repository for all office objects, such as documents and folders, and allow these office objects to be shared concurrently among various applications and office workers. In addition to dealing with persistent object storage, a DBMS provides capabilities for transaction support, recovery, powerful querying mechanism, security, and performance enhancement features. These capabilities together provide robust data management. Thus, not only our office objects are stored within the database, but they are also protected by the security mechanism of the database, and the DBMS guarantees that all operations to the database will leave the office object repository in a consistent state.

The network and hierarchical database models formed the basis for most of the commercial database systems during the 1960s and early 1970s. Both of these data models are primarily navigational. The user started with a node and fetched a sequence of child or related nodes, effectively navigating through the physically stored database of nodes.

In the 1970s, E. F. Codd introduced the simple and elegant relational data model. The underlying theory is based on the mathematically well-founded concepts of relational algebra and first-order predicate calculus. We devoted a large portion of Chapter 4 to the discussion of relational data model. The relational model incorporates a collection of relational operators such as selection, projection, join. This collection of simple yet powerful operators forms the basis for most of the relational query languages such as SQL, which has been accepted by all relational database vendors as the common database definition and manipulation language.

Relational database management systems are typically implemented in client/server architectures. The database search is performed on the "server," and the access to the server is performed through "client" nodes.

Besides the basic relational and distributed database capabilities, SQL-based relational systems are starting to incorporate a number of "intelligent" database functionalities such as inferencing, object orientation, support of multi-media data types, and so on.

Intelligent office systems will utilize the current generation and the next generation of relational database systems to store and manipulate office objects. The database system not only will store office objects, but it will guarantee office objects' consistency and their safety. In addition, database systems' concurrent access capabilities permit sharing of office objects among as many users as possible. The next generation of intelligent database engines will integrate more diverse data types. It will become possible to store heterogeneous information types about office objects, such as an actual video or voice message. The deductive capabilities of intelligent databases will allow rules to be associated with various intelligent office object types.

■ 12.4 FULL-CONTENT RETRIEVAL

Databases are used to organize documents by their attributes. These might include name, author, creation date, and description, among others. As the quantity of documents to be searched becomes larger, there need to be other ways to find relevant information from among them. These other methods use the content of the documents as search criteria.

If the content of a document is used to identify it, this information needs to be in as useful a form as possible. Data refinement is the process of structuring the information contained within a document. It takes raw data at the lowest level and uses recognition to identify the elements of which it is composed. A higher level of structure is achieved by attempting to understand the contained information and converting it into a semantic net of objects and relationships. Data refinement, from raw data to recognized elements typically reduces the amount of data much more than data compression does.

Before the particular information can be searched, a domain must be specified. The domain is a subset of all the documents available to the worker and is defined by listing sources and areas within these. This subset is a document collection to which a query can be applied.

Full-text retrieval is the most developed of content retrieval disciplines. It deals with words and phrases, referred to as terms. The most frequent and the least frequent terms are not useful for searching, as they would either appear in a vast quantity of documents or none at all. A table of term frequencies within the document collection is used to find the terms that are useful for searching, and these are then used as the attributes that define the document content. Words can be reduced to their stem, where all information about such details as tense, gender, and number is removed. Words can be organized in dictionaries, either to define equivalent terms or as a list of common words to be ignored for the purposes of retrieval. A thesaurus groups terms with the same or similar meaning to increase the power of a search to include equivalent terms. Concepts are groups of terms which the worker defines as being related, so that a search for one concept can encompass a number of related terms.

There are a number of ways to index documents for full-text retrieval. Inversion of terms associates a list of terms within a document collection with pointers to the documents which contain them. Clustering assigns a vector to each document, defining a vector space where proximity between documents reflects similarity of content. Signature extraction converts each term to a "signature"; these are then combined to define a document.

A query on a document collection can be defined in various ways. One of the most useful ways is to specify a Boolean expression of terms, combined with AND, OR and NOT predicates. The Boolean expression indicates the terms the user wants to see in the document. The expression can also include proximity searches (for example, a term WTHIN a paragraph of another term) and weight (specifying the importance of some of the search terms). The returned set of qualifying documents satisfy the Boolean search criteria. To help the office worker in the search, some systems also indicate the relevance of a document to the search. As the quantity of data available to a worker increases, full-content retrieval provides the power necessary to navigate through it to find useful information.

12.5 IMAGING SYSTEMS

Imaging systems evolved at a time when most desktop workstations were not powerful enough to cope with the tasks of image display, volume scanning, indexing, archive, and retrieval. Proprietary systems were developed to cope with the task of imaging, using both hardware and software to augment or replace standard systems. A number of components are necessary for an imaging system, including various peripherals and add-in boards to standard systems. These are combined with software to create an imaging system.

Scanners are available from simple, low-speed flatbed models and hand-held units through mid-range to large, high-speed units. They consist of optical, mechanical, and digital subsystems for reading, feeding, and processing images.

A compression board is an add-in card that can be used in a workstation to speed up display of compressed images. It can also be used to drive an attached scanner or printer, usually with a daughter board attached.

A high-resolution monitor makes it possible to display a letter-size image without zooming. Most letters are in black and white, so a monochrome display is sufficient. As standard displays reach higher resolutions, specialized displays become less important.

Optical character recognition (OCR) is the process of recognizing text within an image. It holds character descriptions and attempts to match them against a bitmap image. There are many methods for OCR; some require hardware assistance. As workstations have become more powerful, this function has migrated to software implementations.

Fax boards are used to send and receive images electronically. They can act as a remote scanner and printer for an imaging system. Fax capability in the intelligent office is extremely useful, as it extends the reach of a system to any location where there is a fax machine.

Voice capability can be added to a computer, from simple voice annotation to speech recognition. The former requires simple voice digitization while the latter involves recognition and understanding of the digitized input.

There is a trend toward providing more multi-media functions to the workstation, notably video. A video board can display live video in a window, it can be used to overlay computer-generated images and to display animation scenes.

Laser printers are becoming more common in the office environment. They provide high-quality output for printing documents retrieved from the system archive, as well as those created by the office worker.

An imaging system combines the technologies of networking, databases, image compression, and mass storage to provide a solution to the high-volume paper throughput and archive situations in the office. As the underlying technology has improved and new devices and techniques have become available, so more powerful workstation networks can be used to aid the office worker in many other ways. Presentations can include video animation and digital stereo music. Elaborate work flows can be organized and kept track of automatically. Searching for archived information can be performed with greater intelligence. The intelligent office will allow the worker to spend less time on searching for information and administrating schedules and more time on the job at hand.

■ 12.6 OBJECT ORIENTATION

One of the most important characteristics of intelligent offices is their ease of use. This ease of use results from representing two key aspects of the office to the office worker as directly as possible: the items (objects) in the office and the way in which the worker interacts with those items. Direct representation is made possible by the concept of object orientation, which is the basis for software technologies in the intelligent office.

Object orientation permeates all aspects of the intelligent office environment. It allows the office worker to interact with the environment in a more natural way: through sending messages to office objects. This is very similar to the way office workers interact with one another or with other "physical," and nonelectronic office objects.

Object orientation is defined as follows:

Object orientation = Abstract data typing + Inheritance + Object identity

Each of these concepts provides various advantages to the modeling and implementation of intelligent office environments.

12.6.1 Abstract Data Typing

Abstract data typing models various classes of intelligent office objects, where each class instance has a protocol: a set of messages to which it can respond. Thus, there are classes for office workers, office peripherals, folders, documents, and so on. With abstract data types, there is a clear separation between the external interface of a data type and its internal implementation. The implementation of an abstract data type is hidden. Hence, alternative implementations could be used for the same abstract data type without changing its interface.

In most object-oriented programming languages, abstract data types are implemented through classes. A class is like a factory that produces instances, each with the same structure and behavior. A class has a name, a collection of operations for manipulating its instances, and a representation. The operations that manipulate the instances of a class are called methods. The state or representation of an instance is stored in instance variables. The methods are invoked through sending messages to the instances. Sending messages to objects (instances) is similar to calling procedures in conventional programming languages. However, message sending is more dynamic.

Abstract data typing allows the construction of complex software systems through reusable components: the classes. Thus, through abstract data typing, programming becomes modularized and extensible. Abstract data typing supports a much more natural representation of real-world problems: the dominant components are the objects rather than the procedures. Abstract data typing allows objects of the same structure and behavior to share representation (instance variables) and code (methods).

12.6.2 Inheritance

Inheritance allows a class to inherit the behavior (operations or methods) and the representation (instance variables or attributes) from existing classes. Inheriting behavior enables code sharing (and hence reusability) among software modules. Inheriting representation enables structure sharing among data objects. The combination of these two types of inheritance provides a most powerful modeling and software development strategy.

Inheritance is achieved by specializing existing classes. Classes can be specialized by extending their representation (instance variables) or behavior (operations). Alternatively, classes can also be specialized through restricting the representation or operations of existing classes. When a class $C2$ inherits from a class $C1$, then the instance variables and the methods of $C2$ are a superset of the instance variables and methods of $C1$, respectively. The subclass $C2$ can override the implementation of an inherited method or instance variable by providing an alternative definition or implementation.

Inheritance organizes the classes of intelligent office objects in inheritance class hierarchies. It models the hierarchies of office workers, peripherals, folders and other office items and allows representation, protocol, and implementation to be inherited from superclass to subclass. Inheritance also organizes the classes of the intelligent office environment.

12.6.3 Object Identity

The third fundamental concept of object orientation is object identity. The inheritance hierarchies organize the object-oriented code and support extensibility and code reusability. Object identity organizes the objects or instances of an application in arbitrary graph-structured object spaces.

Identity is a property of an object that distinguishes the object from all other objects in the application. In programming languages, identity is realized through memory addresses. In databases, identity is realized through identifier keys. User-specified names are used in both languages and databases to give unique names to objects. Each of these schemes compromises identity.

In a complete object-oriented system, each object will be given an identity that will be permanently associated with the object, immaterial of the object's structural or state transitions. The identity of an object is also independent of the location or address of the object. Object identity provides the most natural modeling primitive to allow the same object to be a sub-object of multiple parent objects.

With object identity, objects can contain or refer to other objects. Object identity clarifies, enhances, and extends the notions of pointers in conventional programming languages, foreign keys in databases, and file names in operating systems. Using object identity, programmers can dynamically construct arbitrary, graph-structured composite or complex objects, which are constructed from subobjects. Objects can be created and disposed of at run time. In some cases, objects can even become persistent and be reaccessed in subsequent programs.

Object identity organizes the instances of intelligent office classes (that is, the objects) in graph-structured object spaces. It allows objects to be referentially shared: for instance, the same document can be referenced in multiple folders. All the attributes of intelligent office objects (folders, peripherals, policies, procedures, and workers) reference other objects directly, thus constructing compound object spaces. These object spaces are most natural and direct in intelligent office environments.

■ 12.7 GRAPHICAL USER INTERFACES

The modern user interfaces are revolutionizing the application of computers by users with diverse needs and backgrounds. One of the main goals of modern user interfaces is to simplify and reduce commands required to perform tasks. Command-driven user interfaces are being replaced with windows, menus bars, pull-down menus, and dialog boxes. The mouse is used as the primary pointing device to select commands from a list of menu choices.

In the 1960s, projects at SRI International, MIT, and other universities led to the invention of pointing devices and windowing systems. In the 1970s, researchers at Xerox

PARC were busy designing powerful new workstations armed with graphical user interfaces. Their experiments concentrated on applying the associative memory of the end user combined with direct manipulation capabilities. The basic assumption of these new workstations was that one user could have a powerful desktop computer totally dedicated to that user's personal task. Thus, the computer not only is used to perform the user task but can also provide a much more intuitive and easy-to-use environment. For user interfaces, both the Xerox Star workstation (also developed at PARC) and its predecessor prototype, the Alto, influenced the design and look-and-feel of Apple's Macintosh, Aldus's PageMaker desktop publishing software, and Microsoft's Windows.

In the 1990s, computer systems will include much more powerful processors, higher-resolution displays, and more memory. A larger portion of the computing power of the future machines will be used to make computers more aesthetically pleasing. The user interfaces in the 1990s will be characterized by being more intuitive, by handling diverse types of objects, and by providing visual environments.

Emerging technologies such as Digital Video Interactive (DVI), optical disk drives, and digital signal processors will permit the end user to interact with multi-media applications. Object orientation will be exploited to integrate diverse sets of objects, ranging from text and voice to images and video. Apple HyperCard, Asymetrix ToolBook, and other hypermedia tools will be used more often to interconnect these disparate objects.

There are a number of popular GUI environments, including Microsoft Windows and the Macintosh Toolbox. The GUIs provide programming interfaces that allow users to create screen objects, draw screen objects, monitor mouse activations, and report screen events to the user. Communication about the state of the screen objects is accomplished through messages to be sent between the application and the user interface engine.

Object orientation comes to the rescue of the software engineer by lightening the burden of user-interface development. Development environments such as MacApp, Actor, and NeXT provide libraries composed of object hierarchies. Each class within the hierarchy defines the attributes necessary for its object, in addition to inheriting features from its superclasses. Each object within the hierarchy communicates with other objects in the system through transmission of messages. User interface designers can further extend the class hierarchy by adding their own screen object designs. These new screen objects can inherit properties from existing classes. In addition, they can refine old properties or define new properties as needed. In addition, the NeXT user interface development environment demonstrates how direct manipulation can come to the rescue of programmers and application developers. The NeXTStep clearly shows the future of user-interface design. This tool permits the developer to design the user interface directly on the screen.

HP's NewWave provides an object-oriented user-interface environment available to the end user. NewWave applies the desktop metaphor and object orientation throughout its environment. This environment permits end users to directly manipulate objects that are familiar to them, such as folders and documents. Also, the NewWave Object Management Facility allows creation and manipulation of compound documents composed of text, graphics, and images.

Graphical user interfaces will play a dominant role in the intelligent office environment. As discussed in this book, there are many tasks that require an intelligent office to function appropriately. The main task of graphical user interface is to provide a visual environment to make the execution of these office functions through computers much more intuitive. Concepts such as direct manipulation and the desktop metaphor will change the computer to behave as a natural extension of an office. In addition, the composition and management of compound documents will be made much easier with the current generation of graphical user interfaces.

12.8 MULTI-MEDIA DATA TYPES AND PERIPHERALS

The advent of multi-media technology has made the concept of the intelligent office possible. No longer is the office worker limited to using simple computer data types for the expression of information. Multi-media provides the foundation for a new paradigm in information processing.

The basic concept of multi-media is the marriage of voice, text, image, and video data types within an application to enhance the output. Multi-media combines traditional data processing with graphics, speech, animation, audio, video, and synthesis. The standard emphasis of multi-media is to enhance presentation software for corporate users.

The concept of multi-media under the intelligent office is a much broader and more useful paradigm. The goal of multi-media in the intelligent office is to enhance the productivity of the user by improving traditional office data-processing techniques through expanding both the types of data processed and the methods used for processing the data. Intelligent offices combine the typical multi-media types of text, image, video, and sound with full-text, hypertext, and pattern recognition processing methods to provide a phenomenal improvement in the usefulness and quality of corporate data.

The intelligent office's multi-media capabilities are based on an object-oriented paradigm. This approach increases the ability of the intelligent office to correctly model real-world office environments (for example, each multi-media object or peripheral can be defined as an instance of a class). The combination of multi-media types in conjunction with advanced object methods such as inferencing allows the term "multi-media" to be redefined, bringing it out of the realm of the computer enthusiast and into the office. The term "multi-media information processing" (MMIP) is perhaps a more useful description of the functionality of the intelligent office multi-media environment.

Only recently has the underlying technology been in place to allow multi-media to become a viable part of the intelligent office. The availability of mass storage on optical media has been particularly critical in the development of multi-media information systems. The storage demands of multi-media information are exacerbated when that information is linked into hypermedia systems that may include versioning or retention of the previous history of the database (Copeland and Khoshafian, 1987). Fortunately, the availability of mass storage has kept pace with the demand, largely due to the impact of optical storage.

The basic reason for introducing multi-media data types into the intelligent office is productivity. The rich set of data types provided by multi-media contain more information, and are far more expressive, than the simple numeric and ASCII data types provided by the typical MIS application.

The ability of multi-media to provide more information through the combination of data types such as image, text, voice, and video allows the office worker to be more productive by obtaining more information in a shorter period of time. In effect, multi-media "compresses" the information into a more manageable or understandable format by using voice annotation, video clips, text, animation, and so on. The incorporation of multi-media into the office will change forever the way we interact with computers.

■ 12.9 INTELLIGENT OFFICES: A PRESCRIPTION FOR THE OFFICE OF THE FUTURE

This book concentrated on the integration of the aforementioned enabling technologies into advanced next-generation office automation systems called intelligent offices. We are already witnessing the emergence of numerous products that are offering affordable solutions to the corporate world using many of the elements of intelligent offices.

Although the number of software products and various platforms has mushroomed in the past decade, nevertheless the next-generation computing environments continue to provide better integration capabilities across applications. By the same token, the cost of hardware continues to steadily decrease. Furthermore, better internetworking solutions are proving the viability of distributed client/srever architectures.

These technological advances, together with the propagatioon of multi-media computing and object-oriented graphical user interfaces culminate in the next-generation office environments, which we have labeled "intelligent" offices.

Many of the concepts, and even the notion of integrating some of these technologies in next-generation systems, are neither new nor original to intelligent offices. Many terms, such as "intelligent information management," "intelligent document management," and "intelligent databases" describe similar concepts and "visions." Nevertheless, intelligent offices provide a cohesive model attempting to address two most crucial problems in the corporate world:

1. How to efficiently model, organize, and search the vast amounts of heterogeneous information in the office environment

2. How to facilitate cooperative computing, communication, and group work in the office

Intelligent office environments address these issues through providing a uniform object-oriented model of the office. The intelligent office environment contains at least four categories of objects:

1. *Information:* First and foremost is information from different sources, stored in different formats. Information is almost always persistent and should be under versioning and transaction control. Any concurrently shared information should also be under the transaction-based concurrency control provided by an underlying database management system. In an intelligent office environment, the multi-media, textual, tabular, and object-oriented databases are concurrently shared in dynamic client/server architectures.

2. *Office workers:* Office workers hold certain relationships to other workers and to other office objects. Two fundamental relationships exist with respect to other workers: the inheritance relationship (a Sales Manager is also a Sales Person; a Sales Person is also an office worker), and the organizational relationship (the VPs report to the president; the president reports to the CEO). Office workers also have various ownership and access privileges for other office objects (such as documents and peripherals).

3. *Office tools, resources, devices, and peripherals:* The office environment includes tools (such as an electronic mail system), resources (such as storage space), devices, and peripherals, all of which are objects. Chapter 10 discusses the container object aggregates, such as offices, folders, and cabinets, that are constructed using the multi-media data types and peripherals.

4. *Policies and Procedures:* Intelligent offices also include policy and procedure objects, which could be instantiated and executed in the office environment. A policy or procedure is an object in the sense that it has attributes (instance variables), which can be read, searched, or updated. Policies and procedures also have operations (methods) associated with them, which can be used to activate the procedure or policy.

In terms of containment hierarchies and "localities," these categories of intelligent office objects are organized in an overall office environment involving buildings, floors, offices, desktops, peripherals, and other office objects. The office workers are assigned to various departments and groups, and the departments are assigned to various office floors. Thus, the intelligent office model office enables workers and corporations to organize the following:

- The object spaces (information, peripherals, processes and procedures) of individual office workers, providing various levels of privileges and supporting the notion of localities for combining objects with the same privileges and ownerships in the same "office"

- The object spaces of the entire corporation, with shared libraries and common areas represented iconically and visually, and allowing office workers access (check-out/check-in) and interaction with various objects in these shared environments using familiar metaphors

- The office worker hierarchies (inheritance and organizational), with the allotment of various privileges and relationships to other workers or other office objects

And what is "intelligent" about intelligent offices? The "intelligence" in intelligent offices can be summarized through the following:

1. A uniform object-oriented Model
2. Distributed processing. An important aspect of "intelligence" is the ability to access distributed information bases uniformly, as if the information resided in a

single (logical) database. The intelligent office environment provides a distributed database model for office data.

3. Integration of heterogeneous data. A true intelligent office environment blurs the distinction between record management, document imaging, and database management systems. Through a single integrated intelligent office environment, office workers can manipulate any type of data.

4. Programming the flow of information and office policies. The intelligent office environment incorporates office policies and procedures as objects, which can be instantiated and can respond to their "interface" or protocol. As a result, they can be manipulated by office workers.

5. Support of the intelligent office versus the intelligent desktop model. Most existing desktop products do not have an icon representing office objects, the interconnection between offices, the organization of information in offices, or the allocation of office workers to offices. By contrast, an intelligent office model must provide a direct representation of the "real-world" office environment.

6. Expert system rules with office objects. Rules can be associated with any object within the intelligent office environment and can be used to filter messages, prioritize electronic mail, trigger work flow, and so on. Office workers use high-level declarative rules to "build" expert systems in the intelligent office.

Intelligent offices. An idea whose time has come? Perhaps. As mentioned earlier, there are numerous companies (including heavyweights such as IBM, DEC, and UNISYS) who are providing document-imaging and other GUI object-oriented systems and solutions with similar capabilities as intelligent offices. However, the widespread acceptance and propagation of the intelligent office "blueprint," providing an intelligent, object-oriented model for all office objects and the "intelligent" organization, as well as the communication of these objects, is yet to be seen. In the meantime, we have phone calls to make, meetings to attend, and file cabinets to search. . . . please excuse us. . . .

REFERENCES

Abrial, J. R. (1974). "Data Semantics." In J. W. Klimbie and K. L. Koffeman (eds.), *Data Base Management*. New York: North-Holland.

Agha, G., and Hewitt, C. (1987). "Concurrent Programming Using Actors." In A. Yonezawa and M. Tokoro (eds.), *Object-Oriented Concurrent Programming*. Cambridge, MA: MIT Press.

AIA/ATA. (1990). "SFQL: Structured Full-Text Query Language." AIA/ATA Subcommittee 89-9C Specification, December 1989, revised February 1990.

ANSI SQL 89. (1989). *Database Language SQL*. New York: American National Standards Institute.

Apple Computer. (1985–87). *Inside Macintosh* (volumes 1–5). Reading, MA: Addison-Wesley.

Apple Computer. (1987). *MPW Pascal Reference Manual*. Cupertino, CA: Apple Computer Inc.

Apple Computer. (1988). *The MacApp Interim Manual*. Cupertino, CA: Apple Computer Inc.

Astrahan, M. M., et al. (1976). "System / R: A Relational Approach to Data Management." *ACM Transactions on Database Systems*, 1(2), pp. 97–137.

Asymetrix. (1989). *Using OpenScript*. Bellevue, WA: Asymetrix Corporation.

Asymetrix. (1990). *Using ToolBook*. Bellevue, WA: Asymetrix Corporation.

Atkinson, M., Bancilhon, F., DeWitt, D., Dittrich, K., Maier, D., and Zdonik, S. (1989). "The Object-Oriented Database System Manifesto." *First International Conference on Deductive and Object-Oriented Databases*. Kyoto, Japan: Elsevier.

Backus, J. (1978). "The History of FORTRAN I, II and III." *ACM Sigplan Notices*, 13 (8), 165–180.

Bancilhon, F., et al. (1983). "VERSO: A Relational Back-End Data Base Machine." *Proc. of 2nd International Workshop on Database Machines,* D.K. Hsaio, ed. Englewood Cliffs, NJ: Prentice Hall, pp. 1–18.

Bancilhon, F., Briggs, T., Khoshafian, S., and Valduriez, P. (1987). "FAD—a Simple and Powerful Database Language." *Proceedings of VLDB 1987*.

Bancilhon, F., and Khoshafian, S. (1986). "A Calculus for Complex Objects." *ACM International Symposium on PODS* (March).

Bancilhon, F., and Khoshafian, S. (1989). "A Calculus for Complex Objects." *Journal of Computer and System Sciences*, 38(2), 326–340.

Bancilhon, F., and Ramakrishnan, R. (1986). "An Amateur's Introduction to Recursive Query-Processing Strategies." *ACM SIGMOD International Conference on Management of Data*, pp. 16–52.

Barnes, J. G. P. (1980). "An Overview of Ada." *Software Practice and Experience*, Vol. 10, 851–8.

Barth, P. S. (1986). "An Object-Oriented Approach to Graphical Interfaces." *ACM Transactions on Graphics*, 5(2), 142–172.

Berg, B., and Roth, J. P. (1989). *Software for Optical Storage*. Westport, CT: Meckler Publishing Corporation.

Bobrow, D. G., *et al.* (1988). "Common Lisp Object System Specification." X3J13 Document 88-002R (June).

Bobrow, D. G., *et al.* (1986). "CommonLoops Merging Lisp and Object-Oriented Programming." *Proceedings of OOPSLA-86*.

Booch, G. (1986). *Software Engineering with Ada* (second edition). Menlo Park, CA: Benjamin/Cummings.

Brachman, R. J. (1985). "I Lied about the Trees—Or, Defaults and Definitions in Knowledge Representation." *AI Magazine,* 6(3), 80–93.

Brown, A. (1991). *Object-Oriented Databases*. London: McGraw-Hill.

Brown, J. R., and Cunningham, S. (1989). *Programming the User Interface. Principles and Examples*. New York: John Wiley and Sons, Inc.

Burstall, R. M., and Goguen, J. A. (1977). "Putting Theories Together to Make Specifications." *Proceedings of ICJAI-77*.

Cardelli, L. (1987). *Building User Interfaces by Direct Manipulation*. Palo Alto, CA: Digital Equipment Corporation, Systems Research Center (October).

Cardenas, A. F. (1979). *Data Base Management Systems*. Boston, MA: Allyn and Bacon.

Cattell, R.G.G. (1991). *Object Data Management*. Reading, MA: Addison-Wesley.

Chang, C. L., and Walker, A. (1986). PROSQL: A Prolog Programming Interface with SQL/DS. In L. Kerschberg (ed.), *Expert Database Systems, Proceedings from the First International Workshop*. Menlo Park, CA: Benjamin/Cummings, Inc., pp. 233–246.

Chen, P. P. (1976). "The Entity-Relationship Model—Toward a Unified View of Data." *ACM Transactions on Database Systems,* 1(1).

Cinnamon, B. (1988). "Optical Disk Document Storage and Retrieval Systems." Silver Spring, MD: AIIM Publication.

Cobb, A., and Weiner, J. (1989). "Examining NewWave, Hewlett-Packard's Graphical Object Oriented Environment." Redmond, CA: *Microsoft Systems Journal* (November), 1–18.

CODASYL. (1971). *CODASYL Data Base Task Group Report*. New York, ACM.

Codd, E. F. (1970). "A Relational Model for Large Shared Data Banks." *Communications of the ACM*, 13, 377–387.

Codd, E. F. (1979). "Extending the Database Relational Model to Capture More Meaning." *ACM Transactions on Database Systems,* 4, 397–434.

Codd, E. F. (1985). "Is Your DBMS Really Relational?" *Computer World*, October 14.

Condon, C. (1990). "Networked Cooperative Work: Usability Issue of MILAN." *Proceeding of Telmatics '90,* Bremen (December).

Conklin, Jeff (1987). "Hypertext: a Survey and Introduction." *IEEE Computer,* 20(9), 17–41.

Conrac Corporation. (1980). *Raster Graphics Handbook*. New York: Van Nostrand Reinhold.

Copeland, G. P. (1980). "What If Mass Storage Were Free?" *Proceedings of the Fifth Workshop on Computer Architecture for Non-Numeric Processing*. Pacific Grove, CA.

Copeland, G. P., and Khoshafian, S. (1987). "Identity and Versions for Complex Objects." *Proceedings of Persistent Object Systems: Their Design, Implementation, and Use*. University of St. Andrews, Scotland, Research Report No. 44.

Copeland, G. P., and Maier, D. (1984). "Making Smalltalk a Database System." *Proceedings of the SIGMOD Conference*. ACM, Boston.

Cox, B. (1986). *Object-Oriented Programming: An Evolutionary Approach*, Reading, MA: Addison-Wesley.

Cox, B., and Hunt, B. (1986). "Objects, Icons, and Software ICs." *BYTE* (August).

Dahl, O-J., and Nygaard, K. (1966). "SIMULA—An ALGOL-based Simulation Language." *Communications of the ACM*, 9, 671–678.

Dahl, O-J., Myhrhaug, B., and Nygaard, K. (1970). *The SIMULA 67 Common Base Language*. Publication S22, Oslo: Norwegian Computing Centre.

D'Alleyrand, M. R. (1989). *Image Storage and Retrieval Systems*. New York: McGraw-Hill.

Date, C. J. (1986a). *An Introduction to Database Systems (in Two Volumes)*. Reading, MA: Addison-Wesley.

Date, C. J. (1986b). *Selected Writings*. Reading, MA: Addison-Wesley.

Date, C. J. (1987). *A Guide to SQL Standards*. Reading, MA: Addison-Wesley.

Dewdney, A. K. (1989). *The Turing Omnibus: 61 Excursions in Computer Science*. Rockville, MD: Computer Science Press.

Diettrich, K. R. (1986). "Object-Oriented Database Systems: The Notion and the Issues." *Proceedings of the International Workshop on Object-Oriented Database Systems*, Pacific Grove, CA, September 1986.

Ehrig, H., Kreowski, H., and Padawiz, P. (1978). "Stepwise Specification and Implementation of Abstract Data Types." *Proceedings of the 5th ICALP*.

Englebart, D., and Lehtman, H. (1988). "Working Together." *BYTE* (December).

Eswaran, K. P., et. al. (1976). "The Notions of Consistency and Predicate Locks in a Database System. *Communications of the ACM*, 19, 624–633.

Faloustos, C. (1985). "Signature Files: Design and Performance Comparison of some Signature Extraction Methods." *Proc. ACM SIGMOD*, Austin, TX.

Faloustos, C., and Christodoulakis, S. (1984). "Signature Files: An Access Method for Documents and Its Analytical Performance Evaluation." *ACM Transactions of Office Information Systems*, 2 (4).

Florence, D. (1989). *LAN: Local Area Networks, Developing Your System for Business*. New York: John Wiley and Sons.

Folk, M. J., and Zoellick, B. (1988). *File Structures: A Conceptual Toolkit*. Reading, MA: Addison-Wesley.

Glover, G. (1990). *Image Scanning for Desktop Publishers*. Blue Ridge Summit, PA: Windcrest Books.

Goguen, J. A., Thatcher, J. W., Wegner, E. G., and Wright, J. B. (1975) "Abstract Data Types as Initial Algebras and Correctness of Data Representation." *Proceedings of the Conference on Computer Graphics, Pattern Recognition and Data Structures*.

Goldberg, A. (ed.) (1988). *A History of Personal Workstations*. NewYork: ACM Press.

Goldberg, A., and Robson, D. (1983). *Smalltalk-80: The Language and its Implementation*. Reading, MA: Addison-Wesley.

Goldstein, I. P., and Bobrow, D. G. (1984). "A Layered Approach to Software Design." In D. Barstow, H. Shrobe, and E. Sandewall (eds.), *Interactive Programming Environments*. New York: McGraw-Hill, 387–413.

Gonzalez, R. C. (1987). *Digital Image Processing*. Reading, MA: Addison-Wesley,

Goodman, D. (1987). *The Complete HyperCard Handbook*. New York, Bantam Books.

Gray, J. (1978). "Notes on Database Operating Systems." *IBM research report RJ2188*. San Jose, CA: IBM Research Center.

Greif, I. (1988). *Computer-Supported Cooperative Work: A Book of Readings*. San Mateo, CA: Morgan Kaufman.

Grochow, J. M. (1991). *SAA: A Guide to Implementing IBM's System Application Architecture*. Englewood Cliffs, NJ: Yourdon Press.

Gupta, R., and Horowitz. (1991) *Object-Oriented Databases with Applications to CASE, Networks, and VLSI CAD*. Englewood Cliffs, NJ: Prentice-Hall.

Guttag, J. (1977). "Abstract Data Types and the Development of Data Structures." *Communications of the ACM*, 20.

Hall, P. A. V., Owlett, J., and Todd, S. J. P. (1976). *Relations and Entities. Modeling in Data Base Management Systems* (G.M. Nijssen, ed.). New York: North-Holland Publishing Co.

Hämäinen, H., and Condon, C. (1991). "Form and Room: Metaphors for Groupware." *ACM Proceedings of Organizational Computing Systems,* Atlanta, November.

Hammer, M., and McLeod, D. (1981). "Database Description with SDM: a Semantic Database Model." *ACM Trans. Database Syst.*, 6(3).

Hayes, F., and Baran, N. (1989). "A Guide to GUI." *Byte* (July), 250–257.

Henderson, D. A., and Card, S. K. (1986). "Rooms: The Use of Multiple Virtual Workspaces to Reduce Space Contention in a Window-Based Graphical User Interface." *ACM Transactions on Graphics*, 5(3) (July).

Hewitt, C. (1977). "Viewing Control Structures as Patterns of Passing Messages." *Artificial Intelligence,* 8(3).

Hewlett-Packard. (1988). *HP NewWave Enironment General Information Manual*. Cupertino, CA.

Hughes, J. G. (1991). *Object-Oriented Databases*. New York: Prentice Hall.

Johnson, J., Roberts, T., Verplank, W., Smith, D. C., Irby, C. H., Beard, M., Mackey, K. (1989). "The Xerox Star: A Retrospective." *IEEE Computer* (September), 11–26.

Katz, R. H. (1987). *Information Management for Engineering Design*. Berlin: Springer-Verlag.

Katz, R. H., and Lehman, T. J. (1984). "Database Support for Versions and Alternatives of Large Design Files." *IEEE Transactions on Software Engineering,* SE-10(2).

Kaye, R. A., and Karam, G. M. (1987). "Cooperating Knowledge-Based Assistants for the Office." *ACM Transactions on Office Information Systems*, 5(4), 297–326.

Khoshafian, S., Chan, A., Wong, A., and Wong, H. (1992). *Guide to Developing Client/Server SQL Applications*. San Mateo, CA: Morgan Kaufmann.

Khoshafian, S. (1989). "A Persistent Complex Object Database Lanaguage." *Data and Knowledge Engineering*, 3.

Khoshafian, S. (1990). "Insight into Object-Oriented Databases." *Information and Software Technology,* 32(4), 274–289.

Khoshafian, S. (1991a). "Intelligent SQL." *Computer Standards and Interfaces*, Vol. 13, Issues 1–3.

Khoshafian, S. (1991b). "Modeling with Object-Oriented Databases." *AI Expert* (October).

Khoshafian, S., and Abnous, R. (1990). *Object Orientation*. New York: John Wiley and Sons.

Khoshafian, S., Blumer, R., and Abnous, R. (1990b, 1991). "Inheritance and Generalization in Intelligent SQL. *ANSI OODBTG Standardization Workshop*, October 1990 (also appeared in *Computer Standards and Interfaces*, Vol. 13, Issues 1–3).

Khoshafian, S., and Briggs, T. (1988). "Schema Design and Mapping Strategies for Persistent Object Models." *Information and Software Technology* (December).

Khoshafian, S., and Copeland, G. (1986). "Object Identity." *Proceedings of OOPSLA-86*, Portland, OR.

Khoshafian, S., and Frank, D. (1988). "Implementation Techniques for Object Oriented Databases." *Proceedings of the Second International Workshop on Object-Oriented Database Systems*, Germany (September).

Khoshafian, S., Franklin, M. J., and Carey, M. J. (1990a). "Storage Management for Persistent Complex Objects." *To Information Systems*, 15(3).

Khoshafian, S., and Thieme, L. (1991). "Declarative Reasoning Extensions to Commercial SQL Database Management Systems." COMPCON 91, San Francisco.

Khoshafian, S., and Valduriez, P. (1987a). "Persistence, Sharing, and Object Orientation: a Database Perspective." *Proceedings of the Workshop on Database Programming Languages*, Roscoff, France, 1987.

Khoshafian, S., and Valduriez, P. (1987b). "Parallel Execution Strategies for Declustered Databases." *Proceedings of IWDM 1987*.

King, R., and McLeod, D. (1985). "Semantic Database Models." In S. B. Yao (ed.), *Database Design*. New York: Springer-Verlag.

Klausner, A., and Goodman, N. (1985). "Multi-relations—Semantics and Languages." *Proceedings of VLDB* 1985.

Knor, E. (1990). "Software's Next Wave: Putting the User First. *PC World* (January), 134–143.

Knuth, D. E. (1973). *Sorting and Searching*. Reading, MA: Addison-Wesley.

Krasner G. E., and Pope, S. T. (1988). "A Cookbook for Using the Model-View-Controller User Interface Paradigm in Smalltalk-80." *Journal of Object Oriented Programming* (August/September), 26–49.

Kulkarni, K. G., and Atkinson, M. P. (1986). "EFDM: Extended Functional Data Model." *The Computer Journal*, 29(1).

Kung, H. T., and Robinson, J. (1981). "On Optimistic Methods for Concurrency Control." *ACM TODS*, Vol. 6, No. 2 (June).

Kuper, G. M., and Vardi, M. Y. (1984). "A New Approach to Database Logic." *Proceedings of the ACM International Symposium on PODS*, Waterloo, Canada.

Kurzweil, R. (1990). *The Age of Intelligent Machines*. Cambridge, MA: MIT Press.

Lai, Kum-Yew, Malone, T. W., and Yu, Keh-Chiang (1989). "Object Lens: A 'Spreadsheet' for Cooperative Work." *ACM Transactions on Office Information Systems*, Vol. 6, No. 4 (October).

Lanford, A. G. (1991). *Choosing the Right Imaging System*. Silver Spring, MD: Micro Dynamics.

Lecluse, C., and Richard, P. (1989). "The O2 Database Programming Language." *Proceedings of VLDB*.

Ledbetter, L., and Cox, B. (1985). "Software-IC's." *Byte* (June).

Lee, E. S., and McGregor, J. N. (1985). "Minimizing Menu Search Time in Menu Retrieval Systems." *Human Factors*, 27, 157–162.

Lieberman, H. (1981). "A Preview of Act 1." *MIT AI Lab Memo* No. 625.

Lieberman, H. (1986). "Using Prototypical Objects to Implement Shared Behavior in Object-Oriented Systems." *Proceedings of OOPSLA-86*, Portland, OR.

Lieberman, H., and Hewitt, C. (1983). "A Real-Time Garbage Collector Based on the Lifetimes of Objects." *Communications of the ACM*, 26(6).

Lindley, C. A. (1991). *Practical Image Processing in C: Acquisition, Manipulation, Storage*. New York: John Wiley and Sons.

Liskov, B., Snyder, A., Atkinson, R., and Schaffert, C. (1977). "Abstraction Mechanisms in CLU." *Communications of ACM*, 20(8).

Liskov, B., and Guttag, J. (1986). *Abstraction and Specification in Program Development*. Cambridge, MA: MIT Press; New York: McGraw-Hill.

Liskov, B., and Zilles, S. M. (1975). "Specification Techniques for Data Abstractions." *IEEE Transactions on Software Engineering*, SE-1.

Livney, M., Khoshafian, S., and Boral, H. (1987). "Multi-Disk Management Algorithms." *Proceeding of SIGMETRICS*, pp. 69–77.

Lockwood, L. (1990). *The IMS/VS Expert's Guide*. New York: Van Nostrand Reinhold.

Lundgren, T. D., and Lundgren, C. A. (1989). *Records Management in the Computer Age*. Boston: PWS-KENT Publishing Company.

Maier, D. (1983). *The Theory of Relational Databases*. Rockville, MD: Computer Science Press.

Maier, D., and Stein, J. (1986). "Indexing in an Object-Oriented DMBS." *Proceedings of 1986 International Workshop on Object-Oriented Database Systems*, Pacific Grove, CA.

Martin, J., Chapman, K. K., Leben, J. (1990). *IBM Office Systems Architectures and Implementations*. Englewood Cliffs, NJ: Prentice Hall.

Mazer, M.S., and Lochovsky, F.H. (1989). "Logical Routing Specification in Office Information Systems." *ACM Transactions on Office Information Systems*, 2(4), 303–330.

McCarthy, J., et al. (1965). *LISP 1.5 Programmer's Manual*. Cambridge, MA: MIT Press.

Metaphor Computer Systems. (1988). *Workstation Tools*. Mountain View, CA.

Meyer, B. (1988). *Object-Oriented Software Construction*. Englewood Cliffs, NJ: Prentice Hall.

Michalski, G. P. (1991). "The World Of Documents." *Byte*, (April).

Moon, D. A. (1986). "Object-Oriented Programming with Flavors." *Proceedings of OOPSLA-86*, Portland, OR.

Murray, S. M., and Lochovsky, F. H. (1984). "Logical Routing Specification in Office Information Systems." *ACM Transactions on Office Information Systems*, 2(4) (October).

Mylopoulos, J., Bernstein, P. A., and Wong, H. K. T. (1980). "A Language Facility for Designing Database-Intensive Applications." *ACM Transactions on Database Systems*, 5(2).

Nance, B. (1990). *Network Programming in C*. QUE Corporation.

Newcombe, R. M. (1991). "Why Workflow." *INFORM* (June).

Nunamaker, J. F., Dennis, A. R., Valacich, J. S., Vogel, D. R., George, J. F. (1991). "Electronic Meeting Systems to Support Group Work." *Communications of the ACM*, 34(7).

Otten, K. (1987). *Integrated Document and Image Management*, Silver Spring, MD: AIIM.

Parnas, D. L. (1972). "On the Criteria to Be Used in Decomposing Systems into Modules." *Communications of the ACM*, 12 (December).

Parsaye, K., Chignell M., Khoshafian S., Wong, H. (1989). *Intelligent Databases*. New York: John Wiley and Sons.

Perin, C. (1991). "Electronic Social Fields in Bureaucracies." *Communications of the ACM*, 34(12), 75–82.

Perry, T. S., and Voelcker, J. (1989) "Of Mice and Menus: Designing the User-friendly Interface." *IEEE Spectrum,* (September), 46-51.

Pertzold, C. (1990). *Programming Windows*. Redmond, WA: Microsoft Press.

Pfaff, G. E. (Ed.) (1985). *User Interface Management Systems*. New York: Springer-Verlag.

Podovano, M. (1991). "AFS Widens Your Horizons in Distributed Computing." *System Integration* (March).

Popek, P., *et al.* (1981). "LOCUS: A Network Transparent, High Reliability Distributed System." *Proceedings of the Eighth Symposium On Operating Systems Principles* (December).

Quillian, M. R. (1968). "Semantic Memory." In M. Minsky (ed.) *Semantic Information Processing*. Cambridge, MA: MIT Press, pp. 227–270.

Ranade, S., and Ng, J. (1990). *Systems Integration for Write-Once Storage*. Westport, CT: Meckler Publishing Corporation.

Randell, B., and Russell, L. (1964). *ALGOL 60 Implementation*. New York: Academic Press.

Rimmer, S. (1990). *Bit-mapped Graphics*. Blue Ridge Summit, PA: Windcrest Books.

Rose, C. G. (1990). *Programmer's Guide to Netware: A Complete Guide to Novell's Client API's*. New York: McGraw-Hill.

Roth, J. P. (1990). *Converting Information for WORM Optical Storage*. Westport, CT: Meckler Publishing Corporation.

Roussopoulos, N., Faloustos, C., and Sellis, T. (1988). "An Efficient Pictorial Database System for PSQL." *IEEE Transactions on Software Engineering*, SE-14(5).

Saffady, W. (1986). *Optical Disks for Data and Document Storage*. Westport CT: Meckler Publishing Corporations.

Salton, G. (1989). *Automatic Text Processing*. Reading, MA: Addison-Wesley.

Salton, G., and McGill, M. J. (1983). *An Introduction to Modern Information Retrieval*. New York: McGraw-Hill.

Schaffert, C., Cooper, T., Bullis, B., Kilian, M., and Wilpolt, C. (1986). "An Introduction to Trellis/Owl." *OOPSLA-86 Proceedings*, 9–16.

Schawderer, W. D. (1988). *C Programmer's Guide to NetBios*. Carmel, IN: Howard W. Sams and Company.

Schek, H. J., and Scholl, M. H. (1986). "The Relational Model with Relational Valued Attributes." *Information Systems*, 11(2).

Schmucker, K. J. (1986). *Object Oriented Programming for the Macintosh*. Hasbrouck Heights, NJ: Hayden Book Co.

Schnaidt, P. (1990). *LAN Tutorial with Glossary of Terms*. San Francisco: Miller Freeman Publications.

Schneiderman, B. (1987). *Designing the User Interface*. Reading, MA: Addison-Wesley.

Servio Logic. (1989). *Programming in OPAL*. Beaverton, OR: Servio Logic Development Corporation.

Seymour, J. (1989a). "The GUI: An Interface You Won't Outgrow." *PC Magazine* (September), 97–109.

Seymour, J. (1989b). "GUIs for DOS and OS/2." *PC Magazine* (September), 111–131.

Shibayama, E., and Yonezawa, A. (1987). "Distributed Computing in ABCL/1." In A. Yonezawa and M. Tokora (eds.), *Object-Oriented Concurrent Programming*. Cambridge, MA: MIT Press.

Shu, N. C. (1988). *Visual Programming*. New York: Van Nostrand Reinhold Company.

Snyder, A. (1985) *Object-Oriented Programming for CommonLisp*. Hewlett-Packard Technical Report ATC-85-1.

Stefik, M., Foster, G., Bobrow, D. G., Kahn, K., Lanning, S., and Suchman, L. (1988). "Beyond Chalkboard: Computer Support for Collaboration and Problem Solving in Meetings." In Irene Greif (ed.), *Computer Supported Cooperative Work: A Book of Readings*. San Mateo, CA: Morgan Kaufmann Publishers.

Stonebraker, M., and Rowe, L. A. (1986). "The Design of Postgres." In *ACM SIGMD Record*, 15(2). (June) 340–355.

Stonebreaker, M., Wong, E., Kreps, P., and Held, G. (1976). "The Design and Implementation of INGRES." *ACM Transactions on Database Systems*, 1, 189–222.

Stroustrup, B. (1986). *The C++ Programming Language*. Reading, MA: Addison-Wesley.

Schnaidt, P. (1990). *LAN Tutorial. A Complete Introduction to Local Area Networks*. San Francisco: Miller Freeman Publications, Inc.

Simson, D. (1990). "SNMP: Simple but Limited." *Systems Integration* (October).

Sybase. (1990a). *Learning TRANSACT-SQL*. Emeryville, CA: Sybase Inc.

Sybase. (1990b). *SQL Server Language Reference*. Emeryville, CA: Sybase Inc.

Sybase. (1990c). *SQL Server Programmer's Reference*. Emeryville, CA: Sybase Inc.

Sybase. (1990d). *SQL Server System Administrator's Guide*. Emeryville, CA.: Sybase Inc.

Symbolics, Inc. (1988). *Statice*. Cambridge, MA: Symbolics.

Tanaka, M., and Ichikawa, T. (1988). "A Visual User Interface for Map Information Retrieval Based on Semantic Significance." *IEEE Transactions on Software Engineering*, SE-14, 666–671.

Tenopir, C., and Soon Ro, J. (1990). *Full Text Databases*. New York: Greenwood Press.

Tsur, S., and Zaniolo, C. (1986). "LDL: A Logic Based Data Language." *Proceedings of VLDB '86*.

Ullman, J. D. (1980). *Principles of Relational Database Systems*. New York: Computer Science Press.

Ullman, J. D. (1987). "Database Theory—Past and Future." *Proceedings of 6th PODS*, San Diego.

Ullman, J. D. (1988). *Principles of Database and Knowledge-Base Systems*. Rockville, MD: Computer Science Press.

Veith, R. H. (1988). Visual Information Systems: The Power of Graphics And Video. Boston, MA: G.K. Hall and Co.

Wallace, P. E., Schubert, D. R., Lee, J. A., and Thomas, V. S. (1987). *Records Management: Integrated Information Systems*. New York: John Wiley & Sons.

Wang (1989). *Wang On Imaging*. Lowell, MA: Wang Laboratories Inc.

Webster, B. F. (1989). *The NeXT Book*. Reading, MA: Addison-Wesley.

White, G. M. (1983). "The Desktop Metaphor." *Byte* (December).

Whitewater Group. (1989a). *Actor Language Manual*. Evanston, IL: The Whitewater Group.

Whitewater Group. (1989b). *Whitewater Resource Toolkit for Windows*. Evanston, IL: The Whitewater Group, Inc.

Wiederhold, G. (1983). *Database Design*. New York: McGraw-Hill.

Wilson, P. (1991). *Computer Supported Cooperative Work*. Oxford, England: Intellect.

Winograd, T. (1988). "Where the Action Is." *Byte* (December).

Winograd, T. (1987/88). "A Language/Action Perspective on Design of Cooperative Work." *Human-Computer Interaction*, 3(1).

Winograd, T., and Flores, F. (1991). *Understanding Computers and Cognition*. Reading, MA: Addison-Wesley.

Winston, P. H. (1984). *Artificial Intelligence*. Reading, MA: Addison-Wesley.

Wong, H. T. (1983). *Design and Verification of Information Systems*. Ph.D thesis, University of Toronto.

Wulf, W. A., London, R. L., and Shaw, M. (1976). "An Introduction to the Construction and Verification of Alphard Programs." *IEEE Transactions on Software Engineering*, SE-2.

Yokote, Y., and Tokoro, M. (1987). "Concurrent Programming in ConcurrentSmalltalk." In A. Yonezawa and M. Tokoro (eds.), *Object-Oriented Concurrent Programming*. Cambridge, MA: MIT Press.

Yonezawa, A., *et al.* (1987). "Modeling and Programming in an Object-Oriented Concurrent Language ABCL/1." In A. Yonezawa and M. Tokoro (eds.), *Object-Oriented Concurrent Programming*. Cambridge, MA: MIT Press.

Young, R. L. (1987). "An Object-Oriented Framework for Interactive Data Graphics." *OOPSLA '87 Proceedings*, 78–90.

Zaniolo, C. (1983). "The Database Language GEM." *Proceedings of the ACM SIGMOD Conference*, San Jose, CA.

Zdonik, S., and Maier, D. (1990). *Readings in Object-Oriented Database Systems*. San Mateo, CA: Morgan Kaufmann.

Zdonik, S., and Wegener, P. (1986). "Language and Methodology for Object-Oriented Database Environments." *Proceedings of the Nineteenth Annual Hawaii International Conference on System Sciences*.

INDEX

ABCL/1, 204
Ablative recording technique, 23, 24
Abstract data typing, 7, 88, 120–121, 202, 207–208, 233, 265, 398
   advantages of, 214
   constraints on, 213–214
Access time, 31
Action, 372
Act 1, 204
Actor, 204, 240, 265–277
   class hierarchy, 267–276
   control classes, 271
   dialog classes, 271–272
   existing dialog class hierarchy, 272–276
   extending the class hierarchy, 276–277
   overview of, 265–267
   window classes, 269–271
Ada, 89, 202, 205, 210
AD/CYCLE, 333
Adjacency, 346
Advanced Program to Program Communications (APPC), 63
ALGOL, 201, 202
Allophone, 175–176
Alphanumeric information structure, 5
Alphard, 202
Alto, 203
American National Standards Institute (ANSI), 313
Amiga (Commodore), 176, 323
Andrew File System (AFS), 79
Animation, 7, 177, 321–322, 397, 402
Application-specific device driver, 41
Applications programming interface (API), 45, 109
Appointment Schedulers and Calendars, 370, 380–381
Archive Server, 74

Archiving, 1, 73–74, 185, 191–192
ARPANET, 63
ASCII (American Standard Code for Information Interchange), 158, 172, 312–313, 401
Association of Information and Image Management (AIIM), 15
Associative links, 17
Attributes, 86, 90, 91, 123–124, 310, 316
Authorization, *see* Security
Automatic sector reallocation, 33

Back-file conversion, 194
Backup, 73–74
Banyan Vines, 47, 69
Bar codes, 187
Batch systems, 236
Bayer dithering, 316
Bernoulli principle, 50
Bimetallic alloy medium, 25
Bit-mapped displays, 243, 256, 313
BLOBs (Binary Large OBjects), 131, 141, 158, 309, 311
Boolean base type, 230
Boolean query, 153, 154
Bridge, 77–78
B-trees, 38, 132
Burkes dither, 316
Buttons, 254

C, 88, 104, 120, 211, 240, 258
C++, 89, 204, 206, 210, 215, 258, 286
Caching, 35, 36, 76
Calculus of Complex Objects (CCO), 90, 118
Cartesian product, 93
CCITT Group 3/Group 4, 167, 172–173, 190, 311, 315
CD-ROMs, 18–21, 31, 49, 131, 393
Centralized database model, 368

416 ■ Index

Charge-coupled device (CCD), 165
Child windows, 253–254
Classes, 7, 201, 208–209, 398. *See also* Object orientation
  extensions, 210–211
Class inheritance hierarchies, 7
Client/server architecture, 9–10, 64–65, 109–111, 368–369, 394
Clipping, 190
CLOS (Common List Object System), 89, 205–206
CLU, 202
Clustering, 34–35, 202
Coarse seek, 32
Coaxial cables, 56, 57
COBOL, 104, 201
Codd, E. F., 85, 91, 395
COKES (Carleton Office Knowledge System), 372
Colab, 371
Collaborative work. *See also* Groupware; Workflow
  intelligent collaboration, 374
  models of, 368–369
Collision overflow, 37
Command-driven interfaces, 235, 236, 399
CommonLoops, 205
Common Management Information Protocol (CMIP), 71
Communication, 2, 8–9
Communications servers, 77–78
Compact disc (CD), 18
Complex object models, 86, 88
Compression, 141, 166–167, 178, 314–316, 395
Compression boards, 166–167, 397
CompuServe, 314
Computer-aided design (CAD), 89, 190
Computer-aided manufacturing (CAM), 89
Computer-aided software engineering (CASE), 89
Computer-supported collaborative work (CSCW), 367, 369. *See also* Groupware and Work flow
Concept indexing, 133–134, 137–138, 316
  indexing domain, 152
  techniques and strategies for, 150–152
Concurrency, 83, 204, 330–331
Conditional branching, 201
Conference on Data Systems Languages (CODASYL), 84–85
Constant angular velocity (CAV), 27
Constant linear velocity (CLV), 27, 31
Convolution, 190
CorelDRAW!, 238, 243, 244
Creeping, 33
Crude concept index, 134
Cursor-based operations, 103
Cyclic Redundancy Check (CRC), 33

Database management systems (DBMSs), 394–395
  capabilities of, 82–84
  concurrent access, 83
  evolution of, 84–90
  intelligent databases, 114–128
  object-oriented capabilities in, 88–89
  performance of, 84
  persistent storage, 82
  query languages, 83
  recovery, 83
  relational data model, 90–114
  security, 84
  transactions, 82–83
  uses of, 81
Database servers, 76–77
Data Base Task Group (DBTG), 84
Data definition language, 83
Data hiding, 265
Data independence, 91
Data manipulation, 92–95, 99–104
Data manipulation language, 83
Data modeling, 84
Data refinement, 135, 141, 159, 395
dBASE, 120, 296
DB2, 85
Decision Support Center (IBM), 381
Declarative constraints, 107–108
Declustering, 38–39
Decompression, 190
Deductive object-oriented data (DOOD) model, 118–128
  deductive rules and SQL, 118–120
  object-oriented constructs in intelligent SQL, 120–125
Desktop conferencing, 382
Desktop metaphor, 235, 238, 244, 249
Dialog boxes, 243, 247, 256, 263, 264, 271, 304, 399
Digital Equipment Corporation (DEC), 52, 205, 235, 393, 404
Digital paper, 50
Digital Video Interactive (DVI) boards, 176, 323, 324, 400
Directed acyclic graph (DAG), 221, 231
Directory structures, high-performance, 36–38
Direct read after write (DRAW) technology, 33, 34
Direct read during write (DRDW) technology, 33, 34
DIS, 203, 239, 242, 373
Disk servers, 75
Dithering, 316
Document management systems, 6
  work flow in, 382–383
Document retrieval:
  anarchic use, 133
  bibliographic mode, 132
  concept-based indexing, 133–134
  database support for, 156–158
  data refinement, 135
  dictionary, 156
  document collections, 141
  document object descriptors, 157

    document storage, 157
    expectations of, 133
    full-text, 131, 142–156, 159
    implementation techniques using frames, 158
    index storage, 157
    intelligent content retrieval, 137–140
    inverted indexing, 132, 133
    origins of, 131–132
    production and maintenance of documents, 132
    quality of information, 134–140, 159
    rare word list, 157
    raw data, 135
    recognition, 135–136
    signature indexing, 132, 133
    stop word list, 156
    understanding, 136–137
Domain, 70, 90, 141
Domain constraints, 108
DOS, 67, 69, 223
Dye-polymer technology, 25–26, 31
Dynamic binding, 211–213
Dynamic data exchange (DDE), 290
Dynamic link libraries (DLLs), 290

Eiffel, 205, 206, 213–214, 215
Electronic document interchange (EDI), 162, 188
Electronic fund transfer (EFT) systems, 375
Electronic mail, 75, 367, 370
Electronic meetings, 370, 381–382
Electronic messaging systems, 6, 371–372, 374–379
    in intelligent offices, 376–378
    launchers, viewers, and object linking, 378
    message filtering, 378–379
    message forwarding, 379
Electronic publishing, 17
Elevator seeking, 35
Encapsulation, 120, 201, 205, 239
Enterprise Model of the Repository Manager, 333
Entity, 85–86
    entity-relationship (ER) diagram, 86, 105, 354
    entity-relationship model, 86
    integrity, 91, 96
Erasable optical disks, 28–31, 393
    dye-polymer technology, 31
    future of, 49, 50
    history, 28–29
    magneto-optic technology, 29–30
    performance of, 31
    phase change technology, 30–31
Error correction codes (ECCs), 32–33, 43
Error detection and correction (EDAC) circuitry, 32
Ethernet, 55, 57–59, 78
Expert systems, 118, 374
Extended Binary Coded Decimal Interchange Code (EBCSDIC), 313
Extended Edition Database Manager, 85
Extended Industry Standard Architecture (EISA), 76

Extension, 86
External data representation (XDR), 78

FAD, 87
False drop, 143
Fax boards, 172–173, 397
Fiber optic cables, 56, 57
Fields, 84, 131
File allocation tables (FATs), 37, 42
File:
    servers, 75–76
    striping, 38–39
    system drivers, 45
    system kernel, 44
    System Switch, 45
FileNet, 192, 372, 383
    seek, 32
Flavors, 205
Floating-point numbers, 230
Floyd-Steinberg dither, 316
Fonts, 256
Foreign key, 91
Foreign key constraints, 108
FORTRAN, 202
Fourier transform, 171
Fragmentation, 34, 35, 36
Frame(s), 137, 152
    amorphous frame support, 158
    fixed frame support, 158
    frame compression utility, 158
    rules and goals, 158
FreeStyle computer system, 180
Frequency domain recording, 49
Full-text retrieval, 134, 312, 395–396. *See also* Document retrieval
    automatic indexing, 143
    clustering, 152–153, 309
    document parsing, 142
    indexing methods, 143–153, 309
    in the intelligent office, 159
    organizing words, 142–143
    origins of, 131
    query definition, 153–156
Functional dependency (FD), 107
Fuzzy query, 153

Gateway, 78
Gbase, 88
GEM, 88, 314
GemStone, 88, 3353
Generalized file routines, 84
GIF, 314
Global naming service, 69
Glossary, 346
Goldberg, Adele, 203
Graphical user interfaces (GUIs), 6–7, 70, 399–401
    bit-mapped displays, 243
    defined, 249, 304
    desktop metaphor, 244, 249

418 ■ Index

Graphical user interfaces (GUIs), (*continued*)
    dialog boxes, 243, 247
    direct manipulation, 244
    evolution of, 236–241
    goals of, 235
    icons, 243–244, 248
    in imaging systems, 180, 197
    main task of, 401
    menus, 243, 246
    on personal computers, 249–264
    pointing devices, 241, 243
    windows, 156, 243, 245
Graphics Device Interface (GDI), 257–258
Groupware, 6, 367, 392
    defined, 369
    features of, 369
    overview of, 369–372
    research, 371–372

Hashing, 37
Hewlett-Packard, 235, 295
Hierarchical data model, 84, 85, 395
High-resolution display monitors, 167–168, 397
High Sierra format, 20
Holography, 322
Huffman encoding, 315
HyperCard, 290, 346, 400
Hyperlink, 346
Hypermedia, 159, 200, 306, 342, 401. *See also* ToolBook
    links, 344–346
    nodes in, 342, 344
Hypertext, 10, 17, 159, 342

IBM, 52, 63, 109, 111, 235, 393, 404
Icons, 6, 238, 239–240, 242, 243–244, 248, 256, 304
ICOT, 89
Identifier keys, 225–226
Image data types, 313–318
    dithering, 316
    image compression, 314–316
    image file formats, 313–314
    images in the intelligent office, 317–318
    neural network technology, 317–318
    optical image recognition, 317
Images, 7, 127–128
Imaging systems:
    accounting applications, 196–197
    advantages of, 161–162
    archiving images, 191–192
    banking applications, 194–195
    closed, proprietary systems, 161
    compression boards, 166–167, 397
    database interface, 185
    database server, 182
    decision to purchase, 194
    engineering applications, 197
    fax boards, 172–173, 397
    fax service, 184, 193
    forms and, 184
    government applications, 195–196
    high-resolution display monitors, 167–168, 397
    host access, 184
    host interface, 192–193
    image decompression, 190
    image manipulation, 190
    image workstation, 180–181
    imitating paper flow, 192
    indexing, 186–188
    input format, 188
    insurance applications, 194
    and the intelligent office, 197–198
    laser printers, 178–179, 397
    markup and editing, 190–191
    multi-component systems, 179–180
    need for, 163
    OCR (optical character recognition) systems, 168–171, 184, 193, 397
    origins of, 161
    print service, 183–184
    purposes of, 162–163
    reporting, 188–189
    retrieval software, 189–193
    scanners, 163, 164–166, 396
    scan station, 181–182, 186
    searching, 185
    single-workstation systems, 179
    sound capability, 180
    storage requirements, 182–183
    turnkey systems, 179–184
    video boards, 176–178, 397
    voice boards, 163, 173–176, 397
IMG, 313–314
Impedance mismatch, 88
Index-end concept indexing, 134
Indexing, 1, 4, 97, 132–134
    automatic, 143
    bar codes, 187
    clustering, 152–153
    concept, 133–134, 137–138, 150–152, 316
    crude concept, 134
    full-text, 309
    in imaging systems, 186–188
    index-end concept, 134
    inversion of terms, 144–147
    inverted, 132, 133, 142, 144–147, 148, 157
    machine-readable input, 188
    methods, 143–153
    OCR (optical character recognition) technology and, 187–188
    query-end concept, 134
    removing words, 145
    signature, 133, 134, 147–150
    storage, 157
Industry standard architecture, 76

Index ■ 419

Inferencing, 10–11, 90, 119, 159, 306, 395
Inferencing database models, 89
Information backlog, 3–5
Information explosion, 17, 132
Information hiding, 203
Information management:
   in an intelligent environment, 2, 3, 391
   in a nonintelligent environment, 1, 11–13, 391
Information Management Systems (IMS), 85
Informix, 312
INGRES, 85
Inheritance, 7, 88, 120, 121–123, 201, 205, 214–223, 233–234, 265, 346, 398–399. *See also* Object orientation
   advantages of, 223
   code sharing/reusability, 216, 398
   defined, 214–215
   hierarchies, 348, 399
   instance variables, 217–218
   and the interface, 222–223
   method(s), 218–219
   method overriding, 219–220
   multiple, 220–221
Integer, 230
Integrity constraints, 105, 106, 107–109, 112
Intelligent database(s), 10–11, 90, 114–128, 395
   architecture of, 116–118
   deductive object-oriented data (DOOD) model, 118–128
Intelligent database repository, 368
Intelligent office:
   characteristics of, 13–14, 199
   collaboration, features to support, 374
   communication and information flow in, 2, 8–9
   document management systems in, 6
   example of, 14–16
   integrating technologies for, 5–11, 392
   intelligence in, 403–404
   modeling and organization of information in, 2, 4–5, 333
   prescription for the future of, 402–404
Intelligent SQL, 89, 90, 118
   object-oriented constructs in, 120–125
Interbase, 312
International Standards Organization (ISO), 60
Internetwork Packet Exchange (IPX), 63
Inverted indexing, 132, 133, 142, 144–147, 148, 157
   creation of, 146–147
ITASCA, 88
Iteration, 201

Joystick, 236
JPEG, 316

Kerr effect, 30
Keyboard accelerators, 256
Keyword, 152

Knowledge base, 3, 137, 159
Kurzweil K52000 system, 171

Language(s). *See also* SQL
   object-oriented, 89, 204–205
   programming, 88, 201–206
   query, 88, 94, 154–156
LANMAN, *see* Microsoft LAN Manager
Laser printers, 178–179, 397
Latency time, 31
Lazy allocation, 36, 37
LDM, 88
Least-recently-used (LRU) algorithm, 36, 42
Links, 84–85, 152, 344–346, 383
LISP, 202, 205, 206
Local area networks (LANs), 5, 9–10
   application of, 367
   backup, 73–74
   bus structure, 55, 57
   cabling, 56–57
   client/server architecture, 9–10, 64–65
   data transport protocols, 63–64
   defined, 53, 394
   electronic mail and, 375
   Ethernet, 55, 57–59, 78
   features of, 53
   growth rates of, 53–54
   hierarchical, 55
   imaging systems, 179–180
   in the intelligent office, 65–66
   internetworked, 367
   multi-point, 55
   networking topologies, 54–56
   network management software, 70–72
   network servers, 74–79
   operating systems, 66–69
   OSI/ISO models, 60–61, 62
   peer-to-peer architecture, 9–10, 65–66
   point-to-point, 55
   productivity problems in, 79–80
   ring structure, 55–56
   security and authorization, 72–73
   SNA (System Network Architecture) model, 61–63
   star architecture, 55
   token ring, 59–60, 78
Locality, 73, 328, 329–330, 332, 403
Logical data independence, 91
Logic-based database models, 89
Logic-based Data Language (LBDL), 90
Long-distance codes, 32
Lotus 1-2-3, 296
LZW, 315

MacApp, 240, 277–284, 400
   capabilities of, 277–278
   extensibility, 283–284

MacApp (*continued*)
  user interface class hierarchy, 278–283
  view subclass, 280–282
Machine-readable input, 188
Macintosh computers, 67, 69, 109, 176, 203, 235, 400
Macintosh Programmer's Workshop (MPW) language, 258, 277
Macintosh Toolbox, 258–264, 400
  Control Manager, 261–263
  Dialog Manager, 263
  functional overview, 258
  Menu Manager, 260–261
  QuickDraw, 261, 263
  Resource Manager, 260
  Scrap Manager, 263
  Window Manager, 258–260
MacPaint, 313
Magneto optics, 29–30
Management information base (MIB), 71
Mastering, 19, 26
MCC, 89
Memo field, 158
Menus, 243, 246, 256, 304, 399
Message handling service (MHS), 75
Methods, 201, 310, 398
Microchannel Architecture (MCA), 76
Microfiche, 1, 50, 183
Microfilm, 50, 131, 183
Microsoft LAN Manager, 68–69, 70
Microsoft Manager, 243
Microsoft Windows, 8, 203, 235, 244, 249–258, 378, 400
  benefits of, 250
  creation and manipulation of a window, 250–252
  Graphics Device Interface (GDI), 257–258
  pop-up and child windows, 252–255
  resources, 256–257
  scroll bars, 254
  voice in, 319
Microsoft Word, 243, 246, 378
MILAN (Multimedia Interactive LAN), 329
Modem, 172, 173
Monitors, *see* High-resolution display monitors
Morphological analysis, 150
Motion Picture Experts Group (MPEG), 178, 316
Mouse, 235, 236, 243, 399
MS-DOS, 42, 43, 44, 47
Multi-function optical drives, 49
Multi-media data types, 125–128, 310–312, 395, 401–402
  graphics, 311
  image data, 127–128
  sound, 311
  symbols, 310–311, 312
  text data, 126–127, 312–313
Multi-media information processing (MMIP), 306, 401

Multi-media information structure, 5, 7–8
  defined, 305
  evolution of, 306–307
  goal of, 305–306
  object-oriented nature of, 310
  storage demands, 306
Multi-media objects:
  categories of, 307–308
  on the client side, 308
  structure and interactions of, 309–310
Multiple inheritance, 220–221
Multi-volume sets, 39

Nested relationship models, 87
NETBIOS (Network Basic Input/Output System), 63, 66
Network File System (NFS), 45, 78
Network file systems, 78–79
Networking, *see* Local area networks (LANs)
Network model, 84
Network operating systems (NOS), 66–69
  Banyan Vines, 69
  methodologies for creating, 66–67
  Microsoft LAN Manager, 68–69
  Novell NetWare, 67–68
Network repeater, 57
Network servers, 74–79
Network trunk cable, 57–58
Network view, 84
Neural networks, 171, 317–318
NewWave, 89, 239, 242, 295–304, 400
  advantages of, 296
  Agent Facility, 299
  Application Programming Interface, 299
  architecture, 297–300
  compound objects, 300–301
  computer-based training (CBT) facility, 299–300
  container objects, 300
  context-sensitive help facility, 300
  data-passing links, 303, 304
  links and views, 301–304
  Object Management Facility (OMF), 297, 299, 300–304, 400
  office tools and systems objects, 300
  simple links, 302, 303
  software, overview of, 296–297
  user objects, 300
  visual links, 303, 304
NeXT computers, 173, 176, 205, 284–290, 400
  Application Kit, 285, 286–287
  applications supported by, 285
  Interface Builder, 285, 287–290
  software, overview of, 284–285
  user interface, 285
  voice in, 319
  Window Server, 285
NeXTStep, 8, 241, 249, 400
NLS/AUGMENT, 371
Nodes, 342, 344

Index ■ 421

Non-null constraints, 108
Normalization, 106–107, 123
Novell NetWare, 47, 67–68, 70

Object hierarchies, 240, 400
Object identity, 88, 120, 124–145, 399. *See also* Object orientation
   advantages of, 231–233
   built-in, 228
   defined, 233
   through identifier keys, 225–226
   object spaces with, 230–231
   path names in operating systems, 223–225
   type-state-identify trichotomy, 227–230
   user-defined names, 223
Objective-C, 205, 206, 286
Objectivity/DB, 88
Object Lens, 6, 371
Object Management Group, 206
Object orientation, 5, 395, 397–399, 401
   benefits of, 199–200
   defined, 199, 239–240
   evolution of, in programming languages, 202–206
   object-message paradigm, 206–214
Object-oriented database systems (OODBS), 7, 87–89, 90
Object-oriented user interfaces, 265–290
   Actor, 265–277
   MacApp, 277–284
   NeXT, 284–290
Object Pascal, 277
Object repository, design of, 352–361
   accessing objects in the current folder, 357–358
   accessing objects in the document database, 358
   folder navigation, 357
   locking shared objects, 360–361
   maintaining object numbers, 356
   populating the database, 356
   query forms, 357
   relational database for, 353, 354–356
   updating objects, 359–360
Object spaces, 230–231
ObjectStore, 88, 353
Odesta's Document Management Systems (ODMS), 383
Office objects:
   buildings and corporations, 333–337
   cabinets/drawers/folders/documents, 338–347
   categories of, 331–332, 402–403
   change management, 361–363
   check-out/check-in, 363–365
   collaborative work, 331
   concurrent sharing, 330–331
   floor/department, 338
   heterogeneous information, 330
   in the intelligent office environment, 328–333
   object repository for, 352–361
   the office as object, 347–348
   office workers and, 330, 348–351
   organizing the office environment, 332–333
   procedures and policies, 331, 335–337
   security, 332, 335
   types of, 327
OfficeVision, 89, 373
Office workers, 330, 348–351
OLE, 378
Omnifont systems, 169–170
On-line information, 1
OOPSLA (Object-Oriented Programming Systems and Languages), 206
OpenScript, 294–295
Open Systems Interconnection (OSI) Reference Model, 60–61, 62
Optical character recognition (OCR) systems, 2, 15, 136, 168–171, 397
   and imaging systems, 184
   for indexing, 187–188
   preserving format, 171
   recognizing a character, 170–171
Optical device drivers, 41–43
Optical disks, 8. *See also* Erasable optical disks
   advantages of, 392–393
   characteristics of, 17–18
   drawbacks, 18
   in imaging systems, 183
   multi-platter systems, 49
Optical file server, 76, 77
Optical floppy disk, 50
Optical image recognition, 317
Optical jukeboxes, 39, 47–48, 49, 74–75, 183
Optical media, 24–27
   CLV *vs.* CAV, 27
   digital paper, 50
   error correction, 32–33
   media format, 26–27
Optical scanning, 17
Optical storage, 10, 392–393
   advantages of, 17
   backup and, 73–74
   CD-ROMs, 18–21, 31, 48–49, 131, 393
   disk software format, 39
   erasable optical disks, 28–31, 49, 50, 393
   floppy disks, 50
   in the future, 48–51
   general-purpose transportable optical file system, 44
   in intelligent offices, 51
   nontransportable optical file system, 43–44
   optical device drivers, 41–43
   optical jukeboxes, 39, 47–48, 49, 74–75, 183
   optical tape, 50
   performance characteristics of, 31–40
   tape emulation, 40–41
   WORM (write-once, read-many) technology, 21–28, 31, 49, 393
Optical tape drives, 50

Oracle, 111, 185
OS/2, 8, 42, 43, 45, 67, 69, 295
Overhead(s), 35, 37, 38, 39, 42, 143, 144
Overloading, 211–213

PageMaker (Aldus), 203, 400
Paper, information on, 1, 4, 50, 131, 163, 391
 managing, 351–352
Parallelism, 204
Parent window, 269
Pascal, 202, 205, 211, 258
Passwords, 72
PC-LAN, 63
PC Paintbrush, 313
PCX, 313
Peer-to-peer architecture, 9–10, 65–66, 368–369
Persistent information, 104–105
Persistent objects, 82
Phase change technology, 30–31
Physical data independence, 91
PL/I, 88, 104
PM, 89
Pointing devices, 241, 243
Polymorphism, 265
Pop-up windows, 252–253
POSTGRES, 89
Preallocation, 35, 37, 39
Primary key, 91, 108
Privilege, *see* Security
Product codes, 32
Programmable read-only memory (PROM), 41
Program Manager, 244
Programming language, 88, 201–206
Prolog, 89–90
PROSQL, 90
Protocol, 5
PSQL (Pictorial SQL), 128
Pull-down menus, 243, 399

QUEL, 95
Quantization, 166
Query, defined, 153, 159
Query-end concept indexing, 134
Query language, 88, 94, 154–156

Raster-to-vector (R-V) conversion, 136, 190
Recognition, 135–136
Redundancy, 33
Reed-Solomon code, 32, 33
Referential integrity, 91, 108
Referential sharing, 7, 124, 225, 331, 332, 339
Relational database management systems, 85, 90–114
 client/server architecture, 109–111
 data independence, 91
 data manipulation, 92–95
 design, 104–109
 entity and referential integrity, 91
 relational algebra, 92–95, 100–101, 395
 SQL language, 95–104
 SQL server, case study of, 111–114
Relational query languages, 94–95
Relationship, 86
Remote File System (RFS), 45, 79
Remote procedure calls (RPC), 45, 78
Resource script, 257
Rooms windows manager, 329
R-trees, 38

Sampling, 174
Sap, 201
SASI (Shugart Associates Standard Interface), 20
Scanners, 163
 color, 165
 document-feed, 164
 flatbed, 164
 gray-level, 165
 hand-held, 165
 non-gray-level, 165
 overhead, 164–165
 and photographs, 166
Scan station, 181–182, 186
Scroll bars, 254
SCSI (Small Computer Systems Interface), 20, 35, 39, 40, 46
Security, 72–73, 75, 98, 332, 335
Seek time, 31
Semantic Data Model, 86
Semantic data models, 85–86, 88
Semantic gap, 88
Semantic net, 137, 159
Semantic networks, 215
Semantic structuring, 135
Sequenced Packet Exchange (SPX), 63
Sets, 87
Set-and-tuple models, 231
SFQL, 126, 154
Sigma Design, 192
Sigma Imaging Systems, 383
Signature indexing, 133, 134, 147–150
 character string signatures, 148
 creation of, 148–150
 storage, 157
 word-based signatures, 147–148
SIM, 88
Simple Network Management Protocol (SNMP), 71
SIMULA, 201–202, 205, 215
SLD resolution, 90
Smalltalk, 89, 203, 204, 210, 215, 217, 258, 265
Smalltalk MVC, 249
Sneaker net, 75
Soap, 201
SPARC-station, 170, 173
Spare area, 33

Index ■ 423

Spatial orientation, 323
Speaker independence, 320
Speech:
   potential uses of, 320–321
   recognition, 176, 319–320
   understanding, 320
Speech Transaction Manager and Generator firmware, 320
Spin coating, 25
Sputtering, 24
SQL, 77, 88, 89, 95–104, 154
   cursor-based operations, 103
   data definition, 96–99
   data manipulation, 99–104
   deductive rules and, 118–120
   embedded SQL, 104
   extending, advantages of,118
   indexes, 97
   relational algebra, support for, 100–101
   retrieval, 101
   security and privilege, 98–99
   tables and data types, 96–97
   view, 97–98
SQL/DS, 85
SQL Gupta, 111
SQL Server, 111–114
   command processing, 114
   dblibrary, 113–114, 115
   results processing, 114
   TRANSACT-SQL, 112–113
SQL2, 95
SQL3, 121, 353
Star workstation, 203
Statice, 88
STEELMAN, 202
Stored procedures, 112
Streettalk, 69, 70
Structured query language, *see* SQL
Structure of management information (SMI), 71
Stucki dither, 316
Super servers, 75–76
Sybase, 312
Sybase SQL Server, 69
System Application Architecture (SAA), 235
System Network Architecture (SNA), 61–63
System/R, 85
System 7 (Apple), 8

TAXIS, 86
Tellurium oxide medium, 24–25
Template,152
3-COM operating system, 47
Thresholding, 190
TIFF, 314
Timesharing systems, 236
Token ring, 59–60, 78
ToolBook, 290–295, 400
   books, 290, 291, 292–293
   buttons, 294

fields, 294
graphics, 294
identifiers, 291
links, 290, 291
objects, 291–294
OpenScript language, 294–295
pages, 290, 291, 293
script, 292
visual style properties, 291
Topic (full-text retrieval system), 150
Transactions, 82–83
TRANSACT-SQL, 112–113, 120
Transmission Control Protocol/Internet Protocol (TCP/IP), 63
Trellis/Owl, 205
Triggers, 108–109, 112
Trunk segment cable, 57
Tuple(s), 86, 87, 90, 123–124
Twisted-pair cables, 56–57
Type, 227

Unique constraints, 108
UNISYS, 52, 88, 393, 404
Universal Optical File Systems (UOFS), 44–47
UNIX, 36, 42, 43, 45, 57, 69, 79, 109, 223, 295
User-defined functions, 120
User-defined resources, 256

Variable rotation, 190
VAX Rdb, 111
Vbase, 88
Vector images, 313
Versioning, 306
Version management, 361–363
VERSO, 87
Video, 7, 321–325
   animation, 7, 177, 321–322
   boards, 176–178
   compression, 178
   digital, 322
   full-frame, 321–322
   and the intelligent office, 323, 325
   still-frame, 321, 322
   video capture and overlay, 177
Video annotation, 325, 402
Video conferencing, 325
Video disk, 22, 321
View, 97–98
Virtual File System (VFS), 45
Voice, 318–321, 397, 402
   boards, 163, 173–176
   digitizing sound, 174–175
   potential uses of speech, 320–321
   speech recognition, 176, 319–320
   voice synthesis, 175–176
Voice data, 7
Voice synthesis, 175–176

WANG, 52, 180, 372, 393
Whitewater Resource Toolkit, 265
Wide area networks, 375
Winchester drives, 21, 25, 30, 31
Winchester emulation, 41–43
Windows, 156, 243, 244, 399. *See also* Microsoft Windows
Word recognition, 320
Work flow, 367, 372–373, 392
   components of, 387–388
   in document management systems, 382–383
   dynamic, 386–387
   in intelligent offices, 383–385
   mechanisms for specifying, 386
   sample diagram for, 383, 384
   static diagrams, 386

WORM (write-once, read-many), 21–28, 393
   dedicated file systems for, 43–44
   future of, 49
   history of, 21–22
   in imaging systems, 183
   in the intelligent office, 27
   optical media, 24–27
   performance of, 31
   technology for, 22–24

Xerox Network Standard (XNS) packet protocol, 63
Xerox Palo Alto Research Center (PARC), 203, 204, 236, 329, 400
Xerox Star, 235, 400
X Windows, 249